Contemporary
Musical Expressions
in Canada

Contemporary Musical Expressions in Canada

Edited by
Anna Hoefnagels, Judith Klassen, and Sherry Johnson

McGill-Queen's University Press
Montreal & Kingston | London | Chicago

© McGill-Queen's University Press 2019

ISBN 978-0-7735-5879-3 (cloth)
ISBN 978-0-7735-5880-9 (paper)
ISBN 978-0-2280-0014-3 (ePDF)
ISBN 978-0-2280-0015-0 (ePUB)

Legal deposit fourth quarter 2019
Bibliothèque nationale du Québec

Printed in Canada on acid-free paper that is 100% ancient forest free (100% post-consumer recycled), processed chlorine free

This book has been published with the help of a grant from the Canadian Federation for the Humanities and Social Sciences, through the Awards to Scholarly Publications Program, using funds provided by the Social Sciences and Humanities Research Council of Canada.

We acknowledge the support of the Canada Council for the Arts.

Nous remercions le Conseil des arts du Canada de son soutien.

Library and Archives Canada Cataloguing in Publication

Title: Contemporary musical expressions in Canada / edited by Anna Hoefnagels, Judith Klassen, and Sherry Johnson.
Names: Hoefnagels, Anna, editor. | Klassen, Judith, editor. | Johnson, Sherry, editor.
Description: Includes bibliographical references and index.
Identifiers: Canadiana (print) 20190160128 | Canadiana (ebook) 20190160136 | ISBN 9780773558809 (paper) | ISBN 9780773558793 (cloth) | ISBN 9780228000143 (ePDF) | ISBN 9780228000150 (ePUB)
Subjects: LCSH: Folk music—Canada—History and criticism. | LCSH: Music—Canada—21st century—History and criticism. | LCSH: Dance—Canada. | LCSH: Multiculturalism—Canada. | LCSH: Canada—Civilization—1945-
Classification: LCC ML3563.6 .C761 2019 | DDC 781.620097109/051—dc23

Set in 11/14 Sina Nova with Futura
Book design & typesetting by Garet Markvoort, zijn digital

To Beverley Diamond for her legacy of ethical and relational scholarship and contributions to ethnomusicology in Canada, and especially for her inspiring mentorship and guidance.

Contents

Figures and Table   xi

Foreword   xv
Gordon E. Smith

Acknowledgments   xix

Introduction   3
Judith Klassen, Anna Hoefnagels, and Sherry Johnson

1 The Study of Music in Canada: Ethnomusicological Sources and Institutional Priorities   13
Anna Hoefnagels, Judith Klassen, and Sherry Johnson

Part One | Transforming Musical Traditions

Introduction   39
Anna Hoefnagels

2 *Le bon vieux temps*: The *Veillée* in Twentieth-Century Quebec   43
Laura Risk

3 Kathak in Canada: Classical and Contemporary   87
Margaret E. Walker

4 Taking the Piss Out: Presentational and Participatory Elements in the History of the Cape Breton Milling Frolic   114
Heather Sparling

5 Improvising on the Margins: Tradition and Musical Agency in les Îles-de-la-Madeleine   145
Meghan C. Forsyth

6 The Continuities and Legacies of English Song Traditions in Nova Scotia   177
Chris McDonald

Part Two | Rethinking Genres and Artistic Practices

Introduction   205
Sherry Johnson

7 Metis (Style) Fiddling: From Historical Roots to Contemporary Practice   209
Monique Giroux

8 War Drums in Chinatown: Chinese Canadian Lion Dance Percussion as Martial Art   242
Colin P. McGuire

9 "Holy jeez, I can hear *everything*": Liveness in Cape Breton Fiddle Recordings   275
Ian Hayes

10 Fantastic Voyage: The Diasporic Roots and Routes of Early Toronto Hip Hop   305
Jesse Stewart and Niel Scobie

11 Identity, Aesthetics, and Place in Medicine Dream's "In This World"   335
Janice Esther Tulk

Part Three | Heterogeneity, Diversity, and the Possibility of Alternatives

Introduction   357
Judith Klassen

12　A View from Toronto: Local Perspectives on Music Making, Ethnocultural Difference, and the Cultural Life of a City　361
Louise Wrazen

13　Re-imagining the Nation: The CBC as a Mediator of Ethnocultural Encounter in St John's, Newfoundland and Labrador　386
Rebecca Draisey-Collishaw

14　Music, Mimesis, and Modulation among Mennonites in Rural Manitoba　417
Judith Klassen

15　Ukrainian Catholic Congregational Singing in Canada: Sounds in Service and Celebration　453
Marcia Ostashewski

16　(Re)Presenting Indigenous Activism in the Nation's Capital: Signifying Resistance across Time and Place through Music in Alanis Obomsawin's *Trick or Treaty?* (2014)　477
Anna Hoefnagels

Accompanying Video and Audio Examples　503

Contributors　511

Index　517

Figures and Table

Figures

2.1 List of stage furnishings for *veillées* in Ottawa, 5–7 May 1920. Image courtesy of the Canadian Museum of History (fonds Marius Barbeau, B340, f1)   51

3.1 The author performing a kathak solo at the DANs/cE KAPITAL Festival in Ottawa, Ontario, in 2006. © Lorne Finley, Photographer   91

3.2 Kathak exponent Manisha Gulyani with accompanists, 2014. Licensed under the Creative Commons CC0 1.0 Universal Public Domain Dedication   95

3.3 Invitation to solo kathak debut performance. Used with permission   96

3.4 Publicity photo for *Paratopia*. Used with permission   103

4.1 Waulking cloth in Eriskay, 1934. Photograph by Werner Kissling. School of Scottish Studies Archives, F102_30, University of Edinburgh. Used with permission   120

4.2 Transcription of "Hé Mandu" by author   124

4.3 Cape Breton Milling Frolic, c. 1958. Photograph by Abbass Studios Ltd. A-3107.1, Beaton Institute, Cape Breton University. Used with permission   127

5.1 Map of the Magdalen Islands. Map by Wilco van Eikeren, 2011   146

5.2 Map of Atlantic Canada and Maritime Quebec. Map by Wilco van Eikeren, 2011   147

5.3　Jam, Parc du Gros-Cap, L'Étang-du-Nord. Courtesy of Noémie Guédé, 2012　150

5.4　A traditional music session at Café de la Grave, Havre-Aubert. Pascal Miousse (centre, fiddle) and Pastelle LeBlanc (accordion). Courtesy of Dana Whittle, 2013　150

5.5　Avila LeBlanc. Courtesy of Alain LeBlanc　154

5.6　*Les Pêcheurs*, sculpture by Roger Langevin (1990). Site de La Côte, L'Étang-du-Nord. Courtesy of Annik Martin, 2018　154

5.7　"Reel à Jean-Joseph à Avila" (traditional), Part A, as played by Bertrand Déraspe in the local style. Transcription by author, 2012　158

5.8　"Reel à Jean-Joseph à Avila" (traditional), Part A, as played by Bertrand Déraspe in his interpretation of a straight version of the tune. Transcription by author, 2012　158

5.9　"Paddy on the Turnpike" (traditional), Part A, as played by Bertrand Déraspe in the local style. Transcription by author, 2012　158

5.10　"Paddy on the Turnpike" (traditional), Part A, as played by Bertrand Déraspe in his interpretation of a straight or standard version of the tune. Transcription by author, 2012　158

5.11　Author's transcription of Bertrand Déraspe tune transcription (title unknown), from the notebook of Alain Cummings. Photo by author, May 2008　164

7.1　Clogging rhythm in duple metre　224

7.2　Garry Lepine, "Andy Roussin Reel," performance at Metisfest 2012. Transcription by author　228

7.3　Shawn Mousseau, "Buck Skin Reel," performance at Metisfest 2012. Transcription by author　229

7.4　JJ Lavallee, "Buffalo Gals," performance at Metisfest 2012. Transcription by author　231

8.1　Hong Luck lion dance team. Photo by author　250

8.2 Left to right: Jeung Fei, Lau Bei, and Gwan Gong lion heads at Hong Luck. Photo by author   252

8.3 Location of Sei Yap in Guangdong, China. Image by Fang Guofu, used under CC Attribution-Share Alike 3.0   256

8.4 Banner featuring Southern-style lion, Dundas Street West, Toronto. Photo by author   260

8.5 Notation of Hong Luck lion dance walking beat variant. Transcription by author   264

12.1 Józef Podczerwiński, Józef Ratułowski, and Franek Mrowca in 1985. Photo by author   370

12.2 The ensembles Biały Orzeł and Harnasie presenting the Podhale region in 2011. Photo by author   375

13.1 Program for Come By Concert 1   399

13.2 Program for Come By Concert 2   401

13.3 Program for Come By Concert 3   403

14.1 Villages of the West Reserve Mennonite settlement in southern Manitoba. Map used with permission from CMU Press   418

14.2 Mennonite youth in Halbstadt (Molotschna, Ukraine), 1914. Photo credit: Mennonite Archives of Ontario (M2004F 70)   423

14.3 Mennonite circle games at a wedding in southern Manitoba, 2008. Photo courtesy Lori Dueck   425

14.4 Jacob K. Schwartz with the *Brommtopp* he built for Neubergthal's centennial celebration in 1976. Photo courtesy Jolanda Schwartz Friesen   431

14.5 *Brommtopp* troupe from Amsterdam School District near Rosenfeld, Manitoba, in the late 1920s. Photo courtesy Marge Friesen   437

15.1 Interior, Holy Ghost Ukrainian Church, Sydney, Nova Scotia, 12 July 2012. Photo by author   454

15.2 Facsimile of Joseph Roll's transcription of the First Resurrectional Antiphon (Roll 1984)   463

15.3 Facsimile of The Divine Liturgy of St John Chrysostom (Synod 1987)   464

16.1 Musicians, demonstrators, flags, and drums at an Idle No More march in Ottawa. Image from *Trick or Treaty?* (2:23). *Trick or Treaty* ©2014 National Film Board of Canada. All rights reserved. Used with permission   480

16.2 Women musicians in an Idle No More march in Ottawa. Image from *Trick or Treaty?* (2:31). *Trick or Treaty* ©2014 National Film Board of Canada. All rights reserved. Used with permission   487

Table

16.1 Timeline of key Idle No More events   478

Gordon E. Smith

Foreword

I am pleased and honoured to contribute the foreword to *Contemporary Musical Expressions in Canada*. Writings about music in Canada extend from carvings on rocks and the bark of trees by inhabitants of Turtle Island in pre-contact times, through colonial diaries and travel and missionary accounts by newcomers in the colonial eras, to a substantial growth of research and writing dating from the mid-twentieth century to the present. Scholarship in this field has proliferated over the past seventy years, stimulated and supported by the establishment of music programs in public institutions such as schools, colleges, universities, museums, and community organizations. Paralleling the growth of research and scholarship, musical performance across multiple genres, styles, and cultures has become part of the Canadian social fabric. In the past several decades, new digital technologies have played a major role in the dissemination of musical expressions. Importantly, digital technologies have facilitated critical intersections between music scholarship and performance, often regarded before the twentieth-first century as separate, at times, contested spaces. Simultaneously, the oral traditions that have run alongside and through writings about music in Canada for centuries continue to shape our collective understandings of musical expression and experience.

The sixteen chapters in *Contemporary Musical Expressions in Canada* provide fresh understandings of the histories and cultural diversity that are embedded in this country's musical heritage and are part of contemporary expressive practices. At the same time, these chapters frame exciting and innovative approaches to musical creation, articulating multiple perspectives on a range of contemporary music and dance practices. The chapters engage with contextual and theoretical issues that will be of interest to both scholars and performers, and the volume will serve as a valuable new source for teaching and learning about music in Canadian contexts.

xvi | Foreword

Organized into three interrelated sections – "Transforming Musical Traditions," "Rethinking Genres and Artistic Practices," "Heterogeneity, Diversity, and the Possibility of Alternatives" – the book's layout provides the reader with a helpful structural trajectory, moving from historically embedded concepts such as tradition and the search for identity in musical practices, through problematizing musical genres and different contexts, to exploring current critical themes around the plurality of contemporary musical expressions.

The first chapter in the volume, "The Study of Music in Canada: Ethnomusicological Sources and Institutional Priorities," serves as an update of developments in ethnomusicology across the country, as well as an introduction to key themes in the interpretation of historical and contemporary music practices in Canada. In addition to reviewing ethnomusicological sources and assessments of the "emergence" of ethnomusicology in Canada, a couple of pivot points that are critical turns in this emergence should be highlighted. These include the historical and musical source study research of such librarians and musicologists as Helmut Kallmann, Maria Calderisi, George Proctor, Marie-Thérèse Lefebvre, Carl Morey, Robin Elliott, and Elaine Keillor, from the 1960s through to the first decades of this century. A second pivot point occurred in the final decades of the twentieth century and the turn of this century – the emergence of new critical approaches to music in Canada, led by such scholars as Jean-Jacques Nattiez, Regula Qureshi, and Beverley Diamond, along with many of their students. The move toward interdisciplinary approaches in understanding music as a social as well as historical process is now an important theme in the teaching and research of music in universities across Canada. In innovative ways, post-secondary institutions such as the University of British Columbia, the University of Alberta, the University of Toronto, York University, Wilfrid Laurier University, L'Université de Montréal, L'Université Laval, Memorial University of Newfoundland, and Cape Breton University have introduced programs that move past traditional models of music study. These include drawing on fields such as folklore, popular music studies, gender studies, media and digital technology studies, and emergent approaches to interpreting history. Most recently, these approaches have included conversations around Indigenization and decolonizing curriculum in the academy and wider communities, promising to bring exciting and timely trajectories in music and expressive practices.

The chapters in *Contemporary Musical Expressions in Canada* reflect these shifts and the range of new and emerging directions in ethnomusicology in

Canada. Each of the editors did graduate work with Beverley Diamond and were inspired by her. They emphasize the impact of Diamond's work in the book's first chapter, pointing out that she articulated fresh pathways for researching and interpreting music in Canada, exploding notions of history and applying concepts that are variously inspired by critical theory and Indigenous ways of knowing. Microhistories, counter-narratives, storytelling, alliances and collaborations, are some of the pivotal trans-disciplinary areas that Diamond has introduced and inspired others to follow. The chapters in *Contemporary Musical Expressions in Canada* embrace these pathways, drawing on a range of perspectives, and the book can take its place as a welcome addition to the substantial number of valuable collaborative publications that have come to be a defining hallmark of Canadian ethnomusicology.

Contemporary Musical Expressions in Canada thus inspires us to participate in the ongoing process of questioning what ethnomusicology is within and without borders, as well as what distinguishes us as researchers and practitioners of *musical expressions* in Canada. Fluid concepts such as relationality and relationships, respect and responsibility – essential themes throughout the history of ethnomusicology as a field of study – are foundational to this understanding. Linked to collaborative practices and community engagement, these concepts connect in powerful ways with Indigenous ways of knowing, which are increasingly being seen and heard as part of our research. Within this frame, what stand out for me in *Contemporary Musical Expressions in Canada* are the voices in the collection. Individually and collectively, they are powerful affirmations of the capacity of music to tell the stories of our diverse landscapes.

On a personal note, I congratulate the three editors of *Contemporary Musical Expressions in Canada*, Anna Hoefnagels, Judith Klassen, and Sherry Johnson, whom I have known as students, colleagues, and friends over many years. Their complementary areas of research expertise and their collective commitment to exploring and experiencing expressive musical cultures have provided a valuable contribution to knowledge about music in Canada. I know the readers of this volume will join me in thanking Anna, Judith, and Sherry for their extraordinary collaborative effort on this project.

Acknowledgments

It is the expressive work of performers, music-makers, dancers, and memory-holders that makes a project like this one meaningful. Thank you to each musician and tradition-bearer who has inspired and contributed to this collection – for your time, for your insight, for welcoming new ways of thinking about artistic practices and communities, and, of course, for your music.

Thank you to each contributor for entrusting us with your work and for your patience with the process that brought this project to fruition. We hope that, like us, you feel both fulfillment and potential when holding the final manuscript in your hands.

To Gordon Smith, who gave guidance and feedback throughout the preparation of this collected edition and who graciously agreed to write the foreword, we extend our deepest gratitude. Our appreciation of your generosity and your influence on ethnomusicology (and ethnomusicologists) in Canada cannot be overstated.

We would like to thank the anonymous reviewers of early chapter drafts and of the manuscript as a whole; this collection is richer for your careful reading of individual contributions, as well as your invaluable engagement with the project's big idea.

Thanks to Jonathan Crago, Kathleen Fraser, Finn Purcell, and the team at McGill-Queen's University Press for guiding us throughout the publication process and for offering helpful suggestions for improvement. Special thanks to our copyeditor Kate Merriman and our indexer Ruth Pincoe whose thorough engagement with the texts and attention to detail have contributed immensely to the strength of this volume.

To our institutional homes of the Canadian Museum of History, Carleton University, and York University, and to the colleagues and friends who animate them: thank you for your encouragement and for offering support throughout the course of this project.

Finally, for seeing us through various waves of heavy lifting, for listening to myriad ponderings and reimaginings of theoretical scaffoldings and grammatical minutiae, and for understanding that the textual guest in our respective homes was temporary, we offer our families profound thanks.

This book has been published with the help of a grant from the Federation for the Humanities and Social Sciences, through the Awards to Scholarly Publications Program. Additional financial support was provided by the School for Studies in Art and Culture, The School for Indigenous and Canadian Studies, and the Office of the Dean, Faculty of Arts and Social Science at Carleton University, the Office of the Vice-Dean, Faculty of Arts and Science, Queen's University, and a SSHRC Exchange-KMB Grant from York University.

All proceeds from the sale of this manuscript will be donated to the Student Paper Prize of the Canadian Society for Traditional Music / La Société canadienne pour les traditions musicales.

Contemporary
Musical Expressions
in Canada

Judith Klassen, Anna Hoefnagels,
and Sherry Johnson

Introduction

Public discourses around contemporary musical expression in Canada[1] often take diversity, multiculturalism, and cross-cultural exchange as fundamental points of reference. From these vantage points, diverse artistic practices, song forms, genres, geographies, and performance contexts become tools through which deeper understanding and cohesion across perceived cultural divides are possible. While the recognition of multiple and diverse lived experiences within a "multicultural Canada" is valuable, it is worth considering the deeper implications of this logic. As Caitlin Gordon-Walker writes, "Using the concept of cultural diversity to define cultural difference inevitably reifies culture and leads to the perception of different cultures as relatively cohesive and bounded units" (2016, 21).

Contemporary Musical Expressions in Canada engages microhistories as a means of rethinking bounded conceptions of expressive culture. Grounded in ethnomusicological inquiry, its chapters provide substantial examinations of contemporary musical expressions in Canada, recognizing the transnational nature of many communities and the impact that long-established music and dance practices have on new generations. Through the chronicling of historical and contemporary practices, it becomes clear that artistic expressions are not linear in their impacts, functions, and meanings; rather, the work of performers and culture-bearers resonates outward, charting continuity, disjuncture, intersection, and interplay. This collection is especially timely at a historical moment when identity politics, multiculturalism, diversity, immigration, and border crossings are topics of debate in Canada and around the world. While some chapters address the diasporic transplantation of expressive practices, others reconsider conceptual frameworks through which cultural forms are viewed and understood; still others examine and critique policies meant to encourage cross-cultural sharing, or analyze ways in which deep-rooted practices have changed to reflect new contexts and audiences for performance. In bringing these works together, we do not wish to reinstate a canon through the use of topical measures (e.g., genre, region) as organizing tools, nor do we seek to weave this volume into a cohesive national narrative. Instead, by juxtaposing detailed snapshots of historically situated musical practices – practices that shape engagement with myriad cultural identities in Canada – this volume serves to place microhistories into dialogue at a critical contemporary moment.

Themes and Theories: Nationhood and Multiculturalism

Conceptions of Canadian nationhood have changed drastically since Confederation, shaped in part by waves of immigrants from regions outside Britain and France. Often renewed and refocused in response to explicit or implicit threats – first from British colonialism, then Quebec separatism and American imperialism, and currently from an escalation in transnational mass media and migration – changing ideas about Canadian nationhood reflect the "realities of maintaining a national project in a changing world" (Edwardson 2008, 6). Additionally, domestic awakenings such as the increasing public recognition of Indigenous experience, knowledge, and power are forcing the reconsideration of "nationhood" within the Canadian context.[2]

Historian Ryan Edwardson suggests that the construction of a national idea involves "an active employment of myths, symbols, and other identifiers valued for reifying a sense of nationhood" (2008, 7). In Canada, one such myth is multiculturalism, resulting in an ongoing nation-building project that might best be described as multicultural nationalism (Kernerman 2005). Contrasted with more assimilationist models, multicultural nationalism "combin[es] the unifying intentions of nationalism with the pluralizing ambitions of multiculturalism" and "is extolled as a form of inclusive civic nationalism, in opposition to more outwardly violent, exclusionary or assimilationist nationalisms" (Gordon-Walker 2016, 15). The tensions implicit in this model have been variously experienced and interpreted, particularly vis-à-vis the implementation of multiculturalism through government policy.

Canada's official Multiculturalism Policy was introduced in 1971; it was followed by the Multiculturalism Act in 1988, in which the federal government officially recognized "the diversity of Canadians as regards race, national or ethnic origin, colour and religion as a fundamental characteristic of Canadian society" (Minister of Justice 2017). Through the Multiculturalism Act, the rights of all Canadians, regardless of language, custom, religion, etc., are guaranteed, and since its introduction, perceptions of the country's cultural fabric have expanded from a primarily Euro-Canadian (French/English) society, to one that includes other settler and immigrant communities and increasingly recognizes First Peoples cultures. As with concepts of nationhood, however, there are many "different discursive articulations and uses of multiculturalism" (Bannerji 2000, 5); as an epistemology that shapes social behaviour, it can be both divisive and exclusionary as well as unifying and inclusionary, depending on how it is used, by whom, and for what reasons. Many scholars have critiqued official multiculturalism for the fragmented ascription of "core" and "periphery" that it enables vis-à-vis cultural communities and belonging (see, for example, Bannerji 2000; Bissoondath 1994; Brown 2006; Day 2000; Gordon-Walker 2016; Hage 2000). Indeed, Himani Bannerji describes official multiculturalism as a "device for constructing and ascribing political subjectivities and agencies for those who are seen as legitimate and full citizens and others who are peripheral to this" (2000, 6).[3] She proposes an alternative, popular framing of multiculturalism, one that "would not engage in fetishized and essentialized traditions. It would speak to multiplicities of tradition and power differences within the space of the nation, as well as in multinationalities" (Bannerji 2000, 5).

Debates about multiculturalism and belonging continue in contemporary Canada, and their links to music, dance, and other forms of cultural expression take on increasing weight following Canada's 2017 sesquicentennial celebrations. We are challenged to consider how Canada and Canadians are defined, and by whom. How have diasporic musics found expression in Canadian communities and contexts? What long-standing traditions from earlier settlers continue to be performed, and how have they changed over time? What about Indigenous musics and cultural practices that continue to be celebrated, particularly in the spirit of "reconciliation" following the 2015 report of the Truth and Reconciliation Commission? What do these questions, and our responses to them, suggest about how identities are understood and performed in contemporary Canada? While not all of the chapters in this collection engage with these questions directly, together they constitute a strong sample of the musics, practices, priorities, and agendas of culture-bearers at the start of the twenty-first century.

Music Scholarship: Querying Narratives and Engaging Alternatives

Music scholars in Canada continue to grapple with the ways in which musical practices and related notions of Canadian identity are represented in print sources, and many have challenged the dominant narratives that characterize early texts, with their focus on Anglo- and Franco- folk musics, musicians, and performers (Diamond 1994).[4] While these traditions are an integral part of Canadian music history, contemporary scholarship expands its range to acknowledge additional, less-studied communities and their cultural forms; it also recognizes that music and dance practices frequently associated with particular cultural communities are not static, contained, or homogeneously experienced.

Microhistories, especially those based in ethnography, are powerful tools in subverting cultural analyses that take imagined homogeneous cultural groups as their point of reference. Ethnography reveals the multivalence of cultural practices, as well as the multiple identities of individual participants in those practices – and their vitality. "Subjects" are given voice in constructing their own subjectivities, and shed light on their own agency in dealing with ideological points of reference (e.g., multiculturalism in Canada) that frame their participation in local, regional, and national spheres. We do not pretend that the voices of ethnographers are absent from the microhistories presented in this volume, nor deny that fieldwork is "a power-laden process" involving "socially situated actors" (Koskoff 2010, 102). We do, however, contend that "when the multiply voiced texts are on display, they offer the reader far more interpretive possibilities than are present when the interpretation comes through the inflection of a single voice" (Titon 2003, 178). By considering the experiences of people living in Canada who engage in cultural practices that link to multiple identities and subject positions, it is possible to recognize both confluence and heterogeneity, and to complicate static, reified portrayals of "culture" and its expressive forms.

Within this context – recognizing contested narratives vis-à-vis "Canadian music" and the importance of microhistories and counter-narratives – scholars must nevertheless contend with the implicit canon formation that can result from music practice and scholarship built and disseminated through performances, recordings, publications, conference panels, radio programming, fieldwork, the building of archival and material collections, and other means. This tension reflects the processual nature of scholarship: ethnomusicological study is necessarily tied to specific moments, people, and places. But what are the implications of bringing microhistories together under a framework of "contemporary musical expressions in Canada"? When we place them in dialogue, do we implicitly weave related processes and relationships into regional or national narratives?

Beverley Diamond has written extensively on the discipline and practice of ethnomusicology in Canada, and her work offers a valuable point of departure for these considerations. She has repeatedly urged critical reflection regarding what is meant by ethnomusicology, how it is distinct in Canada, and what narratives have been – and are being – created about music cultures in Canada.[5] Putting ethnomusicology into context vis-à-vis historical reference points and the interpretation of broader social issues, Diamond writes, "In Canada, the separate social and intellectual worlds of not just English, French, and others, but also the fragile tensions between these worlds, lead us to fear grand narratives, and this has perhaps been one of the reasons we have gravitated to microhistories" (2006, 331–2).

Most recently, in a 2013 special issue of *Intersections*, Diamond returned to questions around historiographical narratives in "The Power of Stories: Canadian Music Scholarship's Narratives and Counter-Narratives." Here, Diamond emphasizes the importance of storytelling – articulating individual experiences in defiance of "erasures" of narratives – in considering the interplay between grand histories and ideas of nationhood and the lived experience of everyday people. The article ends with a sense of optimism for the future of Canadian music scholarship, "[recognizing] the multiplicity of meanings that music inevitably generates and its unique capacity to be a space for contested points of view, multiple narratives, and different aesthetically defined politics" (2013, 162).

The works in this collected edition build on the multiplicity of meanings, points of view, and narratives articulated above. Methodologically, this volume comprises a collection of microhistories that were brought into conversation as a result of a call for papers; each contribution was developed to examine contemporary practice (meaningfully placed in historical context) in order to appeal to a broad readership and allow for the individual voices of authors and their consultants to be heard.[6] Individually, chapters engage microhistories to provide thick descriptions that challenge generalizations often associated with specific musics and communities. In their juxtaposition as a collection, these same chapters are placed into dialogue and work to mitigate the superficial use of commonly referenced concepts such as "diversity" and "multiculturalism" vis-à-vis expressive culture in Canada. In various ways and to varying degrees, these collected works address questions of (re)presentation, racism, heterogeneity, and identity in practice. Through ethnography, analysis, and diverse modes of storytelling, the multiplicity of local and transnational experience is highlighted, creating important space for the "contested points of view, multiple narratives, and different aesthetically defined politics" to which Diamond calls attention (2013, 162).

Anthology Overview

This volume is organized into three broad sections, the result of much discussion and experimentation by the editors. In early conversations, we considered diverse framing tools, including those that were regional, historical, thematic, genre-based, organological,[7] and narrative. Seeking to avoid artificial boundaries between sections, we nevertheless wanted to create a structure that would enhance relationships between chapters and assist readers in entering a substantial collection. The framework we chose brings chapters together under the umbrellas of "Transforming Musical Traditions," "Rethinking Genres and Artistic Practices," and "Heterogeneity, Diversity, and the Possibility of Alternatives." This structure links contributions thematically, drawing connections across regional, generic, and temporal lines. Additional theoretical and thematic connections can also be drawn among chapters, crossing sectional boundaries and demonstrating the presence of multiple entry points into the collection.

In the first section, "Transforming Musical Traditions," authors engage with processes of continuity and change, demonstrating how music and dance practices, in addition to conceptions of those practices, can transform in relation to changing audiences, participants, and platforms for performance. These contributions challenge readers to query "tradition," and consider the implications of shifting expectations and performance contexts. Laura Risk's and Heather Sparling's chapters reveal some of the ways in which historical cultural practices are reimagined by performers and presented to contemporary audiences, reflecting the changing meanings and purposes of music and its accompanying activities. Whereas Risk examines the varied conceptualizations and enactments of the *veillée* in twentieth-century Quebec, Sparling demonstrates the continued valuing of Gaelic milling songs' participatory nature, despite alterations in function and performance contexts. The concept of tradition is problematized in Margaret Walker's chapter on kathak dance, as she illustrates how this syncretic and hybrid dance form from North India challenges common understandings of authenticity and innovation in its practice and presentation to Canadian audiences. Shifting to an examination of tradition and individual agency, Meghan Forsyth carefully documents a fiddle tradition in les Îles-de-la-Madeleine, characterized by improvisation and tune variability. Finally, Chris McDonald's study of English song traditions in Nova Scotia engages with issues of cultural continuity, commercialism, and tourism, as he examines the collection and promotion of folkloric materials in the construction of Nova Scotian identity.

The second section, "Rethinking Genres and Artistic Practices," challenges bounded conceptions of genre, revealing connections between musical expression, cultural identity, and place. Chapters in this section expand existing research on long-standing expressive forms in Canada, and also address previously underdocumented practices from diasporic communities. Monique Giroux's chapter repositions Metis (style) fiddling as a resurgent practice, highlighting varying historical and contemporary styles and contexts for performance, and examining their social and political significance. Colin McGuire's work on the Chinese lion dance engages directly with questions of genre and identity. Recognized as an art form, the lion dance has distinct roots in Chinese martial arts; McGuire traces the development of the lion dance in Toronto, illustrating its role in fostering cultural pride and identity among Chinese Canadians. Drawing attention to the links between genre, performance contexts, and recording aesthetics, Ian Hayes demonstrates the ways in which Cape Breton fiddlers and sound engineers harness varied sound technologies in the process of recording to negotiate multiple and sometimes conflicting audience and performer expectations. Jesse Stewart and Niel Scobie examine the work of pioneer hip hop artists who were instrumental in the genre's emergence in Canada, highlighting the contributions of key Toronto-based musicians who articulated diasporic roots through distinct musical choices. Finally, Janice Tulk investigates the careful negotiation of identity through musical and visual cues for Mi'kmaw musician Paul Pike and his band Medicine Dream; the group is based in Alaska, geographically far removed from Pike's home in Newfoundland. Together the chapters in this section demonstrate the dynamic nature of particular genres and practices, their links to expressions of identity, and the shifting meanings and interpretations to which they are connected.

The final section, "Heterogeneity, Diversity, and the Possibility of Alternatives," considers the multiplicity of musical practices within specific communities and how music is used to affirm diverse cultural identities and creative agency. These studies grapple with the ways in which contemporary music idioms in Canada articulate important social, political, and cultural issues in rural and urban settings. The first chapter draws on Louise Wrazen's ongoing work with the Polish community in Toronto. Wrazen challenges readers to recognize how public discourses of diversity can lead to the erasure of some communities from local histories and larger narratives. Also engaging public discourse and presentation, Rebecca Draisey-Collishaw examines a concert series organized by CBC St John's that sought to facilitate cross-cultural exchange by bringing together musicians from diverse backgrounds. Draisey-Collishaw considers related questions of policy and programming, and the ways in which multiculturalism is imagined, and belonging negotiated. Shifting to community practice, Judith Klassen's chapter explores the permeability of boundaries among Mennonites in rural Manitoba. Through an analysis of musical practices that demonstrate heterogeneity and cosmopolitanism, her research challenges portrayals of Mennonite communities as insular, homogeneous, and conservative. Also engaging ideas of community and identity, Marcia Ostashewski examines contemporary congregational singing practices in the Ukrainian Catholic Church in Canada; Ostashewski's work reminds readers of the power of music to create community and reinforce cultural identities, in this case, through congregational singing responses. The final chapter in this section, by Anna Hoefnagels, examines the music featured in Alanis Obomsawin's documentary *Trick or Treaty?* In this documentary Obomsawin explores the conditions around historic treaty negotiations and their connection with Idle No More. Hoefnagels demonstrates the centrality of music to historical and contemporary Indigenous activism, linking Indigenous activists across time and place. Together the chapters in this section illustrate the heterogeneity of musical practices frequently perceived as singular, and the ways in which identity is negotiated, performed, and created, often unsettling commonly held views of specific communities and musics.

This collection presents a snapshot of contemporary ethnomusicological research in Canada at the start of the twenty-first century, reflecting current trends in ethnomusicology, folklore studies, and Canadian studies. Following Diamond's engagement with microhistories in lieu of grand narratives, the authors provide detailed descriptions and analyses of musical expressions that are currently practised in various regions throughout Canada. These rich descriptions are illustrated in the YouTube videos that are referenced in each chapter and included on a playlist. While not comprehensive, the collection is expansive: the ways in which the authors engage with questions of identity, belonging, alliances, survival, adaptation, and change are valuable models for readers as they consider expressive culture and related identities in Canada. Indeed, the means through which the authors grapple with constructs such as multiculturalism, cultural tourism, mediation, and representation are broadly applicable to music and dance expressions within and beyond those presented in this collection.

Notes

1 Like many scholars, we frame the work in this collected edition within the context of music in Canada, rather than "Canadian music." While the latter implies the possibility of a music that is definitively "Canadian," we prefer to think about musics that are created within the borders of Canada, recognizing that borders are continually crossed, even contested, and that resulting exchanges are often manifested through hybridity, syncretism, and other expressive processes.
2 Consider grassroots movements such as Idle No More and federal initiatives such as the Truth and Reconciliation Commission, to name only two contemporary examples.
3 For a related critique vis-à-vis identity, heritage, and artistic expression in Canada, see Bakht, 2012.
4 For further reading, see "The Study of Music in Canada: Ethnomusicological Sources and Institutional Priorities," chapter 1 in the current volume.
5 As co-authors of the entry on the history of ethnomusicology in Canada for the second (1992) edition of the *Encyclopedia of Music in Canada*, Diamond and James Robbins each wrote articles discussing the decisions involved in the creation of this encyclopedia entry. While Robbins interrogated the who, what, how, and why questions around selecting contents for the EMC entry (1992), Diamond challenged readers to consider the boundaries and definitions that are assumed in the terms "ethnomusicology" and "Canada," and whose music is thereby included/excluded (1993). Throughout the 2000s Diamond continued to champion ethnomusicology in Canada and ethnomusicological research by Canadians. Speaking at the fiftieth anniversary roundtable of the Society for Ethnomusicology in 2005, Diamond asked, "Is there anything distinctive about the work of Canadians, and does it matter?" (2006, 326–7). This address was later published in *Ethnomusicology* (2006).
6 We had no misconception that this volume would provide a comprehensive survey of the diversity of music traditions across Canada, or that it would represent the wide variety of work being done by Canadian ethnomusicologists and scholars of Canadian music. Instead, the resulting chapters showcase the research of contemporary scholars, working from an ethnomusicological perspective, on some aspect of music in Canada, and who responded to a call for works to be included in this publication. Similarly, many music cultures are not represented in this collection although they are integral to many local music scenes across the country and are the focus of contemporary ethnomusicological inquiry. The privileging of English as the language of this collection highlights the linguistic base from which authors (and the editors) are working. Notwithstanding its obvious limitations, we hope that readers will use this collection as a jumping off point to pursue literature found elsewhere that likewise seeks to expand narratives and demonstrates the diversity of contemporary musical expressions and their cultural resonances across Canada and beyond.
7 Organology is the study of musical instruments.

References

Bakht, Natasha. 2012. "Mere 'Song and Dance': Complicating the Multicultural Imperative in the Arts." In *Pluralism in the Arts in Canada: A Change Is Gonna Come*, edited by Charles C. Smith, 13–26. Ottawa, ON: Canadian Centre for Policy Alternatives.

Bannerji, Himani. 2000. *Dark Side of the Nation: Essays on Multiculturalism, Nationalism, and Gender*. Toronto, ON: Canadian Scholars' Press.

Bissoondath, Neil. 1994. *Selling Illusions: The Cult of Multiculturalism in Canada*. Toronto, ON: Penguin Books.

Brown, Wendy. 2006. *Regulating Aversion: Tolerance in the Age of Identity and Empire*. Princeton, NJ: Princeton University Press.

Day, Richard J.F. 2000. *Multiculturalism and the History of Canadian Diversity*. Toronto, ON: University of Toronto Press.

Diamond, Beverley. 1993. "Lessons Learned, Questions Raised: Writing a History of Ethnomusicology in Canada (II)." *Canadian Folk Music Journal* 21: 49–54.

— 1994. "Narratives in Canadian Music History." In *Canadian Music: Issues of Hegemony and Identity*, edited by Beverley Diamond and Robert Witmer, 139–71. Toronto, ON: Canadian Scholars' Press; reprinted in *Taking a Stand: Essays in Honour of John Beckwith* (1995), edited by Timothy McGee, 273–305. Toronto, ON: University of Toronto Press.

— 2006. "Canadian Reflections on Palindromes, Inversions, and other Challenges to Ethnomusicology's Coherence." *Ethnomusicology* 50 (2): 324–36.

— 2013. "The Power of Stories: Canadian Music Scholarship's Narratives and Counter-Narratives." *Intersections: Canadian Journal of Music / Revue canadienne de musique* 33 (2): 155–65.

Edwardson, Ryan. 2008. *Canadian Content: Culture and the Quest for Nationhood*. Toronto, ON: University of Toronto Press.

Gordon-Walker, Caitlin. 2016. *Exhibiting Nation: Multicultural Nationalism (and Its Limits) in Canada's Museums*. Vancouver: University of British Columbia Press.

Hage, Ghassan. 2000. *White Nation: Fantasies of White Supremacy in a Multicultural Society*. New York, NY: Routledge.

Kernerman, Gerald. 2005. *Multicultural Nationalism: Civilizing Difference, Constituting Community*. Vancouver: University of British Columbia Press.

Koskoff, Ellen. 2010. "Is Fieldwork Still Necessary?" In *Music Traditions, Cultures & Contexts*, edited by Robin Elliott and Gordon E. Smith, 101–12. Waterloo, ON: Wilfrid Laurier University Press.

Minister of Justice. 2017. *Canadian Multiculturalism Act*. Accessed 24 January 2018. http://laws-lois.justice.gc.ca/PDF/C-18.7.pdf.

Robbins, James. 1992. "Lessons Learned, Questions Raised: Writing a History of Ethnomusicology in Canada." *Canadian Folk Music Journal* 20: 3–8.

Titon, Jeff Todd. 2003. "Textual Analysis or Thick Description?" In *The Cultural Study of Music: A Critical Introduction*, edited by Martin Clayton, Trevor Herbert, and Richard Middleton, 171–80. New York, NY: Routledge.

Anna Hoefnagels, Judith Klassen,
and Sherry Johnson

Chapter 1

The Study of Music in Canada: Ethnomusicological Sources and Institutional Priorities

The development of ethnomusicology is closely tied to its sister disciplines, including anthropology, musicology, folklore, and cultural studies, among others. The struggle to define what ethnomusicology is – and where it fits in the academy – has occupied generations of scholars. The Society for Ethnomusicology defines ethnomusicology as "the study of music in its cultural context. Ethnomusicologists examine music as a social process in order to understand not only what music is but what it means to its practitioners and audiences" (2018). While monikers such as "comparative musicology" reflect research priorities at particular times, more recent branches of ethnomusicology, such as "applied ethnomusicology," "archiving," "ecomusicology," "economic ethnomusicology," "medical ethnomusicology," and "sound studies," demonstrate the variety of approaches, concerns, genres, and issues with which ethnomusicologists engage. For many, ethnomusicology is characterized by its interdisciplinarity, its prioritizing of field research methodologies, and an emphasis on the understanding of music and sound. Defining "ethnomusicology in Canada" is even more difficult than defining the discipline itself: it is important to recognize the Canadian scholars who do research in their own (very large) backyard but also those whose work focuses on music cultures in other parts of the world, as well as ethnomusicologists from outside Canada who engage with communities in Canada.

Beverley Diamond has written extensively on ethnomusicological trends and priorities in Canada, and she cogently summarized many of the opportunities and challenges in Canadian ethnomusicology as part of a roundtable at the fiftieth annual meeting of the Society for Ethnomusicology. In a special anniversary issue of *Ethnomusicology* (2006), Diamond offered a regional perspective from Canada on the history of ethnomusicology, starting with the work of numerous collectors in the nineteenth century, the institutional recognition of ethnomusicology in the academy starting in the late 1960s, and highlighting the close relationship between ethnomusicological trends and debates in Canada and those in the United States. Drawing on the work of historian Marlene Shore, she asserted that "Canadian history is marked by a lack of consensus about the desirability or even the possibility of studying Canada as a nation" (2006, 328). Consequently, Diamond argued, Canadian ethnomusicologists have "a curious relationship with history" (331), informed by tensions among citizens from various cultural groups in Canada, which has resulted in an avoidance of grand narratives.

The prioritization of microhistories in Canadian ethnomusicology is in stark contrast to historical surveys of music in Canada, many of which omitted the music of Indigenous peoples and minority groups. As noted by Diamond in 1994, foundational texts on music in Canada tended to privilege Anglo-/Franco-Canadian cultures, with a geographic focus on music created, taught, and performed in major urban centres. Attention to rural musics and "folk" traditions started with folksong collecting in the late nineteenth century (mirroring the collecting that was taking place throughout Europe). Collectors were also interested in "preserving" Indigenous musics prior to their anticipated demise, and some scholars carefully documented musical practices and repertoires of then-newer immigrants, such as those from eastern Europe and Asia, although those microhistories were often excluded from "grand narratives" of music in Canada.

Histories of music in Canada, as well as the understanding of ethnomusicology itself, are marked by a diversity of approaches.[1] Building on previous bibliographies of music scholarship in Canada (e.g., Morey 1997; Elliott 2004), as well as surveys of writings about particular ethno-cultural communities (e.g., Diamond 2012) and genres (e.g., anonymous 1973, 1978, 1983), in this chapter we identify recent scholarship (i.e., since c. 1990) and its scholarly context. Following a brief review of some key materials that serve as points of departure for studies on ethnomusicological research in Canada, we turn our attention to recent research and publication trends, and the music communities and artistic practices that inform related scholarship. This is followed by a survey of institutional engagement with ethnomusicology as a discipline of study to demonstrate its value not only within the academy but also in broader public spheres and communities.

Key Sources on Ethnomusicology in Canada

Perhaps the most comprehensive survey of music cultures and ethnomusicological research trends in Canada is the *Garland Encyclopedia of World Music: The United States and Canada*, edited by Ellen Koskoff (2001). Unlike most music encyclopedias, which frequently use alphabetically organized entries of individual artists and genres, the complete *Garland Encyclopedia of World Music* reference collection is made up of ten volumes, organized geographically, with entries written by specialists. The third volume, *The United States and Canada*, includes a great deal of material related to Canada. Beverley Diamond provides a theoretical framework for the study of music cultures in Canada in "Identity, Diversity, and Interaction," followed by a detailed survey of cultural policy issues, the music industry, and regional history in her "Overview of Music in Canada" (Diamond 2001a and b). Although not comprehensive, the subsequent entries on various music cultures, complemented by case studies of specific music communities (e.g., "Musical Life in Montréal's Judeo-Spanish Community" by Judith R. Cohen and "Caribana" by Annemarie Gallaugher), provide interested readers with a solid launching point for their own research on and understanding of music practices in Canada.

The *Encyclopedia of Music in Canada* (EMC) was the first reference publication to focus on music cultures in Canada, and is an important precursor to the *Garland*. First published in 1981 (edited by Helmut Kallman, Gilles Potvin, and Ken Winters), and released in French as *Encyclopédie de la musique au Canada* in 1983, EMC provides information about diverse musicians, genres, and music practices among specific cultural communities.[2] Beginning in 2003, EMC was moved online with *The Canadian Encyclopedia* (now managed by Historica Canada). Bilingual content, as well as continuously updated entries, make it a significant contemporary resource.

One of the most recent monographs to address music in Canada is Elaine Keillor's *Music in Canada: Landscape and Diversity* (2006). An almost encyclopedic volume, this book is organized chronologically, and uses a vignette approach to highlight specific musical examples, with a strong focus on Anglo- and Franco-Canadian traditions. Keillor's textbook follows the practice of many earlier historical studies, in which ethnomusicological topics are addressed within a larger narrative of Anglo- and Franco-Canadian development and change, with an early chapter dedicated to "Traditional Musical Expressions of the First Peoples." Keillor intersperses her historical narrative with sections devoted to "other" cultural groups (e.g., "New Cultures on the Canadian Scene," "Music of Cultural Communities"), specific topics (e.g., "New Direction in Opera"), and descriptions of music communities and practices (e.g., "Fiddling in Prince Edward Island"). The themes of this book – landscape and diversity – draw attention to the ways in which Canadian music and culture are often characterized, highlighting commonly invoked connections between land, environment, and one's surroundings to the creation and performance of music, while acknowledging the diversity of cultures and musics within Canada's borders.

A number of publications focus specifically on ethnomusicological research in Canada, reflecting the significant growth of ethnomusicology as a respected discipline in Canadian universities in the 1980s and 1990s. Robert Witmer's *Ethnomusicology in Canada* (1990), for example, includes abstracts and conference papers from a 1988 gathering of over one hundred scholars that is often considered the first ethnomusicology conference in the country.[3] The contents of this collection are grouped thematically around issues (e.g., "'Not Knowing': Dilemmas in Musical Ethnography," "Transmission Processes"), musics (e.g., "Canadian Native Traditions," "Latin American and Caribbean Musical Cultures"), and broader considerations of ethnomusicology in Canada (e.g., "Doing Ethnomusicology in Canada: Focus and Community," "Ethnomusicology in Canada: Institutional Concerns"). As a snapshot of ethnomusicological research and areas of inquiry in the late 1980s in Canada, this publication demonstrates the growth of the discipline in terms of both variety of musics studied and interest in critical issues such as representation and research ethics during a pivotal time in Canadian music studies.

Beverley Diamond and Robert Witmer's *Canadian Music: Issues of Hegemony and Identity* (1994) was a landmark publication due to its explicit integration of critical theory into Canadian music scholarship. The collection offers new perspectives on issues in Canadian music, with some focus on particular ethno-cultural communities (Caribbean and Indian music communities in Toronto are just two examples). The collection as a whole queries the power dynamics that shape and influence music practices in Canada, as well as those that inform choices in music research, and many chapters engage with questions of identity at national, community, and individual levels.

Two additional collections include the special themed issue of the *Canadian University Music Review*, "Canadian Perspectives in Ethnomusicology" (1999), edited by Diamond and Witmer, and Anna Hoefnagels and Gordon E. Smith's *Folk Music, Traditional Music, Ethnomusicology: Canadian Perspectives, Past and Present* (2007). Both works expand papers presented at ethnomusicology conferences held in Canada; the Diamond/Witmer issue showcases research from the 1996 meeting of the Society for Ethnomusicology in Toronto, and the Hoefnagels/Smith publication is based on conference presentations at the fiftieth anniversary meeting of the Canadian Society for Traditional Music/La Société canadienne pour les traditions musicales (CSTM/SCTM) that took place in 2006 in Ottawa.[4] Both sources feature works that are specific to particular music communities (e.g., Mennonite, First Peoples), and address genre-specific considerations (e.g., definitions, transmission) and ethnographic issues (e.g., research positionality, media representation). In addition to these published collections, *MUSICultures*[5] and *Canadian Folk Music* (the journal and magazine, respectively, of the CSTM/SCTM) publish English- and French-language articles on topics connected to ethnomusicology, traditional music research, and popular music studies in Canada. For many ethnomusicologists and folklorists, these sources are both home to their own research and points of departure for discussions about and engagement with musical expression in Canada.

Complementing these key reference and overview publications are numerous sources that address specific musical traditions and cultures in Canada. While a comprehensive bibliography is beyond the scope of this chapter, what follows is a cross section of some musics that have received scholarly attention since the heightened engagement with ethnomusicological research that began in earnest in the late 1980s. This sampling of research does not include the work of the great number of ethnomusicologists in Canada conducting research internationally.

First Peoples' Musics

Documenting the music and cultures of First Peoples in North America has been of interest to scholars since the emergence of ethnomusicology in the late nineteenth century. But with Indigenous studies flourishing as a discipline in the mid-2010s, more recent scholarship on Indigenous music includes the interests and priorities of musicians and tradition-bearers themselves, and is informed by collaborative engagement with Indigenous communities and peoples in Canada. *Aboriginal Music in Contemporary Canada: Echoes and Exchanges* (2012), for example, edited by Anna Hoefnagels and Beverley Diamond, brings together the voices of academics and musicians by incorporating scholarship, interviews, and creative writings by Indigenous musicians and non-Indigenous allies. It showcases research priorities and interests at the start of the twenty-first century, a period marked by increased awareness of Indigenous peoples and their histories in Canada. Diamond's literature review, "Recent Studies of First Nations, Inuit, and Métis Music in Canada," surveys major trends and writings about Indigenous music since 1988;[6] here, we build on this by focusing on materials published since 2008.

A number of publications, such as Victoria Lindsay Levine and Dylan Robinson's *Music and Modernity among First Peoples of North America* (2019), Tara Browner's *Music of the First Nations: Tradition and Innovation in Native North America* (2009) and *The Encyclopedia of Native American Music of North America* (2013), co-written by Elaine Keillor, Tim Archambault, and John M.H. Kelly, include materials that focus on music traditions found in Canada, within the broader context of Indigenous music studies in North America. These sources complement earlier publications with a North American focus, such as Brian Wright-McLeod's 2005 compendium of Indigenous music recordings, *The Encyclopedia of Native Music: More than a Century of Recordings from Wax Cylinder to the Internet*.

Contemporary research with Indigenous communities is often inspired by social justice issues and initiatives, including the Truth and Reconciliation Commission (2008–15), Idle No More (which reached its peak in the winter of 2012–13), the National Inquiry into Missing and Murdered Indigenous Women and Girls (which began in 2015), and more recent attention to the history and impacts of the '60s Scoop. The Truth and Reconciliation Commission (TRC) examined the intergenerational effects of the abuses suffered by Indigenous children and youth who were forced to attend state-sanctioned and -funded Indian Residential Schools. The resultant Calls for Action are informing approaches and priorities for researchers, educators, and institutions across Canada. Dylan Robinson, Beverley Diamond, and Byron Dueck have written about the TRC hearings and encourage readers to consider what it means to witness, to hear, and to listen, while drawing on their experience at these hearings (see individual chapters in Robinson and Martin 2016).

Many contemporary researchers explore public celebrations and festivals that showcase Indigenous music and dance (Scales 2012; Giroux 2016), Metis fiddling and dance (Dueck 2013; Giroux 2015b; Lederman 2009, 2010, 2013; Quick 2008, 2010), and traditional community-based gatherings (Audet 2013), querying topics such as belonging and definitions of tradition, identity, and difference. Others analyze and discuss popular music idioms and music made in urban contexts, demonstrating, in many cases, the energy and passion of Indigenous youth for their futures and cultural identities (Przybylski 2017; Marsh 2009). Various authors focus on the music making of Indigenous women, examining their negotiations as muscial creators, leaders, and cultural survivors (for example, Diamond 2010; Harrison 2013;

Hoefnagels 2012a and b). New research on Inuit music and communities demonstrates the survivance and industriousness of Inuit and their interconnections with settler culture (Gordon 2007; Van den Scott 2014; Artiss 2014); Sophie Stévance's work with Inuk singer Tanya Tagaq illustrates the ways in which traditions can be altered while still serving the interests of community, allowing for creative expression (2017). Stó:lō scholar Dylan Robinson (2011) and Beverley Diamond (2011) engage in critical discussions around intercultural music involving Indigenous music idioms, challenging us to consider the power dynamics in cross-cultural creations and to think critically about ownership and appropriation of Indigenous music and culture. These and other scholars encourage us to consider important movements within Indigenous studies in Canada and internationally, and the ways that music shapes and is shaped by contemporary challenges for Indigenous and settler peoples.

Anglo- and Franco-Canadian Traditional/Folk Music Studies

In Canada, English and French "folk" or "traditional" musics have historically received the greatest amount of scholarly attention, including the building of song collections and analyses of repertoires, performers, and performance contexts. Much of this work has been and continues to be grounded by local histories and influences, with some regions receiving more attention than others; research priorities are often determined by proximity to research centres, universities, and related resources (e.g., grants and connections with community). This is the case in Newfoundland, for example, where folklorists and ethnomusicologists have produced myriad studies documenting music in the province (for example, Colton, Diamond, and Hillier 2007; Gregory 2004, 2006; Guigné 2014; Clarke and Hiscock 2009; Narváez 1995; Rosenberg 1994; Thorne 2007); they have also built an impressive archive of sound recordings. Anna Kearney Guigné has evaluated the work of some of Newfoundland's early folk song collectors (2007, 2012, 2016); moving outside of Newfoundland, others, such as Croft (1999), Gregory (2000, 2004) and Savard (2015), have offered (re)appraisals of other early collectors. Some regional studies examine particular repertoires and genres, for example, disaster songs in Atlantic Canada (Narváez 1997; Sparling 2017), Québécois folk songs (Bouthillier 2017; Perron 2004), and protest (MacKinnon 2008) and labour songs (MacKinnon and MacKinnon 2012) in Cape Breton. More recent trends include examining how younger generations of musicians use long-time musical practices and repertoires to negotiate past and present (Finch

2011; Turnbull 2009, 2016), to express their own heterogeneous identities (Forsyth 2012; Keough 2007; Labelle 2009; McDonald and Sparling 2010; Osborne 2015), and to attract new audiences (Everett 2016; Forsyth 2013). Several scholars have researched major Canadian folk festivals, including Mariposa (Hill 2017; Tsai 2011; Tsai and Hillhouse 2017) and Winnipeg (MacDonald 2008; Tsai 2007-08).

Because of the unique histories of immigration and subsequent development according to particular contexts, influences, and individuals, scholarly work on Canadian fiddling is almost always focused on regional or ethnic styles (see, for example, Johnson 2012a). In addition to exploring the construction of and boundaries surrounding those styles (Patterson 2015; Patterson and Risk 2014; C. Smith 2007; Trew 1996),[7] fiddle scholars are interested in questions of technology (Osborne 2007), creativity (Johnson 2008; Quigley 1995), technique (Duval 2010; Risk 2013), and how the work of fiddlers impacts particular communities (Risk and Patterson 2014).

Perhaps because of the popularity experienced by Cape Breton fiddling during the Celtic Boom of the 1990s, there has been an explosion of scholarly work on this tradition (e.g., Doherty 2015; Graham 2006), including at least eleven masters theses and doctoral dissertations in the last two decades. Scholars are exploring issues such as intellectual property rights (Hayes 2011), technology (Hayes 2012; Thompson 2006), identity (Alexander 2016; Dorchak 2010), and performance (Garner 2015; Herdman 2010). In light of the interest in Cape Breton fiddling, it is perhaps not surprising that scholars are now also paying attention to the unique Cape Breton piano accompaniment style (MacKinnon 2009; McDonald 2017; McDonald, MacKinnon, and Campbell 2016). Although there is some research on accordion (Hiscott 2000; Le Guével 1999) and piping (Gibson 1998; Shears 2008), most instrumental folk music, besides fiddle, is underresearched.

Scholarly interest in the vernacular percussive dancing that accompanies these instrumental traditions began much later; for several of the traditions – for example, Acadian (Forsyth 2015, 2016), Ontario Old-time (Johnson 2015), and Ottawa Valley (Johnson 2010, 2012b) step dancing, and Metis jigging (Giroux 2015a; Quick 2015) – research is still in its beginning stages. Other traditions, such as Newfoundland (Harris Walsh 2008, 2015) and Cape Breton (Gibson 2017; Melin 2013, 2015; Sparling 2015) step dancing, and *la gigue* in Quebec (Chartrand 2004–05, 2009), have received significantly more attention. Step dancing in northern Canada and social dancing to vernacular traditional musics across the country have been minimally documented or examined, with a few exceptions (e.g., Harris 2002; Tremblay and Voyer 2001).

Later Diasporic Musics

In addition to the substantial body of research examining English and French song and dance practices are studies that focus on later diasporic musics in Canada. The work of Marcia Ostashewski (2014, 2001a and b), Brian Cherwick (1995), Andriy Nahachewsky (2002), and Robert B. Klymasz (1999, 1989, 1972), for example, has expanded understandings of Ukrainian music and dance vis-à-vis performance practice, identity, and change. Louise Wrazen's research in southern Poland and in the Polish diaspora (2013, 2010, 2007a and b) has examined song and dance through lenses of transnationalism, transmission, and gender, while Muriel Smith has considered regional Polish ensembles within the context of globalization and larger diasporic currents and transatlantic cultural flows (2013). Bulgarian folk musics in Canada have received attention from scholars such as Irene Markoff (2014) and Yves Moreau (1990), who have considered the transmission, adoption, and adaptation of Bulgarian folk music and dance within the context of Canadian pluralism. Research on other transplanted European traditions includes, for example, Scots in Cape Breton (e.g., Sparling 2011, 2014) and Italians in Toronto (e.g., Del Giudice 1994).

The practices of relocated religious communities have also been examined, including among others, Hutterites, Doukhobors, and Mennonites. In addition to song transmission within the context of worship and community life (Berg 2002; Martens 1972, 2002), scholars have explored links between individual and collective song practice, identity, and belief (see, for example, J. Dueck 2008, 2011, 2017; Epp et al. 2005, 2009; D. Klassen 1989, 1995, 2010; J. Klassen 2005; Mealing 2001; Peacock 1970; and Weaver et al. 2015). Cohen's research on transplanted repertoires and the role of music in the Jewish diaspora (1996, 2001, 2007, 2011, 2012) and Wolters-Fredlund's examinations of Jewish song practice and identity within the context of Canadian multiculturalism (2002, 2005) are also pertinent.

Studies of Asian musics and cultures as practised in Canada have tended to focus on Chinese, Japanese, and Indian diasporic communities. Margaret Chan (2001) and Kim Chow-Morris (2009), for example, explore how Chinese composers and musicians adapt their practices to Canadian audiences and musical contexts in Toronto and Montreal respectively; more recently, Colin McGuire's case study of the Hong Luck Kung Fu Club in Toronto examines the relationship between martial arts, lion dance, and percussion music (2015). Research on Japanese music in Canada has focused almost exclusively on taiko drumming, with particular interests in gender (Kobayashi 2006), sexuality (Ahlgren 2016), and ethnicity (Izumi 2001). Both bhangra music and dance (Gosselin and Girn 2011/12; Mooney 2008; Warwick 2000) and Afro-Asian fusion musics (Hirji 2015) are examined as sites of intercultural meaning-making and identity negotiation for second- and third-generation South Asian Canadian youths.

Microhistories associated with diverse song practices and cultural communities in Canada have expanded significantly in recent decades. For example, Carolyn Ramzy (2015) is doing research among Egyptian Coptic Christians addressing historical and contemporary diasporic practice in Canada, and Ameera Nimjee has examined the exhibition of South Asian and Islamic sound and music within the context of several Canadian museums (2015). Studies of diasporic music making in particular communities is also emergent, including, for example, Rebecca Draisey-Collishaw's work on intercultural music making in St John's (2012), Kati Szego's exploration of reinterpretations of instrument practices in new locations (2015), and Mike Anklewicz's work on klezmer in Toronto and Montreal (2012). Latin American and African Canadian music genres proliferate in major cities across the country, yet an online search for publications on these traditions in Canada yields few results; exceptions include Gauthier Mercier on Brazilian music in Toronto (2007/2008) and Provost on West African drum making in Montreal (2015). Some of this writing reflects the increase in ethnomusicological research and education at Canadian universities. Unfortunately, however, while many graduate students in Toronto, Montreal, Edmonton, St John's, Vancouver, Ottawa, and elsewhere conduct research in local communities, resulting studies have rarely been published. With the growth of ethnomusicology at post-secondary institutions in Canada at the start of the twenty-first century, there promises to be opportunity for additional research and publications. This edited collection is one forum in which new research from both emerging and more established ethnomusicologists in Canada is being made available to readers.

Institutional Engagement with Ethnomusicology in Canada[8]

The ways in which post-secondary institutions engage with the musics of Canada in their course and program offerings has commanded the attention of many musicologists, ethnomusicologists, composers, and Canadian music advocates. Perhaps in response to John Beckwith's compelling provocation in "About Canadian Music: The P.R. Failure" (1969), in which he bemoaned the lack of attention given to Canadian contemporary music on the international music scene, scholars from a variety of disciplines have discussed how to better promote knowledge of Canadian music. Although many authors have advocated for more attention to newly composed art and experimental music,[9] others have turned their attention to questions around the discipline of ethnomusicology, as it is taught at Canadian universities, and particularly courses that focus on musical traditions practised in Canada. Considerations of ethnomusicology programs that began at Canadian institutions in the 1960s and 1970s[10] were highlighted in the 1988 roundtable présentation "Ethnomusicology in the Canadian University" and the ensuing group discussion (Beaudry et al. 1990). In this discussion, participants identified major challenges confronting ethnomusicologists in universities in Canada in terms of programs, course offerings, institutional support, and understanding ethnomusicology as an area of study within a music program; many of the challenges outlined in 1988 remain relevant today.[11]

Updated surveys of ethnomusicological course offerings and degree specializations at post-secondary institutions in Canada have yet to be conducted. There are, however, established graduate programs in ethnomusicology at a number of post-secondary institutions, including the Université de Montréal, Memorial University, York University, the University of Toronto, the University of Alberta, and the University of British Columbia. Many university programs that include ethnomusicology in their course offerings also offer "world music" ensembles, including African drumming and dancing, gamelan, Chinese orchestra, Balkan singing, Celtic music, and Latin jazz, among others. There are also a significant number of ethnomusicologists at institutions without dedicated graduate programs in ethnomusicology, and ethnomusicologists with faculty positions in sister disciplines such as Indigenous studies and community studies; others are in senior administrative roles in their universities, and still others are in positions at national institutions as curators, arts administrators, etc.

Numerous universities are also home to research centres, archives, and research labs that support ethnomusicological research. Memorial University's Research Centre for the Study of Music, Media and Place (MMaP) engages with local music communities in the area of St John's, Newfoundland, producing annotated recordings and inviting guest musicians and speakers to participate in events that bring academic and public communities into conversation. The University of Alberta boasts both the Moses and Frances Asch Collection of Folkways Records and the Canadian Centre for Ethnomusicology;

these centres hold archival recordings, musical instruments, and research resources. The Institute for Canadian Music at the University of Toronto has a mandate for "promoting, supporting, and producing scholarship in all areas of Canadian music studies" (Institute for Canadian Music 2018), while Cape Breton University's Centre for Sound Communities "fosters interdisciplinary collaboration and community engagement on sound, movement, and performance" (Centre for Sound Communities 2018). In Quebec, various research labs are sites for ethnomusicological inquiry; for example, the Université de Montréal houses the Laboratoire musique, histoire et société (LMHS) and the Laboratoire de musicologie comparée et anthropologie de la musique (MCAM). Université Laval also boasts a number of research labs, including the Laboratoire audionumérique de recherche et de création (LARC) and the Groupe de recherche-création en musique (GRECEM); they are also part of the cross-university research consortium comprising various universities in Quebec, Observatoire interdisciplinaire de création et de recherche en musique (OICRM). At the University of Regina, the Interactive Media and Performance (IMP) Labs are housed in the Faculty of Fine Arts and engage with local youth and community members. University-housed archives have also been a source for rich research by ethnomusicologists, including Memorial University's Folklore and Language Archive (MUNFLA), Cape Breton University's Beaton Institute and Archives, the Archives de folklore et d'ethnologie at Université Laval, and the Mariposa Folk Festival's archives housed at York University.[12]

Complementing these university-based resources are a great number of public museums, archives, and research centres that support ethnomusicologically oriented research. The largest archive of field recordings associated with ethnocultural communities in Canada is located at the Canadian Museum of History.[13] Representing over a century of fieldwork and comprising more than 100,000 recordings, these holdings include song, narrative, dance, and oral histories connected to First Nations, Inuit, Metis, French, and English practices in the early twentieth century, expanding over time to document Canada's increasingly multicultural population. The museum's music collection also includes material culture (musical instruments, etc.) that documents historical practice, cultural diversity, popular music, and craftsmanship in Canada. In 2018, the Canadian Museum of History, together with MMaP (Memorial University), the Sound Studies Initiative (University of Alberta), and Smithsonian Center for Folklife and Cultural Heritage (through its

Smithsonian Folkways Recordings) announced the creation of the Cultures of Sound Network. This cross-sector collaboration encourages research and public engagement in areas of music and sound through increased access to historical recordings, outreach and educational initiatives, and other projects. Library and Archives Canada holds an important collection of commercially released sound recordings, as well as the archival fonds of composers, musicians, industry professionals, and other actors within Canada's music spheres in the twentieth and twenty-first centuries. The archives of the Canadian Broadcasting Corporation and the Hudson's Bay Company hold collections that support contemporary and historical research, while regional archives house valuable research collections, such as the Helen Creighton Collection at the Nova Scotia Archives and Record Management, and Centre Mnémo in Quebec. The Canada Science and Technology Museum, the Glenbow Museum, and the Royal Ontario Museum hold music-related materials that connect to their respective institutional collecting priorities. Collections at the National Music Centre in Calgary include material culture and archival materials; the centre's programming provides musicians with access to unique instruments and recording equipment, as well as a commercial recording studio. Many of these museums and archives are actively engaged with families and communities to enable access to and repatriate materials; they are also digitizing collections and increasing awareness of those collections outside institutional and academic circles, despite such challenges as aging formats.

Closing Thoughts

The collection and documentation of expressive culture and musical experience throughout Canada has been a priority for researchers in many institutional contexts; this work continues in earnest, and scholars and musicians are engaging diverse modes of distribution to share their work, including websites, annotated CD compilations, documentary films, and various social media platforms. The breadth of possible subject matter is extensive, as are the theoretical and conceptual frameworks through which increasingly diverse – and at the same time frequently interwoven – musical spaces might be explored. Still, the music cultures of many communities within the borders of Canada have not been documented. Changing governmental and institutional policies and agendas mean that certain priorities dominate public discourse, but as ethnomusicologists, we have particular lenses – and tool kits – to engage with and support all community-based musicians whose songs, dances, and traditions enrich Canada today.

The ongoing augmentation of archival holdings, the priorities of research centres, and the work of individual ethnomusicologists, as researchers, performers, and teachers, will continue to contribute to the understanding and awareness of the complex diversities of music in Canada.

Notes

1 There are several bibliographies on music in Canada, including Helmut Kallmann's 1972 article "Toward a Bibliography of Canadian Folk Music," the reference lists on Canadian folk music published in the *Canadian Journal for Traditional Music* (Anonymous 1973, 1979, 1983), George Proctor's "Sources in Canadian Music: A Bibliography of Bibliographies" (1979), Carl Morey's *Music in Canada: A Research and Information Guide* (1997), and Robin Elliott's "A Canadian Music Bibliography 1996–2004" (2004). Gordon Smith examined the representation of Canadian materials in various academic journals, specifically the *Canadian Journal for Traditional Music*, *Ethnomusicology*, the *Journal of American Folklore*, and *Canadian Folklore Canadien/Ethnologies* (2005, 2007).
2 Second editions of the EMC were subsequently published: in English in 1992, and in French in 1993.
3 See Jay Rahn's report on this gathering, in which he asserts that the event "officially" brought together "for the first time ethnomusicologists from all over Canada" (1988, 55). However, according to Witmer, "the Centennial Workshop on Ethnomusicology held at the University of British Columbia in June of 1967 probably deserves [the] distinction" of the first conference on ethnomusicology in Canada (1990, xi).
4 For historical accounts and contemplations about the history of and future directions for the Canadian Society for Traditional Music at its fiftieth anniversary conference, see the final section of Hoefnagels and Smith (2007).
5 This journal has had two name changes. Originally, it was titled the *Canadian Folk Music Journal* (1988–96); it was subsequently renamed the *Canadian Journal for Traditional Music / La Revue de musique folklorique canadienne* (1996–2009), mirroring the society's name change and the renaming of the International Council for Traditional Music (the parent organization of the CSTM/SCTM). The journal has been named *MUSICultures* since 2007/2008. For an overview and analysis of the contents of *MUSICultures* over its first thirty years in print, see Smith (2005).
6 Diamond identifies 1988 as a year marked by a series of pivotal writings in Indigenous studies, as well as the year in which various meetings with an ethnomusicological focus were held, including the First Conference on Ethnomusicology in Canada (Diamond 2012, 11); it is also the year in which the editors for the *Garland Encyclopedia of World Music* convened.
7 The significant work on Indigenous fiddling by scholars such as Giroux, Lederman, Dueck, Quick, etc., has been discussed above.

8   For a review of ethnomusicological programming with a focus on American post-secondary institutions, see Stone (2014).
9   See *Celebration: Essays on Aspects of Canadian Music* (Ridout and Kenins 1984) for articles about modern music published in honour of the twenty-fifth anniversary of the Canadian Music Centre. See also *Hello Out There!: Canada's New Music in the World, 1950–85* (Beckwith and Cooper 1988) for conference proceedings on new music in Canada in which various composers and scholars address the reception of and needed advocacy for contemporary music; *The Fifth Stream* (Hatch and Beckwith 1991) discusses new directions in compositional practice in Canada. R. Murray Schafer advocates for Canadian modern music in "Canadian Culture: Colonial Culture" (1984), and John Beckwith revisits his 1969 musings on "The P.R. Failure" in 1986, among other reflections on contemporary music and composers in Canada (see Beckwith 1997). The publication of these materials in the 1980s and early 1990s reflects the heightened interested in new music of Canada at this time.
10 See, for example, Carlisle (1972) and Qureshi (1986).
11 Although not focused specifically on ethnomusicology, there have also been surveys on Canadian music course offerings (see, for example, Diamond 1991; Elliott 2003).
12 Part of the University of Toronto Libraries, the University of Toronto's Media Commons Archives houses collections associated with Canada's music industry, as well as Canadian film/video, broadcasting, and media studies.
13 The Canadian Museum of History has roots in the Geological Survey of Canada, which established the (then) Province of Canada's first museum in the 1850s. It became known as the National Museum of Canada in 1927, then the National Museum of Man (1968), the Canadian Museum of Civilization (1986), and, most recently, the Canadian Museum of History (2013).

References

Ahlgren, Angela K. 2016. "Butch Bodies, Big Drums: Queering North American Taiko." *Women & Music* 20 (1): 1–26.

Alexander, Kathryn. 2016. "Cape Breton Girl: Performing Cape Breton at Home and Away with Natalie MacMaster." *MUSICultures* 43 (1): 89–111.

Anklewicz, Mike. 2012. "Extending the Tradition: KlezKanada, Klezmer Tradition and Hybridity." *MUSICultures* 39 (2): 83–102.

Anonymous. 1973. "A Reference List on Canadian Folk Music." *Canadian Folk Music Journal / Revue de musique folklorique canadienne* 1: 45–56.

–   1978. "A Reference List on Canadian Folk Music." *Canadian Folk Music Journal / Revue de musique folklorique canadienne* 6: 41–56.

–   1983. "A Reference List on Canadian Folk Music." *Canadian Folk Music Journal / Revue de musique folklorique canadienne* 11: 43–60.

Artiss, Tom. 2014. "Music and Change in Nain, Nunatsiavut: More White Does not Always Mean Less Inuit." *Études Inuit Studies* 38 (1/2): 33–52.

Audet, Véronique. 2013. *Innu nikamu – L'Innu chante: Pouvoir des chants, identité et guérison chez les Innus*. Québec: Les Presses de l'Université Laval.

Beaudry, Nicole, Beverley Diamond Cavanagh, Virginia Garrison, Regula Burckhardt Qureshi, George Sawa, and Robert Witmer. 1990. "Round Table Discussion: Ethnomusicology in the Canadian University" and "Discussion 21." In Witmer, *Ethnomusicology in Canada: Proceedings of the First Conference, Toronto, 1988*, 349–69.

Beckwith, John. 1969. "About Canadian Music: A P.R. Failure." *Musicanada* 21: 4–7, 10–13.

– 1997. *Music Papers: Articles and Talks by a Canadian Composer 1961–1994*. Ottawa, ON: The Golden Dog Press.

Beckwith, John, and Dorith R. Cooper. 1988. *Hello Out There! Canada's New Music in the World, 1950–85*. Toronto, ON: Institute for Canadian Music.

Berg, Wesley. 2002. "Songs of the Germans from Russia: The Old Colony Mennonite Perspective." *Lied und populäre Kultur / Song and Popular Culture: Jahrbuch des Deutschen Volksliedarchivs* 47: 59–76.

Bouthillier, Robert. 2017. *Temporel / Intemporel: 29 chansons de tradition orale du Québec et d'Acadie*. Compact disc, Quebec: Independent release, Robert Bouthillier et Éva Guillorel, RBEG 01.

Browner, Tara. 2009. *Music of the First Nations: Tradition and Innovation in Native North America*. Urbana: University of Illinois Press.

Carlisle, Roxane C. 1972. "The Current Ethnomusicology Curriculum in Canadian Universities." *Ethnomusicology* 16 (3): 488–98.

Centre for Sound Communities. 2018. "Centre for Sound Communities." Accessed 24 January 2018. http://soundcommunities.org/about/.

Chan, Margaret. 2001. "East Meets West at Chinese Festivals in Toronto." *Canadian Journal for Traditional Music / Revue de musique folklorique canadienne* 28: 1–14.

Chartrand, Pierre. 2004–5. "Le quiproquo de la gigue au Québec." *Canadian Folk Music Bulletin / Bulletin de musique canadienne* 38 (4): 1–4.

– 2009. "La gigue québécoise dans la marge de celle des Îles britanniques." *Bulletin Mnémo* 12 (1). Accessed 25 February 2018. http://www.mnemo.qc.ca/spip/spip.php?article150.

Cherwick, Brian. 1995. "Ukrainian Tsymbaly Performance in Alberta." *Canadian Journal for Traditional Music / Revue de musique folklorique canadienne* 23: 20–8.

Chow-Morris, Kim. 2009. "'Small Has No Inside, Big Has No Outside': Montreal's Chinese Diaspora Breaks Out/In Music." *MUSICultures* 36: 49–82.

Clarke, Sandra, and Philip Hiscock. 2009. "Hip-Hop in a Post-insular Community: Hybridity, Local Language, and Authenticity in an Online Newfoundland Rap Group." *Journal of English Linguistics* 37 (3): 241–61.

Cohen, Judith L. 1996. "A Bosnian Sephardic Woman in Kahnewake, Quebec (Nina Vuckovic)." *Canadian Woman Studies* 16 (4): 112–13.

– 2001. "Musical Life in Montréal's Judeo-Spanish Community." In Koskoff, *The Garland Encyclopedia of World Music*, 3: 1201–6.

– 2007. "Three Canadian Sephardic Women and Their Transplanted Repertoires: From Salonica, Larache and Sarajevo to Montréal and Kahnawá:ke." In Hoefnagels and G. Smith, *Folk Music, Traditional Music, Ethnomusicology*, 150–62.

- 2011. "Selanikli Humour in Montreal: The Repertoire of Bouena Sarfatty Garfinkle." In *Judeo-Espaniol: Satirical Texts in Judeo-Spanish by and about the Jews in Thessaloniki*, edited by Rena Molho, H. Pomeroy, and E. Romero, 220–42. Thessaloniki: Ets Ahaim Foundation.
- 2012. "The Role of Music in the Quebec Sephardic Community." In *Contemporary Sephardic Identity in the Americas: An Interdisciplinary Approach*, edited by Margalit Bejarano and Edna Aizenberg, 202–20. New York, NY: Syracuse University Press.

Colton, Glenn, Beverley Diamond, and Jim Hillier, eds. 2007. *Newfoundland and Labrador Studies: Music Issue* 22 (1).

Croft, Clary. 1999. *Helen Creighton, Canada's First Lady of Folklore*. Halifax, NS: Nimbus.

Del Giudice, Luisa. 1994. "Italian Traditional Song in Toronto: From Autobiography to Advocacy." *Journal of Canadian Studies – Revue d'études canadiennes* 29 (1): 74–89.

Diamond, Beverley. 1991. "Canadian Music Studies in University Curricula." *Newsletter of the Association for Canadian Studies* 12 (3): 16–18.
- 1994. "Narratives in Canadian Music History." In Diamond and Witmer, *Canadian Music: Issues of Hegemony and Identity*, 139–71. Reprinted in *Taking a Stand: Essays in Honour of John Beckwith* (1995), edited by Timothy McGee, 273–305. Toronto, ON: University of Toronto Press.
- 2001a. "Identity, Diversity, and Interaction." In Koskoff, *The Garland Encyclopedia of World Music*, 3: 1056–65.
- 2001b. "Overview of Music in Canada." In Koskoff, *The Garland Encyclopedia of World Music*, 3: 1066–100.
- 2006. "Canadian Reflections on Palindromes, Inversions, and other Challenges to Ethnomusicology's Coherence." *Ethnomusicology* 50 (2): 324–36.
- 2010. "Native American Contemporary Music: The Women." *World of Music* 51 (1–3): 387–415.
- 2011. "Decentering Opera: Early Twenty-First-Century Indigenous Production." In *Opera Indigene: Re/presenting First Nations and Indigenous Cultures*, edited by Pamela Karantonis and Dylan Robinson, 31–56. Burlington, VT: Ashgate Publishing Limited.
- 2012. "Recent Studies of First Nations, Inuit, and Métis Music in Canada." In Hoefnagels and Diamond, *Aboriginal Music in Contemporary Canada*, 10–26.
- 2016. "Resisting Containment: The Long Reach of Song at the Truth and Reconciliation Commission on Indian Residential Schools." In Robinson and Martin, *Arts of Engagement*, 239–66.

Diamond, Beverley, and Robert Witmer, eds. 1994. *Canadian Music: Issues of Hegemony and Identity*. Toronto, ON: Canadian Scholars' Press.
- 1999. "Introduction: Canadian Perspectives in Ethnomusicology." *Canadian University Music Review* 19 (2): 1–4.

Doherty Elizabeth A. 2015. *The Cape Breton Fiddle Companion*. Sydney, NS: Cape Breton University Press.

Dorchak, Gregory J. 2010. "The Exported Cape Breton Fiddler: A Hermeneutic Study of the Meaning of Cape Breton Fiddle Music outside of Cape Breton." In Russell and Guigné, *Crossing Over*, 3: 130–47.

Draisey-Collishaw, Rebecca. 2012. "'Fusions and Confusions': Reflections on Intercultural Collaboration, Musical Hybridity, and the Intersubjective Nature of Reality." *MUSICultures* 39 (2): 61–82.
Dueck, Byron. 2013. *Musical Intimacies and Indigenous Imaginaries: Aboriginal Music and Dance in Public Performance*. New York, NY: Oxford University Press.
– 2016. "Song, Participation, and Intimacy at Truth and Reconciliation Gatherings." In Robinson and Martin, *Arts of Engagement*, 267–81. Waterloo, ON: Wilfrid Laurier University Press.
Dueck, Jonathan. 2008. "Mennonite Choral Music Recordings of the West Coast Mennonite Chamber Choir." *Journal of American Folklore* 121 (481): 348–60.
– 2011. "Binding and Loosing in Song: Conflict, Identity, and Canadian Mennonite Music." *Ethnomusicology* 55 (2): 229–54.
– 2017. *Congregational Music, Conflict and Community*. London, UK: Taylor and Francis.
Duval, Jean. 2010. "Les 'tounes croches' du Gramophone virtuel." *Bulletin Mnémo* 12 (3). Accessed 4 February 2018. http://mnemo.qc.ca/bulletin-mnemo/article/les-tounes-croches-du-gramophone.
Elliott, Robin. 2003. "Survey of Canadian Music Courses." *Institute for Canadian Music Newsletter* 1 (1): 9.
– 2004. "A Canadian Music Bibliography, 1996–2004." *Institute for Canadian Music Newsletter* 2 (3). Accessed 12 October 2017. http://sites.utoronto.ca/icm/vol02no3.pdf.
Epp, Maureen, and Carol Ann Weaver, eds. 2005. *Sound in the Land: Essays on Mennonites and Music*. Kitchener, ON: Pandora Press.
Epp, Maureen, Carol Ann Weaver, Doreen Helen Klassen, and Anna Janecek, eds. 2009. *Sound in the Lands: Mennonite Music across Borders*. Kitchener, ON: Pandora Press.
Everett, Holly. 2016. "Do You Play Newfoundland Music? Tracking Traditional Music in the Tourist Imaginary." *MUSICultures* 43 (1): 112–31.
Finch, Marc. 2011. "Experiencing Authenticity and Bluegrass Performance in Toronto." *MUSICultures* 28: 191–204.
Ford, Clifford. 1982. *Canada's Music: An Historical Survey*. Agincourt, ON: GLC Publishers.
Forsyth, Meghan. 2012. "Performing Acadie: Marketing Pan-Acadian Identity in the Music of Vishtèn." *Journal of the Society for American Music* 6 (3): 349–75.
– 2013. "Staging La Francophonie: Tradition, Tourism and Acadian Musical Spaces on Prince Edward Island." *MUSICultures* 40 (2): 65–93.
– 2015. "Dansez! Acadian Percussive Dance on Prince Edward Island, Past and Present." *Canadian Folk Magazine / Musique folklorique canadienne* 49 (2/3): 30–5.
– 2016. Exhibition, *Dansez! Acadian Dance Traditions on Prince Edward Island, Past and Present*. Bilingual museum and web exhibition. Le Musée acadien de l'Île-du-Prince-Édouard. 19 June–31 December 2016. Accessed 5 February 2018. http://danseacadienne.ca.
Gallaugher, Annemarie. 2001. "Caribana." In Koskoff, *The Garland Encyclopedia of World Music*, 3: 1207–9.
Garner, David Kirkland. 2015. "That Driving Sound: Use of Tempo in Traditional Cape Breton Fiddle Performance." *MUSICultures* 42 (2): 55–78.

Gauthier Mercier, Catherine. 2007/2008. "Interpreting Brazilianness: Musical Views of Brazil in Toronto." MUSICultures 34/35: 26–46.
Gibson, John G. 1998. *Traditional Gaelic Bagpiping, 1745–1945*. Montreal & Kingston: McGill-Queen's University Press.
— 2017. *Gaelic Cape Breton Step-Dancing: An Historical and Ethnographic Perspective*. Montreal & Kingston: McGill-Queen's University Press.
Giroux, Monique. 2015a. "An Interview with Simone Blais." *Canadian Folk Magazine / Musique folklorique canadienne* 49 (2/3): 45–8.
— 2015b. "Singing for Frog Plain." *Ethnologies* 37 (1): 43–64.
— 2016. "'Giving Them Back Their Spirit': Multiculturalism and Resurgence at a Metis Cultural Festival." MUSICultures 43 (1): 64–88.
Gordon, Tom. 2007. "Found in Translation: The Inuit Voice in Moravian Music." *Newfoundland and Labrador Studies* 22 (1): 287–314.
Gosselin, Viviane, and Naveen Girn. 2011/12. Exhibition, *Bhangra.me: Vancouver's Bhangra Story*. Museum of Vancouver. Vancouver, British Columbia. 5 May 2011–1 January 2012.
Graham, Glenn. 2006. *The Cape Breton Fiddle: Making and Maintaining Tradition*. Sydney, NS: Cape Breton University Press.
Gregory, David. 2000. "Maud Karpeles, Newfoundland, and the Crisis of the Folk Song Revival, 1924–1935." *Newfoundland Studies* 16 (2): 151–65.
— 2004. "Newfoundland Traditional Song: The Legacy from the English West Country." MUSICultures 31: 50–65.
— 2006. "Vernacular Song, Cultural Identity, and Nationalism in Newfoundland, 1920–1955." *Canadian Folk Music / Musique folklorique canadienne* 40 (2): 1–14.
— 2010. "Vernacular Folk Song on Canadian Radio: Recovered, Constructed, and Suppressed Identities." In *How Canadians Communicate*. Vol. 3, *Contexts of Canadian Popular Culture*, edited by Bart Beaty et al., 281–318. Edmonton, AB: Athabasca University Press.
Guigné, Anna Kearney. 2007. "'The Folklore Treasure There Is Astounding': Reappraising Margaret Sargent McTaggart's Contribution to the Documentation of Newfoundland Folksong at Mid-century." *Ethnologies* 29 (1–2): 171–214.
— 2012. *Maud Karpeles (1885–1976): A Retrospective of Her Newfoundland Fieldwork, 1929 and 1930*. St John's, NL: Centre for the Study of Music, Media and Place.
— 2014. "'Old Brown's Daughter': Re-contextualizing a 'Locally' Composed Newfoundland Folk Song." In *Street Ballads in Nineteenth-Century Britain, Ireland, and North America: The Interface between Print and Oral Traditions*, edited by David Atkinson and Steve Roud, 245–62. Burlington, VT: Ashgate Publishing Limited.
— 2016. *The Forgotten Songs of the Newfoundland Outports: As Taken from Kenneth Peacock's Newfoundland Field Collection, 1951–1961*. Ottawa, ON: University of Ottawa Press.
Harris, Kristin. 2002. "'From the Kitchen to the Stage': Recontextualization of Set Dance in Newfoundland and Labrador." *Theatre Research in Canada* 23 (1): 83–100.
Harrison, K. 2013. "Music, Health, and Socio-economic Status: A Perspective on Urban Poverty in Canada." *Yearbook for Traditional Music* 45: 58–73.

Harris Walsh, Kristin. 2008. "Irish-Newfoundland Step Dancing and Cultural Identity in Newfoundland." *Ethnologies* 30 (1): 125–40.

– 2015. "Irishness and Step Dancing in Newfoundland and Labrador." In *Global Movements: Dance, Place, and Hybridity*, edited by Olaf Kuhlke and Adam Pine, 25–37. Lanham, MD: Lexington Books.

Hatch, Peter, and John Beckwith. 1991. *The Fifth Stream*. Toronto, ON: Institute for Canadian Music.

Hayes, Ian. 2011. "'You Have to Strike That Balance between Sharing and Charging': Cape Breton Fiddling and Intellectual Property Rights." *Ethnologies* 33 (2): 181–201.

– 2012. "'Our Fiddles Sound Big. That's the Way I Think It Should Be': Cape Breton Fiddling and Amplification Practices." *MUSICultures* 39 (2): 161–80.

Herdman, Jessica. 2010. "'Old Style' Cape Breton Fiddling: Narrative, Interstices, Dancing." In Russell and Guigné, *Crossing Over*, 3: 130–47.

Hill, Michael. 2017. *The Mariposa Folk Festival: A History*. Toronto, ON: Dundurn Press.

Hirji, Faiza. 2015. "Jamming in the Third Space: South Asian Fusion Music in Canada." *Popular Music and Society* 38 (3): 318–36.

Hiscott, Jim. 2000. "Inuit Accordion Music – A Better Kept Secret." *Canadian Folk Music Bulletin / Bulletin de musique folklorique canadienne* 34 (1/2): 16–19.

Historica Canada. 2003. *Canadian Encyclopedia*. Accessed 31 August 2018. https://thecanadianencyclopedia.com/en/.

Hoefnagels, Anna. 2012a. "Aboriginal Women and the Powwow Drum: Restrictions, Teachings, and Challenges." In Hoefnagels and Diamond, *Aboriginal Music in Contemporary Canada*, 109–30.

– 2012b. "One Strong Woman: Finding Her Voice, Finding Her Heritage." In Hoefnagels and Diamond, *Aboriginal Music in Contemporary Canada*, 194–205.

Hoefnagels, Anna, and Beverley Diamond, eds. 2012. *Aboriginal Music in Contemporary Canada: Echoes and Exchanges*. Montreal & Kingston: McGill-Queen's University Press.

Hoefnagels, Anna, and Gordon Smith, eds. 2007. *Folk Music, Traditional Music, Ethnomusicology: Perspectives Past and Present*. Newcastle, UK: Cambridge Scholars Press.

Institute for Canadian Music. 2018. "Institute for Canadian Music." Accessed 12 January 2018. http://sites.utoronto.ca/icm/.

Izumi, Masumi. 2001. "Reconsidering Ethnic Culture and Community: A Case Study on Japanese Canadian Taiko Drumming." *Journal of Asian American Studies* 4 (1): 35–56.

Johnson, Sherry. 2008. "'I Don't Want to Sound Like Just One Person': Individuality in Competitive Fiddling." In *Driving the Bow: Fiddle and Dance Studies from around the North Atlantic*, edited by Ian Russell and Mary Anne Alburger, 2: 166–84. Aberdeen, Scotland: Elphinstone Institute.

– 2010. "Step Dancing to Hip Hop? Reconsidering the Interrelationship between Music and Dance in the Ottawa Valley Step Dancing Community." In Russell and Guigné, *Crossing Over*, 130–47.

– ed. 2012a. *Bellows & Bows: Historic Recordings of Traditional Fiddle & Accordion Music from across Canada*. St John's, NL: Centre for the Study of Music, Media and Place.

- 2012b. "Dancing outside the Box: How Ottawa Valley Step Dancers Conceive of Space." In *From Field to Text & Dance and Space: Proceedings for the 24th Symposium of the ICTM Study Group on Ethnochoreology*, edited by Elsie Dunin, Anca Giurchescu, and Csilla Konczei, 183–6. Cluj-Napoca: The Romanian Institute for Research on National Minorities.
- 2015. "Ontario Old-time Step-Dancing: Piecing Together a History through Ethnography." *Canadian Folk Magazine / Musique folklorique canadienne* 49 (2/3): 39–44.

Kallmann, Helmut. 1960 (1987). *A History of Music in Canada, 1534–1914.* Toronto, ON: University of Toronto Press.
- 1972. "Toward a Bibliography of Canadian Folk Music." *Ethnomusicology* 16 (3): 499–503.

Kallmann, Helmut, Gilles Potvin, and Kenneth Winters, eds. 1981 (1992). *The Encyclopedia of Music in Canada.* Toronto, ON: University of Toronto Press.
- eds. 1983 (1993). *Encylopédie de la musique au Canada.* Montreal, QC: Éditions Fides.

Keillor, Elaine. 2006. *Music in Canada: Capturing Landscape and Diversity.* Montreal & Kingston: McGill-Queen's University Press.

Keillor, Elaine, John M.H. Kelly, and Tim Archambault. 2013. *Encyclopedia of Native American Music of North America.* Santa Barbara, CA: Greenwood Press.

Keough, Sara Beth. 2007. "Constructing a Canadian National Identity: Conceptual Explorations and Examples in Newfoundland Music." *Material Culture* 39 (2): 43–52.

Klassen, Doreen Helen. 1989. *Singing Mennonite: Low German Songs of the Mennonites.* Winnipeg: University of Manitoba Press.
- 1995. "From 'Getting the Words Out' to 'Enjoying the Music': Musical Transitions among Canadian Mennonite Brethren." In *Bridging Troubled Waters: The Mennonite Brethren at Mid-twentieth Century*, edited by Paul Toews, 227–46, 285–90. Fresno, CA: Historical Commission, Mennonite Brethren Church.
- 2010. "'I Guess We Should Use Some Drums': Negotiating Applied Ethnomusicology in a Mennonite Intercultural Context." In Epp et al., *Sound in the Lands*, 67–101.

Klassen, Judith. 2005. "Rebel with a Cause: Innovation and Grace in the Music of a Reinfeld Boy." In Epp and Weaver, *Sound in the Land*, 112–24.

Klymasz, Robert B. 1972. "'Sounds You Never Before Heard': Ukrainian Country Music in Western Canada." *Ethnomusicology* 16 (3): 372–80.
- 1989. *The Ukrainian Folk Ballad in Canada.* New York, NY: AMS Press.

Klymasz, Robert B., and Canadian Museum of Civilization. 1999. *Musique et chansons ukrainiennes de l'ouest canadien / Ukrainian Folk Music from Western Canada.* Hull, QC: Canadian Museum of Civilization.

Kobayashi, Kim Noriko. 2006. "Asian Women Kick Ass: A Study of Gender Issues within Canadian Kumi-Daiko." *Canadian Folk Music Bulletin / Bulletin de musique folklorique canadienne* 40 (1): 1–11.

Koskoff, Ellen, ed. 2001. *The Garland Encyclopedia of World Music*, Vol. 3, *The United States and Canada.* New York, NY: Garland Publishers (available electronically).

Labelle, Ronald. 2009. "La chanson traditionnelle dans l'Acadie contemporaine." In *Acadians and Cajuns: The Politics and Culture of French Minorities in North America,* edited by Ursula Mathis-Moser and Gunter Bischof, 183–90. Innsbruck, Austria: Innsbruck University Press.

Lederman, Anne. 2009. "Métis Fiddling: Found or Lost?" In *Histoires et identités: homage à Gabriel Dumont / Métis Histories and Identities: A Tribute to Gabriel Dumont*, edited by Denis Gagnon, Denis Combet, and Lise Gaboury-Diallo, 365–75. Winnipeg, MB: Presses universitaires de Saint-Boniface.

– 2010. "Aboriginal Fiddling in the North: The Two Traditions." In Russell and Guigné, *Crossing Over*, 3: 130–47.

– 2013. "Aboriginal Fiddling: The Scottish Connection." In *Irish and Scottish Encounters with Indigenous Peoples*, edited by Graeme Morton and David A. Wilson, 223–41. Montreal & Kingston: McGill-Queen's University Press.

Le Guével, Yves. 1999. "L'implantation de l'accordéon au Québec: Des origines aux années 1950." *Bulletin Mnémo* 4 (1). Accessed 4 February 2018. http://www.mnemo.qc.ca/spip/spip.php?article33,

Levine, Victoria Lindsay, and Dylan Robinson. 2019. *Music and Modernity among First Peoples of North America*. Middletown, CT: Wesleyan University Press.

MacDonald, Michael. 2008. "'The Best Laid Plans of Marx and Men': Mitch Podolak, Revolution, and the Winnipeg Folk Festival." *Ethnologies* 30 (2): 73–91.

MacKinnon, Ian. 2008. "Protest Song and Verse in Cape Breton Island." *Ethnologies* 30 (2): 33–71.

MacKinnon, Richard. 2009. *Discovering Cape Breton Folklore*. Sydney, NS: Cape Breton University Press.

MacKinnon, Richard, and Lachlan MacKinnon. 2012. "Residual Radicalism: Labour Song-Poems of Industrial Decline." *Ethnologies* 34 (1/2): 273–98.

Markoff, Irene. 2014. "Bulgarian Music in Canada." *The Canadian Encyclopedia*. Accessed 14 January 2018. http://www.thecanadianencyclopedia.ca/en/article/bulgaria-emc/.

Marsh, Charity. 2009. "'Don't Call Me Eskimo': Representation, Mythology, and Hip Hop Culture on Baffin Island." *MUSICultures* 36: 110–29.

Martens, Helen. 1972. "The Music of Some Religious Minorities in Canada." *Ethnomusicology* 16 (3): 372–80.

– 2002. *Hutterite Songs*. Kitchener, ON: Pandora Press.

McDonald, Chris. 2017. "From Stride to Regional Pride? Cape Breton Piano Accompaniment as Musical and Cultural Process." *Ethnomusicology Forum* 26 (2): 193–214.

McDonald, Chris, Richard MacKinnon, and Darcy Campbell, dirs. 2016. *Doug MacPhee and Cape Breton's Celtic Piano Style*. Sydney, NS: Novastream Media.

McDonald, Chris, and Heather Sparling. 2010. "Interpretations of Tradition: From Gaelic Song to Celtic Pop." *Journal of Popular Music Studies* 22 (3): 309–28.

McGee, Timothy J. 1985. *The Music of Canada*. New York, NY: W.W. Norton.

McGuire, Colin. 2015. "The Rhythm of Combat: Understanding the Role of Music in Performances of Traditional Chinese Martial Arts and Lion Dance." *MUSICultures* 42 (1): 1–12.

Mealing, F. Mark. 2001. "Music of the Doukhobors." In Koskoff, *The Garland Encyclopedia of World Music*, 3: 1267–71.

Melin, Mats. 2013. "Step Dancing in Cape Breton and Scotland: Contrasting Contexts and Creative Processes." *MUSICultures* 40 (1): 35–56.
– 2015. *One with the Music: Cape Breton Step Dancing Tradition and Transmission.* Sydney, NS: Cape Breton University Press.
Mooney, Nicola. 2008. "Aaja Nach Lai [Come Dance]: Performing and Practicing Identity among Punjabis in Canada." *Ethnologies* 30 (1): 103–24.
Moreau, Yves. 1990. "Observations on the Recent Widespread Adoption and Adaptation of Bulgarian Folk Music and Dance in North America and Elsewhere." In Witmer, *Ethnomusicology in Canada*, 113–19.
Morey, Carl. 1997. *Music in Canada: A Research and Information Guide.* London and New York: Routledge.
Nahachewsky, Andriy. 2002. "New Ethnicity and Ukrainian Canadian Social Dances." *The Journal of American Folklore* 115 (456): 175–90.
Narváez, Peter. 1995. "Newfoundland Vernacular Song." In *Popular Music: Style and Identity*, edited by Will Straw, Stacey Johnson, Rebecca Sullivan, and Paul Friedlander, 215–19. Montreal, QC: Centre for Research on Canadian Cultural Industries and Institutions.
– 1997. "'She's Gone, Boys': Vernacular Song Responses to the Atlantic Fisheries Crisis." *Canadian Journal for Traditional Music / Revue de musique folklorique canadienne* 25: 1–13.
Nimjee, Ameera. 2015. "Exhibiting Music: Case Studies in Imagining, Performing, and Collecting Sound." *Ethnologies* 37 (1): 153–73.
Osborne, Evelyn. 2007. "Fiddling with Technology: The Effect of Media on Newfoundland Traditional Musicians." *Newfoundland and Labrador Studies: Music Issue* 22 (1): 187–204.
– 2015. "The Most Irish Place in the World? 'Irishness' in the Recorded Folk Music of Newfoundland and Labrador." *MUSICultures* 42 (2): 79–102.
Ostashewski, Marcia. 2001a. "Identity Politics and Western Canadian Ukrainian Musics: Globalizing the Local or Localizing the Global?" *TOPIA: Canadian Journal of Cultural Studies* 6: 63–82.
– 2001b. "Women Playing the Bandura: Challenging Discourses of Nationhood." *Ethnologies* 23 (1): 123–46.
– 2014. "A Song and Dance of Hypermasculinity: Performing Ukrainian Cossacks in Canada." *World of Music* 3 (2): 15–38.
Patterson, Glenn. 2015. "Fiddle Music and the Constitution of Musical Affect on (and away from) the Gaspé Coast: Interpreting Musical Affordance, Motion, and Emotion through Turino's Peircian Framework." *MUSICultures* 42 (2): 19–54.
Patterson, Glenn, and Laura Risk. 2014. "Digitization, Recirculation and Reciprocity: Proactive Archiving for Community and Memory on the Gaspé Coast and Beyond." *MUSICultures* 41 (2): 102–32.
Peacock, Kenneth. 1970. *Songs of the Doukhobors.* Ottawa, ON: National Museum of Man.
Perron, Mathieu. 2004. "Jacques Labrecque et la diffusion de la chanson traditionnelle: Quand le répertoire folklorique prend des airs d'opéra." *Ethnologies* 26 (2): 79–105.

Proctor, George. 1979. *Sources in Canadian Music: A Bibliography of Bibliographies / Les sources de la musique canadienne: une bibliographie des bibliographies*. Sackville, NB: Ralph Pickard Bell Library.

Provost, Monique. 2015. "L'expression matérielle québécoise du djembé africain de culture mandingue: Étude de la fabrication locale d'un objet mondialisé." *Ethnologies* 37 (2): 161–83.

Przybylski, Liz. 2017. "Customs and Duty: Indigenous Hip Hop and the US–Canada Border." *Journal of Borderlands Studies*, 1–20. Online only: https://doi.org/10.1080/08865655.2016.1222880.

Quick, Sarah. 2008. "The Social Poetics of the Red River Jig in Alberta and Beyond: Meaningful Heritage and Emerging Performance." *Ethnologies* 30 (1): 77–101.

– 2010. "Two Models of Métis Fiddling: John Arcand and Andy Dejarlis." In Russell and Guigné, *Crossing Over*, 114–29.

– 2015. "Red River Jigging: 'Traditional,' 'Contemporary,' and in Unexpected Places." *Canadian Folk Magazine / Musique folklorique canadienne* 49 (2/3): 49–53.

Quigley, Colin. 1995. *Music from the Heart: Compositions of a Folk Fiddler*. Athens: University of Georgia Press.

Qureshi, Regula. 1986. "Canada." *Bulletin of the International Council for Traditional Music* 69: 20–3.

Rahn, Jay. 1988. "First Conference on Ethnomusicology in Canada." *Canadian Folk Music Journal* 16: 55–6.

Ramzy, Carolyn. 2015. "Modern Singing Sons of the Pharaohs: Transcriptions and Orientalism in a Digital Coptic Music Collection." *Ethnologies* 37 (1): 65–88.

Ridout, Godfrey, and Talivaldis Kenins. 1984. *Celebration: Essays on Aspects of Canadian Music*. Toronto, ON: Canadian Music Centre.

Risk, Laura. 2013. "The Chop: The Diffusion of an Instrumental Technique across North Atlantic Fiddling Traditions." *Ethnomusicology* 57 (3): 428–54.

Risk, Laura, and Glenn Patterson, co-producers. 2014. *Douglastown: Musique et chanson de la Gaspésie*. Compact disc, Douglas Community Centre DOUG001.

Robinson, Dylan. 2011. "Peaceful Surface, Monstrous Depths: Barbara Pentland and Dorothy Livesay's *The Lake*." In *Opera Indigene: Re/presenting First Nations and Indigenous Cultures*, edited by Pamela Karantonis and Dylan Robinson, 245–57. Burlington, VT: Ashgate Publishing Limited.

Robinson, Dylan, and Keavy Martin, eds. 2016. *Arts of Engagement: Taking Aesthetic Action in and beyond the Truth and Reconciliation Commission of Canada*. Waterloo, ON: Wilfrid Laurier University Press.

Rosenberg, Neil. 1994. "The Canadianization of Newfoundland Folksong; or the Newfoundlandization of Canadian Folksong." *Journal of Canadian Studies* 29 (1): 55–73.

Savard, Louis-Martin. 2015. "Joseph-Thomas LeBlanc et les 'vieilles chansons acadiennes.'" *MUSICultures* 42 (2): 1–18.

Scales, Christopher A. 2012. *Recording Culture: Powwow Music and the Aboriginal Recording Industry on the Northern Plains*. Durham, NC: Duke University Press.

Schafer, R. Murray. 1984. "Canadian Culture: Colonial Culture." In *On Canadian Music*, by R. Murray Schafer, 75–94. Bancroft, ON: Arcana Editions.

Shears, Barry William. 2008. *Dance to the Piper: The Highland Bagpipe in Nova Scotia*. Sydney, NS: Cape Breton University Press.

Smith, Christina. 2007. "Crooked as the Road to Branch: Asymmetry in Newfoundland Dance Music." *Newfoundland and Labrador Studies: Music Issue* 22 (1): 139–64.

Smith, Gordon E. 2005. "*The Canadian Folk Music Journal / The Canadian Journal for Traditional Music – La Revue de musique folklorique canadienne*: Reflections on Thirty Years of Writing about Folk and Traditional Music in Canada." *Canadian Journal for Traditional Music* 32: 1–11.

– 2007. "*The Canadian Folk Music Journal / The Canadian Journal for Traditional Music – La Revue de musique folklorique canadienne*: Some Retrospectives on Writing about Folk and Traditional Music in Canada." In Hoefnagels and G. Smith, *Folk Music, Traditional Music, Ethnomusicology*, 251–61.

Smith, Muriel. 2013. "The Polish Folk Ensembles of Winnipeg: Shaped by Atlantic Cultural Currents." *MUSICultures* 40 (1): 144–77.

Society for Ethnomusicology. 2018. "About Ethnomusicology." Accessed 31 August 2018. https://www.ethnomusicology.org/page/AboutEthnomusicol.

Sparling, Heather. 2011. "Cape Breton Island: Living in the Past? Gaelic Language, Song, and Competition." In *Island Songs: A Global Repertoire*, edited by Godfrey Baldacchino, 49–63. Lanham & Toronto: Scarecrow Press.

– 2014. *Reeling Roosters & Dancing Ducks: Celtic Mouth Music*. Sydney, NS: Cape Breton University Press.

– 2015. "History of the Scotch Four: A Social Step Dance in Cape Breton." *Canadian Folk Magazine / Musique folklorique canadienne* 49 (2/3): 11–18.

– 2017. "Sad and Solemn Requiems: Disaster Songs and Complicated Grief in the Aftermath of Nova Scotia Mining Disasters." In *Singing Death*, edited by Helen Dell and Helen Dickey, 90–104. Abingdon, UK: Routledge.

Stévance, Sophie. 2017. "From Throat Singing to Transcultural Expression: Tanya Tagaq's Katajjaq Musical Signature." In *The Routledge Research Companion to Popular Music and Gender*, edited by Stan Hawkins, 48–62. New York, NY: Taylor and Francis.

Stone, Ruth M. 2014. "Ethnomusicology at the Bend in the Road." *College Music Symposium* 54. https://www.jstor.org/stable/26574371.

Szego, Kati. 2015. "Technology of Inclusion: Redefining and Gendering the 'Ukulele in Atlantic Canada." *MUSICultures* 42 (1): 41–65.

Thompson, Marie. 2006. "The Myth of the Vanishing Cape Breton Fiddler: The Role of a CBC Film in the Cape Breton Fiddle Revival." *Acadiensis* 35 (2): 5–26.

Thorne, Cory. 2007. "Gone to the Mainland and Back Home Again: A Critical Approach to Region, Politics, and Identity in Contemporary Newfoundland Song." *Newfoundland and Labrador Studies* 22 (1): 51–73.

Tremblay, Gynette, and Simone Voyer. 2001. "Quadrille, cotillon, reel, brandy ... : Tout le monde danse!" *Cap-aux-Diamants* 67: 38–44.

Trew, Johanne. 1996. "Ottawa Valley Fiddling: Issues of Identity and Style." *British Journal of Canadian Studies* 11: 339–44.

Tsai, Sija. 2007/08. "Electric Picking, Ethnic Spinning: (Re)Defining the 'Folk' at the Winnipeg Folk Festival." *MUSICultures* 34/35: 71–94.

– 2011. "Public Policy and the Mariposa Folk Festival: Shared Ideals in the 1960s and 1970s." *MUSICultures* 38: 147–58.
Tsai, Sija, and Andrew Hillhouse. 2017. "The Mariposa Folk Festival and the Canadian Singer-Songwriter Tradition." In *The Singer-Songwriter's Handbook*, edited by Justin Williams and Katherine Williams, 147–64. London, UK: Bloomsbury Publishing.
Turnbull, Gillian. 2009. "'Land of the In Between': Nostalgia and the Gentrification of Calgarian Roots Music." *MUSICultures* 36: 22–48.
– 2016. "Authorship and Nostalgia in Contemporary Cowboy Repertoire." *Cultural Studies, Critical Methodologies* 16 (1): 58–67.
Van den Scott, Jeffrey. 2014. "Affirming Identity through Musical Performance in a Canadian Arctic Hamlet." *Canadian Folk Music / Musique folklorique canadienne* 48 (2): 1–5.
Warwick, Jacqueline. 2000. "'Make Way for the Indian': Bhangra Music and South Asian Presence in Toronto." *Popular Music and Society* 24 (2): 25–44.
Weaver, Carol Ann, Doreen Helen Klassen, and Judith Klassen, editors. 2015. *Sound in the Land: Music and the Environment*, special issue of *The Conrad Grebel Review* 33 (2).
Witmer, Robert, ed. 1990. *Ethnomusicology in Canada: Proceedings of the First Conference, Toronto, 1988*. Toronto, ON: Institute of Canadian Music.
– 1990. "Preface." In Witmer, *Ethnomusicology in Canada*, xi–xiii.
Wolters-Fredlund, Benita. 2002. "Leftist, Jewish, and Canadian Identities Voiced in the Repertoire of the Toronto Jewish Folk Choir, 1939–1959." *Canadian Journal for Traditional Music / Revue de musique folklorique canadienne* 29: 19–31.
– 2005. "'We Shall Be Better Canadians by Being Conscious Jews': Multiculturalism and the Construction of Canadian Identity in the Toronto Jewish Folk Choir." *Intersections* 25 (1–2): 187–201.
Wrazen, Louise. 2007a. "Privileging Narratives: Singing, the Polish Tatras, and Canada." *Intersections* 27 (2): 60–80.
– 2007b. "Relocating the Tatras: Place and Music in Górale Identity and Imagination." *Ethnomusicology* 51 (2): 185–204.
– 2010. "Daughters of Tradition, Mothers of Invention: Music, Teaching, and Gender in Evolving Contexts." *Yearbook for Traditional Music* 42: 41–61.
– 2013. "Marysia's Voice: Defining Home through Song in Poland and Canada." In *Women Singers in Global Contexts: Music, Biography, Identity*, edited by Ruth Hellier, 146–60. Urbana: University of Illinois Press.
Wright-McLeod, Brian. 2005. *The Encyclopedia of Native Music: More than a Century of Recordings from Wax Cylinder to the Internet*. Tucson: University of Arizona Press.

Part One

Transforming Musical Traditions

Introduction
Anna Hoefnagels

"Tradition" is a term that has generated much discussion – and disagreement – among academics and artists. Often imbued with a sense of long-standing history and connections between generations, traditions are also recognized as responsive to cultural, geographic, and temporal changes. In ethnomusicological inquiry, as in many other fields, scholars have engaged in research examining various music "traditions" and genres. Inspired by the work of Eric Hobsbawm and Terence Ranger on "invented traditions" (1983), these scholars have queried the origins of these cultural expressions and their designation as "traditional" (see, for example, Coplan 1991, Finnegan 1991, Phillips and Schochet 2004). As David Coplan wrote in 1991, "Tradition is a core concept common to ethnology, folklore, and ethnomusicology, and its use has remained current and indispensable despite its inherent contradictions, doubtful empirical status, and ideological entanglements" (36).

Although many cultural expressions and practices in Canada have a long-standing history in this country, earning them the moniker "traditional," others have arrived with more recent immigrants. Performers and audiences alike conceive of and consume these artistic practices in various ways, considering them to be traditional, new, or innovative, and mixtures of old and new, local and "from away." As the chapters in this section demonstrate, internal and external factors continually shape the cultural expressions found in Canada and the ways that we understand and think about those practices. These chapters query the ways in which music and dance have been showcased and performed for different audiences, and together they demonstrate the transformations that various music and dance practices have undergone, presently and historically.

Contemporary musical practices in Canada are very much influenced by changes in technology, media, and audience demographics. Expectations around a musical performance and presentation of a particular repertoire can have a standardizing effect, yet as the chapters in this section demonstrate, it is through modifications and reconfigurations that songs and dances, whether heard and experienced live or over the airwaves, continue to resonate with audiences young and old; changes in media and advances in technology have also shaped the ways in which music and dance are both performed and consumed across Canada. The chapters featured in this section engage with processes of continuity and change, demonstrating how music and dance practices can transform in relation to changing audiences and platforms for performance.

The first chapter in this section, Laura Risk's "*Le bon vieux temps*: The Veillée in Twentieth-Century Quebec," focuses on the *veillée*, an informal social gathering common in rural Quebec, that has also been idealized in staged performances to represent traditional French-Canadian identity. Risk argues for the *veillée* as a culturally resonant space that, in the late nineteenth century, served as a representation of an idealized rural lifestyle associated with a conservative national identity and, in the twentieth, grouped a diverse collection of musical materials (themselves associated with that idealized lifestyle) under the genre of folklore. The chapter historicizes the *veillée* in twentieth-century Quebec through three case studies: early staged *veillées* in Montreal in the 1910s and 1920s; informal music-making on the Gaspé peninsula in the mid-century; and the popular television show *Soirée Canadienne*, which ran from 1960 to 1983. Risk demonstrates how a historical social gathering has become iconic of "traditional" Québécois culture and how its transformations have been shaped according to different agendas.

In "Kathak in Canada: Classical and Contemporary," Margaret Walker engages directly with questions of "tradition," examining the ways in which Kathak, the "classical" dance of North India, is presented to Canadian audiences as an "authentic" art form, even as it continues a long history of syncretism and hybridity. She explores tensions between tradition, innovation, classicism, and authenticity, particularly vis-à-vis so-called mainstream genres, in the work of performers and choreographers of Canadian-based Kathak, who often struggle to be considered professionals. Kathak dance has been part of the Canadian cultural scene since the 1970s, yet its syncretic origins and flexible movement vocabulary, and its South Asian, Canadian, and transnational connections, continue to complicate the classification and marketing of this genre.

Heather Sparling's chapter, "Taking the Piss Out: Presentational and Participatory Elements in the History of the Cape Breton Milling Frolic," provides another example of how historical cultural practices are reimagined and presented to contemporary audiences. Engaging with Thomas Turino's model of participatory/presentational music practices (2008), Sparling reflects on the changing meanings and purposes of music and its accompanying activities through a case study of Cape Breton milling frolics (a labour activity with Scottish roots at which songs were sung to accompany the pounding of cloth). Documenting changes in practice over the last one hundred years from a women-only labour activity, to one involving both women and men, to a tourist attraction, to the primary public context for Gaelic socializing, Sparling assesses whether and how Cape Breton milling frolics have shifted from primarily participatory to presentational events.

Through her careful analysis of a vibrant fiddle tradition that blends Acadian, Scottish, and Québécois elements, Meghan Forsyth examines the intricate web of influences and cultural alliances that define both the lived experience of the Acadian inhabitants of les Îles-de-la-Madeleine, Quebec and its traditional fiddling practices. Cultivated in private settings and, increasingly, in the public sphere, this music is renowned for its tune variability and improvisatory embellishments. Forsyth's "Improvising on the Margins: Tradition and Musical Agency in les Îles-de-la-Madeleine" examines the motivations behind, and expectations of, creativity in contemporary performance, as well as the sociocultural and socioecological factors – from the sea-faring life to the global market – that have contributed to a culture of creativity and individual agency.

Similarly engaging with questions of history, tradition, and transformation is the final chapter in this section, Chris McDonald's "The Continuities and Legacies of English Song Traditions in Nova Scotia." Through an exploration of the legacy of English folk song collecting in Nova Scotia, McDonald assesses the political and social reasons for collecting and promoting folkloric music in the province, with attention to the roles this music played in building tourism and heritage discourses, and reconstructing affirmative identities in the face of economic decline. McDonald describes how several generations of Nova Scotian musicians have used this folk song legacy, as well as the east coast's reputation for its preservation of folk traditions, at various times emulating the canon for cultural reasons, exploiting its value as a recognizable and marketable commodity, and rejecting it entirely.

Each chapter in this section articulates a specific history and musical practice associated with a particular cultural community in Canada. Together these microhistories engage with notions of tradition, transformation, performance choices, and audience expectations, demonstrating the wide range of considerations for performers and scholars of various musical practices. These case studies challenge readers to query "tradition," audience expectations, and reception, as well as the implications of changing contexts and goals for performance.

References

Coplan, David B. 1991. "Ethnomusicology and the Meaning of Tradition." In *Ethnomusicology and Modern Music History*, edited by Stephen Blum, Philip V. Bohlman, and Daniel M. Neuman, 35–48. Urbana and Chicago: University of Illinois Press.

Finnegan, Ruth. 1991. "Tradition, but What Tradition and for Whom?" The Milman Parry Lecture on Oral Tradition for 1989–90. *Oral Tradition* 6 (1): 104–24.

Hobsbawm, Eric, and Terence Ranger, eds. 1983. *The Invention of Tradition*. Cambridge, UK: Cambridge University Press.

Phillips, Mark Salber, and Gordon Schochet, eds. 2004. *Questions of Tradition*. Toronto, ON: University of Toronto Press.

Laura Risk

Chapter 2

Le bon vieux temps: The Veillée in Twentieth-Century Quebec

31 December 2008, 11 pm: Radio-Canada Television's live broadcast of "Bye Bye 2008" (Morrisette and Cloutier 2008)

A clock tolls as the iconic rhythm of traditional Québécois music – quarter-eighth-eighth, quarter-eighth-eighth – ramps up. Centre stage is a long table with a roast on a platter and tall candles. A glissando from an invisible piano leads into a fast I-V-I-V vamp and some of the dozen "guests" around the table start to tap their feet double-time; others clap and whoop. A fiddler, the only on-stage musician, plays a fast A minor break and the host, actress Véronique Cloutier, rises. "Ce sont les gens de ce pays,"[1] she sings, and everyone responds, "Ce sont les gens de ce pays," as two circus artists walk on their hands on the tabletop and do simultaneous backflips.

The song is "Mettez votre parka," by the legendary poet and songwriter Gilles Vigneault; the off-stage backup band is La Bottine Souriante, with its distinctive mix of fiddle, accordion, rhythm section, and brass section. Next are brief sung cameos by the humorist Cathy Gauthier, Marie-Élaine Thibert of Star Académie fame, television animator Joël Legendre, and actress Sylvie Moreau. Moreau sings over a fast-paced disco groove while sinuous, upside-down circus artists grasp at her with their legs, then Olympic diver Alexandre Despatie backflips into a shallow pool of water and dances heavily from one foot to the other, elbows out. The band repeats an eight-bar fragment behind a video montage of Véronique Cloutier dancing: in a restaurant with a fiddler and pianist, her mouth in an "O" of surprise; with firefighters; on top of the Mont-Royal; with babies; in a bookstore; onstage at a rock concert; by a mall Christmas tree; outside at night with *revellers in Santa Claus hats. Everywhere the dancing is the same: exaggerated stomping, elbows out and swinging, lots of turns by the elbow.*

Back at the live show, seven people dance on the tabletop and the pop duo Alfa Rococo sings. Many of the guests have taken off their shoes and are thwacking them together in time as "Bob la Cuillère" (Robert Gauthier, a 2008 finalist on the French show "Incroyable Talent") step-dances out from the wings and plays spoons on his legs, Véronique Cloutier's lap, and comedian Jean-François Mercier's head.

For over a century, the term *"veillée"* has had a dual meaning in Quebec. On the one hand, it is an informal gathering at which family, friends, and neighbours play cards, share news, sing, play music, dance, and generally entertain one other. On the other, it is an idealized performance of those gatherings and, as such, a powerful means of representing traditional French-Canadian identity. In this chapter, I argue that the *veillée* is a culturally resonant space that, in the late nineteenth century, served as a symbol of an idealized rural lifestyle associated with a conservative national identity and, in the twentieth, grouped a diverse collection of musical materials (themselves associated with that idealized lifestyle) under the genre of folk, or traditional, music.[2] I historicize the *veillée* in twentieth-century Quebec via two case studies: early staged *veillées* in Montreal in the 1910s and 1920s; and informal music making on the Gaspé peninsula in the mid-twentieth century.

"Bye Bye" is an annual New Year's Eve broadcast of sketch comedy on Radio-Canada Television. The *veillée* that opened "Bye Bye 2008" is, in many regards, a compendium of caricatured clichés of traditional Québécois music: the holiday season setting, the excessive jolliness, the incessant and uncoordinated foot-tapping, the out-of-tune group singing on the *chansons à répondre* (call-and-response songs), the party-happy fiddler, the repetitive melodic fragment that accompanies the video montage, the ungainly dancing itself. This is traditional music restricted to the short spectrum from ossified to ludicrous: a farcical backdrop to a variety show of circus acts and pop, television, and sports stars. Yet even as "Bye Bye 2008" excited controversy in the early days of 2009 – Cloutier and head writer Louis Morrisette eventually issued a formal apology for several sketches deemed racist (Radio-Canada 2009) – this opening *veillée* was unremarked upon. Why this sort of caricatured representation of a traditional *veillée* is not only accepted in Quebec but often expected is a central concern of this chapter.

The opening sketch of "Bye Bye 2008" sits squarely in a tradition of staged *veillées* that began in Montreal in 1919 and was grounded in the nationalist literary movements of the late nineteenth and early twentieth centuries. These early *veillées* launched a century of commercial representations of rural music making on stage, radio, television, and in recordings. A photo of the set of *Les bonnes soirées canadiennes* on CHRC radio (Quebec City, c. 1939) shows several generations dressed in old-fashioned clothing and gathered around a long table, a fiddler and an accordionist to one side (Du Berger, Mathieu, and Roberge 1997, 143). The 1964 LP *Noël et le jour de l'an avec la famille Soucy* opens with the clink of dishes and a child's voice asking for more roast, before launching into an A side of *chansons à répondre* and a B side of dance tunes (Fernando Soucy et al., Dominion 48013). The television shows *Chez Isidore* (CFTM Montreal, 1960–62) and *Soirée Canadienne* (CHLT Sherbrooke, 1960–83) were both set as *veillées* (Labbé 1995, 17–18, 229; "Soucy, Isidore" 2007); "Bye Bye 2008" neatly prefaced Joël Legendre's cameo with a video clip of a ten-year-old Legendre singing the same song on *Soirée Canadienne*. Richard Handler (1984) describes a folk dance show at the 1978 Quebec City Winter Carnival that featured "family revellers" in a "traditional farmhouse interior, dominated by a painted chimney, hearth, and grandfather clock" – all on stage at one end of a hockey arena (58).

This long history of staged *veillées* has resulted in a wealth of associated imagery, including the exaggerated elbow swinging and comical spoons playing shown in "Bye Bye 2008." Kitsch media representations aside, however, the *veillée* remains a touchstone of participatory traditional music activity. "S'il y a une affaire qu'on a essayé de démontrer ici dans le festival, c'était justement [que] tout le monde pouvait faire de la musique,"[3] declared organizer André Gladu at the opening of "La Veillée des veillées," the final concert of the 1975 Montreal folk music festival "Les Veillées d'automne" (Gosselin 1976; see also Berthiaume 2006). The Montreal-based Société pour la promotion de la danse traditionnelle québécoise runs an amateur music school called L'École des arts de la veillée[4] that currently offers weekly instructional courses in fiddle, accordion, song, harmonica, accompaniment guitar, dance calling, step dance, and social dance (SPDTQ 2015). In March 2015, the Quebec minister of culture and communications designated the *veillée de danse* – an evening of square sets and other group social dances in a public venue – an official item of intangible cultural heritage in the province (CQPV [Conseil québécois du patrimoine vivant] 2015).

Today's traditional musicians and dancers ground their work in the musical and extra-musical traits of the *veillée* in order to push the genre in new directions. Québécois touring bands such as Le Vent du Nord, De Temps Antan, Genticorum, and La Bottine Souriante perform the repertoire of the idealized *veillée* – a combination of songs (primarily *chansons à répondre*) and instrumental dance tunes – in a professional, festival-ready format; their choice of repertoire grounds them in the genre of traditional Québécois music even when their arrangements reference other styles. The quartet Maz goes further, combining the rhythmic and melodic structures of traditional music with sounds and techniques from jazz, electronica, and contemporary art music: electric guitar, synthesizers, programming, sound manipulation, complex chord progressions and intricate formal structures, riff-based composition, spoken word, and improvised solos. In an interview for *Le Nunavoix*, bandleader Marc Maziade describes the band's music as "une multiplication de points de vue":[5] an exploration of, and investment in, traditional music in Quebec that presumes a repertoire open to new melodic, harmonic, and textural forms; new formal arranging techniques; and improvisation (15 June 2016, 1). This understanding of tradition as a creative resource is a far cry from "Bye Bye 2008," which might be taken as an extreme example of what Maziade terms the "folklorisation" of traditional music (Maziade and Godbout-Castonguay 2014).[6]

In this chapter, I historicize staged *veillées* in Quebec as a first step toward understanding how such dissimilar, yet linked, uses of traditional music and dance as "Bye Bye 2008" and Maz may coexist in the early twenty-first century. I argue that early staged *veillées* shaped cultural understandings of traditional music in Quebec and laid the foundations for a century of mediated representations of traditional music and dance. The first part of this chapter describes staged *veillées* from 1919 to 1922. This narrow date range includes the first staged *veillées*, organized primarily by Édouard-Zotique Massicotte, Marius Barbeau, and the Quebec Section of the American Folklore Society, and concludes just after the start of Conrad Gauthier's long-running series, the "Veillées du bon vieux temps."[7] I document over two dozen staged *veillées* and related events. Many of these theatrical performances referenced what we might term the "prototypical *veillée*": a rural gathering of family and neighbours, all likely subsistence farmers, fishermen, lumbermen, or homemakers, who entertained themselves with stories, songs, fiddle tunes, step dances, and group social dances. Such gatherings existed both in fact (I document several in the second part of this chapter) and in the cultural imagination.

I argue that writers, folklorists, and promoters used the imagery of the *veillée* to articulate[8] – to use Stuart Hall's term – a variety of musical repertoires to ideologically charged discourses of tradition and national identity.

The repertoires of early-twentieth-century staged *veillées* – songs, social and step-dancing, instrumental dance tunes, and stories and legends – were not all associated with discourses of tradition and identity at the same time. I argue that text-based materials (songs, stories, and legends) were articulated to national identity in the mid-nineteenth century, whereas dancing and the accompanying instrumental music took most of the second half of the nineteenth century to shift from morally suspect behaviours to celebrated traditions. Although these articulations were made manifest in the staged *veillées* of the late 1910s and 1920s, I argue that they originated in the literature of the late nineteenth and early twentieth centuries.

Running parallel to this commercial activity were non-commercial, rural social gatherings centred on music and dance – that is, *veillées*. In the second part of this chapter, I draw on ethnographic interviews to describe several such "unstaged" *veillées* on the Gaspé Peninsula from the 1940s through the 1970s. My intent is not to position these gatherings as somehow more sincere than staged *veillées*, or as some sort of survival of an earlier era. Rather, I interrogate the nearly nonexistent boundary between what we would retrospectively term folk and popular repertoires at these unstaged *veillées*.

Citationality

Traditional music evokes the (imagined) musical past of a given locale; in Quebec, that past has been encapsulated in the *veillée* for over a century. Yet the sounds and contexts of the genre have changed dramatically over that time. How do we square this ongoing flux with the implied stability of a traditional music linked to a presumably fixed point of origin?

David Brackett (2016) argues for citationality – the possibility of being cited – as requisite to the formation of a musical genre. A listener interprets and categorizes a new musical text through its musical and contextual references to existing genres, and this process shifts (perhaps imperceptibly) the borders of those genres. This model of genre as iterative belies any attempt at locating a genre's origins; since every potential prototype for a genre cites previously existing genres, "the attempt to establish a prototypical example of a genre that functions as a point of origin then appears as an act of constant deferral." Certain genres do reference such prototypical points of origin, as this chapter demonstrates. However, as Brackett notes, the designation of a "text or a group of texts" as the "origin of a genre" is always a retrospective act; a prototypical point of origin is "figured on the basis of its citation as the origin in the present" (13). When musicians and listeners in the field of traditional music point to the prototypical *veillée* as a point of origin for the genre, it tells us next to nothing about how the actors in those prototypical *veillées* understood themselves, their actions, and their music making. Rather, it indicates a collective agreement by present-day musicians and listeners to associate certain sounds, lyrics, images, performer personae, and musical rhetoric – all associated with the prototypical *veillée* – with the generic label "traditional" or "folk."

The *veillée* is thus shorthand for a diverse mix of repertoires (*chansons à répondre*, fiddle tunes); instrumentation (fiddles, accordions, foot-tapping); dance forms (step dances, certain group social dances); playing styles (certain vocal styles, fiddle and accordion techniques); and extra-musical markers (oral transmission, physical setting). To use at least some of those generic markers is to affiliate a musical sound or an event with the prototypical *veillée*, and so to stake out space within the generic boundaries of folk or traditional music. Conversely, it is the stability of the *veillée* as a generic referent and the richness of its musical and extra-musical evocations that have allowed the genre of folk or traditional music to include such a wide range of musical, performative, and participatory contexts. Beyond the generic markers of the *veillée*, most everything else – harmonic language, additional instrumentation, accompaniment, and arrangement style – is up for grabs.

Veillées on Stage and on the Printed Page

Several scholars have recently addressed early staged *veillées* in Montreal. In search of the origins of the present-day concept of "patrimonialisation," Diane Joly documents the behind-the-scenes negotiations between Massicotte, Barbeau, and Victor Morin, president of the Société historique de Montréal, for the first staged *veillées* in Montreal, at the Bibliothèque Saint-Sulpice on 18 March and 24 April 1919 (2012, 357–63). Joly also briefly contrasts the staged *veillées* of the Quebec Section of the American Folklore Society and those produced by actor and singer Conrad Gauthier (369–72). Daniel Guilbert argues that these two sets of *veillées* were substantially different in intended audience and musical content: the Quebec Section *veillées* targeted an elite, educated audience and promoted folk melodies as fodder for a new nationalist school of art music composition, whereas Gauthier's *veillées* were populist recreations of rural folkways for an urban, working-class audience (2010–12). Luc Bellemare documents Gauthier's *veillées* from 1922, focusing on connections between the stage show, the Montreal radio station CKAC, and the local sponsor, Living Room Furniture (2012).

In the following sections, I use archival sources to deepen these descriptions and correct some misconceptions.[9] The table in the appendix lists all staged *veillées* from March 1919 to November 1922 for which I have documentary evidence.

Early Staged Veillées

Massicotte proposed the *veillée* concept to Barbeau after a presentation by the latter to the Société historique de Montréal on 29 May 1918. Other members of the society were also keen on the idea and they formed a small organizational team, with Barbeau consulting from afar. Massicotte was charged with finding performers. The first *veillée* was originally scheduled for St Catherine's Day, 25 November 1918, but was delayed to March of the following year, in part because of Barbeau's initial unresponsiveness (Joly 2012, 357–8; "Les Mémoires de Marius Barbeau," Canadian Museum of History Archives, fonds Carmen Roy, Box 624, f9, 67–8).

For Barbeau, Massicotte, and the Quebec Section of the American Folklore Society, this first *veillée* was both an outreach activity and a fundraising opportunity. Between May 1918 and early 1919, Barbeau had collected 1,300 song variants, fifty-five fiddle tunes, eight sung dances, twenty-two stories, and forty anecdotes, and Massicotte had collected some 460 songs, expressions, and popular rhymes (Barbeau 1919, 182; *La Presse*, 27 March 1919, 9). The American Folklore Society had published one French-Canadian issue per year in 1916 and 1917, and would do so again in 1919 and 1920, but these required financial support from the Quebec Section (Nowry 1995, 176–7, 192). Too much material and not enough money – the solution was to go public with their findings.

The target audience for the March 1919 *veillée*: the educated classes who, "mieux avertie, partagerait peut-être notre profonde appréciation des trésors cachés du terroir canadien, et nous aiderait à triompher de résistances qui nuisent au progrès de nos travaux folkloriques."[10] Such support was by no means assured, however. More typical, according to Barbeau, were "l'indifférence générale" and "l'hostilité hautaine" of certain intellectuals, including an unnamed colleague of the Royal Society of Canada who had reproached Barbeau for seeking to preserve "ces niaiseries" that others had sought to do away with for decades[11] (Barbeau and Massicotte 1920, 1).

In spite of these naysayers – or perhaps to win them over – Massicotte and Barbeau filled the program with *exécutants du terroir*: singers, a fiddler, and a dancer, all with no formal training and from agricultural or working-class backgrounds (ibid., 4, 8–11).[12] Barbeau was concerned about the reception of these performers, whose style he described as rough, naive, and harsh. Would an untoward gesture or unusual musical ornament shock an audience accustomed to the conservatory and the opera? He considered their performance style akin to slag in an ironworks, a sort of residual waste that could be burned off to leave behind the pure metal of the musical texts (ibid., 2–3). He and Massicotte thus proceeded cautiously. They hired a professional monologist rather than risk "un vrai conteur du crû"[13] (ibid.). They included artists "qui sauraient rehausser le ton du programme":[14] trained singers and pianists performing art music arrangements of folk melodies, or *folklore artistique* ("Les Mémoires de Marius Barbeau," Canadian Museum of History Archives, fonds Carmen Roy, Box 624, f9, 68). The overwhelmingly positive audience reaction to the first soirée seems to have taken them quite by surprise.

Massicotte and Barbeau set the scene to transport the audience out of the city and into an idealized and endangered past, and the crowd signed on wholeheartedly. With the stage furnished as a rustic home interior and the singer of voyageur songs dressed as a lumberman, the "résurrection du passé" was complete, and many felt "un ravissement complet"[15] as the evening re-awakened childhood memories (Barbeau and Massicotte 1920, 3). Reviewer Louis Claude later recalled the first *veillée* audiences as "conquise, emballée même"[16] and applauding frenetically. In response to public demand, Massicotte and Barbeau organized a second *veillée* on 24 April 1919. Large numbers were turned away at the door on both evenings (*La revue moderne*, 15 July 1920, 23).

Following on these successes, Massicotte and Barbeau organized over a dozen additional *veillées* between 1919 and late 1920 (appendix). Massicotte usually took the lead on Montreal *veillées*, held at the Monument-National from June 1919, and Barbeau on out-of-town *veillées*, including performances in Quebec City, Ottawa, and New York City (figure 2.1).

For St Catherine's Day, 25 November 1920, Massicotte planned the most ambitious *veillée* to date on the theme "La vie des voyageurs." The first half of the program used song to follow lumbermen from hiring and departure,

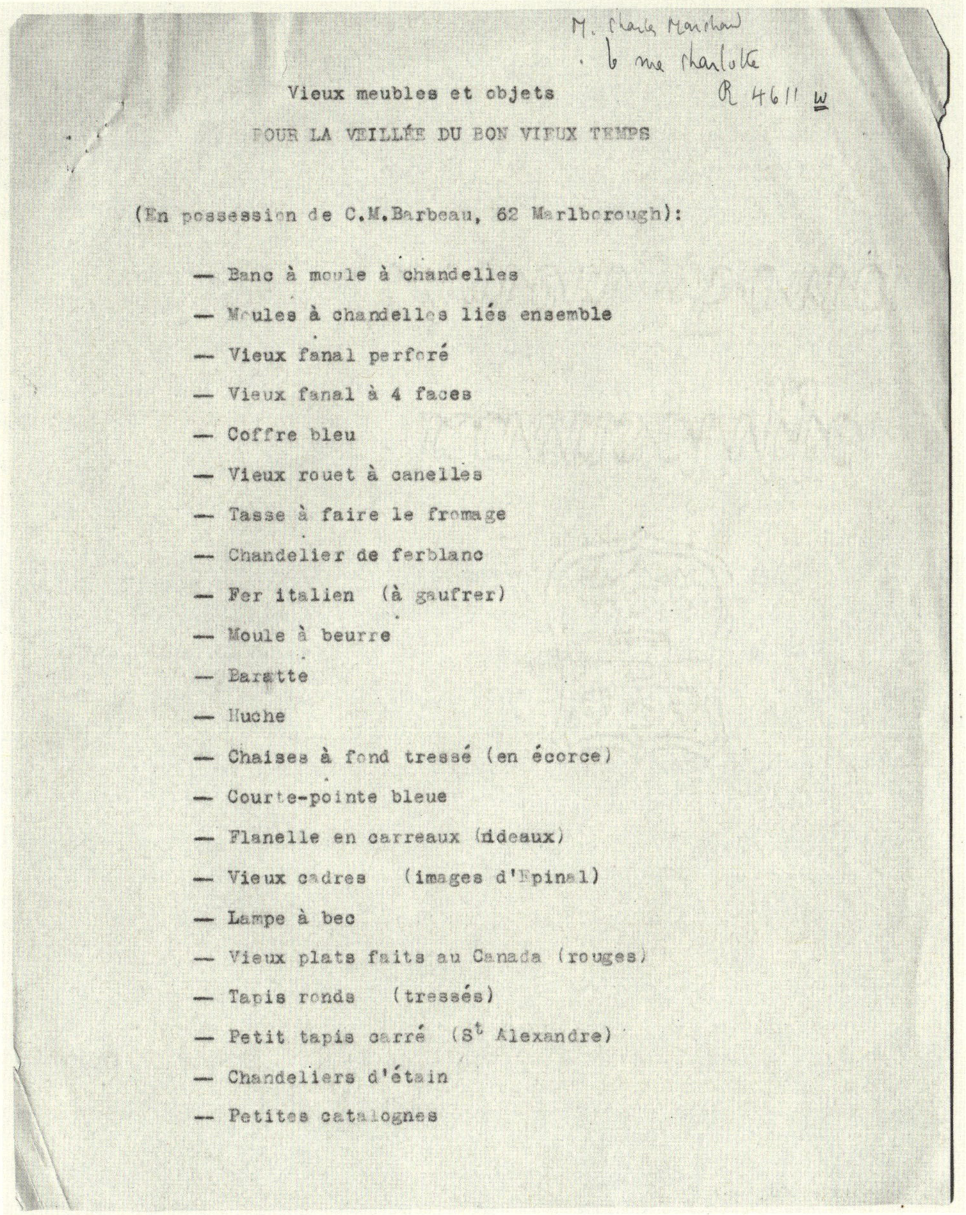

M. Charles Marchand
6 rue Charlotte
R 4611 W

Vieux meubles et objets

POUR LA VEILLÉE DU BON VIEUX TEMPS

(En possession de C.M.Barbeau, 62 Marlborough):

— Banc à moule à chandelles
— Moules à chandelles liés ensemble
— Vieux fanal perforé
— Vieux fanal à 4 faces
— Coffre bleu
— Vieux rouet à canelles
— Tasse à faire le fromage
— Chandelier de ferblanc
— Fer italien (à gaufrer)
— Moule à beurre
— Baratte
— Huche
— Chaises à fond tressé (en écorce)
— Courte-pointe bleue
— Flanelle en carreaux (rideaux)
— Vieux cadres (images d'Epinal)
— Lampe à bec
— Vieux plats faits au Canada (rouges)
— Tapis ronds (tressés)
— Petit tapis carré (St Alexandre)
— Chandeliers d'étain
— Petites catalognes

Figure 2.1 | List of stage furnishings for *veillées* in Ottawa, 5–7 May 1920.

through the measured rhythm of rowing, to Saturday night in the lumber camp and the return home. The second half featured twelve Gaspesians performing group dances from their home parishes of Rivière-Madeleine, Rivière-au-Renard, L'Anse-au-Griffon, and Percé. The program was repeated on 2 December 1920, and the 800-seat theatre filled to capacity both evenings: a measure, according to *La Presse*, of the number of people "qui ont reçu la leçon de patriotisme qui se dégage des évocations des choses du passé, des chansons, des contes et des danses de nos pères"[17] (3 December 1920, 13). Audience members at the 25 November show ingested this "patriotic lesson" not only metaphorically through sound and sight, but literally, as they ate free St Catherine's Day taffy (*tire*) distributed by Montreal businessman Ludger Gravel.

What began as an experiment had turned into a highly successful theatrical formula. "Retentissantes ... " wrote Gustave Baudouin, "partout, on désire les entendre et l'accueil est enthousiaste"[18] (*L'action française*, March 1921, 167). The Monument-National *veillées* attracted a cross-section of the urban population well beyond Barbeau and Massicotte's original target of the educated elite. Some spectators were young and hoped to learn about the customs of their forebears, while others were older and recalled times gone by. *La Presse* describes a raucous, presumably working-class crowd that enthusiastically tapped out the rhythms of the fiddle tunes and songs with their heels in April 1920 and required a police presence at entrances and exits in November 1920. Yet the audience also contained many lovers of art music who applauded enthusiastically for the *folklore artistique* portions of the evening. I explore these divergent audiences and interests further in the "*Folklore artistique*" and "*Imitations burlesques*" sections below. First, however, I ask how the diverse elements presented on stage at the *veillées* – song, stories, dance, instrumental dance music – all came to be subsumed under the label folklore.

Prior to 1919 the term "folklore" rarely occurred in Quebec periodicals.[19] Within two years, however, and presumably as a result of the Quebec Section's *veillées*, folklore was an established genre in the cultural imagination of Quebec's literate classes. Henri Miro's arrangement of the song "Veillée rustique" was a "chanson du terroir" in *Le Passe-temps* in 1913 and 1915 but a "Chanson du folklore canadien" in 1920 (1 February 1913, 21; 18 December 1915, 481; 11 December 1920, 533). On 29 November 1919, *Le Passe-temps* invited readers to submit "folklore" to a new feature entitled "Le Coin des poètes" (489). By July-August 1921, the women's magazine *La Canadienne* had rhetorically set the preservation and performance of folklore as "une œuvre patriotique"[20] (8).

That the genre of folklore coalesced so quickly and with no documented opposition suggests the extreme legibility of the label "folklore" as a means of grouping together these texts. Using Brackett's framework of citationality, we might say that these staged *veillées* invited audiences to relate "sounds, lyrics, images, performer personae, [and] musical rhetoric" to the generic label folklore (2016, 13); that educated audiences did so with such enthusiasm and ease suggests that the genre already existed in some sense in their cultural imagination (though not necessarily as "folklore"). In the following section, I argue that this pre-existing genre was neither on the stage nor in the rural home, but on the printed page.

The Veillée in Literature

Beginning in the mid-nineteenth century, French-Canadian songs and legends were collected, published, and reworked as the textual embodiment of a national, language-based identity. Publications such as Henri-Raymond Casgrain's *Légendes canadiennes* (1861), Joseph-Charles Taché's *Forestiers et voyageurs, mœurs et légendes canadiennes* ([1863] 1884), François-Alexandre-Hubert LaRue's book-length "Les Chansons populaires et historiques du Canada" (1863–65), and Ernest Gagnon's *Chansons populaires du Canada* (1865–67) were the French-Canadian expression of a Western European collecting movement that presumed that folk texts had been shaped by the physical attributes of the land and the character of the people who inhabited it. As such, folk songs and stories were ideal carriers of national identity within literary contexts. From the mid-nineteenth century until well into the twentieth, French-Canadian authors incorporated or referenced folk texts in nationalist writings celebrating the beauties of the countryside, the healthful purity of agricultural labour, the wholesome innocence of rural values and traditions, and – at a time of massive French-Canadian out-migration – the importance of remaining on the land (Smith 1995; Lemire and Saint-Jacques 1996, 413; Lemire and Saint-Jacques 1999, 381, 385; Saint-Jacques and Lemire 2005, 382–91).

Unlike songs and stories, instrumental music and dance had no part in this text-based expression of national identity. In mid-nineteenth-century texts, fiddles are sometimes simply part of the decor but are more often viewed with suspicion. In *Charles Guérin* (Chauveau [1846] 1853), two fiddles hang next to horsewhips, fishing gear, and hunting rifles but never sound, even during the Mid-Lent house dance (117, 124–5). An 1859 moralistic essay by Paul Stevens uses folk songs as the wholesome entertainment of honest and sober rural folk but the fiddle as the accessory of a debauched lifestyle (*L'Echo du Cabinet de lecture paroissial de Montréal*, 1 May 1859, 152–3).

Such attitudes shifted gradually, but by the last decades of the nineteenth century, authors were penning long, rose-coloured descriptions of rural fiddling and social dancing. Narcisse Faucher de Saint-Maurice's *À la veillée* (1879) opens with an evening of fiddling and dancing hosted by the endearing lumberman Jérôme Tanguay, "*un vrai Canadien du pays*" who is almost vaudevillian in his excesses, his devil-may-care attitude, and his irrational belief that he was born to be a gentleman (5–9, italics in original). Napoléon Legendre's "Le voyageur" includes a description of four homesick lumbermen at a Christmastime *veillée*: "On a vu plusieurs fois, vers la fin de la soirée, ou plutôt vers le commencement de la matinée, toute une horde de danseurs enthousiasmés se mettre aussi à turluter en *battant à quatre,* et les *jouars,* poussés comme par un ressort, entrer eux-mêmes en danse avec une énergie incroyable"[21] (*Nouvelles soirées canadiennes*, July 1887, 318–19, italics in original). This is a far cry from the sparse and moralistic descriptions of the 1860s; texts such as "Le voyageur" worked to place rural dance and instrumental music on par with songs and legends as literary indicators of French-Canadian identity.

In the first two decades of the twentieth century, facing a "future shock" of massive emigration, rapid urbanization, and industrialization, many in Quebec looked backwards to an idealized past. The early twentieth-century *régionaliste* movement advocated an autonomous French-Canadian literature that would celebrate the natural landscape, the heroic past, legends, and the morals and lifeways of rural folk, or habitants (Hayward 2006, 20, 33).

One of the prime architects of *régionalisme* was the Société du parler français au Canada, founded in Quebec City in 1902, which advocated a linguistic, and later literary, approach to preserving the faith, language, and traditions of French Canada. Speaking at the society's annual public meeting in 1904, Camille Roy called for a new "nationalisation de la littérature" and outlined the agenda that would dominate French-Canadian letters until the Second World War: "Traiter des sujets canadiens, et les traiter d'une façon canadienne"[22] (Marcotte and Hébert 1979, 65).

To treat French-Canadian subjects in a French-Canadian manner required a French-Canadian vocabulary. Each issue of the society's journal, the *Bulletin du parler français*, included a lexicon of French-Canadian terms and expressions, and the society encouraged authors to use this vocabulary in their writings (see Mercier 2002).

In May 1908 J.-E. Prince, a lawyer, professor at Laval University, and frequent contributor to the *Bulletin du parler français*, drew a parallel between the collecting of linguistic artifacts from the far reaches of Quebec and the collecting of fiddle tunes. He called on his colleagues to study instrumental dance music with the care and attention previously given only to songs, legends, and idiomatic expressions, and used his own essay in the journal to make a start on such a study, describing the processes and products of amateur luthiers in Quebec, listing typical tune types, and naming several locally celebrated fiddlers (330–7). No one responded to his call, however, and the collection of instrumental dance music in Quebec would have to wait nearly a decade, until the cylinder recordings of Marius Barbeau and Édouard-Zotique Massicotte (for example, Canadian Museum of History Archives, fonds Marius Barbeau, 1916–17, Box 224, Tapes 37 and 38).

The texts cited above are a small percentage of the nationalist writings of the late nineteenth and early twentieth centuries. Even in these works, music and dance are only rarely the primary focus. Yet taken together, these occasional references seem to have been enough to define the prototypical rural *veillée* for Quebec's literate classes.

In December 1917, Émile Chartier penned a "petite histoire" of rural life in Quebec for the nationalist magazine *L'action française*. He concluded with a description of the *veillée* as a formulaic event with a standardized repertoire of card games, fiddle tunes, dances, songs, and stories. Most remarkable is Chartier's complete reliance on literary sources, as in his description of the stock characters – fiddler, singer, storyteller – required for any "honest" *veillée*:

> M. Prince, dans le *Bulletin du parler français* ..., et Van Dyke, dans la *Gardienne de la lumière,* ont célébré le caractère unique de notre violoneux, incapable souvent de répondre à l'attente parce qu'il n'était pas *chaussé pour*! Le chanteur enfilait à perte d'haleine le répertoire recueilli par Gagnon dans ses *Chansons canadiennes* et par le docteur Larue dans le *Foyer canadien* de 1864 ... Quant au conteur, dont Taché

a dit la faconde dans ses *Trois légendes* ou ses *Forestiers,* comme Van Dyke dans la *Gardienne,* ou bien il redisait des récits appris ou bien il en inventait de toutes pièces. M. Barbeau est en train de ressusciter le genre par ses contributions à *l'American Folk-lore.*[23] (365, italics in original)

Chartier's imagining of the prototypical rural *veillée* is more idealized fiction than factual account and is largely constructed through the citation of literary works with which he presumed his readership would be acquainted. His wide-ranging literary source list (only partially reproduced in the citation above) suggests an easy conflation of early folk song and legend collections (Gagnon, LaRue, Taché), nineteenth-century literature (Louis Fréchette, Ernest Choquette), contemporary folklore scholarship (Barbeau), early-twentieth-century regionalists (Adjutor Rivard, Prince), and even American short fiction (Henry Van Dyke [1901] 1906). The prototypical rural *veillée* as he defines it is standardized, rooted in both fiction and fieldwork, and legible to a literate elite.

A detailed investigation of the professional and ideological connections between the early folklorists, such as Barbeau and Massicotte, and contemporaneous literary circles is beyond the scope of this chapter.[24] Chartier was clearly aware of Barbeau's contributions to the *Journal of American Folk-Lore,* however, and his casual treatment of his literary sources, including Barbeau's writings, presumes that these sources were also familiar to readers of *L'action française.* Whether or not Barbeau and Massicotte had read Chartier's "petite histoire" before organizing their first staged *veillées* two years later, their target audience of the educated elite likely understood these performances as citations not only of actual rural *veillées* but also of idealized *veillées* as imagined by the writers of the time.

Folklore artistique *and* exécutants du terroir

Barbeau justified his own collecting activities and the Quebec Section's staged *veillées* much as the Société du parler français justified the collection and publication of linguistic idioms. The society had advocated for a new nationalist literature rich in the detail of rural life; Barbeau promoted the collections of the Quebec Section as a repository of such detail and the staged *veillées* as outreach to those French-Canadian authors (the "exoticists"; see Hayward 2006) who had turned toward French impressionist or "ultramoderne" writings for inspiration (Barbeau and Massicotte 1920, 2). Similarly,

Barbeau advocated – at a time when the classical music culture of Quebec was still young (see Thompson 2015) – for a new national art music based on rural French-Canadian musical texts; the *folklore artistique* performances at every *veillée* were intended to demonstrate the compositional potential of the *terroir* repertoire (see Willis and Kallmann 2007).

To incorporate rural spoken idioms into literature, or fiddle tunes into art music, is to reach across social class and economic circumstance. Both the *Bulletin du parler français* and Barbeau and Massicotte's *veillées* used the language of uplift: they collected linguistic and musical texts with the goal of extracting those texts from rural cultural life and relocating them within high art. Just as authors writing for the *Bulletin du parler français* surrounded italicized idiomatic expressions with proper French, so Barbeau and his colleagues carefully situated *terroir* performances within a museum-like framework, beginning most *veillées* with a lecture on popular traditions and introducing each *terroir* performer by age, place of origin, and occupation, and each song, dance, story, or tune with historical and technical details. This information was intended to raise the perceived value of the *terroir* performers and repertoire (*La Canadienne*, July–August 1921, 8).

While these introductions provided important contextualization, the broader discourse – of *terroir* performances as raw material for art music – worked to devalue the *exécutants du terroir* by positioning them as temporary, and unsuitable, carriers of musical texts that rightly belonged to the nation as a whole. Yet Massicotte and Barbeau's programming decisions suggest that the *terroir* performers were the primary draw for many audience members. Many of the *veillées* after April 1919 featured only one *folklore artistique* soloist, even as the number of *exécutants du terroir* rose – to nineteen for the "Vie des voyageurs" evenings. (In general, Barbeau hired fewer *exécutants du terroir* for out-of-town *veillées* than did Massicotte for the Montreal *veillées*.)

Barbeau and Massicotte intended their *veillées* as a glimpse into an idealized past with the goal of rejuvenating French-Canadian art music in the future, and likely never anticipated the profound emotional reactions that their stagings would provoke. *La Presse* described an audience nearly swooning over the rustic stage set, which included objects such as a cradle, a bench, a bed, and wool carders. "À chaque objet que M. Marius Barbeau montrait, le public trépignait de joie et chacun répétait le nom de l'objet: 'Ah! regardez-moi donc ça! Un vrai rouet!'"[25] (30 April 1920, 7). In such a context, the *veillée*'s *exécutants du terroir*, many of whom were septuagenarians and octogenarians, were both object – living antiquities, akin to the stage props – and guide, able to lead a willing public deep into an imagined place and time.

Les imitations burlesques

In July–August 1921, *La Canadienne* concluded its profile of the Quebec Section with a warning to readers: "Il ne faut pas confondre les soirées que [la Section du Québec] organise avec les imitations, qui prêtent plutôt au burlesque qu'à l'exposé fidèle et vécu des touchantes traditions de notre population"[26] (9). This most likely referred to the "Veillées du bon vieux temps" organized by actors and singers Conrad Gauthier and Arthur Lapierre. Their *veillées* borrowed heavily from those of the Quebec Section but were unashamedly populist.

Gauthier produced his "Veillées du bon vieux temps" at the Monument-National through the early 1940s. (Lapierre's involvement ended in the mid-1920s; see Thérien 1998.) These stagings held little appeal for the city's cultural elite and a March 1925 review in *La Lyre* called for an end to "cette ridicule et inutile parade de 'canayens' en perruques carotte, en pantalons rapiécés, en chemises d'étoffe du pays, et en souliers de bœuf"[27] (Fabio, "Le Mois Théatral," [11]). Yet it was Gauthier's *veillées* that endured. Within a few years he had in place a younger generation of *exécutants du terroir* who made their names not only on the stage but also via radio and recordings, and in the process defined much of the core repertoire of Quebec folk music. Musical icons from Isidore Soucy, Donat Lafleur, and Alfred Montmarquette to Mary Travers, aka La Bolduc, would all perform in Gauthier's "Veillées du bon vieux temps" (Labbé 1995, 142, 182, 231; Bellemare 2012, 169–75). In this section, I focus on the early years of these *veillées* as they competed with, and ultimately replaced, Barbeau and Massicotte's *veillées*.

Gauthier and Lapierre produced their first "soirée de folklore canadien," entitled "À la bonne franquette," at the Salle Ste Brigide in Montreal. Most of the *terroir* performers they hired for this and subsequent *veillées* in 1921 and 1922 were Barbeau and Massicotte's finds (see appendix). They also copied repertoire and props with impunity and even treated spectators to *tire* on St Catherine's Day (*La Presse*, 19 November 1921, 4).

Gauthier and Lapierre's *veillées* had fundamentally different aims than those of Massicotte and Barbeau. The latter balanced amusement and edification; the former were pure entertainment and likely influenced in format and characterizations by contemporary vaudeville and minstrel shows. The latter presented *exécutants du terroir* as museum pieces; the former incorporated their performances into a theatrical framework. The latter segregated artistic and *terroir* performers and promoted the composition of art music based on folkloric elements; the former eliminated *folklore artistique* entirely.

For "À la bonne franquette," repeated at the Monument-National on 21 April 1921, Gauthier penned a series of scenes evoking bygone French-Canadian life. He played the lead role and hired a small group of professional actors, but the star performers were the *terroir* singers, dancers, storytellers, and fiddlers, and Gauthier seems to have constructed his scenes around their repertoires (*La Presse*, 22 April 1921, 21).

Gauthier's subsequent *veillées* similarly placed *terroir* repertoire within theatrical representations of rural festivities, usually linked to the performance date: Mardi Gras, Christmas, a fall corn husking, a springtime sugaring-off. For the 24 November 1921 *veillée*, for instance, he authored a two-act comedy entitled "La Sainte-Catherine." The first act borrows liberally from "Consultations gratuites," a farce by Régis Roy in which a young Montreal dentist reconciles with his estranged habitant father. In the second act the father hosts a *veillée* in his home village of Saint-Jacques-de-l'Achigan. There, Gauthier's *terroir* performers danced the "danse du matelot" (featured the previous St Catherine's Day at the Quebec Section's *veillée*), minuets, and country dances; two actresses danced the "Ballet des roses." Gauthier performed traditional French-Canadian songs and Lapierre and actors Sylva Alarie and Armand Lefebvre sang Ernest Gagnon's "Soirées de Québec" (*La Presse*, 25 November 1921, 14). These latter performances were neither *terroir* nor *folklore artistique*, but probably best understood in the context of the growing number of professional singers, such as Charles Marchand, who, in the wake of the Quebec Section's successful *veillées*, performed recitals of folk songs in dialect and wearing costume (De Surmont 2005; Potvin 2007).

Barbeau and Massicotte had only contempt and disapproval for Gauthier and his *veillées*. In an article summarizing the work of the Quebec Section, Barbeau alludes to "ceux qui se mirent, pour des fins purement personnelles, à le vulgariser et à l'exploiter sans discernement"[28] (*La Presse*, 25 February 1922, Saturday supplement, K, M). In his private correspondence, Massicotte was even more direct: "Faudrait empêcher Gauthier de récolter ce que nous avons semé," he wrote to Barbeau on 27 March 1922. "Il se fait passer pour le représentant accrédité du folklore canadien."[29] Nearly a decade later, Massicotte's rancour had not diminished; in a 3 January 1930 letter to Barbeau, he regrets that "certains types se sont acquis une renommée que je crois surfaite et ils ont présenté nos vieilles choses d'une façon qui m'humilie. On ne vise qu'à faire de l'argent et à faire parler de soi"[30] (Archives de Folklore de l'Université Laval, fonds Édouard-Zotique Massicotte). As this letter makes clear, Massicotte's long-lasting resentment and even humiliation was due not to Gauthier's unauthorized borrowings but to his framing of those borrowings.

A crucial difference between the Quebec Section's and Gauthier's *veillées* was the use of language. The former carefully restricted popular language to song and story texts, and surrounded those with learned explanations in proper French. Working-class audiences likely found such explanations dull – why else would a reviewer for *La Presse*, a working-class daily, need to repeatedly justify the *veillées*' pedagogical elements (26 November 1920, 13) – but for educated members of the audience, this framing offered the frisson of peering over a socioeconomic divide from the safety of privilege. At Gauthier's *veillées*, by contrast, according to a critical review by Fabio in *La Lyre*, a cultural magazine, "on y parle une langue farcie des plus atroces anglicismes"[31] (March 1925, [11]). Dialect was an instant identifier of social class – in "Consultations gratuites," the rough-spoken father interprets his son's erudite French as a sign of material success in the city – and Gauthier's extensive use of popular idioms likely indicated to educated spectators that they were not his target audience. Disagreement over the merits of Gauthier's *veillées* centred not on musical repertoire, but on language: *La Presse* condoned the use of popular idioms, arguing that it served to "rendre plus complète l'illusion" (7 November 1922, 21) while in *La Lyre*, Fabio wrote in a tone of disgust and dismay that "si vraiment nos pères avaient cette grossièreté de langage et de tenue, je demanderais à M. Conrad Gauthier d'en priver désormais la scène canadienne-française."[32] If, to the educated classes, using popular idioms in a carefully regulated context had been a step toward a national literature, allowing those idioms free rein threatened the idealized national identity that that literature had so carefully constructed. Yet it was this quasi-burlesque staging of folklore that endured twenty years and, in many ways, shaped the imagery of traditional music to the present day. Following the staged *veillée* through theatre, radio, recordings, television, film, and other media is, however, well beyond the scope of this chapter. Rather, I turn to an alternative understanding of the genre of folklore as constructed through the *veillée*.

"It Was All Folk Music": Unstaged *Veillées* in the Mid-twentieth Century

Although Barbeau and Massicotte sought textual purity and Gauthier and Lapierre popular amusement, both used the stage to draw borders around the genre of folklore. Early staged *veillées* defined a generic reference point – the prototypical *veillée* – that has held steady through to the present.

The following paragraphs look beyond these staged *veillées* to what might be called unstaged *veillées*: actual rural social gatherings centred on music and dance. It should be noted that staged and unstaged *veillées* were mutually influential in twentieth-century Quebec: while staged *veillées* presented commercialized, idealized representations of unstaged *veillées*, unstaged *veillées* were at times shaped by their participants' understanding of folk music as mediated by staged *veillées* (Risk 2017, 295–6).

I describe two sites of rural music making on the Gaspé peninsula in the mid-twentieth century: the childhood *veillées* of Sister Henriette Essiambre, and music and dance in the home of pulpwood contractor William McDonald. These sections are based on fieldwork and recent interviews. (Note that some interviewees requested anonymity.) I use these examples to argue for an alternative understanding of the generic boundaries of folk music.

This case study focuses on the Gaspé peninsula for several reasons. The Gaspé has long been celebrated for the strength of its cultural traditions: Barbeau collected folksongs there on several occasions (Nowry 1995, 180–6, 210, 305–6); the "Vie des voyageurs" *veillées* featured over a dozen Gaspesian dancers and fiddlers. My research was also guided by practical considerations: from 2010 to 2014, I visited the Gaspesian village of Douglastown regularly to work on a community CD project (Patterson and Risk 2015; Patterson, Risk, and Chaput 2014) and that project led, directly or indirectly, to most of the interviews cited below. The informal music making that I describe here was by no means limited to the Gaspé peninsula, however; there were similar gatherings in many rural communities, and urban areas, across Quebec, in New England, and elsewhere in eastern Canada (see, for instance, Bennett 2009; Bronner 1987; Forsyth 2011; Forsyth 2014; Graham 2006; Perlman 2015).[33]

Family Veillées

Sister Henriette Essiambre was born in 1935 and grew up in the village of Saint-Godefroi on the southern Gaspé coast, along the Baie-des-Chaleurs. She worked as a schoolteacher, principal, and educational consultant in many locales in eastern Canada until her retirement in 1994. We first met in August 2014 at a weekend traditional music camp where I was teaching fiddle and she was a student.

Sister Essiambre's parents "had a little farm" and her father earned additional income working in the woods in the winters. She is the fifteenth child of the family and when she was five or six years old, several of her older brothers went to work in lumber camps in either Quebec or Ontario. No one in the family had played music previously but in the camps her brothers learned to play fiddle, guitar, and mandolin. They brought instruments home and Sister Essiambre recalls learning to play "by listening to my brothers" (interview, 16 August 2014, Sayabec, QC).[34]

The Essiambre family's music making attracted local community members who would "come to our place and learn from us and have their instruments tuned by us." When I asked Sister Essiambre if she remembered *veillées* in her youth, she replied emphatically: "Oh yeah. Yes. We often had them at home ... Probably when one of my brothers was coming back from work or – you know, we'd get together and play a lot and invite people and dance" (ibid.).

Sister Essiambre's brothers played violin and she accompanied them on guitar, on tunes such as "St Anne's Reel," "Money Musk," "Soldier's Joy," and "La Grondeuse." "It was mostly square dance[s] when I was young," she recalled, although there was also "lots of step-dancing" and some waltzes. She also learned a piece on the guitar to accompany "boogie-boogie" dancing, and her brother Donat played a piece on violin for "rock 'n' roll" dancing.[35] The assembled family members and neighbours also sang songs, including "Western songs" learned from the radio (ibid.).

In many ways, the details of Sister Essiambre's childhood *veillées* fit neatly into the prototypical *veillée*: a small village in rural Quebec; an agricultural economy supplemented by wintertime lumber work; fiddlers, square dancers, and step dancers. Yet she and her brothers also played boogie-boogie and rock 'n' roll. This might seem to suggest that the generic boundaries of folk music, which both defined and were defined by staged *veillées*, were of little or no importance at the Essiambre family *veillées*. In fact, Sister Essiambre's definition of folk music was quite different from that promoted by staged *veillées*:

LAURA RISK: Was there some of the music that you played [at *veillées*] that you thought of as traditional music, or as folklore?
HENRIETTE ESSIAMBRE: Yes, all of it.
LR: The fiddle tunes.
HE: Yes.
LR: What about the Western songs?
HE: Oh yes, those were folklore too. Folk music.
LR: What about when you played [boogie-boogie] and rock 'n' roll, later on?

HE: [*wrinkles her brow, purses her lips, and pauses*] Yes, that was folk music too. It was all folk music.
LR: Was there any music that you played that wasn't folklore, or folk music?
HE: Yes, for instance now I play some songs in church. I play with the choir. (Conversation transcribed from field notes, 16 August 2014, Sayabec, QC)

This exchange suggests that the generic boundaries of folk music regulated the repertoire of the Essiambre family *veillées* just as they did the repertoire of early staged *veillées*, but that those boundaries were defined quite differently for the two. Sister Essiambre describes folk music as any non-religious participatory music. In practice, this meant that the folk music she and her siblings played included both commercially popular songs and instrumental music for a range of popular dance forms that reached rural Quebec from the turn of the twentieth century on.

A similarly broad definition seems to have been in place in the Gaspesian village of Douglastown (where, coincidentally, Sister Essiambre worked in the 1970s). Although Douglastown was, until recently, primarily English-speaking and Irish-identified, the generation born in the early twentieth century used the word "*veillée*" to refer to an evening visit among family or friends; later generations spoke of "house parties," "kitchen parties," or "cottage parties," depending on the venue, or a "sing-song," a gathering of only singers.[36] *Veillées* in Douglastown were organized along lines of kinship and affinity and, like the *veillées* of the Essiambre family, included a wide range of participatory music. John McDonald (born 1963) is the youngest son of Douglastown pulpwood dealer William McDonald. He recalls musical gatherings in his childhood home:

It would be in the summer, winter, didn't matter when it was, but they'd decide, OK, we're gonna have some people in this weekend ... I remember taking the table out of the kitchen and putting it outside. And there'd be chairs all around that little kitchen and they'd have square dances. You'd think the floor was gonna go through, you know, the floor was gonna break ... They'd play a bunch of fiddle music and then they'd all start singing these old Irish songs [often learned from Bing Crosby recordings] and gospel songs and country songs, old

Hank Williams songs and stuff, and Jimmy Reeves songs. And then they'd dance again. (Interview, 26 October 2013, Brampton, ON)

Later in the interview, I asked John McDonald about local understandings of musical genre:

> LAURA RISK: One of the things I love about Douglastown is the way people were into all kinds of music. I mean, they were into country music and older Irish songs and fiddle tunes. Did people ever talk about ...
> JOHN MCDONALD: It all kind of blended, you know.
> LR: ... the different styles of music.
> JMD: Yeah. Like when I was young, I couldn't really tell the difference between any of that music. I just thought it was music. Church music was different. But the fiddle music and the country music and the Irish music, it all kind of blended for me ... It was just music. It was how people entertained themselves. But then as you got older, you kind of figure out, OK this is Irish, this is – you put things in place. (ibid.)

I am struck by the similarities in how Sister Essiambre and John McDonald classify the music of their childhoods. Both describe only two categories, both essentially functional: music for church and music for entertainment. The latter category could be subdivided into fiddle music (equivalent to dance music) and songs, which could in turn be categorized by theme (Irish songs), source (Hank Williams, Jim Reeves), or mainstream genre classifications used on radio and television (country, rock 'n' roll). When family and neighbours gathered at the Essiambre or the McDonald house, however, only the highest level of categorization – music for religious purposes versus music for entertainment – affected the choice of repertoire.

Informal Music-Making in the Pulpwood Economy

John McDonald's father, William McDonald, was a pulpwood dealer who hired men to cut wood on public land under contract with the government. He also purchased cut wood from local landowners, often small-scale farmers or fishermen, who cut on their own property. From 1962 to 1964, and again in the 1980s, Norma McDonald (née Gaul, no relation) worked for William McDonald as a live-in housekeeper and "jack-of-all-trades" (interview with

Norma McDonald, 3 August 2012, Douglastown, QC). I first met her in 2010 at Douglastown's annual music festival and have since spent many enjoyable hours playing music with her and listening as she and her husband, Brian McDonald, described the culture of music and dance that once flourished in the village.

Norma McDonald's memories of her years at William McDonald's are studded with small-scale musical encounters: fiddler Joe Howell stopping by on a Sunday afternoon to play a few tunes and sing songs; singer Dick Hatch playing William McDonald's pump organ to accompany himself on Irish songs and "Jamaica Farewell"; the family sending for fiddler James Henry Conley, then in his seventies, to play for William McDonald's bedridden mother. Norma McDonald sometimes accompanied visiting singers, fiddlers, and dancers on guitar. She would sing the first few bars of a tune to get a fiddler started when necessary (ibid.).

Some of the men who cut wood for William McDonald were fiddlers or dancers and he would on occasion request a tune or a few steps when they came to pick up their cheques. Recalls his eldest son Alban McDonald, "[Gérard Durette would] phone my father and tell him he was coming to get paid. 'Bring your fiddle.' [*laughs*] 'You're not gonna get paid that easy, chum!'" (interview, 5 August 2014, Douglastown, QC). Norma McDonald remembers fiddler Ralph Lucas similarly playing for his cheques in the early 1960s (phone conversation, 15 May 2013). William McDonald would occasionally sing the fiddle tunes "St Anne's Reel" and "The Old Man and the Old Woman" for step-dancer Joe Girard, who drove a truck and cut wood, when he came for his cheque. Norma McDonald describes these Friday afternoons as moments of release after a week of hard labour: "He'd come to get paid, and now William would say, 'We're gonna have a drink of gin, you're gonna dance a tune.' [William would] start stamping his feet [and singing the tune]. And Joe Girard, after working hard loads all week, would get up and make the nicest steps over there in the kitchen. Just like that, and they were satisfied then" (interview, 3 August 2012, Douglastown, QC).

These were not lengthy evening entertainments, in the home or on the stage, but rather brief daytime moments of musical exchange grounded in an economic exchange. As such, they propose an alternate understanding of the social function of fiddle music and step dance in rural Quebec in the later twentieth century. Fiddle music and dance were at times public entertainment in Douglastown (at the annual St Patrick's Day concerts, in the dance halls of neighbouring villages, or, for an earlier generation, at summertime picnic dances) and at times semi-private (at *veillées* among families and neighbours), but they also worked to smooth everyday economic interactions, such as picking up a paycheque.

Taken together, the varied music and dance activities described by Henriette Essiambre, Norma McDonald, and William McDonald's sons paint an alternative portrait of participatory music in rural Quebec to that defined by the staged *veillée* or by French-Canadian literature. *Veillées* were not simply open houses; people moved within their own musical circles of kinship and affinity. The lumber industry created social contexts for music making at remote, male-dominated camps, as in "La vie des voyageurs," but also in village homes, where both male (woodcutters and truck drivers) and female (the live-in housekeeper) employees participated. Fiddle tunes and step dancing were used as social lubricant in economic interactions. At evening gatherings – unstaged *veillées* – and in small-scale daytime music making, generic boundaries were broad and repertoires were linked by function rather than origin.

Conclusion

In this chapter, I argue for the *veillée* as a particularly efficient focal point for the genre of folk or traditional music in Quebec and a means of articulating specific musical repertoires to discourses of tradition and national identity. The *veillée* is a culturally resonant space that encompasses place, people, and music; my goal has been to historicize our imaginings of that space and to examine the ongoing dialogue between those imaginings and musical practice. Although I restrict my discussion to folk or traditional music in Quebec, I believe this chapter will be of interest to scholars of other musical traditions with similarly evocative spaces, such as the kitchen party in maritime Canada or the ceilidh in Scotland. This chapter also contributes to growing bodies of scholarship on the construction of musical genre in the early twentieth century (Hagstrom Miller 2010, Brackett 2016), and on folk music as an ideologically charged genre constructed from popular styles (Gelbart 2007).

This chapter uses contemporary periodical sources to describe early staged *veillées* and ethnographic sources to describe a sampling of mid-twentieth-century unstaged *veillées*. Many questions remain, however. How typical were the unstaged *veillées* in Saint-Godefroi and Douglastown? How influenced were amateur musicians by commercial *veillées* on radio, record, and later television? How stable were the repertoire and format of staged and unstaged *veillées* over the twentieth century? This chapter interrogates and complicates the construction of the genre of folk or traditional music in Quebec; how musicians and audiences then worked out the possibilities of that genre, however, remains an open question.

For well over a century, folklorists, writers, illustrators, producers, and performers have selected aspects of rural musical gatherings to celebrate, elevate, and, sometimes, caricature. Professional musicians and dancers today may choose to adopt, adapt, or challenge that imagery to sell their own work. They cannot, however, simply ignore it: audiences understand folk and traditional music by its citation of previous iterations of the genre, and in Quebec that chain of citations leads through a maze of staged *veillées* to the prototypical *veillée*.

Non-professionals, on the other hand, have a choice. Genre identifiers are necessary only if musicians or listeners need to distinguish between musical texts that belong to a genre and those that do not. When music making is in the service of strengthening social bonds, however, other qualities may take precedence; for example, is it participatory? is it enjoyable? is it new / old / associated with a special person? I do not mean to suggest that generic boundaries somehow disappear in unstaged *veillées*, but rather that participants don't necessarily restrict their music making according to those boundaries, or that they adopt an extremely broad definition of "folk music." In unstaged *veillées*, multiple chains of citation point outward toward a wide range of participatory musics, including commercially mainstream styles.

The music making at Henriette Essiambre's home, or William McDonald's, was not a staging intended for public consumption (although much of the repertoire can be traced to commercial sources), and was in certain cases inseparable from day-to-day economic activities. In writing the second half of this chapter, I have taken on the task of slicing those gatherings out of larger cultural narratives and representing them to an outside public as contained events – of, in essence, staging elements of cultural life in Saint-Godefroi and Douglastown in the mid-century. Staging cultural practices – cultural objectification – is how our society creates cultural heritage (although heritage itself may be staged in various guises, including the kitsch of Radio-Canada's "Bye Bye 2008"). Cultural heritage in turn delineates a set of generic markers that may serve modern-day musicians as creative resources. In that sense this chapter is an attempt to shift, if ever so slightly, our modern-day understanding of the *veillée*, and therefore of traditional music. I propose a chain of citation that leads back not only to the earliest staged *veillées* and from there to imagined prototypical *veillées*, but also to informal, unstaged musical gatherings that were as much about family and community as they were about music or dance; that prized intimate music making; that included both men and women and were both francophone and anglophone; and that reached out willingly to other styles for accessible, participatory music.

Acknowledgments

This research was supported by Bibliothèque et Archives nationales du Québec and the Social Sciences and Humanities Research Council of Canada. Many thanks to Marc Bolduc, David Brackett, Luc Chaput, Jean Duval, Sister Henriette Essiambre, Daniel Guilbert, James Lambert (Archives de folklore et d'ethnologie at Université Laval), Alban and Trina McDonald, Norma and Brian McDonald, John McDonald, Glenn Patterson, the late Francine Reeves, Benoit Thériault (Canadian Museum of History), and the staff at McGill's Humanities and Music libraries.

Appendix: List of all staged veillées from March 1919 to November 1922 for which documentary evidence has been located

Date	Title and Location	Organizations and Organizers	Performers [square brackets indicate performers listed in previews but absent from program or reviews]	Sources of Information (LP = La Presse, fMB = fonds Marius Barbeau, fCR = fonds Carmen Roy, both at the Canadian Museum of History)
18 March 1919	"Soirée des traditions populaires canadiennes," Bibliothèque Saint-Sulpice, Montreal (coincides with second annual meeting of the Quebec Section of the American Folk-Lore Society; "Veillée du bon vieux temps" title assigned retroactively by Barbeau and Massicotte [1920])	Société historique de Montréal, American Folk-Lore Society (Quebec Section); Édouard-Zotique Massicotte, Marius Barbeau	*Du terroir*: Vincent-Ferrier de Repentigny (song), Adolphe Tison (song), Médard Bougie (violin), François-Xavier Baulne (step dance) *Artistique*: Mme. J.-Émile Dionne (solo piano), Yvonne Montet (song), Sarah Fisher (song), R.-H. Duhamel (story), choir of architecture students with P.-E. Corbeil (acc. piano), [Alice Valiquette (song), Julie Fortin (acc. piano)] *Lectures*: Victor Morin on popular traditions, Marius Barbeau on Quebec art and architecture (with lantern slides)	Barbeau and Massicotte 1920, 8–9 (full program); *LP* 1919-3-11, 9; *LP* 1919-3-12, 17; *LP* 1919-3-15, 46; Joly 2012, 357–69; Nowry 1995, 186–9; fCR B624 f9 p. 68–70
24 April 1919	"Soirée des traditions populaires canadiennes," Bibliothèque Saint-Sulpice, Montreal ("Veillée du bon vieux temps" title assigned retroactively by Barbeau and Massicotte [1920])	Société historique de Montréal, American Folk-Lore Society (Quebec Section); Édouard-Zotique Massicotte, Marius Barbeau	*Du terroir*: Vincent-Ferrier de Repentigny (song), Adolphe Tison (song), Médard Bougie (violin), Joseph Rousselle (story), Philéas Bédard (story), Famille Dagenais (dialogue song, dance): Catherine Dagenais-Major (also jaw harp), Israël Dagenais, Jean-Baptiste Dagenais, Olivier Dagenais	Barbeau and Massicotte 1920, 10–11 (full program); *LP* 1919-4-17, 15; *LP* 1919-4-21, 17 (full program); *LP* 1919-4-25, 17; Joly 2012, 357–69; Nowry 1995, 186–9; fMB B340 f4

Date	Title and Location	Organizations and Organizers	Performers	Sources of Information
24 April 1919/ cont'd			*Artistique*: Loraine Wyman (song) with Mme A. Laurendeau (acc. piano) *Lectures*: Victor Morin on popular traditions, Marius Barbeau on Quebec art and architecture (with lantern slides)	
24 June 1919	"Veillée de folk-lore," Monument-National, Montreal (Saint-Jean-Baptiste celebration)	Société Saint-Jean-Baptiste de Montréal; Édouard-Zotique Massicotte	*Du terroir*: Isaïe Leroux (dance, story), Famille Dagenais (song, dance), Vincent-Ferrier de Repentigny (song) with Jeanne Ladouceur (acc. harmonium), Adolphe Tison (song), Philéas Bédard (song, story), Médard Bougie (violin), Arsène Jarry (violin), Henri Groulx (dance), Joseph Rousselle (story) *Artistique*: Yvonne Montet (song) with Mme. J.-Emile Dionne (acc. piano) *Lecture*: Victor Morin; lantern slides projected by Edgar Gariepy during songs	*LP* 1919-6-25, 3 (full program); Joly 2012, 357-69
11 Dec. 1919	"La soirée des ancêtres," Monument-National, Montreal	Société Saint-Jean-Baptiste de Montréal, for the profit of "quelques groupes minoritaires"	*Du terroir*: Vincent-Ferrier de Repentigny (song), Adolphe Tison (song) with Michel Renaud (piano), Elie Ménard (dance), Isaïe Leroux (dance, short stories), Médard Bougie (violin), Joachim Simard (accordion), Famille Dagenais (dance, jaw harp as above), Joseph Roussel (story), Philéas Bédard (song, story)	*LP* 1919-11-29, 5; *LP* 1919-12-12, 10; *Le passe-temps* 25, no. 645 (1919-12-13), 494; *La Canadienne* 3, no. 5 (July-August 1921), 8-9; Joly 2012, 357-69; fMB B219 f36

		Artistique: J.-P.-L. Bérubé and Auguste Paquette (song) with Aldéa Lussier; trio of Bérubé, Paquette, and Hercule Lavoie (song) *Lecture*: Victor Morin	
25 April 1920	"Old French Traditions (Folk-songs and Folktales) as They Survive in Canada," Cosmopolitan Club, New York City	Loraine Wyman and Marius Barbeau	*Du terroir*: Vincent-Ferrier de Repentigny (song), Philéas Bédard (song) *Artistique*: Loraine Wyman (song), Ruth Emerson (piano) *Lecture*: Marius Barbeau (with slides) *Staging*: No props; de Repentigny is dressed as a lumberjack, Bédard is dressed as an habitant	*LP* 1920-4-27, 19; *LP* 1920-4-30, 24; Nowry 1995, 190; fCR B624 f9 p. 71-2
26 April 1920	"Old French Traditions (Folk-songs and Folktales) as They Survive in Canada," Columbia University, New York City (matinée for students)	Loraine Wyman and Marius Barbeau	*Du terroir*: Vincent-Ferrier de Repentigny (song), Philéas Bédard (song) *Artistique*: Loraine Wyman (song), Ruth Emerson (piano) *Staging*: No props; de Repentigny is dressed as a lumberjack, Bédard is dressed as an habitant	*LP* 1920-4-27, 19; *LP* 1920-4-30, 24; Nowry 1995, 190; fMB B340 f5
29 April 1920	"Veillée du bon vieux temps," Monument-National, Montreal	American Folk-Lore Society (Quebec Section), sponsored by *La Presse*; Édouard-Zotique Massicotte, Marius Barbeau	*Du terroir*: Roméo Jetté (song), Louis Leduc (story, jaw harp, "rouette"), Caïus Benoit (violin), Edouard Giroux (violin), Oscar Durocher (violin), Vincent-Ferrier de Repentigny (song), Isaïe and Honoré Leroux (dance), Philéas Bédard (story, song), Joachim Simard (accordion), [Joseph Dion (story), Philippe Lambert (violin)] *Artistique*: Ruth Emerson (solo and acc. piano), Loraine Wyman (song)	*LP* 1920-4-9, 23; *LP* 1920-4-10, 5 (soliciting participants); *LP* 1920-4-21, 5; *LP* 1920-4-23, 25, 27; *LP* 1920-4-26, 11; *LP* 1920-4-27, 1; *LP* 1920-4-28, 1; *LP* 1920-4-30, 7, 27 (majority of program); Joly 2012, 357-69; Nowry

Date	Title and Location	Organizations and Organizers	Performers	Sources of Information
29 April 1920/ cont'd			*Format*: Included "concours de violon" between Caius Benoit, Edouard Giroux, and Oscar Durocher *Lecture*: Barbeau on popular traditions and Quebec art and architecture [Arts et architecture populaires, Reliques d'art français au Canada, Ancienne maîtrises d'art] (with lantern slides)	1995, 190; fMB B340 f5 and f6 (program)
2 May 1920	"Veillée du bon vieux temps," L'Auditorium, Quebec City (matinée and evening performances; coincides with annual meeting of the Quebec Section of the American Folk-Lore Society)	Marius Barbeau, American Folk-Lore Society (Quebec Section), profits to the Société du Terroir (directed by Marquis and Damase Potvin)	*Du terroir*: Ulric Pageau (violin), Jérôme Cloutier (dance, song), Honoré Leroux (dance, song), Luc April (song), Ovide Soucy (song), Achille "Ti-Chille" Fournier (story), [Philéas Drolet (dance)] *Artistique*: Loraine Wyman (song) with Ruth Emerson (acc. piano) *Lecture*: Barbeau on Quebec landscapes along the St Lawrence, incl. Beaupré, Charlevoix (with lantern slides)	*L'événement* 1920–5–3 (fMB B340 f7); *LP* 1920-4-24, 7; *LP* 1920–5–5, 25; Nowry 1995, 191; fCR B624 f9 p. 73
5 May 1920	"Veillée du bon vieux temps," Salle Ste.-Anne, Ottawa (French-speaking audience)	Jules Tremblay, Marius Barbeau, American Folk-Lore Society (Ontario Section), Cercle Social Sainte-Anne d'Ottawa. Assistance from Charles Marchand.	*Du terroir*: Vincent-Ferrier de Repentigny (song), Olivier de Repentigny (violin), Philéas Bédard (story, song), Isaïe Leroux (dance, story), Honoré Leroux (dance) *Artistique*: Ruth Emerson (solo and acc. piano), Loraine Wyman (song) *Lecture*: Barbeau on popular traditions	fMB B340 f1 (full program); *LP* 1920–5–7, 6; Nowry 1995, 191–2; fCR B624 f9 p. 74–5

Date	Event	Organizers	Content	Sources
6 May 1920	"Veillée du bon vieux temps," Russell Theatre, Ottawa (matinée for schoolchildren plus evening performance)	Jules Tremblay, Marius Barbeau, American Folk-Lore Society (Ontario Section)	*Du terroir*: Vincent-Ferrier de Repentigny (song), Édouard Giroux (violin), Philéas Bédard (song), Isaïe Leroux (dance), Honoré Leroux (dance) *Artistique*: Ruth Emerson (solo and acc. piano), Loraine Wyman (song) *Lecture*: Barbeau on popular traditions and Quebec art and architecture (with lantern slides)	fMB B340 f1 (full program); Nowry 1995, 191–2; fCR B624 f9 p. 75–6
7 May 1920	Morning Music Club, Ottawa (concert)	Marius Barbeau, American Folk-Lore Society (Ontario Section), Morning Music Club	*Du terroir*: Philéas Bédard (song) *Artistique*: Loraine Wyman (song) with Ruth Emerson (acc. piano) *Format*: No props, majority *folklore artistique*	fMB B340 f1; Nowry 1995, 191–2
15 May 1920	"Séance de folklore," Monument-National, Montreal (matinée for schoolchildren)	Édouard-Zotique Massicotte, Société Saint-Jean-Baptiste de Montréal, American Folk-Lore Society (Quebec Section)	*Du terroir*: Joseph Rousselle (story), Vincent-Ferrier de Repentigny (song), Adolphe Tison (song), others *Format*: Children from two orphanages (Saint-Henri, Soeurs Grises of Sainte-Cunégonde) perform dances including a minuet and sung *ronde*	*LP* 1920–5–11, 13; *LP* 1920–5–14, 9; *LP* 1920–5–15, 11; Joly 2012, 357–69
12 and 14 Oct. 1920	"Veillée de campagne: Une noce du bon vieux temps chez le père Hubert Perron," Monument-National, Montreal	Parish of Sainte-Cécile, with the patronage of Montreal mayor Médéric Martin	*Du terroir*: unnamed dancers and instrumentalists *Format*: Representation of a rural wedding	*LP* 1920–10–04, 7; *LP* 1920–10–05, 3 (negative preview); *LP* 1920–10–13, 10, 22; July 2012, 369

Date	Title and Location	Organizations and Organizers	Performers	Sources of Information
25 Nov. 1920	"La vie des voyageurs," Monument-National, Montreal	Édouard-Zotique Massicotte, American Folk-Lore Society (Quebec Section)	*Du terroir*: Vincent-Ferrier de Repentigny (song), Adolphe Tison (song), Philéas Bédard (song), F.-X. Blache (song), Joseph Rousselle (story), Jean Bourgeois (dance), Eugène Bourgeois (dance, violin); Gaspesian dancers: Paul Curadeau (violin), Mme. S. Curadeau, Mlle. A. Curadeau, Mme. Charles Blanchette, Charles Blanchette, Mme. M. Thériault, Hervé Samson, Mme. Hervé Samson, Salomon Samson (violin), Mme. Salomon Samson, Luc Samson, Ludger Côté *Artistique*: Stanley Gardner (piano), Alice Bélanger (poetry reading), Lucienne-B. Laliberté (song) with Alfred Laliberté (acc. piano) *Lecture*: Victor Morin on voyageurs *Poetry*: "Connaissez-vous la Gaspésie?" by Blanche Lamontagne-Bauregard, recited by Alice Bélanger *Format*: First half follows "la vie de voyageur" via song; also includes the "Pantomime du barbier." Second half features Gaspesian dances: Gigue des anciens, Reel des matelots, Spandy. Distribution of St Catherine's Day *tire*, sponsored by Ludger Gravel	*LP* 1920–11–15, 11; *LP* 1920–11–16, 12; *LP* 1920–11–17, 21; *LP* 1920–11–20, 34; *LP* 1920–11–23, 9; *LP* 1920–11–25, 13; *LP* 1920–11–26, 13, 27 (detailed description of program); *Le passe-temps* 26, no. 671 (1920–12–11), 551; *La Canadienne* 3, no. 5 (July–August 1921), 8–9; Joly 2012, 357–69; Nowry 1995, 192; Bellemare 2012, 90, 394; fMB B340 f6
2 Dec. 1920	"La vie des voyageurs," Monument-National, Montreal	Édouard-Zotique Massicotte,	Repeat of 25 November 1920 *veillée*, though with slight differences in programming: Gaspesian dances include	*LP* 1920–11–20, 34; *LP* 1920–12–3, 7, 13 (detailed

	American Folk-Lore Society (Quebec Section)	Grand cotillion, Stanley Gardner opens the second half rather than the first; the first half opens with a "concours de violoneux" between Bourgeois, Curadeau, and Samson	description of program); *Le passe-temps* 26, no. 671 (1920–12–11), 551; *La Canadienne* 3, no. 5 (July–August 1921), 8–9; Joly 2012, 357–69; Nowry 1995, 192; fMB B340 f6
c. March 1921	"Veillée du bon vieux temps: 'À la bonne franquette,'" Salle Sainte-Brigide, Montreal	Conrad Gauthier and Arthur Lapierre	*Du terroir*: M. and Mme. Charles Blanchette, Mme. Curadeau, Isaïe Leroux, Honoré Leroux [and others?] *Artistique*: unknown *Format*: A comedy. Two acts of "scènes canadiennes"	Letter from É.-Z. Massicotte to M. Barbeau, 1921-3–21 (Archives de folklore et ethnologie à l'Université Laval, fonds Édouard-Zotique Massicotte); *LP* 1921–4–9, 5
April 1921?	Trois-Rivières	Édouard-Zotique Massicotte, Société historique de Montréal	At the request of Albert Tessier?	Joly 2012, 365; *L'action française*, March 1921, 167
9 April 1921	"Souper du bon vieux temps," Chalet, Cartierville	Club de raquette le Montagnard	*Du terroir*: Unnamed fiddler, accordion players, dancers Includes a supper "du vieux temps"	*LP* 1921–4–9, 15
21 April 1921	"Veillée du bon vieux temps: 'À la bonne franquette,'" Monument-National, Montreal	Conrad Gauthier and Arthur Lapierre, under the auspices of M. l'abbé Victor Geoffrion	*Du terroir*: Isaïe Leroux, Honoré Leroux, M. and Mme. Casaubon, M. and Mme. [Charles] Blanchet[te], Mme. and Mlle. Curadeau, MM. Côté (father and son), Ovila Desrochers	*LP* 1921–4–9, 5; *LP* 1921–4–20, 3; *LP* 1921–4–22, 21

Date	Title and Location	Organizations and Organizers	Performers	Sources of Information
21 April 1921/ cont'd			*Actors*: Conrad Gauthier (principal actor), Arthur Lapierre, Armand Lefebvre, Alcide Boivin, Mlle. Whillhelmy [Boivin?] *Format*: A comedy. Two acts of "scènes canadiennes"	
24 Nov. 1921	"Veillée du bon vieux temps:' La Sainte-Catherine,'" Monument-National, Montreal	Conrad Gauthier and Arthur Lapierre	*Du terroir*: M. Durocher (violin) and others. *Dancers*: Isaïe Leroux, Mme. Curadeau, Mlle. Curadeau, Catherine Dagenais (also jaw harp), Charles Blanchette, Mme. Blanchette, M. Côté père, M. Côté fils *Actors and singers*: Arthur Lapierre, Conrad Gauthier, Sylva Alarie, Armand Lefebvre, Mme. Chailler, Mme. [Wilhelmy-]Boivin [dance], Mme. Laurendeau-Chailler [dance], Pauline Gravel (6 months) *Format*: A two-act play. The first act, in Montreal, reproduces portions of "Consultations gratuites" by Régis Roy; the second act is a *veillée* in the village of Saint-Jacques-de-l'Achigan. An orchestra was to play "airs canadiens" between the acts, but played "American music" instead (ragtime and jazz). Distribution of St Catherine's Day *tire* sponsored by the evening's president, Ludger Gravel	*LP* 1921–11–19, 4; *LP* 1921–11–25, 14; *LP* 1922–2–25, 8
29 Nov. 1921	"Veillée du bon vieux temps:' La Sainte-Catherine,'" Monument-National, Montreal	Conrad Gauthier and Arthur Lapierre	Repeat of 24 November 1921 *veillée*	*LP* 1921–11–25, 14

24 Nov. 1921	"Veillée du Bon Vieux Temps," Notre-Dame du Perpetuel-Secours, Montreal	La Conférence de St-Vincent de Paul, profits to help the poor	*Du terroir*: Vincent-Ferrier de Repentigny, Philéas Bédard, J.E. Bourgeois and others *Format*: Free sweets distributed to the audience	*LP* 1921–11–19, 4, 6
27 Feb. 1922	"Veillée du bon vieux temps: 'Le Mardi-Gras,'" Monument-National, Montreal	Conrad Gauthier and Arthur Lapierre	*Du terroir*: François-Xavier Baulne, Famille Dagenais, Isaïe Leroux (dance), Ovila Desrochers (violin), Mme. Curadeau *Actors and singers*: Conrad Gauthier, Arthur Lapierre, Armand Lefebvre, Joseph Cadieux, C.-A. Vallerand, Mlle. Albertine Martin, Mlle. Jeannette Teasdale, Mme. A. Gravel, Pauline Gravel (9 months), [Mme. Wilhelmy-Boivin] *Format*: "Le Mardi-Gras" (Conrad Gauthier and Napoléon Tellier) is in two acts and is set at a rural *veillée*. The performers *du terroir* are all in the second act. During the entr'acte: a staging of the poem "Le Drapeau de Carillon" (Octave Crémazie); national songs (*chansons du pays*) performed by Arthur Lapierre; "Les Echos Laurentiens" performed by the Orchestra Larose	*LP* 1922–2–18, 7; *LP* 1922–2–25, 8; *LP* 1922–2–28, 14
10 March 1922	"Folk Song Recital," Russell Theatre, Ottawa	Marius Barbeau and G. Lanctot. Patrons: Governor General Baron Byng of Vimy	*Du terroir*: William and Omer Mallette (violin), M. Vaive, M. Carisse, Mme. Desjardins and others (dancers), Philéas Bédard (songs and *Le pari du silence*, "a folk tale with songs") *Artistique*: Loraine Wyman performing arrangements of folk songs from England, the American South, France	fMB B340 f8; Nowry 1995, 192

Date	Title and Location	Organizations and Organizers	Performers	Sources of Information
11 March 1922	"Veillée du bon vieux temps," Russell Theatre, Ottawa	Marius Barbeau and G. Lanctot	*Du terroir*: William and Omer Mallette (violin), Ulric Carisse (violin), Philéas Bédard (songs, stories), Fidèle Vaive, Jérémie Carisse, Samuel Carisse, Argentine Desjardins, Eleanor Moreau (dancers), Trefflé Bigras and Mme. Joseph Tremblay (songs) *Artistique*: Loraine Wyman performing arrangements of folk songs from France, Louisiana, Canada	fMB B340 f8; Nowry 1995, 192
24 May 1922	"Une veillée chez nos gens"	Le club Gouin	*Du terroir and actors*: Mme. Moïse Raymond (song), Mme. Joseph Godard (song), Joseph Godard (song, dance, role of habitant), M. and Mme. A. Levesque, Henri Watier (violin), Mme. François-Xavier Baulne, Aldéric Pleau, Percy Trevelyan	*LP* 1922–05–20, 9
6 Nov. 1922	"Veillée du bon vieux temps: 'Lépluchette de blé-d'Inde,'" Monument-National, Montreal (Action de grâce)	Conrad Gauthier and Arthur Lapierre; Ludger Gravel, president of the evening	*Du terroir*: Isaïe Leroux, Mme. Caradeau, Stanislas Laporte, Oscar Durocher, Paul Lajoie, Léo Vallières, André Laurendeau (8 years old). Includes songs (*chansons à répondre, chansons de chantier*), dances, monologues, stories. Performers on violin, jaw harp, accordion, harmonica *Actors and singers*: Conrad Gauthier, Arthur Lapierre, Paul Coutiée, Mme. Laurendeau-Challier, Claire Vast, Jeannette Teasdale, Hector Charland, Armand Dumouchel, Oscar Laparé, [Albertine Martin, Mlle. Chayer]	*LP* 1922-10-14, 12; *LP* 1922-10-21, 42; *LP* 1922-10-28, 42; *LP* 1922-11-4, 8, 27, 41; *LP* 1922-11-7, 21 (detailed description of program, including distribution of roles)

8 Nov. 1922	Salle Sainte-Brigide, Montreal (concert)	Concert given by Albert Larrieu	*Format*: Act 1: "Un marriage à la gaumine" (Louis Guyon); Act 2: "Une épluchette de blé-d'Inde" (Hervée Gagnier), set in 1875 and including performances *du terroir*. An orchestra plays "airs canadiens" between the acts. *Singers*: Albert Larrieu, France Ariel Duprat, Armand Duprat *Format*: Part 1 is "Une veillée bretonne"; Part 2 is "Une veillée canadienne" (songs *du terroir* composed by Albert Larrieu: "Au bon vieux temps," "La légende de la feuille d'érable," "En traineau," "Une querelle de vieux"). A student choir sings "Le pain Gagnée" (words by Rév. Père Lalande, music by Albert Larrieu) between parts.	*LP* 1922–11–9, 12
Nov. 1922	Sainte-Catherine's Day performance	unknown	*Du terroir*: Vincent-Ferrier de Repentigny	*LP* 1922–11–2, 16 (profile of Vincent-Ferrier de Repentigny)

Notes

1. "It is the people of this country." This and all subsequent translations by author.
2. This chapter engages with vocal and instrumental repertoires that, since the mid-nineteenth century, have variously been termed *national, populaire, du terroir, folklore, folk, traditionnel,* or *trad*. The French-speaking population of Quebec were "French-Canadian," *canadien(ne)s français(es),* or simply *canadien(ne)s* until the Quiet Revolution of the 1960s and 1970s, when they became *québécois(es).* I use contemporary terminologies throughout this chapter.
3. "If there is one thing that we tried to show here in the festival, it was that everyone can make music."
4. "The Society for the promotion of traditional Québécois dance"; "The school of the arts of the *veillée*"
5. "a multiplication of viewpoints"
6. See Seitel (2001) and McDowell (2010) for more on the concept of "folklorization."
7. *Veillées* "of the good old times."
8. Stuart Hall describes society as composed of multiple "regimes of truth" that "define an ideological field of force" through structural relations of power and resistance (see Foucault [1980, 131] for more on regimes of truth). Hall theorizes this field, including the linkages between people and ideologies, via the concept of articulation: "the form of the connection [between two parts] that *can* make a unity of two different elements, under certain conditions" (Grossberg 1996, 136, 141, italics in original). Such connections are never necessary, or pre-determined, though once established they may be hard to break. Hall takes an overtly activist stance: articulations might be broken and remade otherwise, meaning that people may choose to articulate to an alternate ideology to advance their cause. Note that in Hall's formulation, a person or group of people articulate other people, objects, discourses, or actions "to" one another. See Grossberg for more on the concept of articulation (1996, 141ff); see Gelbart for a historicization of tradition as an ideological discourse within Western music (2007).
9. For instance, Bellemare erroneously states that Gauthier assumed direction of the Quebec Section *veillées* and was "seconded" by Massicotte (2012, 89). Guilbert reports that the Quebec Section staged only two *veillées* (2010–12). Note that Jean Duval's recent dissertation on crooked tunes in traditional music in Quebec mentions early staged *veillées* only briefly (2012).
10. "better informed, would share our profound appreciation of the hidden treasures of the French-Canadian land [*terroir*] and help us overcome the [material] obstacles that hinder the progress of our folklore projects."
11. "the general indifference"; "the haughty hostility"; "this nonsense." Barbeau gives no clues, unfortunately, as to the identity of this colleague.
12. "Exécutants du terroir" might be rendered as "performers of the land," "of the region(s)," or "of the soil." I do not translate "terroir" in the remainder of this chapter.
13. "a real, raw storyteller"
14. "that would know how to elevate the tone of the program"
15. "resurrection of the past"; "a complete rapture"
16. "conquered, even thrilled"

17 "who received the patriotic lesson that is released by the invocation of the things of the past, of the songs, of the stories, of the dances of our forefathers."
18 "Resounding ... Everywhere, people want to hear them and the welcome is enthusiastic."
19 Based on a text search of digitized periodicals available via Bibliothèque et Archives nationales du Québec, http://www.banq.qc.ca/collections/collection_numerique/journaux-revues/index.html.
20 "a patriotic duty"
21 "We've seen many times, near the end of the evening, or rather near the beginning of the morning, an entire hoard of enthusiastic dancers begin to sing the tunes while foot-tapping double-time [*battant à quatre*] and the *players* [musicians], pushed as if by a spring, enter the dance themselves with an incredible energy." Legendre was a lawyer and journalist originally from Nicolet, Quebec (Boivin 1994).
22 "nationalization of literature"; "treat French-Canadian subjects, and treat them in a French-Canadian manner"
23 "Mr Prince, in the *Bulletin du Parler français*, and Van Dyke, in *Gardienne de la lumière*, celebrated the unique character of our fiddlers, often incapable of meeting the expectation [that they would play] because they were not *wearing the proper shoes*! The singer would spin out non-stop the repertoire collected by Gagnon in his *Chansons canadiennes* and Dr LaRue in the 1864 *Foyer canadien* ... As for the storyteller, whose loquaciousness Taché has described in his *Trois légendes* or his *Forestiers*, as Van Dyke did in his *Gardienne*, either he retold stories he knew or he invented some from scratch. Mr Barbeau is in the process of resuscitating this genre through his contributions to [the *Journal of*] *American Folk-lore*."
24 I am presently studying these connections as part of the project "Folklore, *Régionalisme*, and Discourses of Language in Quebec, 1902–1942." This project is funded by the Fonds de recherche du Québec – Société et culture and is in association with Dr Micheline Cambron (Département des littératures de langue française, Université de Montréal) and the Centre de recherche interuniversitaire sur la littérature et la culture québécoises.
25 "With each object that Mr Marius Barbeau indicated, the public was bursting with joy and each repeated the name of the object: 'Ah! Will you look at that! A real spinning wheel!'"
26 "One must not confuse the soirées organized [by the Quebec Section] with the imitations, which borrow from burlesque rather than give an authentic presentation of the touching traditions of our population."
27 "this ridiculous and useless parade of 'canayens' in carrot-coloured wigs, patched pants, homespun shirts, and [traditional French-Canadian] boots."
28 "those who set out, for entirely personal ends, to vulgarize and exploit [the concept of staged *veillées*] without discernment."
29 "Gauthier must be prevented from reaping what we have sown ... He passes himself off as the accredited representative of French-Canadian folklore."
30 "certain fellows acquired a renown that I think is overrated, and they presented our old things in a manner that humiliates me. They have no aim but to make money and to get people talking about them." Note, however, that Gauthier and Massicotte exchanged polite correspondence in 1931 regarding Massicotte's play "Les Cousins du Député." In

letters dated 18 and 23 September, Massicotte authorized Gauthier to use the play for the "Veillées du bon vieux temps" provided that he (Massicotte) was not credited as the author, but only for having "compilée et adoptée" the work (Archives de Montréal, fonds Edouard-Zotique Massicotte).

31 "they speak a language stuffed full of the most atrocious anglicisms."
32 "render the illusion more complete"; "if our forefathers really had such rudeness of language and of conduct, I would ask Mr Gauthier to spare the French-Canadian stage [from such language and behaviour] from now on."
33 In an article paralleling certain aspects of the present chapter, Forsyth (2014) describes Acadian "kitchen parties" on Prince Edward Island as discursive referents for the commercialized presentation of Acadian music.
34 Sister Essiambre is a native French speaker but is equally at home in English after many years of working in anglophone communities. This interview was conducted in English.
35 I understand Sister Essiambre's "boogie-boogie" as equivalent to boogie-woogie.
36 For more on musical traditions in Douglastown, see Patterson and Risk 2015; Patterson, Risk, and Chaput 2014; Patterson 2013–14; Risk 2013. Rural social gatherings centred around music, song, and dance were common in many parts of North America as well as in Ireland and Scotland and went by a variety of names (Bennett 2009, 1–20; Bronner 1987, 6; Doherty 2015, 192–3, 208; Perlman 2015, 19–46, esp. 41–3).

References

Barbeau, Marius. 1919. "Notes et enquêtes: La première séance annuelle de la Section de Québec." *The Journal of American Folk-Lore* 32 (123): 181–3.

[Barbeau, Marius, and Édouard-Zotique Massicotte]. 1920. *Veillées du bon vieux temps à la Bibliothèque Saint-Sulpice, à Montréal, les 18 mars et 24 avril 1919 sous les auspices de la Société historique de Montréal et de la Société de folklore d'Amérique*. Montreal: G. Ducharme.

Bellemare, Luc. 2012. "Les réseaux des 'Lyriques' et des 'Veillées': une histoire de la chanson au Québec dans l'entre-deux-guerres par la radiodiffusion au poste CKAC de Montréal (1922–1939)." PhD diss., Université Laval.

Bennett, Margaret. 2009. *Dìleab Ailein: The Legacy of Allan MacArthur: Newfoundland Traditions across Four Generations*. Ochtertyre, Scotland: Grace Note Publications.

Berthiaume, David. 2006. "Les Veillées d'automne à Montréal (1975)." *Bulletin Mnémo* 10 (1). Accessed 23 November 2015. http://www.mnemo.qc.ca/spip/bulletin-mnemo/article/les-veillees-d-automne-a-montreal.

Boivin, Aurélien. 1994. "Legendre, Napoléon." In *Dictionary of Canadian Biography*, vol. 13. University of Toronto/Université Laval, 2003. Accessed 30 November 2015. http://www.biographi.ca/en/bio/legendre_napoleon_13E.html.

Brackett, David. 2016. *Categorizing Sound: Genre and Twentieth-Century Popular Music*. Berkeley: University of California Press.

Bronner, Simon J. 1987. *Old Time Music-Makers of New York State*. Syracuse, NY: Syracuse University Press.

Casgrain, Henri-Raymond. 1861. *Légendes canadiennes*. Quebec: J.T. Brousseau. http://bibnum2.banq.qc.ca/bna/numtexte/174730.pdf.

Chartier, Émile. 1917. "Notre petite histoire." *L'action française* 1 (12): 353–67.

Chauveau, Pierre J.O. 1853. *Charles Guérin: Roman de mœurs canadiennes*. Montreal: John Lovell. Originally published in 1846 in *Revue canadienne*. Digital book from Sabin Americana. http://galenet.galegroup.com/servlet/Sabin?af=RN&ae=CY102916129&srchtp=a&ste=14.

CQPV. 2015. "La veillée de danse comme patrimoine immatériel." Conseil québécois du patrimoine vivant. Accessed 23 November 2015. http://patrimoinevivant.qc.ca/2013/03/soutien-a-la-designation-de-la-veillee-de-danse/.

Doherty, Liz. 2015. *The Cape Breton Fiddle Companion*. Sydney, NS: Cape Breton University Press.

Du Berger, Jean, Jacques Mathieu, and Martine Roberge. 1997. *La Radio à Québec 1920–1960*. [Sainte-Foy, QC]: Les Presses de l'Université Laval.

De Surmont, Jean-Nicolas. 2005. "Marchard, Charles." In the *Dictionnaire biographique du Canada* 15. Université Laval/University of Toronto, 2003. Accessed 29 November 2015. http://www.biographi.ca/fr/bio/marchand_charles_15F.html.

Duval, Jean. 2012. "Porteurs de pays à l'air libre: jeu et enjeux des pièces asymétriques dans la musique traditionnelle du Québec." PhD diss., Université de Montréal.

Fabio. 1925. "Le Mois Théatral." *La Lyre* 3 (29): 11.

Faucher de Saint-Maurice, Narcisse. 1879. *À la veillée: contes et récits*. Quebec City: C. Darveau. Digital copy by Google Books.

Forsyth, Meghan. 2011. "*De par chez nous*: Fiddling Traditions and Acadian Identity on Prince Edward Island." PhD diss., University of Toronto.

– 2014. "Staging *La Francophonie*: Tradition, Tourism and Acadian Musical Spaces on Prince Edward Island." MUSICultures 40 (2): 65–93.

Foucault, Michel. 1980. "Truth and Power." Interview with Alessandro Fontana and Pasquale Pasquino. In *Power / Knowledge: Selected Interviews and Other Writings, 1972–1977*, edited by Colin Gordon, 109–33. New York, NY: Pantheon Books.

Gagnon, Ernest. 1865–67. *Chansons populaires du Canada*. In six installments. Quebec City, QC: Bureaux du Foyer canadien.

Gelbart, Matthew. 2007. *The Invention of "Folk Music" and "Art Music": Emerging Categories from Ossian to Wagner*. Cambridge, UK: Cambridge University Press.

Gosselin, Bernard. 1976. "La veillée des veillées." National Film Board of Canada film, 95: 29. https://www.onf.ca/film/veillee_des_veillees.

Graham, Glenn. 2006. *The Cape Breton Fiddle: Making and Maintaining Tradition*. Sydney, NS: Cape Breton University Press.

Grossberg, Lawrence, ed. 1996. "On Postmodernism and Articulation: An Interview with Stuart Hall." In *Stuart Hall: Critical Dialogues in Cultural Studies*, edited by David Morley and Kuan-Hsing Chen, 131–50. London, UK: Routledge.

Guilbert, Daniel. 2010–12. "La légende des 'Veillées du bon vieux temps.'" In four parts. *Bulletin Mnémo* 12 (4); *Bulletin Mnémo* 13 (1); *Bulletin Mnémo* 13 (4); *Bulletin Mnémo* 14 (1). Accessed 19 August 2019. http://mnemo.qc.ca/bulletin-mnemo/

article/la-legende-des-veillees-du-bon; http://mnemo.qc.ca/bulletin-mnemo/article/la-legenge-des-veillees-du-bon; http://mnemo.qc.ca/bulletin-mnemo/article/la-legende-des-veillees-du-bon-227; http://mnemo.qc.ca/bulletin-mnemo/article/la-legende-des-veillees-du-bon-vieux-temps-4e-partie-suite-et-fin.

Hagstrom Miller, Karl. 2010. *Segregating Sound: Inventing Folk and Pop Music in the Age of Jim Crow*. Durham, NC: Duke University Press.

Handler, Richard. 1984. "On Sociocultural Discontinuity: Nationalism and Cultural Objectification in Quebec." *Current Anthropology* 25 (1): 55–64.

Hayward, Annette. 2006. *La querelle du régionalisme au Québec, 1904–1931: vers l'autonomisation de la littérature québécoise*. Ottawa, ON: Le Nordir.

Joly, Diane. 2012. "(En)Quête de patrimoine au canada français 1882–1930: Genèse du concept et du processus de patrimonialisation." PhD diss., Université Laval.

Labbé, Gabriel. 1995. *Musiciens traditionnels du Québec (1920–1993)*. Montreal, QC: VLB.

LaRue, François-Alexandre-Hubert. 1863–65. "Les Chansons populaires et historiques du Canada." In two parts. *Foyer canadien* 1 (1863): 321–84; *Foyer canadien* 3 (1865): 5–72.

Lemire, Maurice, and Denis Saint-Jacques. 1996. *La vie littéraire au Québec*. Vol. 3, 1840–69. Saint-Foy, QC: Presses de l'Université Laval.

– 1999. *La vie littéraire au Québec*. Vol. 4 (1870–94). Saint-Foy, QC: Presses de l'Université Laval.

Marcotte, Gilles, and François Hébert. 1979. *Anthologie de la littérature québécoise*. Vol 3, *Vasseau d'or et croix du chemin*. . Montreal, QC: La Presse.

Maziade, Marc, and Gabriel Godbout-Castonguay. 2014. Interview by Jordan Dupuis, Claire Moeder, and Caroline Rousse. Le Quartier Général, CIBL. 23 October. Podcast audio. Accessed 31 October 2014. http://www.cibl1015.com/le-quartier-general.

McDowell, John H. 2010. "Rethinking Folklorization in Ecuador: Multivocality in the Expressive Contact Zone." *Western Folklore* 69 (2): 181–209.

Mercier, Louis. 2002. *La Société du parler français au Canada et la mise en valeur du patrimoine linguistique québécois. (1902–1962): Histoire de son enquête et genèse de son glossaire*. Quebec City, QC: Les Presses de l'Université Laval.

Morissette, Louis, head writer, and Véronique Cloutier, producer and host. 2008. "Bye Bye 2008." Live broadcast 31 December. Télévision de Radio-Canada. Accessed 31 October 2014. http://video.veroniquecloutier.com/2654311170001/Ouverture_-_Bye_Bye_2008.

Nowry, Laurence. 1995. *Marius Barbeau: Man of Mana, a Biography*. Toronto, ON: NC Press Ltd.

Patterson, Glenn. 2013–14. "The Gaspé Sound: Fiddle Music from Two Anglo-Gaspesian Villages." *Canadian Folk Music* 47 (4): 14–24.

Patterson, Glenn, and Laura Risk. 2015. "Digitization, Recirculation and Reciprocity: Proactive Archiving for Community and Memory on the Gaspé Coast and Beyond." *MUSICultures* 41 (2): 102–32.

Patterson, Glenn, Laura Risk, and Luc Chaput. 2014. Liner notes to the compact disc *Douglastown: Musique et chanson de la Gaspésie*. Douglastown Community Centre DOUG-001.

Perlman, Ken. 2015. *Couldn't Have a Wedding without the Fiddler: The Story of Traditional Fiddling on Price Edward Island*. Knoxville: University of Tennessee Press.

Potvin, Gilles. 2007. "Charles Marchand." In *The Canadian Encyclopedia*. Article published 9 May. Accessed 23 November 2015. http://www.thecanadianencyclopedia.ca/en/article/charles-marchand-emc/.

Prince, J.-E. 1908. "Les violons d'autrefois: essai de folklore musical." *Bulletin du parler français* (May): 330–37.

Radio-Canada. 2009. "Bye Bye 2008: Excuses et explications | Plus | Radio-Canada.ca." 9 January. Accessed 31 October 2014. http://ici.radio-canada.ca/arts-spectacles/PlusArts/2009/01/09/002-cloutier-morissette.asp.

Risk, Laura. 2013. "Douglastown: Les traditions musicales d'un village gaspésien." *Bulletin Mnémo* 14 (2): 1–6.

– 2017. "*Veillées*, Variants, and *Violoneux*: Generic Boundaries and Transnational Trajectories in the Traditional Instrumental Music of Quebec." PhD diss., McGill University.

Saint-Jacques, Denis, and Maurice Lemire. 2005. *La vie littéraire au Québec*. Vol. 5, 1895–1918. Saint-Foy, QC: Presses de l'Université Laval.

Seitel, Peter. 2001. "Proposed Terminology for Intangible Cultural Heritage: Towards Anthropological and Folkloristic Common Sense in a Global Era." International Round Table, "Intangible Cultural Heritage" – Working Definitions, UNESCO, Piedmont, Italy. www.unesco.org/culture/ich/doc/src/05297-EN.pdf.

Smith, Gordon E. 1995. "The Genesis of Ernest Gagnon's *Chansons populaires du Canada*." In *Taking a Stand: Essays in Honour of John Beckwith*, edited by Timothy J. McGee, 221–37. Toronto, ON: University of Toronto Press.

"Soucy, Isidore." 2007. In *The Canadian Encyclopedia*. Article published 3 April. Accessed 23 November 2015. http://thecanadianencyclopedia.ca/en/article/isidore-soucy-emc/.

SPDTQ. 2015. "Espace Trad | SPDTQ." Société pour la promotion de la danse traditionnelle québécoise. http://espacetrad.org.

Stevens, Paul. 1859. "Lecture de Mr Paul Stevens, le 15 Mars 1859, Esquisses de mœurs, influence des mauvaises liaisons, effets désastreux de l'intempérance." *L'Echo du Cabinet de lecture paroissial de Montréal* 1 (10): 152–3.

Taché, Joseph-Charles. 1884. *Forestiers et voyageurs, mœurs et légendes canadiennes*. First published in 1863. Montreal: Librairie Saint-Joseph, Cadieux & Derome. Digital copy by Google Books.

Thérien, Robert. 1998. "Arthur Lapierre, Singer, Folk Musician, and Actor *(circa 1888–?)*." Library and Archives Canada. Accessed 23 November 2015. http://www.collectionscanada.gc.ca/gramophone/028011-1078-e.html.

Thompson, Brian Christopher. 2015. *Anthems and Minstrel Shows: The Life and Times of Calixa Lavallée, 1842–1891*. Montreal & Kingston: McGill-Queen's University Press.

Van Dyke, Henry. 1906. *La Gardienne de la lumière et autres histoires canadiennes*. Originally published in English in 1901. French adaptation by E. Sainte-Marie Perrin. Paris, France: Calmann-Lévy.

Willis, Stephen C., and Helmut Kallmann. 2007. "Folk-Music-Inspired Composition." In *The Canadian Encyclopedia*. Article published 20 August. Accessed 23 November

2015. http://www.thecanadianencyclopedia.ca/en/article/folk-music-inspired-composition-emc/.

Archival Collections

Archives de Folklore de l'Université Laval. Fonds Édouard-Zotique Massicotte.

Bibliothèque et Archives nationales du Québec. Revues et journaux québécois. Online digital collection, including many with full text-search option. http://www.banq.qc.ca/collections/collection_numerique/journaux-revues/index.html

Canadian Museum of History Archives. Fonds Marius Barbeau and fonds Carmen Roy. Select items available online at http://www.historymuseum.ca/research-and-collections/library-and-archives/archival-collections/

McGill University Library. Periodicals collection (on microfilm).

Margaret E. Walker

Chapter 3

Kathak in Canada: Classical and Contemporary

Ta - Thei - Thei - Tata - A - Thei - Thei - Tata - Ta — *At the Hindu Society of Manitoba's Diwali holiday celebration, some audience members chat in the darkened hall while others watch two young women on a makeshift stage dance together in graceful synchronized movements. Using recorded music and visual effects, three dancers from the QuébéAsia Dance Collective present a new choreography based on an ancient Vedic story. In a Toronto dance theatre, musicians on tabla and piano improvise a jazz interpretation of Beethoven's* Moonlight Sonata *as a single dancer performs classic moves to the spellbound audience. In community centres, dance schools, and home studios from St John's to Vancouver, students change into salwar kameez outfits and tie on ankle bells in preparation for the strenuous footwork sessions that will begin their dance classes. This is kathak dance in Canada.*

Kathak is one of eight dances of India categorized as "classical."[1] Virtuosic, professionally performed, and inextricably linked to Indian music, these dances differ considerably in their accompanying instruments, movement vocabulary, and geographical origins. Kathak is the dance associated with North India and in particular with the states of Uttar Pradesh and Rajasthan.[2] A syncretic genre that includes influences from male and female, Muslim and Hindu, and aristocratic and vernacular practices, its movement vocabulary reflects its hybrid history. Dressed in colourful costumes of overshot silk, wearing dramatic black eyeliner, brass ankle bells, and, in the case of the women, glittering jewelry, kathak dancers combine graceful flowing gestures, vigorous rhythmic pieces, narrative sections, and spectacular sequences of spins on the left heel in an often seamless progression of dance items.[3] Although some of the more nuanced facial expressions and hand gestures are best experienced in smaller performance venues or salon concerts, kathak dance today is most often performed in large theatres with sophisticated sound systems and lighting displays. By this point in the early twenty-first century, kathak has become thoroughly globalized while simultaneously remaining a marker of Indian culture, and it is not difficult to find professional dancers and dance troupes touring and performing in most large cities of the world.

Like other Indian classical performing arts, kathak has strong links to Indian nationalism and the cultural revival that accompanied independence from Great Britain in 1947. In seeking a truly "Indian" culture that could be reclaimed after almost two hundred years of British and East India Company rule, nationalist cultural reformers embraced Orientalist narratives of ancient and devotional cultural origins, an "invented history" that sought to erase or at least minimize British and Islamicate influence.[4] In kathak's case, the invented history linked the syncretic dance of the mid-twentieth century to a narrative of ancient religious storytellers and thus "Hindu" origins, in spite of its obvious connections to the Mughal courts of North India. My previous historiographic work has revealed that there is little if any reliable evidence that supports a connection to the remote past, although it has uncovered examples of choreographic fragments related to today's dance. These fragments, which date from between the thirteenth and seventeenth centuries and include characteristic movements such as rhythmic footwork, spins, and poetic interpretation, were danced by diverse groups of people in quite different contexts and identified by a variety of names. In the documentation from the eighteenth and nineteenth centuries, one finds descriptions of female performers who sang and danced with graceful gestures, and men who danced complex rhythmic genres or performed in rural theatre. Historical forces including colonialism, changing patronage, and resultant migrations gradually brought performers and their practices together through the nineteenth century and the final fusion into a dance called kathak occurred during the early decades of the twentieth century. What dance anthropologist Pallabi Chakravorty (2008) terms the "dominant narrative" of kathak, the claim that the dance has roots in ancient temple practice, was invented during the nationalist revival in the first half of the twentieth century and reinforced in the postcolonial period (for further information about kathak and its history see especially Walker 2014a, but also Chakravorty 1998, 2006, and 2008 and Walker 2009/10, 2010, and 2014b).

The phenomenon of invented traditions and their links to nationalism is of course not uncommon and most often connected to colonial and postcolonial societies (Hobsbawm and Ranger 1983). Both inside and outside India, the belief in the performing arts as expressions of ancient devotion can be strongly embedded and often gives rise to rather fixed ideas about what "traditional" music and dance are or should be. In migrant or diasporic communities, the resultant "imported invented traditions" can become yet further exaggerated and result in tensions between ideas about which aspects of art and culture should be preserved as traditional and which aspects may be modified in the interest of individual expression. Both migrant and host peoples can hold firm beliefs about what is "authentically" representative of a given community and also how far artistic creations can stray from these ideals while still maintaining a sense of cultural integrity. For kathak in Canada, the opposition between traditional and innovative can be further complicated by the context of official multiculturalism, including audience expectations, requirements of funding agencies, and resultant categorization of practice.[5]

These tensions give rise to a number of questions concerning professional artistry, questions that, while explored with reference to kathak dance in this paper, can also be applied to studies of other styles and genres of performance in Canada. In contexts where kathak is by and large classified as a multicultural or ethnic dance representing Indian culture, for example, how can Canadian kathak dancers[6] explore innovative and contemporary expressions of personal artistic agency while still performing kathak? How do they dance, literally and figuratively, between their own conceptions of traditional and innovative kathak? Finally, should kathak dance in Canada be seen primarily as a cultural import, representing Indian or South Asian arts in the Canadian multicultural mosaic, or can it be understood as a transnational art form, distinctly capable of making its "traditional" elements a current and exciting part of Canadian contemporary performing arts?

In this chapter, I approach these questions largely through the works and words of Canadian kathak dancers themselves. One can find South Asian communities in Canada in almost every urban area and meet Canadians of South Asian origin or descent in all walks of life. The largest communities, however, and thus potential dance students, audiences, and patrons, are found in the lower mainland in and around Vancouver in British Columbia, and the Greater Toronto Area in Ontario, particularly in the urban areas of Mississauga and Brampton just west of the city. Nevertheless, one can easily locate kathak dancers and dance schools in many other Canadian cities including Calgary, Winnipeg, Ottawa, and Montreal. The research that I draw on for this paper focuses largely on dancers based in Toronto and Ottawa whom I have known for many years. This is not because they are necessarily better placed to represent kathak dance in Canada than other dancers, but rather because my research and interview questions grew out of lessons I took, performances I saw, and many informal conversations I had with these dancers over the last two decades. From my colleagues in the Canadian kathak world, I learned not only how to dance, but also about the importance of classical kathak as a living tradition and contemporary art form.

Kathak in Canada

I discovered the world of kathak in 1995 when I saw Toronto-based kathak dancer Joanna de Souza (then Joanna Das) give a lecture demonstration at the University of Toronto's Faculty of Music. I was immediately drawn to how the dance embodied and expressed the music that accompanied it; indeed, as de Souza and tabla player Ritesh Das, who performed with her, emphasized, music and dance are one in kathak, sharing structures, repertoire items, and an oral notation system.[7] A year later, I enrolled in my first classes, beginning ten years of kathak dance study first at M-Do Studio in Toronto with de Souza, followed by lessons with dancer-choreographer Deepti Gupta in Toronto and New Delhi, further study with Saveeta Sharma at the Upasana School of Dance in Ottawa, and for a short while, with Ashok Chakravorty, a teacher at the New Delhi Kathak Kendra national dance school. My experiences of intensive practice, aching muscles, blistered feet, and the occasional performance (see figure 3.1), were accompanied by a wide-ranging study of historical literature, archival material, iconography, and music as I explored and absorbed this fascinating and compelling dance genre. My doctoral and postdoctoral research also took me to India, where I had the honour of meeting, interviewing, and observing the performances and classes of many of India's top kathak dancers. Nevertheless, through my teachers in Canada and ongoing relationships with other Indo-Canadian choreographer-dancers such as Rina Singha, Bageshree Vaze, and Sudeshna Maulik, I have long been interested in kathak's Canadian life.

Figure 3.1 | The author performing a kathak solo at the DANs/CE KAPITAL Festival in Ottawa, Ontario, in 2006.

My introduction to kathak was in a university setting, where it was presented as a classical art form as demanding and profound as ballet or Beethoven, rather than "exotic," "ethnic," or "multicultural." Indian dance, however, has generally been most visible in Canada through what religion and society scholar Paul Bramadat calls "ethnic cultural spectacles": the multitude of folk, ethnic, and multicultural festivals held across the country where various groups present and represent themselves to their own and other communities (2001, 3). The performing arts often play a key role in uniting diasporic groups in their host countries, particularly through their centrality in holidays, religious occasions, and rites of passage (Dietrich 2004), and can also be used by groups who are heterogeneous in their geographical place of origin to present strategic cultural homogeneity in their new locale (Bramadat 2001, 6). In the Canadian context, however, the conflation and overlap of North and South Indian music systems or the varieties of Indian dance can take place simply because of the availability of good teachers in a given town or region. For example, both Natasha Bakht (2011) and Bageshree Vaze (described below) began their dance training in the South Indian genre of bharatanatyam despite their North Indian heritage. Furthermore, the importance of the performing arts in postcolonial nation building in India, in addition to a more recent sense of transnational South Asian identity, has made almost any genre of South Asian performing arts – from rural vernacular songs to Bollywood dancing – equally able to represent a homogeneous national Indian culture at home or abroad. These links to Indian national identity are frequently explained as expressions of Indian tradition, and although most visible in public performance, they are also an important part of dance training and, indeed, often a reason why parents enrol their second- or even third-generation children in classes here in Canada (Varghese 2008, Dhiman 2013, and Thobani 2017c).

In their research on Indian dance in Canada, both Meera Varghese and Palak Dhiman focus on identity creation in the diaspora, yet also draw attention to the tension between traditional or ethnicized enactments of culture and creative artistic innovation. Natasha Bakht, in her article on multiculturalism and the arts, lays the responsibility for this friction squarely at the feet of "the rhetoric of multiculturalism in Canada," pointing out that "it has not allowed us to be unpredictable because it has insisted upon categorizing us, usually inaccurately" (2011, 183). While this is undoubtedly true in many situations, other Canadian kathak dancers with whom I have spoken have pointed out that sometimes Indo-Canadians can be restrictive in their own ways. Some of the experiences they shared with me included performing for community organizations that support dance primarily as a balm for homesickness, or being criticized for their innovative choreographic work by fellow professional Indian dancers.

A further tension is found in the equating of traditional with classical in South Asian performing arts. A quick Google search for "traditional dance" leads predominantly to sites from around the world that present or define self-identified "folk" genres, yet the keywords "traditional Indian dance" produce page after page of hits linked almost exclusively to Indian classical dance websites. Such categories are, of course, problematic and have in many cases been broken down in our postmodern world, but the descriptors "traditional" and "classical" continue to be used by dancers and event organizers both within India and in the diaspora. Kathak is properly categorized, like modern dance or ballet, as a virtuosic concert dance rather than a folk dance, but, along with the South Indian dance genre bharatanatyam, it has been an important representative of "traditional" Indian culture at folk festivals and multicultural pavilions across Canada. I remember, during my initial years of study, being surprised to learn that my teacher's dance company was performing at a fringe festival.[8] I quickly learned, however, that my understanding of kathak as a "high" art form was not necessarily shared, and a folk, fringe, or multicultural festival was in fact a far more likely setting at that time to experience a kathak performance in Canada than Toronto's Hummingbird Centre for the Performing Arts.[9] There are vigorous criticisms of multicultural events and their presentations of racialized "otherness" to hegemonic white Canadian culture (Bisoondath 1994 and Bakht 2011 among others), but these contrast with arguments interpreting these types of displays as discursive and dialogic places where the participants negotiate their (multi)cultural identities with full agency and awareness (Bramadat 2001; see also Ramnarine 2007 and Dhiman 2013). This emphasis on agency is particularly apt in the study of kathak in Canada, as the dancers who perform in festivals like Winnipeg's Folklorama, Toronto's now defunct Caravan, fringe, folk, and multicultural festivals across the country, or the various Canada Day extravaganzas are often the same ones who perform in local Indo-Canadian Mahotsavs,[10] dance school recitals, and also on the concert stage.

Recognition of individual agency and choice is also particularly important when looking at the work of professional dancers. Canadian performing artists who specialize in non-European genres like kathak often find themselves at odds with concepts of tradition that link music and dance with national essences, multicultural colour, and diasporic nostalgia, even if they were introduced to their art form through these contexts. Such artists can find that they struggle to be accepted as professionals who create and perform artistic works that are as original and relevant as those in the so-called mainstream genres. For kathak dancers, this sense of disconnect can occur equally with members of South Asian communities, non-Indian dancers or audiences, and the administrators of professional performance venues and funding organizations. Difficulties can arise as easily from a dancer's choice of music as from the presentation of a potentially controversial theme or topic in a new work. Stretching the boundaries of choreography or costume design might result in disapproval, but paradoxically a dancer might also be criticized in wider professional circles for adhering too closely to the parameters of "traditional" kathak. Yet, in spite of these frictions and frustrations, I have found that my colleagues in the Canadian kathak world have long been negotiating these seeming oppositions of classical and traditional, traditional and contemporary, and Indian and Canadian with full agency and understanding.

Traditional Kathak

In the international kathak world there is no controversy surrounding the conflation of traditional and classical, and the characteristics of kathak dance are well established. Whether in India, Canada, or elsewhere, what is understood as traditional kathak is performed as a solo by a male or female dancer with a small ensemble of accompanying instrumentalists (figure 3.2). The performance will often begin with a devotional number, most frequently an invocation to a Hindu deity like Saraswati or Ganesh expressed through a sung Sanskrit poem.[11] Ideally accompanied by a live singer, but outside India often by a recording, the dancer strikes iconic postures and chooses movements that evoke the deity's appearance and characteristics. Next, the dancer usually moves through a series of composed dances that are smoothly linked together by improvised movement sequences called *thaat*[12] that express the nuances of the *tal* or rhythmic cycle and mark important beats with arresting postures. *Amad* or entry, *salami*, featuring the Muslim greeting *salam*, and *rang manch*, which is a symbolic salutation to the stage, flow gracefully over the accompanying tabla drums and the *nagma*, a repeated melody that marks the time cycle. Matching the gradual increase of tempo also found in North Indian instrumental music, the kathak performance will next shift into a medium pace, and then finally arrive at the fast, virtuosic finale with its rhythmic footwork and breathtaking sequences of spins. During this progression, the dancer presents a variety of composed rhythmic pieces, most commonly *tukras* or *parans*,[13] which she or he will often recite using the dance's syllabic oral notation before dancing. Other items include the virtuosic footwork called *tatkar*, rhythmic variations called *leri*, three-fold cadential patterns called *tihais*, and captivating sequences called *gat nikas*, which illustrate evocative characters through an iconic stance or series of gestures enhanced by a gliding walk. An audience favourite, which also illustrates kathak's bond with its music, is *sawal-jawab* or *jugalbandi*, where dancer and drummer engage in a playful competition of improvised question and answer phrases.[14]

Although it dates only from the post-independence period of the 1950s, this performance sequence forms the core of "traditional" kathak all over the world. Yet, since some of the repertoire items, in particular the footwork,

Figure 3.2 | Kathak exponent Manisha Gulyani with accompanists, 2014.

spins, and the gliding walk, are documented in treatises that date back to between the thirteenth and seventeenth centuries, it is not inaccurate to understand this as a twentieth-century artistic framework that juxtaposes and links together older material.[15] Perhaps more importantly, it is the choreographic material in the solo, including footwork, spins, rhythmic variations, and composed dance pieces like *amad*, *tukra*, *paran*, and *rang manch*, that forms the core of kathak training in both Indian and Canadian dance classes. Mastering not only the often-short dance items themselves, but more crucially their musical fundamentals, movement vocabulary, and characteristic postures and gestures, is essential to proper kathak training. In some diasporic classes, students present a substantial solo performance as a graduation recital (figure 3.3),[16] and it is the solo material that is taught and tested in diploma and certificate programs, where they exist. Furthermore, advanced training as a soloist will also lead to a deep understanding of the dance's musical and kinesthetic grammar including not only the structure of the dance repertoire

Figure 3.3 | Invitation to solo Kathak debut performance.

but also improvisation and the creation of new compositions or movement sequences, which are fundamental skills and part of kathak's aesthetic. If tradition can be understood as forming an established foundation for current creative production, rather than as something unchanging or ancient that needs to be preserved for its own sake, then the solo repertoire, its structure and grammar, and accompanying expressive skills inarguably form one of the traditional pillars of kathak.

The other pillar of kathak is its story-telling aspect. The name kathak is cognate to the Sanskrit or Hindi term *katha* meaning a story or tale. While an important part of the claim to ancient origins is this etymological link supposedly connecting today's dance to a Vedic story-telling practice, there are also more convincing and recent connections between kathak and various forms of vernacular theatre (Walker 2006). In performance, the narrative or dramatic sections of the kathak solo are often separated from the sequence described above and include pantomimed accounts largely from Hindu mythology called *gat bhav* and stories from the youth of the Hindu God Krishna often enacted in illustration of songs such as *thumri*. In solo performances, these dramatic presentations can easily be presented by one dancer, who uses single turns called *paltas* to change from one character to another, playing several roles as he or she conveys a well-known tale. The same stories, however, can also be used for group choreographies or even large-scale "ballet" productions that include scenery and dramatic costumes. Somewhat ironically, although strongly connected to the dominant narrative and its claim that kathak originated in the activities of ancient storytellers, it has been this aspect of the twentieth-century dance that has commonly provided opportunities for new choreography, allowing kathak dancers and choreographers to express contemporary themes and tell current stories rather than revisiting Hindu mythology.

The frequent separation of the narrative portion from the flow of solo material facilitates such creative opportunities. Many of the kathak performances I have seen in Canada are organized to begin with a version of the traditional solo in the first half of the program, followed by a new solo or group choreography after the intermission. Although the ensemble number is sometimes a reinterpretation of a previously choreographed work, it is also just as often a premiere of a new creation. This structure is also sometimes followed in student recitals, with each class or level presenting a pre-composed ensemble version of beginner, primary, or intermediate repertoire using the same shifts in tempo and mood as a professional solo, followed by new group work in the second half of the presentation. In both expert and student versions, the initial presentation of traditional kathak functions in large part to demonstrate the dancers' or teacher's artistic proficiency and expertise before moving into anything that might be more contemporary or controversial. Although the second half may still rely on presentations of Hindu mythological material, perhaps with inventive instrumentation or some new use of lighting or sound, it is also frequently an occasion for much more adventurous material and ideas.

Contemporary Kathak

New choreographic creations using kathak movement vocabulary range from quite conservative retellings of familiar portions of epics or scenes from mythology to experimental recombinations of gestural cells and courageous explorations of social or political themes. Such work is certainly not confined to Canada or other parts of the South Asian diaspora. Kathak dancer-choreographers within India include ground-breaking pioneers such as Kumudini Lakhia and current innovators like Aditi Mangaldas, in addition to many world-renowned artist-teachers such as Birju Maharaj, Rajendra Gangani, and Saswati Sen.[17] Furthermore, artists like Daksha Seth and Madhu

Nataraj have reached beyond the standard classical repertoire in their contemporary Indian dance productions, which can combine influences from South Asia with global inspirations and state-of-the-art technological effects.[18] Tensions between conservative and inventive approaches can nonetheless be found even at the heart of professional kathak in New Delhi, as a vigorous debate about whether all female kathak dancers should be required to wear the conservative *dupatta* or veil recently demonstrated (Mangaldas et al. 2013). Strange as such a requirement may seem to those unconnected with the kathak world, the invocation of the importance of so-called traditional attire in the definition of the dance itself speaks directly to the issues of postcolonial national identity and essence alluded to above. In Canada, where "Indian" identity and essence are not only originally imported but also rub shoulders with other migrant, settler, and Indigenous identities and art forms, negotiations regarding the importance of tradition and its relevance to artistic creation have given rise to a variety of approaches to new choreography. Three such approaches to original production can be seen as characteristic of new kathak choreography in Canada, each using kathak's traditional features in different ways, while also variously interacting with the Canadian context.

The first of these manifestations, and arguably the most conservative of the three, is the creation of new choreographic productions that continue to reinforce kathak's links to real and imagined past culture. I have argued elsewhere that the account that places kathak's origins in a performance practice from the remote past is an invented history with origins in the nationalist cultural revival that largely took place in the first half of the twentieth century. Nevertheless, stories from epic narratives like the *Ramayana* and *Mahabharata* and mythological tales like those concerning youthful exploits of Krishna continue not only to form important teaching material but also to provide ongoing inspiration for new work. A related and popular subject is the portrayal of Indian history, and in particular the development of kathak as it supposedly moved from Hindu temple to Muslim court. While new dance creations in India may be moving beyond the ubiquitous retellings of tales from the epics and portrayals of Vedic society, the role of kathak in reinforcing South Asian identity as a unique part of the mosaic can still make these choices common in Canada. There are many examples of recent productions, including the Mississauga Taal Academy's 2010 production *Utkranti – Evolution of Kathak* (taalacademy.com) and Toronto-based Hemant and Vaishali Panwar's 2014 creation *Shakuntala*,[19] which depicts "the social context of ancient India" and is based on a story from the *Mahabharata* (panwarmusicanddance.com).

A further reason for the popularity of mythological and historical topics is the function of dance classes in some contexts for the dissemination of information about "Indian culture" to second- or third-generation Indo-Canadian children (Varghese 2008, 30–2 and Dhiman 2013, 73–4) or even for the "promotion, preservation and propagation of ... South Asian heritage" in Canada (panwarmusicanddance.com).

Some professional dancers and teachers distance themselves from these ideas and emphasize that they are first and foremost creating dance and dancers rather than offering classes in religious and cultural education (see also Varghese 2008, 30–2). Yet artistic creation is obviously influenced by experience, and thus the second prominent aspect of kathak dance in Canada has been the creation of original productions that reflect the migrations, chance encounters, and multicultural realities of the dancers themselves. The work of Toronto-based kathak dancer Rina Singha, who came to Canada in 1965, provides a number of significant and illustrative examples, including expressions of her Christian faith in *Yesu Katha* (1988), stories of various aspects of migration in *Becoming – A Song from Exile* (1994) and *Manzilen – A Journey* (2007), and adventurous cross-cultural fusions and collaborations such as *The Seekers* (1997) and *Agony and Ecstasy* (1999). Some of Indo-Canadian kathak dancer Deepti Gupta's creations explore similar themes. *Collision/Collusion* (2007) presented a series of four dance pieces that explored the chance artistic encounters that have been an important feature of her Canadian creative life, juxtaposing and blending kathak with jazz and other styles.[20] Similarly, Ottawa-based kathak and odissi dancer Saveeta Sharma has explored the multicultural relationships Canada provides both through her own original choreographies and her annual DANs/cE KAPITAL – Revolution in Movement festival, which presents both international and Canadian dancers in a multiplicity of styles from around the world. Kathak's choreographic vocabulary provides another, perhaps more direct, path to intercultural dialogue, as *Firedance*, Joanna de Souza's collaboration with flamenco dancer Esmeralda Enrique, illustrates.[21] Flamenco and kathak share a number of postures and fluid hand gestures as well as dynamic footwork, and kathak's rhythmic patterns also invite less formal fusions or collaborative presentations with step dancing and even breakdancing.[22]

Sharma, Singha, Gupta, and de Souza have all nonetheless remained firmly connected to their foundations in classical kathak and their transnational relationships to India. All these Canadian professional dancers pursued advanced training in India, although at slightly different points in their lives, and all still perform and teach solo traditional kathak in addition to choreographing new works. Gupta still travels frequently between Canada and India and has taught kathak dance and theory to Indian students in New Delhi, and Sharma's senior students regularly win scholarships to pursue advanced study in India. One of Singha's most influential and enduring projects since 2008 has been the Kathak Mahotsav Canada, a festival of classical kathak performances by visiting Indian and Canadian dancers. As Palak Dhiman asserts in her work on Canadian multicultural dance, "living a particular culture is not about preserving something from the past, but rather about making it relevant to the present. This also does not mean that one must in some way force oneself to become Canadian by giving up elements of one's culture" (Dhiman 2013, 109).

There are kathak dancers in Canada, however, for whom the opposition of "Canadian" and "Indian" has by and large lost any real meaning, at least in an artistic if not in a personal sense. Although choreographic works that combine different dance styles or create kathak dance numbers to non-Indian music may reflect the variety of artistic encounters in multicultural Canada, such creations still largely stand outside mainstream Canadian dance performance practice. The third face of contemporary kathak dance in Canada is therefore the emergence of kathak as a valid, professional dance art, neither more nor less "multicultural" than ballet or modern dance, yet still firmly rooted in its own aesthetic. The increasing number of kathak dancers in Canada includes not only artists who migrated here as adults, such as Rina Singha, but also those who were born in Canada or migrated here as small children, who grew up in other parts of the South Asian diaspora before coming to Canada, who are the children of such double migrants, and who are of mixed descent or not of Indian descent at all. This range of backgrounds and origins continues to complicate and challenge notions of "South Asian," "Indian," and "Indo-Canadian" identity. Furthermore, although one does not have to be of a certain ethnicity in order to adopt or become devoted to its traditions, the importance of preserving one's own identity through artistry connected to a supposed ancient Indian past can fade in this more transnational context. I suggested above that traditional kathak might be most productively defined by the choreographic and musical foundations achieved through established pedagogies that form the core of its artistic vocabulary, rather than a sense of national or exotic essence. This is also the hope of many Canadian kathak dancers – ranging from the established doyenne Rina Singha to the multi-talented Bageshree Vaze – that kathak lose its multicultural label and join mainstream, serious classical art in Canada.

Bageshree Vaze and Pratibha Arts

Reaching beyond restrictive labels and concepts of tradition has long been important to Indo-Canadian musician and dancer Bageshree Vaze.[23] Born in Pune, a city in the North Indian state of Maharashtra, Vaze migrated to Canada with her parents as a small child in the 1970s, and the family settled in St John's, Newfoundland. Initially trained in the South Indian dance bharatanatyam, Vaze also studied North Indian singing with her father and subsequently pursued training in multiple South Asian and Western dance genres, both in India and North America. She moved to Ontario in 1996, and had by 1998 picked kathak as her dance of choice. This was, as she has explained to me several times, in large part because of its close links to North Indian classical music, and most of her public performances continue to feature kathak in both classical and innovative presentations. After further professional study in both kathak dance and Hindustani (North Indian) vocal music, Vaze settled in Toronto where she is based with her musician husband, tabla player Vineet Vyas, and their two children.

Vaze describes herself as a "product of Canadian culture," and credits not only former prime minister Pierre Trudeau's multicultural policies, but also funding agencies like the Shastri Indo-Canadian Institute, Chalmers Foundation, and Canada Council for her artistic education and evolution (personal communication 2010). Although some of her earliest choreographic creations, such as *The Rebel Goddess* (1999), explored combining and contrasting dance genres (Dandekar 2004), Vaze is also dedicated to the presentation of traditional kathak on Canadian stages and in professional venues. Facing the programming challenges openly, she asserts not only "if there's enough room for all kinds of ballet, there should be room for all kinds of classical and fusion South Asian dance," but also "contemporary dance has changed and is changing and should include people like me" (personal communication 2013).

Bageshree Vaze believes that one of the difficulties complicating kathak's recognition in Canada as a professional dance genre as mainstream as ballet is the scarcity of Canadian-based professional-level training. I have observed this phenomenon too; although there are an increasing number of kathak schools, teachers, and attendant dance companies in Canada, dancers interested in pursuing advanced study still typically go to India, most often to study with their teacher's *guru*.[24] One of the barriers to advanced training in Canada can be funding; although grants for education and performance production are available, dancers seeking support for non-Western genres have as a rule needed to apply through multicultural or community channels rather than be considered for support similar to a professional ballet or modern dance company (Bakht 2011, 177). Furthermore, although many Canadian kathak dancers have engaged in successful and creative collaborations, Vaze is particularly interested in developing what she sees as a more integrated approach to cross-cultural dance. "To really do fusion, you really have to have training in both genres," she explained to me. She then once again emphasized the necessity for anyone dancing kathak to have a deep understanding of North Indian musical structure and grammar and to retain that connection even in multidisciplinary initiatives (personal communication 2013).

To achieve these ends, Bageshree Vaze formed Pratibha Arts in 2011, a comprehensive organization aiming "to enhance and advance the cultural fabric of Ontario and Canada through the production, education and performance of and about arts, particularly dance and music styles originating from South Asia" (http://www.bageshree.com/pratibhaarts). Equally dedicated to producing and presenting high standard performances in a variety of venues and to providing workshops and training sessions for emerging dancers and musicians, Pratibha Arts also pursues partnerships with other Ontario music and dance organizations through its Raagini Dance Company. With financial support from the Ontario Arts Council's Aboriginal and Culturally Diverse Dance Training fund, Raagini's mandate now includes the provision of the type of intensive professional training Vaze has long wished to see in Canada. Pratibha Arts has already created a number of new performances, choreographies, and student workshops, largely presented through Toronto's culturally diverse Harbourfront Centre. In 2015, Pratibha Arts took an important step forward when the Toronto contemporary dance organization DanceWorks commissioned Vaze and Raagini to create and perform a new production to be presented as part of Harbourfront's Next Steps Dance Series. The new work, *Paratopia*, premiered at Harbourfront on 23 April as the closing performance of the Mainstage Season, a series normally dedicated to Western contemporary dance (figure 3.4).

The performance, which I saw on 25 April 2015, was presented in two sections, not unlike the characteristic "traditional/innovative" division described above. The first four pieces, *In My (Dis)Place, Dhamaru/Dhamaar, Navarasas,* and *Tarana*, were drawn from earlier original productions by Vaze. All solo performances, and danced either by Vaze or Anuj Mishra, a kathak dancer from Lucknow in India, these works intriguingly covered most of the approaches and themes I identify above as characteristic of other new Canadian

Figure 3.4 | Publicity photo for *Paratopia*.

kathak choreographies. *In My (Dis)Place* explored themes of migration and personal artistic searching, issues Vaze also grappled with in her 1999 work *The Rebel Goddess*.[25] *Damaru/Dhamaar* was an example of pure dance or *nritt*, and other than a few gestures that evoked the Hindu deity Shiva as Nataraj or Lord of the Dance, the choreography focused on rhythm, improvisation, and kathak's connection with the tabla drums. *Navarasas*, an excerpt from a much longer presentation entitled *Avatar (9)*, was the most "traditional" in its links to the ancient artistic theory of nine aesthetic emotions, but was set to music composed and sung by Vaze herself. The final solo number, *Tarana*, also used music performed by Vaze, in this case a selection from her 2007 album also entitled *Tarana*, which contains North Indian classical songs she specifically arranged and adapted for dance.[26] The choreography itself aimed to celebrate "the setting and origins of Kathak dance in the ... royal court" (Program Notes, DW211 Bageshree Vaze). Although not conforming precisely to the sequence of the traditional solo performance, these four pieces were nonetheless closely tied to classical kathak not only by their use of kathak vocabulary such as footwork, spins, and classic postures, but also through their inclusion of many recognizable complete dance items such as *thaat*, *amad*, and *vandana* and their accompanying music.

It was *Paratopia*, the group work ending the evening, that broke new ground. In the darkened theatre, the performance began with the amplified sound of a metronome marking a steady beat. A male voice began to recite kathak *bols*, the oral notation syllables used for both dance movements and drum strokes: Dha - - - Dha - - - Dha tit dha - - - Dha - - - Dha tit dha - treke dha. Projected on the screen at the back of the stage, these syllables appeared in Devanagri script as they were articulated: धा - - - धा - - - धा तति धा - - - धा - - - धा तति धा - तृक धा |. Bageshree Vaze entered the stage dressed in a simple black dress rather than the usual colourful costume, veil, and jewelry. She was wearing sunglasses, ankle bells, and rendering the *bols*, which continued to be recited and to float across the screen, with her feet. As the recitation and her footwork became faster and more virtuosic, she moved through classical footwork patterns playing with sounds, patterns, rhythmic density, and cross-rhythms, and finally settled into the well-known eight-beat pattern "takita takita dhinne." Until this point, although the sound and setting, including Vaze's costume and the projected *bols*, were not what one would expect in a kathak solo, Vaze's dance technique and rhythmic choices were entirely in keeping with kathak's traditional vocabulary. She was then joined on stage by three more dancers, who were also wearing sunglasses and dressed in black. Danny Gomez, Danny McArthur, and Samantha Schlesse are all Toronto-based professional dance artists and experts in multiple styles including hiphop, house, ballet, modern, contemporary, jazz, and types of ballroom dance. Joining Vaze in dancing the eight-beat pattern, which had taken on the characteristic of a rhythmic groove, they played with it, exploring its 3+3+2 ostinato with moves from their own dance vocabulary. As the four dancers then synchronized their movements, conforming to the classical kathak footwork pattern for "takita takita dhinne" with which Vaze had begun, they were joined by another performer, beatboxer Cj Mairs, who uses the professional name Killabeatz. The rhythmic energy that had been building through the performance increased even further as Killabeatz's driving vocal percussion combined with the sounds of the tabla played by Vineet Vyas and the precise rhythms of Vaze's feet and ankle bells. Sound and movement came to a climax as modern, urban, and jazz dance vocabularies mingled, then united with the performance's overarching kathak aesthetic, and philosophical quotes from T.S. Eliot, Abraham Lincoln, and Stephen Hawking floated across the screen.

The evening's performance showed clearly how Vaze's innovative work, while certainly aware of the aesthetics of modern or contemporary dance, stays faithful to the traditional movement vocabulary of classical kathak and its musical structures. In *Paratopia*, she took this basic elemental artistic integrity a step further by seeking "an interaction between different dance styles ... using kathak dance language [performed by] dancers who are not trained in kathak dance, but ... are taking on kathak language and interpreting it through their own bodies" (Vaze 2015). Although new choreography can often involve some degree of collaborative creation with the dancers who will perform the new work, Vaze expanded this cooperative process to include an educational element, training her dancers in classical kathak. Yet, after teaching the traditional footwork, musical structure, and basic repertoire to her company, she then encouraged them to reclaim the vocabulary they had learned and dance it through their own professional styles. In a publicity video for the Next Steps Dance Series published on YouTube shortly before the premiere, Vaze placed her work firmly in both the trajectory of classical kathak and the Canadian context, explaining that kathak dance is "evolving with the different collaborators in this program as a product of Toronto, as a product of Canada, and with very versatile dancers and artists from different backgrounds" (Vaze 2015).

In this intention and presentation Vaze's kathak is inarguably a "Canadian" dance art. In all her explanations and her publicity material, she presents herself as an artist – a musician, choreographer, and dancer – whose creations arise from her experiences and personal expression as a globalized Canadian rather than from a need to be "multicultural," "traditional," or representative of transplanted identity. She is not alone in these goals. Many of the kathak dancers I have already drawn attention to, and others not addressed here, perform Canadian kathak, not as an expression of nostalgia rooted in ancient Indian traditions but as a transnational art form with its own ongoing traditions. As Palak Dhiman put it, "Indian diasporas all over the world ... contribute significantly to the innovation and growth of Indian classical dance forms such as kathak ... in a way that is not just about cultural preservation or nationalist tropes, but about these art forms themselves and their own continuous development" (Dhiman 2013, 137).

Classical and Contemporary

I have drawn attention above to the difficulties sometimes faced by professional kathak dancers and choreographers in Canada due to tensions between expectations about "traditional" kathak and contemporary creative works. The term "traditional" has, of course, been thoroughly problematized in the past few decades, and even an incomplete list includes work on colonialism and postcolonial nationalism (the "imagined communities" of Anderson 2006 and the "invented traditions" of Hobsbawn and Ranger 1983; see also Phillips and Schochet 2004); anthropology, folklore, and oral history (Finnegan 1991; Bronner 2000; Noyes 2009); and revival and hybridity (Briggs 1996; Anklewicz 2012; Ronström 2014). Indeed, as social anthropologist David Coplan asserted in his chapter entitled "Ethnomusicology and the Meaning of Tradition," "the concept of tradition ... [has by now been] reified, manipulated, and stretched entirely out of analytical shape" by well-meaning scholars seeking to re-examine the obvious (1991, 47). Yet, as Coplan and others point out, the word and the concept have "remained current and indispensable despite [their] inherent contradictions, doubtful empirical status, and ideological entanglements (Coplan 1991, 36). Certainly, the term "traditional kathak" not only has currency and cultural weight in India, Canada, and elsewhere; it connects with little question or controversy to a recognizable and transnational performance style, including a body of repertoire and an established choreographic and musical vocabulary used in composition and improvisation.

I have also drawn attention to the conflation of the terms "traditional" and "classical" in the Indian music and dance world. My consultants for this article and my other work on kathak dance over the years have largely used the two words interchangeably, as I have to some extent in this chapter. Certainly they appear as equivalents on websites and other publicity material. In academic discourse, however, the word "classical" can seem as problematic as the term "traditional": it is "deeply multivalent and slippery," according to cultural historian Katherine Schofield, and "particularly problematic when applied to non-Western traditions" (Schofield 2010, 484). Yet, as I outlined above and Schofield goes on to clarify, the shift to modernity, independence, and postcolonial nation-state in India included a reconfiguration of the performing arts as existing court and temple practices were adapted for urban centres of patronage. Central to the changes was a process of classicization that included the creation of a canon of musical and choreographic competencies,[27] the adoption of an institutionalized curriculum for their dissemination, and gradual gentrification as new generations of performing artists were drawn from the middle and upper-middle classes rather than communities of hereditary performers. Although this resulted in the marginalization of lower class or caste performers, the (re)creation of court music and dance as "classical" national culture provided the independence movement with cultural ammunition with which to confront colonial accusations of inferiority or barbarism (Moro 2004, Bakhle 2005, Kippen 2006, and Subramanian 2007). The association of the classicized arts with tradition, particularly ancient "Hindu" tradition, was part of the revival and gave rise to the invented history connecting the classical performing arts with pre-Islamicate devotional practices. India, of course, has hundreds more "traditional" performance practices beyond those considered classical. These are, perhaps predictably, categorized as "folk" or *lok* (meaning literally "people") and are closely associated with rural and local cultures.[28] It is largely the classical genres that represent the nation on the global stage, however, and their connections with "Indian traditional culture" play a significant role in their publicity and presentation.

Kathak is inarguably accepted as classical, as Sunil Kothari's widely known book *Kathak: Indian Classical Dance Art* (1989) proudly declares. Although one occasionally hears lingering doubts expressed about kathak's "Hindu-ness," given its association with the North Indian Mughal courts, it is certainly never considered a folk dance, nor does it have a place in Peter Manuel's concept of the "intermediate sphere" of Indian performing arts that lie between classical and folk (Manuel 2015). Yet, in oral and written discourse about kathak and other South Asian dance genres, classical is used interchangeably with traditional, which marks these practices not only as virtuosic "high art," but also as ancient, ancestral, and timeless. This equates Indian concert dances with many of the qualities that Euro-American society idealistically ascribes to "traditional" or "folk" culture, and seems to have, in some contexts, produced artistic barriers for kathak dancers that are not necessarily there for contemporary, modern, or ballet dancers. This hegemonic division between the dances of "West" and the "rest" is nothing new, as Joann Keali'inohomoku addressed in her seminal article from 1970, "An Anthropologist Looks at Ballet as a Form of Ethnic Dance." Although she did not focus on non-Western genres of theatre dance or the concept of classical in any detail,[29] Keali'inohomoku's incisive analysis culminates in a recognition that our use of labels like "ethnic," "primitive," "folk," or "exotic" (or arguably "traditional") are reflective of the "pan-human trait to divide the world into 'we' and 'they'" (Keali'inohomoku 2001, 41). If, in Canada, kathak is considered a traditional dance, while ballet and modern are not generally categorized that way, one can easily understand the tension and occasional frustration of professional dancers who feel constrained by the assumptions made about the resultant "ethnicity" of their dance. But, on the other hand, as audiences in Canada increasingly experience kathak dance through professional productions in both classical and contemporary idioms, it seems inevitable that kathak will finally be recognized as a transnational classical art form, and one particularly capable of contemporary expression through its traditional foundation.

For some Canadians, kathak will largely remain a marker of Indian or Indo-Canadian identity. Certainly, the dance's global presence as one of India's cultural exports is indisputable. Furthermore, kathak's role in identity construction by second- or third-generation Indo-Canadians is clearly important, as is its significance in community events and festivals. Yet the need for professional recognition has been present for decades. Rina Singha, speaking of the opening of Harbourfront's Premiere Dance Theatre in 1983, told me she immediately became a subscriber: "Because I wanted to see dance. How they danced professionally. I wanted to see this mainstream that I'm not supposed to be" (personal communication 2013). Since then, however, Singha and other professional kathak dancers have become increasingly visible on the Canadian stage, not only as representatives of Indian or South Asian tradition, but as creative artists in their own right, and one can see kathak's musical and movement vocabulary communicating an increasingly broad spectrum of meaning to an increasingly cosmopolitan audience. The dance's syncretic history and hybrid origins can facilitate this expansion as the dance evolves without losing sight of foundations that are traditional, not in the sense of Orientalist or neo-Hindu ancient origins, but in their centrality and role in maintaining integrity in training including transmitting its canonic repertoire and music (cf. Noyes 2009, 247). As Vaze and many of her colleagues point out, it is as important that traditional kathak be performed in Canada, funded and received as an established classical dance, as it is that contemporary kathak continue to evolve and interact with other genres.

It remains to be seen if kathak will eventually shed its multicultural and exotic labels and become only as glamorous or ethnic as ballet or any other theatrical dance in Canada. It has, nevertheless, a growing artistic presence on mainstream stages in both traditional and contemporary manifestations that is as much a face of Canadian kathak as folk festivals or student performances. The dance's syncretic roots have provided it with a flexible repertoire and vocabulary, which allow it to symbolize ancient India to some while simultaneously communicating transnational artistry to others. Kathak's hybridity, strong connection with music, and crucial creative component allow it – in the hands and feet of a capable professional artist – to interact or even fuse with other dance genres without losing its integrity. It is this core, rather than the invented history or multicultural colour, that is kathak's foundation and future in Canada and beyond.

Notes

1 Other dances of India officially deemed classical are bharatanatyam, kathakali, kuchipuri, odissi, manipuri, mohini attam, and sattirya.
2 South Asian classical dances, and in particular kathak, have also been part of Pakistani culture since partition in 1947, and in some pre-Independence literature about kathak dance, Lahore is listed as a stylistic centre (Banerjee 1942). Research regarding the life of kathak in Pakistan, however, is still emergent. While I recognize that this is a part of the dance's cultural history, I shall be referring to kathak as an "Indian" dance genre and to my consultants as "Indo-Canadian."
3 In using the term "items" for the various composed or improvised parts of a kathak performance, I follow the work of Hindustani music and dance aesthetics scholar Sushil Kumar Saxena, who called this stream of elements "items" or "intra-forms" (1991). Some of these items are standard pieces in the dance repertoire, others are newly created compositions, yet others consist of improvised strings of footwork or rhythmic cadences. The individual items can be performed as stand-alone cameo pieces and re-ordered in performance to suit individual dancers' strengths or preferences.
4 A detailed explanation of the re-examination of the revivalist narrative is beyond the scope of this paper. Significant work in the historiography of the performing arts in this period may be found in Soneji (2012), Peterson and Soneji (2008), Kippen (2006), and Bakhle (2005) among others.
5 Sitara Thobani's recent fieldwork in Canada and the United Kingdom also explores nationalist reconstruction, essentialized identities, and how dance in the diaspora "continues to be constructed as the descendent of an ancient tradition" (2017b, 165; see also Thobani 2017a and 2107c).
6 I use the modifier "Canadian" here to mean both kathak dancers based in Canada and those kathak dancers who self-identify as Canadian.
7 Oral notations use recited or sung syllables to represent sound or movement rather than the graphic symbols used in written notations. Both kathak and tabla notations use *bols* (from the Hindu/Urdu verb *bolna* meaning to speak), which are recited syllables representing dance steps or drum strokes.
8 My surprise was due to my expectations of suitable venues for "classical" arts. I would have been equally startled to hear that my Royal Conservatory piano teacher was performing in a folk festival.
9 Now the Sony Centre for the Performing Arts.
10 *Mahotsav* is generally translated as festival. Dance *mahotsavs* in India usually feature several evenings of performances plus daytime seminars and discussions. Canadian versions are generally less lavish.
11 The most common Sanskrit poetic genre used in a kathak performance is the *vandana*, but other genres such as *stuti*, *stotra*, or *sloka* may be similarly presented.

12   I have omitted diacritical markings or doubled vowels from romanized Hindi words with the exception of *thaat* as it can be confused with the English word "that."
13   A *tukra*, which means a "piece" or a "fragment," is a short, often flashy, rhythmic composition. A *tora* is similar. A *paran* is often longer and uses a different variety of movements. There are also *tukras* and *toras* composed specifically for tabla, whereas *parans* are compositions shared with the large, barrel drum called the pakhawaj.
14   Written description of performance obviously falls far short of experience, and the reader is urged to seek out live presentations of kathak by local or touring artists. There are also many excerpts of recorded performances. A performance on YouTube by Sanjay Bhattacharya (see https://youtu.be/BBycSHTaT7A) provides a ten-minute example of a "traditional kathak solo" beginning with an invocatory Sanskrit piece (in this case a *stotra* praising the Hindu God Ram), followed by the string of *nritt* or non-representational dance items described above, and ending with an expressional item or *abhinaya* telling a well-known story of the Hindu God Krishna teasing a maiden who is fetching water. One can see examples of *thaat* at 1:56, composed rhythmic items beginning at 2:57, footwork at 4:45, and *gat nikas* at 5:57. An excerpt from the end of a longer performance by Mukta Joshi with Kishore Pane on tabla provides a good example of a *jugalbandi*, with the tabla player responding to the patterns of the kathak dancer's feet. The video ends with footwork and a *tihai* that finishes with the characteristic left-heel spins (see https://youtu.be/rS1OBXT7Eec).
15   Although none of this material is verifiably from an ancient temple dance or the activities of Vedic storytellers, one can find documentation of kathak-like dance vocabulary in Sanskrit works like *Sangitratnakara* (c. 1240) and *Nartananirnaya* (c. 1500), and Indo-Persian material including *Ghunyat al-Munya* (1374–75) and *Muraqqa'-i Delhi* (1738–41). See Bose 1998; Walker 2009/10 and 2014a.
16   This type of graduation recital parallels the *aurangetram* debut performance in bharatanatyam, but is not as ubiquitous in kathak training.
17   This list could easily be expanded to include innovative kathak dancers based in Pakistan, Bangladesh, the United Kingdom, United States of America, and many other countries with South Asian diasporic communities.
18   In her work on Indian dance in the UK, Sitara Thobani contrasts contemporary South Asian dance and dancers with the classical/traditional performance. Contemporary South Asian dance, as a "genre related to but distinct from Indian classical dance," is much less common in Canada than in the UK and thus not addressed here (Thobani 2017a, 12 and 2017b).
19   This performance is presented at https://youtu.be/6J8V5MtppmU.
20   Another intriguing example of blending genres is in the Manohar Performing Arts Dance Company of Winnipeg's 2002–03 presentation of Marius Petipa's *La Bayadère* with original kathak and bharatanatyam choreography and new music in lieu of the 1877 score by Ludwig Minkus (www.manohardance.com).
21   See https://youtu.be/FoNjpIezVVQ; see also Fellay-Danbar 2013.
22   Two examples are Saveeta Sharma and some of her students performing with Irish step dancers, breakdancers, and popular fusion group Delhi2Dublin on Canada Day at Parliament Hill, Ottawa in 2007 (see https://youtu.be/AcFWOdDg_rk), and April Verch,

Ilsa Godino, and Amika Kushwaha performing Ottawa Valley step dancing, flamenco, and kathak in an improvised *sawal-jawab* or question and answer selection at the Vancouver Island Music Festival in 2008 (see https://youtu.be/rcEiSV1fFqA).

23   I have chosen to focus on Vaze with the recognition that there are many significant kathak dancers in Canada whose work reaches beyond "multicultural" pigeonholes.

24   The role played by advanced training in India to "authenticate" the artistry of diasporic and non-Indian dancers is explored at length in Thobani's essay "Training in the Homeland."

25   *The Rebel Goddess* premiere in 1999 at the Music Gallery in Toronto was, incidentally, the first time I saw Vaze dance.

26   *Tarana* is also the name of a dance item in classical kathak.

27   Including repertoire but also lists of *rags*, *tals*, and types of improvisation.

28   South Asian popular music, including but not limited to material from Bollywood films, is yet another category. It often includes dance, and, as in the West, is far more widely disseminated and consumed than either classical or folk forms. It is not seen as "traditional," however, and thus is beyond the scope of this paper.

29   Interestingly, Keali'inohomoku's only mention of India comes in a brief discussion of the terms "ethnic" and "ethnological" when she writes, "When the term ethnic began to be used widely in the [nineteen] thirties, there apparently arose a problem in trying to refer to dance forms which came from 'high' cultures such as India and Japan, and the term 'ethnologic' gained its current meaning for dance scholars" (41). To my knowledge, the term ethnologic is no longer in widespread use.

References

Anderson, Benedict. 2006. *Imagined Communities: Reflections on the Origin and Spread of Nationalism*, revised edition. London: Verso.

Anklewicz, Michael. 2012. "Extending the Tradition: KlezKanada, Klezmer Tradition and Hybridity." *MUSICultures* 39 (2): 81–102.

Bakhle, Janaki. 2005. *Two Men and Music: Nationalism in the Making of an Indian Classical Tradition*. Oxford and New York: Oxford University Press.

Bakht, Natasha. 2011. "Mere 'Song and Dance': Complicating the Multicultural Imperative in the Arts." In *Home and Native Land: Unsettling Multiculturalism in Canada*, edited by May Chazan, Lisa Helps, Anna Stanley, and Sonali Thakkar, 175–83. Toronto, ON: Between the Lines.

Banerjee, Projesh. 1942. *Dance of India*. Allahabad, India: Kitabistan.

Bissoondath, Neil. 1994. *Selling Illusions: The Cult of Multiculturalism in Canada*. Toronto, ON: Penguin Books.

Bose, Mandakranta. 1998. "An Early Textual Source for Kathak." In *Dance of India*, edited by David Waterhouse, 49–59. Toronto, ON: The Centre for South Asian Studies.

Bramadat, Paul A. 2001. "Shows, Selves and Solidarity: Ethnic Identity and Cultural Spectacles in Canada." *Ethnocultural, Racial, Religious, and Linguistic Diversity and Identity Seminar*. Halifax: Department of Canadian Heritage. http://canada.metropolis.net/events/ethnocultural/publications/shows_shelves.pdf. Accessed December 2014.

Briggs, Charles L. 1996. "The Politics of Discursive Authority in Research on the 'Invention of Tradition.'" *Cultural Anthropology* 11 (4): 435–69.

Bronner, Simon J. 2000. "The Meanings of Tradition: An Introduction." *Western Folklore* 59 (2): 87–104.

Chakravorty, Pallabi. 1998. "Hegemony, Dance and Nation: The Construction of the Classical Dance in India." *South Asia* 21 (2): 107–20.

— 2006. "Dancing into Modernity: Multiple Narratives of Indian's Kathak Dance." *Dance Research Journal* 38 (1 and 2): 115–36.

— 2008. *Bells of Change: Kathak Dance, Women and Modernity in India*. Calcutta, India: Seagull Books.

Coplan, David B. 1991. "Ethnomusicology and the Meaning of Tradition." In *Ethnomusicology and Modern Music History*, edited by Stephen Blum, Philip V. Bohlman, and Daniel M. Neuman, 35–48. Urbana and Chicago: University of Illinois Press.

Dandekar, Sarala. 2004. "The Rebel Goddess: An Investigation of the Shift in Narrative in Indian Classical Dance." In *Canadian Dance: Visions and Stories*, edited by Selma Landen Odom and Mary Jane Warner, 435–45. Toronto, ON: Dance Collection Danse.

Dhiman, Palak. 2013. "Multiculturalism and Identity Formation among Second Generation Canadian Women of South Asian Origin through Indian Classical Dance." Master's thesis, University of Manitoba.

Dietrich, Gregory. 2004. "Dancing the Diaspora: Indian Desi Music in Chicago." In *Identity and the Arts in Diaspora Communities*, edited by Thomas Turino and James Lea, 103–15. Warren, MI: Harmonie Park Press.

Fellay-Dunbar, Catalina. 2013 *Firedance: Sharing a Flame between Flamenco and Kathak*. Canadian Dance Studies Conference 2012 Proceedings, http://www.csds-sced.ca/English/proceedings.html. Accessed August 2013.

Finnegan, Ruth. 1991. "Tradition, but What Tradition and for Whom?" The Milman Parry Lecture on Oral Tradition for 1989–90. *Oral Tradition* 6 (1): 104–24

Hobsbawm, Eric, and Terence Ranger, eds. 1983. *The Invention of Tradition*. Cambridge, UK: Cambridge University Press.

Keali'inohomoku, Joann. 2001. "An Anthropologist Looks at Ballet as a Form of Ethnic Dance." In *Moving History/Dancing Cultures: A Dance History Reader*, edited by Ann Dils and Ann Cooper Albright, 33–43. Middletown, CN: Wesleyan University Press.

Kippen, James. 2006. *Gurudev's Drumming Legacy: Music, Theory and Nationalism in the Mrdang aur Tabla Vadanpaddhati of Gurudev Patwardhan*. SOAS Musicology Series. Aldershot, Hants, England: Ashgate Publishing.

Kothari, Sunil. 1989. *Kathak: Indian Classical Dance Art*. New Delhi, India: Abhinav Publications.

Mangaldas, Aditi, et al. 2013. "Roses and Thorns: Turning Down Sangit Natak Akademi Award." http://www.narthaki.com/info/rt/rt53.html. Accessed April 2013.

Manuel, Peter. 2015. "The Intermediate Sphere in North Indian Music Culture: Between and beyond 'Folk' and 'Classical.'" *Ethnomusicology* 59 (1): 82–115.

Moro, Pamela. 2004. "Constructions of Nation and the Classicisation of Music: Comparative Perspectives from Southeast and South Asia." *Journal of Southeast Asian Studies* 35 (2): 187–211.

Noyes, Dorothy. 2009. "Tradition: Three Traditions." *Journal of Folklore Research* 46 (3): 233–68.
Peterson, Indira Vishwanathan, and Davesh Soneji, eds. 2008. *Performing Pasts: Reinventing the Arts in Modern South Asia*. New Delhi, India: Oxford University Press.
Phillips, Mark Salber, and Gordon Schochet eds. 2004. *Questions of Tradition*. Toronto, ON: University of Toronto Press.
Program Notes. *DW211 Bageshree Vaze* (Toronto) 2014/15 Mainstage Series.
Ramnarine, Tina K. 2007. "Musical Performance in the Diaspora: Introduction." In *Musical Performance in the Diaspora*, edited by Tina K. Ramnarine, 1–17. London and New York: Routledge.
Ronström, Owe. 2014. "Traditional Music, Heritage Music." In *The Oxford Handbook of Musical Revival*, edited by Caroline Bithell and Juniper Hill, 43–59. New York, NY: Oxford University Press.
Saxena, Sushil Kumar. 1991. *Swinging Syllables: Aesthetics of Kathak Dance*. New Delhi, India: Sangeet Natak Akademi.
Schofield, Katherine Butler. 2010. "Reviving the Golden Age Again: 'Classicization,' Hindustani Music, and the Mughals." *Ethnomusicology* 54 (3): 484–517.
Soneji, Davesh. 2012. *Unfinished Gestures: Devadasis, Memory, and Modernity in South Asia*. South Asia across the Disciplines. Chicago and London: University of Chicago Press.
Subramanian, Lakshmi. 2007. "The Master, Muse and the Nation: The New Cultural Project and the Reification of Colonial Modernity in India." *South Asia* 23 (2): 1–32.
Thobani, Sitara. 2017a. *Indian Classical Dance and the Making of Postcolonial National Identities: Dancing on Empire's Stage*. New York, NY: Routledge.
— 2017b. "Projects of Reform: Indian Classical Dance and Frictions of Generations and Genre." *MUSICultures* 44 (1): 163–86.
— 2017c. "Training in the Homeland: Negotiating Artistic Travel between Canada and India." In *Engaging India and Canada*, edited by Suchorita Chattopadhyay. Delhi, India: Indo-Canadian Shastri Institute.
Varghese, Meera. 2008. "Ascending the Canadian Stage: Dance and Cultural Identity in the Indian Diaspora." Master's thesis, University of Alberta.
Vaze, Bageshree. 2015. *Next Steps 2014–15 – Bageshree Vaze*. Published on 20 April 2015. Accessed May 2015. https://www.youtube.com/watch?v=uFO8MUZO86o.
Walker, Margaret E. 2006. "Ancient Tradition as Ongoing Creation: The Kathavacaks of Uttar Pradesh." *MUSICultures* 33: 48–63.
— 2009/10."Kathak *Log ya* Kathak *Nrtya*: The Search for a Dance Called Kathak." *Journal of the Indian Musicological Society* 40: 168–90.
— 2010. "Revival and Reinvention in India's Kathak Dance." *MUSICultures* 37: 171–84.
—2014a. *India's Kathak Dance in Historical Perspective*. SOAS Musicology Series. Aldershot, Hants, England: Ashgate Publishing.
— 2014b. "Postcolonial Hybridity and National Purity in India's Kathak Dance Revival." In *The Oxford Handbook of Musical Revival*, edited by Caroline Bithell and Juniper Hill, 205–27. New York, NY: Oxford University Press.

Heather Sparling

Chapter 4

Taking the Piss Out: Presentational and Participatory Elements in the History of the Cape Breton Milling Frolic

One of Cape Breton's most celebrated Gaelic activities is its milling frolic, a distinctive activity during which a group of people mill wool while singing Gaelic songs. "Milling," as it is known in Nova Scotia, or "waulking," as it is known in Scotland, came to the island with Gaelic-speaking immigrants from Scotland's Highlands and Islands who arrived largely between the late eighteenth and mid-nineteenth centuries. It is a process by which woven cloth is beaten in order to shrink it. By beating the cloth, the weave becomes tighter, shrinking the fabric and avoiding later shrinkage during washing. At the same time, the woolen fibres become fuller through the beating process, with the "fluff" filling the spaces in the weave and making the resulting fabric more resistant to wind and rain. Consequently, "waulking" and "milling" are also sometimes known as "fulling." The beating of the wool is a communal labour activity conducted in time to Gaelic songs. The milling frolic continues to be practised in Cape Breton, even though it is no longer regularly practised in Scotland.[1] It is widely admired for its continuity, a folk tradition that has persisted despite industrialization, urbanization, and migration. But just how "continuous" has it been as a practice? What at first glance appears to be a continuous activity turns out, with careful analysis, to have changed in almost every imaginable regard: it has changed in terms of its purpose, its participants, its song repertoire, and its venue. It no longer takes place at the same time of year as it once did, nor for the same length of time.

One of the changes that I treat as emblematic in this chapter is the move away from soaking the milling cloth in stale urine prior to milling it. *Mais-*

tir, as the stale urine is known in Gaelic, is essentially homemade ammonia that took the oils out of the wool, helped the dye to set, and softened the fabric. But as the need to mill cloth declined in the early part of the twentieth century, so did the need to use *maistir*. At the same time, changing ideas about cleanliness, hygiene, privacy, and bodily functions meant that *maistir* became a less and less appealing ingredient in the milling process. Although the milling cloth still needs some kind of liquid solution to keep the wool dust and fibres from releasing into the air during the beating process, plain water has been used for decades.

This chapter's title phrase "taking the piss out" is a British colloquialism that means to tease or make fun of someone. Teasing and humour are fundamental parts of the traditional milling frolic, as I note below. However, in this case, the colloquial meaning of the phrase is less important than its literal meaning, which serves as one memorable example of the many changes to the milling frolic over the twentieth century, along with its British (more specifically, Scottish) associations. It doesn't usually take long for those new to milling to discover the history of the stale urine. Those "in the know" tend to tell its history with glee in order to get a reaction from unsuspecting newbies. It is therefore a well-known historical aspect of the milling frolic, and the change in liquid from maistir to water is generally acknowledged with relief. As a widely recognized change to the milling frolic – unlike many of the other changes (to be discussed) that largely go unmarked – it serves as a vivid, representative symbol of the numerous changes to the milling frolic over the last hundred or so years.

Change, of course, is inevitable. In this chapter I demonstrate that milling frolics in Cape Breton remain participatory despite the introduction of paying tourist audiences, and I also highlight the importance of milling songs and frolics as tools for language and cultural retention for Gaels. The milling frolic remains an important cultural practice that marks Gaelic culture as distinct to Gaels and tourists alike. I use ethnomusicologist Thomas Turino's concept of "participatory vs presentational performance" to reflect on the significance of changes to waulkings and milling frolics over time, as well as to consider how today's locals and tourists engage with these practices differently than their predecessors. In *Music as Social Life* (2008), Turino focuses on a relatively static understanding of participatory vs presentational performance from the perspective of its cultural practitioners. In this chapter, I use Turino's framework to explore shifts from participatory to presentational music-making elements in the milling frolic over time and the way in which a given music-making tradition engages different kinds of audiences. As Turino defines his terms, "*Participatory performance* is a special type of artistic practice in which there are no artist-audience distinctions, only participants and potential participants performing different roles, and the primary goal is to involve the maximum number of people in some performance role. *Presentational performance*, in contrast, refers to situations where one group of people, the artists, prepare and provide music for another group, the audience, who do not participate in making the music or dancing" (2008, 26; italics in the original). Before briefly reviewing Turino's framework and describing a traditional waulking in Scotland and its evolution into today's Cape Breton milling frolic, I provide some context for this study.

One of the valued features of milling songs is their Gaelic texts; as a threatened language in Cape Breton – and globally – Gaelic remains a marker of cultural distinction. Gaelic was once the dominant language throughout the Highlands and Islands of Scotland. However, as the courts and the nobility adopted the Norman French, Scots, and English languages (starting around the eleventh century), Scottish Gaelic began its steady decline. Various forms of legislation were enacted over several centuries to establish English as the language of the aristocracy, government, education, and the court system. Events such as the Reformation, the failure of the Jacobite cause in 1746, and the Clearances in the nineteenth century all contributed to the decline of Gaelic. The number of Gaelic speakers decreased from 254,415 in 1891 to 57,375 in 2011 (1.1 percent of the Scottish population). There are no longer any monolingual Gaelic speakers (all Gaelic speakers also speak English) and many areas that were once predominantly Gaelic speaking are now predominantly English-speaking.[2]

In Canada, at the time of Confederation in 1867, Gaelic was the third most spoken language after English and French (Dembling 2006, 209) and it was the dominant language on Cape Breton Island and in eastern areas of the Nova Scotia mainland. In 1901, approximately 90,000 Canadians spoke Gaelic, of whom about 50,000 lived in Nova Scotia (ibid). Unofficial tabulations in the 1930s suggest that the Gaelic-speaking population of Canada's three Maritime provinces (Nova Scotia, New Brunswick, and Prince Edward Island) was somewhere between 30,000 and 50,000 (Campbell 1990, 33, 41). However, the language has declined quickly since then. Although there are still a handful of first-language Gaelic speakers according to the 2011 Census, most of the 1,200 plus Gaelic speakers in Nova Scotia today are learners who've achieved varying degrees of fluency. Despite substantial language loss, there are presently significant efforts to revitalize the language and its associated culture. The Nova Scotia government established an Office of Gaelic Affairs in 2006 and numerous institutions and organizations, along with individuals and informal community groups, are engaged in documenting, promoting, and teaching the language along with Gaelic cultural expressions, including songs.

I am a relatively fluent Gaelic learner who has been conducting fieldwork with Gaelic speakers and singers in Cape Breton since 1998. I moved permanently to Cape Breton in 2005. I have taught Gaelic language classes in Toronto and Cape Breton, and I regularly interact with Gaelic speakers, learners, and organizations through formal and informal contexts as well as at traditional activities and events, including milling frolics. Although I am conscious of myself as a "come from away," I consider myself to be part of the local Gaelic community.

Surprisingly little literature exists about the milling song genre (on defining genres, see Sparling 2008) and the milling frolic as an activity, despite the fact that milling songs are regularly celebrated as one of the more distinctive song genres in Scottish Gaelic culture. Their celebrated status can be seen in the large number of published milling/waulking song collections (see, for example, Tolmie 1910–13; Campbell and Collinson 1969–81; MacCormick and Campbell 1969; Shaw 1977 [1955]; Comunn Gaidhealach Leodhais 1998 [1982]; Campbell 1990; Shaw 2000). The large number of milling/waulking descriptions also indicates that authors felt they were distinctive enough to warrant commentary and description (many early descriptions are quoted at length in Campbell and Collinson 1981). Unfortunately, many of these descriptions are relatively short and, by nature, they tend to be descriptive rather than analytical or critical.

Participatory and Presentational Musics

Turino argues that, in any given social group, live music making tends to be either predominantly participatory or predominantly presentational. Even when a social group as a whole or a particular musical activity incorporates elements of each, one will predominate. Turino emphasizes that presentational and participatory performance are equally valid and equally "good"; however, presentational performance tends to dominate in the Anglo-American capitalist-cosmopolitan formation (2008, 29, 35, 92), causing participatory music, by contrast, to be misunderstood and often denigrated.

Turino argues that the different goals of each kind of music necessitate different elements, and that it is inappropriate to judge participatory performance according to the values of presentational performance and vice versa.

The point of participatory music making is to make it possible for anyone to join, regardless of ability or experience. Although there are many forms of musical participation, including listening, Turino uses the term "in the restricted sense of actively contributing to the sound and motion of a musical event through dancing, singing, clapping, and playing musical instruments when each of these activities is considered integral to the performance" (2008, 28). Presentational performance, by contrast, is meant to entertain an audience and is therefore generally restricted to skilled musicians, often trained and certainly experienced.

To make it easy to participate, the basic participatory form tends to be short, predictable, full of repetition, and with virtually no structural contrast that could confuse an unskilled and/or unrehearsed participant. Variation does, however, occur within these parameters. For example, "Celtic" instrumental music involves ornamentation of a basic, repetitive melodic framework, making it possible for sessions – groups of musicians who come together to jam – to incorporate musicians of varying abilities. As long as the musicians are capable of playing the basic melody at the group's tempo, they can join in. The better musicians will employ advanced ornamentation and playing techniques, but these do not impair anyone else's ability to participate. Meanwhile, presentational music tends to be the opposite: forms can be much longer and less predictable. Repetition is limited to avoid boring the audience, while contrast creates interest. Presentational performance also allows for greater variation and unpredictability in all facets in order to maintain the attention of the audience. Finally, while presentational performance is judged for the quality of sound – it is treated as a sound or art object – participatory performance is judged for the extent and quality of participation.

As will quickly become clear, waulkings and milling frolics are designed to be participatory, and waulking and milling songs exhibit most of the participatory musical characteristics that Turino identifies. However, as I also explain, the Nova Scotian milling frolic has changed over the past century. Despite increasingly attracting non-participatory audiences (especially tourists), and despite many changes to the repertoire, participants, venue, and context in which the milling frolic is enacted, it remains a participatory music-making activity. It is its ongoing participatory orientation that, I argue, allows the milling frolic to be conceived as a continuous practice and tradition despite its many changes.

Waulking in Scotland and Its Move to Nova Scotia

Keeping participatory and presentational music-making characteristics in mind, I turn now to the milling frolic as it was practised in Scotland and, presumably, in Cape Breton since Gaelic-speaking immigrants first brought the practice to the region. In many parts of Europe, water-powered fulling mills replaced the manual labour of waulking by the thirteenth and fourteenth centuries (see Shaw 1984; Lucas 2005). Water mills were late coming to the Scottish Hebrides, however, and so cloth was waulked manually far longer there than elsewhere (Shaw 1984); in parts of the Highlands and Islands of Scotland, mechanization did not replace manual labour until the late twentieth century. A number of lengthy descriptions of waulkings exist from as early as 1772, a time when it was fashionable for the wealthier classes in Britain to travel throughout the United Kingdom as well as continental Europe, and to publish their experiences as travel writing (see Campbell and Collinson 1981, 3). Some Gaelic songs also describe waulkings, and waulking songs themselves offer us some evidence of how waulkings were historically practised.

Sheep would be shorn in the spring; wool would be carded, spun, and woven in the fall; and waulkings would be held in the winter when the cold weather and short days meant that little could be accomplished outdoors anyway. The labour required to waulk the wool was long and tedious, so it became an opportunity for group work and the creation of a social event at which song was used to coordinate labour and alleviate its tedium. In Scotland, a waulking was for women only, and there are stories of men who were teased and roughly handled should they inadvertently enter a waulking (see, for example, Campbell and Collinson 1981, 13).

All the women within the community would be invited to a waulking, and it would last for hours. The hostess would ensure that there was ample food and drink for all the participants. The women would sit around a large table, sometimes made specifically for the waulking, with grooves in the top to facilitate the beating and to allow the excess moisture to run off (see figure 4.1). But it was just as likely that a door would be taken off its hinges and used (Campbell and Collinson 1981, 13).[3]

To pass the time and coordinate their efforts, the women sang waulking songs.[4] They would beat and pass the cloth around the table in time to the song to ensure an even and thorough shrinking. Waulking songs are structured in a call-and-response format, with each woman at the table taking a turn leading a song and singing the verses while the remaining women joined her on the choruses. Songs could be about any number of topics, including

Figure 4.1 | Waulking cloth in Eriskay, 1934.

clan chiefs and community heroes, hunting, love relationships, and laments for the dead. Not surprisingly, given the gender exclusivity of the group, the subjects of waulking songs also deal with women's issues, including love (requited and not), rape, and pregnancy. Some of the songs were set up as teasing songs in which different men would be proposed as potential partners for one of the young women present, and she would refuse all but the one in whom she was most interested (Dunn 1991 [1953], 40–1).[5]

The song below is an example of a waulking song that addresses a woman's issue from a woman's perspective. In this song, a woman is left with a young son, struggling to support him, while the father of the child ignores her; the blame she lays on the father indicates that she may have been raped. The fact that the father rides a horse suggests that he comes from a higher class than she.

"Gura Mise Tha Fo Mhulad" ("It Is I That Am Sorrowful")[6]

Séist	Chorus [vocables]
Ho ro ho ì, hó ro nan	*Ho ro ho ì, hó ro nan*
Ho ro chall éile	*Ho ro chall éile*
Ho ro ho ì, hó ro nan	*Ho ro ho ì, hó ro nan*

Rannan	Verses
Gura mise tha fo mhulad	It is I that am sorrowful
Air an tulaich, 's mór m' éislein.	On the little hillock, and great is my grief.
Chunna mise mo leannan,	I saw my sweetheart
Cha do dh'aithnich e 'n dé mi.	And he didn't recognize me.
Cha do d'fhidir, 's cha d'fharraid,	He did not perceive, he didn't ask
Cha do ghabh e dhiom sgeula.	He would not listen to my story.
Chunna mise dol suas thu	I saw you going up
Gu buaile na spréidhe.	To the cattlefold.
'S ann a ghabh e orm seachad	He passed me
Air each glas nan ceum eutrom.	On a grey horse with a light step
Air each glas nan ceum lùthmhor	On the grey horse of the nimble step
A ghearradh sunndach an fhéithe.	Lively at jumping the bog.
Tha mo leanabh 'nam achlais,	My babe is in my arms
'S mi gun taice fo'n ghréin dha.	And I without sustenance under the sun for him.
Cha bu mhise bu choireach,	I was not to blame,
'S ann bu choireach e fhéin ris.	It was himself that was at fault.
Mar a théid mi 'nam ònar	As I go alone
Ag iarraidh lòn air gach té dha.	Seeking food of every woman for him.

One of the foremost experts on waulking songs, John Lorne Campbell, suggests that they were initially extemporized although they had become fixed songs by the time waulkings began to be documented (Campbell and Collinson 1981, 18–19). The evidence, he argues, comes from the often disjointed nature of the verses; the sudden changes in rhyme scheme that suggest that either different songs were brought together or that a singer was unable to continue a particular rhyme and so changed it; the "woven" structure of many waulking songs in which the last line of one verse becomes the first line of the next, buying the singer time to make up new words; and the formulaic lines that reappear in multiple songs describing figures and situations (Campbell and Collinson 1969, 21), typical of many oral song traditions. The songs were often long to help pass the time. After a number of songs, one of the women would measure the cloth with her finger to determine whether it was sufficiently shrunk. If not, she would suggest how many more songs would be required before it was ready (Campbell and Collinson 1981, 15).

Older waulking song choruses tend to consist of vocables, as in the song above, sometimes combined with a few semantically meaningful words. The vocable choruses, however, are fixed – these were not improvised by the singers, but were rather carefully transmitted and learned (see "The Meaningless Refrain Syllables and Their Significance" in Campbell and Collinson 1969, 227–37 for an analysis). The verses, by contrast, consist of words, although the short phrases and distorted grammar often mean that the overall meaning of the lyrics can be difficult to decipher.

An excellent example of an older waulking song is "Hé Mandu." It is still well known, largely thanks to its appearance on *Music from the Western Isles* (1992), an LP of archival recordings later launched as a cassette and then CD in the Scottish Tradition series initially developed by the University of Edinburgh's School of Scottish Studies.[7] It is an example of what I call a "split chorus" song, in which the chorus and verses are interwoven. According to Collinson and Campbell, half-line verses, such as those in "Hé Mandu," were rarely written after about 1700 (Campbell and Collinson 1969, 227–8).[8] It is difficult to translate because the verse text is abbreviated and disjointed.

"Hé Mandu"

Hé Mandu	*Vocables*
'S truagh nach tigeadh	It's a pity that [subject missing] would not come
Hé Mandu	*Vocables*
Sud 'gam iarraidh	That [thing/person] yonder fetching me
Hé Mandu	*Vocables*
Gille 's litir	Lad and letter
Hi ri o ro	*Vocables*
Each is diallaid	Horse and saddle

Hé Mandu	*Vocables*
Hi ri o ro	*Vocables*
Hò rò bù ò	*Vocables*[9]

Na'm bitheadh agam / If I were to have
Sgiath a' ghlaisein / Wing of the sparrow
Iteag an eòin / Feather of the bird
Spòg na lachainn / Foot of the duck

Iteag an eòin / Feather of the bird
Spòg na lachainn / Foot of the duck
Shnàmhainn na caoil / I would swim the narrows
Air an tarsuinn / Across them

Shnàmhainn na caoil / I would swim the narrows
Air an tarsuinn / Across them
An cuan Ileach / The Sound of Islay
'S an Caol Arcach / And the Orkney Sound

An cuan Ileach / The Sound of Islay
'S an Caol Arcach / And the Orkney Sound
Rachainn a-steach / I would go inside
Thun a' chaisteil / To the castle

Rachainn a-steach / I would go inside
Thun a' chaisteil / To the castle
'S bheirinn a-mach / I would take outside
Às mo leannan / My darling

'S bheirinn a-mach / I would take outside
Às mo leannan / My darling
'S chan fhoighnichinn / I would not ask
Có bu leis i / Whose she was

'Se mo Dhòmhnall / It's my Donald
Fhuair an togail / Who was raised
Cha b' ann le burn / Not with water
Gorm a' lodain / That was blue-green from the pond

Figure 4.2 | Transcription of "Hé Mandu."

Cha b' ann le burn	It wasn't with water
Gorm a' lodain	That was blue-green from the pond
Ach le bainne	But rather with milk
Nam ban donna	Of brown-haired women.[10]

The split chorus format is quite typical of older waulking songs, as is the chorus consisting of vocables and the woven form, in which the last two lines of one verse become the first two lines of the next. The woven form extends the song while also allowing the lead singer time to think of the next lines. Such split chorus songs were apparently known in Cape Breton at one time. Cape Breton tradition bearer and singer Lauchie MacLellan (1910–1991), for example, from whom ethnologist John Shaw collected a large number of songs in the 1970s (Shaw 2000), had several split chorus songs in his repertoire. However, in my experience, split chorus songs are today rare at Cape Breton milling frolics, if they are performed at all.

"Hé Mandu's" melody also aids participation (see figure 4.2). We might call this pentatonic tune atonic, with a modal frame constructed through the pendular alternation between intervals of a fourth with G and C emphasized in odd-numbered measures, and, except at the end, A and E in even-numbered measures.[11] There is no sense of functional tonality here, given that there are almost no clear triads. Just as the short, fragmented verse lines alternate with lines from the refrain, the melodic motives associated with verse and refrain also alternate, never developing into phrases or establishing clear cadences. There is therefore no sense of a tonal centre, nor a sense of a satisfying conclusion. The pendular fourths, together with the lack of a tonal centre, are ideal for a call and response format, facilitating the melodic movement between soloist and chorus, as well as facilitating as much repetition as desired.

The song's octave range is comfortable for most singers and typical of many waulking songs. In addition, the melodic motion is mostly by 2nds, 3rds, or 4ths. Such a controlled range, together with relatively small and manageable intervals, ensures that everyone can sing together, whatever their musical abilities or vocal range.

Returning to Turino's framework of presentational vs participatory performance, it is clear that the waulking tradition is predominantly participatory. The point of singing is not to entertain an audience but rather to facilitate work and to pass time. The songs are not short overall, but the form is, and the songs are highly repetitive melodically and textually: the chorus repeats both melodically and lyrically; stock phrases are found in multiple songs; and woven song structures, when used, repeat one verse's text in another's. Historically, some creativity was required when the song lyrics were extemporized, but even then, stock phrases and situations meant that less creative singers could still participate (Campbell and Collinson 1981, 21).

Traditionally, everyone at the table participates in the singing. Each person is expected to lead songs by turn, as well as to participate in the singing of the choruses. The singing is not meant to be judged for its "beauty," which people who documented it in the past make clear. For example, in an 1814 description, John Gibson Lockhart reports, "We heard the women singing as they waulked the cloth by rubbing it with their hands and feet and screaming all the while in a sort of chorus. At a distance, the sound was wild and sweet enough, but rather discordant when you approached too near the performers" (quoted in Campbell and Collinson 1981, 7). Clearly, Lockhart valued presentational music, focusing on the sound rather than its participatory aspects. The purpose of the waulking songs is not exclusively participation – after all, the overall purpose of the event was to shrink the cloth. But musical participation was the means by which the larger goal was achieved.

Cape Breton Milling Frolics[12]

We know that the waulking tradition came to Cape Breton with immigrants in the late eighteenth and early nineteenth centuries, but we have no records of the practice prior to the twentieth century. While waulkings are generally no longer practised in Scotland except as occasional historical re-enactments, milling frolics are still a vibrant part of Gaelic Cape Breton cultural life. They have, however, changed considerably over the twentieth century. For one, the

English name changed. Although the Gaelic term remains the same in Scotland and Cape Breton, *luadh*, the English translation in Cape Breton became "milling frolic," apparently so-named for the mills that did the work elsewhere (Campbell and Collinson 1969, 3).

At some point – we don't know exactly when or why – milling frolics began to be attended by men as well as women, and this had a profound impact on the tradition. Charles Dunn suggests that men began participating in Cape Breton milling frolics at the turn of the twentieth century (1991 [1953], 38).[13] The North Shore Gaelic Singers, a group of milling singers initially formed to participate in a 1920s exhibition in Baddeck, Cape Breton, consisted primarily of men (MacDonald 1988–89, 14), so men's involvement was clearly acceptable by this time. There are many possible reasons for the inclusion of men (see Sparling 2006, 225–6). Perhaps the distances between houses were greater in Canada than in Scotland. Assuming that men drove their wives to a frolic and had nothing else to do while the frolic was on, and since more people involved meant easier and quicker work, men may have started joining in. Another theory is that, because the winters are harsher in Canada, men would have had to stay indoors during the coldest months, whereas they might still get outdoor work done in Scotland. Even in the coldest month of February, the average daytime temperature in the Hebrides is about 7°C while nighttime temperatures typically remain above freezing. Snow is rare in such temperatures and short-lived when it does fall. Meanwhile, temperatures below freezing, snow storms, and gusting winds are the norm in February in Cape Breton. Alternatively, men may have become involved simply because milling frolics were "the social occasion for singing par excellence" (Shaw 2000, 19).

When men started joining the milling frolics, they did not know traditional waulking songs, so they brought their own songs to the table, songs that were originally designed to facilitate other kinds of labour, such as sailing or hoeing fields (MacDonald 1988–89, 14; Shaw 2000, 16).[14] These songs still worked in the milling context since they were also participatory in nature, with short, predictable, and highly rhythmic forms, repeated as needed. At the same time, women participants were less inclined to sing songs about women's issues in mixed company and so some of the traditional waulking songs were dropped from the repertoire.[15] The newer (men's) songs are generally easy to identify as they usually do not include vocables, their choruses appear in an ABA format both melodically and textually, and the verses tend to consist of longer lines in patterns of one, two, or four lines each. However,

Figure 4.3 | Cape Breton Milling Frolic, c. 1958. Note the predominance of men at the table, the formal attire (suggesting its social rather than work function), and the location in a large building (perhaps a barn) rather than someone's home. Note also the audience surrounding the table.

importantly, the newly introduced songs still include choruses that allow the continuation of call-and-response singing.

"Ged a Sheòl Mi air M' Aineol" ("Although I Sailed to Foreign Countries") offers an excellent example of a "new" milling song. It is believed to have been composed by Roderick Morrison of Drummondville, Cape Breton (Creighton and MacLeod 1964, 25; Morrison's dates not known), which is supported by the North American perspective evident in the lyrics. It has been popular in Cape Breton for several decades, having been collected by folksong scholar and collector Helen Creighton in the first half of the twentieth century, and is still regularly heard at milling frolics today. The form is typical of more modern milling songs: the chorus is in an ABA form with two-line verses. It is not in a split chorus format, nor is the form woven. The song has no vocables and the text is about sailing, from a sailor's perspective; sailing was, of course, historically a male domain.

"Ged a Sheòl Mi air M' Aineol" ("Although I Sailed to Foreign Countries")[16]

Séist	Chorus
Ged a sheòl mi air m' aineol	Although I sailed to foreign countries
Cha laigh smalan air m' inntinn	Sadness did not linger in my mind
Ged a sheòl mi air m' aineol.	Although I sailed to foreign countries.

Rannan	Verses
'S ann á Boston a sheòl sinn	We sailed from Boston
Dol air bhóidse chun na h-Ìnnsean.	On a voyage to the Indies
Rinn sinn còrdadh ri caiptean	We came to an agreement with a skipper
Air a' bhàrc a bha rìomhach.	Of a handsome ship
Trì là roimh 'n Nollaig	Three days before Christmas
Thàinig oirnn an droch shìde.	Bad weather descended upon us.
Shéid e cruaidh oirnn le frasan	The wind blew strongly with rain-showers
'S clach-mheallain bha millteach.	And stinging hailstones.
Cha robh ròpa 's robh òirleach	When the inch-thick ropes
'N uair reòth e nach robh trì ann.	Froze they became three inches in girth.
Chaill sinn craiceann ar làmhan,	We lost the skin of our hands
'S bha ar gàirdeanan sgìth dheth.	And our arms were tired of the struggle.
Bha còignear nan seasamh	Five of the crew members were standing
'S bha seachdnar nan sìneadh.	And seven were prone.
Trì là is trì oidhche	I spent three days and three nights
'S mi ri cuibhl' ri droch shìde.	At the wheel during the storm.
Sin nuair labhair an caiptean	That is when the skipper said,
"Illean tapaidh na dìobraibh."	"Do not yield stout-hearted lads."

"'N uair a ruigeas sibh caladh	"When you reach port
Bidh ur drama dhuibh cinnteach."	Your dram will be certain."
Dh'fhalbh an "rigging" o'n "bhowsprit"	The rigging and the bowsprit were washed away
Leis an tonn a bha dìreadh.	By the rising wave.
Dh'fhalbh 'n seòl-mullaich 'n a shròicean	The top-sail was torn to shreds
Chan e spòrs a bhi 'g a innse.	It is no fun to tell about it.
'N uair a ruitheadh i 'm fuaradh	When the ship would veer to windward
'S ann a bhuanaicheadh i mìltean.	She would gain many leagues.
Tha lionn dubh air mo mhàthair,	My mother is dejected
Agus dùil aic' nach till mi.	Because she does not expect me to return.

By the 1920s and 1930s, there was little practical need to mill cloth manually in Cape Breton. Industrialization meant that mass-produced cloth and clothing became cheaper to buy. With the introduction of department store catalogues, families could easily purchase cloth or clothing even in rural areas, rather than make it themselves. Women began working outside the home, resulting in less time for weaving and milling, but more money for store-bought goods. Homes became better insulated, decreasing the need for heavy blankets (Bennett 1998, 217). In 1978, Ron Caplan, editor of *Cape Breton Magazine*, published an article about milling frolics, based on interviews with a number of elderly native Gaelic speakers and singers from the North Shore area of Cape Breton. They remembered attending traditional milling frolics as children, sometimes as many as three or four in a week (Caplan 1978, 39). But the Second World War marked a definitive break in the tradition. The last documented "traditional" milling frolic on the North Shore was held in 1941, and no milling frolics were held for about ten years after that (MacDonald 1988–89, 12).

Outmigration also affected the milling frolic. Before the Second World War and even more so afterward, many Cape Bretoners migrated elsewhere in search of work, moving to places like Toronto, Detroit, and especially Boston. These ex-pat Cape Bretoners regularly returned home for visits during the summer and wanted to participate in the distinctive cultural activities that they remembered from their youth. As a result, milling frolics began to be held in the summer instead of the winter, at least in part to allow returning Capers to re-experience a Gaelic cultural activity, rather than for the purpose of milling woven wool cloth (MacDonald 1988–89, 16; Shaw 2000, 20; Kennedy 2001, 133, 238–9). The event was shortened since it no longer had to continue until the wool was completely milled. And because the wool didn't have to be milled, the same cloth began to be used over and over again. Not surprisingly, one of the first things to go was the stale urine solution. Instead, the wool was soaked in warm water largely as a means to keep the wool fibres from shedding and creating a cloud of dust and fibres that is uncomfortable to breathe.[17]

Milling frolics began to be held in public venues, such as church and community halls, instead of in private homes. The participants consisted of a mix of returning Cape Bretoners and locals. Significantly, the Gaelic language was quickly declining in Cape Breton at that time, and whereas the language of earlier millings was exclusively Gaelic, English increasingly became the language of conversation, although the songs themselves remained in Gaelic.

Once milling frolics came to be located in public rather than private venues, and held in the summer rather than the winter, they began attracting tourists.[18] Some hotels began hiring Gaelic singers to hold milling frolics specifically for their guests. Milling frolics shortened further, often lasting only a couple of hours whereas earlier milling frolics lasted much longer, with socializing afterward lasting into the wee hours of the morning. Organizers began to charge admission, particularly in community venues, often used to fundraise for community needs such as building renovations. As the Gaelic language declined further, reducing the opportunities and contexts in which to sing Gaelic songs, the songs at the table changed too. Almost any Gaelic song came to be acceptable as long as it was sung at an appropriate tempo and had a chorus in which the group could join. This meant that textually complex songs, which used to be sung in other contexts that were by then declining in popularity, came to be used at the milling table. These complex songs were more difficult for people to pick up orally on the spot. Meanwhile, not everyone who sat at the table could lead a song, and so core Gaelic singers were often hired to ensure a successful frolic. Although anyone could choose to lead a song and everyone at the table was encouraged to do so, the core Gaelic singers provided the majority of the frolic's songs. Another interesting change was that men became the primary tradition bearers of this once women-only tradition.

Today, milling frolics are still held by and for the Gaelic-speaking community as the primary public cultural event at which Gaelic language and culture is foregrounded. They have largely replaced the once-common *céilidh*[19] as the main context in which Gaelic is spoken and Gaelic culture is performed and transmitted. Indeed, many people point out that the milling frolic is *the* primary Gaelic social event.

A Continuous Participatory Tradition

I would argue that part of what has allowed the milling frolic to persist despite substantial change to many features is the fact that it remains participatory. In fact, changes such as the integration of men and the increasing use of English among people around the milling table have actually increased the inclusivity of milling frolics. Although it is not possible to prove, I would suggest that if there had been any change in purpose from participation to presentation — because it would involve a fundamental shift in the ideologies underlying the activity — this change would have resulted either in the decline of the milling frolic tradition, or its reconceptualization as a different tradition entirely.

I argue here that milling frolics have a continuous history of participation; but what, then, do we make of tourists and non-Gaelic speakers who attend? They are rarely able to participate in a traditional manner and often sit around the perimeter of the table, watching. Has this spectatorship transformed the milling frolic from a primarily participatory genre into a primarily presentational one? I would argue that it has not, which is both a draw and a challenge for tourists. It is important to recognize that very few concessions are made to tourists. Milling frolics are almost never explained to attendees, nor is any background or contextual information provided to attendees in any printed form, such as a brochure or handout. There is no master of ceremonies coordinating the event, and there is no pre-planned program of songs or slate of singers (aside from the few singers who may be hired to ensure there will be enough songs to constitute a milling frolic). Whoever shows up, shows up and whatever they sing, they sing. Songs are not translated or summarized, let alone taught. Songs are not provided in written form: people who want to sing along must either already know the song or pick it up orally. The singers are rarely introduced. The singers remain inwardly facing around a table rather than oriented toward the non-participants. The milling table is always set up on the floor, never on an elevated stage. Although English is used at the milling table, so is Gaelic, and a Gaelic conversation is rarely translated for the benefit of the non-speaker, nor will Gaelic speakers necessarily shift to English to accommodate non-speakers.

The persistent emphasis on traditional participation means that milling frolics continue to be largely participatory in function and nature. This is, of course, part of the reason that they attract tourists: this is the "real deal," not a staged presentation. As many tourism scholars have argued, tourists are often frustrated by presentations of what tourist scholar Dean MacCannell calls "staged authenticity" (1976). Performers in staged presentations make stylized versions of their cultural practices to be consumed by tourists as entertainment and education. But this means that what might otherwise be a participatory performance necessarily becomes presentational. The milling frolic, for all its changes, has not become stylized. It has not adopted presentational elements and continues to emphasize participation as its raison d'être. In maintaining their participatory function, milling frolics continue to attract locals from the Nova Scotian Gaelic community, just as they always have. Local Gaelic speakers and learners are especially valued at milling frolics and are strongly encouraged to participate. As such, milling frolics are not examples of "tourist realism" designed for tourists to seem like an "authentic" Nova Scotian Gaelic experience (Bruner and Kirshenblatt-Gimblett 2005, 49); rather they are held by and for the Nova Scotian Gaelic community. Tourist interest offers organizers increased admission revenues and the potential of government subsidies, but milling frolics are rarely staged for or aimed at tourists. They remain important practices that are distinctly Gaelic to both cultural insiders and outsiders alike. Of course, while tourists get an "authentic" experience, it also means that they may well leave a milling frolic frustrated, understanding neither the songs nor the activity as a whole. Then again, the ever-increasing use of mobile devices means that much information is readily available at tourists' fingertips.

The participatory aspect of milling frolics is fundamental to Gaelic identity politics, particularly insofar as it offers a contrast to the emphasis on presentational music in the dominant Anglo-American culture perceived by many Gaels.[20] Folklorist Roger Abrahams documents the conditions under which "identity" became increasingly important within academic scholarship and in public discourse: "The mid-1960s witnessed a social upheaval that was paralleled by a shift in the central words and metaphors of public discourse … To prove one's humanity, one wanted to demonstrate the existence and the uniqueness of one's culture and one's folklore. Every group came to be designated in terms of its distinct lifeways, a habit of argument that is still very much with us in popular discussions of everyday life" (Abrahams 2003,

210; see also Alba 1990, 1–2). A new emphasis on "uniqueness" in public discourse is key here. Nova Scotian Gaels are, today, all "bicultural" in that they have lived their entire lives in English Canada while having participated to various degrees within Nova Scotian Gaelic culture. There are no longer any monolingual Gaelic speakers; all can speak English fluently and, in fact, Gaelic is often a second language for them. However, despite the fact that Nova Scotia Gaels live simultaneously as Anglo-Canadians, they often draw clear lines between what they consider to be two distinct cultures.

A common perception among Gaelic-speaking settlers in Cape Breton is that, both provincially and nationally, there is an English-speaking, primarily urban hegemony (what Turino frequently calls the capitalist-cosmopolitan formation) that has largely been responsible for shaping education, economy, and language, among other domains. Many believe that hegemonizing institutions and practices have structured life in a way that has fundamentally altered their experiences, forcing many to learn English, industrialize, and urbanize. The cultural damage is not, of course, limited to Gaelic-speaking communities, but has also affected Acadian, Mi'kmaq, and other minority groups. Accompanying the Gaelic community's language and cultural revitalization efforts is their belief that Anglo-provincial or Anglo-Canadian hegemony exists and needs to be resisted. Folklorist Burt Feintuch argues that a strong sense of identity and culture exists in Cape Breton, whatever the postmodernist critiques:

> In his well known work *Modernity at Large*, Arjun Appadurai (1996:140) critiques what he terms "the primordialist argument" regarding identity as including these features: "All group sentiments that involve a strong sense of group identity, of we-ness, draw on those attachments that bind small intimate collectivities, usually those based on kinship or its extensions. Ideas of collective identity based on shared claims to blood, soil, or language draw their affective force from the sentiments that bind small groups." Appadurai intends his characterization as a critique, but it might well have been written as a description of Inverness County [in Cape Breton], where the matter of identity seems more straightforward than much contemporary cultural criticism would comfortably admit. (Feintuch 2004, 78–9)

For many Nova Scotian Gaels, a centuries-long history of cultural oppression is central to their understanding of Gaelic identity. During the height of imperialism, the British royalty and government believed that Britain and its colonies were best served if all its citizens shared a common language and culture. Consequently, countless laws, policies, and practices over the centuries were designed to eradicate Gaelic, or at least to "encourage" the adoption of English norms and culture. Archaeologist Simon James (1999) has written persuasively about how the concept of Celtic identity became politically expedient among speakers of Celtic languages (Irish Gaelic, Scottish Gaelic, Manx Gaelic, Welsh, Cornish, and Breton) in the eighteenth century: a unified "Celticness" offered disparate peoples spread along the peripheries of the British Isles a distinct linguistic and cultural identity that could be asserted against the dominant Anglo-British culture. Johann Gottfried Herder's conceptualization of the essential relationship between a nation and its "folk" was also influential, as it meant that the various Celtic countries and regions in the British Isles each warranted their own language and culture, and that this was, in fact, essential for each nation's health (see, for example, Wilson 1973).

The legacy of cultural distinction remains important among many Nova Scotian Gaels today, who regularly make a point of highlighting how Nova Scotian Gaelic and Anglo-Canadian cultures differ. For many Nova Scotian Gaels, difference is key to their identity, and a significant part of Gaelic cultural history and mythology centres on its struggle to survive in the face of English cultural and linguistic hegemony. Nova Scotia Gaelic scholar Michael Kennedy, for example, writes critically of English (i.e., Anglo-British and Anglo-Canadian) hegemony and its impact on Gaelic culture and identity in both Scotland and Nova Scotia: "English culture is playing an increasingly important role in charting the direction for Gaelic culture and for setting its cultural definitions and priorities. Assimilation is a fact of life for all Gaels ... Enormous social change ... encourages internal redefinition of the minority culture ... to make it fit more comfortably into mainstream (in this case, English) definitions of respectability and to align it with mainstream goals" (2001, 4). Cape Breton Gaelic culture scholar John Shaw warns that "combined with other recent agents of cultural change, the [decline of Gaelic in favour of English] has effectively altered the social context for singing – interrupting the lines of transmission and changing the community's internal concepts of such fundamental aspects as function, performance, occasion, and composition" (2000, 52). The Gaelic cultural publication *Am Bràighe,* published quarterly in Nova Scotia for ten years (1993–2003), offers a number of articulate statements on the differences between Gaels and mainstream anglophones. For example, editor Frances MacEachen writes, "Assimilation has hazed the

Gaels' awareness of their tongue and culture. Without the independent stamp of language that distinguishes Gaels from the English speaking majority, where we've come from and who we are becomes increasingly obscure. This is the reality of Anglicization" (1994).

At the same time that advocates for Nova Scotia Gaelic language and culture emphasize their differences from the Anglo-Canadian majority, they have rejected notions of differences imposed upon Gaelic culture from outside the community, seeking to choose the terms by which they are differentiated and defined:

> Many ... external characterizations ... are the primary source of information available to English-speaking society today regarding Celtic history and culture. The major reason that they tend to offer such a confused and contradictory picture of the "inherent" nature of Celts or Celtic culture is that they generally make no reference to existing Celtic communities, to living Celtic cultures, or the best available Celtic scholarship. In fact, attempts to suggest that these should be the first sources of authority for the interpretation and representation of Celtic culture are often met with scepticism and even open hostility ... The minority culture, then, is marginalized through repression and romanticism and then, finally, by an outright rejection of its authority over the interpretation of its own culture. (Kennedy 2001, 7–8)

The emphasis on a perceived differentiation between participatory Gaelic culture and presentational Anglo-Canadian culture is part of a cultural complex that positions not just music but just about everything in Nova Scotian Gaelic culture as diametrically opposite to Anglo-Canadian culture. Many Nova Scotian Gaels regularly frame their culture as informal, social, and non-competitive, whereas they frame Anglo-Canadian culture as the opposite: institutional, hierarchical, competitive, and individualistic.[21] I use the term "framed" to clarify that community members construct such differences rhetorically; they are not necessarily essential qualities. Culture and identity are, of course, complex and rarely conform to simple characterizations and definitions.

Many Nova Scotia Gaels take pride in informal and intergenerational transmission of traditional and cultural knowledge and skills, and a large number of Nova Scotia Gaels value face-to-face social interactions at informal events such as ceilidhs or more formal milling frolics. I regularly hear, for example,

Cape Bretoners lament the loss of ceilidhs or "visiting culture," and many Gaelic learners make a conscious effort to visit fluent speakers, not only to give themselves opportunities to improve and practise their language skills, but in order to reclaim and revive traditionally valued ceilidh culture.[22] Frances MacEachen brings these contrasts to the fore in an editorial in *Am Bràighe* entitled "Our Heroes":

> Something really bothers me when we speak about the importance of the Gaels' contribution to provincial, or even national society. Credibility so often attaches itself to those whose professional successes are measurable in anglophone terms of reference: politicians, doctors, teachers and so on ... Identifying our culture's champions requires us to reflect on what Gaels themselves consider to be important and valid in their lives. Material wealth and social prominence don't seem too high on the list, compared to fundamental community values and appreciation for creativity, tradition and art. (MacEachen 1996)

Nova Scotia Gaels profess to be non-competitive[23] and collaborative (see, for example, my analysis of attitudes toward competitions in Gaelic Cape Breton in Sparling 2011), evident historically in a variety of communal work "frolics" (which included not just milling, but barn raisings and spinning frolics, for example) and in the modern-day largely unspoken expectation that neighbours and friends help one another with tasks ranging from the making of traditional foodstuffs to the shoveling of snow. As in many other participatory-focused musical traditions, many Nova Scotia Gaels maintain that they value all singers regardless of ability, and that what matters is participation, not skill. Song is regularly integrated into language instruction, implying that anyone who can speak the language can also sing it. Although some milling frolic singers are known for their conventionally beautiful voices (with "beautiful" understood in terms of mainstream presentational aesthetics), the majority have untrained voices, and a significant number are unable to project their voices, or they sing out of tune,[24] do not enunciate lyrics clearly, or otherwise perform in a manner not conventionally recognized as "beautiful." That these latter singers are just as welcome as the former clearly demonstrates the value accorded to participation over skill. By contrast, the perception held by many Gaels is that Anglo-Canadian society privileges presentational music, with the glorification of musical stars; musical value judgments based on technique, skill, and complex musical forms; and the expectation that music is meant to be performed for an audience, supported by performance venues featuring stages that separate performers from audiences and by the recorded music industry.

The milling frolic is itself a unique practice not found in Anglo-American culture. It not only differentiates Gaelic culture from mainstream culture, but it also differentiates Nova Scotia Gaelic culture (where milling frolics are still held today and play a significant role in Gaelic social and cultural life) from Scottish Gaelic culture (where they rarely are). Further, I would argue that, for the purposes of defining cultural identity, the milling frolic's participatory elements are even more important than its distinct visual and sonic elements or its particular history as a practice. Nova Scotia Gaels' privileging of participatory over presentational music may be seen to differentiate them from Anglo-Canadians along ideological, philosophical, and aesthetic lines. It is the apparent "everydayness" (Del Negro and Berger 2004) of participatory music-making in Nova Scotia Gaelic culture that contrasts with the "everydayness" of presentational music-making in the perceived dominant culture that creates the conditions in which non-Gaels experience milling frolics, and by extension, Gaelic culture, as special or different.

The inclusion of tourists at a milling frolic may appear to complicate its definition as either presentational or participatory, particularly if the audience resolutely remains in an observing – rather than a participating – role. Turino acknowledges that musical ensembles and performances may involve both participatory and presentational features, but suggests that "one or the other orientation will ultimately emerge as more fundamental for decision making and practice" (2008, 55). As Turino defines participatory performance, the audience's approach to a performance does not define it as either presentational or participatory. A person who stops to watch a participatory performance does not, by his or her observing presence, change the participatory performance into a presentational one. Rather, participatory and presentational performance are defined by "the goals, values, practices, and styles of actors within a given field ... shaped by their conceptions of the *ideologies and contexts of reception* and the purposes of music within that field" (Turino 2008, 27; italics in the original). In other words, the performers' underlying beliefs regarding the purpose of the music-making activity, and the sonic and behavioural characteristics that emerge to facilitate that purpose, will define the music-making activity as either primarily presentational or participatory. Tourists may well approach milling frolics with a presentational frame of mind, especially those that come from societies in which "'real' or at least successful musicians and music are largely conceptualized in relation to professional presentations, recordings (both video and audio), or (usually) some combination of the two" (Turino 2008, 25). Their predominant experience of music in their everyday lives – and probably within tourist contexts as well – is that music is presentational, requiring their attention but not their participation. The milling frolic accommodates such attendees, but its predominant orientation, as illustrated in all the features described earlier, is toward participation. It is the milling frolic's resiliently participatory orientation that enables it to continue serving an important social bonding role while representing and providing the conditions for enacting a distinct Gaelic Nova Scotian identity.

Conclusions

If you were to drive to Cape Breton and take Highway 4 up the east side of the Bras d'Or Lakes, you'd drive through Johnstown. As is true for many communities in Cape Breton, there isn't much to mark it other than a church and church hall. But within the Gaelic community, it is famous for its annual milling frolic, held every August. In fact, it is probably the longest running milling frolic in Canada, and its age is regularly highlighted; 2018 marked the eighty-fifth annual Johnstown milling frolic. Noting that the Johnstown milling frolic has been running continually for almost a century implies that the event today is pretty much the same as it was when the milling frolic was first organized in 1933. Indeed, I would suggest that the implication is that it is much the same as much older waulking events in Scotland, evident from numerous websites that proclaim with amazement that waulking the cloth can "still" be seen in Cape Breton. It is true that people still take turns singing traditional Gaelic songs in a call-and-response format. A woven blanket is still moistened and pounded on a rough-hewn table in time to the singing. But despite these similarities to descriptions of earlier milling frolics, a remarkable number of aspects of the milling frolic have changed over time. They are no longer held during the winter in people's homes by women only. The milling song repertoire includes more than just waulking songs, and some traditional waulking songs were dropped from the milling repertoire when men began participating. They are performed in public spaces during the summer months for audiences that include tourists as well as locals, and, based on my personal observations, more non-Gaelic speakers than Gaelic speakers. The same milling blanket is reused repeatedly, and plain water has replaced the solution of stale urine to soak the cloth. Milling frolics are no longer necessary to process cloth intended for blankets and clothing. Instead, they have become one of the pre-eminent social contexts within the Nova Scotia Gaelic community, where Gaelic learners and speakers come together to visit and enjoy sharing traditional culture among themselves and with others.

However, despite this extensive list of changes, participation remains central to milling frolics. It could have easily happened that they became showpieces, representing historical performance rather than current practice. Openness to tourists could have meant the literal staging of milling frolics, separating tourist audiences from specialized local performers. Instead, they remain resolutely participatory. Everyone is welcome (or at least tolerated) at the milling table, whether they speak Gaelic or not, can sing well or not, know a suitable Gaelic song or not. It is true that tourists may experience a milling frolic without a clue as to what it is since explanation is rarely offered. But it is also true that tourists experience the "real deal"; the milling frolics they attend are the same frolics that locals look forward to attending all year. It is this participatory aspect of milling frolics that enables the framing of milling frolics as "continuous" despite extensive changes.

Notes

1 According to the *Dictionary of Cape Breton English* (Davey and MacKinnon 2016), "frolic" is a term that means "a gathering of neighbours to work voluntarily on a specific task, frequently followed by a meal and entertainment" and is usually preceded by a range of modifiers, including barn, carding, chopping, cutting, digging, haying, hooking, house, mowing, planting, ploughing, quilting, reaping, rolling, spinning, stumping, tucking, weaving, and wood. However, "milling frolic" is by far the most common kind of frolic referenced in Cape Breton.
2 For a brief and accessible history of the Gaelic language in Scotland, see http://www.undiscoveredscotland.co.uk/usscotfax/society/gaelic.html.
3 Although this photograph shows a waulking taking place out of doors and therefore presumably during a mild season (rather than inside during the winter), it was likely staged. At the time this photograph was taken in 1934, natural light would have been required for both film and photography. In fact, prolific photographer and Gaelic song scholar Margaret Fay Shaw, active in Gaelic communities at about the same time, apparently once described an (indoor) waulking in detail but was unable to take a picture due to the low light levels (personal correspondence with Fiona MacKenzie, Canna House archivist, 14 June 2016).
4 I encourage readers to listen to waulking and milling songs online. Many can be found by searching for "waulking" or "milling song" in YouTube. For a video of South Uist women performing a waulking in 1970, see http://vimeo.com/20467842.

5 See also journalist Francis Campbell's description of courting songs at Cape Breton milling frolics (1993, 15). Interestingly, the tradition of pairing people romantically in a milling song or at a milling frolic continued in a modified manner even after men started participating in Cape Breton (see Caplan 1978, 46; Dunn 1991 [1953], 40).
6 These lyrics and their translation come from Margaret Fay Shaw's book, *Folksongs and Folklore of South Uist* (1977 [1955], 228–9).
7 Several contemporary versions of "Hé Mandu" can be found online, in both video and audio format. iTunes carries *Music from the Western Isles* and readers can listen to a preview of "Hé Mandu" there to get a sense of the song in its traditional guise.
8 I use the term "split chorus" instead of "half line verses," which is the term Collinson and Campbell use, for several reasons. I think that "split chorus" better describes the interweaving of verse and chorus that I consider essential to the form; furthermore, the term "half line verses" refers to individual lines of text, not to overall song forms. Since "half line verses" is no more a vernacular term than "split chorus," I feel justified coining a term that, for my purposes, better represents the overall form.
9 Italics are used in the English translation to differentiate the refrain from the verse. The refrain repeats in the same place in each of the subsequent verses.
10 Unless otherwise noted, all translations are mine.
11 Musicologist Peter van der Merwe suggests using the term "atonic" for pieces that have no tonal centre, and suggests using the term "modal frame" to refer to "significant notes [that] form a sort of frame on which the melody is constructed" (van der Merwe 1989, 102).
12 It is worth noting that milling frolics were not, apparently, limited to Nova Scotia in North America, nor, apparently, even to Gaelic diasporas. A National Film Board film, *Songs in Nova Scotia* (1958) shows an Acadian milling frolic, known in Acadian French as a "foulerie." It appears similar to the Gaelic frolic except that people are standing rather than sitting around a table and consequently the cloth is thrown down with more force than in the Gaelic context. They are also, of course, singing in French rather than in Gaelic. Folklorist Margaret Bennett documented the Gaelic traditions of Newfoundland's Codroy Valley, including milling frolics, in the early 1970s. Intriguingly, various ethnic and settler communities, which held separate milling frolics at one time, gradually came together so that Codroy Valley milling frolics eventually involved songs in multiple languages and sometimes macaronic songs (Bennett 1980). It is not clear whether the milling tradition was once a more widespread phenomenon than hitherto assumed and practised in several immigrant communities, or whether the Gaelic tradition spread to other groups as a result of intercultural contact in North America.
13 Interestingly, men were involved in Newfoundland's Codroy Valley milling frolics as well (Bennett 1980, 100). One of Bennett's primary consultants, Allan MacArthur, a Gaelic speaker born in Newfoundland in 1884 who had participated in many milling frolics, only ever remembered both men and women at the table. Bennett also found a reference dating from 1830 to men participating in a Quebec milling (Bennett 1998, 214). Many Gaelic speakers settled in the eastern townships of Quebec; Bennett documents the Gaelic traditions there in her book *Oatmeal and the Catechism: Scottish Gaelic Settlers in Quebec* (1998).

14 Rosemary MacCormack, a Gaelic speaker from Scotland who lived for many years in Cape Breton and who researched Gaelic songs and song practices, noted, however, that some men learned traditional women's waulking songs from their mothers and continued to sing them at the milling table. She gave Malcolm Angus MacLeod from the North Shore area of Cape Breton as an example (interview with author, 13 June 1998).

15 Rosemary McCormack hypothesized that women would have stopped singing songs about women's intimate affairs when men joined the frolics (interview with author 13 June 1998; see Sparling 2006, 226–7); we don't have any direct evidence that women made a conscious decision to stop singing particular songs because of the gender orientation of the lyrics, other than the lack of these songs in the active milling song repertoire.

16 These lyrics and their translation come from Creighton and MacLeod (1964, 24–5). Several versions can be heard online; I particularly recommend recordings by Julie Fowlis of Scotland, as well as the archival recording held at the Beaton Institute at Cape Breton University (http://www.beatoninstitutemusic.ca/gaelic/ged-a-sheol-mi-air-maineol.html) (note that this version is atypical in that different people take turns singing the verses). I also recommend the recording of this song on *A Tribute to the North Shore Gaelic Singers* (1996).

17 Margaret Bennett also observed the use of water, rather than stale urine, at Newfoundland milling frolics in the 1970s. In fact, Newfoundlanders were shocked to hear of the use of urine in Scotland (Bennett 1989, 155). By contrast, Bennett discovered that the practice of using urine at milling frolics continued far longer in Gaelic-speaking communities in Quebec (Bennett 1998, 216).

18 The word "tourist" is a challenging term in this context. It may be assumed to refer to a particular kind of person (i.e., someone who visits an area once and has little knowledge of the culture and community) whereas the reality is much more complex in Cape Breton. Gaelic event "tourists" may include returning ex-pats, Gaelic learners who return to Cape Breton annually and are embedded in the Gaelic community, Gaelic-speakers from Scotland, Cape Bretoners who don't really know anything about Gaelic culture, and so on. Based on my observations, today's milling frolics generally attract locals predominantly but with some tourists "from away" as well.

19 *Céilidh* (pronounced KAY-lee) literally means "visit" in Gaelic, although it has come to refer in English to concerts or parties. The Gaelic spelling includes an accent, but the word has entered the English language where it is typically spelled without an accent (all subsequent iterations of the word in this chapter therefore do not have an accent). Historically and traditionally, a ceilidh involved impromptu house visits, and the sharing of news, songs, stories, dance, and music, as well as food. Ceilidhs could involve a small number of people, or many.

20 I use the term "Anglo-American" where others might use the term "Western" since Gaels are also "Western" but believe themselves to have different cultural ideologies, values, practices, and identity than English-speakers in "the West," as I clarify in the remainder of the chapter. In my use of the term, "Anglo-American" refers to people from English-speaking British and North American regions, recognizing that a history of British colonization inflected a great deal of present-day North American culture. Thus, "Anglo" in

"Anglo-American" refers to both language (and, by extension, culture and identity) and geographical region, while "American" refers to all of North America. By extension, I use the terms "Anglo-Canadian" and "Anglo-Nova Scotian" in the ways that many Gaels conceive of them: mainstream, English speaking, and hegemonic cultural formations within Canada and the province.

21 Turino also notes this contrast within the capitalist-cosmopolitan formation: "Participatory music making/dancing is the most democratic, the least formally competitive, and the least hierarchical. As such, participatory performance does not fit well with the broader cultural values of the capitalist-cosmopolitan formation, where competition and hierarchy are prominent and profit making is often a primary goal" (2008, 35). For an excellent example of these binaristic characterizations of culture in action (individual vs social, hierarchical vs egalitarian, presentational vs participatory) in Nova Scotia, see the extensive response to Highland dancer Kelly MacArthur's letter to the editor, posted on 9 December 2011 to the Cape Breton events website, *What's Goin On* (http://www.whatsgoinon.ca/letter-to-the-editor-the-end-of-an-era-at-the-gaelic-college). Respondents debated whether or not Highland dancing should be cut from Cape Breton's Gaelic College curriculum, and whether a long-standing Highland dance competition should be cancelled.

22 In 2018, for example, Nova Scotia's Gaelic Affairs initiated a new language program, *Cum Sìos* (a Gaelic phrase traditionally used to invite people in and stay for a visit/ceilidh), designed to support language learners wanting to visit fluent and native Gaelic speakers. Members of another group with which I am involved, the "Gaels Jamily," regularly express a desire to do more visiting, and occasional initiatives have been taken to help support other members with visiting (e.g., by making introductions, accompanying each other on visits, etc.). Visiting is seen as a traditional Gaelic practice, but not part of modern mainstream society.

23 It is worth noting that the trope of non-competitiveness in Nova Scotian Gaelic culture is also used to distinguish between it and other diasporic forms of Scottish culture in Canada. The Ottawa Valley fiddle and step dance tradition, for example, is organized around a competition circuit in which performers travel to competitions throughout Ontario on most weekends during the summer season. Ontario pipers and Highland dancers regularly perform at and compete in Highland Games that are held throughout the province during the summer as well. Of course, many people enjoy these activities as social activities even as they engage them in a competitive capacity.

24 Of course, notions of "in tuneness" may vary between cultural traditions. However, when I use the term "out of tune," I am speaking of tuning that goes beyond internally defined conventions.

References

Abrahams, Roger D. 2003. "Identity." In *Eight Words for the Study of Expressive Culture*, edited by B. Feintuch, 198–222. Urbana: University of Illinois Press.

Alba, Richard D. 1990. *Ethnic Identity: The Transformation of White America*. New Haven, CT: Yale University Press.

Bennett, Margaret. 1980. "A Codroy Valley Milling Frolic." In *Folklore Studies in Honour of Herbert Halpert*, edited by K.S. Goldstein and N.V. Rosenberg, 99–110. St John's, NL: Memorial University of Newfoundland.
– 1989. *The Last Stronghold: Scottish Gaelic Traditions in Newfoundland*. St John's, NL: Breakwater Books.
– 1998. *Oatmeal and the Catechism: Scottish Gaelic Settlers in Quebec*. Edinburgh and Montreal: John Donald Publishers; McGill-Queen's University Press.
Bruner, Edward M., and Barbara Kirshenblatt-Gimblett. 2005. "Maasai on the Lawn: Tourist Realism in East Africa." *Cultural Anthropology* 9 (4): 435–70.
Campbell, Francis. 1993. "Old-Fashioned Romance." *Am Bràighe*, Autumn, 15.
Campbell, John Lorne. 1990. *Songs Remembered in Exile*. Aberdeen, Scotland: Aberdeen University Press.
Campbell, John Lorne, and Francis Collinson. 1969. *Hebridean Folksongs*. 3 vols. Vol. 1. Oxford: Clarendon Press.
– 1981. *Hebridean Folksongs*. 3 vols. Vol. 3. Oxford: Clarendon Press.
Caplan, Ronald. 1978. "A Milling Frolic on the North Shore." *Cape Breton's Magazine*, 39–46. Accessed 13 January 2019. http://capebretonsmagazine.com/modules/publisher/item.php?itemid=820.
Comunn Gaidhealach Leodhais. 1998 [1982]. *Eilean Fraoich: Lewis Gaelic Songs and Melodies*. Stornaway, Scotland: Acair Earranta.
Creighton, Helen, and Calum MacLeod. 1964. *Gaelic Songs in Nova Scotia*. Ottawa, ON: National Museum of Canada.
Davey, William J., and Richard MacKinnon. 2016. *Dictionary of Cape Breton English*. Toronto, ON: University of Toronto Press.
Del Negro, Giovanna P., and Harris M. Berger. 2004. "New Directions in the Study of Everyday Life: Expressive Culture and the Interpretation of Practice." In *Identity and Everyday Life: Essays in the Study of Folklore, Music, and Popular Culture*, edited by H.M. Berger and G.P. Del Negro, 3–22. Middletown, CT: Wesleyan University Press.
Dembling, Jonathan. 2006. "Gaelic in Canada: New Evidence from an Old Census." In *Cànan & Cultar / Language & Culture: Rannsachadh na Gàidhlig*, vol. 3, edited by W. McLeod, J.E. Fraser, and A. Gunderloch, 203–14. Edinburgh, Scotland: Dunedin Academic Press.
Dunn, Charles. 1991 [1953]. *Highland Settler: A Portrait of the Scottish Gael in Cape Breton and Eastern Nova Scotia*. Wreck Cove, NS: Breton Books.
Feintuch, Burt. 2004. "The Conditions for Cape Breton Fiddle Music: The Social and Economic Setting of a Regional Soundscape." *Ethnomusicology* 48 (1): 73–104.
James, Simon. 1999. *The Atlantic Celts: Ancient People or Modern Invention?* Madison: University of Wisconsin Press.
Kennedy, Michael. 2001. *Gaelic Nova Scotia: An Economic, Cultural and Social Impact Study*. Report. Halifax: Nova Scotia Museum, Nova Scotia Department of Culture and Tourism. Accessed 13 January 2019. http://gaelic.novascotia.ca/sites/default/files/files/Gaelic-Report.pdf.
Lucas, Adam. 2005. "Industrial Milling in the Ancient and Medieval Worlds: A Survey of the Evidence for an Industrial Revolution in Medieval Europe." *Technology and Culture* 46 (1):1–30.

MacCannell, Dean. 1976. *The Tourist: A New Theory of the Leisure Class.* New York, NY: Schocken Books.

MacCormick, Donald, and John Lorne Campbell. 1969. *Hebridean Folksongs: A Collection of Waulking Songs.* London, UK: Oxford University Press.

MacDonald, Marilyn. 1988–89. "Milling Frolics on the North Shore: A Look at the Past, Present and Future." Unpublished manuscript, Beaton Institute.

MacEachen, Frances. 1994. "Invisible Minority." *Am Bràighe,* Autumn, 4.

– 1996. "Our Heroes." *Am Bràighe,* Summer, 4.

Shaw, John. 1984. *Water Power in Scotland: 1550–1870.* Edinburgh, Scotland: J. Donald.

Shaw, John, ed. 2000. *Brìgh an Òrain.* Montreal & Kingston: McGill-Queen's University Press.

Shaw, Margaret Fay. 1977 [1955]. *Folksongs and Folklore of South Uist.* Oxford, UK: Oxford University Press.

Sparling, Heather. 2006. "Song Genres, Cultural Capital and Social Distinctions in Gaelic Cape Breton." PhD diss., York University.

– 2008. "Categorically Speaking: Towards a Theory of (Musical) Genre in Cape Breton Gaelic Culture." *Ethnomusicology* 52 (3):401–25.

– 2011. "Cape Breton Island: Living in the Past? Gaelic Language, Song, and Competition." In *Island Songs: A Global Repertoire,* edited by G. Baldacchino, 49–63. Lanham and Toronto: Scarecrow Press.

Tolmie, Frances. 1910–13. "Frances Tolmie Collection." *Journal of the Folk-Song Society* 4 (16):143–276.

Turino, Thomas. 2008. *Music as Social Life: The Politics of Participation.* Chicago, IL: University of Chicago Press.

van der Merwe, Peter. 1989. *Origins of the Popular Style: The Antecedents of Twentieth-Century Popular Music.* Oxford, UK: Clarendon Press.

Wilson, Wiliam A. 1973. "Herder, Folklore and Romantic Nationalism." *Journal of Popular Culture* 6 (4):819–35.

Discography

North Shore Gaelic Singers. 1996 [1986]. *A Tribute to the North Shore Gaelic Singers.* B&R Heritage Enterprises BRCD 0005. CD.

Various artists. 1992 [1971]. *Music from the Western Isles.* Vol. 2 of the Scottish Tradition Series. Greentrax CDTRAX 9002. CD.

Meghan C. Forsyth

Chapter 5

Improvising on the Margins: Tradition and Musical Agency in les Îles-de-la-Madeleine

There is a popular belief on les Îles-de-la-Madeleine (the Magdalen Islands) of Quebec that the rhythmic pulse of a fishing boat engine can be felt in the rhythms of the islands' traditional fiddle music.[1] Located in the south-central portion of the Gulf of Saint Lawrence, this small archipelago boasts a vibrant tradition of music making that blends French Acadian, Scottish, and Québécois traditions, reflecting the intricate web of influences and cultural alliances that define the lived experience of its Acadian inhabitants. While Madelinots[2] – residents of the islands – celebrate a rich musical lineage that is audible in their repertoire and stylistic choices, the tradition's flexible style parameters, including tune variability and fiddle improvisations, promote a culture of individual musical agency that is becoming recognized within and beyond the archipelago as a marker of the islands' traditional music.

In this chapter, I examine the role of improvisation in madelinot fiddling and how improvisatory musical practices, as well as broader ideas about musical agency, have shaped and been shaped by tourism and the global market. While I discuss what and how fiddlers play, I am primarily concerned with how they listen to, understand, and enact their relationships to material culture and the physical environment, and how these connections play out musically. After a brief introduction to the people, place, and history of the islands, I turn to broader questions of the role of improvisation in traditional music, particularly in Western musical traditions, illustrating how we might conceive the creative agency of musicians in the context of the Magdalen Islands' tradition. I examine sociocultural and socioecological factors, such as

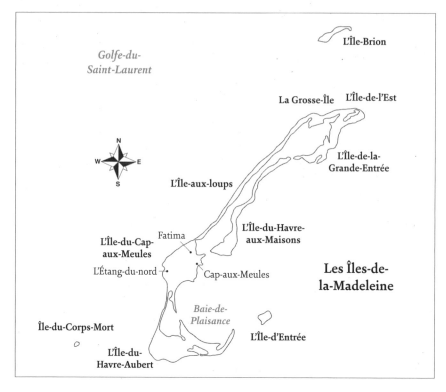

Figure 5.1 | Map of the Magdalen Islands.

radio transmission and maritime economy, that have contributed to a culture of creativity and individual agency within this tradition. Finally, in light of the increasing global visibility of some of the islands' traditional musicians and the transnational networks within which they work, I consider the motivations behind, and expectations of, creativity in contemporary practice that has come to characterize musical expression in this community.

"Islands Beat by the Waves": People, Place, History

The archipelago of the Magdalen Islands, with its characteristic fishhook shape, comprises a dozen islands and islets, of which seven are inhabited and six are connected by long, narrow sand dunes.[3] The sixty-five-kilometre road extends from the southwesterly tip at Havre-Aubert to the northeasterly tip at Grande-Entrée. A seventh island, l'Île d'Entrée, can be reached only by ferry from the island of Cap-aux-Meules, the administrative and business centre

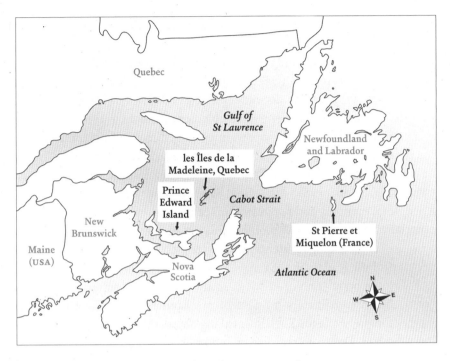

Figure 5.2 | Map of Atlantic Canada and Maritime Quebec.

of the municipality (figure 5.1). Archaeological evidence suggests that coastal First Nations[4] had fished and hunted from the islands for hundreds of years prior to the arrival of Basque, Breton, and Norman fishermen, and other European settlers (Rowdon 1994, 21; Martijn 2003; McCaffrey 1986). The archipelago's geographic position directly in the path of the great trade routes between Europe and the historic province of Upper Canada (now the province of Ontario), and the abundance of fish and walrus in the surrounding waters, meant that the natural resources of the islands were coveted and exploited by European and American merchants, particularly with the increase of commercial trade around the end of the eighteenth century (figure 5.2).

Two linguistic groups – French and English – have shared the archipelago from its early settlement. French-speaking Acadians of the islands are direct descendants of 250 Acadians who arrived in the late eighteenth century from the French outpost of Saint-Pierre et Miquelon, where they had sought refuge during *le Grand Dérangement*, the deportations of thousands of francophone Acadians from what are now known as the Maritime Provinces by the British government between 1755 and 1763 (Halliday 1973, 9).[5] With the signing of the Treaty of Paris in 1763, which resulted in new territorial divisions of the Canadian Maritime region, the Magdalen Islands were annexed to the British colony of Newfoundland (Béland 1987) and, subsequently, to Quebec by the British North America (Quebec) Act in 1774. This "double dependency" (Miller 2007, 17) status as dependent islands of Newfoundland and, later, Quebec,[6] while both were dependent colonies of Britain, contributed to the marginalization, political disempowerment, and dire economic conditions of the island community in the century that followed the deportations. In his history of material and social life in the Magdalen Islands, Anselme Chiasson, a pioneer folklorist in the region, writes that this period was marked by a poor local economy and poor communication with off-island communities, especially during the winter months. This isolation arguably favoured an intense social life among residents and the creation and maintenance of a rich popular culture (Chiasson 1981, 19).

Today, the population of 12,781 is scattered in small communities across the island. Approximately 95 percent of islanders speak French as their mother tongue, while the English-speaking population makes up the remaining 5 percent. Drawn to the developing trade industry and fertile hunting grounds, English-speaking families began to settle on the islands in 1790, and in greater numbers after 1828, when several families of British (largely Scottish) descent from Nova Scotia bought property on Entry Island and Grosse-Île. The municipality of Grosse-Île, located on the east end of the archipelago, and Entry Island, the only inhabited island not attached to the main island (Île du Cap-aux-Meules), remain the predominant English-speaking communities in the islands, with approximately 550 of the 695 native English speakers (Statistics Canada 2012).[7]

While the islands are currently under the administrative control of the province of Quebec, they are recognizably Acadian in collective popular consciousness, from the traditional colourfully painted clapboard houses to the Acadian flags proudly displayed across the islands. The islands' residents distinguish themselves culturally from their mainland Québécois neighbours, an identification that is evident in the several localized dialects and the numerous stories, legends, songs, and tunes transmitted orally from generation to generation that document the local history and distinct way of life.[8] As the cultural and linguistic majority of the islands, francophone Acadians are in a position distinct from that of most other Acadian communities throughout the global Acadian diaspora, for whom loss of cultural forms and a legacy of discrimination based on language, religion, and social class mark the collective Acadian experience. The relative isolation of the archipelago and linguistic support from Quebec have resulted in less encroachment from the dominant anglophone presence in eastern Canada, and the islanders have experienced, for the most part, an uncontested preservation of their French Acadian dialect and culture.

Island Economies, Island Music

In recent years, the government of Quebec has created many local public service jobs to encourage educated islanders to remain in the archipelago (Cayo 1991, 40, in Burke 1999, 2). Many Madelinots choose to pursue traditional industries of fishing and farming, and the fishery remains a mainstay of the economy, cementing Madelinots' strong attachment to the landscape. The island community has experienced challenges similar to other parts of Atlantic Canada with regard to a declining fishing industry, an aging population, and a consistent exodus of youth, particularly since young people frequently leave to continue their education and to find work on the mainland. Mirroring trends in other Maritime communities, Madelinots have confronted these obstacles by promoting their burgeoning tourism and ecotourism industries, both of which are becoming important components of the region's economic plan. Nevertheless, the fishing industry and its calendar dominate daily activities: life seems to ebb and flow to the rhythms of the various fishing seasons[9] and fishermen's schedules, and the influence of the fishery is palpable in maritime cuisine, old nautical terms that are incorporated into the local dialects, and the numerous active fishing ports.

Tourism is the second most important industry in the region and has grown steadily since the early 1970s. These visitors triple the island population in the summer months, hailing predominantly from the Montreal area, drawn to the relaxed way of life and relative isolation the islands offer (LeBlanc 2012). Cultural events play an important role in drawing and entertaining both visitors and locals. Numerous concert halls and bars (many of them seasonal) feature a wide range of theatrical and musical performances – particularly by Québécois singers and country music bands – on a regular basis throughout the summer and early fall.

There is a popular saying in the islands' tourism literature that those who know the islands know that in each house we can find a musician, if not a whole family of musicians, and that there is a good chance they are all fiddlers (Rivière 2005, 16). While there are several prominent musical families,

Figure 5.3 | Jam, Parc de Gros-Cap, L'Étang-du-Nord.

Figure 5.4 | A traditional music session at Café de la Grave, Havre-Aubert. Pascal Miousse (centre, fiddle) and Pastelle LeBlanc (accordion).

wild stories about music making as a pastime during "storm stays," and a strong tradition of instrumental music, traditional music plays a relatively minor role in public life. Indeed, in contrast to neighbouring Prince Edward Island and Cape Breton Island, where traditional fiddle music dominates promotional material and is featured regularly and publicly in ceilidhs and concerts, there are few formal or informal public events at which one can hear performances of traditional music and song. Nevertheless, traditional song and instrumental music thrive in more private settings where they are cultivated, celebrated, and shared aurally between family, friends, and the occasional lucky visitor. In recent years, some local enthusiasts have endeavoured to bring their traditions further into the public light by organizing events such as the *Festival de musique traditionnelle*, a festival featuring local musicians and dancers, and, since 2011, weekly musical gatherings during the summer months in Parc de Gros-Cap, which draw large crowds of participants and observers (figure 5.3). Lastly, Café de la Grave, a café/restaurant located in the historic site of La Grave[10] in Havre-Aubert, draws locals and visitors for its local cuisine, friendly atmosphere, family-style dining, and informal, participatory traditional music sessions (figure 5.4).

Creativity, Tune Variability, and Western Traditional Music

Scholarship on musical improvisation[11] has been dominated by studies of jazz and non-Western musical traditions in which improvisatory performance predominates or exists alongside pre-composed music.[12] Increasingly, scholars have sought to extend these subject boundaries and broaden our understanding of musical creativity *as* culture in a broader context (Solis and Nettl 2009). Improvisation, in particular, has been underrepresented in scholarship on modern Western classical and traditional or folk music. Notable exceptions include Hill's work on creative freedom in contemporary Finnish folk music pedagogy and performance (2005; 2009), O'Suilleabhain's analyses of ornamentation and melodic improvisation in Irish traditional music (1990), and essays on improvisation in Western art music by Levin, Mattax Moersch, Hatten, Kinderman, and Temperley in Solis and Nettl's volume *Musical Improvisation: Art, Education, and Society* (2009). While not focused on improvisation per se, several scholars have examined musical creativity in relation to compositional processes of individual musicians (Quigley 1995; O'Suilleabhain 1978) and the social influences that shape folk music traditions (Burman-Hall 1978; Cowdery 1990; Turino 2008).

Musicians make extemporaneous decisions constantly in most Western traditional music contexts in relation to physical gestures (eye contact, facial expressions), social gestures (taking turns as leader for a set of tunes or adjusting one's playing to create a more unified group experience in the context of a session, for example), or musical gestures (such as variations in melodic, rhythmic, or chordal elements). Nonetheless, improvisation in such traditions tends to operate, as Solis has noted, "in an unacknowledged way" (2009), and is often framed under the rubric of tune variation or local aesthetic, instead of creative agency. Why do discourses about Celtic folk and traditional music avoid addressing these musical aspects in terms of improvisation and creative practice? While processes and degrees of improvisationality (Sawyer 2003, 158; 1996, 273) may differ between genres and between musicians, common definitions of improvisation set up a false dichotomy between improvisation and "pre-composition"[13] (see Spring; Nettl and Russell 1998; Solis and Nettl 2009) and a separation of composition from performance, particularly in the context of Western classical music (Toynbee 2003, 108). In Celtic folk music, such dichotomies are often based on an oversimplification of the tradition that focuses on the common binary structure (AABB) of traditional instrumental tunes; the transmission of tunes at the intersection of written and oral traditions; and the standardization of many aspects of traditional music performance through shared repertoire and the global proliferation of Celtic musics. Nevertheless, as the case study at the heart of this chapter seeks to demonstrate, players generally work from predetermined tune models, which are modified per their "aural lineage" – a term used by fiddler Stan Chapman to describe the stylistic influences or repertoires developed from listening to radio, recordings, or live performance, or learned through formal or informal instruction (Chapman, in Lavengood 2008, 183) – or which are modified in the course of performance. Both practices are evident in the fiddling tradition of the Magdalen Islands, as they are in many other practices around the world in which players are expected to memorize patterns or a set of "obligatory features" (Nettl et al. 2001).

Building on Hill's and Nettl's suggestions that musical activities such as "composing, improvising, arranging, varying, embellishing, and interpreting" (Hill 2012, 88) fall along a continuum of creativity (Nettl 1974, 6), I base my approach to the musical processes of improvisation and transmission at play in the Magdalen Islands on an understanding of improvisation and composition as "linked processes" (Solis 2009). Here, Hill's definition of musical creativity as "the process of using divergent thinking and exercising volition in the creation of a sound product that does not conform to an entirely predetermined model" (Hill 2012, 88) is useful, as the phrase "not entirely predetermined" can include the processes of tune variation and aural composition at the heart of this musical tradition.

"It Sounds like the Waves ... Calm Playing and Then Wild"

The traditional instrumental music that I discuss in this chapter is predominantly fiddle-based. Historically, madelinot fiddlers most often played alone, accompanied by the rhythmic tapping of their feet, but it is now common for fiddlers to be accompanied by guitar or piano. In some newer contexts, such as the aforementioned gatherings in Parc de Gros-Cap, a group-playing format has become more common, likely influenced by session formats found in Prince Edward Island. The dominant fiddle repertoire heard on the islands comprises local variants of Scottish Cape Breton tunes, especially those on the widely disseminated recordings of prominent Scottish Cape Breton violinists Winston "Scotty" Fitzgerald and Angus Chisholm from the 1930s and 1940s.[14] The Cape Breton Island repertoire played by older fiddlers in the Magdalen Islands is described by several musicians as having a "homemade" quality to it, in that musicians frequently modify the melody (often referred to as the "setting"), ornamentation, key, and mode of well-known tunes to suit individual aesthetics. Scottish Cape Breton tunes exist alongside older, locally composed madelinot tunes, some of which are based on songs. These older tunes are generally reels and cotillions, many of which have been championed by fiddler and singer Bertrand Déraspe and disseminated widely through his teaching on- and off-island, performances, and recording projects. Fiddler Lisa Ornstein has documented a type of tune known as *rabostan*, of which a number were composed by blind fiddler and storyteller Avila à Alfred Leblanc (1914–2010), a lobster and herring fisherman and respected oral historian from Gros-Cap (a community in Cap-aux-Meules). *Rabostan*, meaning "the very last" or "leftover," is a type of short dance tune with a set of associated, and often humorous, lyrics (Naud 2011; Ornstein, 2013).

The button accordion has long been a part of the local music scene as an instrument dominated by male players, but it is often in the shadow of the fiddle. In recent years, the piano accordion has gained popularity as a solo instrument, particularly among young women, and is featured regularly at musical sessions, such as those at the Café de la Grave, where café owner and accordionist Sonia Painchaud has led this instrumental revival. Despite

Figure 5.5 | Avila LeBlanc.

Figure 5.6 | *Les Pêcheurs*, sculpture by Roger Langevin (1990). Site de La Côte, L'Étang-du-Nord.

the trend toward a dominance of female fiddlers in neighbouring regions since the 1990s – and, indeed, globally, in Celtic fiddling traditions – the madelinot fiddle has remained firmly in the domain of men, with only a few women fiddlers referenced in the course of my research.

The natural and material culture of sea-faring life permeates islanders' daily lives and collective imagination, and underpins the rich heritage of the islands. Never far from one's sight, the sea is heard everywhere: old nautical terms colour the local Acadian French dialect, musicians and artists cite their experiences of the physical environment as inspiration for creative expression, and listeners relate the rhythms and movements of madelinot fiddlers to the rolling of the waves and the syncopated *toc-a-toc* rhythms of the old one-lung "Make-and-break" twin-cylinder fishing boat engines. Louis Charles Vigneau describes the distinct feel of madelinot fiddling:

> It's typical in the Maggies. Because of the fish ... the fish bring people to the Maggies, it was very prosperous, rich. And the men from the beginning were sailing and working on boats. Little ones and bigger ones like today. You know that kind of roll you have on the sea? Sometimes bad weather, sometimes calm. A guy from home told me that in the fiddle style the rolling [also corresponded to] the sea. Because many fiddlers were looking out the window to the sea and playing, just trying to forget about the bad day they had, but they still have the rolling in their heads when they come back from the sea. So, always rolling. And also they move a lot, like the bounce of the waves. (2009)

In his introduction of Félix LeBlanc, madelinot fiddler and member of the acclaimed traditional band Suroît, at a 2009 performance during the Jamboree atlantique des violoneux/Atlantic Fiddlers' Jamboree, hosted by the town of Abrams Village (PEI), the emcee described Félix's style in similar terms: "son style est littéralement imprégné par la mer" ("his style is literally infused by the ocean"). The group Vent'arrière[15] highlighted this connection between expressive and material cultures on the first track of their self-titled CD (1998), which begins with the syncopated rhythm of the engine. Without missing a beat, the fiddler, Bertrand Déraspe, takes up this rhythm and launches into the "Reel à Célestin à Jos," maintaining the momentum of the motor's rhythm to the end. This sonic connection is frequently highlighted in music, lyrics, and conversation. Legends and extraordinary stories of seafaring life abound in the oral tradition, many of them stemming from a time when the islands were far more isolated than they are today. These local discourses about music making reveal particular ways of listening to music and an intimate relationship to the physical environment that is understood and experienced sonically.

Individuality and Tune Variability in Contemporary Performance

One evening during a research trip on Prince Edward Island in 2008, I found myself in a cozy tune shed, a well-known venue for informal music making behind a house in the Région Évangéline of western PEI. As the rain poured down outside, I sat with friends on old wooden chairs lining the shed's walls as Patricia Richard, a young Acadian woman and noted singer, performed some old French songs and jazz standards, accompanied by a small ensemble of snare drum, keyboard, and electric bass. Pascal Miousse (b. 1971), a multi-instrumentalist from the Magdalen Islands and member of the Acadian group Vishtèn,[16] joined the ensemble and began improvising a fiddle harmony under the vocal line. There was some applause as Patricia finished her song and, thanking the musicians, drifted away from the circle. Pascal had not stopped playing, the soulful melody gradually increasing in volume, speed, and melodic complexity until both his legs pounded up and down on the wooden floor, beads of sweat stood out on his forehead, and hair fell from his bow. By the time he had completed numerous repetitions of the single tune, what had begun as a relatively simple reel had morphed into a fiery and highly ornamented improvisation. With each repetition of a phrase, accents migrated to different beats, the rhythm was pushed and pulled, notes added, changed or dropped, and left-hand (fingered) and bowed ornaments flavoured the melody in new and sometimes surprising ways until, eventually, he cycled back to the original.

While Pascal's playing is often perceived by both Madelinots and other listeners as particularly virtuosic, this kind of performance has, in recent years, become common among a generation of predominantly male, professional madelinot fiddlers, now in their early forties and fifties, who have become active participants in national and international musical networks. In light of the growing visibility of these musicians, the flexible style parameters of the tradition and the improvisatory aspects of performance are increasingly recognized both locally and internationally as markers of local practice. At the same time as the virtuosic playing of some professional musicians is bringing greater awareness of madelinot traditional music, my conversations with older musicians suggest that these flexible style parameters have deep roots in local culture and reflect broader ideas about music making that are influenced by a variety of sociocultural and environmental factors. Pascal's style can be understood as a contemporary extension of the traditional, improvisatory practice that has shaped and is shaped by festival and tourism culture.

The oral history of the islands is replete with anecdotes about learning Scottish fiddle music via radio broadcasts that featured traditional music from neighbouring Cheticamp (Cape Breton Island) and Antigonish, Nova Scotia in the 1940s and 1950s, as well as via the dissemination of tunes and sound recordings by sea-faring traders and fishermen. Older Madelinots recount that they and their families would listen on their prized battery radios to the musical shows aired daily at 6 p.m., directly after the broadcast of a nightly religious message. Thus, many fiddlers' styles and repertoires are heavily influenced by the Cape Breton tradition. For example, the playing style of Bertrand Déraspe, the archipelago's most celebrated fiddler, borrows the bowed triplet ornaments ("cuts"), drones, and left-hand ornaments, such as grace notes and turns, common to the Cape Breton style. At the same time, it is differentiated from neighbouring traditions by its emphasis on rhythmic aspects over melodic notes. This is achieved by the use of double-stops, dropping notes, and accenting the off-beats at the end of a phrase by changing bow pressure or dynamics; the result is a rhythmic emphasis that typically falls on the up-bow. Both techniques of dropped notes and accenting create a syncopated rhythm similar to, but generally more emphasized than, the "shuffle" bowing style played by Acadians in other regions (particularly western Prince Edward Island, see Forsyth 2012) and Gaspesian fiddlers (Patterson and Risk 2014). Transcriptions of Bertrand playing "Reel à Jean-Joseph à Avila"[17] and "Paddy on the Turnpike" (figures 5.7 and 5.9) illustrate the prominent rhythmic elements of this distinct regional style. Figures 5.8 and 5.10 illustrate Bertrand's interpretation of how non-Madelinots might play the tunes in a straight manner without the rhythmic nuance of the madelinot style. While the "Reel à Jean-Joseph à Avila" is locally composed, "Paddy on the Turnpike" is a well-known tune in Scottish and Irish repertoires. Figure 5.7 illustrates the dropping and accenting of notes to create a syncopated rhythm. Dropped or muted notes are depicted by an alternate note-head. In figure 5.9, the off-beats at the end of the phrase are accented. Bertrand demonstrates a different "turn" (sequence) of the notes at the end of the second and fourth measures, the second and fourth eighth-notes of which are prominently accented. The frequent three-note slurs from the fourth eighth-note of

Figure 5.7 | "Reel à Jean-Joseph à Avila" (traditional), Part A, as played by Bertrand Déraspe in the local style.

Figure 5.8 | "Reel à Jean-Joseph à Avila" (traditional), Part A, as played by Bertrand Déraspe in his interpretation of a straight version of the tune.

Figure 5.9 | "Paddy on the Turnpike" (traditional), Part A, as played by Bertrand Déraspe in the local style.

Figure 5.10 | "Paddy on the Turnpike" (traditional), Part A, as played by Bertrand Déraspe in his interpretation of a straight or standard version of the tune.

one grouping into the second eighth-note of the following grouping shifts the rhythmic accent of the measure.

Madelinot fiddlers and enthusiasts articulate some common ideas about the evolution of this syncopated style. First, there is a rhythmic link between the sound of the old fishing boat motor, as exemplified in the Vent'arrière example described above. Second, several fiddlers believe that this local style developed as a direct result of learning tunes via battery-operated radio, since it was common that the radio signal would cut out, missing notes or phrases.

Narratives surrounding the experience of listening to music via these radios and learning the tunes from this medium often reference the emergence of a syncopated rhythmic pattern; this rhythm was subsequently mimicked as tunes were memorized and transmitted to others, and eventually it became part of a local aesthetic.[18]

While this mode of transmission *may* account for the heavily accented traditional style, many fiddlers with whom I spoke also noted that it has led to a level of variability and individual interpretation, both melodic and ornamental, within the tradition that is widely accepted among fiddlers and listeners. Several older fiddlers described their process of learning tunes via radio broadcasts, emphasizing that they had had to recreate the tune from memory after hearing it only a couple of times through.[19] Thus, a certain degree of instant composition was necessary to fill in missing notes and phrases. Fishermen also talk about long days on the sea contributing to the creation of their own versions of songs and instrumental tunes. They often frame this as experimenting with tunes, whether they had instruments with them or not, since they would jig tunes that they knew and improvise new settings.[20] In my conversations with musicians, an important distinction emerges between older generation fiddlers who tend to have maintained fixed versions – albeit their own, unique versions – of tunes, and the first generation of professional fiddlers and their contemporaries, who are known for the more improvisatory renditions and are more apt to incorporate a wide range of ornamentation and effects in the course of a performance.

The notion of a spectrum of variability in folk music has been examined by several scholars who emphasize, as has folklorist Richard Bauman in relation to oral texts, that "completely novel and completely fixed texts represent poles of an ideal continuum" (Bauman 1977, 40); Bauman later expands on this statement, writing that "all but the most ideally stereotyped of performance events will have discernibly variable features of act sequence and/or ground rules for performance. The emergent structures of performance events are of special interest under conditions of change, as participants adapt established patterns of performance to new circumstances" (41–2). Within the broader category of Celtic music, many traditional musicians personalize the tunes in their repertoire, but it is the extent to which a musician is permitted to change a tune, while staying within the perceived boundaries of tradition, that is noticeably more flexible in the Magdalen Islands than elsewhere. In the Cape Breton fiddle tradition, for example, melodic variation was historically applied in a more formal manner and many composed sets of variations on traditional and popular tunes were published (MacQuarrie 1940; Dunlay and Greenberg 1996). Both personal style and creativity are valued in Cape Breton fiddling, but they are generally expressed in ways other than by creating new variations or altering tunes in other ways, such as musicians' choices of the tunes that make up a set, danceability, and technical skill. In his study of performance practice in contemporary Cape Breton fiddling, Ian Hayes notes, "there is little melodic improvisation done by the fiddler. Bowing and ornamentation may be improvised or change from one performance of a tune to the next, but the melody of a tune is often reproduced note for note. 'Correctness' is highly valued in the Cape Breton tradition, and this fixity of melody is a palpable example of that" (Hayes 2014, 28). In contrast, madelinot fiddlers can change a tune more radically, while staying within the boundaries of tradition. There is a conscious move away from a fixed or "correct" idea of a tune and value placed on one's ability to improvise embellishments, melodic variation, and rhythm. In fact, among some fiddlers, tune variation is not only *promoted* but there is also a degree of expectation that fiddlers will take creative liberties and vary their renditions of tunes "on the fly."

While madelinot and Cape Breton Island traditions are highlighted here, individuality (making a tune one's own through melodic and rhythmic variation, among other possible musical expressions of individuality) is also valued and encouraged in other fiddle traditions within the bounds of the respective traditions. Several authors have related shifts in performance context – specifically, a shift from music for dancing to music for listening – to increases in melodic and rhythmic variation. Writing about American contest fiddling, Goertzen notes that melodic variation on early American fiddle recordings was a widespread practice, but the variations themselves were minor so as not to distract the dancers (1988, 111). As the American contest/ Texas style developed, the style shifted from dance venues to concert stages, resulting in an increased focus on technical proficiency and variation.[21] Johnson writes that fiddlers in the Ontario old-time fiddling tradition perform their individuality through melodic creativity, ornamentation, tune choice, and tune composition (2006, 424–8), even in the context of fiddle competitions. While one might expect the competitive context to stifle creativity in favour of other musical considerations, Johnson notes that "increased individuality in fiddling performances is *shaped by* a combination of the competitive process, individual preferences, and audience appeal" (Johnson 2006, 406; my emphasis).[22]

The Irish traditional music scholar Breandán Breathnach explains that tune variation involves "a degree of instant composition" in which a group of notes or bar is varied. In some cases, "perhaps only the skeleton of a phrase is ... retained. Each time the part is played some grouping is varied, no performance ever being the same" ([1977] 1993, 98, quoted in Dunlay 2009). This kind of variation is admired in the Irish tradition Breathnach describes, and some players are highly regarded for their abilities to improvise.[23] Moreover, many Irish musicians and aficionados distinguish between musicians who are recognized for having extensive talent for instant composition and those who have worked out a series of small variations that can be applied seemingly spontaneously (Breathnach [1977] 1993; Berthoud 2011, 26). Many Madelinots make a similar distinction, placing greater esteem on fiddlers who can improvise spontaneously. This ability to vary each rendition of a tune is particularly valued among a young generation of madelinot fiddlers who are carving out a reputation for madelinot fiddling in professional folk music circles and in festival circuits.

This focus on tune variation has influenced several features of madelinot fiddle performance. First, the abundance of tune variants and individual interpretations has favoured solo performance over group playing. Fiddler Alexandre Déraspe, now in his thirties, notes that because playing solo enables more flexibility in timing and ornamentation, which he calls "adding individuality," it is challenging to play with multiple other fiddlers; he feels that the loss of individuality results in "less interesting" music (2012). Second, related to this propensity toward individual playing, variation within the tradition privileges a culture of listening over participatory music and dance, and individual twists and variations are commended. Musical dexterity undoubtedly also plays a role in one's ability to apply variations and improvisations to a passage of music, and several of the best-known fiddlers have some formal, classical training and/or began their music careers playing fiddle or other instruments in touring rock, country, and folk bands. Finally, instead of sets of three or four tunes each played two or three times, which is the prevalent formal structure of a performance in many Euro-American and Canadian fiddling traditions, it is more common in the Magdalen Islands for tunes to stand alone and be played numerous times with increasingly complex variations.[24] There is no consistency in how many times a tune is played, although it is rare to hear a tune repeated less than three times. Regardless of the extent to which a performance incorporates variation or embellishment of musical elements, there seems to be an unspoken preference among my informants to return to the original or model tune in the final repetition of the tune as a kind of *homage* to the tune itself or to the playing of the fiddler from whom the tune was learned.

Wong writes that the "real-time nature [of improvisation] defies the very possibility of music analysis despite the fact that any improvised performance can be pinned down and fixed through recording technology" (2004, 288). Given the spontaneous nature of the performance, the following comments are necessarily broad and descriptive, as opposed to a note-by-note analysis. A methodological challenge in studying and writing about improvisation within the Magdalen Islands' tradition stems from the fact that such performances are rarely recorded. Furthermore, on most iconic archival recordings of madelinot fiddlers, the pieces are much shorter, with a limited amount of variation and improvisation, than those the same musicians are likely to have played in more informal or spontaneous contexts. The dearth of recordings that represent the improvisatory aspects of this tradition, and the challenge of writing about it, speaks to the irony of "fixing" a spontaneous creation versus the experience of a live performance.[25]

While improvisation and tune variation vary greatly from player to player, tune to tune, and performance to performance, the following description of a recent performance by Pascal Miousse of the Québécois reel "Reel du pendu" (Hanged Man's Reel) at the *Festival Chants de Vielles* in 2011 (Montérégie, QC) will serve as an example of Pascal's ability to incorporate variation and embellishments.[26] His virtuosity on the fiddle is most readily audible in his phrasing and use of the bow to create varied effects. The tune is widely known among French-Canadian fiddlers as a showcase tune that is commonly played with the violin cross-tuned (*scordatura*) in the key of A as AEac#[27] instead of the standard GDae violin tuning. Myriad versions and variations of the tune exist, and there are numerous well-known recordings by fiddlers Isidore Soucy (1927), Joseph Allard (1928), and Jean Carignan (1973), among others.[28] According to Ornstein, the tune "typically features a nuclear melody which is followed by a number of short strains based on arpeggiated motifs which gradually descend from the upper to the lower octave; many versions include the use of left-hand pizzicato on the open strings ... virtually all versions are characterized by the AEac# scordatura and by an associated story which credits the composition of the tune to a prisoner condemned to be hanged" (Ornstein 1985, 132).[29]

As in Ornstein's description, Pascal's rendition of the tune follows a basic (or skeletal) tune model, described by Nettl as a "series of obligatory musical events that must be observed, either absolutely or with some sort of frequency, in order that the model remain intact" (1974, 52). The fiddler follows the common four-part structure of the tune and the melody of each part is recognizable in some form. In addition to steady drones, which are common to the madelinot style, he incorporates progressively varied rhythms and bowed ornamentation with each rendition of the tune (which he plays in total four times). This is accomplished by using a wide range of bowing techniques that are more commonly associated with Western classical violin practices than traditional music, such as *spiccato* (horizontal bouncing bow), *sautillé* ("flying spiccato" or rapid bouncing stroke), *ricochet* or *jeté* (technique of "throwing" the bow on to the string in the upper third of the bow so that it bounces, producing a series of rapid notes), and suppressed strokes such as *sul tasto* ("on the fingerboard") and *sul ponticello* ("on the bridge").[30] This mix of strokes unfolds generally by playing a short phrase with the bow in full contact with the string, followed by the same phrase using a lighter bow stroke, or more accented strokes, to accomplish a variety of different effects. In other instances, a pattern of four eighth notes is replaced by a run of sixteenth notes, an arpeggiated major chord is played in the minor or with the addition of a minor seventh, notes are variably added or dropped (either silenced completely or played with a suppressed stroke), and the rhythm is pushed and pulled differently in each repetition of a phrase. All the while, the tempo remains constant and the tune retains enough major pillars of the original melody that it is recognizable as "Reel du pendu."

There are several factors that contribute to the development of the flexible stylistic parameters I have described. First, and most obviously, the tradition is almost exclusively an oral tradition. But the madelinot tradition differs from some other oral traditions, such as the Norwegian fiddle tradition documented by Goertzen (2007), in which "rote memorization" and "note for note fidelity" (to borrow Bauman's terms) emerge as central features. I describe this as an *almost exclusively* oral tradition because Bertrand Déraspe has developed his own shorthand for transcribing tunes for his students, and this method has been adopted by some other players in the region. In Déraspe's method, pictured in figure 5.11, specific notes are identified by means of a fraction with the appropriate finger as the top number of the fraction and the French term for one of the four fiddle strings (from highest to lowest string: mi, la, ré, sol) as the bottom solfège syllable. Therefore, the notation of the fraction 2/la indicates the note C or C# above middle C. The key below outlines specific fingerings and strings:

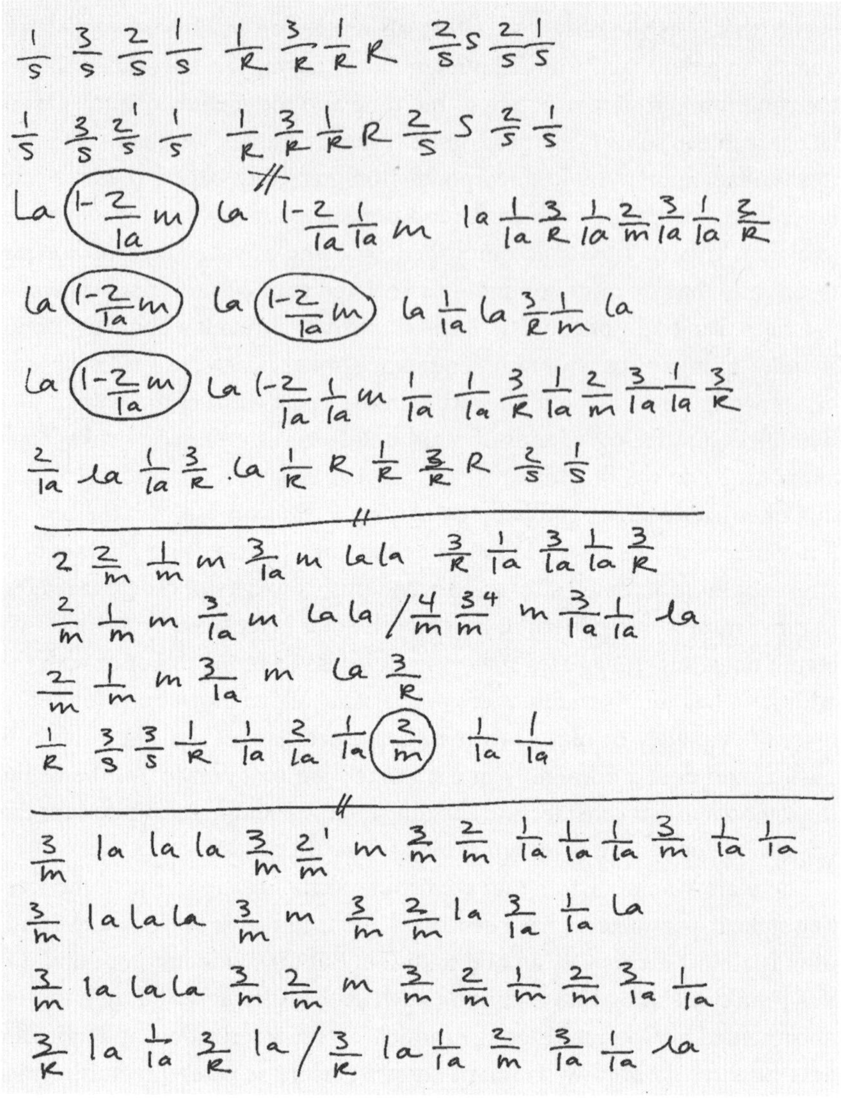

164 | Meghan C. Forsyth

Figure 5.11 | Author's transcription of Bertrand Déraspe tune transcription (title unknown), from the notebook of Alain Cummings.

Left hand:
Pointer finger = 1; Middle finger = 2; Ring finger = 3; Pinky finger = 4
String:
S (or sol) = open G; R (or ré) = open D; L (or la) = open A; M (or mi) = E

On some occasions, an arrow up or down beside a number indicates a sharp or flat note. As one might imagine, there is much room for interpretation using this method of learning. The key of a tune is not generally indicated, nor are specific rhythms, although with some consistency shorter-value notes such as eighth or sixteenth notes are indicated by a circle around two fractions. Therefore, players require significant knowledge of a melody in order to reproduce even its skeletal version. There is much room for personal interpretation using this method of learning, and the transcriptions function as memory aids rather than note-for-note guides.

Through the formal transmission of traditional fiddle music by Bertrand and others, a number of locally composed tunes and variations of older Cape Breton tunes have entered the common local fiddle repertoire alongside contemporary tunes. While the combination of written and aural methods that fiddlers use creates the perception of individuality, some local musicians are critical of contemporary performance practice, arguing that there is sometimes a false perception of creativity and individualization in the repertoire; that is, Bertrand's students tend to play in his idiosyncratic style and they learn his settings of tunes.

Extra-musical Enablers of Musical Creativity

In addition to these musical processes, islanders point to extra-musical elements that promote local creativity and a vibrant artisanal community, often suggesting links between their physical environment and creative practice. Even within the close regional boundaries of the archipelago, communities were fairly isolated from each other and still are to some extent in the winter and when the dunes upon which the highway is built flood during storms. This isolation has resulted in particular versions of tunes and stylistic differences developing in different families, which in turn has contributed to a broader acceptance of tune variability and personal expression. Other musicians with whom I spoke were more poetic, connecting creativity to landscape, environmental conditions, and the changing of the seasons. In our interview, one young man described at length how he felt that the constant view of the sea and the horizon inspired him to compose new settings of fiddle tunes. This kind of inspiration was echoed by others, such as Carole Painchaud, a well-known interpreter of old songs, who talks about "les moments propice" (roughly translated as "favourable moments"), such as the winter months, when the light is different than in other seasons, the islands are more isolated (and less focused on tourism), and the weather is more volatile; these aspects, she explains, lend themselves to creative practices such as composing and trying new things (2012). Echoing a connection between his performance and compositional styles to the sense of space on the islands, Pascal Miousse relates his extensive use of improvisation to a sense of creative freedom that he associates with playing the fiddle, noting in a press release that he "enjoys taking part ... in the osmosis that occurs during a musical moment, in the freedom of a fiddle, in the improvisation on an instrument that touches the soul" (Oklahoma City Community College, 2012). This connection of creativity to place, both on land and on sea, came up frequently in my conversations with islanders, many of whom emphasized the creative or artistic community of the islands, a community and way of life heavily influenced by the physical surroundings, and that attract a wide array of artists and promote artistic endeavours.

The municipal and provincial governments support the growing artistic industry through touring grants, residencies, small business grants (through which several musicians have established successful recording studios), and promotional materials. As a career as a professional fiddler becomes an increasingly viable way to make a living, a distinct discourse about madelinot musical identity has emerged that positions madelinot fiddlers in contrast to their Québécois, Acadian, and Scottish Cape Breton neighbours, and seeks to set them apart on the world stage. This kind of discourse has given individual fiddlers and traditional bands an advantage in securing gigs, especially at festivals, where they can position themselves as simultaneously francophone, Acadian, Québécois, and Celtic, or any number of these categories, depending on the context, as well as tradition-bearers of a distinct, often romanticized and mythologized, musical tradition. The labeling of madelinot fiddlers and groups under the umbrella of "Québécois music" (a label that grates many islanders who identify more strongly with their Maritime Acadian ancestry than with their mainland Québécois neighbours) has been slowly changing as several madelinot groups, such as the band Suroît, have garnered attention for their distinct style of playing. Increasingly, bands are articulating this difference in their stage talk, bios, and album liner notes. This difference extends not only to musical style and language, but also to the experience of being Acadian – with all the history that comes with that ancestry – in an increasingly anglicized professional industry and environment.

Conclusion

Personal expression is highly valued in contemporary madelinot fiddling, and this has fostered attitudes and expectations about musical performance that privilege variation and improvisatory embellishment. These attitudes frame how madelinot music is played locally and presented to cultural outsiders, particularly by touring professionals and in the context of national and international folk music festivals. Improvisation and other creative practices have emerged as central to defining and positioning madelinot traditional music in relation to the region's dominant (mainland Québécois and Scottish Cape Breton) musical traditions. More broadly, these practices further a prominent local discourse about Acadian cultural identity that is increasingly shaped and articulated through musical performance.

The case of the fiddle tradition of the Magdalen Islands represents just one point along a continuum of creative practices that includes improvisation and variation, composition, and other forms of musical agency. A complex spectrum of why music is created and what is valued in musical performance shapes the nature and range of creative opportunities that are desirable in the community. But innovation and traditional forms hang in a delicate balance. Critical local listeners valorize an older aesthetic that draws on strong, syncopated rhythms and Cape Breton-influenced ornamentations over other Maritime regional styles. Some critics of the more virtuosic interpretations of the tradition suggest that, while there is a perception of creativity and an openness to variation, the extent to which some professional musicians incorporate improvisatory aspects into their performances is not representative of all players in the tradition. Yet, increasingly, these younger, professional fiddlers are setting expectations both locally and beyond for this kind of practice through their performances and recordings. Time will tell, but the tradition appears to be gradually shifting and, in another generation or two, perhaps improvisation will be widely recognized as a hallmark of madelinot fiddling.

Notes

1 Les Îles-de-la-Madeleine is the official name of the archipelago, but, among English speakers, the colloquial name for the islands is the Magdalen Islands. In this chapter, for ease of reading, I use the English name the Magdalen Islands.

2   A Madelinot(e) (n., m/f) is a resident of the islands. Madelinot (adj.) refers to something that is of the islands.
3   The archipelago is located 215 km southeast of the Gaspé Peninsula coast, 105 km north of Prince Edward Island (PEI), and 95 km northwest of Cape Breton Island. The islands are accessible by plane (to mainland Quebec), by a multi-day cruise from Montreal, or by a five-hour ferry from the town of Souris, at the eastern tip of PEI. Quebec Route 199 is built on the long stretches of sand dunes that link the islands.
4   In this region, the coastal First Nations comprised Abenaki, Mi'kmaq, and Montagnais. The Mi'kmaq called the islands *Munagesunok*, "islands beat by the waves" (Mailhot and Dubois 2006). While the broader economic region of Gaspésie–Îles-de-la-Madeleine has two First Nation reserves and one Mi'kmaq community, there are currently no Indigenous people on the islands.
5   The Acadians are descendants of the first French settlers in eastern Canada in the seventeenth century. The Acadians who arrived in the Magdalen Islands from Saint-Pierre et Miquelon had been exiled from Nova Scotia. When the French Revolution of 1789 reached the islands of Saint-Pierre et Miquelon, dividing the loyalties of its inhabitants, the Acadians fled to the Magdalen Islands (Halliday 1973, 9).
6   The Magdalen Islands were annexed to Quebec in 1895.
7   The remainder of the English-speaking population is spread across the inhabited islands. Of the 695 native English speakers, 470 are considered to speak English only (Statistics Canada 2012).
8   See Chiasson 1981 and 2004.
9   Lobster remains the primary species fished around the islands. The lobster fishing season opens in May and runs for nine weeks. Other species fished in and around the islands, mainly in the summer months, include snow crab (April or May), northern shrimp, molluscs (scallops, mussels, clams; March to July), pelagic fish (mackerel, herring), and ground fish species (Atlantic and Greenland halibut and cod). Ground fish were considered the mainstay of the fishing industry until the beginning of the 1990s but moratoria were imposed on ocean perch and cod due to overfishing (Tourisme Îles-de-la-Madeleine). The sealing industry shut down in the 1980s and has made a weak recovery since the mid-1990s.
10 The name "La Grave" comes from the French term *grève*, meaning pebbled or sandy terrain. La Grave was the site of the islands' first settlement, which extended over and around its pebble beach, and also the centre of the archipelago's early fishery. Now a bustling, bohemian community from April to October, with restaurants, cafés, museums, a marina and theatre, Havre-Aubert was designated as a historical site by Quebec's minister of cultural affairs in 1983.
11 In this chapter, I use the term improvisation to refer to an aspect of a broader conceptualization of creativity. Similarly, in his introduction to *Musical Improvisation: Art, Education, and Society*, Solis defines improvisation as "one of many tools creative musicians use to make new music" (2009, 2).
12 Ernst Ferand's 1938 study, which focused largely on Baroque improvisation and nineteenth-century improvised organ fugues, is widely considered the first substantial book on improvisation. Nettl notes that the study of improvised performances gained

momentum in the late 1960s and 1970s with a marked increase in publications devoted to the topic (1998, 2–3; see, for example, Rycroft 1962; Lord 1965; Jairazbhoy 1971; Nettl 1974; Berliner 1978; Malm 1975; Viswanathan 1977; Elkholy 1978). Early work during this period on creativity in jazz focused on techniques and performances of individual musicians (Smith 1983; Owens 1974; Stewart 1979), jazz improvisation theory (Wang 1973; Tirro 1974), and pedagogical approaches to jazz improvisation (Baker [1969] 2005; Coker 1964). There is also a substantial body of literature on the histories of jazz in and beyond the United States. Since the 1970s, improvisation has been the focus of numerous ethnographic case studies of individual musicians and musical cultures in which improvised performance plays a central role (see, for example, Kippen 1988; Brinner 1995; Monson 1996; Slobin 2000; Gray 2016). Texts by Bailey (1992), Moore (1992), and contributors to Solis and Nettl's volume *Musical Improvisation* (2009) have illuminated key issues in the study of improvisation in the context of Western art music. For a useful survey of the literature on improvisation, see Nettl and Russell 1998.

13 Howard Spring (n.d.) uses the term "pre-composition" – the act of composing a piece of music prior to performance – to distinguish it from the more commonly used term "composition," arguing that improvisation is also a form of composition.

14 While further research is needed to sonically map the diverse influences and musical styles of the islands, my interviews with local fiddlers also suggest that the Down East style frequently attributed to fiddler Don Messer was particularly popular on the east side of Grand-Entré and the island of Havre-aux-Maison.

15 The group Vent'arrière takes its name from a sailing term for a tail wind that disrupts the flow of air over the sails, reducing the speed of the boat and often causing sailors to shift the sail of a vessel from one side to the other (a manoeuvre known as a "jibe").

16 See Forsyth 2012 for a discussion of this group's music and their marketing of Acadian traditional music.

17 In the Magdalen Islands, tunes are typically named after a musician known for playing them or passing them on to others; in this case the tune is associated with Jean-Joseph, son of Avila.

18 Further research is needed about the use of these battery-operated radios, the listening experience, and the musical programming to gain a more complete understanding of this aspect of local history and this narrative about musical life that has become local lore.

19 Transmission of tunes via radio has been documented in several other fiddle contexts; see, for example, Forsyth (2011) and Perlman (2015) on PEI fiddling; Osborne (2007) and Russell (2000) on Newfoundland fiddling; and Favreau (1997) on fiddling in the Sherbrooke region of Quebec.

20 The term "jig" here refers to mouth music or *turlutte*, singing dance tunes with full rhythmic nuance. This practice is also known as chin music, *musique à bouche*, and diddling.

21 See also Houle 2014 for an analysis of stylistic variation and evolution in Texas contest-style fiddling.

22 Cooley notes a high degree of virtuosic playing and improvisation in Polish Górale fiddling in Chicago, which accompanies athletic dancing (2002). Métis fiddling is also known for creativity and variation (see, for example, Giroux 2013).

23 Such privileging of creativity has been observed in a variety of ethnomusicological studies around the world. Hood, for example, observed that in Javanese gamelan group improvisations, both performers on instruments that hold the ensemble together, as well as those that depart most drastically from the model, are held in high esteem (1964, 34–8).

24 This style of performance featuring numerous renditions of a tune with increasing melodic and rhythmic complexity is also found in the Texas fiddle contest style (see Goertzen 1988; Houle 2014). Deeper comparison between the two traditions requires further research and analysis than has been conducted to date.

25 The relationships between improvisation and composition, and live performance and studio recording, in the context of jazz and bebop are discussed by Whyton (2013), DeVeaux (1988, 132), and Giddens and DeVeaux (2009).

26 Miousse also recorded "Reel du pendu" in a live performance for Vishtèn's 2009 *Live* CD. While some improvisation in rhythmic and melodic embellishments is evident in both versions, I have based my description of his interpretation of the tune on his solo performance at the Festival de Chants Vielles and not the version on the *Live* CD, in which he is accompanied on guitar by his father, Bernard Miousse.

27 To avoid confusion, lower-case letters indicate that the notes are an octave higher than their upper-case counterparts, i.e., 'a' is an octave above 'A.'

28 As noted above, "Reel du pendu" is a Québécois tune known for individualized and, sometimes, virtuosic, variations, including (depending on the player) various bowed articulations, some of which are described here. "Reel du pendu" is neither a madelinot tune nor is the improvisatory nature of the performance of this tune exclusive to the Magdalen Islands' tradition. Because a large portion of the Magdalen Islands' fiddle repertoire comes from Cape Breton Island or Quebec, it is common to hear fiddlers playing and/or adapting these popular tunes. I chose to focus on this particular tune because Pascal's performance of it exemplifies numerous techniques found in the improvisatory style of the Magdalen Islands and also because the commercially available recorded version on the *Live* CD can be consulted as an approximate reference. Pascal's basic melody of "Reel du pendu" is close to that recorded by fiddler Joseph Allard on the Victor record label in 1928 (Risk 2016, 154–9).

29 The most common version of the legend of the "Reel du pendu" relates that, while standing on the gallows, a man condemned to death by hanging was given a badly tuned fiddle and, despite never having touched a fiddle before, played this tune from memory so expertly that he was granted his freedom.

30 Few madelinot fiddlers would recognize and name these bowing techniques, which are commonly used, in various combinations, by fiddlers of other traditions when playing this tune. Fiddlers learn the bowing techniques aurally from recordings or from versions passed down through generations. Interestingly, because much of the non-Magdalen Islands' repertoire was learned aurally from recordings and players were unable to see the original recorded performers, the execution of the bowed techniques, or fingerings, are often improvised in their own right.

References

Bailey, Derek. 1992. *Improvisation: Its Nature and Practice in Music*. London, UK: Moorland Publishing.

Baker, David. (1969) 2005. *Jazz Improvisation: A Comprehensive Method for All Musicians*. Rev. ed. Chicago, IL: Alfred Music.

Bauman, Richard. 1977. *Verbal Art as Performance*. Prospect Heights, IL: Waveland Press.

Béland, Bibiane. 1987. "Ethnographie de l'île d'Entrée (Îles-de-la-Madeleine)." Master's thesis, Université de Montréal.

Berliner, Paul. (1978) 1993. *The Soul of Mbira: Music and Traditions of the Shona People of Zimbabwe*. Chicago, IL: University of Chicago Press.

Berthoud, Philip. 2011. *Irish Fiddle Playing*. Fenton, MO: Mel Bay Productions.

Breathnach, Breandán. (1977) 1993. *Folk Music and Dances of Ireland*. Dublin and Cork, Ireland: Mercier Press.

Brinner, Benjamin. 1995. *Knowing Music, Making Music: Javanese Gamelan and the Theory of Musical Competency and Interaction*. Chicago and London: University of Chicago Press.

Burke, Brian. 1991. "The Spatial Dimensions of Landscape and Cultural Identity: A Case Study of the Magdalen Islands, Quebec." Master's thesis, Carleton University.

Burman-Hall, Linda. 1978. "Tune Identity and Performance Style: The Case of 'Bonaparte's Retreat.'" *Selected Reports in Ethnomusicology* 3 (1): 77–97.

Cayo, Don. 1991. "Islands in the Gulf: Quebec's Iles de la Madeleine." *Canadian Geographic* Oct/Nov: 29–40.

Chiasson, Anselme. 1981. *Les Îles de la Madeleine: Vie matérielle et sociale de l'en premier*. Ottawa, ON: Éditions Leméac.

– 2004. *Les légendes des Îles de la Madeleine*, 3rd ed. Montreal, QC: Planète Rebelle.

Coker, Jerry. 1964. *Improvising Jazz*. Englewood Cliffs, NJ: Prentice-Hall.

Cooley, Timothy. 2002. "Music of the Polish Górale Community in Chicago." In *American Musical Traditions* 4, edited by Jeff Todd Titon, 72–6. New York, NY: Schirmer Reference.

Cowdery, James R. 1990. *The Melodic Tradition of Ireland*. Kent, OH: Kent State University Press.

Déraspe Alexandre. 2012. Interview with author.

DeVeaux, Scott. 1988. "Bebop and the Recording Industry: The 1942 AFM Recording Ban Reconsidered." *Journal of the American Musicological Society* 41 (1): 126–65.

Dunlay, Kate. 2009. Essay published in the booklet accompanying MacKinnon's Brook, *Traditional Fiddle Music of Cape Breton* 4. Rounder CD 7040.

Dunlay, Kate, and David Greenberg. 1996. *The Dungreen Collection – Traditional Celtic Violin Music of Cape Breton*. Toronto, ON: DunGreen Music.

Elkholy, Samha. 1978. *The Tradition of Improvisation in Arab Music*. Giza, Egypt: Rizk.

Favreau, Eric. 1997. "The Transmission of Traditional Music via Radio Broadcasts." *Bulletin Mnémo* (June and September). Accessed 2 May 2014. http://www.mnemo.qc.ca/html2/97(11)a.html.

Ferand, Ernst. 1938. *Die Improvisation in der Musik*. Zurich, Switzerland: Rhein-Verlag.

Forsyth, Meghan. 2011. "'*De par chez nous*': Fiddling Traditions and Acadian Identity on Prince Edward Island." PhD diss., University of Toronto.

— 2012. "Performing *Acadie*: Marketing Pan-Acadian Identity in the Music of Vishtèn." *Journal of the Society for American Music* 6 (3): 349–75.

Giddens, Gary, and Scott DeVeaux. 2009. *Jazz*. New York, NY: W.W. Norton & Company, Inc.

Giroux, Monique. 2013. "Music, Power and Relations: Fiddling as a Meeting Place between Re-settlers and Indigenous Nations in Manitoba." PhD diss., York University.

Goertzen, Chris. 2007. *Fiddling for Norway: Revival and Identity*. Chicago, IL: University of Chicago Press.

Gray, Nicholas. 2016. *Improvisation and Composition in Balinese Gendér Wayang: Music of the Moving Shadows*. London, UK: Routledge.

Hall, Roger. 2006. "Upper Canada." *The Canadian Eycyclopedia*. Accessed 12 November 2014. http://www.thecanadianencyclopedia.ca/en/article/upper-canada/.

Halliday, Hugh. 1973. "The Lonely Magdalen Islands." *Canadian Geographic* 36 (1): 1–13.

Hatten, Robert. 2009. "Opening the Museum Window: Improvisation and Its Inscribed Values in Canonic Works by Chopin and Schumann." In Solis and Nettl, *Musical Improvisation*, 281–95.

Hayes, Ian. 2014. "'It's a balancing act. That's the secret to making this music fit in *today*': Negotiating Professional and Vernacular Boundaries in the Cape Breton Fiddling Tradition." PhD diss., Memorial University of Newfoundland.

Hill, Juniper. 2009. "Rebellious Pedagogy, Ideological Transformation, and Creative Freedom in Finnish Contemporary Folk Music." *Ethnomusicology* 53 (1): 86–114.

— 2012. "Imagining Creativity: An Ethnomusicological Perspective on How Belief Systems Encourage or Inhibit Creative Activities in Music." In *Musical Imaginations: Multidisciplinary Perspectives on Creativity, Performance and Perception*, edited by David Hargreaves, Dorothy Miell, and Raymond McDonald, 87–104. Oxford, UK: Oxford University Press.

Hood, Mantle. 1964. "Improvisation as a Discipline in Javanese Music." *Music Educators Journal* 50 (4): 34–8.

Houle, Laura. 2014. "Carrying on the Tradition: A Performance Practice Analysis of Stylistic Evolution in Texas Contest Style Fiddling." Master of Music thesis, Texas Tech University.

Jairazbhoy, Nazir A. 1971. *The Rāgs of North Indian Music*. London, UK: Faber and Faber.

Johnson, Sherry. 2006. "Negotiating Tradition in Ontario Fiddle Contests." PhD diss., York University.

Kinderman, William. 2009. "Improvisation in Beethoven's Creative Process." In Solis and Nettl, *Musical Improvisation*, 296–312.

Kippen, James. 1988. *The Tabla of Lucknow: A Cultural Analysis of a Musical Tradition*. Cambridge, UK: Cambridge University Press.

Lavengood, Elizabeth. 2008. "Transnational Communities through Global Tourism: Experiencing Celtic Culture through Music Practice on Cape Breton Island, Nova Scotia." PhD diss., Indiana University.

LeBlanc, Gabrielle. 2012. Interview with author.

Levin, Robert. 2009. "Improvising Mozart." In Solis and Nettl, *Musical Improvisation*, 143–9.
Lord, Alfred B. 1965. *The Singer of Tales*. New York, NY: Athenaeum.
MacQuarrie, Gordon. 1975. *The Cape Breton Collection of Scottish Melodies for the Violin*. Medford, MA: J. Beaton.
Mailhot, Pierre, and Jean-Marie Dubois. 2006. "Îles de la Madeleine." In *The Canadian Encyclopedia*. Accessed 12 November 2014. http://www.thecanadianencyclopedia.ca/en/article/iles-de-la-madeleine/.
Malm, William P. 1975. "Shoden, A Study in Tokyo Festival Music: When Is Variation an Improvisation?" *Yearbook of the International Folk Music Council* 7: 44–66.
Martijn, Charles A. 2003. "Early Mikmaq Presence in Southern Newfoundland: An Ethnohistorical Perspective, c. 1500–1763." *Newfoundland and Labrador Studies* 19 (1): 44–102.
Mattax Moersch, Charlotte. 2009. "Keyboard Improvisation in the Baroque Period." In Solis and Nettl, *Musical Improvisation*, 150–70.
McCaffrey, Moira. 1986. "La préhistoire des Îles de la Madeleine: bilan préliminaire." In *Les Micmas et la mer*, edited by Charles A. Martijn, 99–162. Montreal, QC: Recherches amérindiennes au Québec.
Miller, Rebecca. 2007. *Carriacou String Band Serenade: Performing Identity in the Eastern Caribbean*. Middletown, CT: Wesleyan University Press.
Moore, Robin. 1992. "The Decline of Improvisation in Western Art Music: An Interpretation of Change." *International Review of the Aesthetics and Sociology of Music* 23 (1): 61–84.
Monson, Ingrid. 1996. *Saying Something: Jazz Improvisation and Interaction*. Chicago, IL: University of Chicago Press.
Naud, Chantal. 2011. *Dictionnaire des regionalisms des Îles de la Madeleine*. Montreal, QC: Québec Amérique.
Nettl, Bruno. 1974. "Thoughts on Improvisation: A Comparative Approach." *Musical Quarterly* 60 (1): 1–19.
Nettl, Bruno, and Melinda Russell, eds. 1998. *In the Course of Performance: Studies in the World of Musical Improvisation*. Chicago, IL: University of Chicago Press.
Nettl, Bruno, Rob Wegman, Imogene Horsley, Michael Collins, Stewart Carter, Greer Garden, Robert Selectsky, et el. 2001. "Improvisation." *Grove Music Online. Oxford Music Online*. Oxford University Press. Accessed 10 October 2014. https://doi.org/10.1093/gmo/9781561592630.article.13738.
Oklahoma City Community College. 2012. "Enjoy New-Traditional Acadian Music March 27." Press release published 13 March 2012. Accessed 28 June 2012. http://www.occc.edu/news/communicator/vishten.html.
Ornstein, Lisa. 1985. "A Life of Music: History and Repertoire of Louis Boudreault, Traditional Fiddler from Chicoutimi, Québec." Master's thesis, Université Laval.
– 2013. "Rabostans and Reels: The Musical Legacy of Avila Leblanc, Fiddler." Presentation at the Acadian and Celtic Crossroads Conference, Cape Breton University, Sydney, NS, 13 October 2013.

Osborne, Evelyn. 2007. "Fiddling with Technology: The Effect of Media on Newfoundland Traditional Musicians." *Newfoundland and Labrador Studies* 22 (1): 187–204.
O'Suilleabhain, Michael. 1978. "Innovation and Tradition in the Music of Tommy Potts." PhD diss., The Queen's University of Belfast.
– 1990. "The Creative Process in Irish Traditional Music." In *Irish Musical Studies*. Vol. 1, *Musicology in Ireland*, edited by Gerard Gillen and Harry White, 117–30. Dublin, Ireland: Irish Academic Press.
Owens, Thomas. 1974. "Charlie Parker: Techniques of Improvisation." PhD diss., University of California, Los Angeles.
Painchaud, Carole. 2012. Interview with author.
Patterson, Glenn, and Laura Risk. 2014. Liner notes of *Douglastown: Music and Song of the Gaspé Peninsula*. Douglastown Community Centre.
Perlman, Ken. 2015. *Couldn't Have a Wedding without a Fiddler: The Story of Traditional Fiddling on Prince Edward Island*. Knoxville: University of Tennessee Press.
Quigley, Colin. 1995. *Music from the Heart: Compositions of a Folk Fiddler*. Athens: University of Georgia Press.
Risk, Laura. 2016. "*Veillées*, Variants, and *Violoneux*: Generic Boundaries and Transnational Trajectories in the Traditional Instrumental Music of Quebec." PhD diss., McGill University.
Rivière, Sylvain. 2005. *Têtes de violon*. Outremont, QC: Éditions du Passage.
Rowdon, Larry. 1994. *Hidden Bounties: Memories of Pioneering on the Magdalen Archipelago*. Manotick, ON: Nine Pines Publishing.
Russell, Kelly. 2000. *Kelly Russell's Collection: The Fiddle Music of Newfoundland and Labrador, Vol. 1, Rufus Guinchard and Émile Benoit*. St John's, NL: Pigeon Inlet Productions.
Rycroft, David. 1962. "The Guitar Improvisations of Mwenda Jean Bosco." *African Music* 3: 86–102.
Sawyer, R. Keith. 1996. "The Semiotics of Improvisation: The Pragmatics of Musical and Verbal Performance." *Semiotica* 108: 269–306.
– 2003. *Group Creativity: Music, Theater, Collaboration*. New York, NY: Psychology Press.
Slobin, Mark. 2000. *Fiddler on the Move: Exploring the Klezmer World*. Oxford, UK: Oxford University Press.
Smith, Gregory E. 1983. "Homer, Gregory, and Bill Evans? The Theory of Formulaic Composition in the Context of Jazz Piano Improvisation." PhD diss., Harvard University.
Solis, Gabriel. 2009. "Introduction." In Solis and Nettl, *Musical Improvisation*, 1–20.
Solis, Gabriel, and Bruno Nettl. 2009. *Musical Improvisation: Art, Education, and Society*. Urbana and Chicago: University of Illinois Press.
Spring, Howard. n.d. "Improvisation and Ethnomusicology." Accessed 2 November 2014. http://www.improvcommunity.ca/sites/improvcommunity.ca/files/research_collection/627/Ethnomusicology_Improvisation.pdf.
Statistics Canada. 2012. Les Îles-de-la-Madeleine, Quebec (Code 2401023) and Les Îles-de-la-Madeleine, Quebec (Code 2401) (table). Census Profile. 2011 Census. Statistics

Canada Catalogue no. 98-316-XWE. Ottawa. Accessed 24 October 2014. http://www12.statcan.gc.ca/census-recensement/2011/dp-pd/prof/index.cfm?Lang=E.
Stewart, Milton L. 1979. "Some Characteristics of Clifford Brown's Improvisational Style." *Jazzforschung/Jazz Research* 11: 135–64.
Temperley, Nicholas. 2009. "Preluding at the Piano." In Solis and Nettl, *Musical Improvisation*, 323–42.
Tirro, Frank. 1974. "Constructive Elements in Jazz Improvisation." *JAMS* 27: 285–305.
Tourisme Îles-de-la-Madeleine. "Fisheries." Accessed 3 November 2014. http://www.tourismeilesdelamadeleine.com/en/discover-the-islands/unique-features-of-the-region/fisheries/.
Toynbee, Jason. 2003. "Music, Culture, Creativity." In *The Cultural Study of Music: A Critical Introduction*, 2nd ed., edited by Martin Clayton, Trevor Herbert, and Richard Middleton, 102–12. New York, NY: Routledge.
Turino, Thomas. 2008. *Music as Social Life: The Politics of Participation*. Chicago, IL: University of Chicago Press.
Vigneau. Louis Charles. 2009. Interview with author.
Viswanathan, Tanjore. 1977. "The Analysis of Raga Alapana in South Indian Music." *Asian Music* 9: 13–71.
Wang, Richard. 1973. "Jazz circa 1945: A Confluence of Styles." *Musical Quarterly* 59 (4): 531–46.
Whyton, Tom. 2013. *Beyond a Love Supreme: John Coltrane and the Legacy of an Album*. Oxford, UK: Oxford University Press.
Wong, Deborah. 2004. *Speak It Louder: Asian Americans Making Music*. New York and London: Routledge.

Discography

Allard, Joseph. 1928. "Reel du pendu" His Master's Voice Victor 263527. Available from *Bibliothèque et Archives nationales*, Quebec. Accessed 3 December 2014. MP3.
Boudreault, Louis. c. 1974. *Portrait du vieux Kébec*, vol. 12, Louis "Pitou" Boudreault, violoneux. Le Tamanoir TAM-512. LP.
Carignan, Jean. 1973. *Jean Carignan*. Philo Fl-2001. LP
Déraspe, Bertrand. n.d. *Auteurs de mer*. CD.
– 1997. *Contre vents et marées*. GBGA Radio-Canada. DC-112. Compact disc.
– 2007. *Pêcheur de tradition*. Îles-de-la-Madeleine, QC: Independent. CD.
Rebels (Steve Poirier and Jean-Eudes Turbide). 2010. *Influences*. Quebec, QC: J.E.T. Musique. CD.
Soucy, Isidore. 1927. "Reel du pendu." Starr 15330. Available from *Bibliothèque et Archives nationales*, Quebec. Accessed 3 December 2014. MP3.
Suroît. 1977. *Suroît*. Les Discques Biplan Inc., DB-2861. CD.
– 1993. *Suroît*. Suroît Musique, SURC-997. CD.
– 1998. *Bootleg*. Suroît Musique, SURC-990. CD.
– 2000. *Salue la Bolduc*. GSI Musique, SURC-554. CD.
– 2001. *Les Grandes Marées, 1992–2000*. GSI Musique, SURC-553. CD.

- 2002. *Prends le temps*, Octant Musique, OCCD-9199. CD.
- 2005. *En concert à l'Anglicane de Lévis*, Editions Sud-Ouest, B000C6WV36. CD.
- 2006. *Chouche*. Suroît Musique, B01K8MH0CU. CD.
- 2009. *Mi-Carême*. Suroît Musique, SURC-99B. CD.
- 2014. *Bercer l'amer*. Suroît Musique, GOCD-1401. CD.
- 2017. *La r'visite*. Go-Musique, B073X1P96Z. CD.

Vent'arrière (Bertrand Déraspe, Patrice Déraspe, and Carole Painchaud). 1998. *Vent'arrière: Chansons et musiques de folklore acadien des Îles-de-la-Madeleine*. TB-225. CD.

Vishtèn. 2004. *Vishtèn*. Moncton: Distribution Plages, VISH0104. CD.
- 2007. *11:11*. Moncton: Distribution Plages, CD999–DB10. CD.
- 2009. *Live*. Independent publication, VISH0308. CD.
- 2012. *Mosaïk*. PTVISH04. CD.
- 2015. *Terre Rouge*. PTVISH05. CD.
- 2018. *Horizons*. PTVISH18. CD.

Chris McDonald

Chapter 6

The Continuities and Legacies of English Song Traditions in Nova Scotia

Nova Scotia's celebrated folklorist and song collector Helen Creighton (1899–1989) was once asked why she collected folksongs, ballads, and tunes from the farmers and fishers of her home province. She replied, "I've always thought that my job as collector is to provide the raw material for our writers and musicians," and added, "It's always a great thrill when one of our songs comes back to me in another form" (quoted in Davies 2001). Like other collectors working in eastern Canada – Kenneth Peacock and Maud Karpeles in Newfoundland, Louise Manny in New Brunswick, and Edith Fowke in Ontario – Creighton subscribed to the idea that the vernacular song traditions of rural people, the last vestiges of pre-industrial society, were the authentic basis of national and regional cultures. This was a widespread and influential idea in the United States, Britain, and Europe through much of the late 1800s and early 1900s; during the second and third quarters of the twentieth century, it was an idea whose time had come in Nova Scotia.

The songs Creighton collected and published would be used, initially, as repertoire to be taught in Maritime schools and as source material for choral and other types of compositions. Through later incarnations on radio, television, records, revivals, and festivals, the folk repertoire Creighton and others collected continued to reverberate in Nova Scotian culture, and was tied in various ways to the image of the Maritimes that came to be marketed for tourists. Critics of Creighton have argued that the selective biases that informed her collecting did much to help build an image of Nova Scotia as a pastoral land of farmers, fishers, and handicraft artisans, carrying the treasures of a deeply rooted folk culture – an image that stands in marked contrast to the turbulent heavy industrialization that transformed the province in the late 1800s. Ian McKay (2009) offers a particularly pointed critique of ways in which Nova Scotia was framed as a pre-modern, predominantly Scottish province beginning in the 1930s, arguing that Creighton's collections were an invaluable contribution to this framing.

This chapter explores the legacy of English folksong tradition in Nova Scotia, as it was first established by folk collectors like Creighton and W. Roy MacKenzie, and reinforced by the provincial government and other cultural and political actors. But my central interest is in how each generation of Nova Scotian musicians responded to the potentials, problems, and ambivalences that the province's folksong canon brings, and how it has been mobilized or resisted in each era since the early 1960s. As I will show, musicians in the province have, at times, used the idea of Nova Scotia as a hotbed of folksong tradition very strategically and successfully to authenticate their offerings and to connect with audiences, as well as with communities both real and imagined. However, it is also a problematic legacy, and has proven a burden at times: artists whose music falls outside the lineage of folk tradition have to fight against the centrality of the Maritime "folk" stereotype. Nevertheless, the legacy of Nova Scotia's folksong canon continues to resonate widely in terms of musical style, musicians' backstories, and the cultural infrastructure that animates large parts of the Nova Scotia music and tourism industries, as seen in the Lunenburg Folk Harbour Festival, Cape Breton's Celtic Colours International Festival, and the Stan Rogers Folk Festival held yearly in Canso.

I acknowledge at the outset that the term "folk" has a complicated and problematic history. Folksongs, as discussed in this chapter, are partly those songs that were in oral circulation among rural populations when MacKenzie and Creighton collected them. Creighton would have considered songs traceable to the Child Ballad canon as the only real folk songs when she began her collecting; she later expanded her definition (albeit reluctantly) to include songs that were regionally composed, as well as songs from other ethnic and language groups. In context-specific cases, I also use the term "folksong" to describe newer compositions by professional and semi-professional performers and songwriters who link their work in some ways to the styles or repertoires found in folksong canons like Creighton's or MacKenzie's. This linkage underlies the formation of the commercial genre of "folk" as it emerged from the North American folk revivals of the late 1950s and beyond.

From Settlement to a Folksong Canon

W. Roy MacKenzie's and Helen Creighton's song collections emphasize English-language balladry in Nova Scotia, although Creighton's collecting efforts went beyond this repertoire to include Gaelic, Acadian French, and Mi'kmaq songs. The emphasis on English-language balladry no doubt traces back to the work of Francis Child (1898), Cecil Sharp (1916), and other pioneers who established the orally transmitted ballad as a treasured repertoire of folk literature. When evidence arose that such balladry had survived and been passed down in North America, there was a rush of interest in collecting and documenting the versions and variants that existed in the United States and Canada, with collectors like John Lomax (1910) leading the charge. During the decades on either side of 1900, a time when North America's once agrarian society was shifting to an urban and industrial one, there was a keen desire to keep a sense of deeply rooted English-language culture alive and to serve as a reminder of what the English ethnic identity had been. MacKenzie's and Creighton's collections and publications should be understood against this background. Their collections would be revisited as a source of English-Canadian cultural heritage, with greater emphasis on its potential for constructing national and regional (Maritime-Canadian) identities.

But who were the English settlers who brought these ballads with them, and when and from where did they come? Permanent English-language settlement of Nova Scotia dates from the colonial wars with France over control of the area in the 1740s. There had been abortive attempts to colonize the region in the 1630s, but the founding of Halifax in 1749 marked the first permanent settlement of the British in the Nova Scotian peninsula. Prior to this, the Mi'kmaq and French Acadian settlers formed the primary population base. The largest English-speaking influx of settlers came from the American colonies. A wave of "New England Planters" arrived between 1759 and 1768, as the New England colonies had become land-scarce (Choyce 2007, 140–1). A much larger influx of American settlers, the United Empire Loyalists, arrived around 1783, escaping persecution after the American War of Independence. About 30,000 Loyalist settlers arrived in Maritime Canada, with about 17,000 in Nova Scotia alone, representing the region's most significant influx of English-speaking settlers (MacKinnon 1986, 31–2).

Smaller groups of settlers arrived as well, with the British colonial government particularly interested in settling the Nova Scotian peninsula with a population that was not just English speaking but also Protestant.

The government doubted the loyalty of the largely Catholic and French- or Mi'kmaq-speaking population, and sought to balance them demographically (Plank 2004, 87, 91). This led to settlement drives in 1761, which brought English-speaking Protestant settlers from the Derry area of Northern Ireland, and between 1772 and 1775, which primarily brought a few hundred English settlers from Yorkshire and Northumberland. Even earlier, a colonization drive brought German-speaking Protestants to the colony around 1752, underscoring how much importance the government placed on displacing and outnumbering the largely Catholic Acadian and Mi'kmaq populations with Protestants, regardless of their origin. Further English-speaking population was provided by the British army, navy, and merchant forces that garrisoned the colony and drove its growth. The primary focus of the colonization was on the South Shore, including Halifax, which is the area where Creighton would collect many of her ballads. Other English-speaking settlements were established in the Annapolis Valley, and the North Shore, opposite Cape Breton, where MacKenzie did much of his collecting. Cape Breton itself received some Loyalists and discharged British soldiers in the vicinity of Sydney at the time of the city's founding (1784), but the existing population of Acadians, and subsequent and extensive settlement by Gaelic-speaking Scots (beginning in 1785), ensured that song collecting on the island would not only be in English; Creighton and others would also look to Cape Breton for its Gaelic and French traditions.

This pattern of settlement led Ian McKay to critically question the "rebranding" of Nova Scotia as foremost a Scottish province, which took place during the premiership of Angus L. MacDonald between the 1930s and the 1950s (1992, 19). As heavy industry in the province began to falter, MacDonald looked to tourism as a potential growth area, and felt the province needed a distinct and appealing identity to attract tourists; the idea of a tartan-clad province with deeply rooted Celtic traditions gained traction. As McKay notes, at the time of MacDonald's "tartanization" project, the province's population balance was definitely tilted in favour of English rather than Scottish background, especially on the mainland (1992, 8). Indeed, this does much to explain why MacKenzie and Creighton were able to find so much English-language folksong to collect.

Folksong Collection and Nova Scotia Identity

Prior to MacDonald's Scottish rebranding of Nova Scotia, the province's cultural and economic profile was not a simple matter to pin down. Certainly, an agrarian and fishing economy existed, and the many small communities that sustained these also maintained a number of traditional folkways, the diversity of which reflected the complex settlement pattern of the province. But industry and business in Halifax had been developing from early in the nineteenth century, and by 1900, heavy industries in mining, shipbuilding, and steelmaking were firmly established. Immigration from Central and Eastern Europe, as well as the Caribbean, further diversified the province's larger cities. Contemporary media and popular culture were as much part of Nova Scotia's urban experience as they were in other industrial towns across central Canada and the American northeast, to which the province was strongly connected.

These facts seemed to weigh on the ballad-collecting efforts of W. Roy MacKenzie, a Harvard-educated professor of English and philology who had grown up in Pictou County, on the north shore of Nova Scotia. Inspired to collect folk balladry by his mentor, the eminent folklorist and professor George Lyman Kittredge, MacKenzie found Pictou County a suitable place for his fieldwork. His collecting efforts in that district, starting in 1908, led to two publications, *The Quest of the Ballad* (1919) and *Ballads and Sea Songs of Nova Scotia* (1928). MacKenzie foregrounded the lyrics of these folksongs in a manner appropriate to a literary and philological scholar, but he also included some melody transcriptions in a short appendix, which appear to be his own. His ballad publications spoke of his conviction that Nova Scotia, which had once been fertile ground for the English-language ballad tradition, was modernizing and quickly losing touch with its traditions. He was not interested in framing what Nova Scotian culture *is*, but documenting what it *had been* for the purpose of study, observing that "as this ancient custom approaches its dissolution the more need there is that one should hasten to record something of its operation [for] ... we shall have left only a few printed versions of their lore, dry bones from that great body of song and story that once lived [here]" (1919, 18).

Nevertheless, his account of ballad collection along Nova Scotia's North Shore in *The Quest of the Ballad* painted a vivid picture of the traditional singer, which greatly contrasted the Ivy-League educated, patrician character of MacKenzie himself (whose father and grandfather had run a successful shipbuilding business). Though a purported lover of balladry, MacKenzie confessed a great deal of social distance from his subject: "Those of us who are sophisticated may be heartily entertained by such amusements [as ballad singing], but we cannot accept them in the spirit of the persons for whom they were originally planned" (1919, 12). He cast the folksinger from whom he collected as an isolated rustic: "It is axiomatic that he who reads the newspaper shall cease to be a perpetuator of folklore. The *sine qua non* of the latter, in our time at least, is an aloofness from the world of progress, a mellow retirement where the events of a bygone day are rather more near and familiar than are the noises of the great city" (1919, 1).

MacKenzie's statements speak to the ways in which social class informed the folkloristic scholarship of the time, as many folklorists were middle or upper-middle class and well educated, while the folk ballads they collected were presumed to be "relics" which were orally preserved by the rural labouring class. There is also an element of romanticism in this quest to preserve oral texts, which was common in folklore studies of the time. Just as oral culture seemed to be in danger of disappearing from rural districts in the face of urbanization and the growth of mass media, it suddenly (and ironically) became precious, even sacred (Abrahams 1993, 37). The belief that illiterate, rural populations carried the vestiges of a more organic and authentic culture, tied to the land and to antiquity, was foundational to the kind of folklore that Johann Gottfried Herder (1744–1803) proposed in Europe during the late eighteenth century. Herder felt that these vestiges, in the forms of folksong, proverb, and other texts, could be used to frame new national identities, which he thought had become submerged by the cosmopolitan high culture of the early modern era (Wilson 1973, 820, 822). These notions of the folk, folklore, and folk music clearly left their mark on North American folklore collectors, like MacKenzie and Helen Creighton, but as we will see, these collectors did not necessarily assume Herder's racially essentialist relation between the folk and their expressive culture.

This lack of "national" or "racial" essentialism was evident in MacKenzie's discussion of his collection of balladry. Although they were in the English language, MacKenzie identified these ballads as Scottish in origin. MacKenzie collected in the Pictou region of Nova Scotia, which was heavily settled by Gaelic-speaking Highland Scots. Yet he never mentions Gaelic, leaving open many questions about how and when his informants learned their songs. Interestingly, he credits the descendants of the French Acadians with enthusiastically picking up the ballads of their Scottish neighbours and passing them on more faithfully than the Pictou County Scots themselves. For MacKenzie, the singing culture of Nova Scotia's north shore seemed to be tied to region, lifestyle, and occupation rather than simple ancestry.

It should be noted, furthermore, that *Quest of the Ballad* was a surprisingly reflective and critical text for its time, despite MacKenzie's sometimes patronizing tone. Rather than compiling an anthology of collected texts, as so many ballad scholars did, MacKenzie seemed genuinely interested in the context of the music, and he confesses the complexities and contradictions involved in his fieldwork. Contrary to Herderian notions of folk culture having racial origins, he did not portray ballad singing on Nova Scotia's North Shore simply as an organic oral tradition of the folk; he acknowledged that the English ballads were carried by Scots, and picked up by French neighbours. He also noted that some recent Scottish immigrants were still having commercially published broadside ballads mailed to them from the old country. MacKenzie seemed to understand that he was documenting a singing culture that urbanization and industrialization were destroying, but was not entirely in thrall to romantic notions of "pure" oral traditions.

In any case, MacKenzie shared origins in high society with his successor, Helen Creighton, who was born into a well-to-do family in Dartmouth, Nova Scotia, with roots in the Halifax business sector dating back to the late 1700s. Creighton, who had ambitions to be a freelance journalist, fell into the practice of collecting folksongs at the suggestion of Nova Scotia's minister of education, Henry Munro. Following the publication of MacKenzie's *Ballads and Sea Songs of Nova Scotia*, Munro suggested that folksong collecting could make a good, timely topic for the young writer. Not long after locating some traditional singers in the vicinity of Halifax – Enos Hartlan and Ben Henneberry – Creighton found herself collecting surprising amounts of material, especially given MacKenzie's assumption that ballad singing was nearly extinct. Despite lacking any formal training in folklore or music, Creighton decided to dedicate her career to folksong collecting. Over the next sixty years, Creighton collected over 4,000 songs. Published collections, including *Songs and Ballads of Nova Scotia* (1932), *Maritime Folksongs* (1962), *Folk Songs of Nova Scotia* (1968), and several others, established a folksong canon that secured for her an international reputation.

Despite the social distance between Creighton and her informants, she proved adept at approaching Nova Scotian farming and fishing communities and cajoling the locals into sharing their songs with her. After collecting more than one hundred songs in the late 1920s from people like Henneberry on Devil's Island, a fishing community in the mouth of Halifax harbour, Creighton needed to figure out what to do with the songs. Selling them commercially to folk festivals was one option she explored, though the takers were few and the money sparse. Another avenue was to publish a collection like MacKenzie's, focusing on Nova Scotia's South Shore. This, too, proved difficult until Creighton, with some effort, was able to track down someone with reliable musical training to transcribe the melodies correctly. She also needed to find a publisher. A publishing deal with J.M. Dent and Sons was leveraged by Henry Munro's contract to buy 250 copies of *Songs and Ballads of Nova Scotia* for the Nova Scotia school board (Croft 1999, 41). This was a significant start for Creighton as a public advocate for the folk arts, since these songs would become part of the education of Nova Scotian school children (Sircom 1993, 28).

Creighton was sometimes denounced as an amateur and a "popularizer" by academic folklorists in her day, who lamented the bias and lack of critical analysis and context she brought to her work (see Croft 1999, 227–33). Diane Tye argues that this dismissal was somewhat unfair. First, Creighton was aware of the work and methods of academic folklorists (some of whom admired Creighton's sensitive fieldwork techniques). Second, as a woman coming of age in the 1920s and 1930s, she would have had little access to the male-dominated academic world of the time, and had to promote her work through the popular media (Tye 1993, 109–10). In some ways, this popular media attention was good for folklore studies, and Creighton's high degree of media visibility and the positive way in which she portrayed folk culture raised the profile of the discipline among the general public (Posen 2012, 139). Indeed, Creighton's ability to build a media persona through outlets such as CBC radio and the National Film Board of Canada (NFB) was crucial in making links between the types of songs populating her collections and Nova Scotia's regional identity at large. For example, arrangements derived from some of the songs she collected were scored for NFB films depicting Atlantic Canada,[1] which suited Creighton's idea that folk music should serve as a kind of raw material for new cultural works. A short film centring on Creighton, *Songs of Nova Scotia*, appeared in 1958 and actualized her vision of the province's folk culture and her own position with respect to it by staging interactions between a well-dressed and benevolent-looking Creighton and her farmer and fisherman informants, casually dressed, singing as they worked.

It was this kind of image that historian Ian McKay critiqued in *Quest of the Folk* (1994), arguing that it was typical of the kind of "brand" Nova Scotia was courting during the middle decades of the twentieth century. Pushed along by the provincial premier, Angus L. MacDonald (in office 1933–40; 1945–54), the government looked to tourism as a way to supplement the ailing industrial economy of the region, and work like MacKenzie's or Creighton's (but not limited to them) helped to paint the province as scenic, historic, and home to artifacts and living traditions evoking a pastoral, nobler past (McKay 1994, 31–2). According to McKay, Nova Scotians working in the arts were happy to buy into this "antimodern" thrust to the province's identity because it gave them an appealing commercial angle and allowed them to find a niche in a globalizing cultural marketplace (1994, 35). Thus, Nova Scotia was imagined as the home of the "Folk," "the lost, authentic producers of our culture," a people who were different, because of their rural isolation, from the rest of "us" in urban, industrial Canada, but were also *more* essentially English Canadian or Nova Scotian for possessing deeply rooted cultural traditions (McKay 1994, 29).

It follows from McKay's critique that Creighton's work is more directly influenced by Herderian romantic nationalism than MacKenzie's. The idea of rural communities as vestiges of a more "organic" and balanced pre-industrial order is essential to Creighton's idea of the folk. While other collectors, like Edith Fowke, were willing to collect occupational and protest songs from industrial workers, such as miners, Creighton had no interest in this, even though mining and other heavy industries were very important to Nova Scotia's economy. When offered union songs by one Cape Breton informant, Creighton noted, "They made me shiver, for they were all very red ... I could see how these songs would pierce deeply into the consciousness of a dissatisfied people. They frightened me" (quoted in Croft 1999, 119). For a middle-class folk collector, the reassuring idea of more pastoral, non-threatening "folk" could be the basis for "our" larger provincial culture, and a repertoire that could be shared or appropriated across class lines. But the same could not be said of industrial protest songs. Moreover, Creighton's assertion that "my job as collector is to provide the raw material for our writers and musicians" echoes Herder's idea that folklore – though comprising texts from the past – should be the basis for creating a nation's future culture. Wilson explains, "Herder taught that each nation is by nature and by history a distinct organic unit with its own culture [and] ... must cultivate this national culture along lines laid down by past experience" (1973, 832).

Creighton made a quite "Herderian" comment during one of her CBC radio broadcasts in the late 1930s, surmising that, "If you study art music, you see at once that German music is quite different from Italian music ... Each nation has built up a distinctive music because it [has] been founded on the songs and dances of its folk ... Nothing is so national in character as a folk song. And there's nothing that expresses quite so well the soul of each nation. Perhaps we've discovered our folk music too late to develop a school that expresses the soul of our nation. It will take time to find out" (quoted in Webb 1992, 166). About twenty years later, the eminent Canadian composer R. Murray Schafer argued that it was indeed too late, because the English Canadian public at large had abandoned its folk music, which was derivative of old world folk music anyway. Canada, he thought, would never produce a nationalist composer like Bedřich Smetana (1984 [1961], 9–10). He singled out Quebec and the Maritimes as the only places where "one can still be astonished at the alacrity with which folk songs are sung" (ibid., 11).

In any case, the fact that Creighton was collecting in North America and not Europe made a full embrace of essentialist ideas from Herderian nationalism impossible. She understood something of the plurality of musical traditions in Nova Scotia, and she collected French, Mi'kmaq, Gaelic, German, and African-Canadian songs as well as English folklore. However, the hegemony of white English folklore in the province is borne out in her publications, as she published more English ballads and promoted them more than the other material she collected. Nevertheless, much of what she collected had been transplanted to Nova Scotia no more than 200 years previous, so no argument could be made about English folksong being a "native" expression of the land.

Yet, ironically, English Nova Scotian folksongs were put to use in framing the Canadian nation at large around the mid-twentieth century. In this, Nova Scotian folksong canons share much with their counterparts in Newfoundland. Neil Rosenberg demonstrates that, very quickly after the province joined Canada in 1949, Newfoundland folksong was heavily appropriated as English Canadian heritage, helped along by national radio broadcasts, published folksong collections, and its incorporation into English Canadian school curricula. Rosenberg points to the 1954 publication of *Folk Songs of Canada*, edited by Edith Fowke and Richard Johnston, as an example: twenty-two of its seventy-seven songs came from Newfoundland – a number that was far out of proportion with the province's population relative to the rest of Canada (Rosenberg 1994, 63). The book also contains fifteen songs from Nova Scotia, many from Creighton's collection, significantly more than those originating in Ontario or the Canadian west (eight songs for each region). As a popular canon, *Folk Songs of Canada* is a great example of the reframing of regionally collected songs which, although they did not lose all their regional associations, were recontextualized as part of a broader, "Canadian," folk canon.

Nova Scotian Song and the Folk Revival

As popularized folksongs entered the mass media, a new phase began for folk revivalism. Helen Creighton hosted radio shows in the 1930s and 1940s that were heard throughout Nova Scotia, and were directed at both urban and rural audiences. The shows featured folksongs sung by a mix of her informants, professional singers, and arranged for string quartet, giving some media profile to the kind of Nova Scotian folksongs that she collected (Webb 1992, 162). But the advent of the commercial folk revival beginning in the late 1950s gave folksong in general a mainstream media presence and currency with the public that the previous generation of collectors and enthusiasts could have scarcely anticipated. In the English Canadian media, variety television shows based on folk music, country, and gospel began running at this time, and CBC's Halifax station was particularly successful in launching nationally popular shows such as *Don Messer's Jubilee* (1957–69) and *Singalong Jubilee* (1961–74), with the latter establishing the careers of artists such as Anne Murray, Catherine MacKinnon, and Ken Tobias. MacKinnon's version of "The Nova Scotia Song" (also known as "Farewell to Nova Scotia") became *Singalong Jubilee*'s signature song, and the most widely recognized song in Creighton's collection. Creighton and her associate, Doreen Senior, had collected the song reluctantly from in an informant, Ann Greenough, in West Petpeswick in 1933. They felt that the song, seemingly a recent local composition, was not as desirable as the ancient Child ballads they sought; however, they felt that they could not refuse Greenough's offer of the song, since she had extended such hospitality to the weather-stranded folk collectors (Croft 1999, 50). Nevertheless, thanks to MacKinnon and *Singalong Jubilee*, "Farewell to Nova Scotia" became an iconic folksong representing the province.

Creighton recognized the importance of *Singalong Jubilee* in popularizing the traditional songs of the region, but had an ambivalent relationship with the show. While popularizing a number of songs that were in her collection, the versions sung on TV were not always the Nova Scotian variants she collected; Creighton also did not care for the emphasis the show put on singer-songwriters performing newer material (Croft 1999, 164). But programs like *Singalong Jubilee* and *Don Messer's Jubilee* did much to establish the sense of interrelationship between an older repertoire of folksong and newer music on the East Coast, whether it came from singer-songwriters (known to some as "folk entrepreneurs") or the kind of country singer produced in Nova Scotia whose roots in rural and small-town contexts were parlayed into images of wholesome, naturally talented folk from the countryside. Performing side-by-side, professional folksingers like Catherine MacKinnon and Clary Croft, singer-songwriters like Ken Tobias, and country-pop singers like Anne Murray may have been singing different music, but they came to represent a rural East Coast folksiness that did much to promote the province's cultural "brand."

One erstwhile *Singalong Jubilee* performer, Cape Bretoner John Allan Cameron, was a pivotal figure in the evolution and mediation of the Nova Scotian folksong tradition. Although he struggled to rise above minor celebrity status in the mainstream Canadian music market, his television appearances, foregrounding his lilting accent and charming persona, established him as a consummate Nova Scotia folk musician. Cameron's albums from the late 1960s and 1970s encapsulate much of what *Singalong Jubilee* tried to do – mix traditional material with contemporary songs into an eclectic, but recognizably regional blend. Cameron performed Child ballads ("The Four Marys," "The Unquiet Grave"), Gaelic songs ("Chi Mi Na Morbheanna," "Tha Mi Sgith"), songs by Canadian singer-songwriters like Allister MacGillivray and Bruce Cockburn ("Song for the Mira," "Goin' Down the Road"), and Cape Breton fiddle tunes played on Cameron's 12-string guitar.

Through Cameron's repertoire, and similar blends of material on *Singalong Jubilee* and other shows, a process of cultural articulation[2] took place, whereby these eclectic offerings came to seem natural in their juxtaposition, even related. Acoustic singer-songwriters were prevalent by the early 1970s, but in the Maritimes, local singer-songwriters seemed connected somehow to deeper wellsprings of folksong, whether playing their own music, or the music of others, in a recognizably Maritime flavour in terms of accent and instrumentation. In some cases, newly written songs gained credibility and a sense of being placed within tradition by appearing next to older, vernacular songs on record or in live performance.[3] Although the connections being made were sometimes spurious (Cameron's popular rendition of the Child ballad "The Four Marys" was learned from recordings of American folk revivalists, despite being in the Creighton collection), the articulation of this range of material formed a template for later artists like the Rankin Family and the Barra MacNeils, whose recordings combine canonical English and Gaelic ballads, fiddle tunes, and newly composed songs. Similarly, singer-songwriter Dave Gunning acknowledged his debt to Cameron by recording an album of the late singer's material, and mounting a tour with Cameron's former band members (Gunning 2010).

The influence that both Creighton and Cameron exerted on subsequent Nova Scotian music shares some important similarities in timing and significance. Sheldon Posen observes that Creighton's collecting and popularizing of folksong came along at exactly the moment when regional rural and occupational cultures, which had been considered backward and even embarrassing, were suddenly rehabilitated and celebrated as examples of a broader "English Canadian heritage." Moreover, "her selection and presentation of folk materials helped to paint a rosy picture of a romantic folklore past that was highly attractive to mainstream North America in the second half of the twentieth century" (2012, 139). Meanwhile Neil Rosenberg notes of John Allan Cameron that "you have to tie his popularity, I think, to the fact that these were the early Trudeau years which were years of strong national pride and a reaction against the American model. John Allan stressed the region, the religion, and the ethnicity" (quoted in Beaton and Pederson 1992, 94). In this sense, Cameron embodied as a public performer what Creighton's collection sought to represent as the musical heritage of Nova Scotia.

Building on Rosenberg's observation, Cameron's access to the media in the 1960s and 1970s certainly owes something to the proactive stance that Prime Minister Pierre Trudeau's government adopted at the time regarding Canadian cultural nationalism. Bolstering Canada's culture industries and mandating greater amounts of Canadian content in the media were important strategies for Trudeau in combatting both French-Canadian separatism and the overwhelming strength of American media and popular culture (Edwardson 2008, 18). The government's cultural corporations – the CBC, the National Film Board, the Canadian Film Development Corporation – as well as its Canadian content regulations for television and radio, provided the infrastructure and mandate that made regional cultural programming possible and desirable (Edwardson 2008, 19). Moreover, the government's efforts made such regional programming an element of a wider Canadian cultural nationalism, so that Maritime-based TV programs like *Don Messer's Jubilee*, *Singalong Jubilee*, and *The John Allan Cameron Show* became nation-wide broadcasts.

Such exposure did not dilute Cameron's Cape Breton persona, and his role in building a sense of regional pride through music is often remarked upon. The success of his early Canadian tours proved that east coast Celtic music could effectively substitute for American-style country music in bars and taverns throughout the country. His unapologetic presentation of ballad repertoire, Gaelic language, and even Maritime cliché was seen by some as a brave refusal to hide his regional background in order to please deterritorialized, mainstream Canadian popular tastes. It became a common trope in career retrospectives on Cameron that he "dared to be Celtic when Celtic wasn't cool" (e.g., Guy 2005; Szklarski 2006). Even if elements of his act were "corny," including his appearances in a Scottish kilt, the fact that he could draw the attention of a national audience inspired other Maritime songwriters and performers to emphasize a regionally inflected style as a way to build a marketable identity.

Cameron's career – which included an early and sensational appearance on the Grand Ole Opry in 1970 – contrasted with those of previous Nova Scotia singers who were embraced by the country music market. Hank Snow and Wilf Carter are the best known in this regard, and both were raised in the rural, small town context in which Creighton sought her ballads (Brooklyn, Nova Scotia was the hometown of Snow; Port Hilford for Carter). Moreover, Carter's and Snow's highly narrative, strophic songs spoke of a familiarity with ballad form. But their career success, especially in the United States where they flourished, depended on a deterritorialized sound, persona, and repertoire. Carter even adopted the stage name "Montana Slim" to hide his Canadian origins. Although both produced songs at various points in their careers that recalled their roots (Carter's "Moose River Gold Mine" [1936] recounted a mining disaster close to his home town; Snow's "My Nova Scotia Home" [1968] brought his home province into his repertoire), these were not central to their overall audience appeal, whereas Cameron's sense of emplacement in Nova Scotia was crucial to his.

Commercial Folksingers and Singer-Songwriters

The tone set by John Allan Cameron was picked up by some of the younger talent that he helped to nurture. Several performers used this Maritime folksinger identity in creative ways and achieved commercial success. For example, Stan Rogers, whom Cameron supported during the mid-1970s by sharing his stage, became a dominant voice in Maritime music. Rogers was born and raised in Hamilton, Ontario to parents who left Nova Scotia as it began its industrial decline. Rogers clearly identified with his parents' regional roots, and many of his songs were calculated to sound traditional and evoke Maritime history and culture. Like Cameron, Rogers sampled styles historically associated with the Maritimes, including ballads well-known from the Creighton and MacKenzie collections ("The Maid on the Shore"), a cappella songs in the style of sea shanties ("Barrett's Privateers" is the best known), fiddle tunes ("Plenty of Hornpipe"), and disaster songs ("The Wreck of the Jeannie C"). Although much of his repertoire comprised Rogers's own compositions, his talent for emulating traditional styles and Maritime regional flavour was remarkable.

The success of Rogers lay partly in the fact that he was able to capture aspects of Nova Scotia that appealed to both the Nova Scotian and the outsider. Perhaps this was because he was the Ontario-raised son of Nova Scotian parents and could appreciate multiple perspectives. Some of his songs romanticized Nova Scotia as a province of the folk, telling historical and sometimes heroic tales of the sea (e.g., "Barrett's Privateers," "Northwest Passage," or "The Bluenose"), but others lamented the recent collapses of both industry and traditional occupations in Nova Scotia, evident in songs like "Rawdon Hills" and "The Idiot."

The romantic side of Rogers shared much with Creighton's views of the province, and recalled some of Herder's mythic ideas about the folk, whose traditional ways were virtually merged with sea and soil. "Fisherman's Wharf," for example, surveys the skyline of Halifax and laments the loss of the old culture of farmers and fishermen in the face of modern development. As Rogers's protagonist "looks from the Citadel down to the narrows," he sees "Upper Canadian concrete and glass / Right down to the waterline," and asks to sing the old songs with the old-style schooner-sailing fishermen one last time. The ocean tides, once important for the fishing trades, have been replaced by "the single tide of tourists passing through," and Rogers delivers the line "we traded old ways for the new" using a harmonic cadence in which the tonic of A minor is preceded with a B-flat chord – a classic "pathetic" Phrygian cadence, leaving little doubt about the emotional meaning of the lament. Given Nova Scotia's long struggle with population decline and de-industrialization, it may seem odd to find a song lamenting economic development, and Rogers addresses this in the final stanza: "Now you ask, what's this romantic boy / who laments what's come and gone?," noting that the dangerous occupation of fishermen on schooners was not the stuff of pastoral bliss. But Rogers chalks it up to an almost essentialist, biological memory: "But my fathers knew of wind and tide and my blood is Maritime." In the new Nova Scotia, he seems to say, people are no longer following the lifeways that were virtually bred in the bone, and his protagonist seems lost and disconnected from his "true self."

This sentiment certainly recalls Herderian ideas about a nation's folk, including his assertion that a nation must develop along the ways that were established by deep historical experience. For Herder, certain ways of thinking and being were practically "genetic," and the nature of a people was to be sought through their origins (Wilson 1973, 823). Generations of sailing and fishing, for Rogers's protagonist, is literally imprinted on his identity, and the loss of an old lifestyle is a loss of self, even for the offspring of "folk" who never lived in those ways. Rogers digs even more deeply into such ideas in the song "Giant," which stridently romanticizes the Scottish Gaels of Cape Breton. Rogers recasts an outdoor party near Cape Breton's Bras D'Or lakes as a pagan ritual honouring the ancient Scottish-Irish folk hero Fingal (a truncation of the Gaelic name Fionn mac Cumhaill). In the song, young whiskey-drinking Cape Bretoners are sharing stories that are 3,000 years old, carrying "the blood of the Druids," and acting out ancient spiritual activities as if in a drunken state of atavism. These images amplified the kind of experience tourists were encouraged to have in the province, and added an aura of mystery that complemented the usual kitschy run of lighthouses, sailboats, and Scottish tartan crafts that tourists consumed in Nova Scotia. In the song's description – however hyperbolic it may seem – these Cape Breton "folk" are not merely a quaint curiosity; they are bearers of ancient, unchanged folkways literally inscribed in their flesh.

However, Rogers was more than a romanticist, and had a more realistic side to his repertoire; he sang vividly of Nova Scotians struggling in the face of de-industrialization and economic decline. The dilemma of staying in the province or leaving appears in a number of songs, from "Fincher's Complaint" to "The Idiot"; in the latter, Rogers sings, "I bid farewell to the Eastern town / I never more will see / But work I must so I eat this dust / And breathe refinery." Both songs also weigh the desire to stay in the Maritimes against the indignity of thereby becoming a welfare case. Still other songs reminisce about the hopeful industrial expansion Nova Scotia once enjoyed, but which faded wistfully into the past (e.g., "Rawdon Hills," which portrays the one-time site of gold mining north of Halifax). This side to Rogers's repertoire provides a realistic balance to his more nostalgic and romantic portrayal of Nova Scotia. He seemed to see value both in narrating the myths of a rich folkloric past and in giving voice (even if it was a highly stylized and romanticized voice) to the realities of an economically troubled present.

The link that Rogers seems to make here between economic decline and growing, almost defiant, regional pride can be seen broadly during the late 1970s and 1980s. Cape Breton epitomizes this trend during the gradual shutting down of its steel and coal industries. As the island came under greater economic stress, the use of music and other forms of cultural performance provided one way for the community to "circle the wagons" and cope with the loss of its economic base. Turning inward to its own stories, music, and history, communities like Industrial Cape Breton attempted to reclaim and rearticulate their identity as deindustrialization threatened to erase livelihoods and depopulate the region. This process has been observed in many locales; as cultural geographer James Duncan notes, "During times of conflict, when a group feels threatened, cultural production processes which are normally submerged from view and operate at a deep level, rise closer to the surface" (1992, 38).

Such a rising of cultural production can be seen in the theatre scene in Sydney, which experienced a renaissance under the guidance of Liz and Harry Boardmore in the 1970s. It produced a successful series of variety shows called *The Rise and Follies of Cape Breton*, based on local stories and characters, and songs composed by the cast. Comedic presentations of local caricatures were mixed with poignant songs and stories about Cape Breton's landscape, history, and people. *The Rise and Follies*, which ran from 1977 through 1985, helped launch the musical careers of artists like Raylene Rankin and Rita MacNeil, and a number of regional anthems were either composed or popularized by the productions, including "We Rise Again," "The Island," and "Out on the Mira." Some of these songs tied into longstanding Scottish and Irish singing traditions where, for example, the praise of a place was a common theme. Kenzie MacNeil's "The Island" (1977) narrates the history of Cape Breton in three verses, covering the settlers, the industrialization, and the de-industrialization that led to population decline. Although the stories of labour struggles and economic hardship are described in realistic emotional tones, the chorus speaks of Cape Breton's proud people and the island as "the home of our hearts," a sense of people bonded to each other and to the land.

A more direct comparison between traditional folksong and contemporary songwriting can be seen in Allister MacGillivray's "Song for the Mira" (1973), which parallels the style of Gaelic praise songs that have been collected in Cape Breton. Written in praise of the community of Marion Bridge, on Cape Breton's Mira River, the song is essentially non-narrative, depicting nostalgic scenes of contented fishermen in boats, hospitable neighbours, children at bonfires, and storytelling sessions late at night. In the final verse the narrator takes leave of his listeners ("Now I'll conclude with a wish you go well"), presumably to return to the Mira. The refrain bestows high praise on the place: "Can you imagine a place in the universe / More fit for princes and kings? / I'll trade you ten of your cities for Marion Bridge / And the pleasures it brings."

A very similar poetic structure underpins the Gaelic song, "Oran do Cheap Breatainn" ("Song to Cape Breton"), which Creighton collected during her 1944 field trip to the island. The song was composed by the Gaelic bard Dan Alex MacDonald of Framboise around 1917. Again, there is no consistent story unfolding through the verses, but various scenes depicting the island's natural beauty in various seasons are elaborated, as are the joys of each season (weddings, milling frolics, children playing). In the final verse, the singer takes leave of the audience ("Chan urainn dhom-sa leth dhuibh inns' / Na tha mhaisealachd 's an tir / Stadaidh mi bhon tha mi sgith / Beannachd leibh is oiche mhath leibh"; "I can't describe even half of the land's beauty / I will conclude because I'm tired / Blessings be with you and good night"). The refrain praises the island in dramatic terms ("S'e Ceap Breatainn, tir mo graidh ... Tir as aille leinn air thalamh"; "It's Cape Breton, land of my heart ... The most beautiful place on earth").

In his 1989 book *The Nova Scotia Song Collection*, Allister MacGillivray himself comments on the interrelationship between the kinds of songs he writes and the tradition of songwriting in Nova Scotia: "Nova Scotian songwriters have been fashioning 'ballads, songs and snatches' for centuries ... we've produced more than our share. Here is a piece of ground ever abounding with bards, balladeers, pipers, fiddlers, and stepdancers, and so on" (1989, 5). He further recounts, "I have loved folk-oriented songs from the beginning: works which embody the texture and flavour of Maritime life; works which cite the colourful place names and characters; works which speak in our dialects" (1989, 5). His anthology includes ballads from Creighton's collection, country songs by Wilf Carter and Hank Snow, and songs by more recent folksingers and songwriters, like Stan Rogers, Leon Dubinsky, Kenzie MacNeil, Bob Quinn, Rita MacNeil, and former *Singalong Jubilee* cast members Alan Stanbury and Clary Croft. The book, and MacGillivray's framing comments, creates a sense that these recent songs continue a tradition stretching back to the ballads Creighton collected.

"Out on the Mira," "The Island," and "We Rise Again" (1985, a non-specific song about social rebirth, which was popularized by the Rankin Family, and understood in Cape Breton to refer to the reignition of hope after the island's painful period of deindustrialization) are all "vernacular anthems" in the sense described by folklorist Peter Narváez. For Narváez, vernacular anthems are songs in which a particular population has strong emotional investments, so that the songs' significance transcends "specificities of melody, text, and texture." Their popularity with that audience cannot be measured in terms of sales figures (Narváez 2002, 270, 274). Narváez applied these ideas to "Sonny's Dream" (1976), a song by Newfoundland artist Ron Hynes. Narváez found that the narrative, despite being set in outport Newfoundland, was widely claimed throughout Atlantic Canada as a means of working through ambivalent emotions about having to leave the region to find work and prosperity. The Nova Scotian songs discussed above similarly work through conflicted feelings about connection and separation from Nova Scotia, and the desires and myths that characterize home, exile, and return.[4]

Collectively, Stan Rogers's material, the *Rise and Follies* songs, and MacGillivray's song publications may not have been folksongs in the same sense as those collected by MacKenzie and Creighton, but they were extensions of that folk canon in style and themes. In the case of Rogers, some of his material extended an old, romantic folkloristic ideology directly into the songs themselves. As noted above, the process of a community turning inward to its own cultural resources in a time of economic stress is observable in Nova Scotia's musical history.

The Celtic Wave and After

The dramatic rise in commercial popularity enjoyed by Celtic music in Canada between the late 1980s and late 1990s provided a new context for traditional song in Nova Scotia. The "Celtic Wave" made national superstars of Celtic musicians from all over Canada who fused traditional song and instrumental music with pop and rock, including Great Big Sea (Newfoundland), Ashley MacIsaac, Natalie MacMaster, and the Rankin Family (Nova Scotia), La Bottine Souriante (Quebec), Leahy (Ontario), and Spirit of the West (British Columbia). This sudden wave of popularity has never been fully explained, although a number of factors seem to have been involved. First, the establishment and growth of the music industry category known as "world music" or "world beat" provided a niche for East Coast Canadian Celtic music. Moreover, the market cycled through periods where certain "world" categories were dominant (Jamaican and African in the 1970s and 1980s; Latin, Cuban, and Celtic in the 1990s). The early and mid-1990s seem to have been the high point internationally for the Celtic cycle, and in Canada, home-grown artists purveying recognizably "Celtic" sounds were poised to court national, and in some cases, international audiences.

The Canadian music industry reached a critical point in the 1990s as well, with groups like The Tragically Hip, Sloan, the Grapes of Wrath, and other artists able to reach sustainable record and concert ticket sales within Canada alone. Previous generations of Canadian popular artists (The Guess Who, Anne Murray, Rush) generally could not have maintained their careers in the long term without success in the American market, but by the early 1990s, the growth of the Canadian market, Canadian content regulations imposed on the nation's media, support for Canadian music through MuchMusic/MusiquePlus, radio stations embracing the new "alternative rock" format, and networks of independent labels, created conditions favourable for new Canadian acts to build viable nation-wide careers (see Barclay, Jack, and Schneider 2011; Straw 2000, 176). In this sense, the Celtic wave happened at a fortuitous moment, and artists like Ashley MacIsaac and Great Big Sea were successfully marketed through such radio and televisual media. Other supports, like college radio, the university concert circuit, and folk festivals, provided additional opportunities for exposure.

Ethnomusicologist Geoff Whittall suggests that the surge in popularity of East Coast Celtic music in Canada is also tied to English Canadian nationalism.[5] Canadian Celtic music, he notes, was a distinct regional "roots" style that lacked an obvious counterpart in the United States: "this is the first new music to gain major exposure in Canada in many years, where the innovation factor has been driven from within ... Celtic music is the first genre in a long time that we [Canadians] are exporting to the U.S.A., and for which they have no direct, large-scale equivalent" (1998, 28). While American popular culture had fiddlers, folksingers, and other roots styles, the flavour of Maritime Celtic genres was distinct from them, with different fiddling styles and vocal accents, and a closer stylistic relationship to Irish and Scottish antecedents. Atlantic Canada's Anglo-Celtic roots music harkened back to an old cultural heritage for a certain demographic of white, anglophone Canadians, and it provided a cultural touchstone distinct from American models, which may explain some of its appeal. It was a rare moment of regional, but also national, pride.

The role of traditional (or traditional-sounding) English song in all of this is pivotal. The distinct sounds of Celtic music from Atlantic Canada come in good measure from instrumental traditions – fiddling, piping, accordion playing – and in Nova Scotia, the Gaelic song tradition is an important and iconic practice, most prominently promoted commercially during the 1990s by Mary Jane Lamond. But instrumental and "foreign language" recordings are notoriously difficult to market in English Canada with any consistency, and English song has been an important component in the repertoire of most of these Celtic acts. The Rankin Family, for example, wove instrumental tracks, traditional Gaelic songs, and English ballads together with their original songs, which were sometimes written in the style and language of balladry. The title track for the Rankins' *Fare Thee Well Love* album (1990), for example, is their own composition, but it uses an archaic-sounding phrase to evoke the traditional, and it sits well on the album alongside actual ballads like "Fair and Tender Ladies." The group's connection to Nova Scotian folk tradition was further emphasized through Raylene Rankin's appearances in the National Film Board's documentary about Helen Creighton, *A Sigh and a Wish* (2001), in which Rankin introduces a song to her audience as being "from the Helen Creighton collection," and one which she remembers her "mother whistling while she was laying out many lines of wash" (quoted in Davies 2001). Rankin authenticates her version twice, by showing it as being in her family's oral tradition, and also in the "official" Creighton collection.

The up-tempo, rollicking, "ranting-and-roaring" sort of English-language folksong, which had been successful in pubs and bars for John Allan Cameron (e.g., "I'm a Rover seldom Sober" or "Sound the Pibroch"), was another kind of song that worked well during the Celtic wave, in part because it fused well with electric instruments and rock rhythms. When sung with the right Atlantic Canadian accent, it came across as traditional and modern at the same time. Great Big Sea did this kind of song to great effect – their version of "Mari-Mac" (1995) was a rocked up rendition of the same traditional Scottish song that John Allan Cameron had recorded in 1979, and retains Cameron's constantly accelerating tempo. In Nova Scotia, the group MacKeel brought a hard-rocking approach to Celtic ballads and sea songs like "Star of the County Down" and "Drunken Sailor," with bagpipes, fiddles, and tin whistles playing alongside distorted electric guitars in a thoroughgoing Celtic-rock fusion. Natalie MacMaster stands out as a rare Nova Scotian artist who reached international fame with a purely instrumental act;[6] most of the other stars of the Celtic wave abetted their successes by using or emulating the old Nova Scotia folk canon and recording accessible English-language songs during the 1990s.

By 1998, the Celtic wave had largely peaked. According to one industry insider, the Canadian music industry was no longer promoting new "Celtic" artists, and was only interested in profiting from the commercial longevity of acts established earlier in the decade (Jones 2006). Canadian Maritime music was now viewed by the national industry as a trend that had been over-exploited and exhausted. In response, the next wave of Nova Scotia singer-songwriters, such as Gordie Sampson, Bruce Guthro, or Melanie Doane, began playing several sides of the market. The concepts of deterritorialization and reterritorialization, which originate with Deleuze and Guattari (2004 [1972]), and are used in anthropology by Giddens (1990), Tomlinson (1999), Hernàndez (2006) and others, become relevant here. As noted by Hernàndez, deterritorialization and reterritorialization are mutually arising processes; on the one side, "deterritorialization speaks of the loss of the 'natural' relation between culture and the social and geographic territories … which makes it ever more difficult to maintain a stable sense of local cultural identity, including national identity, as our daily life entwines more and more with influences and experiences of remote origin" (Hernàndez 2006, 93). On the other hand, reterritorialization can involve the opposite: people from a particular region taking material from the mass media and making it sound or appear like a local cultural phenomenon, a process Roland Robertson (1995) calls "glocalization."

As the Celtic wave subsided, some Nova Scotian artists began approaching their regional identities and genre associations more flexibly. Their music could be deterritorialized enough to fit into soft rock or adult-contemporary radio formats, or new country. But by emphasizing Maritime themes, accents, or the odd traditional tune, their music could also be reterritorialized, and allow the artists to fit comfortably into folk festivals or venues for tourists. Some of the stars of the Celtic wave tried to rebrand themselves in a similar way in the latter half of the 1990s, with the Rankins and the Barra MacNeils courting American audiences with revamped, deterritorialized new country sounds that put less overt emphasis on their Celtic or Maritime backgrounds (see Hennessy 2015).

Nova Scotian Music beyond the Traditional

At this point, I have discussed how the legacy of traditional English folksongs, as collected by folklorists like W. Roy MacKenzie and Helen Creighton, was used in various ways in the Nova Scotia: it was part of the process of branding the province for tourism, it was taught to school children as part of establishing regional identity, it provided material for Canada's commercial folk revival, it was a source of regional pride and identity-making during the province's industrial decline, and it was a tool in carving out market niches for East Coast artists during Canada's Celtic wave and shortly after. In the repertoire of some singer-songwriters, traditional folksongs provided models of storytelling and musical style that helped to ground their music geographically and legitimize their work as part of a living tradition, when it was advantageous to do so. The "folk inheritance" is still there to be called upon by Nova Scotian musicians, but it is also a legacy some actively resist.

"The Maritimes" (2005) by Halifax-based rapper Luke Boyd (who performs as Classified) is a concise commentary on what is faced by an urban musician who works well outside the expectations and genre classifications so often associated with Canada's East Coast. The song is set against a looped concertina pattern, an instrument associated with sailors, making an aural stereotype of Maritime life the context for his statements. The rap features a clearinghouse of Maritime clichés, like bagpipes, fiddles, coal mines, potatoes, Alexander Keith's beer, Anne of Green Gables, and so on. Classified takes on the myth of the folk – "Welcome to the East Coast, home of the innocents / Still pigeon-holed as a farmer or fisherman" – and goes on to say "I'm trying to shake these stereotypes ... I don't even eat fish and never tried lobster / Can't play the fiddle, and never was a logger." Other parts of the song name musicians in Classified's urban scene, which are nevertheless invisible, or at least unexpected, to visitors to the province.

It is not surprising that such resistance to Maritime stereotypes would surface in Halifax, the largest and most prosperous urban centre in the region. Indeed, the musical life of the city provided a counterpoint during the years of the Celtic wave, as the Halifax alternative rock scene blossomed and produced popular bands like Sloan, Thrush Hermit, Eric's Trip, Hardship Post, and Jale (Hamel 2013, 8). Collectively, these groups were seen as Canada's response to American grunge, and Halifax became known as the "Seattle of the North," a status supported by the Halifax Pop Explosion festivals held since the mid-1990s. Between the Celtic wave and the Halifax alternative rock scene, the province seemed, briefly, to be emerging as a leader in the Canadian music scene across several market categories and genres.

Nevertheless, Nova Scotia's cultural infrastructure at large continues to give strong support to music making that can be grouped under terms like folk or traditional. The province has supported numerous folk festivals over the years – the Stan Rogers Folk Festival (in Canso), the Lunenburg Folk Harbour Festival, the Helen Creighton Folklore Festival of Dartmouth, the Celtic Colours International Festival (in Cape Breton), and Deep Roots Music Festival (in the Annapolis Valley) – which speaks to this folkloric legacy and its cultural and economic importance to the province. The East Coast Music Awards (ECMAs) currently feature terms like folk, roots, and traditional in only four of their twenty-eight awards categories, but artists who are generally classified under the marketing categories of folk or traditional were featured in ten ECMA categories in 2013. The legacy of traditional English song continues to echo in the province's culture and economy.

I have shown that the folksong canons, and their uses by several generations of musicians working in the regional music industry, have an important but ambivalent history. Attempts to argue for a romanticized view of folksong and traditional culture in Nova Scotia were problematic, even for the earliest folklorists and revivalists working in the region. The complex settlement patterns, ethnic diversity, and checkered industrial history of the province made Herderian folk ideology difficult to establish or maintain, even though some desired to do so. However, the province's deindustrialization, and its rebranding as a tourist destination selling natural landscapes, authentic traditional cultures, and living history, has done much to perpetuate that ideology for outsiders. As such, the Nova Scotia folk canon and its later adaptations were of much use in constructing the province as an "imagined state," a territory that exists as much in people's minds as in geography (see Del Giudice and Porter 2001).

The use of a Nova Scotia folk canon, much like those of other provinces, in fostering postwar English Canadian nationalism and cultural industries, also explains the continued reworking and recycling of the canon during and after Canada's folk revival. We have seen how artists working in the popular and roots-based music industry, from John Allan Cameron to the Rankins, used the folk canon, and the ideology associated with it, in incomplete and strategic ways. They used it to express regional pride; they often recognized its usefulness as an appealing selling angle, especially for outsiders and tourists, but knew that constructions of folk authenticity alone would not support all their creative activities. Contemporary East Coast regional artists, working in pop, country, and adult contemporary formats, often find ways to sell themselves as rooted and "downhome" on the one hand, and modern on the other – a commercial balancing act that can be seen in Maritime acts as far back as Don Messer's band (see Rosenberg 2002, 192).

Finally, we saw how the folk canon was used and extended by Nova Scotian communities during the difficult period of industrial collapse in the 1970s and 1980s, in which songs modelled on local traditions were used to reinforce declining communities and give Nova Scotians living away a means to work through the emotions arising from emigration and a way of enacting the "myth of return" to their home communities. The symbolic importance of these musical canons (and newer songs modelled on them), then, has many facets for both insiders and outsiders to the province, and reflects patterns of desire, ideology, and adaptation that are embedded in the cultural and economic history of Eastern Canada over the past century.

Notes

1 See, for example, Eugene Kash's score for Jean Palardy's film *The Rising Tide* (1949).
2 Articulation refers to the contingent and ideological process of joining of meaning to particular cultural expressions or symbols. This was theorized by Gramsci, and applied to music by scholars like Middleton (1990) and Guilbault (1997).
3 The same strategy can be seen in use in Newfoundland, with the group Figgy Duff drawing on Kenneth Peacock's folk collection, while also composing their own material in a similar style (see Guigné 2008, 6).
4 With regard to the role of folk music in fostering a "myth of return" for Maritime expatriots, see Hiller 2009, 338 and Daly Berman 2015.
5 See Kernerman (2005, 62) and Buchignani (1994, 314) for a full description of English Canadian nationalism and English Canada's "refusal to speak its own name." Official multicultural pluralism and regionalism leave English Canada with an indeterminate identity, which many perceive to have been exploited by successive Canadian federal governments as a way of undermining French Canadian national claims about their distinctiveness. The case could then be made that Quebec was just one of many ethno-cultural communities in Canada, rather than a distinct nation-in-waiting.
6 See *In My Hands* (1999) as an example.

References

Abrahams, Roger D. 1993. "Phantoms of Romantic Nationalism in Folkloristics." *The Journal of American Folklore* 106 (419): 3–37.
Barclay, Michael, Ian A.D. Jack, and Jason Schneider. 2011. *Have Not Been the Same: The CanRock Renaissance 1985–1995*. Toronto, ON: ECW Press.
Beaton, Virginia, and Stephen Pedersen. 1992. *Maritime Music Greats: Fifty Years of Hits and Heartbreak*. Halifax, NS: Nimbus Publishing.
Buchignani, Norman. 1994. "Canadian Ethnic Research and Multiculturalism." In *Canadian Music: Issues of Hegemony and Identity*, edited by Beverley Diamond and Robert Witmer, 311–41. Toronto, ON: Canadian Scholars' Press.
Cameron, John Allan. 1969. *Here Comes John Allan Cameron*. Apex AL7-1645. LP.
– 1972. *Get There by Dawn*. Columbia ELS 382/ES-90089. LP.
– 1976. *Weddings, Wakes & Other Things*. Columbia 2-GES 90343. LP.
– 1979. *Freeborn Man*. Glencoe CSPS 1432/GMI-002. LP.
Child, Francis James. 1898. *The English and Scottish Popular Ballads*. New York, NY: Haughton, Mifflin and Co.

Choyce, Leslie. 2007. *Nova Scotia Shaped by the Sea: A Living History*. Lawrencetown Beach, NS: Pottersfield Press.

Classified. 2005. *Boy-Cott-In the Industry*. Urbnet URB-016. CD.

Crabtree, Grant, dir. 1958. *Songs of Nova Scotia*. National Film Board of Canada, 0197033.

Creighton, Helen. 1932. *Songs and Ballads from Nova Scotia*. Toronto, ON: J.M. Dent.

– 1962. *Maritime Folk Songs*. Toronto, ON: Ryerson Press.

– 1968. *Folk Songs of Nova Scotia*. Halifax, NS: Department of Education.

Croft, Clary. 1999. *Helen Creighton: Canada's First Lady of Folklore*. Halifax, NS: Nimbus Press.

Daly Berman, Amanda. 2015. "Repression to Reification: Remembering and Revitalizing the Cape Breton Musical Diaspora in the Celtic Commonwealth." PhD diss., Boston University.

Davies, Donna, dir. 2001. *A Sigh and a Wish: Helen Creighton's Maritimes*. National Film Board of Canada, 9101032.

Deleuze, Gilles, and Felix Guattari. 2004 [1972]. *Anti-Oedipus*. London, UK: Continuum.

Del Giudice, Luisa, and Gerald Porter. 2001. *Imagined States: Nationalism, Utopia and Longing in Oral Cultures*. Logan: Utah State University Press.

Duncan, James. 1992. "Elite Landscapes as Cultural (Re)Productions: The Case of Shaughnessy Heights." In *Inventing Places: Studies in Cultural Geography*, edited by Kay Anderson and Fay Gale, 37–51. Harlow, UK: Longman Chesire.

Edwardson, Ryan. 2008. *Canadian Content: Culture and Question for Nationhood*. Toronto, ON: University of Toronto Press.

Giddens, Anthony. 1990. *The Consequences of Modernity*. Cambridge, UK: Polity Press.

Guigné, Anna Kearney. 2008. *Folksongs and Folk Revival: The Cultural Politics of Kenneth Peacock's Songs of the Newfoundland Outports*. St John's, NL: Institute of Social and Economic Research.

Guilbault, Jocelyne. 1997. "Interpreting World Music: A Challenge in Theory and Practice." *Popular Music* 16 (1): 31–44.

Gunning, Dave. 2010. *Tribute to John Allan Cameron*. Wee House of Music 654367022580. CD.

Guy, Greg. 2005. "Honouring John Allan: Musicians, Friends Get Together to Help Out the Godfather of Celtic Music." *Halifax Chronicle-Herald* (17 May). Accessed 31 July 2015. http://www.scotland.com/forums/music-art/22757-honouring-john-allan-cameron.html.

Hamel, Danielle. 2013. *The Halifax Pop Explosion: Music Scenes, Sloan, and the Case for a Halifax Sound*. Master's thesis, University of Western Ontario.

Hennessy, Jeffrey. 2015. "Deterritorialization and Reterritorialization in Atlantic Canadian Popular Music." *MUSICultures* 42 (1): 66–88.

Hernàndez i Martí, Gil-Manuel. 2002. "The Deterritorialization of Cultural Heritage in a Globalized Modernity." *Transfer: Journal of Contemporary Culture* 1 (1): 92–107.

Hiller, Harry H. 2009. *Second Promised Land: Migration to Alberta and the Transformation of Canadian Society*. Montreal & Kingston: McGill-Queen's University Press.

Jones, Sheri. 2006. Interview with the author, 6 April.
Kernerman, Gerald. 2005. *Multicultural Nationalism: Civilizing Difference, Constituting Community*. Vancouver: University of British Columbia Press.
Lomax, John. 1936 [1910]. *Cowboy Songs and Other Frontier Ballads*. New York, NY: Collier Books.
MacGillivray, Allister. 1989. *The Nova Scotia Song Collection*. Marion Bridge, NS: Sea-Cape Music Ltd.
MacKenzie, W. Roy. 1919. *The Quest of the Ballad*. Princeton, NJ: Princeton University Press.
– 1963 [1928]. *Ballads and Sea Songs of Nova Scotia*. Hatboro, PA: Folklore Associates.
MacKinnon, Neil. 1986. *This Unfriendly Soil: The Loyalist Experience in Nova Scotia, 1783–1791*. Montreal & Kingston: McGill-Queen's University Press.
MacMaster, Natalie. 1999. *In My Hands*. Rounder 11661-7025-2. CD.
McKay, Ian. 1992. "Tartanism Triumphant: The Construction of Scottishness in Nova Scotia, 1933–1954." *Acadiensis* 21 (2): 5–47.
– 2009 [1994]. *The Quest of the Folk: Antimodernism and Cultural Selection in Twentieth-Century Nova Scotia*. Montreal & Kingston: McGill-Queen's University Press.
Middleton, Richard. 1990. *Studying Popular Music*. Milton Keynes, UK: Open University Press.
Narváez, Peter. 2002. "'I Think I Wrote a Folksong': Popularity and Regional Vernacular Anthems." *The Journal of American Folklore* 115 (456): 269–82.
Plank, Geoffrey. 2004. *An Unsettled Conquest: The British Campaign against the Peoples of Acadia*. Philadelphia: University of Pennsylvania Press.
Posen, I. Sheldon. 2012. "Four Songcatchers in Eastern Canada." In *The Ballad Collectors of North America: How Gathering Folksongs Transformed Academic Thought and American Identity*, edited by Scott B. Spencer, 121–49. Toronto, ON: Scarecrow.
Robertson, Roland. 1995. "Glocalization: Time-Space and Homogeneity-Heterogeneity." In *Global Modernities*, edited by Mike Featherstone, Scott Lash, and Roland Robertson, 25–44. London, UK: Sage Publications.
Rogers, Stan. 1976. *Fogarty's Cove*. Borealis BCD213. CD.
– 1978. *Turnaround*. Borealis BCD215. CD.
– 1981. *Northwest Passage*. BCD217. CD.
Rosenberg, Neil V. 1994. "The Canadianization of Newfoundland Folksong: Or the Newfoundlandization of Canadian Folksong." *Journal of Canadian Studies* 29 (1): 55–73.
– 2002. "Repetition, Innovation, and Representation in Don Messer's Media Repertoire." *Journal of American Folklore* 115 (456): 191–208.
Schafer, R. Murray. 1984 [1961]. "The Limits of Nationalism in Canadian Music." In *On Canadian Music*, 9–16. Bancroft, ON: Arcana Editions.
Sharp, Cecil J. 1916. *English Folk Songs, Collected and Arranged with Pianoforte Accompaniment by Cecil J. Sharp*. London, UK: Novello.
Sircom, Hilary. 1993. *Helen Creighton*. Tantallon, NS: Four East Publications.
Straw, Will. 2000. "In and around Canadian Music." *Journal of Canadian Studies* 35 (3): 173–83.

Szklarski, Cassandra. 2006. "Cameron's Vitality Remembered at Music Funeral." *Canadian Press*, 28 November. Accessed 31 July 2015. http://www.ian.davies.com/jacam-profile.htm.

Tomlinson, John. 1999. *Globalization and Culture*. Chicago, IL: University of Chicago Press.

Tye, Diane. 1993. "'A Very Lone Worker': Women-Centred Thoughts on Helen Creighton's Career as a Folklorist." *Canadian Folklore canadienne* 15 (2): 107–17.

Webb, Jeff A. 1992. "Cultural Intervention: Helen Creighton's Folksong Broadcasts, 1938–1939." *Canadian Folklore* 14 (2): 159–70.

Whittall, Geoffrey. 1998. "Fiddle Fast and Loud: The Effects of Popularizing Celtic Music in Canada." Unpublished conference paper, Graduate Colloquium in Music, York University.

Wilson, William A. 1973. "Herder, Folklore, and Romantic Nationalism." *The Journal of Popular Culture* 6 (4): 819–35.

Part Two

Rethinking Genres and Artistic Practices

Introduction
Sherry Johnson

The second section, "Rethinking Genres and Artistic Practices," investigates specific and localized music genres that have taken root and developed in Canada, revealing connections between musical expression, cultural identity, and place. Like "tradition," musical genres are often understood by both audiences and practitioners to be bounded and static (Matsue 2016; Sparling 2008), but of course, in reality, they are "discursively constructed and contested ... [and] shift over time and place" (Sparling 2008, 403); also like "tradition," "genre is always ongoing and therefore always open to reinterpretation, development and mutation" (Mills 2009, 26). Matsue points out that in most recent studies of genre, scholars are interested in "what genre reveals about the processes involved in its production" (2016, 26; see also Lena and Peterson 2008; Lena 2012). Several chapters in this section start with the understanding that musical genres and practices are "embedded in shifting social contexts, [and therefore] remain dynamic, not static" (Devitt 2015, 83); others examine how individual agency, also, can play a role in constructing, reifying, and contesting what constitutes a recognizable genre.

This section begins with Monique Giroux's considerations of an often-misconstrued fiddle genre in "Metis (Style) Fiddling: From Historical Roots to Contemporary Practice." Like many of the musical "traditions" examined in the first section, Metis (style) fiddling is often understood as frozen in the past, and carefully bounded as a body of tunes and set of stylistic practices defined by that past; in reality, of course, it is both emergent and highly relevant to a contemporary Metis Nation. Giroux positions Metis (style) fiddling as a resurgent practice and a practice in revival; as a historical practice and a contemporary practice; and as a style/canon of tunes and an expression of a social and political experience that moves beyond stylistic boundaries.

Next, Colin McGuire challenges readers to reconsider the boundaries that separate music, dance, and other forms of choreographed movement in his examination of martial arts, lion dancing, and percussion music. Together these interrelated practices make up the art of kung fu, which was brought to Canada from southern China's Guangdong Province (and neighbouring Hong Kong) by Cantonese immigrants. Lion dancing and drumming are learned alongside self-defence, which contributes to their distinctively fierce social meanings and positions them as martial arts. In "War Drums in Chinatown: Chinese Canadian Lion Dance Music as Martial Art," McGuire traces the development and uses of these practices in Toronto in relation to their primary social contexts: first, Chinese resistance to racial discrimination in Canada, and later as icons of cultural identity.

While Cape Breton fiddling is celebrated by many of its practitioners and fans for its deep roots and unchanging practice, more recent scholarship reveals the many ways that the practice is shaped not only by the agency of musicians, but also by conflicting expectations and aesthetics of various audiences. In "'Holy jeez, I can hear *everything*': Liveness in Cape Breton Fiddle Recordings," Ian Hayes explores how the concept of liveness, highly valued in Cape Breton fiddle recordings, can be constructed and heard in different, sometimes contradictory, ways: in lo-fi, homemade recordings of a party, as well as hyper-realistic studio recordings. Cape Breton musicians must negotiate these differing definitions of liveness for their own purposes, creating recordings that uphold accepted Cape Breton aesthetics while also satisfying norms and expectations locally and abroad.

In "Fantastic Voyage: The Diasporic Roots and Routes of Early Toronto Hip Hop," Jesse Stewart and Niel Scobie examine hip hop's emergence in Toronto, highlighting the contributions of pioneering musicians who memorialized cultural heritage in their music, while simultaneously constructing and performing hybridized identities. Through a close reading and analysis of selected recordings and videos, Stewart and Scobie examine some of the ways in which these early Canadian hip hop artists articulated hybridized cultural identities rooted in the Caribbean and African diasporas. In so doing, they not only celebrated diasporic history, music, and culture, but also laid the foundations for the future development of hip hop in Canada.

This section closes with Janice Esther Tulk's examination of the links between musical, textual, and visual elements in Indigenous popular music videos in "Identity, Aesthetics, and Place in Medicine Dream's 'In This World.'" Tulk's analysis of the video demonstrates both how music is embedded in mainstream modes of musical expression and how visual elements – images and text – enable and encourage a different way of listening to, and thus understanding, music. Like other authors in this book, Tulk explores how cultural identity is expressed and represented through music and performance, in this case how bandleader Paul Pike signifies his Mi'kmaw identity in this song and video. Considering Pike's work through Mi'kmaw metaphors of a "middle ground" and "two-eyed seeing," Tulk draws attention not only to an inbetween-ness vis-à-vis Mi'kmaw and mainstream identities, but also to Pike's engagement with both of these worlds, challenging readers to listen differently.

Chapters in this section expand existing research on long-standing musical practices in Canada, and also address previously underdocumented practices from diasporic communities. Together they demonstrate the vibrancy of particular music genres and their complex and often shifting meanings for performers and audiences.

References

Devitt, Amy J. 2015. "Genre." In *Keywords in Writing Studies*, edited by Paul Heilker and Peter Vandenberg, 82–7. Boulder, CO: University Press of Colorado.

Lena, Jennifer C. 2012. *Banding Together: How Communities Create Genres in Popular Music*. Princeton, NJ: Princeton University Press.

Lena, Jennifer C., and Richard A. Peterson. 2008. "Classification as Culture: Types and Trajectories of Music Genres." *American Sociological Review* 73 (5): 697–718.

Matsue, Jennifer Milioto. 2016. "Drumming to One's Own Beat: Japanese Taiko and the Challenge to Genre." *Ethnomusicology* 60 (1): 22–52.

Mills, Brett. 2009. *e Sitcom*. Edinburgh, Scotland: Edinburgh University Press.

Sparling, Heather. 2008. "Categorically Speaking: Towards a Theory of (Musical) Genre in Cape Breton Gaelic Culture." *Ethnomusicology* 52 (3): 401–25.

Monique Giroux

Chapter 7

Metis (Style) Fiddling: From Historical Roots to Contemporary Practice

Metis (style) fiddling[1] has long captivated the settler[2] imagination. It has been disparaged as primitive, and treated as a vestige of a wild, uncivilized past; yet it has also been celebrated for its uniqueness and used by settlers to mark the Prairie provinces' difference from the rest of Canada (see Giroux 2013, 64–95; and Quick 2009, 135–6). This appropriation of Metis fiddling has become especially common as fiddling, after several decades of decline, regains popularity among Metis and First Nations youth and becomes an important part of a growing number of Metis-run and -attended festivals. While Metis-run events often centre on fiddling as an expression of contemporary Metis-ness with little (explicit) concern for delineating a distinct style, the mainstream (unmarked) public has a strong interest in difference and boundaries (i.e., a Metis *style* of fiddling); often, particular emphasis is placed on asymmetrical phrases, cross tuning, and clogging,[3] which are then understood within a framework of authenticity. Commenting on the style of fiddling adopted by contemporary Metis youth, ethnomusicologist Anne Lederman writes that "the 'Métisness' of the music seems to go no further than the fact that it is being played by Métis[4] people" (2009, 371). She later notes that it may be "left to white girls like me to play this old crooked music, reveling in its unique beauty, while young aboriginal fiddlers are busy trying to sound as much like everyone else as they possibly can" (2009, 373).

These comments point to the ways in which Metis (style) fiddling has been misconstrued within mainstream spaces; instead of understanding it as emergent and community-based, it is frozen in the past, and carefully bounded as a body of tunes and set of stylistic practices defined largely by past practice. Changes to the style are thus considered inauthentic.[5] This chapter challenges these notions, exploring Metis fiddling's stylistic and social complexity, as well as its contemporary relevance to the people who refer to and understand themselves as members of the Metis Nation. The first section offers a brief history of Metis fiddling, from its roots in the fur trade to its resurgence and revival[6] in Metis, First Nations, and mainstream settler communities. The second section examines two contemporary Indigenous[7] spaces for the propagation and performance of Metis fiddle music, exploring where and how it is learned and shared within the Metis community. The final section provides an overview of the distinct elements of Metis fiddling, both as a historical style and contemporary practice. By addressing Metis fiddling from these varied vantage points, I hope to highlight the diversity within the category "Metis fiddling" and demonstrate its continued significance to the Metis Nation. I ultimately argue that Metis fiddling is a resurgent practice *and* a practice in revival; a historical practice *and* a contemporary practice; and a set of tunes (a canon) and way of playing (a style), *as well as* a social and political experience that has little to do with particular tunes or styles.

An emphasis on social and stylistic complexity has significant implications for our understanding of Metis music and Indigenous musics more generally. As mixed-blood Mi'kmaw scholar Bonita Lawrence notes, "traditional academic understandings of Native identity have been couched in terms of primordiality, a state of existence in contradistinction to modernity" (2004, 1). She later notes that, "engaging in ongoing struggles to challenge the demand for primordiality is necessary work that Native academics must do. Canadian court decisions continue to restrict Aboriginal rights to precontact activities. The Western imagination continues to paint the world as populated by 'endangered authenticities,' always juxtaposed to modernity, always going crazy in the face of the inescapable momentum of progress and change ... There is no future for Native people within these frameworks, other than as 'the Vanishing Race'" (Lawrence 2004, 5). Emphasizing the close relationship between musical practice and the diverse and changing needs of the contemporary Metis Nation challenges the notion of the disappearing or inauthentic Metis. That is, it recognizes that change and diversity are legitimate and indeed authentic aspects of all cultures, including Metis culture. Contemporary Metis fiddling may not always sound like it did thirty (or one hundred) years ago. Metis fiddling has, furthermore, emerged in new contexts and venues, and has developed new social meanings and purposes – some of which may at times seem contradictory. These changes and complexities are not, however, evidence of a "Vanishing Race," but rather, evidence of Metis creativity and vitality.

A Short History of Metis (Style) Fiddling

Little information is available on Canada's earliest fiddle traditions. What is known has been pieced together from fragments uncovered in archives (Lederman et al. 2012) and by retracing connections between Canadian and European styles (e.g., see Lederman 2013 and Rodgers 1980). Ethnomusicologist Anne Lederman notes, for example, that early fiddling in what is now Manitoba was influenced by Scottish players who came into the Prairies via Hudson Bay (Lederman 1988, 208). This is corroborated in an account of a Christmas celebration written by R.M. Ballantyne about his visit to York Factory, Manitoba, in 1843: "the sound of a fiddle struck upon our ears ... On a chair, in a corner near the stove sat a young, good-looking Indian, with a fiddle of his own making beside him. This was our Paganini: and beside him sat an Indian boy with a kettle-drum on which he tapped occasionally, as if anxious that the ball should begin ... we each chose partners, the fiddle struck up and the ball began. Scotch reels were the only dances known by the majority of the guests, so we confined ourselves entirely to them" (cited in Bassett 194, 20–1).

While fiddlers in the northwest had direct connections to Scotland, they were also influenced by French-Canadian fiddlers working as voyageurs and coureurs de bois, who in turn had been influenced by both Scottish and Irish fiddling, and by Indigenous music (Lederman 2010b; 1988, 208). By the mid-1800s, a new style of fiddling had emerged in the northwest (Lederman 2010b). The oldest available recordings suggest that this style featured tunes with short, often asymmetrical and motif-based phrases, and descending melodic lines. It was likely unaccompanied or used clogging as accompaniment, and was highly individualized, with fiddlers performing their own versions of tunes.[8] Although definitive evidence is scarce, it is likely that this style was one among several that emerged along fur trade routes (e.g., compare the stylistic differences heard in the recordings made by Lederman [1987], Mishler [1974], and Vrooman [1984] from Manitoba, Alaska, and North Dakota).

By the late 1800s, immigration to western Canada had begun in earnest; many Indigenous peoples were, as a result, pushed away from European settlements and onto reserves. This physical separation, paired with negative attitudes toward the Metis, shifted the dynamic between Metis and settler styles. As critic for the *Manitoba Free Press* C.W. Handscomb wrote in his turn-of-the-century review of a Winnipeg performance of a Wagner opera, "how this young town of ours away out here in the wild and woolly west does take on metropolitan airs to be sure ... it seems but yesterday that our most classic melodies were those scraped by the Metis fiddler for a Red River Jig" (Handscomb 1906). As suggested by this quote, settlers began associating Metis fiddling with a "primitive" past (Giroux 2013, 64–5, 67–70). This physical and attitudinal distance did not, however, completely eliminate the influence of Metis fiddling on the developing mainstream fiddle style. In fact, throughout the twentieth century, fiddlers who we now know were Metis often performed at settler-run and -attended events, and at least one tune that developed in the Red River prior to the influx of new immigrants, the "Red River Jig," was commonly heard at events held at Winnipeg's posh Royal Alexandra Hotel, at police fundraisers, and at old-time fiddle contests (Giroux 2013, 71–2, 79–80). The presence of a Metis tune and Metis fiddlers in these mainstream spaces points to the complex paths Metis fiddling has followed from the past to the present era.

Beginning in the 1930s and 1940s, the spread of radio technology and increased access to modern means of transportation created new contexts for Metis fiddling (Quick 2009, 152–3). Metis fiddler Andy Dejarlis became particularly well known during this period, borrowing and adapting tunes from the Metis repertoire to create "a smoother ... version of the Métis tradition, now commonly known as the 'Red River' style" (Lederman 2010b). Dejarlis' fame was in large part a result of his adoption of modern technologies; he travelled extensively, regularly performed on the radio, and recorded thirty-two LPs and four 78s (see discography in Mackintosh 2010, 151–6). In doing so, he became a local, and to a somewhat lesser extent, national sensation. Although Dejarlis never represented himself or his music as Metis (Chrétien 2005, 162), his influence was very strong in both Indigenous (Gibbons 1981, 84) and settler communities in Manitoba and elsewhere, and many Prairie fiddlers have adopted his style and his versions of tunes.[9] Other Indigenous fiddlers who took advantage of new technology during the early era of radio include Del Genthon (son of Frederick Genthon whose recording of the "Red River Jig" in 1940 is the earliest known recording of the tune), who was heard over the airwaves on a show called "Le Ranch" (Mackintosh 2010, 37), and brothers Pete, Lawrence, and Gilbert Anderson, members of the Enoch Cree Nation, located near the town of Stony Plain west of Edmonton. The

Anderson brothers had little access to the radio, but by the 1950s they were able to travel by car to Edmonton to advertise evening dances in Enoch.[10]

The 1950s saw a decline in the popularity of fiddling, along with a decline in associated dances such as jigging and square dancing, among Metis, First Nations, and settler peoples (Giroux 2013, 80; Mackintosh 2010, 107; Dueck 2005, 367). This decline has been linked to the rising popularity of commercial genres such as country and western and rock and roll (Mackintosh 2010, 107; and Lederman 1986, 12, 52, 56). Yet even in the midst of this ebb, new venues for fiddling emerged. For example, by the 1970s, fiddling had become an increasingly important part of large events such as treaty days, competitions, multicultural celebrations, and large Metis festivals (see Giroux 2013, 84–5). Friendship centres also began serving as important spaces for fiddling as Indigenous populations moved into urban areas (Quick 2009, 155). In the early 1960s, the Canadian Native Friendship Centre in Edmonton began hosting dance instruction for both children and adults with a live fiddler and square dance caller. By 1963, it was hosting a Native music festival, an event that incorporated fiddling and dancing competitions, with the latter including competitions for the "Reel of Eight," "Duck Dance," and "Red River Jig," and, eventually, a square dance competition (Quick 2008, 82). Despite similar migration to urban areas in Manitoba, the Indian and Métis Friendship Centre in Winnipeg did not begin hosting dances until the 1980s, with live fiddlers added only in the 1990s (Dueck 2007, 346–7).

The emergence of these new venues can be linked to the confluence of several social and legal factors. The Indian Act of 1951 relaxed the rules restricting Indigenous lives and therefore allowed for more open celebration of Indigenous cultures. Although the Indian Act did not directly affect Metis lives, fiddling was often included at First Nations cultural celebrations (Giroux 2013, 84–5), creating new, large-scale venues for fiddling.[11] Other factors that led to the emergence of Metis fiddling in the public sphere included a shift toward multiculturalism as Canadian public policy (including funding for events that supported this re-envisioning of Canadian identity) in the 1970s; and the formation and re-energization of Metis political organizations in the late 1960s.[12] As anthropologist Sarah Quick suggests, Metis organizations were "corroborating with discourse around multiculturalism" (2009, 164), that is, using renewed (mainstream) interest in the ethnic other to support Metis events and raise Metis consciousness (2009, 164). During this period, new dance groups grew out of settlers' desire to see Metis culture represented at multicultural and heritage events (Quick 2009, 162; Gibbons

1981, 2), while Metis-run and -attended cultural events became increasingly important venues for Metis and First Nations fiddlers to hone their skills, and for Metis people to celebrate their culture (Giroux 2013, 112).

In the 1980s and 1990s, the shame imposed on Metis people since the Red River and Northwest Resistances[13] of the late nineteenth century slowly turned to pride, leading to a significant shift in the number of artists representing themselves as Metis (Chrétien 2005, 155). Mel Bedard's album *Metis Fiddler* (1984) is a particularly good marker of this shift, since it is the first fiddle album to use the term "Metis" (Chrétien 2005, 163). During this period, many fiddlers who had been active in the old-time fiddle scene "came out" as Metis (Quick 2009, 165). As fiddler Calvin Vollrath notes, prior to this period, no one referred to Metis fiddling; everything was simply "fiddling" (cited in Chrétien 2005, 149).[14] Since then, Metis people have adopted the term "Metis fiddling" quite broadly to refer to both themselves (i.e., Metis fiddlers, not necessarily Metis *style* fiddlers) (Chrétien 2005, 155) and their unique style. In contrast, since the 1980s settlers have tended to use the term to refer to a particular style of fiddling. The work of Roy Gibbons (1981, 1980) and Anne Lederman (1988, 1986) is especially significant in this regard, providing considerable information on Metis *style* fiddling but little on its social contexts. By identifying and focusing on tunes and stylistic features that demonstrated the greatest difference from the old-time style (i.e., the mainstream style played in the Prairies), this research delimited relatively clear boundaries between each style, thereby solidifying the distinction between Metis and old-time fiddling.

Although it can be difficult to draw a clear line between music for exhibition and music that functions as sociality,[15] in recent years demand for performances of Metis fiddling for a non-participatory rather than participatory audience (i.e., for concert-like performances) has grown. With the increased exhibition of Metis fiddling and dancing, the 1980s and 1990s saw a divide emerge between traditional dance tunes (such as "Drops of Brandy" and "Duck Dance") that were revived and played for exhibition, and tunes played for social dancing (e.g., "St Anne's Reel," "Big John McNeil," "Whiskey before Breakfast," and "Faded Love"). While the "Red River Jig" is an exception since it is played and danced at many Metis social gatherings, traditional dance tunes are now rarely played in social dance settings; instead, they are usually performed in presentational contexts (Quick 2009, 181–2). A tension closely linked to that between fiddling for exhibition and fiddling for social events has also emerged between traditional and innovative approaches to

Metis fiddling. For example, competitors in the traditional Metis category at the John Arcand Fiddle Festival (a Saskatchewan competition run by Metis fiddler and composer John Arcand) must accompany themselves with their feet (i.e., clog) and use specific cross tunings. In contrast, the only rule at the Metisfest contest in Manitoba is that fiddlers must play two tunes (Giroux 2013, 119; Quick 2009, 197). Similarly, fiddlers at the Back to Batoche contest in Saskatchewan do not need to clog or used specified tunings.[16]

The division between traditional and innovative approaches has manifested itself in settler contexts through an increased fascination with authenticity (Chrétien 2005, 116). As far back as 1980, Gibbons noted that the "pure" folk tradition was rapidly disappearing, suggesting that Metis people were unable to withstand outside cultural influences (1980, 47). He was presuming that Metis fiddlers were no longer practising Metis fiddling. More recently, settler-run and largely settler-attended events, such as old-time fiddle contests, have tended to confine the Metis tradition within the parameters of a narrowly defined style that can be (and often is) showcased for outsiders (see Giroux 2013, 267–90; and Dueck 2005, 430, who describes this in the context of Metis dance). Beyond being an inaccurate representation of Metis music, which has always been in flux, this fascination with the "authentic" has helped construct a homogeneous and essentialist view of Metis people. Chrétien is particularly critical of the role of music in this construction of Metis authenticity, noting that "recordings by non-Metis people seem to present a relatively homogenous and essentialist view of the Metis through their emphasis on the past, the Historical Metis of the nineteenth century, who are usually associated with Western Canada" (2005, 154).[17] Metis fiddlers are in fact more diverse musically than often represented (Chrétien 2005, 154); just as importantly, the vitality of Metis fiddling as a living, changing, and modern tradition is emphasized in Indigenous spaces (i.e., spaces claimed for the primary use of Indigenous peoples).

Metis Fiddling in Contemporary Contexts

Fiddling that falls under the umbrella "Metis fiddling" is currently heard in Ontario, across the Prairies (including south of the Canada/US border), and into the Canadian north and Alaska. Although house parties and community events remain important, large-scale, Metis-run cultural festivals and various educational programs are becoming increasingly significant venues. The section that follows explores two of these contemporary Indigenous spaces by providing an overview of the origins and goals of the Frontier Fiddle program, the largest of the Indigenous fiddle education programs, followed by an overview of Metisfest, a Metis rendezvous (i.e., cultural gathering) in Manitoba. These descriptions highlight some of the diverse ways in which Metis (style) fiddling is learned and shared within Indigenous communities.

The Frontier Fiddlers: Educating the Next Generation

The Frontier Fiddle program was started in the mid-1990s in Sherridon, Manitoba, by the principal of Sherridon's school,[18] Blaine Klippenstein (Gluska 2011, 90). It has since become an important part of music education in the Frontier School Division, Manitoba's most northerly school division. Although a southern Manitoban by birth, Klippenstein had a long-standing interest in making schooling a culturally relevant experience for children in the north, who are largely Metis and First Nations.[19] Recognizing the cultural significance of fiddling, Klippenstein started teaching himself, and fourteen of his students, how to play the fiddle (Lederman et al. 2012, 206). Klippenstein and his students eventually connected with Cameron Baggins, a Suzuki violin and fiddle teacher from Winnipeg, inviting him to spend some time in Sherridon to facilitate workshops. This sparked Baggins's interest and, in the years that followed, Baggins started programs in other northern communities with the support of school principals such as Dave Maynard in Duck Bay, Manitoba (Lederman et al. 2012, 206). The Frontier Fiddle program is now offered in thirty-three schools across the division, bringing fiddle instruction to 2200 students (personal communication 2015). Every year, students come together at a jamboree, where fiddle instructors from across Canada facilitate workshops and teach students new tunes. In 2004, the event brought together 175 students; the following year, 550 fiddle students attended (Gluska 2011, 86), and by 2014, 700 fiddlers and guitarists took part in the jamboree.[20]

The Frontier Fiddle program has been particularly successful in nurturing community bonds. Although most of the teachers are non-Indigenous and are not from the north, educator Virginia Gluska argues that it is nonetheless a grassroots movement; northern communities were actively involved in bringing the program to their communities and remain active supporters of the program. Gluska notes, for example, that the need to fundraise has created "space for active community involvement" (2011, 111), and has "add[ed] a dimension of cohesiveness to the communities" (ibid., 134). This cohesiveness has included a strengthening of relations between generations.

As Klippenstein told Gluska, "when students started taking the fiddles home to play for family and friends, the positive response was immediate. I think that had the largest impact on the success of this program. Grandparents and parents were disconnected from education. But they took an immediate interest in the fiddle and encouraged students right from the beginning. The affirmation and accolades kept students interested and excited to play and learn more songs" (quoted in Gluska 2011, 106). Gluska's consultant, Tina, made a similar observation: "the elders in the communities were very, very touched that this was being done ... Now all of a sudden this fiddling came back in and now the old people are back into the lives of the young people. There is definitely a connection and it connects the old to the young people" (quoted in Gluska 2011, 123–4). Gluska's research includes numerous stories about people who remember the fiddle as a central part of their childhood and about how the new program has served to bring together the generations.

The Frontier Fiddle program has also created bonds between remote, often isolated, northern communities. In many cases, students' involvement in the program is their only opportunity to go outside their communities, especially if they are not involved in sports (Gluska 2011, 132). Gluska relates numerous stories about reconnecting with old friends and notes that many new friendships have started at the annual jamborees (2011, 87–9). As one of her consultants told her, "Throughout the years of playing I met so many great friends that shared the love for the fiddle like me. Now when we gear up to go to a workshop it just feels like a family reunion/get together" (quoted in Gluska 2011, 126). While the annual jamboree is a large-scale example of students coming together from across the Frontier School Division, other events, such as concerts in Winnipeg, provide additional opportunities throughout the year to maintain these friendships.[21] Thus, outsiders started the program, but northern communities have upheld its momentum and continued vibrancy. By its twentieth anniversary, the program's graduates had begun returning as teachers (Lederman et al. 2012, 206), in a sense, bringing the program more fully into the hands of the communities it serves.

Although the Frontier Fiddle program has created a link between generations, the approach to learning to fiddle adopted by the program marks a significant shift from past practice. Imitation and learning "by ear" (the traditional approaches) are still important, but a stronger emphasis is now placed on notation via a form of tablature developed for the program. This tablature, along with a desire to facilitate group playing, has led to the standardization of melodies, forms, and bowings, where in the past these aspects of performance were highly personalized (see below for further discussion of style). The teachers also include tunes from a variety of traditions (Lederman et al 2012, 207); while exchange has always been an important part of Metis fiddling, it is now taking place more deliberately and at a faster rate than in the past. Some have in fact criticized the program for the changes cited above, arguing that the unique aspects of the style will be lost as it becomes standardized (Quick 2009, 171). Certainly, these changes raise questions regarding the relationship between formalized teaching and the older tradition (as noted in Gluska 2011, 186), yet it is clear that the program provides a musical and social outlet, as well as at least some "sense of cultural continuity" for youth in the north (Whidden 2007, 42).

Gathering in Celebration at Metisfest

In recent years, a growing number of students and former students of the Frontier Fiddle program have been hired as entertainers at Metis cultural festivals. Back to Batoche Days, an annual festival in Batoche, Saskatchewan, is the longest-running Metis cultural festival of its kind, dating back to 1970 (Quick 2009, 122). Numerous other festivals have been added since the early 2000s, resulting in a summer festival "circuit"[22] that unites the Metis Nation through music, dance, and other cultural activities. This circuit includes festivals in Ontario (e.g., Metis Heritage Celebration in Oshawa), North Dakota (e.g., Keplinfest held on the Turtle Mountain Chippewa Reservation), Manitoba (e.g., Koushkoupayh Days in southwestern Manitoba, and Metis Music Festival in St Laurent), Saskatchewan (e.g., Back to Batoche Days), Alberta (e.g., Métis Fest in Edmonton), and British Columbia (e.g., Louis Riel Day in Vancouver). These festivals keep Metis fiddlers busy throughout the summer months. The section that follows provides an overview of one of these festivals, Metisfest, in order to highlight some key features and priorities of contemporary Metis cultural festivals. Although the account below is based largely on the 2012 event, it is informed by several years of fieldwork at Metisfest and other Metis cultural events in Manitoba, North Dakota, and Saskatchewan.

Metisfest grew out of Metisville, a festival held in Boissevain, Manitoba, from 2006 to 2008 (see Villeneuve 2006, 7). Since many Metis people were coming across the border from Turtle Mountain Chippewa Reservation, North Dakota, for the event, the organizers decided in 2009 to move Metisville to the International Peace Garden, a 9.5 km^2 park that straddles the North

Dakota/Manitoba border, becoming International Metisfest. Using this new venue as a symbol of unity, organizers committed to making the event truly international, inviting performers and working to draw attendees from both Canada and the United States. From 2009 to 2011, the event was promoted as North America's only truly international Metis festival. This changed in 2012 when it was moved to Killarney, Manitoba, just fifty kilometres northeast of the International Peace Garden. Although organizer Dan Goodon referred to the move as "bittersweet," since the festival lost its international status (becoming simply "Metisfest"), the new venue, a large recreation centre, was more accessible to senior event-goers and made financial sense since the town of Killarney donated the space (interview with Goodon 2012). Financial difficulties and volunteer burnout led to its cancellation in 2013 (email communication with Goodon 2013), but similar events in Manitoba and North Dakota have taken its place.

Metisfest attendees often travel[23] a considerable distance to attend the event, hailing from Manitoba, Ontario, Saskatchewan, Alberta, Turtle Mountain Chippewa Reservation,[24] and North Dakota. Since Metisfest is a three-day event, many of the travellers bring RVs, parking them at one of the two nearby campgrounds. Most of the performers (who also often travel significant distances) stay in tents set up outside the recreation centre, creating a small performers' village. The entertainment is heard on several stages. The main stage, set up in a large arena within the recreation centre, features performers from morning until about 10:00 p.m. on the first two days and 5:00 p.m. on the final day. The smaller "udder stage"[25] features music beginning mid-morning and ending at supper, while the half stage (set up in a hallway between the main and udder stages) hosts organized events off and on throughout the day and is used, during the remaining time, as a stage for impromptu performances or jams. In a large room just off the main stage is the "trading post" where vendors display their arts, crafts, books, foods, and other items for purchase. Outside the recreation centre on a grassy stretch is a "rendezvous village," featuring a teepee, fire pit, Red River cart, and an ample supply of furs for attendees to admire.

The majority of the approximately thirty entertainers are fiddlers, with just a few country and gospel singers rounding out the lineup. A house band made up of Indigenous musicians from Winnipeg backs up the performers on the main stage and a rotating lineup of less experienced musicians back up the performers on the udder stage. Perhaps because the fiddlers do not bring their own bands (with the exception of those performing in the evening), many play the same tunes, with the most popular being "Whiskey before Breakfast," "Big John McNeil," "St Anne's Reel," and "Faded Love." Tunes recorded by Anishinaabe fiddler Cliff Maytwayashing (1939–2009) are popular as well. Most of the fiddlers in attendance are in their late teens or early twenties; just a few are in their thirties and one is a senior. The fiddlers notably come from varied backgrounds; some are from reserves or Metis communities, others from settler communities. It is clear that Metisfest organizers do not require performers to be "card-carrying" Metis; rather, as Goodon told me, they choose fiddlers who are accepted as part of the Metis fiddle circuit (interview with Goodon 2012).

Despite the array of available entertainment, the audience (primarily seniors, as is often the case at large-scale Metis gatherings like Metisfest) takes every opportunity to make their way to the dance floor with a partner, dancing the polka, fox-trot, waltz, heel-toe polka, or seven-step; the Red River Jig, played several times throughout the day, also brings some audience members to their feet. While the evening entertainment is structured like a typical old-time Prairie dance (e.g., two tunes of the same tune type, followed by a short pause), almost every performance at Metisfest is an opportunity to join in celebration through dance. The audience does, however, remain in their seats for the three hours (spread over the weekend) when dance troupes, backed by a live fiddler, come to the stage. In contrast to the fiddlers who generally wear casual "street" clothing, female dancers wear colourful dresses with billowing petticoats under knee-length skirts that lift like a blossoming flower to reveal matching undergarments as they twirl across the dance floor; male dancers (and women filling the male role) wear pants and collared shirts that match the women's dresses. Each troupe performs a few sets, and invariably ends with the "Red River Jig," an exciting finale that often brings the audience to their feet cheering in appreciation.

While the description above offers only a glimpse into the event,[26] it points to the two main goals of Metisfest: to promote Metis artists as promulgators of Metis identity, and to create a space for the Metis Nation to celebrate and reconnect as a community. As main organizer Dan Goodon explained to me in an interview, there is a great deal of Metis talent, but many Metis artists are not well-promoted: "we have so much Metis talent and we had one fellow that came, Garry Lepine, and he had been fiddling for forty years, and, you know what … when I Googled his name, nothing was on there! And I said you know what, this is a forty year … veteran of Metis music … and the internet … the world wants to look at [it]. He didn't come up!" (interview with

Goodon 2012).[27] The promotion of Metis fiddlers (and Indigenous fiddlers more broadly[28]) emerges, then, as a key component of Metisfest. In fact, fiddle music (including playing, listening, watching, and dancing to the fiddle) is understood as an expression of Metis identity without necessarily being attached to one particular style.[29] As a result, being an Indigenous fiddler is more important than playing in a specific way. This is true of all the Metis-run cultural events that I have attended, with the exception of the John Arcand Fiddle Festival, which features a clearly delineated traditional Metis fiddle category as part of a larger fiddle competition.[30]

While promotion and recognition of Metis talent is an important goal of Metisfest, Goodon also wants to provide a space for Metis people to gather, to express themselves, and to reconnect as Metis people. Goodon told me with great enthusiasm about the many reunions that took place during Metisfest as people got in touch with their "lost relatives." He further explained that hundreds of people have told him the same story, that "they had a feeling" that they were Metis but only discovered the truth in their later years. During my conversation with Goodon, it was clear that he wants to give Metis people a space to discover this truth about themselves, and to live as Metis people if only for the weekend. In fact, it was the moments where community building was front and centre, moments when he saw lost connections being rebuilt, that were clearly the most memorable for him. As he told me, "that's what you'll see at the festival. You'll see people smiling and laughing, and shaking hands, and hugging, and you know you'll see even crying, but it'll be more tears of joy ... I found a relative I never seen for the last fifty years ... We've made this connection here and you'll see people, they will come back and they'll just continue coming back. They are just kind of drawn to it" (interview with Goodon 2012). Through the festival and his work promoting the festival, Goodon wants "to talk to people, [to] let them know, it's proud, it's okay to be Metis" (interview with Goodon 2012).

The participatory nature of Metisfest is a key aspect of this coming together as a community. Allowing attendees to become performers through dance or informal jam sessions, and indeed valuing their participation, helps enhance social bonding (Turino 2008, 33, 36, 157), creating a sense of cohesiveness as a resurgent nation.[31] In this way, each attendee, whether a performer or audience member, becomes an important part of the Metisfest community over the course of the weekend (cf. Turino 2008, 173). This sense of coming together needs to be understood, furthermore, in the context of multiple Metis events that take place throughout the year. While Metisfest is just three days long, other Metis festivals create a coming together of the Metis Nation several times each summer. Although audiences vary from event to event, many attendees make it out to more than one event, and the entertainers frequently attend several Metis festivals, thus creating continuity among the events.[32] Just as importantly, attendees bring videos and sound recordings purchased at Metisfest home with them, and attend community events featuring performers from Metisfest, allowing them to re-experience the sense of community created at Metisfest throughout the year. As Goodon told me, "Some [attendees] are junkies now ... they have to have the fiddle going; they have to be able to watch a DVD of dancers" (interview with Goodon 2012). Through Metisfest and similar events, Metis people are given the opportunity to reconnect, becoming a united, healthy, vibrant, and resurgent nation.

Metis Style Fiddling

The above section provides an overview of the influences that have shaped Metis fiddling, as well as a synopsis of two contemporary Indigenous spaces where fiddling flourishes. Because these influences and spaces are diverse, and because they have shaped Metis fiddling at different points in its history, it can be difficult to pinpoint the exact boundaries of Metis fiddling as a unique style. As Quick notes, mixing, fusion, and the general transformation of Metis fiddling took place in layers over time, and today this includes a new fusion as the older style of Metis fiddling is revived (2009, 265–6). That is to say, the boundaries of the style shift over time and over space. Yet several unique characteristics have come to be strongly associated with the Metis fiddle style. Part three of this chapter addresses these unique characteristics, exploring the boundaries of Metis fiddling as a distinct style. The first section offers information on the aspects of style most often associated with Metis fiddling – in particular, asymmetry, cross tunings, and clogging – as well as secondary characteristics such as individuality, bowings, melodic line, "double-stringing," and danceability. The second section provides transcriptions and analyses of tunes performed by three contemporary fiddlers who are popular in the Metis fiddle scene. These transcriptions challenge older definitions of the Metis style, and suggest that subtle rhythmic features (instead of asymmetry, altered tunings, and clogging) are now distinguishing the Metis style from other fiddle styles. By positioning a discussion of characteristics most associated with Metis fiddling alongside transcriptions of contemporary performances, the third part of this chapter points to change and diversity within Metis style fiddling and highlights the continued vitality and creativity of Metis fiddlers.

Overview of Form, Tunings, Accompaniment, and Other Characteristics

Asymmetry of form and metre is one of the most referenced and celebrated aspects of Metis fiddling. While the vast majority of Scots-Irish, Anglo-Canadian, and New England fiddle tunes have two sections that can be broken down into two, four, or eight measure phrases,[33] tunes in the Metis style are often "crooked." They might have an odd number of phrases (e.g., three or five) that are of different lengths (e.g., three or five measures); one phrase that is repeated with some variation; phrases that elide (i.e., the last note of one phrase is the first note of the next); cadence notes that lengthen the phrase by one or more beats; or have just one section, or one section plus an extension (Lederman 1988, 209–10).[34] Since these features are all found in the Anishinaabe songs recorded in Minnesota and Wisconsin by Frances Densmore circa 1910, it is possible that the asymmetry found in Metis fiddling was a result of Ojibwe/Chippewa influence, although it may also signal the influence of music from the Shetland Islands (Lederman 2013, 334; Lederman 1988, 209). Asymmetry might alternatively be a result of Norwegian influence (Ellestad and Giroux 2016). Lederman's recordings in six Metis and First Nations communities in western Manitoba provide the largest body of evidence for the importance of asymmetry (1987a, 1987b). Folklorist Nicholas Vrooman's collection of tunes from the Turtle Mountain Chippewa Reservation (North Dakota) provides several additional examples of crooked tunes (1984), as does Craig Mishler's collection of tunes recorded in Gwich'in territory (the Canadian northwest and Alaska) (1974).

Asymmetry remains somewhat common in the more isolated northern regions of Canada (Lederman 2010a, 143–4), but has become uncommon among Metis fiddlers in the Canadian Prairies; in the south it is often relegated to specific tunes such as the "Red River Jig," "Drops of Brandy," and "Duck Dance" (Giroux 2013, 123–33; Quick 2009, 245–6; Gabriel Dumont Institute 2002). In the latter context, asymmetry is no longer an unconscious quality. Rather, it is a feature that is usually consciously adopted as a celebrated aspect of the Metis style, and is therefore often associated with particular tunes (Quick 2009, 245–6). Dueck suggests that the increased use of regular metre and phrases of predictable lengths may be a way for musicians to synchronize their versions of tunes with "as-yet-unknown collaborators"

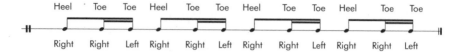

Figure 7.1 | Clogging rhythm in duple metre.

(Dueck 2007, 56). While in the past fiddlers cultivated close, often familial, relationships with collaborators that allowed them to perform unique, asymmetric versions of tunes, increased opportunities to perform with strangers has necessitated structural predictability. Since the 1990s asymmetry is surviving in new contexts, in particular becoming more common in instances of stranger sociability where older fiddlers concerned with the preservation or revival of the older style teach standardized crooked tunes to younger fiddlers (ibid., 47–8).

Altered tunings are a second commonly highlighted feature of the Metis fiddle style. While standard tuning (GDAE from lowest to highest string) is used for the majority of Metis tunes, some are played on a cross-tuned instrument (i.e., a fiddle tuned to something other than the standard). The most common alternate tunings adopted by Metis fiddlers are AEAE, AEAC#, and ADAE. These tunings are used in Quebec, where they may indicate Scottish influence (Lederman 2013, 328). The first two, known as devil's tunings, are used for "Devil's Waltz" (AEAC#) and "Devil's Reel" (AEAC# or AEAE)[35] and sometimes for the "Duck Dance" (Lederman 2010b). The third tuning is commonly referred to as Red River Jig tuning since it is often used when playing that particular tune. Lederman also mentions tunes in BEBF#, GDGD, DDAE (see "G Reel" by Lawrence Flett in Lederman 1987a), DDAD (see "D Reel" by Frank Catchaway in Lederman 2003), and EEAE. The numerous tunings noted in Lederman point to an overall flexibility that is perhaps a more notable stylistic component than specific tunings. Although the devil's tunings and the Red River Jig tuning remain common when performing the "Duck Dance," "Devil's Waltz," "Devil's Reel," and "Red River Jig," contemporary fiddlers frequently play the "Red River Jig" and "Duck Dance" in standard tuning.

Metis fiddlers traditionally performed alone with footwork as accompaniment, a technique that is most often referred to as clogging. All the older fiddlers in Lederman's study clogged when performing in a seated position. Tunes in duple time use the rhythm notated above (figure 7.1). Clogging is still frequently seen in settings where a conscious effort is being made to revitalize or revive older traditions, such as in the "traditional Metis" category at the John Arcand Fiddle Festival in Saskatchewan. It is uncommon at large Metis festivals like Metisfest, where fiddlers usually play in a standing position, although fiddlers still sometimes clog in more informal settings (e.g., on the half stage) during these same events (Giroux 2013, 113). As noted by Lederman, the adaptation of the above rhythm for tunes in compound metre is either no longer practised by contemporary Metis fiddlers or is exceedingly rare (1988, 207).

While clogging is the most often noted accompaniment to traditional Metis fiddling, there is some evidence that Metis fiddlers used to accompany each other by adding two-note chords or drones (Lederman 1986, 112). Lederman notes that this practice was obsolete in the Ebb and Flow/Camperville region of western Manitoba by the time she started her fieldwork,[36] but several examples from North Dakota are found in Vrooman's collection from 1984 (see first three tracks). By the 1940s, the addition of guitar became increasingly common (Lederman 1986, 36, 47–8); in fact, when Lederman began her research in the early 1980s, she found that many fiddlers did not want to play unless they had guitar accompaniment (1986, 21). The style of guitar accompaniment does nonetheless vary from place to place and from player to player, with particularly striking differences heard in Vrooman's collection; a number of the fiddlers are accompanied by simple strumming, whereas Dorothy Azure Page adds a strong bass line. Currently, at large events, Metis fiddlers are most often accompanied by rhythm and lead guitars, bass, and drums. Piano is also used in some contexts (e.g., the collection released by the Gabriel Dumont Institute [2002]), perhaps pointing to the influence of old-time fiddling; piano is not, however, typically the instrument of choice among contemporary Metis fiddlers.

Crooked phrases, altered tunings, clogging, and guitar accompaniment are the most commonly referenced aspects of the Metis fiddle style; yet a number of more subtle features are important in fully understanding the style. First, individual phrases, as well as entire sections, tend to use downward melodic motion; the first section of the tune tends to use the top two strings, while the second section tends to use the lower two strings (Lederman 1988, 211). Second, Metis fiddlers tend to use short bow strokes, with little slurring (ibid., 208); when playing waltzes, they often leave spaces between notes, even lifting the bow off the string (Lederman 2010b). Third, "double-stringing," a region-specific term used to denote the technique whereby a fiddler drones using an open string, is an important feature of the style (Giroux 2013, 114). Fourth, Metis fiddlers put a premium on individuality, with many having their own versions of tunes, including variations in melody, embellishment, and phrase lengths (Lederman 1988, 215–16). New approaches to learning and increased collaboration between fiddlers who are strangers has, however, led to less individualization of tunes in recent years (though it does remain important); in the process, tunes have become more stable (i.e., one version becomes *the* version) (Dueck 2005, 469–70).

Fifth, the use of a one-beat feel where each beat is more or less equally emphasized is an important aspect of the Metis style. This approach is closely tied to metric irregularity; if the single beat is the most important unit, adding or dropping beats, or changing metres is of little importance. The one-beat approach further explains the juxtaposition of irregular metres with the regularity of Metis dance, since this seeming dissonance becomes insignificant for dancers and musicians when the single beat is considered the most important rhythmic unit (Dueck 2005, 423–5). Sixth, Metis fiddling remains closely implicated with dance practices; only rarely does it exist as a practice independent from dance. This was already noted in the preceding discussion of Metisfest, which highlighted social and presentational dancing as fundamental aspects of the gathering. Quick also stressed the importance of dance in establishing the most important repertoire of the Metis style (2009, 230). Whether related to specific repertoire choices or presentational approaches, a strong connection to dance is thus an important feature of the Metis style. These six aspects of style have in some contexts replaced asymmetry, altered tunings, clogging, and guitar accompaniment as the most important elements of the Metis fiddle style.

Analyses of Three Contemporary Metis Fiddlers

The section that follows provides detailed analyses of reels performed by Garry Lepine, Shawn Mousseau, and JJ Lavallee, all well-known fiddlers in the Prairie Metis scene. The transcriptions provided are from live performances that I videotaped at Metisfest in 2012.[37] Given that all three fiddlers are from Manitoba, analyses of their style cannot highlight differences between Metis fiddlers from western Canada and those from Ontario (Chrétien 2005, 151), nor can they highlight differences among Metis fiddlers in Manitoba, the other Prairie provinces, or the north. They can, nonetheless, highlight the "high degree of individualism that characterizes the style" and the diversity of Metis fiddling even within Manitoba (ibid.). When considered alongside the above discussion of the older style of Metis fiddling, the analyses that follow highlight some of the ways in which Metis fiddling has grown and changed to suit the needs of the Metis Nation, becoming in the process a truly contemporary practice. Although these fiddlers use symmetrical phrases and standard tuning, and are accompanied by a band rather than clogging, their playing demonstrates the continued distinctiveness of contemporary Metis fiddling.

Garry Lepine, "Andy Roussin Reel"

Garry Lepine (Metis) was born in 1950 in St Lazare, Manitoba, but has lived most of his life in Portage la Prairie, Manitoba. Lepine never took formal lessons, but his father and other family members, including his mother and sisters, fiddled, placing him in a milieu that allowed him to learn on his own. As Lepine told me, he first had two little sticks that he would rub together in imitation of his father playing the fiddle. His uncle then bought him a tin fiddle from the Salvation Army. Lepine's father added a sound post and put strings on the fiddle, and then showed him how to play "Little Brown Jug" and "Rubber Dolly." By the age of nine, Lepine was playing for dances, receiving a case of Coca Cola as payment for his performances, and, at the age of seventeen, he began competing at old-time fiddle contests. Lepine has recorded five CDs,[38] one of which won him an Aboriginal Music Award, and he was included on the Gabriel Dumont Collection *Drops of Brandy*, a four-CD set featuring Indigenous fiddlers from western and northern Canada. Lepine also provided some of the music for the documentary *How the Fiddle Flows* (Coyes 2002) and can be heard on the film *The Dances of the Metis* (Prefontaine, n.d.). He was inducted into the Metis Music Hall of Fame in 2005 and the Manitoba Fiddle Wall of Fame in 2012.[39] Lepine is well known in the Metis circuit, appearing at various Metis events throughout the year, including regular appearances at Metisfest, an appearance at Batoche, and an appearance at the first annual Keplinfest in August 2012 (interview with Lepine 2012).

Lepine's rendition of "Andy Roussin Reel" (figure 7.2) has several interesting elements. Although the form is not, strictly speaking, asymmetrical, the B part has phrases that elide; that is, Lepine blurs the beginnings and endings of phrases. Lepine's playing is very much groove-based,[40] with a stronger focus on creating forward motion than on melodic content or rhythmic diversity. This is achieved through accented offbeats and a sense of propulsion toward the first beat of every measure. His time-feel (i.e., the underlying beat)

Figure 7.2 | Garry Lepine, "Andy Roussin Reel," performance at Metisfest 2012.

is consistent and continuous with sixteenth notes filling in the beats; he does not allow stopped or longer notes to break the forward motion. This aspect of the tune made it very difficult to transcribe, as the sixteenth notes tend to blur into each other. Lepine nonetheless marks the ends of sections (and sometimes the middle of sections) by using one or two strongly accented notes, longer note values, and long bows (in contrast to the short, smooth, and controlled bows that he uses most of the time) and then resetting the bow on the string at the frog (near his bow hand). This demarcates the ends of sections and creates interest within the context of maintaining continuous motion. It is clear, furthermore, that Lepine is in control of the pulse, expecting the band to follow him and using his foot to push them into his pulse. In addition to these notable rhythmic elements, Lepine uses a great deal of droning that is often difficult to distinguish from the melody, and he plays a highly individualized version of the tune. During his performance, Lepine rarely speaks to the audience, suggesting that he is not putting on a show as much as he is creating music to get people moving; and without exception, he fills the dance floor.

Metis Fiddling: Historical Roots, Contemporary Practice | 229

Figure 7.3 | Shawn Mousseau, "Buck Skin Reel," performance at Metisfest 2012.

Shawn Mousseau, "Buck Skin Reel"

Shawn Mousseau (Ojibwe) was born in 1979 on Lake Manitoba First Nation. He received his first fiddle when he was just three years old and soon after began playing with his great-grandfather, fiddler Willie Mousseau (1903–1985),[41] and grandfather, guitarist Lawrence Mousseau (1931–2004). Feeling that no one could ever replace his great-grandfather, Mousseau quit playing after Willie Mousseau passed away. He was inspired to pick up his fiddle again after hearing Cliff Maytwayashing (1939–2009), also from Lake Manitoba First Nation, play at a social. Mousseau went on to (re)teach himself to play, always trying to play tunes in the traditional way, or, in his own words, to "play them straight" in the way that he remembered hearing them. Mousseau is not a regular at old-time fiddle contests (and has only competed in a few) and is, therefore, not particularly well known in southern Manitoba's contest scene. As he told me over the phone, his great-grandfather did not want him to play at competitions, telling him that his ability to play the fiddle was a gift from the Creator and that he should not use his gift to compete against other fiddlers. Yet this has not stopped Mousseau from becoming a sought-after fiddler,[42] playing for the Asham Stompers at the Vancouver Olympics and at the XV Festival Zacatecas del Folclor Internacional in Zacatecas, Mexico. More locally, he plays for square dance competitions (usually in the context of Indigenous events such as Peguis Days) and for anniversaries, wedding socials, and festivals such as Metisfest in southwestern Manitoba and Stomperfest in Reedy Creek/Kinosota, Manitoba (interview with Mousseau 2012).

Like Lepine's "Andy Roussin Reel," Shawn Mousseau's version of "Buck Skin Reel" (figure 7.3) features strongly accented offbeats. However, Mousseau uses more detached bowings and rhythmic variety than Lepine. For example, he includes stopped notes throughout, or, alternately, allows for more space between notes. This is in part a function of how he is using his right arm, moving it from the elbow rather than from the wrist (as is the case in Lepine's playing). This playing technique allows for "clean" stops, creating a harder edge, and produces a more aggressive and "in-the-string" sound than bow movements that come primarily from the wrist (which have more of a soft bouncing quality). Throughout this performance, Mousseau uses ghosted notes (i.e., notes that are barely audible, marked in the transcription with an x), just hinting at the presence of some notes (usually the first and third notes in a group of sixteenth notes), while accenting the note that follows (usually the second and fourth notes in a group of sixteenth notes). This technique is central to the "feel" of his playing; that is, it gives the music a lilt or "lift" and creates significant forward motion. Many in the Metis fiddle community would understand this lilt as a "danceable" feel. Mousseau also uses a number of ornaments, and, interestingly, uses them consistently in the same place in each section. His playing fits well with the country/rock sound adopted by the backup musicians. This is, in part, because of his use of strong accents and a somewhat aggressive approach. Although he did not clog during this performance, he tapped his foot in a heel-toe motion similar to that used when Metis fiddlers clog.

JJ Lavallee, "Buffalo Gals"

JJ Lavallee (Metis) was born in 1980 and is from the Metis town of St Ambroise, Manitoba. He was born into a musical Metis family (which includes fiddler Darren Lavallee) whom he credits as important influences: "Those guys [his uncles] were a huge influence musically for me. It's something you can't, never goes away, and watching these guys growing up, when I was a little

Figure 7.4 | JJ Lavallee, "Buffalo Gals," performance at Metisfest 2012.

kid, it just stuck with me, and I said I want to do that! Mom, I want to do that! It's been there ever since" (interview on local radio station The Mix). Lavallee is a composer (perhaps best known for his fiddle tune "Metchif Reel"), songwriter, and singer, and plays a variety of instruments including fiddle, guitar, mandolin, bass, and drums. His first CD, *Jimmy's Breakdown* (named for his grandfather), won an Aboriginal People's Choice Music Award for best fiddle album. He has since released a country album titled *Carry On*, and a second instrumental CD titled *A Fiddle Bit of This and a Fiddle Bit of That* (2010). He has opened for well-known country stars including Johnny Reid, Charlie Major, Jesse Ferrell, and Shane Yellowbird. Lavallee is well known in the Metis fiddle scene and is a regular entertainer at Prairie Metis events. He has also built relationships with Metis in Ontario and British Columbia (where he now lives) through performances and workshops. He is not, however, well known in the old-time fiddle contest scene.

One of the most striking aspects of JJ Lavallee's playing is his use of "filler" notes – what one of the Metisfest main stage band members referred to as adding the "jiggy jiggy" (i.e., adding underlying, constant, sixteenth notes). It is so strong in Lavallee's playing that, in some cases, the jiggy jiggy drowns out the melodic line. The B part of "Buffalo Gals" (figure 7.4) provides an interesting starting point to understand this technique. In this section, Lavallee includes many detached eighth notes without the addition of filler sixteenth notes. In contrast, Lavallee adds the jiggy jiggy when he plays the A part (especially the second time through),[43] a contrast that highlights the effect of this technique; the use of continuous sixteenth notes creates constant motion and thus a sense of momentum.[44] The effectiveness of this technique is augmented by the frequent use of ghosted notes followed by accented offbeats, creating a feel of anticipation for the next downbeat. Lavallee's playing is also very percussive (in other words, the bow attacks the string in a percussive manner), more so than the other fiddlers analyzed here. Given that the melody is often buried in the jiggy jiggy, and that drone notes are often played as loudly as the melody, this percussive element of his playing is especially notable. The ends of phrases tend to have the clearest melody since he detaches the notes. All these techniques are clearly heard, in part, because this performance was on the half stage, where there was less ambient noise and no overpowering backup band. Since it was an impromptu performance, Lavallee asked a young child to accompany him (and his drum machine) with wooden spoons, creating the feel of a house party.

Bringing the Old into the New

The above section outlined some of the key aspects of the Metis style, and provided analyses of tunes played by fiddlers who are popular in the Metis fiddle scene. These analyses point to the importance of accented offbeats, ghosted notes, forward motion, continuous motion (through the addition of filler notes), and droning; more generally, they point to an emphasis on rhythmic motion that downplays the melody. The analyses also demonstrate a significant shift in typical accompaniment, likely a result of new (larger) venues and the influence of popular musics. However, these analyses are snapshots of the style that reflect a particular time and place. Whereas in the past many of the more distinctive aspects of the style were downplayed, resulting in the emergence of the Red River style, some Metis fiddlers are now reclaiming and reviving older styles. Quick notes, for example, that John Arcand has worked hard to ensure that the old style is preserved; at the same time, Arcand uses old Metis tunes as models for new compositions, writing tunes with crooked phrases and non-standard tunings (Quick 2010, 125). In this way, the old style is brought into a modern context. Alternately, tunes from other traditions are being integrated into the Metis style in interesting ways. For example, the "Orange Blossom Special" – a tune by Ervin Thomas Rouse that was popularized by Bill Monroe among others – is now often used when jiggers dance the "Red River Jig."[45] At Back to Batoche days, Cajun music is influential as well (Quick 2009, 241), while in the north, country tunes are often turned into instrumental tunes, which can be considered "a signature of contemporary northern practice" (Lederman 2010a, 144). These are just some of the ways that Metis fiddling has changed in recent years, reflecting the needs and priorities of the Metis Nation.

Conclusion

This chapter provides an overview of Metis (style) fiddling. Although it remains connected to the past, Metis fiddling also reflects the needs and enduring vitality of contemporary Metis communities. Stylistic features associated with the "old style," such as asymmetric phrases, altered tunings, and clogging, remain important in contexts of revival and are of particular interest to scholars; yet accented offbeats, ghosted notes, forward motion, continuous motion (through the addition of filler notes), and droning are more widely adopted by the younger generation. In educational venues, as well as at Metis festivals, creating a strong sense of community is a central priority; this sense of community is fostered in part through an intimate connection among fiddling, participatory dance, and jamming, as well as by creating bonds between far flung communities and between generations. Ultimately, what "counts" as Metis fiddling is diverse and dependent on the context and the audience. As the number of young Indigenous fiddlers grows and as cultural events like Metisfest continue to shape the style, the meanings that Metis fiddling has for Metis communities will continue to shift. It is these factors that make Metis fiddling a socially and stylistically complex category, challenging notions that it is vanishing, (only) historical, or that it needs to be saved by white fiddlers and scholars. As the contemporary examples included in this chapter indicate, Metis fiddling, as an emergent and community-based practice, is a thriving, vibrant tradition.

Notes

1 The use of the term "Metis fiddling" is somewhat contentious because, as outlined in this chapter, the tradition is shared by Metis, First Nations, Inuit, and sometimes settler peoples. One scholar who has studied Metis fiddling concludes, for example, that a term such as "Aboriginal fiddling" would be more appropriate (personal communication 2015). While I do not wish to dismiss this critique, I adopt the term "Metis fiddling" because it is commonly used and recognized in Canada, and more importantly because it is the term used by Metis people. Furthermore, this style and repertoire of fiddling is generally considered a *Metis* practice even though First Nations and Inuit fiddlers are vital contributors to the Metis fiddle scene. I place "style" in brackets as a way to recognize that for some fiddlers who are part of the Metis fiddle scene, style is less important than the community connections built through fiddling; that is, it is these community connections (and not particular stylistic features) that make Metis fiddling Metis. However, when referring specifically to stylistic features, I use the term without brackets.

2 I use the term "settler" to refer to all settler-colonizers who immigrated to Turtle Island (what is now known as North America). I use the term "mainstream" or "unmarked" when referring to people or groups whose ethnicity is normalized (i.e., seen as non-ethnic), or spaces that are positioned as non-ethnic. Although both terms are homogenizing, so too is the term "Indigenous" (frequently used in this chapter). These distinctions between settler/Indigenous and mainstream/other are not, however, intended to indicate sameness within each category but rather to highlight a relationship that clearly exists between Indigenous peoples and those who colonized the continent, as well as between white settlers and racialized people in Canada. These distinctions are particularly relevant to discussions of fiddling in the Prairies given that, for many, old-time fiddling is understood as "regular" fiddling to which other traditions – including Metis fiddling – are marked as ethnic (see Giroux 2018). (For further discussion of race and whiteness see Hage 2000, Mackey 2002, and Thobani 2007.) As a settler scholar who has worked with Metis fiddlers for many years, I am keenly aware of this relationship and the privilege that I have as a white settler who is seen as ethnically unmarked, and who has benefited greatly from continued access to Indigenous lands.

3 Cross tuning refers to tuning a fiddle's strings to pitches other than GDAE. Clogging refers to foot accompaniments, usually done by the fiddler as s/he plays. The pattern used is described in more detail in the final section of this paper.

4 Except when quoting authors who use the accent, I adopt the term "Metis" without the acute accent as a way to counter an overemphasis on French ancestry (see Macdougall 2010, 260). For an opposing point of view, see Andersen (2014, 211).

5 Dueck's scholarship on Indigenous fiddling (2013, 2007, 2006, 2005), as well as Quick's work on Metis fiddling (2010, 2009), implicitly challenges this notion, demonstrating the continued vitality of fiddling in Indigenous communities.

6 The difference between music revivals and resurgence has yet to be explored in detail. However, Quick uses the concept of revival in her dissertation on Metis fiddling in Alberta, addressing in particular the moments (e.g., particular performances [2009, 162–3]) when revival is or was valorized (2009, 134; also see 172–6; 198–9; 311; 314–19). This can be compared with my own use of the concept of resurgence, which highlights

the role of fiddling in reconnecting and rebuilding the Metis Nation (Giroux 2016), and Dueck's discussion of asymmetrical tunes and the work of some fiddlers to preserve the old style (2007, 48).

7 While I choose to use the term "Indigenous" because of its global resonance, I also adopt terms such as Aboriginal and Native as used by the authors that I cite. Doing so acknowledges the complexity of naming practices and the problematic nature of umbrella and outsider-imposed terms.

8 A recording of Frederick Genthon from 1940 is the earliest available recorded example of this style (see Johnson 2012, 91). Historian and folklorist Henri Létourneau made a recording of fiddler Frank Poitras from Belcourt, North Dakota in 1974 that demonstrated similar stylistic features (available in the Henri Létourneau fonds at the Centre du patrimoine in St Boniface and online). These recordings can be compared to those made by Lederman (2003, 1987) and Vrooman (1992, 1984).

9 There is no indication that Dejarlis actively tried to hide his Metis identity. In fact, he was known to donate money to the local Friendship Centre (see Watson 2002, 48). However, when writing about his various performances, mainstream newspapers did not, during his lifetime, represent him as Metis (Giroux 2013, 83–4). This recognition has, to my knowledge, only come posthumously.

10 For further information on Gilbert Anderson, see Rod Olstad's *The Northern Alberta Fiddle Project*, 1994–97, which explores the history of fiddling in Alberta. http://streaming.tapor.ualberta.ca/vmctm/en/html/narratives.php?id=10&sec=13.

11 Native Pride Days is a particularly good example. Held in Selkirk, Manitoba, it included a "Great Peoples' Pow-Wow" and a "Red River Hoedown" ("Native Pride Days Ad" 1982, 15).

12 The Lake Nipigon Metis Association was founded in 1965. The Manitoba Metis Federation was founded in 1967, the same year that the Saskatchewan Metis Society amalgamated with the newly formed Metis Association of Saskatchewan (Quick 2009, 161; Weinstein 2007, 30).

13 Although some continue to refer to the battles between the Metis Nation and Canada in the 1800s as rebellions, the term "resistance" is more accurate given that the Metis were resisting unilateral takeover of their land base.

14 In my own work in Manitoba, I found that this shift started to happen in the 1960s and exploded by the 1980s as an increasing number of mainstream newspapers began describing fiddling as a traditional Indigenous practice (Giroux 2013, 84). Nonetheless, it was the scholarship noted above that truly delineated the difference between Metis and old-time fiddling in the Prairies.

15 See Quick (2009, 176) and Giroux (2013, 112, 117) for examples of this overlap in the context of Metis fiddling and dancing.

16 Differences are also notable in Metis dance. Metisfest allows dancers to use metal taps on their shoes (an innovation), whereas John Arcand's competition does not. Similarly, square dance troupes from Alberta typically use a caller (a tradition that harkens back to informal square dancing) whereas groups from Saskatchewan, Manitoba, and North Dakota do not (Quick 2009, 220).

17 The recordings by non-Metis people that Chrétien uses as examples are *Old Native and Metis Fiddling in Manitoba* (Lederman 1987), and *Metis Old Time Dance Tunes* (Vollrath 1995). More recent examples include Sierra Noble's *Spirit of the Strings* (2005), Vollrath's *Métis Style Fiddle* (2005), and Anne Lederman's *Old Man's Table: Tunes from Grandy Fagnan* (2015). Although few in number, these albums have played a substantial role in constructing mainstream understandings of Metis fiddling.

18 Sherridon, Manitoba, is a very small community and thus has only one school, Cold Lake School, serving kindergarten to grade eight.

19 Klippenstein has written a series of children's stories including the popular *Andrea's Fiddle* (2008), the story of a young girl who receives a fiddle from her grandfather.

20 See http://www.mooselakeschool.com/fiddle-jamboree---2014.html (accessed 5 November 2014).

21 See Dueck 2007 for a description and analysis of a concert in Winnipeg.

22 The term "circuit" is commonly used among old-time fiddlers (e.g., see Johnson 2006, 179).

23 I discuss Metisfest in the present tense as a way to highlight the contemporary vitality of Metis cultural gatherings. Although this particular event was cancelled, it should not be seen as an indication that Metis cultural events are dying. In fact, Ryan Keplin's Summer Fest just across the international border from Killarney is growing every year.

24 Although found within the boundaries of North Dakota, Turtle Mountain Chippewa Reservation maintains its distinctness from the state, perhaps most visibly apparent in the unique Turtle Mountain license plates issued to community members. The reservation is particularly important to Metis people because the Chippewa people gave refuge to Metis people displaced after the 1869–70 Resistance. Many descendants of the Metis people who were given refuge still live on the reservation. Members of this community – identifying themselves as such – played a notable role at Metisfest.

25 The name of this stage is a humorous comment on how some Metis people pronounce "other."

26 See Giroux (2013, 105–22) for a more detailed account.

27 I searched "Garry Lepine" using Google on 11 September 2012 and the first result to come up was a video of Lepine playing for the Four Nations dancers at International Metisfest 2011. Although Lepine is still hard to contact since he does not have a website, his performances at Metisfest have given him a significant online presence, and his name and samples of his music are now more broadly accessible to everyone who searches the internet for information on Metis fiddlers.

28 This of course does present somewhat of a contradiction: if a goal of Metisfest is to promote Metis artists, why are First Nations artists included in the line-up? As I have noted elsewhere, events such as Metisfest do not enforce strict divisions between Metis, First Nations, or sometimes even settler peoples because there is considerable cultural overlap between groups, at least on the Prairies, making strict divisions somewhat artificial (Giroux 2013, 136–7).

29 Of course, style was certainly regulated in more subtle ways at Metisfest, such as by the response of the crowd to a particular fiddler or way of playing.

30 As Quick points out, John Arcand's Fiddle Fest puts a "spotlight" on "the traditional features" of Metis fiddling through a traditional Metis category (2009, 242, 250).

31 Resurgence can perhaps be best understood as "a flourishment of the Indigenous inside" (Simpson 2011, 17). In this way, resurgence connects Indigenous peoples with Indigenous ways of being in the world, with their homelands, with cultural memories and cultural practices, and with each other as individuals, families, clans, communities, and nations (Alfred 2005, 36, 256; Alfred and Corntassel 2005, 612; Simpson 2011, 67, 144; and Barker 2015, 153). Resurgence furthermore transcends the colonial state. As Taiaiake Alfred poignantly notes, while his generation was grounded in ideas of changing and restructuring settler society, the younger (resurgent) generation of Indigenous scholars has "a stronger vision of liberation ... they recognize the futility of 'revolution' and turn inward to focus on the resurgence of an authentic Indigenous existence and the recapturing of physical, political, and psychic spaces of freedom for [Indigenous] people" (2008, 11).

32 Compare the sense of community created at old-time contests as described in Johnson (2006, 2–4, 134–76).

33 However, as Christina Smith found, asymmetry of phrases was at one time quite common in Newfoundland fiddling with as many as 68 percent of Newfoundland tunes (depending on period and region) following irregular phrase structures (2007).

34 Lederman estimates that 90 percent of Scots-Irish, Anglo-Canadian, and New England tunes are in the so-called standard form (i.e., 32-bar, AABB form), whereas just one-fifth of the nearly four hundred tunes she recorded in six Metis and First Nations communities in Manitoba (Pine Creek and Ebb and Flow Ojibwe First Nations, and the adjacent communities of Bacon Ridge, Eddystone, Camperville, and Kinosota) were in standard form.

35 In Quebec, "Devil's Reel" is known as "Hangman's Reel."

36 Lederman's recordings include a track with a second fiddle playing the melody an octave below the first fiddle, and a track with second fiddle playing a harmony line (see "Lady Do-Si-Do" and "Homecoming Waltz" performed by Albert Beaulieu, Lawrence Flett, and Lawrence Houle [Lederman 1987a]). These examples, however, are different from the droning or two-note chords she refers to as obsolete in the area.

37 Thank you to Michael Carter for his help with these transcriptions. Although they were completed with as much detail and accuracy as possible (and any mistakes are my own), it was frequently difficult to hear each note played. In some cases (especially in Lepine's performance), the pitches are approximations. Furthermore, despite having video footage, bowings were difficult to see (with the exception of Lavallee's performance); the included bowings nonetheless give a general sense of the bowing patterns and frequency of slurs.

38 The titles of the recordings are *Whiskey before Breakfast* (his first album, recorded in the 1970s), *Metis Hour*, *Drops of Brandy*, *Dancing Fingers*, and *Metis Trails*. Lepine does not remember when he recorded these albums (phone conversation 1 December 2013).

39 The Manitoba Fiddle Association started the Wall of Fame, located in Carman, Manitoba, in 2006. I have not been able to uncover any information about the Metis Music Hall of Fame.

40 I use this term somewhat differently from Charles Keil who focuses on the interaction between musicians in a performance (and hence "participatory discrepancies") (2010). My use of this term is intended to emphasize the sense of forward motion created by

Lepine and the indescribable "feel" that pulls dancers in the fiddle community to their feet and to the dance floor as Lepine plays.

41 Willie Mousseau can be heard on Anne Lederman's collection of field recordings from the mid-1980s (2003, 1986).
42 This points to the fact that there is a strong, First Nations/Metis scene that functions independently from the old-time contest scene where many fiddlers get their "big break."
43 In the transcribed version of the tune included in this chapter, the B part is transcribed as heard the first time through, while the A part is transcribed as heard the second time through.
44 This tune varies a great deal between fiddlers. I have, in fact, heard some fiddlers play more sixteenth notes in the B part than in the A part. This indicates that Lavallee is making a conscious choice to create this contrast; it is not simply part of the structure of the tune (i.e., how it is "supposed to" be played). Although it is somewhat common to add *some* jiggy jiggy to this tune, I have never heard anyone use this technique (on this tune) to the extent heard in Lavallee's performance (especially the second time through the A part). An interesting comparison is a performance of the same tune by Metis fiddler Ivan Spence (son of Emile Spence, a fiddler included in Lederman's fiddle collection), available on YouTube (https://youtu.be/2bLUq5S3V2c) (accessed 10 January 2013).
45 Quick states that this practice was started by Edmonton Metis Cultural Dance Society instructor Brent Potskin (2008, 95). Lederman notes that the "Orange Blossom Special" is commonly used when dancing the Red River Jig on Manitoulin Island (2010b). This practice is also popular in Manitoba (Giroux 2013, 68, 117).

References

Alfred, Taiaiake. 2005. *Wasáse: Indigenous Pathways of Action and Freedom*. Peterborough, ON: Broadview Press.

— 2008. "Opening Words." *Lighting the Eighth Fire: The Liberation, Resurgence, and Protection of Indigenous Nations*, ed. Leanne Simpson. Winnipeg, MB: Arbeiter Ring Publishing.

Alfred, Taiaiake, and Jeff Corntassel. 2005. "Being Indigenous: Resurgences against Contemporary Colonialism." *Government and Opposition* 40 (4): 597–614.

Anderson, Chris. 2014. *Métis: Race, Recognition, and the Struggle for Indigenous Peoplehood*. Vancouver: University of British Columbia Press.

Barker, Adam J. 2015. "'A Direct Act of Resurgence, a Direct Act of Sovereignty': Reflections on Idle No More, Indigenous Activism, and Canadian Settler Colonialism." *Globalizations* 12 (1): 43–65.

Bassett, Harvey. 1941. "Christmas in the Fur Trade." *The Beaver*, outfit 272 (December): 18–22.

Chrétien, Annette. 2005. "'Fresh Tracks in Dead Air': Mediating Contemporary Metis Identities through Music and Storytelling." PhD diss., York University.

Coyes, Gregory, dir. 2002. *How the Fiddle Flows*, produced by Leigh Badgley, Ava Karvonen, Bonnie Thompson, and Jerry Krepakevich. National Film Board of Canada.

Dueck, Byron. 2005. "Festival of Nations: First Nations and Metis Music and Dance in Public Performance." PhD diss., University of Chicago.

- 2006. "'Suddenly a Sense of Being a Community': Aboriginal Square Dancing and the Experience of Collectivity." *Musiké* 1 (1): 41–58.
- 2007. "Public and Intimate Sociability in First Nations and Métis Fiddling." *Ethnomusicology* 51 (1): 30–63.
- 2013. "Public and Intimate Sociability in First Nations and Métis Fiddling." In *Musical Intimacies and Indigenous Imaginaries: Aboriginal Music and Dance in Public Performance*, 34–60. New York, NY: Oxford University Press.

Ellestad, Laura, and Monique Giroux. 2016. "Métis-Norwegian Musical Exchange in the Borderlands." Presentation at the Society for Ethnomusicology Annual Conference, Washington, DC.

Gabriel Dumont Institute. 2002. *Drops of Brandy: An Anthology of Métis Music*. Saskatoon, SK: Gabriel Dumont Institute.

Gibbons, Roy. 1980. "La Grande Gigue Simple and the Red River Jig: A Comparative Study of Two Regional Styles of a Traditional Fiddle Tune." *Canadian Folk Music Journal* 8: 40–8.
- 1981. "Folk Fiddling in Canada: A Sampling." Canadian Centre for Folk Culture Studies. Paper No. 35. Ottawa: National Museums of Canada.

Giroux, Monique. 2013. "Music, Power, and Relations: Fiddling as a Meeting Place between Re-settlers and Indigenous Nations in Manitoba." PhD diss., York University.
- 2016. "'Giving Them Back Their Spirit': Multiculturalism and Resurgence at a Metis Cultural Festival." *MUSICultures* 43 (1): 64–88.
- 2018. "Silencing the Other Within: Metis Music at Manitoba's Old-Time Fiddle Competitions." *Ethnomusicology* 62 (2): 265–90.

Gluska, Virginia. 2011. "Fiddling with a Culturally Responsive Curriculum." Master's thesis, University of Ottawa.

Goodon, Dan. 2012. Phone interview by Monique Giroux, 30 August. Recording in personal collection.

Hage, Ghassan. 2000. *White Nation: Fantasies of White Supremacy in a Multicultural Society*. New York, NY: Routledge.

Handscomb, C.W. 1906. "Grand Opera Festival Brilliantly Opened with Lohengrin – La Boheme This Afternoon and Rigoletto To-Night." *Manitoba Free Press*, 6 March 1906.

Johnson, Sherry. 2006. "Negotiating Tradition in Ontario Fiddle Contests." PhD diss., York University.

Keil, Charles. 2010. "Defining 'Groove.'" *PopScriptum* 11. http://www2.hu-berlin.de/fpm/popscrip/themen/pst11/pst11_keil02.html (accessed 1 March 2019).

Klippenstein, Blaine, with illustrations by Christie Jedele. 2008. *Andrea's Fiddle*. Winnipeg, MB: Loon Books Publishing.

Lawrence, Bonita. 2004. *"Real" Indians and Others: Mixed-Blood Urban Native Peoples and Indigenous Nationhood*. Vancouver: University of British Columbia Press.

Lederman, Anne. 1986. "Old Native and Metis Fiddling in Two Manitoba Communities: Camperville and Ebb and Flow." Master's thesis, York University.
- 1988. "Old Indian and Métis Fiddling in Manitoba: Origins, Structure and Question of Syncretism." *The Canadian Journal of Native Studies* 8 (2): 205–30.
- 2009. "Métis Fiddling: Found or Lost?" *Histoires et identités: homage à Gabriel Dumont/Métis Histories and Identities: A Tribute to Gabriel Dumont*, edited by Denis

Gagnon, Denis Combet, and Lise Gaboury-Diallo. Winnipeg, MB: Presse universitaires de Saint-Boniface.

— 2010a. "Aboriginal Fiddling in the North: The Two Traditions." In *Fiddle and Dance Studies from around the North Atlantic*, edited by Ian Russell and Anna Guigné, 3: 130–47. Aberdeen, Scotland: Elphinstone Institute.

— 2010b. "Fiddling." *Encyclopedia of Music in Canada*, 2nd ed., edited by Helmut Kallman, Gilles Potvin, and Kenneth Winters, 455–7. Toronto: University of Toronto Press.

— 2013. "Aboriginal Fiddling: The Scottish Connection." In *Irish and Scottish Encounters with Indigenous Peoples*, edited by Graeme Morton and David A. Wilson, 223–41. Montreal & Kingston: McGill-Queen's University Press.

Lederman, Anne, Claire White, James Alexander, and Cameron Baggins. 2012. "Passing the Bow: Teaching Fiddle Traditions in the 21st Century." In *Fiddle and Dance Studies from around the North Atlantic*, edited by Ian Russell and Anna Guigné, 4: 199–213. Aberdeen, Scotland: Elphinstone Institute.

Lepine, Garry. 2012. Interview by Monique Giroux, 28 August. No recording.

Macdougall, Brenda. 2010. *One of the Family: Metis Culture in Nineteenth-Century Northwestern Saskatchewan*. Vancouver: University of British Columbia Press.

Mackey, Eva. 2002. *The House of Difference: Cultural Politics and National Identity in Canada*. Toronto, ON: University of Toronto Press.

Mackintosh, Joe. 2010. *Andy Dejarlis: The Life and Music of an Old-Time Fiddler*. Winnipeg, MB: Great Plains Publications.

Mishler, Craig. 1993. *The Crooked Stovepipe: Athapaskan Fiddle Music and Square Dancing in Northeast Alaska and Northwest Canada*. Urbana: University of Illinois Press.

— recorder and ed. 1974. *Music of the Alaskan Kutchin Indians*. Featuring Charlie Peter. Folkways Records FE 4070. LP.

Mousseau, Shawn. 2012. Phone interview by Monique Giroux, 5 September. No recording.

"Native Pride Days Advertisement." 1982. *Brandon Sun*, 16 June.

Olstad, Rod. N.d. "The Northern Alberta Fiddle Project." *Virtual Museum of Canadian Traditional Music*. http://streaming.tapor.ualberta.ca/vmctm/en/html/narratives.php?id=6&sec=1 (accessed 1 March 2019).

Prefontaine, Darren R., dir. n.d. *The Dances of the Metis/Li Dawns di Michif*. Saskatoon, SK: Gabriel Dumont Institute. Videocassette.

Quick, Sarah. 2009. "Performing Heritage: Métis Music, Dance, and Identity in a Multicultural State." PhD diss., Indiana University.

— 2010. "Two Models of Métis Fiddling: John Arcand and Andy Dejarlis." *Crossing Over: Fiddle and Dance Studies from around the North Atlantic*, edited by Ian Russell and Anna Kearney Guigné, 3: 114–29. Aberdeen, Scotland: Elphinstone Institute.

Rodgers, Bob. 1980. *The Fiddlers of James Bay*. Produced by Bob Rodgers, Mark Zannis, and Gail Singer, and directed by Bob Rodgers. National Film Board of Canada. VHS.

Simpson, Leanne. 2011. *Dancing on Our Turtle's Back: Stories of Nishnaabeg Re-creation, Resurgence and a New Emergence*. Winnipeg, MB: Arbeiter Ring Publishing.

Smith, Christina. 2007. "'Crooked as the Road to Branch': Asymmetry in Newfoundland Dance Music." *Newfoundland and Labrador Studies: Music Issue* 22 (1): 139–64.
Thobani, Sunera. 2007. *Exalted Subjects: Studies in the Making of Race and Nation in Canada*. Toronto, ON: University of Toronto Press.
Turino, Thomas. 2008. *Music as Social Life: The Politics of Participation*. Chicago, IL: University of Chicago Press.
Villeneuve, Joanne. 2006. "Culture of 'Métisville' Adds Spice to Boissevain's Homegrown Reunion." *Brandon Sun*, 23 July.
Watson, Franceene. 2002. *Andy De Jarlis: Master of Métis Melodies*. Victoria: Self-published.
Weinstein, John. 2007. *Quiet Revolution West: The Rebirth of Métis Nationalism*. Calgary, AB: Fifth House.
Whidden, Lynn. 2007. *Essential Song: Three Decades of Northern Cree Music*. Waterloo, ON: Wilfred Laurier University Press.

Discography

Bedard, Mel. 1984. *Metis Fiddler*. Winnipeg, MB: Sunshine SSCD 421. CD.
Gabriel Dumont Institute. 2002. *Drops of Brandy: An Anthology of Métis Music*. Saskatoon, SK: Gabriel Dumont Institute GDI001-GDI002. CD.
Lavallee, JJ. 2006. *Jimmy's Breakdown*. Independent recording, sponsored by the Asham Stompers, produced by Tom Dutiaume. Recorded at the Metis Club of Winnipeg PLCD2006. CD.
– 2007. *Carry On*. Independent recording, produced by JJ Lavallee and Tom Dutiaume, Hangar Recording Studios 835. CD.
– 2010. *A Fiddle Bit of This and a Fiddle Bit of That*. Independent recording, produced by JJ Lavallee and Tom Dutiaume. Hangar Recording Studio 1210. CD.
Lederman, Anne. 1987a. Liner Notes from *Old Native and Metis Fiddling in Manitoba*. Vol. 1, *Ebb and Flow, Bacon Ridge, Eddystone and Kinosota*. Falcon Productions FPC-187. LP.
– 1987b. Liner Notes from *Old Native and Metis Fiddling in Manitoba*. Vol. 2, *Camperville and Pine Creek*. Falcon Productions FPC-287. LP.
– 2003. *Les violoneux autochtones et Métis de l'ouest du Manitoba/Old Native and Métis Fiddling in Western Manitoba*. Toronto, ON: Falcon Productions FPCD 387. CD.
– 2015. *Old Man's Table: Tunes from Grandy Fagnan*. Toronto, ON: Falcon Productions FP515. CD.
Noble, Sierra. 2005. *Spirit of the Strings*. Winnipeg, MB: Arbor Records 12312. CD.
Vollrath, Calvin. 1995. *Metis Old Time Dance Tunes*. Edmonton, AB: Triple J Records CV294. Cassette tape.
– 2005. *Métis Style Fiddle*. St Paul, AB: Astromonical Studio CVCD205. CD.
Vrooman, Nicholas, compiler/editor. 1984. *Turtle Mountain Music*. Folkways Records FES 4140. LP.
– 1992. *Plains Chippewa/Metis Music from Turtle Mountain*. Smithsonian Folkways SFW40411. CD.

Colin P. McGuire

Chapter 8

War Drums in Chinatown: Chinese Canadian Lion Dance Percussion as Martial Art

Prelude

Hong Luck Kung Fu Club. "Chinese Lion Dance @ Wedding in Toronto, Ontario, Canada." YouTube video, 4:31. Posted 25 November 2016. http://youtu.be/wAKfjYocBvk[1]

On a Saturday night in Toronto in the summer of 2015, a Chinese Canadian wedding celebration is about to begin in a packed banquet hall. Suddenly, the double doors are thrown wide open and guests turn toward the sound of loud percussion rhythms coming from outside. At the entrance stand a pair of large, multi-coloured, furry "lions"; hidden under each of them are two dancers who bring their Cantonese puppet-costumes to life. The open space of the banquet hall reverberates with the sound of drum, gong, and cymbals as the percussionists enter the room following the lions, filling the hall with a clangour. The taut ping of the drum skin being struck and the simultaneous booming resonance of the drum's wooden body are clear, as are the sharp clicks of the drumsticks playing accents on the rim of the drum. The cymbals sound sustained high frequencies, seeming to fill the gaps in the other two instruments' rhythms. The gong's frequencies are slightly lower than those of the cymbals, but still much higher than the drum. Frequent mutes by the gong player prevent the sound from ringing freely and also provide a staccato contrast to the sustained resonance of the cymbals. As the troupe makes its way to the centre of the room, the energy of the expectant crowd continues to rise.

The two lions begin to dance facing the newlyweds. Their movements are mostly in sync with each other and the percussion rhythms, making it clear that this is a choreographed routine. As they perform, the dancers strive to maintain the illusion of "living" lions by keeping their human faces hidden. While this makes for a more convincing performance, it also makes it difficult for them to see their surroundings during most of the routine. Rather than peering out from under the head, the lion dancers are relying on their ears, guided by sonic cues and rhythm patterns from the drummer. The ability to follow the drumbeats is essential for synchronizing two or more lions. Upon finishing their routine, the lions appear tired and groggily lie down on the floor for a quick "nap," eliciting chuckles from the crowd. Once they wake up, it is time for the highlight of the performance: the bride and groom "feed" one of the lions a head of lettuce that is tied to a string and dangled from a bamboo pole.

Chinese Canadian Lion Dancing

Southern-style *lion dance* (舞獅)[2] is a common sight in Chinese communities across Canada for festive occasions such as weddings, Chinese New Year, and store openings. Two performers animate a large, puppet-like mask with an attached cloth body, and are accompanied by a percussion ensemble consisting of a drum, a gong, and cymbals. The lion dance is traditionally believed to disperse negative energy through the fearsome countenance of the mask, the martial vigour of the movement, and the sonic intensity of the percussion instruments, thus making room for good fortune to flourish. In contemporary times, it is also a form of entertainment and a symbol of identity. In this chapter, I focus on the connection between lion dancing and Chinese martial arts, and I position both these practices within the history of Chinese experience in Canada. More specifically, I contend that the lion dance and percussion performed by diasporic kung fu clubs are in fact martial arts themselves, and that they bear the imprint of Chinese struggles for acceptance in North America.[3]

My research is based on eight years of ethnographic fieldwork at Toronto's Hong Luck Kung Fu Club (康樂武館), which is housed in a three-storey building at 548 Dundas Street West in the Spadina Chinatown.[4] With over two decades of background in various martial arts and some ability to speak Cantonese, I approached the club in the fall of 2008 about doing research on their percussion for my doctoral dissertation (McGuire 2014).[5] The teacher I spoke with was amenable to my fieldwork plans. He explained that the best way to understand their drumming would be by learning to drum myself and that in order to do so, I would need to follow the club's curriculum, starting with basic kung fu training (i.e., footwork, strikes, and defences). I was able to advance quickly, and after three months I received permission to join the lion dance class. There I discovered that Hong Luck's drumming is what Timothy Rice (2003) calls *learned but not taught*, meaning that students absorb the rhythms through lion dancing and must then translate that knowledge onto the drum. Seniors and elders may give pointers, but prospective drummers are largely self-directed in this endeavour.

Hong Luck members guided me toward using apprenticeship as a research method, which can be essential in ethnographic studies of bodily arts (Downey, Dalidowicz, and Mason 2014). Because of my martial arts and language background, I was eventually included in the full range of the club's activities. Nevertheless, my ongoing acculturation required extensive and generous collaboration on the part of my fieldwork consultants since I am of European Canadian heritage. Hong Luck members used their established transmission process in order to teach me, correct my mistakes, and gradually condition me to make culturally appropriate contributions to Chinatown society through performance. Although I began to do low-profile lion dancing within the first year, it was about five years before I was able to play the drum in regular public performances. During this time, I continued to participate in, and observe most of, Hong Luck's other practices. This means I not only attended classes, but also regularly lion danced, played the supporting instruments, and demonstrated kung fu. By the end of 2013, I had improved sufficiently that I was asked to help instruct kung fu classes. Around the same time, at the club's bi-annual election, a combination of elders and seniors nominated me to the position of a lion dance and percussion teacher. During this extended period of fieldwork, relatively little was said about drumming, and the few formal interviews I conducted proved ineffective at eliciting further information about the practice. The gradual, accretive, and non-linear progression of apprenticeship, however, was a fruitful way of getting at embodied meanings that were incompletely verbalized. I cannot claim mastery, but my emergent skills as a performer and the lion's-eye-view subject position I earned as a social agent in Chinatown have given me insight into the complex topic of this chapter.

I engage with kung fu, lion dance, and percussion as a single, integrated genre. The inherent interdisciplinarity of these practices stems from the way they are taught, learned, practised, and performed. Students typically begin with martial arts training before they are allowed to proceed to lion dancing, and only after having established their abilities in the first two areas do they begin to learn drumming. In researching and thinking about these practices holistically, I draw on Clifford Geertz's (1983) idea of *blurred genres*, which originally referred to academic work that crossed disciplinary boundaries.[6] As a blurred genre, kung fu – including lion dance and percussion – can include music, sport, fitness, dance, and performance, as well as spirituality, self-cultivation, and meditation. This blurring of genres gives a distinctively martial character to the drum rhythms and lion dancing.[7] For example, I was instructed to perform lion movements using kung fu stances and stepping, to grip the drumsticks like a pair of swords, and to beat the drum as though striking in combat.

In this chapter, I provide overview histories of kung fu, lion dance, and Chinese experiences in Canada in order to contextualize contemporary lion dance performances in the Greater Toronto Area. Although I generally proceed from the past to the present, the diversity of practices and peoples under consideration precludes a linear chronology. I have also found it important to sometimes write in a performative way that parallels how I was taught (cf. Wong 2008). By recursively adding information, interpretation, and ideas as I return to topics that were not exhaustively treated, I aim to help the reader grasp a multifaceted phenomenon where understanding one aspect is a prerequisite for understanding another, but not all aspects can be pursued simultaneously. I begin with a brief introduction to the Hong Luck Kung Fu Club and their local Chinatown. Next, I discuss the origins of kung fu, lion dance, and their percussion in China; whereas Chinese martial arts are neither unified nor standardized, I also clarify some of the specifics of Hong Luck's style. Then, I provide more details on Chinese Canadian history and the Chinatown system. Finally, I proceed with a case study of the Hong Luck Kung Fu Club's lion dancing that outlines not only performance practice but also embodied and sonic meanings. While I recognize that my long-term fieldwork at Hong Luck has predisposed my findings toward the martial, this bias reflects the concerns, beliefs, and discourses of my research consultants.

Introduction to Kung Fu in a Canadian Chinatown

Hong Luck was founded in 1961 to meet the acute need of Chinese Canadians in Toronto at that time for self-defence against racist aggression, as well as to pass on the traditions that the founders had learned in China to a new generation and to promote general physical fitness. Shortly thereafter, and somewhat paradoxically, Hong Luck's mandate expanded to include using kung fu as a means to connect with non-Chinese peoples in Canada for greater cultural understanding. The club members strategically shared their martial arts, lion dance, and percussion through performance and teaching, thus finding another use for their skills as diplomatic, rather than physical, self-defence.

As Canada has become more inclusive, the social situation has gradually improved. At the dawn of the twenty-first century, Chinese Canadians have become a more integrated and valued part of society. Nonetheless, racism has not been entirely eradicated, as Arlene Chan documents in her history of the Chinese in Toronto (2011, 265). My fieldwork consultants at Hong Luck have sometimes remarked on this lingering culture of discrimination, suggesting that they continue the club's traditions by "educating" people who use ignorant language, such as racial slurs. Canada's legacy of ethnic intolerance has had a lasting impact on the cultural practices of organizations like Hong Luck. In this chapter, I propose that the lion dance and percussion performed by Chinese Canadian kung fu clubs should be understood as martial arts that embody a resistant stance through empowering performances.

Until the late twentieth century, the vast majority of Chinese Canadians (or their ancestors) came from the coastal regions of southern China's Guangdong Province (formerly known as Canton), belonged to the Han ethnic majority group, and spoke variants of Yue Chinese (粵語), of which Cantonese is the prestige dialect.[8] The earliest immigrants arrived in Canada in the 1850s; unfortunately, during their first one hundred-plus years in this country they suffered various types of discrimination (see Li 1998 for a detailed account). Examples of institutional racism included disenfranchisement, enforced segregation of neighbourhoods, and being barred from numerous occupations. Social discrimination meant many European Canadian business owners excluded Chinese immigrants as either employees or customers. There were also ethnically motivated attacks in the forms of racist language, vandalism, and physical violence. After the Second World War, racist laws against Chinese Canadians and immigrants from China began to be dismantled, but society's intolerance of diversity changed more slowly.

The social and institutional pressures faced by Chinese communities in Canadian cities contributed to the formation of ethnic enclaves called Chinatowns (唐人街), which are still found across the nation. At the heart of these neighbourhoods are networks of mutual aid organizations that have provided social, economic, political, and spiritual support to Chinese communities in Canada. Examples of such groups in Toronto's Spadina/Dundas Chinatown include family-based societies like the Wong Association (黃江夏雲山公所) as well as regional/district organizations such as the See Yup Clansman's Association (四邑同鄉會). Over the years, these associations have been of sustained cultural importance, particularly for the Cantonese who until recently were the largest ethno-linguistic group among Chinese Canadians.[9]

To protect themselves from racially motivated violence, some Chinese Canadians have practised a martial art known as *kung fu* (功夫). While self-defence is not the only reason for practising martial arts, it was a particularly strong incentive in Hong Luck's early days. My research consultants reported that other reasons for learning kung fu include a desire to perform, improve physical fitness, pursue self-cultivation, and/or participate in a cultural heritage activity. In addition to barehanded and handheld weapons fighting skills, kung fu includes lion dancing and percussion among its practices.[10] A martial arts framework thus gives the lion dance a distinctively fierce social meaning, manifested by martial characteristics in the movement and percussion that display aggression and the potential for violence. According to my consultants at Hong Luck, their lions embody the fighting spirit of the kung fu club, and so public performances ideally present a powerful warrior symbol – albeit one that is culturally coded. They also see lion dance and percussion not as separate practices but rather as integral parts of their kung fu system. My interpretation of Chinese Canadian lion dance, martial arts, and percussion emerges from my consultants' views and is grounded in the strategies of resistance that have been deployed within the historical context of discrimination against Chinese people in Canada.

Kung Fu Heritage

Contrary to colloquial usage, the term *kung fu* does not technically mean martial arts in standard Chinese. Its more literal translation is "skill achieved through hard work over time," which is a concept that is also applied to other practices, such as calligraphy and cooking. In both English and Cantonese, *kung fu* is commonly used to refer to Chinese martial arts, maintaining the implications of skill, effort, and time. There is a staggering array of kung fu styles that are differentiated by variations according to lineage, geographic origin, and practitioner interpretation. It is therefore difficult to talk about kung fu as a unified phenomenon. Within the framework of this study, I focus on the specifics of the Southern Chinese martial arts of the Hong Luck Kung Fu Club.

Hong Luck's curriculum has varied over time according to the interests and abilities of teachers and students. The two main styles of martial arts currently practised there are Choi Lee Fut (蔡李佛) and Do Pi (道派). Like many other Southern Chinese martial arts,[11] Choi Lee Fut and Do Pi emphasize a wide, stable stance and powerful hand strikes, but also involve some kicking, grappling, joint-locking, and a range of different handheld weapons. Hong Luck's training also includes self-defence drills and free sparring, but much of the current focus is on preserving choreographed sequences of fighting moves known as *forms* (套路). These martial arts routines are vehicles for practising pre-arranged sets of techniques, but during regular training at the club, no percussion rhythms are played. The same forms are also performed for public kung fu demonstrations, at which time they are complemented by percussion instruments, but remain asynchronous to them (McGuire 2015). Within a kung fu club, martial arts form the basic training and core discursive context for lion dance and drumming.

Myths are as important to kung fu as history. In striking an understanding of the past that balances "fiction" and "fact," while recognizing both, I draw on subaltern historian Dipesh Chakrabarty's (2000) argument that ignoring or rejecting people's stories in favour of the so-called "truth" is a type of symbolic violence. He argues instead that myths be treated as valid because they contribute to people's life-worlds; Chakrabarty also advocates presenting such stories alongside historical data that can meet empirical standards. The ideology of resistance imbricated in kung fu through the myths I recount is perhaps more important than the facticity of specific historical claims, a point argued by Thomas Green (2003) in regard to martial arts folk history.

Myth connects most Southern Chinese styles of martial arts to Shaolin (少林寺), a Buddhist temple in northern China's Henan Province that is famous for its warrior monks. Various versions of the tale are found in movies, television, books, on the Internet, and among kung fu practitioners, but a basic normative account is that the Shaolin monks invented kung fu during the early Tang dynasty (618–907 CE) under the guidance of Bodhidharma, mythic founder of the Zen (禪) style of Buddhism. Scholars are critical of the veracity of this origin myth for Chinese martial arts, arguing that combat skills had existed in China since ancient times, that Shaolin kung fu's spirituality-infused approach was not developed until the late Ming dynasty (1368–1644 CE), and that the Bodhidharma origin story was added retroactively

(Henning 1999; Lorge 2012; Shahar 2008). Nonetheless, this myth has had a profound impact on the way contemporary practitioners – and audiences – understand themselves and these styles. The Qing dynasty was established in 1644 by Manchurian conquerors from the North; myth has it that they were suspicious of the Shaolin warrior monks who had used their fighting prowess in support of the previous Ming dynasty. In order to consolidate their power, the new rulers burned down the Shaolin Temple, but five elders escaped and are widely thought to have brought their martial arts with them as they fled south to Guangdong Province, where they began teaching the practice to laypeople.

Contemporary practitioners do not focus their regular training on Shaolin Temple mythology or Qing-era revolutions, but the aura of righteous struggle remains an important element of self-defence philosophy; *martial virtue* (武 德) entails using fighting skills to protect oneself or one's community. The origin myth linking kung fu to the Shaolin Temple constructs an ancient pedigree that adds canonical weight to more recent lineages of fighting skills and can be considered an invented tradition in the sense intended by historians Hobsbawm and Ranger (1983). Notably, Choi Lee Fut was founded during the 1830s by a martial arts master named Chan Heung (陳享祖師) in the rural Xinhui district of Guangdong Province.[12] Do Pi was also created in Guangdong, but its founder Chan Dau (陳斗祖師) was active one hundred years later in urban Guangzhou. Both styles are syncretic blends of local martial arts practices, and attaching them to ancient Shaolin origin stories helped to legitimate them within a Confucian context that privileges respect for maintaining tradition. Shaolin mythology was also important to various anti-Qing revolutionary groups, some of whom practised martial arts;[13] the connection acted as a symbol of their allegiance to the fallen Ming dynasty, which, as previously mentioned, had been supported by the monks. Hong Luck's kung fu is descended from Shaolin in complex ways, but needs to be understood as part of that lineage and its ethos of using martial arts for self-defence.

Lion Dance Origins

Myths, histories, and symbolism help construct Chinese lion dance in terms of protection, resistance, and heroism. One of several mythical origins for the lion dance on the Hong Luck website tells of a "lion" that terrorized villagers at an unspecified time and place in China.[14] In order to protect themselves, the peasants built a lion costume that was meant to scare their antagonist.

Figure 8.1 | Hong Luck lion dance team.

They then paraded around with their lion while beating pots and pans. The fantastical appearance of contemporary Southern lion costumes reflects the myth. Typically, the head is large enough to fit over the entire upper torso of the lead dancer and has moving eyelids, mouth, and ears to help give the illusion of life. Its bamboo and papier-mâché frame is covered with strips of fur and decorated with coloured paint, sequins, and pompoms. The top of the head is adorned by a single, curved horn. The forehead has a mirror, which my teachers at Hong Luck claim is for reflecting the image of *ghosts* (鬼) back at the adversaries, thus frightening them with their own image. A long cape that matches the colour scheme of the head forms the body of the lion by covering the bent back of the person who plays the role of the tail. Myths and beliefs help explain why the Southern lion does not look much like a natural feline (see figure 8.1). As with kung fu, myths continue to imbue the performance of Southern lion dance with an aura of resistance, which in contemporary times refers to resisting ghosts and/or negative energy.

The earliest historical records of a Chinese lion dance are from the Tang dynasty (618–907 CE).[15] Folklorist, historian, and Chinese performing arts scholar William C.C. Hu (1995) claims that a court performance featuring a lion costume was developed in the Tang dynasty and is the ancestor of today's lion dance. An intervening millennium of oral transmission, however, means that the contemporary expression is only distantly related to the ancient practice. For example, a classic Tang dynasty history text, *The Old Book of Tang* (舊唐書, cited in Hu 1995, 69), states that the courtly lion dance was accompanied by a 140-member chorus of singers, as well as musicians playing wind, string, and percussion instruments. A contemporary ensemble, by contrast, consists solely of a drum, gong, and cymbals. Rather than an unbroken or direct lineage to the lion dance of the Tang court, Cantonese lion dancing may be considered part of a larger cultural formation with ancient roots.

Various types of lion dancing are now found throughout East Asia, many of which have a shamanic and/or exorcism function, but do not appear to be associated with martial arts. In the greater China region (i.e., the neighbouring Chinese nations outside the mainland of the People's Republic of China), the flat-faced Hokkien green lion dance found in Taiwan and the Hakka *unicorn dance* (舞麒麟) seen in Hong Kong are both associated with martial arts in a similar way to the Southern (Cantonese) lion dance. Northern Chinese lion dance is less associated with exorcism or martial arts schools, and is instead an acrobatic performance. In a postmodern fusion, a relatively new style of lion dance was developed by diasporic Chinese kung fu clubs for competitions in Southeast Asia. It is referred to as *Southern lion Northern dance* (南獅北舞) because performers use a Southern lion costume combined with acrobatic Northern lion movements.

Adding another layer of martial significance, the three traditional colour schemes (see figure 8.2) of Southern Chinese lion costumes each symbolize one of the warrior heroes of the historical novel *Romance of the Three Kingdoms* (三國演義).[16] The leader of the trio was Lau Bei (劉備), whose lion is multi-coloured and is the most popular among patrons because of its vibrant, cheerful appearance. Hong Luck's club colours, however, are black and red, which are the colours associated with Gwan Gong (關公) and his lion. The cultural importance of Gwan Gong is evident in Hong Luck, which has a large altar devoted to him, as do many Chinese homes, businesses, and temples. The third character in the trio is Jeung Fei (張飛), whose lion is black with green, yellow, and/or white highlights. This colour scheme is the least common today, although in Hong Luck's earlier years it was used regularly for parades because it is a sign of strength and aggression. Contemporary lion makers now use a myriad of different designs, and it is not uncommon to see other dance groups with bright green, blue, or pink lions.[17] Hong Luck owns approximately twenty-five lion heads, most of which engage the symbolism of the heroes from *Romance of the Three Kingdoms*, but the club also

Figure 8.2 | Left to right: Jeung Fei, Lau Bei, and Gwan Gong lion heads at Hong Luck.

has a few red and yellow lions. These are the colours of the flag of the People's Republic of China, and they are also featured prominently in Chinese New Year decorations due to their associations with luck, wealth, and happiness.

The highlight of contemporary performances is the *plucking-the-greens* (採青) sequence, which deploys symbolism that is auspicious while also referencing a historical layer of resistance. As documented by dance scholar Wanyu Liu (1981), myth has it that anti-Qing martial artists incorporated lion dance into their kung fu training in order to work on stances, stepping, and teamwork without fear of reprisal from Qing officials. The lion dance also gave them a way of raising funds for their seditious activities. The plucking-the-greens sequence involves patrons "feeding" a leafy green vegetable to the lion, which is broken up by the head dancer and "spat" back out. This set of actions had a double meaning based on homonyms that are written with different Chinese characters. The word for *vegetable* (*choi*, 菜) sounds similar to the word for *good fortune* (*choi*, 財), which allows the lion to take one piece of "wealth," multiply it by making many pieces out of it, and spit it out in order to spread the prosperity. For anti-Qing revolutionaries, however, the word for *green* (*ching*, 青) sounded like the word for the Qing dynasty (*Ching*, 清), and so when the lion ate the vegetable it was symbolically destroying the hated oppressors. On a more practical level, the greens typically had a red envelope stuffed with money attached to them in order to pay for the performance, which made lion dancing an important source of income for Qing-era kung fu groups. This practice continues today, and Hong Luck still performs the plucking-the-greens sequence for patrons, as do other Southern Chinese lion dance groups.

Features of Kung Fu and Lion Dance Beats

Of particular importance to this chapter is that Hong Luck's martial arts have an integrated musical component, which, as previously mentioned, is used to accompany lion dancing and choreographed martial arts demonstrations. The ensemble that accompanies both lion dancing and kung fu demonstrations is referred to eponymously as *gong and drum* (鑼鼓). The instruments consist of a large, single-sided, barrel drum that is struck with a pair of short, wooden sticks; a medium-sized, shallow, flat-faced, hanging gong that is struck with a knobbed wooden stick; and one or more pairs of medium to large, concussive, hand-held, metal cymbals. None of the instruments has a distinct pitch. At Hong Luck, the drummer acts as the "general" of the ensemble and uses specific rhythms to cue lion choreography.[18] As described in the prelude of this chapter, dancers in turn synchronize their movements to the drumbeats, ensuring that two or more lions can coordinate their steps even though the mask prevents them from seeing each other clearly. While many club members are capable of playing the various instruments and can switch roles during multi-hour parades, an ensemble has three to five performers at any one time: one drummer, one gong player, and one or more cymbalists.

Historically, such gong and drum ensembles functioned as signalling tools for directing troop movements on the battlefield (trans. Cleary 2003, 124–7), and contemporary lion dance percussion maintains this military association. Scholars of Chinese music classify genres and instruments according to the conceptual binary *civil/martial* (文武) (see Jones 1995, 104); the type of percussion used by kung fu practitioners is unsurprisingly on the martial side of the dichotomy.[19] Additionally, the Chinese character for *drum* (鼓) also means *to rouse*, supporting a belief that the loud, insistent rhythms are able to fuel the fire of a warrior spirit. Although kung fu demonstrations are asynchronous to the drumbeats, they still benefit from the energizing function of the percussion.

The martial qualities of kung fu and lion dance percussion help to explain why this practice is not referred to as *music* (音樂), per se, in Chinese. Ethnomusicologists tend to "take a broad view, accepting everything conceivable into their scope of study" (Nettl 2005, 25), and even go so far as to consider music to be what John Blacking (1973) calls *humanly organized sound*. I follow this comprehensive approach, which has proven useful in the study of other sound organizing practices that are not considered "music" by the people that perform them.[20] In doing so, however, I ask the reader to remember that practitioners themselves understand their percussion as *martial sound* rather than music, which is significant for the meanings associated with it. Typically, practitioners refer to their "music" by the names of instruments or simply as *drumbeats* (鼓點). During my time at Hong Luck, classes have been mostly taught in English, but the naming conventions are consistent with those in Chinese; people talk about their practice as drumming or beats, but not usually as music. In discussing this practice musically, one must keep in mind that the cultural values associated with kung fu and lion dance percussion construct it as wholly martial. Interestingly, the word *dance* is used consistently at Hong Luck even though the word *music* is not, which suggests that there is some latent recognition of the musicality of the beats – or at least that one can move in an aesthetically pleasing, rhythmic way to martial drumming.

Chinatowns and the History of Chinese Experience in Canada

The first immigrants from China to Canada were men, who arrived on the west coast of British Columbia in 1858.[21] Sociologist Peter Li holds that the government and European Canadians alike considered them a source of cheap labour, not potential citizens (1998, 30–1). Most of these Chinese men were from the coastal regions of Guangdong Province and came to work as gold miners along the Fraser River; later, they were labourers, building the Canadian Pacific Railway. By 1878, the first Chinese had arrived in Toronto (Lai and Leong 2012), but when the railroad was finished in 1885, many more began heading east looking for work.

The host of discriminatory laws that were passed against Chinese people in Canada had a lasting effect on their communities. This institutional racism made it difficult for Chinese immigrant workers to bring their families with them and forced them to live in Chinese-only neighbourhoods (Lai 2011). The two most infamous of these discriminatory laws were the Chinese Immigration Acts of 1885 and 1923. The first act required immigrants from China to pay a head tax to enter Canada – a fee that was not paid by immigrants from other countries. The second act is also known as the Chinese Exclusion Act of 1923 because it made it nearly impossible for people from China to be granted entry to Canada. In 1947, the Exclusion Act was repealed and Chinese Canadians were granted full citizenship rights, including suffrage. Immigration, however, was primarily restricted to family reunification. The reformed omnibus Immigration Act of 1967 created a universal point system that allowed independent Chinese immigrants to apply for entry to Canada, and finally put an end to this period of institutional discrimination.

Prior to the gradual improvement of their lot after the Second World War, Chinese Canadians had little access to either public or private institutions like banks, police, or social services. Chinatowns were created and inhabited primarily by men who spoke little English. The combination of legal impediments and social exclusion by European Canadians largely restricted their activities to their local neighbourhoods, which were structured around a network of mutual aid associations, also known as *tongs* (from the Chinese word for *meeting hall*, 堂). Tong associations formed the centre of social, political, and economic life. They were fraternal societies organized along the lines of fictive kinship relations, and so everyone in them would be a "brother" or "uncle." Anthropologist Richard H. Thompson summarizes the functions of tongs in Toronto as follows: "(1) ritual – the organization and celebration of traditional Chinese festivals such as New Year, the Ching Ming festival, the Mid-Autumn festival; (2) social – ownership of a house or hall which served as a center for conversation, gambling, games, and for a few individuals, a rooming house; (3) social-welfare – this included caring for the sick, arranging for the burial of deceased members; (4) economic – providing job placement and operating rotating credit associations known as *hui*; (5) political – settling disputes between members, sanctioning their behaviour, and representing them in their infrequent contacts with Canadian authorities" (1989, 75).

Chinatowns today still reflect many of the historical exigencies experienced by Chinese Canadians through the prominence of mutual aid associations.[22] While not as powerful as they used to be, many of the old tongs continue to function and new tongs are being formed. For example, the Wong Association mentioned in the introduction of this chapter celebrated its one hundredth anniversary in 2015, while the Taishan Friendship Association of Ontario (加拿大安省台山同鄉聯合總會) was only founded in 2010. As times have changed, so too has the role of the tongs. They are still involved with festivals and socializing, but are also now places for new and old mem-

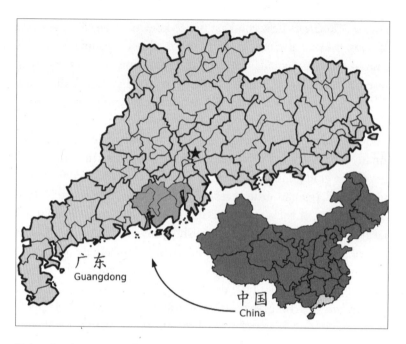

Figure 8.3 | Location of Sei Yap in Guangdong, China.

bers to network for business or political purposes. For some of the functions described by Thompson, however, many Chinese Canadians – particularly those born in Canada and/or who speak an official language fluently – are now more likely to go to a bank, the police, or government social services.

The durability of these benevolent societies is due in part to the fact that much of the immigration from China to Canada in the first one hundred years (1850s to 1950s) was not just from Guangdong Province, but from a small group of counties in Guangdong (see map in figure 8.3) called Sei Yap in Cantonese (Four Counties, 四邑) or the neighbouring Saam Yap (Three Counties, 三邑). The majority of Chinese immigrants in Toronto, for example, came from villages in the Taishan region of Sei Yap (Thompson 1989, 45–9), which ensured a high degree of social, cultural, and linguistic homogeneity, and thus a close-knit foundation for the various benevolent societies. The next major wave of Chinese immigration to Canada came from Hong Kong in the 1970s, 1980s, and 1990s. Dialects from rural Sei/Saam Yap (e.g., Taishanese) as well as Cantonese (as spoken in the cities of Guangzhou, Hong Kong, and Macau) are all part of the same language family, which means that they have some degree of mutual intelligibility. While there were social and dialect differences between the early immigrants and the more cosmopolitan arrivals from Hong Kong, they also shared many cultural similarities as Guangdong people. Immigration from other parts of the People's Republic of China (PRC) has increased since the 1990s, which has diversified the linguistic profile of Toronto's Chinese population. Many of the more recent arrivals speak Mandarin, aka Putonghua (普通話), the official language of the PRC. Increasing diversity in the Spadina/Dundas Chinatown has somewhat diluted the power of the older tongs, but they still remain a significant part of the community.

The Founding of Hong Luck

Immigrants from China have displayed remarkable forbearance in Canada, but not all were willing to quietly endure injustice. The Hong Luck Kung Fu Club was founded as a martial tong in 1961 – the twilight of the institutional discrimination period that technically lasted until the Immigration Act of 1967 came into effect – but racism in society was still a problem for Chinese Canadians. Hong Luck began under the leadership of Master Paul Chan (陳樹郁師傅),[23] and its members were men primarily from Sei Yap or descended from earlier immigrants who were. According to several of the surviving elders (from the original thirteen members) with whom I have spoken, they needed self-defence skills to protect themselves and their community from racial violence. At the same time, lion dancing and drumming were an inseparable part of their kung fu, and they were dedicated to upholding their full lineages. As a martial art, lion dance's protective symbolism was also deployed as a form of self-defence – albeit one of a more supernatural nature with regard to dispersing negative energy.

While some associations are based on surnames or ancestral homelands, Hong Luck acted as a catchall for people of different backgrounds. From the early days, they accepted students of other ethnic heritages, which is indicative of their broader mandate, as spelled out to me by one of the founding elders, Poi Suk.[24] He identified the following four purposes of the organization:

1 to teach kung fu as a pursuit for healthy body and mind
2 to promote the use of kung fu for self-defence only
3 to promote kung fu as a means of bringing together the Chinese and broader Canadian communities in a shared activity for learning, greater cultural understanding, and peace
4 to reach out to all associations for the betterment of Canadian society (personal communication, 24 November 2013).

Hong Luck is now estimated to have over 1,000 members and alumni; it has played a crucial role in preserving and promoting traditional Chinese kung fu, lion dance, and percussion in Canada. Although Master Paul Chan passed away in 2012, the club continued under the guidance of his co-founder, Master Jim Chan (陳振文師傅) until his death in 2016. Hong Luck's new head instructor is a senior member who trained extensively with both the founders and is well prepared to follow in their footsteps.

Masters Paul Chan and Jim Chan were not related and did not meet until their arrival in Toronto. They began their kung fu training as children in Taishan County during the Republican Era in China (1911–49). In that period, the government promoted kung fu as a way of *self-strengthening* (自強) the bodies of its citizens and, thereby, building a stronger nation (Kennedy and Guo 2005, 102–13). This view of kung fu as self-strengthening is a vital part of Hong Luck's ethos, and the idea of building power – physical, spiritual, and national – through martial arts training is in many ways as important as the actual self-defence skills. On an interpersonal basis, however, everyday life in both China and Canada provided many opportunities to put combat skills to use, which Master Paul is reputed to have done very effectively. While it may seem at odds with Poi Suk's delineation of a self-defence mandate for the club, Master Paul believed that the best defence was a good offence.[25] In other words, Hong Luck's founding leader was never afraid to fight when he believed that the situation warranted it. The club's curriculum is deeply marked by these dual imperatives of self-strengthening and self-defence. Understanding the received traditions of kung fu in this context is an essential component for interpreting the meanings of lion dance and percussion.

Cultural insiders know that lion dance performers – both dancers and percussionists – practise kung fu, which in Hong Luck's case is made manifest in a particularly aggressive style of movement and drumming. This aggression is exemplified by the way dancers explosively jerk the mask as though wielding a weapon, and the use of martial arts stances, kicks, and footwork, which demonstrate stability, power, and balance. For informed listeners, the drumming auralizes embodied speed, dexterity, and force as martial qualities that are immanent in the sound of the rhythms. The quick tempo of the percussion rhythms, the ear-splitting loudness of the instruments, and the bellicose timbres of wood pounding skin, or metal crashing into metal, are all hallmarks of the martial style from the aforementioned civil/martial stylistic dichotomy of Chinese music. For those aware of its history and symbolism, the lion dance thus acts as a public expression of fighting spirit. These performances embody what martial arts ethnographer and actor-trainer Phillip

Zarrilli calls a *heroic display ethos*, which he characterizes as "that collective set of behaviors, expected actions, and principles or codes of conduct that ideally guide and are displayed by a hero, and are the subject of many traditional ballads or epics where seemingly superhuman heroes display bravery, courage, and valor in the face of death" (2001, 419).

The fierce power of vigorous lion dancing can boost the morale and pride of audiences. At the same time, lion dance focuses attention on the rhythmic execution of choreography and lively manipulation of the mask as a puppet. While these aesthetic considerations may sometimes conceal or distract from the martial aspects of performance, Hong Luck's lion dancers and percussionists never stray far from their kung fu foundation.

Lions on the Streets, Drumming in the Air

In the twenty-first century, Hong Luck's most common public activity has been lion dancing, which is always accompanied by drumming. The lion is thus literally and figuratively the face of the club, and the drum is the sound of the lion. The Southern lion is also considered a symbol of the Chinese people – particularly in the Cantonese-dominated diaspora – so much so that, for example, the light-posts in the neighbourhood around Hong Luck usually feature a banner with an image of a Southern-style lion and the words "Welcome to Chinatown" (see figure 8.4). In the discussion that follows, I describe the lion dance and percussion in further detail in order to advance a more nuanced view of their meanings.

The most popular occasion for lion dancing is Chinese New Year, although it is also commonly seen at the opening ceremonies of new stores, wedding banquets, and tong anniversary celebrations. During Chinese New Year, the Hong Luck Kung Fu Club is often hired to do lion dance performances for private parties and events, but the highlight of the season is the annual parade through Chinatown. Such processions are typical of many diasporic Chinese communities, as well as those in contemporary southern China. It is not the sort of parade where streets are blocked off and onlookers stand by the side of the road, but rather an interactive event that takes place on the sidewalks and even inside buildings. A lion dance parade thus consists of many individual performances for patrons as the troupe winds its way through the neighbourhood.

In Toronto, the sheer size of the Spadina/Dundas Chinatown means that the parade can last between four and six hours while covering both sides of approximately eight city blocks in a cross shape extending north, south,

Figure 8.4 | Banner featuring Southern-style lion, Dundas Street West, Toronto.

east, and west from the intersection of Spadina Avenue and Dundas Street West. The club sends out two lions and one set of instruments, as well as enough people to be able to rotate positions (including rest) throughout the day, which allows the cavalcade and music to remain continuous for the duration of the event. Non-performing members carry the flags of Canada and China as well as banners emblazoned in Chinese characters with the name of the club and its kung fu styles. For more formal performances like weddings, Hong Luck's percussionists wear matching red silk pants and jackets with standing collars and butterfly buttons, while lion dancers wear a plain Hong Luck branded t-shirt coupled with fanciful pants that match the colour scheme and design of their lion. For the Chinese New Year parade, however, all participants wear layers of warm clothing because it takes place in winter.

The Greater Toronto Area has many kung fu clubs, but during my fieldwork the only other group to do a similar, plucking-the-greens type lion dance parade through the Spadina/Dundas area was the Chinese Freemasons.[26] Also known as the Hongmen (洪門), this group is part of a large, international tong and has their Toronto headquarters down the road from Hong Luck. City bylaws require a permit for lion dance processions, and the two kung fu clubs are not usually allowed to go out on the same day. This scheduling is partly to avoid congestion, but also because – despite cordial relations between the two groups – the authorities are leery of having lions from different martial arts factions meet on the street. Several senior Hong Luck members have speculated that this caution may be due to problems that occurred in Hong Kong in the mid-twentieth century between rival kung fu clubs whose lion dance teams were competing for scarce resources.

Hong Luck's Chinese New Year parades are advertised in advance to the patrons of the Chinatown area; on the day of the event, supporters attract the lion(s) by hanging a vegetable (with a red packet of money attached) from their doorways for a brief performance.[27] As the troupe makes its way through the neighbourhood, a string of individual lion dances is connected by continuous percussion rhythms as the lions travel from patron to patron. Parade routines are usually short (approximately one to two minutes) and stripped down to their basic format, although some businesses or tongs may request more elaborate actions where the lion(s) come inside their premises to bow at one or more altars. The brevity of public parade performances contrasts with the length of private or commissioned events (e.g., banquets), which can last up to thirty minutes and feature more elaborate choreography. Whether on parade or at a staged performance, dancers and patrons can negotiate the specifics of a lion dance according to the requirements of the audience and the space. The typical parts of a Hong Luck routine during the New Year procession are as follows:

1 arriving (walking)
2 greeting (three bows)
3 dispersing negative energy (head up and three rises)
4 plucking-the-greens (approaching, testing, eating, and spitting)
5 farewell (three bows)
6 leaving (walking)

Meanings of Lion Dance at the Intersection of Sound and Movement

Master Jim Chan taught me that the meaning of the dance is built from four components: lion movement, drum rhythms, vocables, and emotion. The first two are fairly self-explanatory, while the second pair requires more elaboration. In terms of movement and sound, Hong Luck lion dancers and percussionists tend to refer to the rhythms according to the choreography that goes with them, which shows the deep integration of lion dancing and drumming.[28] In contemporary practice, most of the names they use are in English, except for a pattern called a *saam sing* (三升) which means "three rises" and involves thrice shooting the head up into the air followed by dropping it down as the lion moves into a low crouching position.

The vocables are onomatopoeic syllables that outline the basic rhythm patterns as they are spoken during training to help lion dancers learn the beats. This practice allows verbal communication of the rhythmic aspects of lion dance, but is fairly informal and underspecified. It also helps to engrain the rhythms into the memories of people who eventually take up the challenge of translating them to drumming.[29] In performance, the vocables are no longer spoken out loud, but remain the internalized foundation or "score" for both movement and beats. Hong Luck's drummers are encouraged to develop their own playing style and interpretation of the standard rhythms, thus allowing them to depart from the simple vocable-based patterns while remaining rooted in them. Individual flair is expressed primarily through the choice of stock patterns and use of ornamentation, but more advanced performers may create their own versions of beats by employing techniques of repetition, variation, expansion, deletion, and insertion. During lion dances, the amount of creative deviation is kept to a minimum in order to allow the dancers to follow the rhythms more easily. However, between parade performances, drummers take the opportunity to mix up their beats while the group walks to the next patron. This type of variation helps to keep things interesting for the performers by providing an opportunity to play rhythms that are not part of the basic plucking-the-greens routine and by allowing them to use more complex rhythms than are appropriate for structured choreography.

The emotions in Master Jim's four-part schema of lion meaning are an important part of what brings the puppet/mask to "life"; they are expressed in the combination of movement and rhythm in relation to the context of choreography. The way these factors work together to express feelings is dynamic and interpretive rather than static and prescribed. Nonetheless, it is also not completely extemporaneous or improvised. "Emotions" signified through the combination of movements and beats include: sleepy, hungry, cautious, excited, happy, playful, coy, respectful, confident, fierce, aggressive, etc.

The appropriateness of different emotions is determined partly by the performers and partly by the context, which can be illustrated with two examples. The first is that a long, continuous roll on the drum is used for both sleeping and eating; lion dancers know how to interpret the beat based on what routine they are doing and/or where they are in the choreography. There is no sleeping during parades, so during a Chinese New Year procession a drum roll would call for showing hunger while cautiously approaching the food. The second example is a situation where drummers and lion dancers have more leeway. When parading down the street, the person playing the drum might keep the energy of the group high with fast loud beats while engaging the attention of both participants and observers with fancy variations and extra ornaments. S/he could also conserve energy by playing basic patterns at medium volume and tempo. In response to complex and energetic rhythms, lion dancers could choose to stomp aggressively down the street while jerking the head sharply and snapping the mouth at pedestrians, or they could opt to strut and swagger in a way that confidently suggests they are the kings/queens of the neighbourhood.[30] For more simple and mid-volume beats, lion dancers might act cautiously by moving the head slowly and stepping gingerly, or they might even take the opportunity to rest a bit by doing a lackadaisical stroll.

Although my consultants at Hong Luck requested that I not publish an exhaustive list of different emotive combinations of choreography, rhythm, and context, I believe it is important to underscore the way that emotional content is generated through the interaction of lion dance and drumming. In general, and befitting Hong Luck's martial heritage, my teachers trained me to display fierceness as my default lion emotion, which I express in sharp head movement, a low stance, and heavy footwork. In general, power is an important touchstone for lion dancing because kung fu lions are supposed to embody a club's strength, a point my teachers and most of the club's senior members emphasized.

Figure 8.5 shows a short-but-rich transcription of Hong Luck's beats in order to clearly illustrate the relationship of vocable *drum texts* (鑼鼓經), percussion variations in performance, lion movement, and emotion. Single-line staffs indicate unpitched percussion and an accent shows the emphasis on the final, strongest beat of each phrase. The lack of time signatures indicates the phrase-based structure of these rhythm patterns, which is an organizing feature of some other types of Chinese percussion as well (e.g., Zhang 1997). The first three parts in figure 8.5 show drum, gong, and cymbal variations for walking, as one might hear them during a lion dance parade. The fourth part renders the vocables for a basic walking beat as lion dancers learn them in class: "chek" specifies a short click on the rim of the drum; "dong"

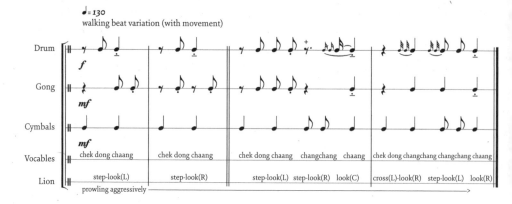

Figure 8.5 | Notation of Hong Luck lion dance walking beat variant.

is used for the first drumbeat after a rest or pause; a short "chang" means an eighth note; and a longer "chaang" indicates a quarter note. I have not transcribed the rhythm of the vocable line because it is rarely heard in performance, except by very inexperienced performers or perhaps an exhausted group of percussionists. In the sample drum part, the chek is omitted entirely and the rhythm is embellished with rests and ornaments, both of which are common variations in performance practice. The last line of the transcription shows lion stepping and head movement where "L" is left, "R" is right, and "C" is centre. In this example, the combination of loud, busy percussion variations on the basic vocables combines with a prowling-type movement to signify an aggressive lion stalking the streets.

Efficacy and Entertainment in Lion Dance

The symbolic logic of Southern Chinese lion dancing is undergirded by its association with martial arts. In addition to the auspicious significance of plucking-the-greens, the lion dance is also used to drive away negative energy, which has been summed up by material anthropologist Heleanor Feltham as the protection of liminal spaces, times, and transitions (2009, 111). The particular types of liminal states that lions preside over are annual cycles (New Year's celebrations and anniversaries) as well as new beginnings (weddings and store openings). Shortly after Chinese New Year 2013, Wing Suk, an elder member of Hong Luck, told me that martial vigour helps "the lion dance disperse nefarious chi energy (舞獅去邪氣)," which explains how it exorcises negativity in order to protect people, places, and events (personal communication, 10 March).[31] Socio-cultural anthropologist Avron Boretz further positions lion dance in terms of the Chinese cosmology that interprets the world as a dynamic interplay of opposites expressed as *yin* (陰 : cold, dark, moon, feminine, dead, etc.) and *yang* (陽 : hot, bright, sun, masculine, alive, etc.). He writes, "the lion, it turns out, is a strongly *yang* creature with the power to drive away or destroy ghosts and other forms of death pollution" (Boretz 2011, 54). This meaning suggests why a martial quality is desirable: in order for a lion dance to protect liminal states, the kung fu training of the performers extends the idea of self-defence into the realm of the supernatural where deleterious energy, ghosts, and even "death pollution" are fought off.

Some people are unaware of the symbolic meanings in the lion dance and are more interested in it as a cultural spectacle rather than anything mystical. This is not unusual, and Richard Schechner has identified a historical continuum for performance that runs from efficacious ritual to entertaining spectacle (1974). I have observed an interest in spectacle over ritual at many weddings where the bride and/or groom are Canadian-born Chinese and are only vaguely informed regarding lion dance symbolism; however, they know from their families that the performance is an important part of a Southern Chinese nuptial celebration. On the far side of Schechner's efficacy-entertainment spectrum would be cultural outsiders, who can still enjoy the boisterous performance without any awareness of its other meanings. Negative reactions are uncommon, and positive encounters tend to create an opportunity for mutual understanding. Given that performers, patrons, and audiences are likely to have different perspectives, Hong Luck's performances can inhabit various points on Schechner's entertainment-efficacy spectrum simultaneously. Such a diversity of perspectives does not detract from the meaning of the lion dance, but rather adds to its value by allowing multiple interpretations.

The commanding sonic presence of a gong and drum ensemble is an important part of lion dance as a performance whose significance need not be supernatural to be efficacious. During Chinese New Year parades, the powerful rhythms fill the air and assert a claim to the Spadina/Dundas neighbourhood as a place, which helps to make it into Chinatown as a space.[32] This phenomenon is consistent with anthropologist Anne Raulin's argument that "in a foreign metropolis, a pluri-cultural one at that, the Lion Dance celebrates

... a sense of territoriality" (1991, 47). She was writing about Paris's Little Asia, but she could have been referring to Toronto – or any number of other multicultural cities with Chinatowns.

The drum, gong, and cymbals together are capable of playing extremely loudly and can reach sound pressure levels of 105 dB in close range (i.e., as loud as a jackhammer breaking concrete). Their military origin means that they are designed so that the sound carries over long distances and cuts through other noise, whether that is across a battlefield or down busy Spadina Avenue. This sonic strengthening of the neighbourhood as Chinatown is all the more necessary in Toronto because the area has little Chinese-influenced architecture, an important visible symbol of Chinese identity in other Chinatowns, such as Vancouver's. Most of the buildings in the Spadina/Dundas area either date from before Chinese Canadians moved into the area or have been built since then in a generically "Canadian" style. In a way, lion dance parades in Chinatown act as a sonic patrol of the neighbourhood that uses the sound of the percussion to rearticulate Chinatown's being during liminal moments.[33] I suggest that the gong and drum ensemble can be thought of as standing in for the lion's roar by claiming territory as far as the beats will carry.

Another use of lion dance percussion is to set the tone for a festive occasion by raising volume and energy levels. Chinese speakers describe ideal social events as *hot and noisy* (熱鬧), which means bustling with people and sound. At banquets featuring a lion dance, for example, the performance usually takes place toward the beginning of the evening – but not until a critical mass of guests has arrived. The brash percussion boosts the liveliness of the room as well as the volume, and people do not sit quietly, but rather continue to talk to each other over the beats. Used in this way, the gong and drum ensemble again harkens back to its martial pedigree. In an ancient Chinese encyclopaedia called *The Spring and Autumn Annals* (呂氏春秋), it is claimed that loud percussion is too extravagant for music, which should instead embody "the harmony between Heaven and Earth, and the perfect blend of Yin and Yang" (trans. Knoblock and Riegel 2000, 138). The proper function of gong and drum is militaristic and should be used "to shock the mental energies, startle the ears and eyes, and agitate the inborn nature" (ibid., 140), which appropriates the rousing quality of martial drumming for non-battlefield use. Plucking-the-greens is still the highlight of any performance, with all its attendant symbolism of spreading good fortune, but the value of kick-starting the evening is also significant. A lion dance draws on the stirring clang and boom of the percussion to act as a catalyst that ensures a properly hot and noisy occasion.

Conclusion: Chinatown in Flux

Chinese Canadians are no longer subject to institutional discrimination in Canada, but the history of racism against them must not be forgotten. On 22 June 2006, then-prime minister Stephen Harper issued an apology for Chinese exclusion and especially for the head tax. At the same time, he formally recognized the important role played by workers from China who built the railroad that united Canada from coast to coast. Acknowledging this history is important for honouring the memory of people whose labour helped connect the nation, as well as for making amends with contemporary Chinese Canadians. The tong system and the existence of Chinatowns across the country, however, still stand as testament to a time when things were not so equitable.

Old-school kung fu clubs like Hong Luck continue to embody the indomitable spirit that helped earlier generations to endure and overcome discrimination. Such martial arts groups promote self-strengthening that is rooted in a steadfast devotion to self-defence, and this fighting spirit contributes to the efficacy of lion dancing as a means to dispel negative energy. I have argued that the fierce character undergirding Cantonese martial arts, lion dance, and drumming can be understood as a form of resistance to oppression in the context of both Chinese and Chinese Canadian history. My position also recognizes the way that these practices act as a form of memory that preserves a commonly shared Chinese cultural heritage, as well as the specific legacy of Chinese communities in Canada.

With the deaths of its two co-founding masters in 2012 and 2016, Hong Luck is at a crossroads. Chinese Canadians are now more integrated into broader Canadian society, and so resistance to domination and reliance on the tong system are no longer as essential as they used to be. A younger generation of kung fu students at Hong Luck may never have to use their fighting skills. The Chinese population in Canada is no longer confined to Chinatowns and now includes immigrants from all over China. The lion dance is being reinterpreted by more and more people as an entertaining cultural performance and less as a type of ritual exorcism with the power to influence preternatural forces.

Hong Luck's half-century tenure in Toronto's largest Chinatown has nurtured several generations of kung fu practitioners, some of whom have gone

268 | Colin P. McGuire

on to start their own schools.[34] Few of these offshoot groups have done things exactly the same way as their alma mater; however, even as the practice has continued to evolve in the hands of a new generation, practitioners remain indebted to their distinct lineage. Hong Luck's kung fu is imbued with the mythic warrior virtues of righteous heroes like Gwan Gong, the Shaolin warrior monks, and anti-Qing rebels. Their practices also bear the indelible imprint of the association's heritage in Canada, which harkens back to the days when self-defence from racial violence was a necessity in Chinatowns across the country.[35] This core meaning of ferocity will continue to undergird lion dancing's symbolic logic, and, no matter how the practices evolve, I am confident that the legacy of clubs like Hong Luck will preserve a record of the strength – tempered with forbearance – that helped Chinese Canadians to fight for their place in Canada.

Notes

1 In this video, I am performing inside the head of the golden lion. The mother of the bride provided me with the videographer's raw files several months after the event so that they could be edited for use on the Hong Luck Kung Fu Club's YouTube channel. Permission has been granted to share this video, which the club is using as promotional material to attract lion dance clients.
2 Where necessary, Chinese terms have been romanized according to convention for common words and/or the preferences of my Chinese Canadian research consultants, who speak English, Cantonese, and/or Taishanese. Where possible, I have translated terms instead, but in either case, I have also included Chinese characters in brackets, which will be legible to literate speakers of any dialect. Official place names in Mainland China use the modern *pinyin* system of Mandarin Chinese romanization.
3 Cantonese opera was long the main form of public entertainment in North American Chinatowns, as documented by Nancy Rao (2017). New works by Chinese Canadian artists have also used combinations of music, drama, dance, and/or martial arts. Some of these creative endeavours address historical injustices, echoing how discrimination against immigrants from China continues to flavour percussion-accompanied lion dance in Canada. Examples of such new works include Paul Yee's Cantonese opera-inspired play *Jade in the Coal* (2010) and Chan Ka Nin's symphonic theatre piece *Harmonious Interest* (2013), both of which deal with Chinese immigrant experiences. Cf. Zheng (2010) on the role of music in the struggles of Chinese Americans to establish themselves in the United States.
4 Toronto has several Chinatowns and the Greater Toronto Area also has several ethnic suburbs with large Chinese populations.
5 When I was considering fieldwork sites for lion dance drumming, I chose Hong Luck based on the advice of Master Henry Lo (盧建雄師傅) with whom I had studied the

Wing Chun style of kung fu (詠春拳) for ten years. He told me unequivocally that he considered Hong Luck's drummers the best in the Greater Toronto Area.

6   This concept has since been applied to the Brazilian dance-fight-game of *capoeira*, first by J. Lowell Lewis (1992) and later by Greg Downey (2002), thus blazing a path for the study of other martial arts that blend hand-to-hand fighting skills with music and dance.

7   There is much more that could be written about these rich areas. Other studies have looked at embodiment of cultural history and identity in Chinese martial arts and lion dance (Chan 2001; Farrer 2011; Johnson 2005; McGuire 2014). Further interesting avenues to explore include: how lion dance relates to the heterodox *Chinese folk religion* (中國民間宗教) (Harrell 1977; Wong 2011; Yang and Hu 2012); discussions of lion dance drumming in relation to other Chinese processional musics (Jones 1995; Mu 2012); and comparisons of drumming and kung fu to percussion and martial acrobatics in Peking Opera (Thorpe 2005; Yao 1990, 2001).

8   In English, the word *Canton* has been used to refer to both southern China's Guangdong Province and its capital Guangzhou. The word *Cantonese* can thus refer to people from that province in general or specifically to the region's lingua franca as spoken in the main city. While not entirely equivalent, I use the ethnolinguistic term *Cantonese* and the ethnogeographic term *Southern Chinese* interchangeably in this chapter to refer to the relatively culturally homogeneous Chinese Canadian population that was established in the nineteenth and twentieth centuries prior to increased immigration from other parts of China in the late twentieth and early twenty-first centuries.

9   Canada's *2016 Census of Population* listed Mandarin as the most spoken language other than English or French, with Cantonese close behind (Statistics Canada 2016). https://www12.statcan.gc.ca/census-recensement/2016/as-sa/98-200-x/2016010/98-200-x2016010-eng.cfm (accessed 25 July 2018). In the *2011 Census of Population* and in previous years, however, Cantonese speakers outnumbered Mandarin speakers (Statistics Canada 2011). http://www12.statcan.ca/census-recensement/2011/as-sa/98-314-x/98-314-x2011003_2-eng.cfm (accessed 28 August 2015).

10 That is to say, the percussion instruments are played by kung fu practitioners rather than by third-party musicians who are neither martial artists nor lion dancers.

11 Generally speaking, Northern styles of kung fu tend to be more focused on agile footwork, acrobatics, and kicks.

12 The names of Choi Lee Fut and Do Pi ancestors are given in the typical Chinese order of surname followed by given name because this follows usage at Hong Luck – even when speaking English.

13 By the end of the Qing dynasty, there was a variety of political, religious, nationalistic, ethnic, economic, and/or dynastic revolutionary groups in China, so the term *anti-Qing* should not be taken as monolithic in its composition or motivation. See Judkins and Nielson (2015) for a discussion of martial arts in relation to Southern Chinese secret societies, militias, and Qing dynasty rebels.

14 For further information on lion dance origin myths, see http://www.hongluck.ca/lion-dance-history.php.

15 Lions are not native to China, although in ancient times some caged specimens were brought along the Silk Road from India or Africa. Since the first century CE, lions have

also appeared in China's religious iconography, where they are depicted as protectors of the Buddha's teachings, as well as in the use of paired stone lion statues as guardians in front of buildings, gates, and temples (see Feltham 2009 and Liu 1981 for examples).

16 *Romance of the Three Kingdoms* is a fourteenth-century book considered one of China's Four Great Classical Novels (四大名著), but the story it tells is older, having been of enduring importance in Chinese culture for nearly two thousand years, with versions now found in storytelling, plays, television, movies, and video games. The classic novel is available online in a public domain translation from http://www.threekingdoms.com/.

17 Lion costumes and percussion instruments are typically imported to Canada from China, Hong Kong, Malaysia, or Singapore.

18 I have observed that some lion dance groups maintain a different relationship to the percussion, where the lion(s) lead(s) and the instrumentalists follow. This approach is more characteristic of Chinese opera performance (Yao 2001, 1990) than military signalling, and Hong Luck members disparage it as sloppy, particularly when there is more than one lion performing. Without following the drum, two or more lions will likely be uncoordinated with each other because the mask obscures their vision.

19 *Literary/martial* (文武) is an old concept drawn from Chinese philosophy that illustrates two sides of the same coin in politics. The idea is well entrenched as a social virtue, and temples devoted to a pair of gods embodying this principle of civil/military balance can be found in Hong Kong, Taiwan, and China.

20 For examples of "non-musics" studied by ethnomusicologists, see Inuit throat-singing games (Nattiez 1999) and cantillation of the Koran among Islamic groups who forbid music (al Faruqi 1978, 1985).

21 The first Chinese people in Canada arrived on Vancouver Island as labourers in 1788, but fell victim to a Spanish attack on the British settlement where they worked (Lai 2011). Immigration did not begin in earnest until the gold rush of the 1850s.

22 The Greater Toronto Area has several older neighbourhoods identified as Chinatowns as well as large, new, suburban areas with primarily Chinese populations that are not called Chinatown per se. Tongs tend to be clustered in the older urban areas, but are also sometimes seen in the newer suburbs.

23 Master Paul had arrived several years earlier in 1950 and was sponsored by his grandfather, who had emigrated from China to work as a labourer many years prior.

24 Poi Suk is literally "Uncle" Poi, properly Ng Ji-Pui (伍梓培).

25 Master Jim, on the other hand, preferred to avoid fights, although he did not turn the other cheek if attacked.

26 It is common for Hong Luck alumni and their students to help during these parades. I have occasionally seen other lion dance groups do processions through the Spadina/Dundas Chinatown for Canada Day (1 July) or China Day (1 October), but these occasions remain on the street and do not involve individual plucking-the-greens performances.

27 Some people might use an orange instead of a vegetable because in Cantonese the word *tangerine* (桔) sounds exactly like the word *lucky* (吉); both are pronounced *gat*. Other patrons hang only a red packet (i.e., without greens or citrus).

28 During a nine-month exchange to Hong Kong in 2011/2012, the two kung fu groups I trained with also referred to rhythms according to the movements they accompany.

29 Perhaps because drumming is learned but not taught, relatively few people have the aptitude or interest to become drummers capable of playing Hong Luck's full repertoire. Apart from my teacher, David Lieu, and myself there was only one other active drummer at the club who could play all the various rhythms for both lion dance and kung fu. While this number of people is very small, many more members could play enough different beats to accompany a lion dance parade routine or kung fu demo.
30 Lion dancers are allowed some freedom in interpreting the rhythms, so two lions parading together might manifest different movements in response to the same drumming.
31 Wing Suk literally means "Uncle" Wing, which is a nickname, but his proper appellation is Chow Lin (周練).
32 See Wrazen (2007) on space and place in diaspora with regard to the music of Toronto's Polish Highlander (Górale) community.
33 Hong Luck does two lion dance parades a year in Chinatown that are focused on plucking-the-greens. One is at Chinese New Year and the other is in August and celebrates the club's anniversary. The annual Chinatown festival in late summer also usually features lion dancing, if not by Hong Luck, then by other kung fu clubs. There are many more lion dances a year in the area, but the rest occur inside tongs, banquet halls, and malls, so the sound of the percussion would not be heard on the street.
34 Descendant groups from Hong Luck who remain in the Greater Toronto Area include JV Martial Arts Studio, Northern Leg Southern Fist, Bamboo Kung Fu, Sammy Cheng Lion Dance and Kung Fu, and Twin Dragon Kickboxing, but there are also alumni with their own schools in British Columbia, New Brunswick, and Florida.
35 For example, in the documentary *Legend of a Warrior* (2012), Edmonton's Frank Lee recounts having had to use his kung fu skills on a regular basis in the 1960s when European Canadian men would come to Chinatown on the weekend to pick fights with Chinese Canadians and cause trouble for Chinatown businesses.

References

al Faruqi, Lois Ibsen. 1978. "Accentuation in Qur'ānic Chant: A Study in Musical Tawāzun." *Yearbook of the International Folk Music Council* 10: 53–68.
– 1985. "Music, Musicians and Muslim Law." *Asian Music* 17 (1): 3–36.
Blacking, John. 1973. *How Musical Is Man?* Seattle: University of Washington Press.
Boretz, Avron. 2011. *Gods, Ghosts, and Gangsters: Ritual Violence, Martial Arts, and Masculinity on the Margins of Chinese Society*. Honolulu: University of Hawai'i Press.
Chakrabarty, Dipesh. 2000. *Provincializing Europe: Postcolonial Thought and Historical Difference*. Princeton, NJ: Princeton University Press.
Chan, Arlene. 2011. *The Chinese in Toronto from 1878: From Outside to Inside the Circle*. Toronto, ON: Dundurn.
Chan, Ka Nin. 2013. *Harmonious Interest*. Performed by the Victoria Symphony. McPherson Theatre, 15 March, https://vimeo.com/71022401.
Chan, Mei Hsiu. 2001. "Transdisciplinary Multicultural Dance Education: Teaching Chinese American Students Chinese Culture through Lion Dancing." PhD diss., Texas Women's University.

Cleary, Thomas, trans. 2003. *The Art of War: Complete Texts and Commentary*. Original by Sun Tzu. Boston, MA: Shambhala Publications.
Downey, Greg. 2002. "Listening to Capoeira: Phenomenology, Embodiment, and the Materiality of Music." *Ethnomusicology* 46 (3): 487–509.
Downey, Greg, Monica Dalidowicz, and Paul H. Mason. 2014. "Apprenticeship as Method: Embodied Learning in Ethnographic Practice." *Qualitative Research* 15 (2): 183–200.
Farrer, D.S. 2011. "Coffee-Shop Gods: Chinese Martial Arts of the Singapore Diaspora." In *Martial Arts as Embodied Knowledge: Asian Traditions in a Transnational World*, edited by D.S. Farrer and John Whalen-Bridge, 203–37. Albany, NY: SUNY Press.
Feltham, Heleanor B. 2009. "Everybody Was Kung-Fu Fighting: The Lion Dance and Chinese National Identity in the 19th and 20th Centuries." In *Asian Material Culture*, edited by Marianne Hulbosch, Elizabeth Bedford, and Martha Chaiklin, 103–40. Amsterdam, Netherlands: Amsterdam University Press.
Geertz, Clifford. 1983. *Local Knowledge: Further Essays in Interpretive Anthropology*. New York, NY: Basic Books.
Green, Thomas A. 2003. "Sense in Nonsense: The Role of Folk History in the Martial Arts." In *Martial Arts in the Modern World*, edited by Thomas A. Green and Joseph R. Svinth, 1–11. Westport, CT: Praeger.
Harrell, Steven. 1977. "Modes of Belief in Chinese Folk Religion." *Journal for the Scientific Study of Religion* 16 (1): 55–65.
Henning, Stanley E. 1999. "Academia Encounters the Chinese Martial Arts." *China Review International* 6 (2): 319–32.
Hobsbawm, Eric, and Terence Ranger, eds. 1983. *The Invention of Tradition*. Cambridge, UK: Cambridge University Press.
Hu, William C. 1995. *Chinese Lion Dance Explained*. San Francisco, CA: Ars Ceramica.
Johnson, Henry. 2005. "Dancing with Lions: (Per)forming Chinese Cultural Identity at a New Zealand Secondary School." *New Zealand Journal of Asian Studies* 7 (2): 171–86.
Jones, Stephen. 1995. *Folk Music of China: Living Instrumental Traditions*. New York, NY: Oxford University Press.
Judkins, Benjamin N., and Jon Nielson. 2015. *The Creation of Wing Chun: A Social History of the Southern Chinese Martial Arts*. Albany, NY: SUNY Press.
Kennedy, Brian, and Elizabeth Guo. 2005. *Chinese Martial Arts Training Manuals: A Historical Survey*. Berkeley, CA: Blue Snake Books.
Knoblock, John, and Jeffrey Riegel, trans. 2000. *The Annals of Lü Buwei* (呂氏春秋). Stanford, CA: Stanford University Press.
Lai, David Chuenyan. 2011. *A Brief Chronology of Chinese Canadian History: From Segregation to Integration*. Burnaby, BC: Simon Fraser University, David See-Chai Lam Centre for International Communication.
Lai, David Chuenyan, and Jack Leong. 2012. *Toronto Chinatowns 1878–2012*. Burnaby, BC: Simon Fraser University, David See-Chai Lam Centre for International Communication.
Lee, Corey, dir. and author. 2012. *Legend of a Warrior*. Corkscrew Media, EnriquePoe Moving Pictures, and the National Film Board of Canada. Film.

Lewis, J. Lowell. 1992. *Ring of Liberation: Deceptive Discourses in Brazilian Capoeira.* Chicago, IL: University of Chicago Press.

Li, Peter. 1998. *The Chinese in Canada.* 2nd ed. Don Mills, ON: Oxford University Press.

Liu, Wanyu. 1981. "The Chinese Lion Dance." Master of Fine Arts thesis, York University.

Lorge, Peter. 2012. *Chinese Martial Arts: From Antiquity to the Twenty-First Century.* New York, NY: Cambridge University Press.

McGuire, Colin. 2014. "Music of the Martial Arts: Rhythm, Movement, and Meaning in a Chinese Canadian Kung Fu Club." PhD diss., York University.

— 2015 "The Rhythm of Combat: Understanding the Role of Music in Performances of Traditional Chinese Martial Arts and Lion Dance." *MUSICultures* 42 (1): 1–23.

Mu, Yang. 2012. "Music and Dance for Interment Rituals in a Chinese Village." *Ethnomusicology* 56 (1): 1–30

Nattiez, Jean-Jacques. 1999. "Inuit Throat-Games and Siberian Throat Singing: A Comparative, Historical, and Semiological Approach." *Ethnomusicology* 43 (3): 399–418.

Nettl, Bruno. 2005. *The Study of Ethnomusicology: Thirty-One Issues and Concepts.* New ed. Urbana and Chicago: University of Illinois Press.

Rao, Nancy Yunhwa. 2017. *Chinatown Opera Theater in North America.* Champaign: University of Illinois Press.

Raulin, Anne. 1991. "The Aesthetic and Sacred Dimension of Urban Ecology: Paris's Little Asia." Trans. Jeanne Brody. *Archives de sciences socials des religions* 36 (73): 35–49.

Rice, Timothy. 2003. "The Ethnomusicology of Music Learning and Teaching." *College Music Symposium* 43: 65–85.

Schechner, Richard. 1974. "From Ritual to Theatre and Back: The Structure/Process of the Efficacy-Entertainment Dyad." *Educational Theatre Journal* 26 (4): 455–81.

Shahar, Meir. 2008. *The Shaolin Monastery: History, Religion, and the Chinese Martial Arts.* Honolulu: University of Hawai'i Press.

Slovenz-Low, Madeline. 1994. "Lions in the Streets: A Performance Ethnography of Cantonese Lion Dancing in New York City's Chinatown." PhD diss., New York University.

Statistics Canada. *2011 Census of Population.* Accessed 28 August 2015, http://www12.statcan.ca/census-recensement/2011/as-sa/98-314-x/98-314-x2011003_2-eng.cfm.

— 2016. *2016 Census of Population.* Accessed 25 July 2018. https://www12.statcan.gc.ca/census-recensement/2016/as-sa/98-200-x/2016010/98-200-x2016010-eng.cfm.

Thompson, Richard H. 1989. *Toronto's Chinatown: The Changing Social Organization of an Ethnic Community.* New York, NY: AMS Press.

Thorpe, Ashley. 2005. "Only Joking? The Relationship between the Clown and Percussion in 'Jingju.'" *Asian Theatre Journal* 22 (2): 269–92.

Wong, Deborah. 2008. "Moving: From Performance to Performative Ethnography and Back Again." In *Shadows in the Field: New Perspectives for Fieldwork in Ethnomusicology*, 2nd ed., edited by Gregory Barz and Timothy J. Cooley, 76–89. New York, NY: Oxford University Press.

Wong, Wai Yip. 2011. "Defining Chinese Folk Religion: A Methodological Interpretation." *Asian Philosophy* 21 (2): 153–70.
Wrazen, Louise. 2007. "Relocating the Tatras: Place and Music in Górale Identity and Imagination." *Ethnomusicology* 51 (2): 185–204.
Yang, Fenggang, and Anning Hu. 2012. "Mapping Chinese Folk Religion in Mainland China and Taiwan." *Journal for the Scientific Study of Religion* 51 (3): 505–21.
Yao, Hai-Hsing. 1990. "The Relationship between Percussive Music and the Movements of Actors in Peking Opera." *Journal of the Society for Asian Music* 21 (2): 39–70.
Yao, Haishing. 2001. "Martial-Acrobatic Arts in Peking Opera: With a Brief Analysis of Fighting Movement in a Scene from 'The Three Forked Crossroad.'" *Journal of Asian Martial Arts* 10 (1): 18–35.
Yee, Paul. 2010. *Jade in the Coal*. Directed by Heidi Sprecht, composed by Jin Zhang, featuring the Guangdong Cantonese Opera Academy First Troupe. Frederic Wood Theatre, 24 November to 4 December.
Zarrilli, Phillip. 2001. "Performing Arts." In *Martial Arts of the World: An Encyclopedia*. Vol. 1, *A-Q*, edited by Thomas A. Green, 417–22. Santa Barbara, CA: ABC Clio.
Zhang, Boyu. 1997. "Mathematical Rhythmic Structure of Chinese Percussion Music: An Analytical Study of *Shifan Luogu* Collections." PhD diss., Turku University.
Zheng, Su. 2010. *Claiming Diaspora: Music, Transnationalism, and Cultural Politics in Asian/Chinese America*. New York, NY: Oxford University Press.

Ian Hayes

Chapter 9

"Holy jeez, I can hear *everything*": Liveness in Cape Breton Fiddle Recordings

Whether at a house party, a dance, or a formal concert, live performance is an integral part of Cape Breton fiddling. An energetic music, it is understood by its participants (both performers and audience members) as a visceral experience that is closely linked to social context. Audio recordings, however, have been part of the tradition since the first commercial Cape Breton fiddle recording in 1928[1] and act as a prominent counterpart to live performances. Folklorist Ian McKinnon asserts that Cape Breton fiddle recordings are related to economics, transmission, and cultural identity: "the Cape Breton fiddle recording has proven itself invaluable as a cultural artifact in the island's cultural process" (1989, 2). This chapter discusses how, for members of the Cape Breton traditional[2] music community, music is marked by shared group experience and live performance, making the aesthetics of Cape Breton fiddle recordings intrinsically linked to notions of "liveness."

I explore the construct of liveness in commercial recordings of Cape Breton fiddling through interviews with professional musicians and audio engineers. For Cape Breton musicians negotiating their position between vernacular and professional music making, the ways in which liveness is presented can be used to create a recording that asserts Cape Breton identity on both local and international levels. Although having a live sound is highly valued by Cape Breton traditional musicians and audience members, liveness is a fluid concept that may be portrayed in different, sometimes contradictory, ways. Liveness can be heard in a homemade recording of a party, but also in a studio recording that consciously constructs a live aesthetic. In one sense, liveness can be presented with a "raw" aesthetic, which draws attention to the social context and performance as a whole. On the other hand, a "polished" aesthetic might be favoured, which stresses intimacy with the performer and the technical detail of a performance. While these two examples of "raw" and "polished" represent seemingly opposite extremes, the aesthetics discussed in this chapter exist on a spectrum between them. Decisions pertaining to microphone placement, how to balance the different frequencies of an instrument, or whether to include extra-musical sounds in the final mix can have profound symbolic meaning. Analyzing the decisions involved in the representation of Cape Breton fiddling on audio recordings provides insight into how musicians conceptualize the tradition and their own playing.

Here, I elaborate on research I have previously conducted on the interplay between structure and agency in Cape Breton fiddling (Hayes 2015; 2013; 2012). Although there are overarching socio-cultural processes and structures that help shape and define Cape Breton fiddling, individual agency creates considerable complexity and unpredictability. The fieldwork that informs this project consists of participant observation and ethnographic interviews with professional Cape Breton traditional musicians (largely between the ages of twenty and thirty-five) who relate to Cape Breton fiddling in deeply personal ways and have tremendous respect for the tradition. As professional musicians, however, they must constantly negotiate how they present their music in vernacular (such as a local square dance or house party), as well as commercial, contexts. Interviews with musicians are complemented by interviews with audio engineers who are responsible for representing this tradition in recordings.

The Performance Practice and History of Cape Breton Fiddling

The expression "Cape Breton fiddling" is generally used to refer to a single, unified tradition, whether it is as a reified construction within the popular imagination or simply out of convenience in everyday speech by tradition bearers. The fiddling of Cape Breton Island has become so entrenched in how the region's culture is imagined that it is inseparable from many aspects of life in the area. Although it is commonly believed to be a virtually unchanged version of the eighteenth-century Highland Scotland fiddle tradition, scholars and others now acknowledge the considerable musical change that has occurred over the past century (Doherty 1996). This musical change has largely been due to the innovation of individual musicians within the region, while explicit outside influence from other musical traditions is most noticeable in the expansion of repertoire.

Relatively self-contained until the twentieth century, Cape Breton fiddling has followed a different course of development from its antecedents and maintains an identity separate from its European and North American counterparts. Extensive face-to-face musical exchange largely occurred with musicians within Atlantic Canada, whose musical practices contained considerable overlap. New repertoire continued to enter the tradition during the eighteenth and nineteenth centuries through European tune book collections that eventually made their way to North America, but the tradition truly began to open to outside influences beyond Atlantic Canada in the early 1900s with Cape Bretoners migrating to Boston and other areas of New England for work. Today, the repertoire consists primarily of Scottish melodies and Cape Breton-composed tunes, along with some compositions from Irish and old-time traditions.

More accurately, however, Cape Breton fiddling is an umbrella term for a collection of distinct, yet closely related, music and dance traditions with overlapping performance practices, aesthetics, and repertoire. In addition to its being a "tradition" that is constructed of a conglomerate of regional or even family-based musical and dance styles, there is also a relatively consistent emphasis on musical individuality, further adding to the potential for variety within the overall genre (Graham 2006). While it is possible to outline some general characteristics, influences, and attitudes that are pertinent to "Cape Breton fiddling," there is enough diversity to create a lack of consensus among tradition bearers regarding even fairly common conventions.

Musicians and audiences typically describe Cape Breton fiddling as aggressive and energetic, closely related to both the square dance and step dance traditions that are commonly performed at local community halls, pubs, and house parties. This aggression and energy, characterized by a fiddler's distinctive tone and articulation, are a result of varied bowing techniques: most notes are played with individual bow strokes, although slurs are incorporated according to individual style; and bow pressure is varied from one stroke to the next (or even within the bow stroke), which creates the percussive, driving sound that is characteristic of the tradition.[3] "Correctness" of the tune is highly valued, resulting in melodic fixity, and is determined by the Cape Breton fiddle community over time (and not always unanimously agreed upon). In some cases, it is the version found in a popular tune book; in others, the "correct" version of a tune might be the way an influential fiddler played the tune on a particular recording.

In addition to differences in repertoire, piano accompaniment and overall aesthetics can be used to identify Cape Breton fiddling. In most current performance contexts, Cape Breton fiddling is typically a duo performance of a fiddler and piano accompanist,[4] although a guitar accompanist may also be present. The Cape Breton piano style has undergone significant changes over the years, but now consistently features walking bass lines constructed in octaves and perfect fifths (often with chromatic approach tones), and syncopated chords in the right hand (McMorran 2013, 16–26). It rose to prominence in the 1930s, after the piano replaced the pump organ as the main instrument for accompaniment (MacKinnon 2009, 32–9).

Commercial audio recordings have played an important role in the development of Cape Breton fiddling. Quickly becoming popular in the 1930s, they were a means of transmitting repertoire, as well as a way for tradition bearers to obtain public recognition and prestige through the regional success of these recordings. Initially, all commercial Cape Breton fiddle recordings were made by record labels in studios, with the majority of recordings released under the Celtic, Banff, and Rodeo record labels between 1935 and 1962. The departure of Rodeo Records owner George Taylor from the Maritimes in 1962 marks the end of this period of recordings.[5] McKinnon attributes the resultant slump in recording to both a lack of interest by record labels and musicians' distrust of the recording business due to the labels' dishonest and exploitative business practices (McKinnon 1989, 93–4, 96). At the same time, the popularity of fiddling in Cape Breton began to wane. Cape Breton fiddling was revived in the 1970s, however, largely in response to the CBC documentary *Vanishing Cape Breton Fiddler* (1971). This documentary, which suggested that the tradition might soon be lost, prompted the establishment of the Cape Breton Fiddler's Association and the Glendale Fiddle Festival, leading to a surge in formal fiddle lessons, particularly among youth (Garrison 1985; Thompson 2003).

Along with the revival came a renewed interest in recording. Dave Miller, an audio engineer from Halifax, began making on-location recordings of Cape Breton fiddle music, resulting in some of the first independent commercial recordings in the Cape Breton fiddling tradition.[6] These independent, on-location commercial recordings afforded greater artistic control to the musicians, in direct contrast to the earlier period of studio recordings. McKinnon asserts that a commercial *studio* recording of Cape Breton fiddling "rarely, if ever, captures the musicians' best performances" because of "the atmosphere within the recording session" (1989, 132). Studio recording sessions are generally divorced from the social context in which most vernacular performances would normally occur, making the session less exciting and inspiring for the musicians. This separation from social performances is particularly true for earlier commercial studio recordings, when performers were required to travel considerable distances to recording studios (Montreal was a common destination) and had little control over the session itself.

While the inadequacies of these earlier studio recordings are notable, the challenges of recording a performance within a social setting such as a party also made them a commercially viable recording option for many years. On-site recordings engender obvious difficulties regarding spatial organization and sound quality, as well as influencing the nature of the performance itself. For instance, an audience can provide desirable ambient sounds but can also be loud enough to interfere with the recording or even crowd the performers. While the quality of such a recording would make it unsuitable for commercial production, home-made recordings, or "dance tapes"[7] – amateur field recordings of dances and house parties originally recorded on reel-to-reel devices – are highly valued within the Cape Breton community because they are believed to be some of the most accurate representations of the tradition. The performers are playing in a relaxed and uninhibited manner, and the extra-musical sounds of the performance context (crowd noise, dancers, etc.) are understood to be representative of place and community, and more broadly, of regional identity.

It is not surprising, then, that McKinnon's informants emphasized the importance of an aesthetic of liveness and a connection to the original social context of the tradition when making a recording. Dave Miller's independent, on-location commercial recordings, usually made at either a house party or a relaxed recording session in a musician's living room, were meant to do this very thing: consciously represent a "live off-the-floor" style of recording that was meant to be directly representative of a particular performance. In addition to having the freedom and agency to record without the influence and control of oppressive labels, independent, on-location recordings from this period also engaged the values and aesthetics of Cape Breton dance tapes.

A new trend of Cape Breton fiddlers becoming recording artists began about a decade into the revival. Jerry Holland's *Master Cape Breton Fiddler* (1982) was the first Cape Breton fiddle recording to have extensive, planned arrangements presented in a highly polished manner, both in regard to the sound quality and the execution of performances. The increasing commercialization of Cape Breton fiddling continued, and reached unprecedented popularity during the Celtic boom of the 1990s. Cape Breton traditional music became an important part of Canadian popular culture in the 1990s, experiencing widespread national and even international commercial success with musical acts such as the Rankin Family, the Barra MacNeils, Natalie MacMaster, and Ashley MacIsaac. They each signed major record deals with commercial companies (EMI, Polygram, Warner, and A&M Records), something that had been unheard of for Cape Breton traditional music acts before that time.

These commercial, staged performances of Cape Breton fiddling represented a new style that was distinct from the semi-improvised "traditional" performances typically associated with a square dance or house party. These recorded performances were carefully arranged, and typically included a drummer, bassist, and electric guitarist, playing rock, country, or even hip-hop grooves to support and accompany otherwise traditional repertoire. This style of Cape Breton fiddling included a great deal of musical experimentation and emphasized innovation rather than previously expected conventions. This new performance style was intended for a broad audience that might not be intimately familiar with Cape Breton fiddling, and it influenced many Cape Breton musicians who followed. Natalie MacMaster and Ashley MacIsaac – probably the most widely recognized fiddlers who are proponents of this style – juxtapose "traditional" with more popular music styles in an effort to position themselves both locally and globally.

Natalie MacMaster has led bands of various sizes, ranging from a "traditional" duo of fiddle and piano to a seven-piece band (fiddle, piano/keyboard, guitar, bass, drums, and percussion). Cape Breton fiddling is always her focus, but she has also explored other musics through fusion experiments with styles such as flamenco, with guitarist Jesse Cooke, and bluegrass, with banjo player Béla Fleck. The distinction between this experimental style and traditional fiddling is clearly demonstrated on MacMaster's album *Live* (2002), which consists of two separate discs – one of her seven-piece band playing a concert at the Living Arts Center in Mississauga, Ontario, and the other of her playing a square dance in Glencoe Mills, Cape Breton. Three of her albums reached gold status in Canada, and she has been the recipient of two Juno awards, as well as the Order of Canada.

Ashley MacIsaac's groundbreaking album, *Hi, how are you today?* (1995), on which MacIsaac is accompanied by a grunge/rock band, also introduced new influences to Cape Breton fiddling. The album was well received commercially, and reached double-platinum status in Canada. Like MacMaster, MacIsaac is also celebrated for his traditional playing, which is featured on his follow-up album, *Fine, thank you very much* (1996). Based on their titles, the two albums were intended to be in dialogue with each other, juxtaposing the two very different aesthetics. MacIsaac went on to combine Cape Breton fiddling with hip hop and electronic dance music in later albums such as *Helter's Celtic* (1999). In this context, MacIsaac cleverly used the general structure of a radio-friendly, popular music recording (complete with hooks, interludes, and audio sampling) to accompany Cape Breton fiddle tunes, performed in an otherwise traditional manner. In many ways his music resembled a typical popular music recording, but instead of the vocal melody of a popular song being the focus of the recording, MacIsaac featured a traditional fiddle melody.

MacMaster and MacIsaac have demonstrated the potential for artistic exploration and experimentation in Cape Breton fiddling, as well as its potential for wide-ranging commercial success. Folklorist and ethnomusicologist Burt Feintuch argues that while their newer, commercial "fusion" style is contentious among traditionalists (Feintuch 2004, 90–3), MacIsaac and MacMaster influenced an entire generation of Cape Breton fiddlers.[8] Their recordings have become required listening for any aspiring fiddler today, and they serve as significant learning tools with regard to style and repertoire. Throughout their careers they have made recordings in a variety of settings, and used different engineering techniques ("raw" aesthetics for more "traditional" recordings and "polished" aesthetics to create more commercial, internationally marketed recordings) to meet the expectations of wide-ranging audiences.

Contrasting Conceptions of Liveness

References to liveness can seem ubiquitous in discussions of contemporary audio recordings, but the concept of liveness has many possible meanings. Musicologist Paul Sanden writes, "Liveness is a perception, guided by the different ways it may be evoked inside cultural discourse and practice ... Liveness exists as a fluid concept among different people and at different times, rather than as a concrete ontological category with well-defined essential characteristics. This very fluidity of the concept of liveness is, in part, what makes this issue so complex and worthy of further scrutiny" (2009, 8). The complex and fluid nature of liveness described by Sanden is exemplified in Cape Breton fiddle recordings. In part, this fluidity is enabled by the absence of formal or specific vocabularies to describe the complex musical aesthetics that characterize these recordings. Various ethnomusicologists, including Thomas Porcello in his study with audio engineers (1991), Steven Feld's work with the Kaluli (1994), and Ingrid Monson's research with jazz musicians (1996), explore how simple descriptors and metaphors are often used as shorthand to discuss complex musical concepts and aesthetics. The discourse around liveness reflects the complexity of this concept; for many, what is meant by liveness is difficult to articulate in a detailed, technical manner.

As I am using the term, liveness is a construct used to compare recorded music to non-recorded musical performances, and engages with attitudes toward technology and authenticity. In his history of sound reproduction, Jonathan Sterne (2003) discusses how audio fidelity, and by extension, authenticity, has been a preoccupation for listeners since the very first audio recordings. Simon Frith (1996) demonstrates that listeners are keenly interested in musical authenticity and may take issue with technological mediation, sound reproduction, and even the musical performance itself.

Thomas Turino (2008) argues that making a live-sounding recording often requires musicians to play in ways that are significantly different from how they would perform in other contexts; furthermore, it may also require significant technological intervention. Elliot Bates documents that a recording of arranged traditional music in Turkey uses "arduous and detailed arrangement and nonlinear editing work that is made feasible through DAW (digital audio workstation) systems" to produce a product that is deemed aesthetically appropriate by knowledgable listeners (2010, 81). Christopher Scales similarly argues in his study of Indigenous powwow recordings that "liveness – which refers to an aesthetic discourse as well as a set of technological and methodological recording practices – is sonically marked on powwow recordings through specific timbral manipulations and nonmusical sonic events, some of which are the natural outcome of a particular recording method, while others are achieved through careful digital manipulation" (2012, 212). These ideas from the broader discourse around liveness are consistent with how the concept manifests in a Cape Breton context in two distinct, yet related, ways: liveness can be related primarily to the audio quality of the recording (audio fidelity), or conversely, to the nature of the performance itself.

Due to the lack of an established vocabulary to describe distinctions in the aesthetics of liveness, I use the terms "raw" and "polished" to distinguish contrasting performance aesthetics, which are associated with different engineering and production processes. A "raw" aesthetic may have a lower audio quality, but it captures the musical performance that is (or at least seems to be) live, uninterrupted, and/or uncut. On the other hand, a "polished" aesthetic focuses on audio fidelity. While a "polished" recording may present a performance that is actively manipulated through audio engineering, the attention given to overall sound quality creates a sense of detail in its sonic replication. It takes little imagination to equate a "raw" recording to a single-track field recording of a house party, perhaps on a reel-to-reel tape recorder. Conversely, a "polished" sound might easily be related to a multi-track studio recording.

Although the above description positions "raw" and "polished" as discrete, even binary, categories, the distinctions are not so simple. Because each aesthetic has a different goal ("raw" focusing on performance context and "polished" focusing on the nuance of the performance itself), it is possible for them to be combined in a single recording. As I outline below, both aesthetics are described indiscriminately as "live" by Cape Breton musicians. Furthermore, all audio recordings are, in fact, engineered, and there is no such thing as unmediated, unmanipulated reproduced sound (i.e., while not all recordings are made by an engineer turning knobs, decisions about how to record a sound are never neutral). Factors such as where a performance is recorded, what equipment is used to record the performance, and where microphones are placed are all decisions that significantly shape the overall recording. While both "raw" and "polished" aesthetics are created through various engineering techniques and active manipulation of sound, they can also both provide the illusion of a live, "natural" sound, free of technological mediation.

The construction of liveness can change significantly from one tradition to another and be presented in different ways. As Turino states, "the aesthetics and conceptions about what live music is among different cultural groups affect the recording and mixing processes" (2008, 72). My discussion of "raw" and "polished" aesthetics relates specifically to Cape Breton fiddling and is shaped by how musicians conceptualize the music they play. At the same time, however, my research with Cape Breton musicians fits into a broader discussion about how audio fidelity and performances are perceived in audio recordings in a variety of styles of music. For instance, both Thomas Porcello (2005) and Louise Meintjes (2003) discuss liveness as a symbol of regional identity in, respectively, Austin, Texas and Johannesburg, South Africa; both studies connect liveness to discourses of authenticity. Based on her research in South Africa, Meintjes writes, "Liveness is an illusion of sounding live that is constructed through technological intervention in the studio and mediated symbolically through discourses about the natural and the artistic. To sound authentically African is to sound live" (2003, 112). Ironically, in many cases for Meintjes' informants, liveness was reliant on mechanical drum machines or MIDI programming, which sharply contrast with a human performance on acoustic instruments.

Meintjes implicitly discusses the difference between "raw" and "polished" liveness in unpacking the different musical aesthetics of South African musicians and engineers. Zulu musicians, on the one hand, conceptualize liveness as a wall of sound, understood through physical experience. White South African engineers, on the other, conceptualize liveness in its recorded form, valuing clarity and separation – a polished aesthetic that they believe is required for success on an international level (2005, 18). In Porcello's work (2005), the "live" aesthetic is understood by Austin musicians as being in direct opposition to the Nashville multi-track studio aesthetic, which relies on greater clarity and separation of individual instruments.

Like the musicians in the two examples above, Cape Breton musicians walk a tightrope between creating recordings that are musically meaningful on a vernacular level but might be too "raw" to be commercially viable, and a highly "polished" recording that accurately presents the intricacies of a performance but may lack regional character and musical values.

Creating Liveness in Cape Breton Fiddle Recordings

Audio engineers in a Cape Breton context construct and manipulate elements of liveness by using an array of techniques, including reverb and other ambient sounds, participatory discrepancies, and hyper-realism. I explore each of these elements and how they are used in the recording process by both performers and audio engineers.

Reverb and Ambient Sounds

Reverb plays a key role in constructing liveness in Cape Breton fiddle recordings by connecting the performance to a particular space, whether it is the "natural" ambient sound of an on-location recording or a recording that is manipulated to mimic aspects of culturally significant performance contexts. Reverb is how we "hear" space. (Because sight also often corroborates such aural information, we may take this for granted.) Reverb provides vital information with regard to the distance and direction of sounds, which we are highly adept at interpreting. Reverb helps determine the distance between a sound and other objects or surfaces; for example, a conversation will sound differently in a small room than in an empty gymnasium. Whether reverb is recorded through the natural sound of a room or is added via other means such as computer processing, to the listener, it is still the expression of space in auditory form.

The ways in which space – both real and imagined – is expressed in audio recordings through echo and reverb are explored by Peter Doyle (2005). The reverberant qualities of the recording space are clearly audible to the listener, aurally communicating information such as the dimensions of a room or the relative location of the musicians within the recording space; for example, Doyle argues that Gene Austin's recording of the Tin Pan Alley hit "My Blue Heaven" combines close-miked vocals with off-microphone musical accompaniment to suggest an intimacy with the vocalist and a physical distance from others (2005, 72–3). In a Cape Breton recording, as with other studio recordings, reverb can be used to construct both "raw" and "polished" aesthetics. For instance, in a "raw" recording, the performers may be playing in the same room, miked at a distance and thereby capturing the ambient sonic reverberation of the room. Although this set-up can create a powerful effect, reminiscent of a house party or early recording, it can also cause challenges with respect to other engineering tasks such as audio editing or equalization, since the more rationalized and isolated each audio track is, the easier it is to manipulate it in post-production. Conversely, the more "polished" sound of a multi-track studio recording would have the musicians in separate rooms with digital reverb added through computer plug-ins.

Space is a key aspect in achieving the desired violin sound on a recording, both in terms of how the fiddler experiences space in relation to his or her distance from a microphone, as well as how studio space shapes the sound of the recording. Fiddler and pianist Kimberley Fraser offers, "I like it if they can get a sound that's a nice room sound where you have some air. As opposed to a very tight, room sound, I don't like ... There are advantages to doing it in the isolation booth, for sure. But if you've got your stuff together and you're well rehearsed ... you can just go in and play it. There's nothing that beats that in my opinion. Getting a nice, big room sound, and playing live where you're not separated from the piano player" (2011). For Fraser, recording in the same room as her fellow musicians not only feels more comfortable, but also documents what she considers to be a more accurate performance. The overall ambience, then, can be important in creating a live-sounding recording, influencing not only audio engineering, but how musicians perform and interact with each other.

In addition to reverb, ambient non-musical sounds related to the performance can contribute to a sense of liveness. In his study of liveness in Glenn Gould recordings, Paul Sanden discusses what he terms "corporeal liveness," sounds of liveness that demonstrate the physicality of the performance, such as the sound of Gould's voice or the creaking of his chair (2009, 21–4). Such sounds make explicit reference to the physical body of the performer and, without them, an audio recording could be heard as divorced from the physical body that performed it. In a Cape Breton recording, this corporeal liveness occurs through extra-musical sounds, such as crowd noise, or the sound of a musician's stomping foot keeping time. The sound of a foot stomp can, in fact, become an integral part of a Cape Breton fiddle recording, which I explore in greater detail later in this chapter.

Participatory Discrepancies

Participatory discrepancies are also particularly important in creating a live sound or human element in music. As ethnomusicologist Charles Keil writes, "The power of music is in its participatory discrepancies ... Music, to be personally involving and socially valuable, must be 'out of time' and 'out of tune'" (1987, 275). In a Cape Breton recording, participatory discrepancies can be created, as I mentioned earlier, by miking a room to record the naturally occurring reverb. Participatory discrepancies are also typically found in the minor rhythmic differences between the fiddler and accompanist or the subtle variation of the fiddler's intonation. Participatory discrepancies may also be manipulated through audio editing – whether they are carefully preserved through careful audio editing or eliminated completely.

Hyper-realism

A "polished" aesthetic of liveness can be expressed through sound quality and the overall detail of a recording, often taken to the point of hyper-reality. Although not the same as liveness, hyper-realism is an important characteristic of a "polished" live aesthetic. This approach captures such intense aural detail that it sounds as if the listener is seated in the same room as the performers; in fact, it creates a much more detailed sound than what a listener would experience in person. Elements of the social context of the performance such as crowd noise may be added in a controlled, rationalized way (e.g., the use of audio sampling), as opposed to capturing these sounds in situ.

An example of the way hyper-reality can be created in the studio is discussed by Porcello in relation to drum-kit miking, where each piece of the kit is miked individually, balanced and equalized in relation to every other piece, and combined to make a composite drum track (2005, 108). In a Cape

Breton recording, a similar sense of hyper-reality can be accomplished by close-miking (and even multi-miking) instruments, which are each recorded to individual tracks, creating a high degree of clarity and separation in the overall mix. Such detail and clarity are particularly important for the fiddle because it is the lead melody instrument; it is commonly recorded in an isolation booth to allow for maximum control in mixing and editing.

Among Cape Breton musicians and fiddle enthusiasts, "raw" liveness is most often equated with the local, vernacular tradition, while "polished" liveness is associated with professionalism and the international music industry. These associations are particularly evident in the contrast drawn between "dance tapes" and commercial recordings. "Dance tapes" encapsulate the experience of a Cape Breton fiddle performance, including the performers' idiosyncrasies and the spontaneity of their performance; professional studio recordings, on the other hand, may be valued for their artistry but are typically seen primarily as commodities that are to be consumed by both the local community and abroad (McKinnon 1989, 132–3; Doherty 2015, 193). While there is a correlation between recording contexts and how liveness is constructed (i.e., a "raw" aesthetic is often linked to on-location recordings and a "polished" aesthetic with multi-track studios), this correlation is not strict, and various aspects of liveness can be combined in seemingly contradictory ways. For instance, in a Cape Breton context, hi-fidelity recordings are often recorded on location (e.g., in someone's home), representing a "raw" liveness that would not typically have the detailed sound quality of a recording studio. It is equally possible (and fairly common), however, to make a hi-fidelity recording in a multi-track studio. Here, a sense of "raw" liveness can be preserved by recording in a "live off-the-floor" manner (using minimal audio editing), while at the same time employing techniques of close-miking and careful equalization that enable a "polished" and "hyper-realistic" liveness. In this way, two seemingly opposed aesthetics can be combined to make a live-sounding Cape Breton fiddle recording.

Liveness in On-Location Recordings

Paul MacDonald is a highly regarded Cape Breton guitarist and audio engineer who has worked on roughly one hundred albums. His recordings represent "raw" liveness in a way that attempts to preserve the original context of the performances, usually made in an on-location, field-recording style. Some of his recordings have enjoyed commercial success; they are most valued by traditionalists and hold considerable currency on a local level. He accomplishes his overall aesthetic through a combination of careful use of reverb, preservation of participatory discrepancies, and choice of a space with good acoustics. Microphone placement, too, is critical, since he employs only a single stereo pair of mics. These mics are mounted on a homemade engineering device consisting of two hinged pieces of plywood, through which he controls the amount of reverb according to the degree that the device is opened or closed. In his own words, "I just want my record to sound like you were sitting there, and that you can have some sort of experience of how much fun was had. The joy of it, the detail of it. What happened at that session, the detail and the joy and the setting" (2011). This method of recording differs deliberately from that of multi-track recordings. MacDonald explains further, "There's something about the way instruments mix in the air that you can't or could never do with a mixing board ... When those instruments are vibrating and playing together, there are special things that happen that you can't make happen through the wires. It's not possible. Only air can do that ... There's a real magic and a soul, I think, that you capture in the air" (2011). Although MacDonald values sound quality in his recordings, his comments reveal that he resists the aesthetic of total clarity and separation that is characteristic of multi-track studio recordings. Instead of recreating liveness through technological studio manipulation, he attempts to create recordings that carefully retain the timbre of the instruments and sound of the room exactly as they were experienced by the musicians and audience.

As I described earlier, a live recording aesthetic is particularly important to the Cape Breton fiddling tradition, although it has only existed as a conscious construction in commercial recordings since musicians took more active roles in shaping their recordings in the 1970s and 1980s. While having a highly polished recording is valued for its ability to present nuances of tone and articulation, Cape Breton musicians and listeners also conceptualize the tradition as one that exists in dance halls or house parties, and reproducing that quality of liveness may take priority over other performance aspects. Non-commercial recordings such as dance tapes are highly valued and sought by local Cape Breton aficionados, and function as the most important musical source for many fiddlers. These amateur field recordings have been MacDonald's main inspiration for his own recordings.

> That Mike Hall record was done in three hours.[9] Had the piano tuned, walked in, stuck that rig in front of the piano and the fiddle, moved it around a bit until I had a nice mix, said "Ok guys, we're

ready," recorded all the music, had a cup of tea, and went home. That's the record. But also, it was a good room, and the other essential ingredient is there – a couple of good listeners. Minnie and Alex MacMaster were there.[10] To me, it's always important too, that when you're making a recording that you're actually making it for people … When you've got Alex and Minnie on the couch, you're playing for Alex and Minnie. You're playing for people, and there's a certain thing between listener and player there. Listener, player, room, microphones, you know? That's really special. Whereas, the other way, ok, well yeah, it's great, it's all polished, everything's perfect. Wonderful. But it's lacking those ingredients, and to me, to have at least one or two good listeners in the room is very important. (2011)

MacDonald's high valuation of an audience pays homage to the "traditional" dance tape conception of a live recording. The inclusion of an audience, even a small one, links the performance to a culturally relevant social context[11] that involves the audience as participants.

MacDonald's preference is realism rather than the idealized perfection of an extensively manipulated studio performance: "Every one of [my recordings] has a wart or two of some sort. Chairs that squeak, you know? On *The Fiddle Tree*[12] at one point, like in one of the most profound parts of a slow air, you can hear this circle fly buzzing himself to death on the floor, right in the middle of the musicians. [laughs] So maybe some of my recordings have a little too much detail" (2011). Although an engineer aiming for a more "polished" aesthetic would opt to use another take or try to edit the recording to mask an imperfection, for Paul MacDonald, a minor imperfection does not necessarily detract from a quality performance.

MacDonald's recordings are similar to dance tapes in another way: he uses audio engineering practices that alter the performance in only very subtle ways. In his view, this is part of preserving the musicians' tone and dynamics, and translates to specific engineering methods: "I've never used compression.[13] I've used reverb only to fix bad sounding rooms that are too dry. I'll put a little touch of reverb on. But I've never used compression. I'll use EQ,[14] again, only to fix a room. I don't use EQ to change an instrument's sound. I use EQ to correct room fluctuations that don't sound that great … I just leave the fiddle exactly like it is. If it's high endy, then it's high endy" (2011). Despite his aesthetics of "realness," MacDonald's recordings are not entirely free of sonic manipulation or modern studio engineering practices. For a commercial recording, he records three takes, and refines the performance by cutting and pasting various takes. In this way, he is willing to manipulate the performance itself to some extent, but not the actual sound quality or tonal aesthetic.

Liveness in Recording Studios

Lakewind Sound Studios and its engineer, Mike Sheppard (locally known as Shep or Sheppy), have been important actors in the development of the accepted sounds and practices of Cape Breton fiddle recordings. Originally established in 1995 for the personal use of founders Gordie Sampson and Fred Lavery,[15] the studio became well known among their friends, who began using the studio as well. Before long, the small, private studio expanded into a full-scale business enterprise. Today, Lakewind is one of the most-respected studios on the east coast, and a high-profile location for Cape Breton fiddle recording.[16] Lavery and I counted over seventy-five traditional Cape Breton CDs that were recorded there (including the majority of the recordings made by my informants), which is a significant number for a relatively niche music market.

Many of my informants pointed to Sheppard's work as an engineer and producer as an important contribution to their recordings. His engineering style is "polished," embracing hyper-reality while using reverb and ambient sounds in a controlled manner. Using terms such as "pristine," "clear," and "crisp" to describe the overall aesthetic of Sheppard's engineering style, my informants felt that a traditional album recorded there had an instantly recognizable sound: full, at times even larger than life, yet still retaining a certain level of intimacy. Cape Breton pianist Jason Roach commented, "Lakewind, the studio itself, is defining [the sound of Cape Breton]. So much of that is Sheppy deciding on a sound" (2010). Lavery also acknowledged Sheppard's influence: "He's assisting in production values all the time, and suggesting ... maybe helping out when things go a little off track or whatever. You know, just giving sound advice to the artist if they're not particularly experienced in the studio. A lot of the time, these people could benefit from a producer, but a lot of times they don't have the money to hire a producer. So that's usually the case. As fiddlers gain more experience they're able to self-produce. They learn how to do it through experience, so it kind of works itself out" (2011). Celebrated locally for his editing abilities, Sheppard routinely isolates individual ornamentations (i.e., cuts, grace notes, trills, etc.), which he then manipulates and repositions within a given track, often rendering punch-ins[17] redundant.

The way Sheppard approaches audio editing is notably different from MacDonald (who tries to minimize the amount of audio editing employed), potentially creating a take that is an elaborate patchwork of heavily manipulated audio files (as is common practice in multi-track studios).

Violin timbre is a crucial part of a recording, and recording engineers can play a key role in shaping the timbre of instruments in the studio. The sound that Sheppard and the fiddler agree upon is not only understood to be a signifier of Cape Bretonness, but also a negotiation between "raw" and "polished": "I try to stay kind of true to the natural sound. That's where I stay. But as soon as you put a microphone anywhere close to a fiddle, everybody would call that the studio sound ... I worked with a couple of Irish fiddlers, and they immediately want to roll the high end off the fiddle. All that top stuff, the clarity part of it, it's not important to them. They just want more kind of a dry, tight sounding fiddle. So, a couple of occasions, that's been the case. And in Cape Breton style, it's trying to get the full spectrum, so as you said before, it sounds like you're sitting in front of the fiddler" (2012). It is significant that Sheppard uses much of the same language to describe his polished live aesthetic as Paul MacDonald does to describe his raw live aesthetic. Both believe their recordings sound as if the listener was physically in front of the performers: "to sound like you were sitting there" (Paul MacDonald 2011) and "sounds like you're sitting in front of the fiddler" (Mike Sheppard 2012). That an ideal can be simultaneously expressed so similarly and constructed so differently underscores the intertextual nature of liveness, and the role that imagination plays in shaping aesthetics.

Creating a live violin sound in the studio is also an issue of context and perspective. While a live studio sound is clearly different from what is heard in a non-recorded performance, it is understood to *represent* a live performance. Perspective is also important. Someone listening to a recording will "hear" a violin sound very differently from someone who is sitting next to the fiddler. Furthermore, the fiddlers themselves "hear" the violin differently than other listeners, as the instrument is held against their bodies, the violin sound vibrating through their head and jaws. Sheppard discusses the difference in these perspectives:

> It's a tough thing, because fiddlers, they have their instrument by their ear. So, what they're hearing coming through the speakers is really two different things [how the fiddler hears the violin and how an audience member hears it]. But you just try to find the middle ground there,

where it sounds as close as it does if they were listening to themselves ... out of body. [laughs] How it sounds to a person standing right in front of them, that's how we try to represent that on the recording ... And of course, some people are used to DI ...[18] like the live sound. Either in a kitchen or on a stage. So, there's a bunch of stuff you have to kind of meet in order to get them happy. (2012)

Any number of violin sounds may be realistic and *interpreted* as live: the sound of an amplified violin, the sound of a violin as the player hears it, or the sound of a violin being played in a hall, etc. The sound that is used on a recording depends on how the musician and engineer wish the listener to experience and understand the recording.

Although raw liveness can hold significant cultural value, in part due to its connection to dance tape recordings, some musicians prefer to present their music with a more polished aesthetic. Fiddler and multi-instrumentalist J.P. Cormier is one such musician:

Although field recordings need to be done, I think it's a detriment to do a field recording of somebody who's not dying – somebody who's quite able to go into a perfectly good studio and make a beautiful record. And you put a field recording out of him? It doesn't make sense to me ... If I ever make another fiddle record, ... I'm going to make a record that's sonically ... syrup. You'll listen to it and just fall over in your chair and melt onto the floor. Now that's what I would go for, for myself. I want to erase all my pimples and freckles, and warts and knobs. I don't want to *exaggerate* them trying to be PBS material. (2012)

Cormier's polished aesthetic does not come as a surprise considering he worked as a session musician in Nashville for much of his early adult life. The highly polished aesthetic that he values references the original performance in a less direct way than MacDonald's, relying more heavily on an imagined perfection that can be constructed in a multi-track studio. The contrast between these aesthetics points to potential distinctions between a recording's function and its target audience. A "raw" recording reminiscent of a dance tape may be highly valued on a local level, but a highly polished studio recording may hold more cultural capital at an international level. Overall, listeners outside the tradition are more familiar with a polished engineering style that is frequently associated with mainstream popular music.

Violin tone is also a highly personal part of a fiddler's musical identity and how she or he conceives of the tradition, as I have demonstrated above. Paul MacDonald shared an anecdote that demonstrates what can happen when the symbolic meaning of timbre is not understood or respected by the engineer, resulting in a conflict in the mixing process:

> So, I had this experience with Jerry [Holland] where we worked really hard just to record him as natural as possible. With no compression, no reverb. No compression, or anything like that. And we were having fun. And we made a couple of good records, you know? And then we went down to do some mastering for his first CD. And in the mastering studio, you know, this very well-intentioned engineer, CBC engineer, hooked it up through these compressors ... and it's really fancy, state of the art for its day – Focusrite EQs and compressors.[19] And the first thing he did was squash Jerry's dynamics and rolled all of the top off his tone. And Jerry got really upset, but he was too shy to ... He felt awkward, you know, because this guy was giving away his free time and doing us a big favour, and he was a bigwig ... you know? What do you say? I could just tell Jerry wasn't happy. And this guy kept saying, "Well, it's my professional opinion that that's too much high end for the public." And finally, Jerry leaves to go smoke, and he was in tears. "Do you hear what that guy's doing to my tone?" ... And we went back in ... Even so, you know, that guy ... we tried to compromise with him and he was such a jerk about it. That's Jerry Holland, man. His zing. The zing. The treble. The zing of his tone. (2011)

In this anecdote, MacDonald demonstrates the significance of violin tone as representing Cape Breton identity, personal identity, and liveness. Although violin tone may be presented in a recording in drastically different ways, both MacDonald and Sheppard agree that capturing a full spectrum of frequencies is a fundamental part of creating a Cape Breton violin tone on a recording. While it may be common in other fiddle styles to limit higher frequencies to some degree in order to create a warmer, mellower sound, in a Cape Breton recording it is important to capture all frequencies (including high end). This results in both a well-defined articulation in the performance, as well as a more accurate production of how the performance would be heard in a natural, unamplified setting. This characteristic Cape Breton violin sound can be expressed using a realistic approach, a more abstract method that takes more artistic liberties in constructing an imagined "live" performance, or a combination of the two.

Microphone placement is a crucial component in any instrument's sound when recording; it affects how specific frequencies are recorded, as well as reverb. Close microphone placement effectively captures low-end frequencies and creates an intimate sound with little natural reverb. The use of close-miking can draw attention to aspects of a performance that are not normally audible, such as lips smacking or the movement of an instrument against a performer's body. Conversely, distance-miking creates a sound with more natural reverb, but less definition. While making it easier to limit and control undesirable aspects of a performance, distance-miking lacks the intimacy of close-miking and may capture unwanted ambient sounds.

Hyper-realism is further exaggerated and more noticeable when multiple instruments are close-miked, and appear on separate, isolated tracks. At a live performance, it is unlikely, even impossible, to hear instruments with the detail and clarity of being inches from each instrument, individually and simultaneously, but it is easy to produce this effect through close-miking in a multi-track studio. J.P. Cormier explains how he relates to a hyper-realistic notion of liveness in recordings:

> Jerry Holland had the best violin sound that I've ever heard on a record. ... He was the first person to ever close-mike a violin. They always thought you had to have a room to record a violin properly. No. He had two ... a stereo pair sandwiching his fiddle ... And there was a third mic there in the corner. So, they mixed these three things together. And I'm telling you, you can hear every single breath, movement of finger. It was so intimate, it was almost unpleasant. The first time you heard it, you went, "Holy jeez. I can hear *everything*." Every scratch, movement of the bow, every single thing he did. You could hear him breathing sometimes. That was the best fiddle sound I ever heard, and that's what I've always done since then. I've always multi-miked my violins. (2012)[20]

In this passage, Cormier provides yet another possible depiction of a recorded Cape Breton violin sound as live. Multi-miking offers a close-up perspective of the instrument's tone, an approach somewhat different from that of Paul MacDonald or Mike Sheppard. MacDonald's approach involves relatively little manipulation of the performance: he does not close-mike musicians, thereby creating recordings that focus on the larger sound of the room and overall social context. Sheppard's recordings, by contrast, provide a close-up sound, though his approach is not as "extreme" as that described by Cormier, and he carefully manipulates the recording to omit any potentially undesirable aspects of the performance. All three work very carefully to achieve the sound that performers want to represent themselves and their understanding of the tradition.

In Cape Breton fiddling, a fiddler's foot stomp typically serves as a percussive accompaniment to the performance. As such, the sound of the foot stomp has become an important signifier of liveness in Cape Breton recordings. There is an element of staging involved here that goes beyond microphone placement; in addition to balancing the foot sound with that of the violin, the interaction between the footwear of the fiddler and the materials of the floor must be considered. If musicians do not feel that the floor has a pleasing sound, it may be necessary to construct an area for the musician to stomp.[21]

The foot stomp is consciously staged as an iconic reference to traditional performance contexts, such as a dance hall or house party. Glenn Graham recounts the deliberate, almost painstaking, process of getting an appropriate foot sound at Lakewind:

> We went all around the studio, different places, just trying different places for the foot sound. Actually, where I recorded most of the CD wasn't actually in one of the isolation booths, it was in a hallway that was between the bathroom and the office of the studio, like in a hallway. Because there was this nice place where when you hit your foot it felt like you were on a stage in a hall, or just on your own kitchen or living room floor. It just had this little bit of give to it. So, to me, it's important, because I tap my foot and without tapping my foot and having a good backing to the fiddling, it just doesn't feel right to me. So, when I do that I want to try to make it, I actually want to try to make the studio sound similar to how it would sound if I was playing it somewhere else, too. I want a live sound to it. If you're going to be listening to me, well, at least the fiddling, and the foot, which I think is a part of my music, should come out maybe in my recording, too. (2011)

Sheppard, the engineer for that recording, recalls, "[Glenn Graham] wanted the hollow floor so that he could stomp. And you can hear that all over the record. I mean, it just sounds like thunder. And it can create energy in a track for sure" (2012). This example demonstrates how musicians can interact in highly specific ways with studio space and the reverberant qualities they possess.[22] Graham actively chose to record in a multi-track studio, but not to use the isolation booth, recreating the sonic character of a space that was culturally and personally meaningful.

Recreating a live feeling through the inclusion of a foot stomp reveals the importance the foot plays in some musicians' conceptions of the music. In a live, non-amplified setting, the sound of a fiddler's foot is often quite loud, and heard by the audience; in a high volume, amplified setting like a dance, however, the sound of a fiddler's foot is considerably less prominent and may not be heard at all. So, including a foot sound in a recording relates not only to the sound of a performance in context, but also to how musicians relate to the music on a physical, experiential basis. The stomp, to a fiddler, is part of the music (whether it is heard by the audience or not), and part of how the music is embodied.

Although the inclusion of a foot sound has become fairly common in the recording studio, it has not always been part of the studio aesthetic; in fact, before the stomp became a sought-after technique in the studio, it was actively avoided. J.P. Cormier explains that avoiding the sound of the feet on a recording was important in early Cape Breton recordings: "Winston Fitzgerald ... cut the four or five LPs ... with two mics. One mic about a foot away from him, a ribbon mic,[23] and one mic sitting between Estwood [Davidson, his guitarist] and Beattie [Wallace, his piano accompanist]. And his shoes off so the mics wouldn't pick up their feet. That's how they made the record" (2012). Kimberley Fraser similarly recalls, "The funny thing, when I first went in, they gave me a carpet so you wouldn't hear the foot sound. Which now, I'd rather hear the foot, I like hearing the foot ... Because it's the way you'd hear it in a live performance" (2011).

The importance of a foot sound, along with sensitivity to the fiddle timbre, has changed over time. Early studio recordings of Cape Breton fiddlers were not necessarily made by engineers who were intimately familiar with their fiddling style, aesthetics, and associated values. As professional quality recording became more accessible to fiddlers, first via on-location recording and then multi-track studios, fiddlers began to take a more active role in the recording process. Moreover, it is now commonplace to record with an engineer from the region, such as Sheppard or MacDonald, who is sensitive to Cape Breton fiddle aesthetics. As this transition occurred, musicians were exposed to the myriad techniques available to shape their fiddle timbre to their own tastes. One could choose to have an intimate, hyper-realistic sound (close-miking), or conversely, a warm sound rich in natural reverb and participatory discrepancies (distance-miking). Such decisions are related to both how musicians choose to represent their musical identity and how the recording might be received in local and international markets.

Liveness and Audio Editing

The possibilities of audio editing in a modern multi-track recording studio can be mind-boggling; from punch-ins to pitch correction and time manipulation, a talented engineer can "fix" many parts of a performance without the musician even realizing it has been altered. At the same time, multi-track studio recordings can enable a musician to project a degree of rawness in the finished product. For example, fiddler Colin Grant prefers to limit audio editing on his recordings, but likes to have such options should he require them: "I also try not to rely too much on fixing things, although I realize that it is a part of [it]. Until I get to the level of Winston 'Scotty' Fitzgerald where I could walk in and play confidently for an afternoon and walk out, with a tape, I can't make a record without relying on a few little fixes and studio tricks... So, when you have the luxury of those studio tricks, then you take things in a slightly different approach. And that approach, a more relaxed approach, I think, is what allows today's musicians to record confidently in the studio. Knowing that they can afford to make little things better with the magic of technology" (2010). In Grant's most recent recording project (2012) with his band Sprag Session, the group attempted to find a compromise between sounding "industrial" and "organic" (2011), terms that relate easily to my own framework of "polished" and "raw." As a group that plays a mix of bars and folk festivals, live performances and audience feedback are integral to the band's identity. Creating a live sound in the studio, then, is a way to connect to the contexts in which the band typically plays. Grant explains how the group tried to retain the natural imperfections and variations of live performance, even when they were in the recording studio: "We were careful not to line up everything so that it wouldn't sound unnatural. The certain ebb and flow where two instruments don't necessarily land exact on the same time goes a long way to make a record sound real" (2011). By "lining up" instruments, Grant is referring to eliminating the participatory discrepancies between instruments; rather, his band deliberately avoids perfect rhythmic unison, keeps instruments slightly asynchronous, and embraces the participatory discrepancies that result.

In relation to this delicate rhythmic balance between sounding overly loose or unnaturally in-time, ethnomusicologist J.A. Prögler discusses the "humanizing" of electronic music by engaging with participatory discrepancies.

Prögler asserts, "Music industry producers and inventors have noted the importance of understanding concepts like swing and groove in their quest to 'humanize' electronically produced musics. No one wants to be the Dr Frankenstein who produces the dreaded Mechanical Man or a music that sounds machine-made" (1995, 22). In a sense, sounding "human," or natural, involves a degree of imperfection. Much like the Austin studio musicians who were Porcello's (2005) informants, the members of Sprag Session value a liveness that celebrates participatory discrepancies, yet still engage in the highly rationalized, polished aesthetic of multi-track studios and popular recordings.

Donnie Calabrese, the bassist for Sprag Session, brings a realist aesthetic of imperfection to the group that is not dissimilar to Paul MacDonald's approach to recording:

> There's usually a lot of compression that goes on those type of records … and people like that. But … I don't like that. I like musicians, and I like people playing music. And it's not perfect; it's never perfect. I like the grit and the personality that comes out in it … I don't know when this obsession or this fascination with like, perfect sounding fiddle records began, but I love those old, dirty recordings. And I feel like what we did on the Sprag Session record is more akin to those old things. We didn't auto-tune anything. What's the point? We go out of tune, and it sounds bad. Yeah! Sometimes we go out of tune and sound bad! [laughs] (2012)

The Sprag Session recording retains a sense of liveness by minimizing processes that would place the recording in the realm of polished, hyper-realistic studio recordings.

The decision of how live a recording should sound in respect to participatory discrepancies is often a group decision. Even on a solo album, fiddlers frequently turn to their fellow studio musicians and engineer to make such a judgment. For this reason, Mike Sheppard is commonly credited as a co-producer on traditional recordings at Lakewind. For Sprag Session, having a group of peers to validate assessments of the recording is an important part of the process. Calabrese explains, "It gets so *strange*, because you don't hear the tunes anymore, after a while. And so … you're being so scientific and pedantic about everything that scrolls by. It becomes a visual line on a screen instead of a song or whatever" (2012). After several hours of intense listening, ears can become tired, and it can be difficult to discern what and what not to edit. Colin Grant comments, "[Deciding when to edit aspects of a recording] is a very difficult thing because only time can really determine that … We would listen back and make notes at certain time points where we thought we heard something. Then we'd listen and often times, we'd hear, 'No … that doesn't really bother me.' But sit in your car and listen to it for a week and things start to jump at you … We all need to be happy with the recording and if something is jumping out at you, screw organic. If it's going to bother you forever, find a way to make it sound organic *and* groovy so that it fits. And it could be a matter of just moving one note. Or tuning one note" (2011). These issues are further complicated by the substantial cost of studio time. When time is money, musicians can feel pressured to avoid unnecessary editing for the sake of efficiency, as well as aesthetics.

Conclusion

The aesthetics of Cape Breton fiddle recordings place a high value on liveness, a quality that links recordings to their social context and frames the tradition as one that is an inclusive group experience for performers and audiences. Some musicians and engineers prefer a live sound that is closely related to a field recording, complete with the microvariations of participatory discrepancies. Others create a very detailed recording that is influenced significantly by the multi-track studio, an imagined performance that is idealized and not replicable in live performance. While elements such as violin timbre, reverb, crowd noise, and even foot stomping take on symbolic value and indicate liveness, their meanings may vary according to context. They are woven together in a complex fashion, drawing on experiences in the listener's imagination.

Drawing on examples from two different recording contexts (on-location recordings and studio recordings), I have demonstrated how conceptions of liveness can vary considerably from field recordings to hyper-realistic studio recordings, and outlined the strategies musicians and engineers employ to reconcile these sometimes contradictory notions of liveness. A "raw" aesthetic of liveness is directly connected to the social context of a performance, embracing participatory discrepancies. A "polished" aesthetic often constructs liveness through hyper-reality, taking greater liberties to create a recording less related to an actual event than an imagined one. Conceiving of these aesthetics as a dichotomy is overly simplistic, however, since each represents overlapping ideas and values. Both aesthetics attempt to create the same thing – a recording that sounds as if the listener was actually there experiencing the performance. "Raw" liveness takes on a particular local meaning through its connection to social performance contexts, while "polished" liveness stresses an almost hyperbolic intimacy with the performer and is generally aimed at broader uses. These aesthetics of liveness also have economic consequences for musicians. A "raw" aesthetic may be particularly important to how a traditionalist views his or her musical identity and may be highly valued on a regional level. Such an aesthetic, however, may not be commercially successful on a broader, international level. Conversely, it can be a challenge for a fiddler who makes highly "polished" recordings and who primarily performs internationally to maintain cultural capital on a regional basis. Cape Breton musicians must negotiate these varied definitions of liveness, creating recordings that uphold accepted Cape Breton aesthetics while also satisfying norms and expectations locally and abroad.

Notes

1. The first Cape Breton fiddle recordings were 78-RPM records by Decca and the Columbia Record Company, recorded in Boston and New York, respectively. These early recordings featured musicians who lived in Boston and New York, such as Dan Hughie MacEachern, Colin Boyd, Alex Gillis, and the Inverness Serenaders.
2. Although "tradition" has various meanings in both scholarly literature and the everyday practice of musical communities, I use it throughout this chapter, as many of my informants do, to reference Cape Breton fiddle music and practice that has its roots in, and continues to reference, an unspecified past.
3. For a detailed explanation of bowing and ornamentation in Cape Breton fiddling, see *Dungreen Collection: Cape Breton Violin* (1996), by Kate Dunlay and David Greenberg.
4. Some solo piano performances do occur as well, usually as a short feature to contrast the more common configuration of fiddle as lead and piano as accompaniment.
5. By this time, the Celtic and Banff record labels were owned by umbrella company Rodeo Records.
6. Some early clients of Dave Miller's Inter-Media Services were Kinnon Beaton, Carl MacKenzie, Winnie Chafe, and Doug MacPhee.
7. The dance tape tradition includes several hundred amateur field recordings, most of which were made between the 1960s and 1990s, and are actively traded and distributed among traditional music lovers. Although they are widely available on a grassroots level, these recordings are not typically accessible to the public via any formal institution or archive.
8. Since there were very few musicians who pursued performance as a means of full-time employment prior to the 1980s (McKinnon 1989), MacMaster and MacIsaac serve as

9   Mike Hall's first Cape Breton fiddle recording, *A Legacy not to be Forgotten* (2010), is an excellent example of "raw" liveness.
10 Alex and Minnie MacMaster (née Beaton) of Troy, Cape Breton, are well-known members of the Cape Breton traditional music scene. In addition to being Natalie MacMaster's mother, Minnie is also an accomplished step dancer.
11 In his work on Indigenous powwow recordings, Scales similarly notes the important role that extra-musical sounds can play in creating a live-sounding recording, explaining that the addition of overdubbed sounds of dancers "indexically link[s] the recorded music to the powwow grounds and the authenticity granted to that performance context" (2012, 216).
12 *The Fiddle Tree* was a recording and book published by Cape Breton luthier Otis Thomas in 2011. The recording features Thomas, Sarah McFayden, Mairi Campbell, Abby Newton, Laoise Kelly, Paul MacDonald, and Claudine Langille. All these musicians play instruments made by Thomas from the wood of the same large sugar maple tree. This recording clearly demonstrates MacDonald's engineering "raw" style, recording in a manner that preserves the natural reverb of the space as well as the participatory discrepancies of the group.
13 Compression narrows the dynamic range of a recording by making quiet sounds louder and louder sounds quieter.
14 Equalization (EQ) refers to the balance of different frequencies on a recording (i.e., bass, mid, treble, etc.).
15 Gordie Sampson and Fred Lavery are Cape Breton musicians and singer-songwriters. Although both have performed extensively with traditional musicians such as Rita MacNeil and Ashley MacIsaac, they now primarily work as producers and songwriters. Lavery is currently responsible for the day-to-day running of Lakewind Sound Studios in Point Aconi, NS, while Sampson is currently based in Nashville where he is a full-time songwriter. Sampson's most successful composition was "Jesus Take the Wheel," recorded by Carrie Underwood in 2005.
16 Over the course of its twenty-two-year history, Lakewind Sound Studios has received numerous music industry awards; in addition, Lavery, Sampson, and Sheppard have received substantial recognition for their individual contributions to the industry, with a collective total of over fifty awards (East Coast Music Awards, Music Nova Scotia Awards, SOCAN, Juno Awards, etc.).
17 A punch-in is a form of audio editing where a portion of a recording is re-recorded or "overdubbed" to replace the original recording. This is most often used to fix small mistakes in an otherwise well-performed take.
18 A DI (Direct Input box) is a preamp used for instruments like violins and guitars in live settings.
19 Focusrite is a company that manufactures high-end audio recording hardware, based in England.

20 The recording to which Cormier refers is *Master Cape Breton Fiddler* (1982), an early and prominent example of "polished" liveness.
21 An area is often prepared for recording a foot sound by putting a rubber mat where the musician's foot hits the ground; other materials may be used, depending on the musician's footwear.
22 The role of space in recording studios has been examined by Paul Théberge, who argues that recording studios have become increasingly rationalized with regard to space, sometimes even existing as "non-places" cut off from the world (1997, 216–22).
23 A ribbon microphone uses a diaphragm of thin foil to convert the air pressure produced by sound waves into an electrical signal.

References

Bates, Elliot. 2010. "Mixing for *Parlak* and Bowing for a *Büyük Ses*: The Aesthetics of Arranged Traditional Music in Turkey." *Ethnomusicology* 54 (1): 81–105.

Doherty, Elizabeth. 1996. "The Paradox of the Periphery: Evolution of the Cape Breton Fiddle Tradition, c. 1928–1995." PhD diss., University of Limerick.

– 2015. *The Cape Breton Fiddle Companion*. Sydney, NS: Cape Breton University Press.

Doyle, Peter. 2005. *Echo and Reverb: Fabricating Space in Popular Music Recording 1900–1960*. Middleton, CT: Wesleyan University Press.

Dunlay, Kate, and David Greenberg. 1996. *Traditional Celtic Violin Music of Cape Breton: The Dungreen Collection*. Toronto, ON: Dungreen Music.

Feintuch, Burt. 2010. *In the Blood: Cape Breton Conversations on Culture*. Sydney, NS: Cape Breton University Press.

– 2004. "The Conditions for Cape Breton Fiddle Music: The Social and Economic Setting for a Regional Soundscape." *Ethnomusicology* 48 (1): 73–104.

Feld, Steven. 1994. "Aesthetics as Iconicity of Style (Uptown Title); or, (Downtown Title) 'Lift Up Over Sounding': Getting into the Kaluli Groove." In *Music Grooves: Essays and Dialogues*, edited by Charles Keil and Steven Feld, 109–50. Chicago, IL: University of Chicago Press.

Frith, Simon. 1996. *Performing Rites: On the Value of Popular Music*. Cambridge, MA: Harvard University Press.

Garrison, Virginia Hope. 1985. "Traditional and Non-traditional Teaching and Learning Practices in Folk Music: An Ethnographic Field Study of Cape Breton Fiddling." PhD diss., University of Wisconsin-Madison.

Graham, Glenn. 2006. *Cape Breton Fiddle: Making and Maintaining Tradition*. Sydney, NS: Cape Breton University Press.

Hayes, Ian. 2012. "'How traditional do you want to sound?': Deconstructing Notions of Traditionalism in Cape Breton Fiddling." In *Eighth International Small Islands Culture Conference Refereed Proceedings*, edited by Henry Johnson and Heather Sparling, 8–16, SICRI (Small Island Cultures Research Initiative).

– 2013. "'Our fiddles sound big. That's the way I think it should be': Cape Breton Fiddling and Amplification Practices." *MUSICultures* 39 (2): 161–80.

— 2015. "'It's a balancing act. That's the secret to making this music fit in today': Negotiating Professional and Vernacular Boundaries in the Cape Breton Fiddling Tradition." PhD diss., Memorial University of Newfoundland.
Keil, Charles. 1987. "Participatory Discrepancies and the Power of Music." *Cultural Anthropology* 2 (3): 275–83.
MacKinnon, Richard. 2009. *Discovering Cape Breton Folklore*. Sydney, NS: Cape Breton University Press.
McKinnon, Ian. 1989. "Fiddling to Fortune: The Role of Commercial Recordings Made by Cape Breton Fiddlers in the Fiddle Music Tradition of Cape Breton Island." Master's thesis, Memorial University of Newfoundland.
McMorran, Jasmine. 2013. "Cape Breton Piano: The Progression and Passing of Innovation and Tradition." Master's thesis, Memorial University of Newfoundland.
Meintjes, Louise. 2003. *Sound of Africa! Making Music Zulu in an African Studio*. Durham, NC: Duke University Press.
Monson, Ingrid. 1996. *Saying Something: Jazz Improvisation and Interaction*. Chicago, IL: Chicago University Press.
Porcello, Thomas. 1991. "The Ethics of Digital-Audio Sampling: Engineers' Discourse." *Popular Music* 10 (1): 69–84.
— 2005. "Music Mediated as Live in Austin: Sound, Technology, and Recording Practice." In *Wired for Sound: Engineering and Technologies in Sonic Cultures*, edited by Paul D. Greene and Thomas Porcello, 103–7. Middletown, CT: Wesleyan University Press.
Prögler, J.A. 1995. "Searching for Swing: Participatory Discrepancies in the Jazz Rhythm Section." *Ethnomusicology* 39 (1): 21–54.
Reynolds, Charles, director. 1971. "Vanishing Cape Breton Fiddler." *30 from Halifax*. Narrated and written by Ron MacInnis. Halifax, NS: Canadian Broadcasting Corporation (television). Recorded 17 November.
Sanden, Paul. 2009. "Hearing Glenn Gould's Body: Corporeal Liveness in Recorded Music." *Current Musicology* 88: 7–34.
Scales, Christopher A. 2012. *Recording Culture: Powwow Music and the Aboriginal Recording Industry on the Northern Plains*. Durham, NC: Duke University Press.
Sterne, Jonathan. 2003. *The Audible Past: Cultural Origins of Sound Reproduction*. Durham and London: Duke University Press.
Théberge, Paul. 1997. *Any Sound You Can Imagine: Making Music/Consuming Technology*. Hanover, CT: Wesleyan University Press.
Thompson, Marie. 2003. "The Rise and Fall of the Cape Breton Fiddler." Master's thesis, St Mary's University.
Turino, Thomas. 2008. *Music as Social Life: The Politics of Participation*. Chicago, IL: University of Chicago Press.

Interviews

Calabrese, Donnie. 2012. Interview by author. Sydney, NS, 7 June.
Cormier, J.P. 2012. Interview by author. Sydney, NS, 8 June.
Fraser, Kimberley. 2011. Interview by author. Sydney, NS, 28 July.
Graham, Glenn. 2011. Interview by author. Judique, NS, 24 June.

Grant, Colin. 2010. Interview by author. Whycocomagh, NS, 15 August.
– 2011. Interview by author. Sydney, NS, 27 August.
Lavery, Fred. 2011. Interview by author. Point Aconi, NS, 21 January.
MacDonald, Paul. 2011. Interview by author. George's River, NS, 6 July.
Roach, Jason. 2010. Interview by author. St Joseph du Moine, NS, October 10.
Sheppard, Mike. 2012. Interview by author. Point Aconi, NS, 7 June.

Selected Audio Recordings

Fraser, Kimberley. 2006. *Falling on New Ground*. Independent KFCD-002. CD.
Graham, Glenn. 2000. *Step Outside*. Bowbeat GG003A. CD.
Hall, Michael. 2011. *A Legacy not to be Forgotten*. Independent. CD.
Holland, Jerry. 1982. *Master Cape Breton Fiddler*. Boot BOS7231. CD.
MacIsaac, Ashley. 1995. *Hi, how are you today?* A&M Records 79602 2001–2. CD.
– 1996. *Fine, thank you very much*. Ancient Music Ltd. 2 70053. CD.
– 1999. *Helter's Celtic*. Loggerhead Records 76974 2192–2. CD.
MacMaster, Natalie. 2002. *Live*. Rounder Records B00006670M. CD.
Sprag Session. 2012. *Sprag Session*. Independent SS001. CD.
Thomas, Otis. 2011. *The Fiddle Tree*. Self-published. CD.

Jesse Stewart and Niel Scobie

Chapter 10

Fantastic Voyage: The Diasporic Roots and Routes of Early Toronto Hip Hop

In addition to being the title of a 1966 science fiction film, *Fantastic Voyage* is also the name of the first radio program in Canada devoted to hip hop. Hosted by pioneering deejay and hip hop promoter Ron Nelson, *Fantastic Voyage* was broadcast on CKLN in Toronto – Ryerson Polytechnical Institute's (now Ryerson University's) campus radio station – on Saturday afternoons between 1983 and 1989. The importance of "Fantastic Voyage," and of Ron Nelson, to the development of hip hop in Canada cannot be overstated. In addition to exposing many Toronto radio listeners to early hip hop recordings by American artists such as Run-D.M.C., Big Daddy Kane, and Boogie Down Productions, *Fantastic Voyage* was crucial to the success of the first generation of hip hop performers from Toronto, many of whom received their earliest exposure on the show. For example, Maestro Fresh-Wes performed live on *Fantastic Voyage* for the first time in 1983 when he was just fifteen years old. He recalls, "It was one of those moments you look back on later, because it turns out to be bigger than you thought. Ron Nelson would go on to be one of my biggest motivators. He was a true rap pioneer, one of the most important individuals in the evolution of Canadian hip hop ... In my mind he is the true Godfather of Canadian hip hop" (Williams 2010, 31).

In addition to its importance to early hip hop music and culture in Toronto, *Fantastic Voyage* provides a resonant metaphor for early Canadian hip hop given the diasporic routes and roots that contributed to its development. Hip hop in Canada, like hip hop culture more generally, is the result of a series of fantastic voyages, the intense circulation of people, music, recordings, and culture that began in the Bronx and then extended to other urban centres in the United States, and eventually to Canada and around the globe. Given hip hop's roots in African diasporic expressive cultures, and given the history of slavery and colonialism that led to the diasporic condition in the first place, we use the term "fantastic" not necessarily in the sense of something positive, but rather to refer to something that is out of the ordinary to the point of being unbelievable, even unthinkable. Indeed, many of the voyages that have made hip hop possible, including those associated with the middle passage – the journey imposed on slaves who were forcibly taken from their homes in West Africa and brought to the "new world" across the Atlantic Ocean – and the subsequent migration of millions of people of African descent, are unknowable to those who, like us (the authors of this paper), have a different family history of migration.

Our understanding of the African diaspora is indebted to Paul Gilroy's influential work. In *The Black Atlantic*, Gilroy (1993) examines the Atlantic Ocean as an avenue for transnational cultural exchange among peoples of African descent in Africa, the Caribbean, Great Britain, and the Americas. He notes that hip hop is too often constructed as a specifically African *American* form, thereby obscuring the important historical influence of Caribbean musical antecedents and the contributions of creative practitioners from around the globe. "The musical components of hip hop," he writes, "are a hybrid form nurtured by the social relations of the South Bronx where Jamaican sound system culture was transplanted during the 1970s and put down new roots." He continues: "In conjunction with specific technological innovations, this routed and re-rooted Caribbean culture set in train a process that was to transform black America's sense of itself and a large portion of the popular music industry as well. Here we have to ask how a form which flaunts and glories in its own malleability as well as its transnational character becomes interpreted as an expression of some authentic African-American essence?" (33–4). The intra-diasporic conversation that Gilroy describes is even richer given that many early proponents of Jamaican sound system culture were heavily influenced by African American musical performers and by American radio shows that featured the fast-paced rhyming of African American radio deejays such as Jocko Henderson.[1] The diasporic dialogue continued when hip hop crossed the border from the United States into Canada in the early to mid 1980s and was adopted by a number of young musicians in Toronto whose cultural ancestry was rooted in the African diaspora and, more specifically, in West Indian and Caribbean communities.

For many members of African diasporic communities in Canada, music has played a vital role in remembering – and maintaining a sense of connectedness to – their cultural heritage, while simultaneously providing opportunities to construct and perform hybridized identities that result from the diasporic condition. As Rinaldo Walcott explains, "post-1960s children of migrants have begun to articulate a belonging to Canada that allows for a cultural expressivity that is both uniquely theirs and simultaneously in conversation with a wide array of cultural expressivity of the black diaspora" (2001, 125). This is particularly true in the case of early Canadian hip hop. Walcott elaborates: "on any Canadian rap album it is not unusual for the performer to shift between recognizable African-American derived musical styles and Caribbean-derived styles and sounds" (136–7). Building on Walcott's important work, the present study examines the diasporic nexus of early Canadian hip hop in Toronto, focusing in particular on the work of Michie Mee, Maestro Fresh-Wes, Dream Warriors, and Devon, as well as Dance Appeal, a "supergroup" of performers associated with the burgeoning hip hop and dance music scenes in Toronto. Through a close reading and analysis of selected recordings and videos, we examine some of the ways in which these early Canadian hip hop artists articulated hybridized cultural identities rooted in the Caribbean and African diasporas, memorializing diasporic history and laying the groundwork for the future development of hip hop in Canada.[2]

Cultural Memory, Signifyin(g), and Code-Switching in Afrological[3] Forms

In addition to the concept of diaspora, the interrelated concepts of cultural memory, Signifyin(g), and code-switching are useful theoretical tools for examining the diasporic underpinnings of early Canadian hip hop. In her introduction to *Acts of Memory: Cultural Recall in the Present*, Mieke Bal writes, "the term *cultural memory* signifies that memory can be understood as a cultural phenomenon as well as an individual or social one ... cultural memorialization [is] an activity occurring in the present, in which the past is continuously modified and redescribed even as it continues to shape the future" (1999, vi, emphasis in original). Similarly, in *How Societies Remember*, Paul Connerton suggests that cultural memory involves "images of the past and recollected knowledge of the past ... conveyed and sustained by (more or less ritual) performances" (1989, 3–4). In African diasporic cultures, music has often been a privileged site for ritualized acts of memory transference, due, in part, to the history and legacy of slavery. Often isolated linguistically and denied access to literacy and formal education, enslaved communities of Africans in the Americas used music and dance to develop and solidify social bonds and to preserve and transmit cultural values, conceptual frameworks, ideologies, and memories rooted in the African diaspora. This shared cultural repertoire continues to impact processes of African diasporic identity formation and their expression in Afrological forms, offering creative life strategies to African diasporic communities that continue to deal with the effects of systemic racism, oppression, and the legacies of colonialism and slavery. This has been particularly true of hip hop cultures, both in Canada and internationally.

Samuel Floyd Jr takes up the issue of cultural memory in relation to Afrological forms in *The Power of Black Music* (1995). For Floyd, cultural memory stretches back beyond the "slave experience in America to Africa" (9). He continues: "The musical retentions and performance practices of African-American music helped and still help to preserve this memory, recalling the mysteries of myth and the trappings of ritual long after they are no longer functional. Whatever its nature and process, cultural memory, as a reference to vaguely 'known' musical and cultural processes and procedures, is a valid and meaningful way of accounting for the subjective, spiritual quality of the music and aesthetic behaviors of a culture" (9). Floyd emphasizes the importance of musical and cultural dialogue – what he designates the "Call-Response" trope – to cultural memorialization in African diasporic musical processes. He goes so far as to describe "Call-Response" as "the master trope, the musical trope of tropes" in African diasporic modes of music making (95). Drawing on the influential work of literary theorist Henry Louis Gates Jr (1988), Floyd writes, "Call-Response functions in black music as Signifyin(g) functions in black literature and can therefore be said to Signify. It implies the presence within it of Signifyin(g) figures (Calls) and Signifyin(g) revisions (Responses, in various guises) that can be one or the other, depending on their context" (1991, 277–8). The term Signifyin(g) (sometimes spelled "Signifyin'" or "signifyin(g)") was coined by Gates to refer to the trope of double-voiced repetition in African American literature and expressive cultures.[4] As Floyd explains, to Signify on something within African diasporic expressive culture "is not the same, simply, as the borrowing and restating of pre-existing material, or the performing of variations on pre-existing material, or even the simple reworking of pre-existing material. While it is all of these, what makes it different from simple borrowing, varying, or reworking is its transformation of such material by using it rhetorically or figuratively – through troping, in other words – by trifling with, teasing, or censuring it in some way" (271). Given the extent to which hip hop music samples and memorializes earlier diasporic modes of music making (particularly soul, disco, and funk), hip hop is a particularly rich site for the kinds of Signifyin(g) calls and responses to which Floyd refers.

The concept of code-switching is similarly useful when examining the diasporic foundations of early Canadian hip hop. In linguistic terms, "code-switching" refers to "the alternative use by bilinguals of two or more languages in the same conversation ... switching sometimes occurs between the turns of different speakers in the conversation, sometimes within a single turn, and sometimes even within a single utterance" (Milroy and Muysken 1995, 7). Code-switching takes place in other modes of creative expression that similarly combine two or more codes to create an example of "border-transcending identity formation" (Sarker et al. 2005, 2060). Both in performance and on record, numerous early Toronto hip hop artists switched between various types of musical and linguistic codes resulting in music that was characterized by its emphasis on diasporic hybridity. This was particularly true of Michie Mee.

"Jamaican Funk – Canadian Style": Code-Switching and Hybridity in the Music of Michie Mee

The career of Michelle "Michie Mee" McCullock offers a particularly clear example of the diasporic underpinnings of early Canadian hip hop and of code-switching in the service of both cultural memory and the performance of a hybridized identity. Born in Kingston, Jamaica, in 1970, McCullock was exposed to the music business early in life. Her father, a concert promoter in Jamaica, regularly worked with Motown recording artists, and was part of a group that brought the Jackson 5 to Kingston to perform on a double bill with reggae superstar Bob Marley (Michie Mee 2013). McCullock's family emigrated from Jamaica to Toronto in 1976. Three years later, The Sugarhill Gang's 1979 international hit "Rapper's Delight" introduced the nine-year-old McCullock to hip hop. During her teens, her frequent trips to visit relatives in New York City elevated her interest in hip hop culture. McCullock explains: "going to New York a lot, my family is from the Bronx, 223rd and Gun Hill Road, and Stardust was a hip hop club where a lot of Zulu Nation people hung out" (Michie Mee 2013). Founded in the 1970s by hip hop pioneer Afrika Bambaataa, the Zulu Nation (now known as the Universal Zulu Nation) began as an Afrocentric organization in the Bronx dedicated to strengthening community through the promotion of the foundational tenets of hip hop culture including DJing, MCing, b-boying/b-girling,[5] and graffiti writing. Unlike many of the other progenitors of Canadian hip hop, McCullock had firsthand exposure to the music and ideas of the Zulu Nation and to early hip hop culture in the Bronx. She summarizes: "back then we didn't have Internet, there was no way of connecting with everyone else ... we actually had to go to Manhattan, go to the Bronx, go to Brooklyn, and be part of the scene, and you know, get in the mix" (Michie Mee 2011).

Through this early access to the burgeoning hip hop scene in New York, McCullock met the duo that would go on to launch her recording career: Scott La Rock (Scott Sterling) and KRS-One (Lawrence Parker), a Bronx-based DJ and MC duo known collectively as Boogie Down Productions (BDP). McCullock first met Scott La Rock and KRS-One outside the famed Manhattan club Latin Quarter. When they questioned her claim that there was hip hop in Canada, she rapped to them on the spot. This initial meeting with the duo would eventually bring them across the border to Toronto for a series of "Monster Jam" concerts and battles[6] organized by Ron Nelson in the mid-1980s that helped lay the foundations for Toronto's emergent hip hop scene.

At one of these battles, Michie Mee significantly increased her local profile by competing against Brooklyn's Sugar Love in an MC battle. She recounts: "I just remember it as New York vs Toronto, and it was just a battle, period. I don't even remember if there was a title to it or whatever. There was a female MC category, there was a DJ category, there was the male MC category, it was like Rumble vs Boogie Down Productions, myself vs Sugar Love, who came with Cutmaster DC. Me, personally, I was fearless. I was like, you know, when she [Sugar Love] was rapping, I was like 'gyal, I'm a Jamaican,' and the whole crowd lost it" (Michie Mee 2009). Michie's rap/reggae vocal blend became widely known within the Toronto hip hop scene because of this battle. Ivan Berry, co-founder of Toronto's pioneering record label, management, and production company Beat Factory, describes the effect of Michie Mee's use of Jamaican cultural signifiers: "Michie would be rappin', rappin', rappin', and the crowd would be into it, and it's a neck and neck battle, tight, and then she would just drop a verse in reggae, and the crowd would lose it ... *lose* it. And she would just win because she did that. American rapper just walks off the stage" (*Love, Props and the T.Dot* 2015).

With Michie Mee's reputation growing as a bona fide battle rapper with a unique ability to switch between linguistic codes,[7] her next step was to enter the studio and record. In 1987, during one of their trips to Toronto, Scott La Rock and KRS-One accompanied Michie Mee (who was sixteen years old at the time) and Toronto DJ L.A. Luv to a Hamilton, Ontario, recording studio to record "Elements of Style" and "Run for Cover" (Michie Mee 2009). "Run for Cover" features her first use of Jamaican Patois[8] on record, one of the first such uses on any hip hop recording.

Michie Mee would go on to include lyrical and sonic signifiers of Jamaican musical and cultural heritage in many subsequent recordings. For example, "Victory Is Calling" (1988) begins with Michie Mee and King Lou (of the group Dream Warriors, discussed below) bantering in Jamaican Patois. In "On This Mic" (1988) Michie Mee shifts from Standard Canadian English[9] to Patois in the third verse, providing a particularly deft example of code-switching. Davies and Bentahila (2006) suggest that code-switching within song lyrics performs two functions. First, it may be used to directly target a specific audience. Using codified words, accents, or gestures aligns the singer with a particular audience (390). In Michie Mee's case, the use of Jamaican Patois targets Jamaican communities in Toronto, Jamaica, and beyond. Second, code-switching can function as a means of opening up a text to a broader audience (390). For example, midway through "On This Mic," Michie Mee breaks into Jamaican Patois for eighteen bars while the underlying groove switches to a dancehall reggae rhythm (or "riddim" as it would be referred to in Jamaican communities) that complements her reggae-style vocals. These coded lyrics help to attract a wider audience to Michie Mee's music, namely reggae fans and the Jamaican community, by appealing to them with coded lyrics and musical signifiers that offer insider status to those that understand and relate to them.

The considerable artistic (if only moderate commercial) success of the singles "Victory Is Calling" and "On This Mic" led Brooklyn-based First Priority Music to release a full LP by Michie Mee and L.A. Luv in 1991, making them the first Canadian hip hop group signed to an American record label. Titled *Jamaican Funk – Canadian Style*, the LP was a mixture of hip hop and reggae. Michie Mee recalls, "One side was hip hop, one side was reggae ... the album was produced by Mikey Bennett and two friends in Jamaica and they did the reggae side, Steele and Clevie. I met Bobby Digital; there was so much people on the record that it was really *reggae*. But hip hop made me who I am"

(2012). Twelve of the fifteen tracks on *Jamaican Funk – Canadian Style* contain either full verses or individual lines in Jamaican Patois, and four songs feature reggae-style instrumentals.

The title track is a remix of an earlier recording by Michie Mee and L.A. Luv titled "Jamaican Funk" that had been released as a single in 1990. "Jamaican Funk – Canadian Style" is considerably slower in tempo than the original, and the backing track draws on a different set of samples: a drum loop from James Brown's "Funky Drummer" blended with a bass line sample from Earth, Wind and Fire's "Fan the Fire." Lyrically, "Jamaican Funk – Canadian Style" begins with guest male vocalists performing an off-key and somewhat humorous vocal interpretation of Stephen Bishop's 1976 hit "On and On," which serves as a tongue-in-cheek nod to Michie Mee's Jamaican background ("Down in Jamaica they've got lots of pretty women").

When Michie Mee begins rapping, she switches between Standard Canadian English and Jamaican Patois, providing another example of code-switching in the construction and performance of a hybridized Jamaican Canadian identity. At one point, she uses Jamaican Patois to tell the audience to raise their hands if they are Jamaican, simulating a dancehall concert setting:

> Push up yu han if yu are Jamaican
> Skin out yu back yu can tek the sun lang
> Bawl it out cause yu a autical don
> Jamaican woman yu hav fi fear, so ah
> Jamaican sweet gal pickney
> Dem dey girl they say dey dem have the whinery
> Wha mek de man dem a run afta she
> Yu neva know sey she a yardie
> Men travel fa miles around they know what's in town
> Jamaican funk!
>
> [Translation (courtesy of Victor Laing)]
> Raise your hand if you're Jamaican
> Bare your back you can take the sun long
> Shout it out because you are in charge
> Jamaican woman you have to fear
> Jamaican sweet gal pickney [child]
> Those girls say they have the whinery [dance]

What makes the men run after her
You didn't know that she is a yardie [a Jamaican living abroad]
Men travel for miles around, they know what's in town
Jamaican funk!

Michie Mee uses several coded forms of Jamaican slang including the word "whinery," a term used in Jamaica to refer to a particular type of dance. She also uses the expressions "pickney" and "yardie" for "child" and "Jamaican person living outside of Jamaica" respectively.

The music video for "Jamaican Funk – Canadian Style" is similarly rich with code-switching, presenting a range of cultural signifiers of both Jamaican dancehall and hip hop culture. Much of the video features Michie Mee and L.A. Luv performing on a raised stage in front of a small audience. Black, green, gold, and red dominate the visual colour palette, primarily due to a towering painted backdrop that depicts abstract images of female figures. Black, green, and gold are the colours of the Jamaican flag, which is prominently on display in front of L.A. Luv's turntables. Although the colour red is not in the Jamaican flag, it is a significant colour in Rastafarian iconography, which often features the colours green, red, and gold.

Michie Mee dons several outfits throughout the video, including clothing inspired by dancehall reggae and "dancehall queen" fashion. The role of the dancehall queen is crucial to dancehall culture. Eschewing the traditional norms associated with Jamaican women's fashion, dancehall queens often wear elaborate, colourful hairstyles, dominatrix-themed clothing, bright make-up, ostentatious jewelry, bra tops, tight dresses, as well as sequined, mesh, and lace clothing (Bakare-Yusuf 2006, 5). Bakare-Yusuf suggests that these brash fashion choices empower women within dancehall culture: "While the aim of dancehall is meant to shock and rebel against the upper- and middle-class and Rastafarian ethos, it cannot be fully understood outside of an attempt to intervene against repressive attitudes towards female sexuality, appearance and comportment. Drawing on motifs of deviant sexuality and symbols of excessive femininity allows dancehall women to express sexual power and affirm their own sexual identification at the same time" (10–11). Dancehall fashion and beauty standards oppose Eurocentric norms concerning femininity and female sexuality, providing instead a space in which women can assert themselves through bodily and sartorial decisions. Admittedly, the line between assertion and exploitation can be thin. But the fact that female dancers dominate the dance floor in Jamaican dancehall culture challenges the notion of the dancehall as a masculine space. By referencing dancehall queen fashion in the video for "Jamaican Funk – Canadian Style," Michie Mee articulates a subject position of a powerful Jamaican Canadian woman. Her empowered subject position is further reinforced by the fact that she is often accompanied by two male back-up dancers, thereby inverting the gender roles found in most hip hop videos.

In addition to dancehall-inspired fashion elements, Michie Mee is shown wearing chunky gold jewellery in the form of bracelets, a chain necklace, and earrings – fashion items that were popular among female rappers of the late 1980s and early 1990s. She dons a variety of other outfits as well: a white and pink sweatsuit, a red dress and heels, and a white jean jacket decorated with silver trim. These sartorial elements, coupled with the piece's linguistic and musical signifiers, constitute a prime example of Michie Mee's use of code-switching to construct and perform a hybridized diasporic subject position, one that articulates not only a sense of Jamaican and hip hop identity and culture, but also a sense of Canadianness.

In addition to references to Jamaican music and culture, Michie Mee regularly references Canadian culture in her recorded output. For example, *Jamaican Funk – Canadian Style* includes tracks titled "A Portion from Up North" and "Canada Large." The latter begins with the words "Step up you wanna know where I come from? Canada is where I conceived the vibe for this album." She goes on to mention several Greater Toronto Area locations including Mississauga, Thornhill, Brampton, Markham, and Scarborough, as well as specific Toronto neighbourhoods such as Regent Park, Jane and Finch, and "Jungle" (Lawrence Heights). By naming Toronto suburbs and locales, she identifies her affiliation with and allegiance to the city. She continues:

> Jamaican born, me and my DJ steppin' on the scene
> You've been warned, you didn't know before talent comes in all forms
> Some claim we try to imitate many Americans
> But like a true Canadian I know I can I know I can
> Be original and mashup the dance
> And many after me will have that same chance

Michie reminds the listener of her birthplace, and highlights her identity as a "true Canadian." She also declares that she and L.A. Luv are not merely mimicking their competition to the south, but represent something unique. She goes on to state that by being original and "mash[ing]up the dance," she is paving the way for subsequent generations of Canadian hip hop performers who will have the same chance to articulate a hybridized cultural identity.

From the earliest days of hip hop in Canada to the present, Michie Mee has articulated a hybridized Jamaican Canadian identity through her multi-faceted performance practice. In doing so, she not only helped pave the way for future international rap/reggae recordings, but also set a standard for how Canadian hip-hop artists with roots in the African diaspora could express themselves through cultural signifiers that recall their homeland as well as Canada. For example, Kardinal Offishall, who was born in Canada to Jamaican parents, articulates a strong sense of Jamaican Canadian identity in his music, lyrics, and videos just as Michie Mee did before him. Similarly, Somalia-born K'naan regularly expresses, and celebrates, his dual Somali Canadian identity through his music and videos. Even Drake, Canada's top-selling rapper and one of the most successful hip hop artists of his generation, celebrates both his African diasporic and Jewish heritage. The roots of such hybridized identities within Canadian hip hop can be traced back to Michie Mee and other pioneers of Canadian hip hop, including Maestro Fresh-Wes.

The "Black Mind Revolutionary Regime" of Maestro Fresh-Wes

The career of Wes Williams (aka Maestro Fresh-Wes and Maestro) sheds further light on early Canadian hip hop in relation to the African diaspora. As the first Canadian rapper to have a top-40 hit with the 1989 single "Let Your Backbone Slide," Maestro helped pave the way for future generations of hip hop artists in Canada and demonstrated that Canadian hip hop could succeed on a national and international level. Furthermore, by critiquing systemic racism in this country and advocating for solidarity and resistance in response to racism, Maestro was a pioneer of socially conscious hip hop in Canada, providing an early example of hip hop's potential to speak out in support of social change.

In his 2010 book *Stick to Your Vision: How to Get Past the Hurdles and Haters to Get Where You Want to Be*, Williams emphasizes the importance of his multi-faceted cultural background to his development as an artist. He explains: "Growing up as an ethnic minority in a country that's overshadowed by the United States, I felt it was (and still feel it is) really important to know my heritage – my Guyanese heritage, my black heritage, my Canadian heritage, my musical heritage. Being an ethnic minority and learning about the various aspects of my heritage has been a lifelong process" (68). Williams understands heritage as an ongoing and multifaceted process of learning and being that includes not only his bi-national identifications (with both Guyana and Canada), but also racial and diasporic identification (his "black heritage"), and cultural identification (his "musical heritage," particularly hip hop).

Born in Toronto in 1968, Williams spent most of his first four years in Guyana with his grandparents (Williams 2010, 22–3). After returning to Canada, his earliest understanding of his heritage and identity was influenced by mediatized representations of the African diaspora. He recalls: "In the summer of 1977, I was blown away by the miniseries *Roots* ... I learned where people who looked like me came from. (I don't know about other schools, but mine sure didn't teach any kind of black history. So this was my first lesson.) ... Watching *Roots* showed me how black people had been abused and stripped of their identity and why I indirectly had a hard time being accepted. I saw the importance of knowing my history although I couldn't fully understand it at the time" (24–5).[10] Musical recordings also played a crucial role in Williams's exposure to, and engagement with, expressive cultures of the African diaspora. "My dad was a huge music fan," he explains, "and he was always playing records by artists like Bob Marley and other reggae, soca, funk, jazz – a lot of jazz like Miles Davis, Duke Ellington, Thelonious Monk, and Count Basie – and soul, like Marvin Gaye and Stevie Wonder. One night in 1979, my dad brought home this record called 'Rapper's Delight' by Sugarhill Gang. I was eleven and it changed my life" (25).

Williams began emulating the rhythmic rhyming that he heard on "Rapper's Delight" and other early hip hop songs. Soon he was performing at his high school in North York, a Toronto suburb. His first success was his appearance at the age of fifteen on Ron Nelson's "Fantastic Voyage" radio show. Known then as "Melody MC," Williams rapped over Vaughan Mason's "Bounce, Rock, Skate, Roll," impressing Nelson, who stated on air, "yo, that's Melody, man, and damn, he's good" (Williams 2013). Williams partnered with Ebony MC (Marlon Bruce) and formed the Vision Crew. The duo began performing regularly in Toronto until 1988 when Williams went solo and rechristened himself Maestro Fresh-Wes. Along with the help of new manager Farley "Flex" Fridal and DJ LTD (Alva Swaby), Williams recorded a demo and produced a video for "I'm Showin' You," which provided his first national exposure on video programs such as *Soul in the City* on MuchMusic.

Williams's next break came after a live performance of "Let Your Backbone Slide" on MuchMusic's *Electric Circus*. The performance impressed American recording artist Stevie B who was in attendance, and who subsequently introduced Williams to executives of New York-based LMR records. Williams soon had a record deal with LMR, with Attic records providing distribution in Canada (Cowie, 2015). In 1989, Williams – as Maestro Fresh-Wes – released his debut album, *Symphony in Effect*, a collection of party-rap and battle-rap oriented tracks including "Let Your Backbone Slide." The album was a runaway success, going platinum in Canada (100,000 copies sold) and earning Maestro Fresh-Wes the first JUNO ever awarded in the rap category (Young and Higgins 2002, 120).

In comparison to *Symphony in Effect*, Maestro's follow-up album, *The Black Tie Affair* (1991), included more politically charged material. In particular, the track "Nothin' At All" offers a frank appraisal of race and racism in Canada, and issues an urgent call for solidarity among peoples of African descent. Maestro begins by challenging the myth of innocence when it comes to racism in Canada: "As we scan this land that we live in / This place with racism / C-A-N-A-D-A / Canada, I'm watchin' it decay everyday / Young minds are being mentally crushed and mushed in / Thanks to men like Rushton / And others who want to smother the dream / Of a black mind revolutionary regime." Maestro's reference to John Philippe Rushton provides an example – and an indictment – of institutionalized racism in Canada: for over twenty-five years, Rushton was a tenured psychology professor at the University of Western Ontario (now Western University) where he conducted research that involved ranking the intellectual capacity of different racial groups. Despite the appallingly racist nature of his research and widespread criticism of his work, Rushton retained his professorship for the remainder of his life, receiving significant external funding, and publishing essays and books that provided academic fuel for the hateful rhetoric of white supremacist groups in Canada and abroad. By condemning Rushton, Maestro critiques institutionally perpetuated racism in Canada.

In response to such forms of racism, Maestro advocates a "black mind revolutionary regime." While there are many ways to exegete this phrase, in our reading, it connotes a sense of solidarity and group consciousness among African diasporic communities, and a radical system of governance (a "revolutionary regime") predicated on a shared commitment to racial equality. In a 2017 email to us, Maestro explained that he was "simply trying to inspire my community to think outside the box and be leaders instead of followers." He continues, "I'm very proud of ['Nothin' At All'] and for years people have told me it means a lot to them. When I continue to record new material, and if I ever have a stumbling block, that song is still one of my greatest points of reference."

The lyrics that follow Maestro's reference to a "black mind revolutionary regime" continue to promote black unity in response to racial oppression: "We gotta redeem ourselves from the chain / By removing all stains of the chain on the brain / We gotta roll with force / Cause the Klan's also movin' on the great white north / We gotta hurdle the system / Cause hate penetrates multiculturalism." Maestro's reference to "the chain" alludes to the history and legacy of slavery, a theme that is reinforced visually in the video for "Nothin' At All" by the presence of chains hanging throughout the studio setting in which Maestro raps. The presence of slavery[11] and white supremacist hate groups[12] in Canada is often omitted from dominant narratives of Canadian history and identity, which tend to posit Canada as a racially tolerant, multicultural society.[13] Even though the Canadian government adopted multiculturalism as an official policy in 1971 and passed the *Canadian Multiculturalism Act* into law in 1988, Maestro highlights the racism and racial violence that continue to exist in Canada.

The lyrics of "Nothin' At All" advocate for solidarity not only among African diasporic communities in Canada but also with other historically aggrieved communities, including Canada's First Peoples. "Listen I want an explanation / Why are Mohawks being kicked out of their reservations?" he goes on to ask, referencing the then-recent Oka Crisis, a 1990 land dispute between the Mohawk First Nation of Kanasatake, near Oka, Quebec and the Canadian government. Calling for social justice, particularly for Indigenous communities, was uncommon in Canadian hip hop at the time.[14] By doing so, Maestro Fresh-Wes provided a trenchant example of politically engaged hip hop that continues to reverberate and inspire to the present day.[15]

"Nothin' At All" advocates for unity and solidarity in other ways as well. For example, George Banton, a Jamaican-Canadian gospel and R&B singer, delivers a soulful version of the song's chorus, which repeats the words "Brother" and "Nothin' at all." His participation adds to the track's articulation of multiple diasporic musical traditions and communities. The lyrics describe the accomplishments of numerous African Canadians including boxers Egerton Marcus and Lennox Lewis, musicians Oscar Peterson and Salome Bey, and fellow Canadian hip hop pioneers Michie Mee and Mr Metro (aka Devon). The lyrics conclude: "Therefore we as a race should support / Black achievement never let society distort / Your mind away from comprehension / Cross-cultural pride is what I'm tryin' to strengthen." Given the lyrics that precede it, we might interpret Maestro's reference to "cross-cultural pride" as encouraging a sense of solidarity among different African diasporic communities and cultures in Canada. However, he clarifies that he is advocating greater recognition of, and support for, the achievements of Canadians of African descent among all Canadians: "To the black, white, yellow and brown / Maestro Fresh-Wes is down / With everyone but I must say loud / Like Trag I'm black and God dammit I'm proud."[16]

By highlighting the accomplishments of African Canadians and critiquing racism in Canada, "Nothin' At All" offers an important counterpoint to dominant narratives surrounding Canadian identity, which often minimize (or omit altogether) the accomplishments and contributions of African diasporic communities. In contrast, "Nothin' At All" offers a powerful representation of African Canadian – and African diasporic – history and identity, memorializing the musical and cultural past for future generations to hear. In this regard, Maestro's music has much in common with another pioneering Canadian hip hop act: the duo known as Dream Warriors.

Signifyin(g) Games and Cultural Memory in the Music of Dream Warriors

Like Maestro Fresh-Wes and Michie Mee, the Toronto hip hop duo Dream Warriors contributed significantly to the development of early hip hop in Canada. Consisting of King Lou and Capital Q, who are of Jamaican and Trinidadian heritage respectively, the Dream Warriors combined abstract lyrics with a wide range of samples drawn largely from Caribbean and African musics. Of the diasporic underpinnings of their music, Capital Q comments, "Some rappers, if they're from the West Indies, seem to forget their heritage ... They just adopt an American style and say they're American. But we stick to our roots" (Smallbridge 1992). On tracks such as "My Definition of a Boombastic Jazz Style," "Ludi," and "Very Easy to Assemble but Hard to Take Apart," the Dream Warriors stick to their roots by memorializing – and Signifyin(g) on – musics and cultures of the Caribbean and African diasporas.

"My Definition of a Boombastic Jazz Style" from the Dream Warriors' 1991 debut album *And Now the Legacy Begins* samples Quincy Jones's "Soul Bossa Nova," a piece that was well known to many Canadians as the theme song to the Canadian television game show *Definition*, which ran from 1974 to 1989.[17] In addition to Signifiyin(g) on Canadian culture and identity via the nod to the *Definition* game show, the piece Signifies on multiple diasporic musics and cultures. "Soul Bossa Nova" is a highly syncretic piece of music that combines elements of jazz, soul, and bossa nova (which is itself a mix of musical elements drawn from jazz and Afro-Brazilian music, notably samba). By sampling and recontextualizing "Soul Bossa Nova" within emergent Canadian hip hop, the Dream Warriors memorialize and Signify on multiple African diasporic musics and cultures, thereby articulating a hybridized subject position. As Kip Pegley notes, the piece "is about being both a Canadian and part of the rich transnational black diaspora" (2008, 74).

The lyrics of "My Definition of a Boombastic Jazz Style" provide further evidence of the group's complex identity politics: "So bob your head, dread, as I kick the funk flow / This rhyme is subliminal yet you don't think so / I walk with a gold cane, a gold brain and no gold chain / Behind the truth lies, there lies a parafix / In the mix is where Dream Warriors go / Define if you will but I know so / There is no definition." In addition to subtly referencing Jamaican culture through the nod to dreadlocks ("So bob your head, dread") and other Afrological musics ("funk flow"), these lyrics complicate dominant understandings of hip hop identity. The "gold cane" to which they refer is not a reference to hip hop "bling." Rather, it is a reference to a six-foot staff made of dried sugarcane stalk that they regularly brought on stage in performance and in music videos including the video for "My Definition of a Boombastic Jazz Style." As one of the main crops associated with the slave trade in the Caribbean, sugarcane symbolically connected the performers to their cultural heritage, including the history of slavery in the West Indies and the history of resistance to slavery.[18]

Their use of the neologism "parafix" also warrants consideration. The term "para" is Greek for "beside." Unlike a prefix or suffix, which refers to bound inflectional elements that come before or after a linguistic base, a "parafix" would stand alongside another word or concept. In addition, the term "para" is sometimes used to describe something that protects against an external force (as a parasol protects against the rain). By stating "Behind the truth lies, there lies a parafix," the Dream Warriors suggest, albeit in a decidedly abstract way, that their understanding and articulation of African diasporic identity in Canada differs significantly from – and perhaps even protects against – misrepresentations of blackness within Canada. On this interpretation, the word "lies" in the line "Behind the truth lies" may not be a verb, but rather part of another neologism, the compound noun "truth-lies," suggesting that dominant understandings and narratives of blackness in Canada that are so often promoted as truth are, in fact, lies promulgated by the mass media and other institutionalized forces surrounding Canadian culture and cultural production. By emphasizing their diasporic background and experience, the Dream Warriors offer an important counterpoint to such "truth-lies." They are more explicit on this point in the lyrics that follow: "In the mix is where Dream Warriors go / Define if you will but I know so / There is no definition." The implication is that there can be no single all-encompassing definition of black identity in Canada or anywhere else. Much like their music, which combines and Signifies on elements from multiple Afrological forms, the Dream Warriors situate their identity firmly "in the mix" of cultures that constitute the African diaspora.

The Dream Warriors' emphasis on the Caribbean and African diasporas in their construction of African Canadian identity is also evident in their song "Ludi." Latin for "games," "Ludi" (sometimes Ludo) is also the name of a board game that is played in the West Indies. The Dream Warriors' "Ludi" Signifies on a sampled groove taken from a Jamaican ska recording, Slim Smith and the Uniques' "My Conversation."[19] The juxtaposition of Jamaican ska and hip hop creates a dialogic space between African and Caribbean diasporic cultures in Canada. This dialogic/diasporic space is reinforced in the lyrics:

> Well my mother wanted me to make another song
> Something brand new so she could dance to, too
> So this one's dedicated to no other than my mother,
> My father, my sisters, and my brother,
> Or you could say the family, or better yet, the families
> Or wait a sec, what the heck, this one's for
> Jamaica, Africa, Dominica, Trinidad and Tobago,
> St Kitts, Bermuda, Antigua, St Lucia, St Martin
> And do not forget Montserrat, Nevis, Aruba
> Grenada, Guyana, and Cuba
> St Vincent, Angola, Bahamas, Puerto Rico, Curaçao,
> Dominican Republic, and Rio,
> Martinique, and Guadeloupe,
> And Virgin Islands for
> Truly this one's for my mother
> When we were playing ludi

By stating that the song is dedicated to "no other than [their] mother," and then expanding the dedication to the majority of Caribbean countries with African populations, the Dream Warriors suggest that a plurality of African diasporic locations and experiences inform their identities as African Canadians. This conception of identity was markedly different from the aggressively nationalistic stance of many African American hip hop artists at the time, and from the Afrocentric paradigm of some hip hop groups that tended to view Africa, not the African diaspora, as the symbolic motherland. In this view, the song's reference to the board game Ludi serves not only as a signifier of Caribbean diasporic cultural memory, but also as an example of the Signifyin(g) games that the Dream Warriors play with respect to constructions of diasporic and black identity in Canada.

The B Side of the "Ludi" single features a piece titled "Very Easy to Assemble but Hard to Take Apart," which was a collaboration between the Dream Warriors and African American jazz singer, pianist, and guitarist Slim Gaillard. Gaillard developed an important antecedent of rap in the 1930s and 1940s, an invented language he referred to as "Vout" or sometimes "Vout-O-Reenie." Musically, the track is underpinned by a two-bar sample taken from Bob James's 1975 jazz-funk recording "Farandole (L'Arlesienne Suite No. 2)." At one point in the middle of the track, King Lou addresses Gaillard: "You know what Slims? You know what? I heard you invented your own language. You know I do the jazz-rap. I do some funk-rap. I do some reggae-rap. Why don't you drop some generation gap?" Gaillard responds with another example of linguistic code-switching, combining English and Vout as he references the history of jazz and his own involvement therein, including his 1938 hit "Flat Foot Floogie (with a Floy Floy)."

This exchange highlights the extent to which the Dream Warriors saw their music, and hip hop more generally, as a Signifyin(g) response to a range of diasporic musics and cultures. King Lou tells Gaillard that he performs "jazz-rap," "funk-rap," and "reggae-rap," thereby emphasizing the connections between rap music and musical expressions that have emanated from other parts of the African diaspora. Moreover, his request that Gaillard "drop some generation gap" indicates that the Dream Warriors saw hip hop as a potent site for cultural memorialization across time as well as space, a way of remembering and honouring African diasporic musical and cultural heritage. As King Lou explains: "A majority of rappers don't understand ... They come on like they're the first person ever to do what they're doing. But you have to look back, look at what came before you. [Gaillard] did this for you. He made you into what you are. You have to learn to put back in what you take out. That's why we did a song with Slim Gaillard: to put back into the jazz what we took out of it. We did a song with Slim Gaillard to say: this is our source. This is what we are speaking about" (quoted in Smallbridge 1992). In light of these comments, as well as the musical and lyrical content of the piece, we are inclined to read the track's title (which also forms the lyrics of the chorus) as referring to African diasporic musics and communities: for the Dream Warriors, they are "Very Easy to Assemble but Hard to Take Apart."

In tracks such as "My Definition of a Boombastic Jazz Style," "Ludi," and "Very Easy to Assemble but Hard to Take Apart," the Dream Warriors memorialized and Signified on multiple expressive cultures associated with the Caribbean and African diasporas. In so doing, they articulated a highly nuanced performance persona and subject position within early Canadian hip hop that was firmly rooted in their understanding of African diasporic experience.

"Mr. Metro": The Cultural Politics of Devon's Nomadic Aesthetic

Like Michie Mee, Maestro Fresh-Wes, and the Dream Warriors, Devon Martin (known professionally as Devon and "Mr. Metro" after his hit of the same name) embodies a diasporic experience in his life and career: born in 1968 to Jamaican parents living in England, he was raised in Malton, now a neighbourhood in the northeastern corner of Mississauga. Early in his career, Devon performed with the reggae band 20th Century Rebels and toured with artists like dub poets Lillian Allen and Clifton Joseph and the Canadian reggae group Messenjah. Rinaldo Walcott describes Devon as the "clearest link between dub poetry and rap music in Canada," emphasizing the "nomadic aesthetic" that characterizes his work (1997, 84), that is, the embrace of creative mobility as a means of reflecting and articulating diasporic experience. Walcott goes on to theorize "nomadology" as an "attempt to think about movement and exile in a fashion which makes those conditions a part of the way in which cultural work is understood and valued" (134). In Devon's case, this means examining the ways in which his practice "reconfigures the nation-state by making links which produce more rich and textured histories/memories of black positionalities across space, time and nation" (90–1).

Devon's nomadic aesthetic is evident in his biggest hit, a track titled "Mr. Metro" that was released as a single in 1989 and again on his JUNO Award winning 1992 album *It's My Nature*. In response to reports of police harassment of black youth – and his own experience of being detained by police in 1989 while on tour in Los Angeles with Lillian Allen (*Canadian Pop Encyclopedia* 2004) – Devon critiques police harassment, an experience that is shared by many members of African diasporic communities. "Mr. Metro" was recorded two years before the widely televised incident of police brutality against Rodney King at the hands of four white Los Angeles police officers.

In it, Devon issues an appeal to the Los Angeles Police Department and the Orange County Sherriff's Department in California, as well as the Royal Canadian Mounted Police, the Ontario Provincial Police, 52 Division of the Toronto Police Service, and the Peel Regional Police in Brampton, Ontario: "No, no, no LAPD," he rhymes, "Ease up RCMP / Ease up Orange County / Ease up / No OPP / Ease up 52 / Ease up Peel Region / Ease up / Don't shoot the youth." As Walcott explains, Devon Signifies on the rock band Queen's hit "Another One Bites the Dust" in order to highlight the growing numbers of black youth killed at the hands of police officers internationally: "The intertextual and intermusical resonances of 'Mr. Metro' ('And another one gone and another one gone / And another one bites the dust') places blackness outside of national boundaries and requires us to theorize blackness as an interstitial space. Devon's signifying and testifying calls up a broader notion of blackness than state narratives would allow, for Devon refuses to reference only one nation in the sonic blackness he constructs. And while he does not lose sense of locality and historicity, his political and artistic identifications exceed national boundaries" (1997, 31). The music video for "Mr. Metro" reinforces a sense of diasporic blackness that crosses national – as well as musical and historical – boundaries in a variety of ways. For example, footage of police officers in Toronto, some of which was blurred in response to the threat of legal action from the Toronto Police Service (*Canadian Pop Encyclopedia* 2004), is interspersed with black-and-white archival footage from Civil Rights-era demonstrations in America including Black Panther Party rallies.[20]

Devon's "nomadic aesthetic" is further evidenced by his embrace of creative mobility and code-switching in "Mr. Metro." For example, the music video references multiple musical traditions: at various points, Devon is shown playing an electronic keyboard; at others, silhouetted figures are shown playing trumpets, trombones, and saxophones – instruments generally associated with jazz, funk, and R&B more so than hip hop. In addition, Devon wears a pork pie hat throughout the video, a sartorial signifier of jazz, blues, and ska music and culture. Devon further emphasizes the diasporic underpinnings of the piece by using a Jamaican accent for much of the song. Unlike Michie Mee, who is known for switching abruptly between Canadian and Jamaican linguistic codes in performance, Devon's Jamaican accent seems to vary by degree from performance to performance and sometimes even within the same song. For example, he raps the opening words of "Mr. Metro" in a relatively thick Jamaican accent: "Metro's number one problem / Is that no one really can trust dem / Causing all of this tension / Some things I won't even mention / Pick up *The Star*; pick up *The Sun* / Headline: 'Metro gets another one.'" By referencing the *Toronto Star* and *Toronto Sun* newspapers, he situates his critique, and his own subject position, in Toronto, while simultaneously gesturing toward his diasporic heritage by adopting a Jamaican accent. Later in the piece, he rhymes the following lyrics with little to no accent: "Yes, the situation is real / Now's the time to show how we feel / I think we get a real bad bad deal / We better have a chat with who? / Mr. Metro." The musical and linguistic nomadicism that characterizes "Mr. Metro," and Devon's creative practice more generally, constructs and performs a hybridized diasporic identity that further articulates the lyrics' call for solidarity among diasporic communities in response to shared experiences of oppression.

"Can't Repress the Cause": Dance Appeal's Articulation of – and Advocacy for – Diasporic Musics and Cultures in Canada

In 1991, Devon participated in another project that emphasized musical and diasporic solidarity, a track titled "Can't Repress the Cause" by a supergroup called Dance Appeal that included many Toronto performers of Caribbean and West Indian heritage. In addition to Devon, Michie Mee, Maestro Fresh-Wes, and the Dream Warriors, the track featured rappers B-Kool, HDV, and Self Defense; reggae artists Leroy Sibbles, Carla Marshall, and Messenjah; dub poet Lillian Allen; as well as singers Dionne, Eria Fachin, Thando Hyman, Jillian Mendez, Lorraine Scott, Lorraine Segato (of Parachute Club fame), Thyron Lee White, and Zama. The project's goal was to advocate for greater inclusion of popular dance musics such as hip hop, reggae, and R&B on commercial radio in Toronto. As the lyrics of the chorus explain, "Whatever they do, they can't stop dance music / Different stations, but they just refuse it." The most pointed critique of the lack of diversity on Toronto radio comes from Maestro Fresh-Wes who states, "The transistor transmits crap / That's the truth, but a predator keeps us trapped / We're pumping out LPs of gold / Still local radio ain't got no soul."

The Dance Appeal project was organized by a group called the "Dance Music Radio Committee" that had been formed to lobby the Canadian Radio-television and Telecommunications Commission (CRTC) on behalf of applicants wishing to start Canada's first urban music radio station.[21] In 1989, the CRTC issued a call for applications to start a new radio station that would broadcast on FM 92.5, the only available frequency in Toronto at the time. Of the eleven applicants, four proposed a "Black or dance or rhythm and blues format" (Tator, Henry, and Mathis 1998, 111–12). In a highly controversial decision known as Decision 90–693, the CRTC awarded the station licence to a country music applicant, noting "the Commission is convinced that a country and country-oriented station would at this time best add to the diversity and provide Toronto FM radio listeners with a true musical alternative" (Canadian Radio-television and Telecommunications Commission 1990). Many Toronto musicians and a number of elected officials including Art Eggleton (then mayor of Toronto), Member of Parliament Howard McCurdy, and Paul M. Tellier, clerk of the Privy Council and secretary to cabinet under Prime Minister Brian Mulroney, criticized this decision. Several members of the Canadian Radio-television and Telecommunications Commission itself went on record condemning the decision, including CRTC chair Keith Spicer who stated that the decision "ignores the principle of broadcasting diversity at its most fundamental: the need to serve today's multicultural, multiracial Toronto" (Canadian Radio-television and Telecommunications Commission 1990). Likewise, many community organizations and groups voiced their dissatisfaction with Decision 90–693, including the Canadian Ethnocultural Council, the Urban Alliance on Race Relations, the National Council of Jamaicans and Supportive Organizations, and the Jane Finch Concerned Citizens Organization (Tator, Henry, and Mathis 1998, 116). The Dance Music Radio Committee lobbied for an appeal, organizing a petition and postcard campaign, as well as the recording session that led to Dance Appeal's "Can't Repress the Cause," which was released as a 12-inch maxi-single on Bruce Bradley's Somersault Record label. Five applicants appealed Decision 90–693, but the commission's decision to grant the licence to a country music station was upheld (117–18).

The push for increased airplay for hip hop, reggae, and R&B in Toronto was part of a larger movement in the 1980s and 1990s aimed at increasing commercial recognition of, and support for, Afrological musics in Canada. Formed in 1984, the Black Music Association of Canada (BMAC) successfully lobbied for greater inclusion of African diasporic musics at the JUNO Awards (Young 2006, 196–7), leading to the introduction of two new award categories in 1985: Best R&B/Soul recording and Best Reggae/Calypso recording. In 1996, the Black Music Association of Canada was replaced by the Urban Music Association of Canada, which became "the lone music industry service provider for urban music in Canada and the work of Canadian urban artists" (Urban Music).

The musically disparate group of performers on "Can't Repress the Cause" all share a connection to dance and the urban club scene. As Eria Fachin and

Thando Hyman sing, "Dance music is the key / It has the groove to set your heart free / No matter what style or form / The beat just makes you wanna dance all night long." Despite the suggestion that the style or form of the music does not matter, and despite the participation of several white performers in the session (Eria Fachin, Lorraine Segato, and Thyron Lee White), the track is clearly advocating for Afrological dance musics specifically, genres that came to be included under the umbrella "urban music" within a few years. For example, rapper B-Kool rhymes, "B, K, double O, L is here to take a stand / Support the cause, cause we're all in the same gang / Hip hop, house, R&B is what we design / Without dance radio, Toronto got left behind." The notion that hip hop, house, and rhythm and blues are "in the same gang" reinforces a sense of diasporic dialogue and solidarity among the musical styles and communities represented on the recording.

It would seem that reggae is part of the same "gang" too, since the track features numerous reggae musicians, notably Leroy Sibbles, who brings significant reggae credentials and history to the project; in addition to his role as the lead singer of the legendary rocksteady/reggae group the Heptones, he was a bassist and arranger at Coxone Dodd's famous Studio One in Jamaica. Sibbles continued to have a successful career after emigrating to Canada in 1973, winning the 1987 JUNO Award for best Reggae/Calypso album. On "Can't Repress the Cause," Sibbles sings "It's been around / The clubs can't survive without the sound." With these lyrics, Sibbles historicizes dance music, reminding the listener of the close connections between hip hop and Jamaican sound system culture, and between music and dance in African diasporic expressive cultures more generally. He also emphasizes the cultural and economic benefits of those forms. Later in the track, Jillian Mendez honours the pioneers of dance music in Canada: "To all the pioneers / We'll say 'word up' and show you how much we care." Lorraine Scott continues, "If it wasn't for musicians like you / The rest of us wouldn't have made it through."

Musically, "Can't Repress the Cause" provides another example of code-switching through its pastiche of musical styles and rhythms. The chorus and opening verses are set against a somewhat generic pop-oriented backing track consisting of synthesizer, bass, and a drum-machine groove. The texture changes abruptly when Michie Mee enters with the words "'Hee haw'? Hell no / That's what you want me to tell the crowd instead of saying 'Ho'?" At this point, the bass and synthesizer drop out leaving only the drum groove and record scratching against her vocals. After returning to the chorus and pop-oriented backing track, the texture changes once again, this time to a

Jamaican dancehall riddim against which Carla Marshall drops a verse in Jamaican Patois. She is followed by Devon, who uses a heavy Jamaican accent (thicker than his accent in "Mr. Metro") to toast with the following words: "Coast to coast and nation to nation / Tell the whole world, say 'we need a dance station.'"

Celebrated Jamaican Canadian dub poet Lillian Allen rounds out the dancehall portion of the track with the words "People around the country ought to know / This part of the culture that always gets the shove / Music is our heart, soul and the struggle / Got to ease up and let the culture bubble." For Allen and her co-performers, "letting the culture bubble" entailed bringing hip hop, dub, reggae, R&B, and other Afrological musics and musicians into contact with one another, celebrating their shared roots in the African and Caribbean diasporas. Crucially, it also meant gaining increased radio play and institutional recognition for the music in order to cultivate a wider audience and support the growth of an urban music industry in Canada. In a 2016 email to us, Allen reflected on the piece, stating that listening to it twenty-five years after it was first released made her remember "how we had to spend so much of our time fighting for every inch of progress ... I know it all seems so 'normal' now and a lot of younger ones take it all for granted; the irony is that in some ways that was what we were fighting for: for those coming up after us to have this space as a normal and natural part of their cultural expression."

Toward the end of the piece, a child rhymes, "Out of the mouths of babes I demand / Give my people dance music on the FM band." His reference to "my people" warrants consideration. On the one hand, this might be interpreted as a reference to young people who were (and who remain) the main audience for dance music in Canada. On the other, we know from the music video that the child, like most of the other participants in the project, is of African descent. So it is possible that his reference to "my people" refers to African Canadian youth specifically, a demographic that had been underrepresented in, and marginalized by, the Canadian music industry historically, making the message in "Can't Repress the Cause" all the more important.

By putting Michie Mee, Maestro Fresh-Wes, Dream Warriors, and Devon – the stars of Canada's nascent hip hop scene – in dialogue with music and musicians from a wider variety of Afrological traditions, the Dance Appeal project highlights the diasporic roots and routes of early Canadian hip hop, articulating an understanding of diaspora that crosses musical, national, generational, gender, and cultural lines. Although "Can't Repress the Cause" was unsuccessful in convincing the CRTC to reverse Decision 90–693, the video received regular airplay on MuchMusic, winning a Canadian Music Video Award for dance music video of the year. The song also played an important role in galvanizing African and Caribbean diasporic communities in Toronto, contributing to a conversation that has brought about significant changes in the musical and cultural landscape in Toronto and, arguably, Canada. Toronto now has two urban radio stations: CFXJ 93.5 FM, which began broadcasting hip hop and other urban musics in 2001; and CKFG 98.7 FM beginning in 2011, which plays R&B, soul, reggae, soca, hip hop, gospel, jazz, and world beat.

A growing number of hip hop artists from Toronto and other parts of Canada – including Drake, Kardinal Offishall, Classified, k-os, K'Naan, Rascalz, Swollen Members, Cadence Weapon, Eternia, Belly, and Shad to name only a few – have achieved considerable critical and commercial success in recent years. Their success was made possible in large measure by the work of pioneering Canadian hip hop artists such as Michie Mee, Maestro Fresh-Wes, Dream Warriors, and Devon, who laid the foundations for hip hop in Canada. By performing, memorializing, and Signifyin(g) on their diasporic heritage, they ensured that hip hop in Canada has been – and continues to be – a fantastic voyage indeed.

Notes

1 Beginning his career in 1952, Jocko Henderson was a popular Philadelphia-based radio disc jockey known for his on-air rhythmic patter between songs. He was also featured on the 1979 rap release "Rhythm Talk," which provided a link between older forms of vernacular African American expressive culture and then-emergent forms of rap.
2 A thorough discussion of hip hop in Canada is, of course, beyond the scope of the present chapter. Much of the academic writing on hip hop in Canada has focused on hip hop within a particular city, region, or cultural group. For example, numerous studies have examined the cultural politics of hip hop in Quebec, including Chamberland (2002), Jones (2011), Ransom (2013), Sarker and Allen (2007), and Sarker and Winer (2006). For a discussion of hip hop in Indigenous communities in Canada, see Manzo and Potts (2013) and Marsh (2009, 2011, 2012). For more general discussions of hip hop in Canada, see Campbell (2014), Chamberland (2001), D'Amico (2015), Haines (1999), Krims (2000), and Walcott (1997). For an online archive of primary materials related to Canadian hip hop culture and history, see Northside Hip Hop Archive at http://www.nshharchive.ca. Charity Marsh and Mark V. Campbell's forthcoming anthology *Hip Hop North of the 49th Parallel* will further our understanding of hip hop cultures across Canada.

3 The terms "Afrological" and "Eurological" were coined by composer/improviser/scholar George Lewis (1996). "These terms," he writes, "refer metaphorically to musical belief systems and behavior which ... exemplify particular kinds of musical 'logic.' At the same time, these terms are intended to historicize the particularity of perspective characteristic of two systems that have evolved in such divergent cultural environments" (93). Like Lewis, we use the term "Afrological" to refer to "historically emergent rather than ethnically essential" systems of musical logic that have developed in African diasporic communities historically (93).

4 The distinctive spellings distinguish Signifyin'/Signifyin(g)/signifyin(g) as theorized by Gates in relation to African diasporic expressive cultures from more general patterns of semiotic signification. In keeping with Gates's and Floyd's nomenclature, we retain the capitalization of the term throughout this chapter as well as the parenthesized "g," unless we are quoting a source that uses an alternative spelling.

5 Within hip hop culture, the terms "b-boying" and "b-girling" are widely used to refer to hip hop dance; outside of the culture, the term "breakdancing" has been more common historically.

6 In hip hop culture, a battle is a competition in which two or more hip hop practitioners (usually MCs, dancers, or DJs) compete with one another by displaying their respective skills. Battle rap typically involves boastful rhymes and verbal insults aimed at the opponent.

7 Although reggae and DJ/sound system culture heavily influenced early hip hop, actual reggae vocal or instrumental styles were not common in 1980s hip hop. Reggae/rap hybrid recordings would become more common in the 1990s. For example, Jamaican artists such as Super Cat, Shabba Ranks, and Cutty Ranks recorded over hip hop style beats and/or collaborated with hip hop artists on rap records. But in the 1980s, the combination of rap and reggae remained isolated to a few recordings. Aside from Michie Mee, Boogie Down Productions was the main exception.

8 Jamaican Patois (sometimes spelled "Patwa") is an English-based hybridized language (with West African linguistic elements) that is widely spoken in Jamaica and the Jamaican diaspora. Although Jamaican Patois is technically a form of English, it can be very difficult for non-native speakers to understand, almost as if it is a different language.

9 See Chambers (2010) for a discussion of the history and salient features of Standard Canadian English. In using this admittedly loaded term, we do not wish to further entrench the hegemony of a particular accent among English speakers in Canada. Rather, we use the term to draw attention to the ways in which Michie Mee strategically employs different linguistic codes to articulate a hybridized Jamaican-Canadian identity.

10 *Roots* was an award-winning television mini-series in 1977 based on Alex Haley's novel *Roots: The Saga of an American Family* which centres on the life of an African slave named Kunta Kinte and the hardships he endures in America under slavery.

11 For a thorough discussion of the history of slavery in Canada, see Marcel Trudel's *Canada's Forgotten Slaves* (2013).

12 For a discussion of the history of racist societies in Canada, including the KKK, see Stanley Barrett's *Is God a Racist? The Right Wing in Canada* (1987).

13 Writing about Canadian literature, Diana Brydon has referred to such narratives as "myths of Canadian innocence, deference, and goodwill" (2007, 5).
14 As Mark V. Campbell notes, "Nothin' At All" was unique within Canadian hip hop of the early to mid-1990s, which otherwise reinforced the "invisibility" of Aboriginal peoples in Canada (2014, 276).
15 In the years since "Nothin' At All" was released, hip hop has assumed a prominent place within many Indigenous communities in Canada, as the work of Marsh (2009, 2011, 2012), Haines (1999), and Manzo and Potts (2013) makes clear. Since 2013, numerous Indigenous hip hop artists have released recordings in support of the Idle No More movement, including Edmonton-based Metis rapper Rellik, who released a track titled "Idle No More." In addition, a growing number of Canadian hip hop artists with roots in the African diaspora have expressed solidarity with Indigenous communities. As Campbell explains, "Today, it is not uncommon for socially conscious hip hop artists and groups to refuse a strictly historical periodization of colonialism and to recognize present day struggles of Aboriginal peoples for self-determination. In recent hip hop music a connection is drawn between the diasporic conditions of immigrants to the very rooted concerns of land, and settler relations by several First Nations in Canada" (276–7).
16 "Trag" (pronounced "Tradj") is short for American rapper Tragedy Khadafi (aka Intelligent Hoodlum) who released a song titled "Black & Proud" on his 1990 album *Intelligent Hoodlum*.
17 Later, "Soul Bossa Nova" was prominently featured in the film *Austin Powers: International Man of Mystery* (Roach 1997) and it was sampled again in 2004 by Ludacris on "Number One Spot" from the album *The Red Light District*.
18 See Sheridan, *Sugar and Slavery: An Economic History of the British West Indies, 1623–1775*.
19 Jamaican Canadian rapper Kardinal Offishall went on to sample "My Conversation" on his 2008 recording titled "Nina," thereby Signifyin(g) on both Jamaican cultural heritage and the Dream Warriors' track, and continuing the diasporic conversation.
20 Since the release of "Mr. Metro," Canadian hip hop artists have continued to address the issue of police brutality in their music. In 2016, numerous Canadian hip hop artists responded to the widely publicized deaths of many African American men at the hands of white police officers, publicly expressing solidarity with the Black Lives Matter movement. For example, Toronto hip hop group Connected by Blood released a track titled "Black Lives Matter"; likewise, Calgary rapper A.Y.E. released a track called "Can I Live." As he explains, "'Can I Live' is meant to pay homage to those gone, and give support [to] the Black Lives Matter Movement worldwide. The idea behind the song was to give an honest account and create a picture of what it's like being a black male or female having to live with fear of being shot dead by law enforcement" (A.Y.E. 2016).
21 "Urban" or "urban contemporary" are radio industry terms used to designate Afrological modes of music making such as soul, rhythm and blues, hip-hop, etc.

References

A.Y.E. 2016. "A.Y.E. supports #BlackLivesMatter with the release of 'Can I Live.'" Accessed 7 October 2016. http://www.hiphopcanada.com/2016/07/a-y-e-supports-blacklivesmatter-with-the-release-of-can-i-live.

Bal, Mieke. 1999. "Introduction." In *Acts of Memory: Cultural Recall in the Present*, edited by Mieke Bal, Jonathon Crewe, and Leo Spitzer, vii–xvii. Hanover, NH: University Press of New England.

Bakare-Yusuf, Bibi. 2006. "Fabricating Identities: Survival and the Imagination in Jamaican Dancehall Culture." *Fashion Theory* 10 (3): 1–24.

Barrett, Stanley. 1987. *Is God a Racist? The Right Wing in Canada*. Toronto, ON: University of Toronto Press.

Brydon, Diana. 2007. "Metamorphoses of a Discipline: Rethinking Canadian Literature within Institutional Contexts." In *Trans.Can.Lit: Resituating the Study of Canadian Literature*, edited by Smaro Kamboureli and Roy Miki, 1–6. Waterloo, ON: Wilfrid Laurier University Press.

Campbell, Mark V. 2014. "The Politics of Making Home: Opening Up the Work of Richard Iton in Canadian Hip Hop Context." *Souls: A Critical Journal of Black Politics, Culture, and Society* 16 (3/4): 269–82.

Canadian Broadcast Corporation News Toronto. *Love, Props and the T.Dot*. 2011. Documentary video, Youtube, 3 July. Accessed 1 May 2015. http://www.cbc.ca/absolutelycanadian/docs/2012/07/14/love-props-and-the-t-dot.

Canadian Pop Encyclopedia. 2004. "Biography for Devon." Accessed 12 October 2016. http://jam.canoe.com/Music/Pop_Encyclopedia/D/Devon.html.

Canadian Radio-television and Telecommunications Commission. 1990. Decision CRTC 90-693. Accessed 16 May 2016. http://www.crtc.gc.ca/eng/archive/1990/DB90-693.htm.

Chamberland, Roger. 2001. "Rap in Canada: Bilingual and Multicultural." In *Global Noise: Rap and Hip-bop Outside the U.S.A.*, edited by Tony Mitchell, 306–25. Middletown, CT: Wesleyan University Press.

– 2002. "The Cultural Paradox of Rap Made in Quebec." In *Black, Blanc, Beur: Rap Music and Hip-Hop Culture in the Francophone World*, edited by Alain-Philippe Durand, 124–37. Lanham, MD: Scarecrow.

Chambers, J.K. 2010. "English in Canada." In *Canadian English: A Linguistic Reader*, edited by Elaine Gold and Janice McAlpine, 1–37. Kingston, ON: Strathy Language Unit. Accessed 13 September 2016. http://www.queensu.ca/strathy/apps/OP6v2.pdf.

Connerton, Paul. 1989. *How Societies Remember*. Cambridge, UK: Cambridge University Press.

Cowie, Del F. 2015. "Maestro Fresh-Wes." *The Canadian Encyclopedia*. Published 30 January 2015. Accessed 15 March 2016. http://www.thecanadianencyclopedia.ca/en/article/maestro-fresh-wes.

D'Amico, Francesca. 2015. "'The Mic Is My Piece': Canadian Rap, the Gendered 'Cool Pose,' and Music Industry Racialization and Regulation." *Journal of the Canadian Historical Association* 261: 255–90.

Davies, Eirlys E., and Abdelali Bentahila. 2006. "Code Switching and the Globalisation of Popular Music: The Case of North African Rai and Rap." *Multilingua* 25 (4): 367–92.

Floyd, Samuel A. 1991. "Ring Shout! Literary Studies, Historical Studies, and Black Music Inquiry." *Black Music Research Journal* 11 (2): 265–87.

– 1995. *The Power of Black Music*. New York, NY: Oxford University Press.

Gates, Henry Louis, Jr. 1988. *The Signifyin' Monkey: A Theory of African-American Literary Criticism*. New York, NY: Oxford University Press.

Gilroy, Paul. 1993. *The Black Atlantic: Modernity and Double Consciousness*. Cambridge, MA: Harvard University Press.

Haines, Rebecca J. 1999. "Break North: Rap Music and Hip-Hop Culture in Canada." In *Ethnicity, Politics, and Public Policy: Case Studies in Canadian Diversity*, edited by Harold Troper and Morton Weinfeld, 54–88. Toronto, ON: University of Toronto Press.

Harriet Tubman Institute for Research on the Global Migrations of African Peoples. 2013. "Performing Diaspora 2013: Toronto's Hip-Hop Practitioners." Video of roundtable panel, 1 June 2013, York University. https://www.youtube.com/watch?v=1somgl6zLoI.

Jones, Christopher M. 2011. "Hip-Hop Quebec: Self and Synthesis." *Popular Music and Society* 34 (2): 177–202.

Krims, Adam. 2000. *Rap Music and the Poetics of Identity*. Cambridge, UK: Cambridge University Press.

Lewis, George. 1996. "Improvised Music after 1950: Afrological and Eurological Perspectives." *Black Music Research Journal* 16 (1): 91–122.

Manzo, John, and Jesse J. Potts. 2013. "Rez Style: Themes of Resistance in Canadian Aboriginal Rap Music." *Canadian Journal of Native Studies* 33 (1): 169–88.

Marsh, Charity. 2009. "'Don't Call Me Eskimo': The Politics of Hip Hop Culture in Nunavut." *MUSICultures* 36: 110–29.

– 2011. "'Keepin' It Real'? Masculinity, Indigeneity, and Media Representations of Gangsta Rap in Regina." In *Making It Like a Man: Canadian Masculinities in Practice*, edited by Christine Ramsay, 149–70. Waterloo, ON: Wilfrid Laurier University Press.

— 2012. "Bits and Pieces of Truth: Storytelling, Identity, and Hip Hop in Saskatchewan." In *Aboriginal Music in Contemporary Canada: Echoes and Exchanges*, edited by Anna Hoefnagels and Beverley Diamond, 346–71. Montreal & Kingston: McGill-Queen's University Press.

Michie Mee. 2009. Interview by Ty Harper. "OTA Live: OTA Talk w/ Michie Mee" (video). YouTube, 17 March. Accessed 1 May 2015. https://www.youtube.com/watch?v=eRxgPh511cg.

– 2011. Interview by Char Loro. "BDC 951: Studio Interview with Michie Mee" (video). YouTube, 26 November 2011. Accessed 1 May 2015. https://www.youtube.com/watch?v=fTvj8QWosmI.

– 2012. Interview by Eddy Bo Williams. "Royalty Radio: Michie Mee Interview and In-Studio Performance" (video). YouTube, 25 July. Accessed 1 December 2014. https://www.youtube.com/watch?v=LaTgtKkvKMQ.

— 2013. Interview by Shaheen Ariefdien. "Performing Diaspora 2013." Accessed 1 May 2015.
Milroy, Lesley, and Pieter Muysken. 1995. "Introduction: Code-Switching and Bilingualism Research." In *One Speaker, Two Languages: Cross-Disciplinary Perspectives on Code-Switching,* edited by Lesley Milroy and Pieter Muysken, 1–14. Cambridge, UK: Cambridge University Press.
Northside Hip Hop Archive. http://www.nshharchive.ca.
Pegley, Kip. 2008. *Coming to You Wherever You Are: MuchMusic, MTV and Youth Identities.* Middletown, CT: Wesleyan University Press.
Ransom, Amy J. 2013. "'Québec History X': Re-Visioning the Past through Rap." *The American Review of Canadian Studies* 43 (1): 12–29.
Sarkar, Mela, and Dawn Allen. 2007. "Hybrid Identities in Quebec Hip-hop: Language, Territory and Ethnicity in the Mix." *Journal of Language, Identity, and Education* 6 (2): 117–30.
Sarkar, Mela, and Lise Winer. 2006. "Multilingual Codeswitching in Quebec Rap: Poetry, Pragmatics and Performativity." *International Journal of Multilingualism* 3 (3): 173–92.
Sarkar, Mela, Lise Winer, and Kobir Sarker. 2005. "Multilingual Code-Switching in Montreal Hip-Hop: Mayhem Meets Method," or "Tout Moune Qui Talk Trash Kiss Mon Black Ass Du Nord." In *Proceedings of the 4th International Symposium on Bilingualism,* edited by James Cohen et al., 2057–74. Somerville, MA: Cascadilla Press.
Sheridan, Richard B. 1974. *Sugar and Slavery: An Economic History of the British West Indies, 1623–1775.* Kingston, ON: Canoe Press.
Smallbridge, Justin. 1992. "The Rhythm Method: The Dream Warriors Spin Some Old Themes into an Altogether New Kind of Rap Music." *Saturday Night.* April. Accessed 27 April 2016. http://justinsmallbridge.com/clips/19920401SNdreamwarriors.html.
Tator, Carol, Frances Henry, and Winston Matthis. 1998. *Challenging Racism in the Arts: Case Studies of Controversy and Conflict.* Toronto, ON: University of Toronto Press.
Trudel, Marcel. 2013. *Canada's Forgotten Slaves: Two Hundred Years of Bondage,* translated by George Tombs. Montreal, QC: Véhicule Press.
Urban Music Association of Canada. "About our UMAC." Accessed 1 May 2016. http://umacgroup.com/index.php/about/.
Walcott, Rinaldo. 1997. *Black Like Who?* Toronto, ON: Insomniac Press.
— 2001. "Caribbean Pop Culture in Canada: Or, the Impossibility of Belonging to the Nation." *Small Axe* 9 (5.1): 123–39.
Williams, Wes. 2010. *Stick to Your Vision: How to Get Past the Hurdles and Haters to Get Where You Want to Be.* Toronto, ON: McClelland and Stewart.
— 2013. Interview by Shaheen Ariefdien. "Performing Diaspora 2013." Accessed 1 May 2016.
Young, David. 2006. "Ethno-racial Minorities and the Juno Awards." *The Canadian Journal of Sociology.* 31 (2): 183–210.
Young, Tony, and Dalton Higgins. 2002. *Much Master T: One VJ's Journey.* Toronto: ECW Press.

Janice Esther Tulk

Chapter 11

Identity, Aesthetics, and Place in Medicine Dream's "In This World"

Indigenous popular music provides a salient space for the study of identity and representation because it often synthesizes elements of traditional and mainstream artistic expression in meaningful ways.[1] Tribal languages, vocables, hand drums, powwow drums, and Native American flutes may be fused with electric guitar, bass guitar, drum kit, pop-style vocal harmonies, and Western-based chord progressions, resulting in musical expressions that are at once nation-specific and mainstream, local and transnational. Thematic content of lyrics may refer to nation-specific histories and broader issues faced by Indigenous peoples, or not refer to these at all. Indigenous popular music is a site of empowerment for Indigenous musicians and their communities, while serving as a bridge to larger social discourse in Canada.

Studies of Indigenous popular musics have largely focused on aural elements in audio recordings and live performances, as well as recording and production practices, to illuminate aesthetic preferences, the relationship between place and music, and the political messages sent and received through song (see, for example, Diamond 2001, 2002; Neuenfeldt 2001, 2002; Scales 1996, 2002, 2012; Tulk 2003, 2004). The visual presentation of such music through the medium of the music video has been addressed less commonly.[2] These expressions, which combine text, music, and moving image, further demonstrate the fusion of generic and cultural influences and elements. Visual imagery complicates the audience's reading of aural elements, reinforcing or contradicting their understandings, while also revealing the continuing importance of authentic representation and Indigenous aesthetic preferences for liveness. Thus, music videos articulate the connections between music, place, and identity in nuanced ways.

In this chapter I examine the links between musical, textual, and visual elements in Indigenous popular music videos through a case study of "In This World" by Medicine Dream, an intertribal pop-rock music group based in Alaska and led by Paul Pike, an Indigenous Canadian of Mi'kmaw descent.[3] In particular, I explore interrelated elements of text, music, symbols, and performance practice to demonstrate how "In This World" is both local and global, nation-specific and "universal" or mainstream at the same time.[4] The connection to place is emphasized through a description of the band and highlights from the life history of Pike that inform the reader's understanding of lyrics and visual elements found in "In This World." I draw on Gow's music video categorization to analyze the formulas employed in the making of the video and demonstrate how the music is embedded in mainstream modes of expression and connects to genre-based idioms, revealing the multivalent nature of the music video when read as a text. The chapter concludes with a discussion of authenticity and the musical representation of Indigenous identity, grounding Paul Pike's approach and lived experience within contemporary Mi'kmaw thought.

Paul Pike and Medicine Dream

Medicine Dream's music combines Indigenous instruments and musical styles with those of mainstream pop and rock. Native American flutes, hand drums, and powwow drums are referred to as "traditional" instruments by Paul and are played alongside electric guitars, bass guitar, keyboard, and drum kit. Song lyrics employ English texts and vocables as a common language among the different Indigenous members in the group, as well as Mi'kmaq (an Eastern Algonquin language) from time to time. Vocal styles include both intertribal (e.g., chanting) and pop style production. Their four albums – *Identity* (independent, 1998), *Mawio'Mi* (Canyon Records, 2000), *Tomegan Gospem* (2002), and *Learning to Fly* (independent, 2007) – establish a musical style that points to the group's intertribal composition and undergirding in Indigenous practice, as well as its mastery of and grounding in mainstream popular music styles, such as country, rock, and pop.[5]

While this paper does not attempt to investigate or problematize the terminology of "traditional" as it pertains to the musical instruments and styles employed by Medicine Dream, it is worth noting that in the context of Indigenous popular music, the use of "traditional" is primarily one of contrast. In relation to more mainstream, Western musical styles and instruments, "traditional" is meant to emphasize the origins of particular musical elements in Indigenous cultures and practices. The term "traditional" does not necessarily imply that something is "ancient" or from a particular historical period, or even from a particular cultural group, nor is it commentary on the acoustic nature of the instruments. It is how Paul Pike refers to the Indigenous component of his music, which often draws on intertribal musical styles.[6]

Medicine Dream's membership is best described as intertribal, but it is also international. While there has been some fluctuation over the past two decades, the group has always been diverse, with members tracing their lineage to several different Indigenous groups, including Mi'kmaq, Aleut, Apache, Chocktaw, Inupiaq, Lakota, Saami, and Yup'ik nations. The group has also included non-Indigenous performers, one of German and Scandinavian heritage and one of Russian-American descent. Members of the group are employed in a variety of careers, including heritage interpretation, addictions counselling, traditional healing, and computer technology, and have recorded albums and performed together in their free time.

Following the death of their close friend K.C. LaFever in 1995, Paul Pike (lead vocals and guitar) formed Medicine Dream in Anchorage, Alaska, with original members Cea Anderson (backup vocals), George Newton (acoustic and electric guitar), and Buz Daney (traditional vocals and percussion[7]).[8] Their first songs, "Lightning Flashes the Sky" and "True Friends," were about and inspired by K.C., but the songs that followed were more diverse in terms of thematic content. Despite the band's location in Alaska, there has always been a strong connection to Newfoundland expressed through their lyrics, and to Mi'kmaw culture through symbols, as a result of Pike's leadership of the group.

Paul Pike was born in Corner Brook, Newfoundland in 1968. As a child, he played drum kit and later guitar, and was self-taught on both instruments. As a young adult, he played in different bands that were predominantly rock-oriented, including Dawn Patrol, Back to Back, and Fear of Flying. He always identified with Indigenous culture but was raised in a Catholic home and attended the local Catholic high school. Throughout his childhood, he enjoyed many of the activities that he associates with traditional Indigenous culture, such as hunting and fishing. In the early 1990s, he went to a local band office to trace his heritage and discovered a genealogy that established that his family is Mi'kmaq.⁹ Since then, he has embarked on a journey to learn more about Mi'kmaw culture with the support of his family.

In 1990, Paul moved to Alaska and performed in many rock-oriented bands there, including Shaker, The Defectors, Chaser, The Cat's Meow, Davinci, and AB Plus. He soon became involved with Indigenous communities and cultures there, while continuing to learn more about his own heritage as a Mi'kmaw from Newfoundland by travelling back to the Atlantic provinces and engaging with Elders and tradition-bearers in Mi'kmaw communities. He taught himself to play Native American flute by sitting with a guitar tuner and trying various fingerings to see which pitches they produced.[10]

Envisioning a fusion of his rock music background and the new intertribal Indigenous music in which he was immersing himself, Paul formed Medicine Dream in 1995. The group often played at the Alaska Native Heritage Center, cultural festivals, and other community events. With a strong message of sobriety, they did not play in bars and over the years had water sponsors instead of beer sponsors for concerts and other events.

Medicine Dream recorded their first album, *Identity*, independently in 1998 at Surreal Studios in Anchorage, Alaska. It featured both music and poetry. In 1999, Paul travelled home to Corner Brook to participate in the opening ceremonies of the Canada Winter Games, representing the Mi'kmaq of Newfoundland. In 2000, the music from *Identity*, along with a few new tracks, was released by Canyon Records[11] on *Mawio'Mi* (Mi'kmaq for "gathering"). By this time, John Field (keyboard and vocals) had joined the group. *Mawio'Mi* was nominated for three Native American Music Awards (known as NAMMYs) and Medicine Dream performed at the awards show in Albuquerque, New Mexico in November 2000. During the summer of 2001, the band travelled to Ireland for World Peace and Prayer Day[12] and performed a successful tour throughout Arizona. That same year, Steven Alvarez (traditional percussion and drum kit) joined the band.

In 2002, the group released their third album, *Tomegan Gospem* (a place in Newfoundland known as Gabriel's Lake). As with *Mawio'Mi*, this album was produced with Canyon Records. Their new music was featured at both their CD release party in Alaska and a concert in Salem, Massachusetts at the Peabody Essex Museum. In February 2003, the band was named Native Artist of the Month on the national radio program Native America Calling.[13] In 2007, the group released their fourth album, *Learning to Fly*, once again as an independent.

While maintaining an active performing career, participating in cultural events, and working in Alaska, Paul expanded his personal mission of Mi'kmaw cultural education in Newfoundland such that he began teaching others. In 1999 and 2000, he returned to Corner Brook to organize and participate in the Elmastukwek Mi'kmaq Mawio'Mi, an annual Mi'kmaw gathering held in the Bay of Islands. He was a guest speaker at Sir Wilfred Grenfell College in Corner Brook, where he spoke to nursing students about providing culturally sensitive care (2001). That same year he travelled around Newfoundland presenting cultural workshops for the Federation of Newfoundland Indians (now Qalipu First Nation). For five years in Alaska, he facilitated cultural education workshops for the Cook Inlet Tribal Council, speaking in numerous venues to a variety of age groups. He then worked as a substance abuse counsellor at the Hudson Lake Healing Camp in Alaska. When possible, he travelled to Miawpukek (Conne River, NL) to participate in the community's annual powwow. He even travelled to St John's, NL, to perform in the annual folk festival. After more than two decades of travelling back and forth between Newfoundland and Alaska, in 2015, Paul decided to return to his hometown of Corner Brook.[14]

A Mi'kmaw in Alaska

While Medicine Dream is physically based in Alaska, the albums *Identity*, *Mawio'Mi*, and *Tomegan Gospem*, in particular, emphasize Paul Pike's Mi'kmaw heritage in both content and design. With few exceptions, the songs performed by Medicine Dream (lyrics and music) are composed by Paul. The artwork for the cover of *Mawio'Mi* is a photograph of a piece of traditional Mi'kmaw quill work displaying a Mi'kmaw eight-point star. Paul made this piece and wears it as part of his regalia when he dances at powwows (see Tulk 2012). Further, the album's liner notes provide extensive background information about the experiences of the Mi'kmaq of Newfoundland. *Tomegan Gospem* makes a political statement about the government of Newfoundland and its treatment of the Mi'kmaw people, addressing issues such as the mercenary myth (colonial powers taught school children until the 1980s that the Mi'kmaq had massacred the Beothuk people) and the view that the only Indigenous people of Newfoundland were the now-"extinct" Beothuk.[15] Some songs employ the Mi'kmaw language and the album includes instrumental works inspired by places in Ktaqmkuk (Mi'kmaq for Newfoundland, meaning "the far shore over the waves"). For example, "Tomegan Gospem" references Gabriel's Lake, "the traditional caribou hunting territory of the Gabriel family" (*Tomegan Gospem*, liner notes). Paul is a descendant of the Gabriel family and the instrumental piece expresses and acknowledges his ancestral relationship to this location.

Referring to specific locales in a song "places" that music; by extension, references to political leaders of an area also locate the music in a particular place. While these types of references may memorialize a historical figure or cultural hero, they may also be more critical. Newfoundland, in particular, is known for its living folksong tradition, which has long included songs critiquing local politicians, governments, and other authorities (see Narváez 1997).[16] In "In This World," Pike references Joey Smallwood, a former premier of Newfoundland and one of the fathers of Canadian Confederation. The lyrics "Joey Smallwood was wrong, he was so wrong. We've been here all along"[17] point to the fact that during the negotiations that led to Confederation, Smallwood did not secure any rights for the Mi'kmaw people of the island. While some Canadians may recognize Smallwood's name, it is unlikely that the Alaskan audience would know the history of Confederation or Smallwood. This reference, then, firmly locates Medicine Dream's music in Newfoundland and is directed at educating the broader listening audience.

Thus, the location in which a specific music is produced is not necessarily the place being invoked. Medicine Dream's music is strongly placed in Newfoundland, with language, themes, and references to locales in Newfoundland all contributing to the particularity of Paul's music. Further, the Alaskan audience that will consume the music in a live context may not be the one for which it was produced or for which it will be most meaningful: that audience (Newfoundland and/or Mi'kmaw) may only be able to interact with it through mediated forms, such as audio and video recordings.

Although this music is placed in Mi'kma'ki (the traditional territory of the Mi'kmaq) and Newfoundland specifically through lyrical markers, it is at the same time placeless. The members of the band often view the messages conveyed through their songs as universal, despite textual references to Newfoundland and the Mi'kmaq. For example, the underlying messages of oppression, according to both musicians and fans, may be understood more universally; other Indigenous and oppressed people can relate to them. When asked how he relates to Paul's music and the themes featured therein, George Newton, a member of Medicine Dream who is of Aleut and Inupiaq heritage, replied that the music speaks to "generally everybody" (Newton, personal communication, 14 June 2002). The concerns expressed in the lyrics – the changes that occurred in Indigenous life after contact with Europeans, and the oppression suffered at the hands of the Europeans – he asserted, are understood by all oppressed peoples. For some listeners, however, the lyrics may be irrelevant; they simply enjoy the pop-rock sound of the music or appreciate a guitar solo. Listeners, then, engage and connect with the music and lyrics in different ways.

Paul's music often addresses issues of oppression and is intentionally political. After he realized that the dominant culture in Newfoundland had subjected him and indeed the entire community to misinformation, for example, the mercenary myth, he was inspired to write from an Indigenous perspective and to affirm his own cultural roots and immerse himself in Indigenous culture. Paul wanted to present an alternative history of the province of Newfoundland and the Mi'kmaw people living there. Many of his songs are a form of political storytelling – "If We Were Wolves," "We Belong," and "Hurtful Stories," to name only a few.[18] Wachowich and Scobie describe the political impact and import of storytelling: "Storytelling is crucial to processes of re-empowerment, for in the act of telling a story we bring experience out of the private consciousness and into the public realm. And by doing this, we bring these experiences under our control. By telling stories, we create the world around us and become social beings" (2010, 99). Syncretic musical styles are another mode of expression by which Indigenous peoples attempt to reassert their identities, often in opposition to one that has been ascribed to them by the dominant culture. Marsh has described Inuit hip hop as "a way to voice past and current lived experiences, a means to challenge stereotypes ... and a cultural practice that illustrates an important relationship between the local and global, as well as the past, present and future" (Marsh 2009, 127). For Paul Pike, the Indigenous pop-rock stylings of Medicine Dream serve a similar purpose.

Certainly, not all Indigenous popular music is composed with the intention of making a political statement, and Medicine Dream does perform songs that are not overtly political (such as "If You Dream of Eagles," written for Pike's sister). However, as Scales's research on musical meaning in Indigenous popular music demonstrates, even music not composed with political intent can become political through audience decoding of musical and textual elements; indeed, in Scales's words, "the *intended* meaning is seldom the *only* meaning" (1996, 23). This decoding of meaning, as demonstrated below in the case of "In This World," can be both clarified and complicated by the addition of visual elements through the medium of a music video.

Making a Music Video: "In This World"

"In This World," with music and lyrics by Paul Pike, was released on the album *Tomegan Gospem* in 2002. A few years later, it became the first (and to date only) song for which Medicine Dream recorded a music video. It is largely strophic, though irregular in that there are additional lines of text at the end of each verse. Lines within the strophes are irregular in length but sung to the same melody. As is common in popular songs, there is a bridge between verses two and three. During this contrasting section, vocables and Mi'kmaq are employed instead of English.[19]

> I've been blessed and I'm grateful
> for the circle of people who've come my way
> I won't forget all their goodness
> that kept me afloat when I felt like drowning
> I thank all my Elders who taught me to pray
> for all my relations at home and away
> You gave me this dream, you showed me what's real,
> and I'm taking this challenge, I've just got to learn how to feel
> In this world.

> Growing up in my homeland
> I had this place I used to go to
> Through the forest, up the stream
> I'd sit on this rock and I'd learn to pray
> I'd dream about singing, I'd dream that I'd travel
> to faraway places and make lots of friends
> When I moved to Alaska, they showed me the dream
> And when it's time to go home, I'll be thankful for all I have seen
> In this beautiful world.
> In this world.

> [Bridge with vocables and Mi'kmaw text]
> [Newfoundland Mi'kmaq. We are Mi'kmaq.]

Born a child of the island
I cannot throw this dream away
Mi'kmaw people, here we stand
We'll never forget, we'll never pretend
We come from this island they call Newfoundland
Indigenous people, our heart's in the land
We cry out for justice, we're praying for peace
And for all those who've wronged us, we pray that you'll cure your disease
Greed, hatred, discrimination
Joey Smallwood was wrong, he was so wrong
We've been here all along
In this world.
In this world.

With such lines as "Mi'kmaw people here we stand" and "We come from this island they call Newfoundland," why would Medicine Dream choose "In This Life" for their first video when the larger audience for their live music, in Alaska, generally has no connection to Newfoundland? Paul explained that the group chose "In This World" because it was on their (then) most recent CD and because it was particularly popular at their shows (Pike, personal communication, 31 October 2005). Indeed, when I attended the Medicine Dream concert in 2002 at the Alaska Native Heritage Center, "In This World," one of their more upbeat tunes, brought members of the audience to their feet, clapping, singing along, and dancing at the back of the auditorium.[20]

Medicine Dream's relationship with the Alaska Native Heritage Center was central to the creation of their first video. The centre is linked to the Peabody Essex Museum in Massachusetts and both are participants in the ECHO partnership – Education through Cultural and Historical Organizations – which seeks "to increase understanding of and respect for the values, perspectives, traditions, forms of creativity, expression, and communication among the peoples of the United States, including Native Americans, Alaska Natives and Native Hawaiians, in order that all may thrive in our increasingly diverse society."[21] One of Medicine Dream's members, Steven Alvarez, worked for the Alaska Native Heritage Center and proposed the project to them. As a result, the live concert portions of the video were filmed at both the Alaska Native Heritage Center and the Peabody Essex Museum, and both organizations provided resources for video production (Paul Pike, personal communication, 31 October 2005).

Performing in the video are Medicine Dream band members from that time period: Paul Pike (lead vocals and guitar), Buz Daney (traditional vocals and percussion), George Newton (acoustic and electric guitar), Chuck Henman (drum kit), John Field (keyboard and vocals), Steven Alvarez (percussion and vocals), and Ralph Sara (bass guitar). The video was produced by Steven Alvarez and directed by Megann C. Lemieux. At the end of the video, credits roll as they would for a film, acknowledging videographers and traditional dancers.[22]

The video primarily consists of the "live" performance of Medicine Dream's music, which, as can be expected, was lip-synced in multiple takes to produce the video. It is not surprising, then, that the events seen at any Medicine Dream concert are reconstructed in this video. For example, the camera zooms in on a young boy standing on stage with the band and playing a hand drum. At a concert I attended in 2002, Paul invited a young boy onto the stage to play and sing with the group during the song "We Belong." The group encourages children to participate and considers it very important; indeed, at the concert in 2002, the keyboard player, John Field, stopped playing and left the stage to take a photograph of the young boy playing with them.

The video opens with Paul playing guitar on a stage outside the Alaska Native Heritage Center. Behind him, a hand drum with a Mi'kmaw eight-point star painted on it is clearly visible. This symbol is featured on the cover of *Mawio'Mi* and also used on posters for upcoming performances and throughout the Medicine Dream website.[23] The Mi'kmaw eight-point star, then, is a symbol of Paul's Indigenous heritage and his homeland, and an important means of maintaining a visible connection to them. It is an iconic element that serves to mark his cultural background as different from those around him, while acknowledging his deep cultural connection to a community of practice that is activated and reactivated as he travels to and from his traditional territory.

Next, the visual frame moves out to encompass the audience, reinforcing for the viewer that this is a "live" performance. Then the frame widens, showing more of the band, as well as dancers preparing for the performance. This is intercut with footage of the group playing a powwow drum in a field (discussed below) and playing an indoor concert at the Peabody Essex Museum. As the first minute of the video progresses, the viewer sees close ups of all of the members of Medicine Dream.[24]

Dancing often takes place at Medicine Dream concerts. However, it is usually informal and spontaneous, and dancers from the audience are not normally dressed in their regalia. In the video, however, dancers in full regalia are featured on stage in front of the band. Paul explained that the group decided to include the dancers in the video because they are a visual cue to and acknowledgment of the tradition in which Medicine Dream's music is based. Paul explained, "They are a visual as to the foundation of our music," which is largely powwow style, First Nation music (Pike, personal communication, 31 October 2005). Thus, the presence of dancers in regalia visually reinforces the sonic elements derived from Indigenous culture – the chanting of vocables in a descending melodic contour and the steady beat of the powwow drum throughout.

"In This World" does not follow a strict narrative form from beginning to end, so the visual elements do not follow a specific order to "tell a story." However, when the second verse, which is more narrative in structure, begins, the images are directly related to the text. When Paul sings "Growing up in my homeland, I had this place I used to go to / Through the forest, up the stream / Sit on this rock and I learned to pray," the imagery moves to a forested area outside Paul's home in Wasilla, AK, where a powwow drum is played, and then on to a rocky stream in Hatcher's Pass. Paul chose this imagery to invoke a place in Corner Brook, NL where he would go and sing while living and visiting there – Margaret Bowater Park (Pike, personal communication, 31 October 2005). As the lyrics proceed to his dream of moving to Alaska and making "lots of friends," we see Paul embracing a fan on stage at the outdoor concert location. Then when he sings of moving home and being thankful for all he has seen, there is footage of a mountain chain in Alaska. These images clarify the intended meaning of the lyrics in concrete ways.

At the bridge in the song, viewers see the aforementioned child on stage with the group playing a hand drum and George Newton playing a guitar solo. George primarily plays acoustic guitar; however, he sometimes switches to electric guitar (for example, for a guitar solo that requires more of a rock aesthetic). In the video we see his typical performance set-up: the electric guitar is mounted in playing position on a stand in front of him so that he does not need to put down his acoustic guitar in order to play the electric one. This adds an air of authenticity for viewers who have seen Medicine Dream in concert, because it replicates Newton's live performance practice. This was clearly a conscious decision on the part of the band, since with multiple takes to record footage for this video, a separate take with just the guitar solo could have been arranged.

The third verse proceeds in a similar vein to the first, with footage of live performances and dancing. The video concludes with the members of the band perched on the rocks in the stream reminiscent of the park in Corner

Brook. As Paul sings the text, "We've been here all along, in this world" for the final time, the band disappears and the rocks remain. This can be read as a poignant, sobering way to end the video, emphasizing that while Mi'kmaw people have been here all along, they were invisible to political powers and treated as if they did not exist when Newfoundland joined Canada. In that light, the video would seem to comment on the plight of many Indigenous peoples who have been oppressed or subject to assimilationist policies by the dominant culture. But according to Paul, "The camera trick [disappearing from the rocks] is just that, a trick" (Pike, personal communication, 31 October 2005).[25] Thus, in this case, the association between images and lyrics can complicate audience decoding of the intended message. This demonstrates the multivalent nature of music video as text. The multiple meanings emerging from a music video depend as much on the creator's intentions as on the audience's interpretations.

While these visual elements of the video highlight Indigenous traditions and Paul's Mi'kmaw background, and emphasize his Indigenous heritage and values, there are also visual cues that directly link to the mainstream pop-rock stylings of Medicine Dream. The live concert concept for the video, along with the shots of the audience, places this music video within a mainstream aesthetic. Furthermore, Paul's postures and stances when playing his guitar are similar to those of many rock musicians. These masculine postures frequently occur during instrumental sections and cadence points moving into new sections. In the most obvious example of this (during the bridge), Paul dramatically flips his head and long hair back while playing acoustic guitar before proceeding to the microphone to sing again. His long hair points both to his cultural heritage (Indigenous) and musical heritage (classic rock and the so-called "hair bands" of the 1980s).[26] Also typical of rock videos is the practice of zooming in on the electric guitar solo. But as a result of his mounted guitar, George Newton's movements are more restricted; he does not adopt the postures usually associated with guitarists during a solo. Again, for those who have seen Medicine Dream live, this is a true representation of the concert experience and in keeping with the aesthetic of "liveness" in the video.

Music Video Formulas and the Promotion of Music

In a survey of top videos from the 1980s, communications scholar Joe Gow noted that most music videos can be divided into two categories: performance and concept (1990, 45). The performance-oriented videos, he suggested, demonstrate that the music itself is the most important element, while concept videos set artists apart from others, as innovators within the new medium, often generating ambiguous meanings. Acknowledging that hybrids of the two are possible, he identified a variety of formulas for music videos. Two of these formulas are relevant for the present study: the enhanced performance and the performance documentary. Gow described enhanced performance videos as those in which "shots of artists lip-syncing and pretending to perform soundtracks are intercut with images which function to illustrate portions of song lyrics, to visually complement moods conjured up by music, to present stories or simply to catch and hold the eyes of viewers" (1990, 62). This is the case for "In This World," with Paul's use of imagery to illustrate the narrative about his childhood in Newfoundland. However, by including shots of the stage, the audience, and the dancers preparing, as well as Paul embracing an audience member on stage, the video also has a documentary feel. With this particular formula, according to Gow, performances do not appear to be "staged" for the camera: "The videomakers are merely documenting events which took place in authentic concert situations" with the goal of realism (1990, 53). "In This World," then, is a hybrid of both the enhanced performance and the performance documentary styles of music videos.

It is perhaps not surprising that the style and formula for "In This World" aligns with those observed by Gow in the survey of videos from the 1980s. MuchMusic, the Canadian station devoted to music videos, was launched in 1984 when Paul was sixteen years old. Paul was influenced by the music and videos popular through the 1980s during his formative musical years, prior to relocating to Alaska and becoming engaged in Indigenous musics. As Pegley notes, MuchMusic became "vital to the consumption, circulation, and articulation of popular culture among youths" (2008, 13). Furthermore, these formulas of enhanced performance and performance documentary have remained popular. And the powwow aesthetic of "liveness" as described by Scales may also be a part of the motivation for the live performance aesthetic of the video. In powwow recording practices, liveness and authenticity are linked, connecting the music to its original live context and collapsing the perception of mediation, thereby allowing a closer connection between the audience and performer (2012). The same processes are at play in enhanced performance and performance documentary videos.

In his discussion of the enhanced performance video, Gow also noted its promotional nature; this formula of music video has as its goal the promotion of the music itself. However, a video's ability to promote a group and its music relies largely on its ability to find an audience. The opportunities for viewing "In This World" in Canada at the time of its release in 2004 were extremely limited. For the first year, the only way to view the video in Canada was to be a part of the informal family and friend network through which it was circulating.[27] Then the video was posted on Medicine Dream's website for personal download, making it available to a much wider audience (a download link is still available there).[28]

In the fall of 2005, I contacted Paul to ask whether the video had aired in Canada, given its connection to Newfoundland and Mi'kma'ki. He had sent a copy to APTN, the Aboriginal Peoples Television Network in Canada, but had not received a response. While APTN featured some music programming, with shows like "Beyond Words," which profiled Indigenous musicians such as Derek Miller and Northern Cree, it did not have a video flow show (Monique Rajotte, personal communication, 30 September 2005).[29] A video like "In This World" could potentially find airtime as "filler" between programs; however, to the best of my knowledge (and Paul's), the Medicine Dream video has never aired on APTN.[30]

Opportunities for viewing the Medicine Dream video in Canada, then, were virtually non-existent in the year following its release. Prior to its posting on the Internet, this video occupied a space similar to that of private recordings made at powwows, circulating among personal networks of family and friends (see Scales 2012). Further, a do-it-yourself approach to distribution and promotion is not uncommon for Indigenous musicians. Scales, for example, explains that artists are often paid (at least partially) with copies of their albums, which they then sell while promoting their music by travelling and singing on the powwow trail (2012). It is also worth restating that the "In This World" music video was produced through the ECHO project and funded by a museum and a heritage centre, not by the record label (Canyon Records), and so distribution and promotion were left to Medicine Dream.

Of course, the video was intended to bring Medicine Dream's music and message to a new medium and new audiences. The video's production values met the quality standards for airing, although it was not as "high-priced and heavily produced" as others often seen on MTV (Pegley 2008, 2). While the video was shot in an atypical aspect ratio of 3:2,[31] this would not have impeded broadcast, since some variation occurs across the medium. Clearly, the biggest impediment to the video receiving airplay was lack of access to the key distribution channels; as an independent group physically located in Alaska, Medicine Dream did not have the required networks to make air play a reality. For the Canadian context, although Paul Pike is a Canadian, the song and music video did not constitute Canadian content.[32] Timing may also have been a complicating factor. As music television has evolved, it has "relied less on music videos and more on series programming with lifestyle shows" (Pegley 2008, 17). With less airtime for videos, there was more competition for spots in video flow programming.

In 2006, "In This World" was nominated for and won a Native American Music Award. On 8 February 2008, Medicine Dream uploaded "In This World" to YouTube, furthering its reach. As of 2 July 2018, it had 14,859 views and 150 likes, while the Medicine Dream channel had 145 subscribers.[33] Since its introduction in 2005, YouTube has quickly become an important means of reaching not only the niche market for Indigenous popular music (as with other niche genres) but also mainstream consumers. As Pegley observes, "Viewers now turn to the Internet for videos-on-demand where they can download music onto computers and MP3 players. User-generated sites ... have lured the public away from television viewing into their own interactive networks" (2008, 18). Indeed, Marsh notes that Inuit rappers Northerners With Attitude launched their 2007 video on YouTube and that this distribution channel was significant for the online discussions that resulted from the interactive medium (2009, 116).[34] Similarly, hip hop artist Wab Kinew disseminates his videos via YouTube,[35] as do many other Indigenous artists today.

Mending Musical Styles – A Middle Ground Approach

In this chapter, I have unveiled some of the meaning embedded and encoded in Medicine Dream's first music video by analyzing the relationships between place, text, music, and image; by communicating with the lead musician to gain a better understanding of his intended meanings; and by describing the video's mode of meaning delivery (formula and distribution). I have referred throughout to Paul's personal life experience, his heritage, and his deep connection to Newfoundland as his homeland. His music is a conscious attempt to fuse diverse experiences, cultures, and influences, while making a political statement by telling his own story and that of the Mi'kmaq in Newfoundland.

From the aesthetic of liveness in the performance video to the stories Paul tells through song, the theme of authenticity – whether implicit or explicit – pervades. Authenticity is, of course, a loaded term that has been problematized in the literature for decades. There have been, and continue to be, many approaches to teasing out its meanings and acknowledging the tensions associated with it. For example, elsewhere I have analyzed the authenticity of Paul's music according to Moore's (2002) notion of authenticity as a process, which he terms authentication (see Tulk 2003). To conclude this chapter, however, instead of applying etic constructs (that is, outsider perspectives), I provide insight into how Paul conceives of his music and how it relates to his identity. I then offer a culturally based perspective through which his musical approach might be understood.

Paul maintains that it is "natural" to combine Indigenous music with pop and rock influences because pop and rock were the musics he listened to while growing up: "You could use blues if that's what you're coming from. It's what you identify with. For myself personally, I grew up listening to and performing a lot of rock music, so it's naturally a part of me. When I implemented my cultural background, this was natural to mend the two. It's part of me, it's a part of my life" (Paul Pike, personal communication, 11 June 2002).

This "mending" of musical cultures and influences is a result of living in and experiencing two worlds; it arises from the double consciousness felt by many Indigenous peoples. In her study of the role and experiences of women in producing contemporary Native music, Diamond noted the double consciousness, or two-ness of identity, that is at the heart of such musical hybridity. She described this as the "in-betweenness of living among different cultural worlds" (2002, 33). In creating music that combines elements resulting from living in two worlds, Paul Pike is authentically representing his lived experience.

Mi'kmaw hereditary chief Stephen Augustine described his own experience of "weaving his life between two societies" (1998, 6). Writing about culturally relevant education, he employed the metaphor of a middle ground that mobilized and combined the best of both Indigenous and mainstream systems to benefit all. Similarly, the guiding principle of two-eyed seeing, developed by Mi'kmaw Elders Murdena and Albert Marshall, provides an Indigenous perspective on processes of experiencing, knowing, understanding, and synthesizing the world around us. As Hatcher and Bartlett explain, "Two-Eyed Seeing is to see from one eye with the strengths of Indigenous ways of knowing, and from the other eye with the strengths of Western ways of knowing, and to use both of these eyes together ... The Two-Eyed Seeing approach mindfully avoids knowledge domination and assimilation" (2010, 16; see also Hatcher et al. 2009).[36] More recently, Elder Albert Marshall emphasized that knowledge is alive; therefore, it is not enough only to engage in two-eyed seeing; rather, the two perspectives must be "cross-pollinated" (see Tulk 2015).

In many ways, these two metaphors – the middle ground and two-eyed seeing – apply to Paul Pike and his music as performed by Medicine Dream. The metaphor of two-eyed seeing acknowledges different ways of knowing and being in the world. Paul expresses this through his music, synthesizing and "cross-pollinating" what he deems to be the best from both musical systems. He weaves musical fabric that expresses the truth of his experience and that of the broader Mi'kmaw community in Newfoundland. Paul's life, like Augustine's, is woven between or stitched together from two societies. This middle ground is a space for the expression of lived experience and for musical innovation. The music of Medicine Dream fuses Western and Indigenous languages, vocal styles, instrumentation, melodic and harmonic structures, and genre-based styles in a way that avoids domination or assimilation. It is the sound of the middle ground.

Notes

1 Segments of this chapter, such as the description of the band, were previously published in *Canadian Folk Music* (see Tulk 2004). My thanks to editor Gillian Turnbull for permission to reproduce that revised content.
2 Marsh 2009 is a notable exception with its discussion of an Indigenous music video produced by participants in the social programming of the Arctic Bay Video Club Project.
3 In the Smith-Francis orthography, Mi'kmaq is the plural noun and language, and Mi'kmaw is the singular noun and adjectival form.
4 Throughout this paper I refer to the concept of "placed" and "placeless," or local and global, or particular and universal. I draw these concepts from various academic discussions on the significance of place in relation to music, including Lipsitz (1994), Leyshon, Mattless, and Revill (1998), and Krims (2000). See Tulk 2003 for ways in which I have applied these notions to Medicine Dreams' output.
5 For an overview of, and commentary on, Medicine Dream's output, see listing on http://cdbaby.com/cd/meddream3, accessed 29 July 2016.
6 For discussion of how the term "tradition" is deployed in the context of Mi'kmaw powwows and its multiple meanings, see Tulk 2008.
7 In this context, traditional vocals refers to chanting and/or northern style powwow singing, while traditional percussion may refer to a powwow drum, a hand drum, or a rattle (i.e., percussion instruments that have their origins in Indigenous culture).
8 Members not referenced in this short history of the group, but active at varying points over the last twenty years include Ralph Sara, Justin Somaduroff, David Helzer, and Chuck Henman.

9 In the 1990s and early 2000s, the Federation of Newfoundland Indians was at the front of a Mi'kmaw cultural renaissance, particularly on the west coast of Newfoundland. Many Newfoundlanders who had for various reasons either hidden or forgotten their Mi'kmaw heritage began to embrace it and lobby for acknowledgment by the federal government. This led to the establishment of a landless band, referred to as Qalipu First Nation, in 2011. For discussion of cultural revitalization efforts, specifically as they pertain to music, see Tulk 2007.
10 While Mi'kmaw culture has a narrative tradition centred on a flute-playing trickster named Mi'kmwesu, it is unclear whether the Mi'kmaq had and/or played flutes historically (see Tulk 2009, 8–11).
11 Canyon Records, located in Phoenix, Arizona, was established in 1951 and specializes in Native American music.
12 See http://worldpeaceandprayerday.com/, accessed 3 August 2016 for information on the prophecy leading to honouring of sacred sites around the world.
13 See http://www.nativeamericacalling.com/, accessed 3 August 2016.
14 The future of Medicine Dream has not yet been determined, but Paul anticipates he will travel back to Alaska on a somewhat regular basis and that the band will perform again on such occasions. Given the current socio-political context in the United States, the reader may question whether such concerns contributed to Pike's decision; however, his decision to return to Newfoundland pre-dated the change in political administration in 2017 and was informed by considerations of a more personal nature.
15 For more on the mercenary myth, see Prins (1998) and Bartels (1988). While the Beothuk no longer exist as a cultural group, it may be erroneous to refer to them as "extinct" as is commonly done. According to Mi'kmaw oral history, the Beothuk intermarried with the Mi'kmaq and several family lines still include Beothuk blood.
16 In Narváez 1997 there is an example of a song critiquing government and politicians (4), as well as one memorializing the great deeds of a politician.
17 Lyrics reproduced with permission of Paul Pike.
18 "If We Were Wolves" makes the point that if Indigenous people were wolves, they would be on an endangered species list, thus pointing to cultural genocide. "We Belong" emphasizes Indigenous peoples' deep connection to the land, which in many cases is now controlled by the governments of Canada and the United States. "Hurtful Stories" addresses the impacts of erroneous and racist narratives shared by the dominant culture about Indigenous peoples.
19 For this chapter, Tulk transcribed the lyrics from the video recording and Pike edited them for accuracy.
20 9 June 2002.
21 For more information on ECHO and its activities, see http://www.echospace.org/about.html, accessed 29 July 2016.
22 Available at https://www.youtube.com/watch?v=BBlzAXobSvY.
23 Some members of the group even wear this symbol on jewellery created for the band by silversmith Don LaVonne.

24 For discussion of the attire of band members and markers of Indigeneity, see Tulk 2004 or Tulk 2003.
25 Paul did indicate, however, that he liked my interpretation of the imagery and thought, upon reflection, that it was a cool idea.
26 It is notable that CD Baby recommends Medicine Dream to listeners who like Bon Jovi, Boston, and the Eagles (https://store.cdbaby.com/cd/meddream3, accessed 29 July 2016).
27 I recall discussing with Paul the possibility of purchasing then-novel bootable business cards (CD-ROMs in the shape and size of business cards) that he could hand out to promote the band and share the music video.
28 Unfortunately, statistics are not available for how many times it was viewed on or downloaded from the Medicine Dream website (https://www.medicinedream.com/).
29 More than a decade later, this is still the case.
30 Pegley notes that part of the reason for the decline of video flow programming is that short formats have lower viewer ratings and cannot attract as much advertising revenue (2008, 17). Additionally, the past decade has seen the proliferation of competing web-based media, such as YouTube and Vimeo.
31 Aspect ratio is the relationship of the width to the height. Typical aspect ratios are TV formats, first 4:3 and now 16:9.
32 As Pegley notes, Canadian involvement is required "in a combination of parameters, including the audio component (the composition or performance of music and lyrics), production (director, producer), or production location" (2002, 110).
33 Medicine Dream has since uploaded two clips from live concerts, but has not fully embraced YouTube as a distribution channel.
34 See also Wachowich and Scobie (2010) regarding Inuit storytelling on YouTube, which references throat singing.
35 See, for example, the video for "Mama Said" at https://www.youtube.com/watch?v=w55EwxH_-4k, accessed 3 August 2016.
36 See http://www.integrativescience.ca/ for more information on this initiative.

References

Augustine, Stephen. 1998. "A Culturally Relevant Education for Aboriginal Youth: Is There Room for a Middle Ground, Accommodating Traditional Knowledge and Mainstream Education?" Master's thesis, Carleton University.

Bartels, Dennis A. 1988. "Ktaqamkuk Iluni Saqimawoutie: Aboriginal Rights and the Myth of the Micmac Mercenaries in Newfoundland." In *Native People, Native Lands*, edited by Bruce Alden Cox, 32–6. Ottawa, ON: Carleton University Press.

Diamond, Beverley. 2001. "Re-placing Performance: A Case Study of the Yukon Music Scene in the Canadian North." *Journal of Intercultural Studies* 22 (2): 211–24.

– 2002. "Native American Contemporary Music: The Women." *The World of Music* 44 (1): 11–39.

Gow, Joe. 1990. "Music Video as Communication: Popular Formulas and Emerging Genres." *Journal of Popular Culture* 26 (2): 41–70.

Hatcher, Annamarie, and Cheryl Bartlett. 2010. "Two-Eyed Seeing: Building Cultural Bridges for Aboriginal Students." *Canadian Teacher Magazine*. May: 14–17.

Hatcher, Annamarie, Cheryl Bartlett, Murdena Marshall, and Albert Marshall. 2009. "Two-Eyed Seeing: A Cross-Cultural Science Journey." *Green Teacher* 86: 3–6.

Krims, Adam. 2000. *Rap Music and the Poetics of Identity*. Cambridge, UK: Cambridge University Press.

Leyshon, Andrew, David Mattless, and George Revill, eds. 1998. *The Place of Music*. New York, NY: Guilford Press.

Lipsitz, George. 1994. *Dangerous Crossroads*. London, UK: Verso.

Marsh, Charity. 2009. "'Don't Call Me Eskimo': Representation, Mythology and Hip Hop Culture on Baffin Island." *MUSICultures* 36: 110–29.

Moore, Allan. 2002. "Authenticity as Authentication." *Popular Music* 21 (2): 209–23.

Narváez, Peter. 1997. "'She's Gone, Boys': Vernacular Song Responses to the Atlantic Fisheries Crisis." *Canadian Journal for Traditional Music* 25: 1–13.

Neuenfeldt, Karl. 2001. "Cultural Politics and a Music Recording Project: Producing Strike Em! Contemporary Voices from the Torres Strait." *Journal of Intercultural Studies* 22 (2): 133–46.

– 2002. "www.nativeamericanmusic.com: Marketing Recordings in an Interconnected World." *The World of Music* 44 (1): 115–26.

Pegley, Kip. 2002. "Multiculturalism, Diversity and Containment on MuchMusic (Canada) and MTV (US)." *Canadian University Music Review* 22 (2): 93–112.

– 2008. *Coming to You Wherever You Are: MuchMusic, MTV, and Youth Identities*. Middletown, CT: Wesleyan University Press.

Prins, Harald E.L. 1998. "We Fight with Dignity: The Miawpukek Mi'kmaq Quest for Aboriginal Rights in Newfoundland." *Papers of the 28th Algonquian Conference*, edited by David H. Pentland, 283–305. Winnipeg: University of Manitoba Press.

Scales, Christopher. 1996. "First Nations Popular Music in Canada: Identity, Politics and Musical Meaning." Master's thesis, University of British Columbia.

– 2002. "The Politics and Aesthetics of Recording: A Comparative Canadian Case Study of Powwow and Contemporary Native American Music." *The World of Music* 44 (1): 41–59.

– 2012. *Recording Culture: Powwow Music and the Aboriginal Recording Industry on the Northern Plains*. Durham, NC: Duke University Press.

Tulk, Janice Esther. 2003. "Medicine Dream: Contemporary Native Music and Issues of Identity." Master's thesis, University of Alberta.

– 2004. "Awakening to Medicine Dream: Contemporary Native Music from Alaska with Newfoundland Roots." *Canadian Folk Music* 38 (4): 1–10.

– 2007. "Cultural Revitalization and Mi'kmaq Music-Making: Three Newfoundland Drum Groups." *Newfoundland and Labrador Studies* 22 (1): 259–86.

– 2008. "'Our Strength Is Ourselves': Identity, Status, and Cultural Revitalization among the Mi'kmaq in Newfoundland." PhD diss., Memorial University of Newfoundland.

- 2009. *Welta'q "It Sounds Good": Historic Recordings of the Mi'kmaq.* CD with liner notes. St John's, NL: MMaP Research Centre, Memorial University of Newfoundland.
- 2012. "Localizing Intertribal Traditions: The Powwow as Mi'kmaw Cultural Expression." In *Aboriginal Music in Contemporary Canada: Echoes and Exchanges,* edited by Anna Hoefnagels and Beverley Diamond, 70–88. Montreal & Kingston: McGill-Queen's University Press.
- 2015. *Report on Sharing Circle of Traditional Knowledge Holders.* Sydney: Purdy Crawford Chair in Aboriginal Business Studies, Cape Breton University.

Wachowich, Nancy, and Willow Scobie. 2010. "Uploading Ourselves: Inuit Digital Storytelling on YouTube." *Inuit Studies* 34 (2): 81–105.

Discography

Medicine Dream. 1998. *Identity.* Independent. CD.
- 2000. *Mawio'Mi.* Canyon Records CR–7039. CD.
- 2002. *Tomegan Gospem.* Canyon Records CR–7048. CD.
- 2007. *Learning to Fly.* Independent. CD.

Part Three

Heterogeneity, Diversity, and the Possibility of Alternatives

Introduction
Judith Klassen

Contemporary public discourse in Canada recognizes – and frequently celebrates – diversity, change, and multiplicity of experience at local and national levels. Still, engagement with what this language implies and how it is played out in lived experience are frequently superficial. Although rarely malicious, this semantic laziness has implications for how heterogeneity, diversity, and difference are conceptualized and perceived, and how understanding across perceived boundaries is navigated, or not.

It is difficult to unravel concepts of "diversity" from those of "difference," interwoven as they are in scholarly and everyday language. Bruno Nettl observes how critical theorists have recognized the use of "differences" to structure worldviews that are frequently predicated on imbalanced binary oppositions (see, for example, Derrida 1982); "*Difference* thus ... becomes a code word for a large number of relationships characterized by unequal power" (Nettl 2005, 419). Recognizing "a deep insecurity, even a fear of confronting and dealing head on with musical and social difference" within the context of ethnomusicology and fieldwork, Ellen Koskoff, too, articulates the importance of "understand[ing] the nature of difference and how to manage its destabilizing power" (2010, 103–4).

Significantly, links between diversity, difference, and imagined homogeneous cultural identities often hinge on related (mis)conceptions of identity: "No sense of play is manifested in discussions of identity, nor is there any recognition of the historical ironies that hover around deliberations of national, social, or individual identities. The discourse on identity carries this burden because it emerges from perceptions of social and cultural difference, seemingly arguing that bounded wholeness can be maintained in a culturally plural environment" (Abrahams 2003, 199). Homogeneous conceptions of culture have long been critiqued in ethnomusicology and related disciplines, with scholars such as Kati Szego pointing to movements in the humanities and social sciences that "critique the notion of cultural totality and attend to the active and variable interpretation of expressive forms within social groups" (2003, 291; see also Noyes 2003). Szego goes on, "for those who study music in culture, the heterogeneities, discontinuities, and contradictions that these movements expose provide an increasingly compelling approach to the investigation of musical meaning" (2003, 291).

The chapters in this section, "Heterogeneity, Diversity, and the Possibility of Alternatives," address related discourses and their implications through lenses of discrete cultural experiences and musical practices. Authors examine public policy and activism, as well as individual and community expressions that reflect permeability and change without an explicit public gaze; collectively, they force the reconsideration of easy shorthands that dilute "local," "multicultural," and "diverse" within the context of expressive culture and experience. Through examples that demonstrate the significance of musical practices in claiming space, affirming (and challenging) cultural identities, and articulating the dynamic multiplicity of experience that makes these expressions meaningful, authors encourage the rethinking of commonly used language and ideas.

The section opens with Louise Wrazen's "A View from Toronto: Local Perspectives on Music Making, Ethnocultural Difference, and the Cultural Life of a City." Reflecting on the music practices of immigrants and newcomers to Canada as a component of public discourses of diversity, Wrazen asserts difference as a central feature of urban life, and uses ethnography to examine the complex layering of cultural activities that contribute to its vitality. Drawing attention to contrasts in performance style, aesthetics, and self-presentation among Highlanders/Górale of southern Poland in Toronto, she not only traces a performative history from newcomer to settled resident in Canada but also destabilizes "tokenistic references to diversity" through a reconceptualization of difference in the local sphere.

Also engaging with policy and discourses of belonging, Rebecca Draisey-Collishaw's "'Re-imagining the Nation': The CBC as a Mediator of Ethnocultural Encounter in St John's, Newfoundland and Labrador," considers the impacts of multicultural policy through a close reading of three concerts produced by CBC St John's and premised on intercultural contact. Contextualized vis-à-vis specific policy pressures, and taking musician and community experiences into account, her chapter looks at production motives and issues of voicing, considering how the concerts contribute to broader discourses of citizenship, (in)equalities, and belonging in Canada.

By contrast, Judith Klassen investigates heterogeneities within contexts frequently perceived as static and insular in "Music, Mimesis, and Modulation among Mennonites in Rural Manitoba." Drawing on fieldwork in southern Manitoba, she examines Mennonite circle games, the *Brommtopp*, and popular song within the context of home to challenge portrayals of rural Mennonite experience as staid, homogeneous, and conservative. While nonconformity has functioned, historically, as a vital aspect of ethnocultural Mennonite identity, Klassen's work demonstrates a "gentle cosmopolitanism" wherein heterogeneity and permeability emerge through active processes of adoption, adaptation, and ongoing negotiations of lived belief.

Marcia Ostashewski draws attention to sacred aspects of musical practice in "Ukrainian Catholic Congregational Singing in Canada: Sounds in Service and Celebration." Her research focuses on changes in Byzantine Ukrainian congregational responsorial music practices, demonstrating a continued vitality in the practice despite declining numbers of practitioners. Underscoring the revered place of Ukrainian sacred music practices in Canada, Ostashewski simultaneously demonstrates the ongoing creation of community in ways that encompass distinctiveness, difference, and change.

Turning to public expressions of resistance and activism, Anna Hoefnagels brings individual, community, and national voices into conversation in "(Re)Presenting Indigenous Activism in the Nation's Capital: Signifying Resistance across Time and Place through Music in Alanis Obomsawin's *Trick or Treaty?* (2014)." Using Obomsawin's film and the Idle No More movement as key points of departure, Hoefnagels examines the historical and contemporary ways in which music has been used as a platform for Indigenous activism. Articulating social, political, and environmental concerns, and the centrality of place in related dialogue and exchange, she underscores the vital role of music in Indigenous empowerment and resurgence in local, national, and global spheres.

Through microhistories that engage with diverse historical and contemporary musical practices, the chapters in this section explicitly name heterogeneous experience and perspective.

By bringing these microhistories together, their respective considerations of policy and lived experience at local, national, and international levels are put into dialogue and readers are encouraged to engage critically with language and concepts that open up alternative understandings.

References

Abrahams, Roger D. 2003. "Identity." In *Eight Words for the Study of Expressive Culture*, edited by Burt Feintuch, 198–222. Chicago: University of Illinois Press.
Derrida, Jacques. 1982. *Margins of Philosophy*. Chicago, IL: University of Chicago Press.
Koskoff, Ellen. 2010. "Is Fieldwork Still Necessary?" In *Music Traditions, Cultures & Contexts*, edited by Robin Elliott and Gordon E. Smith, 101–12. Waterloo, ON: Wilfrid Laurier University Press.
Nettl, Bruno. 2005. "Diversity and Difference: Some Minorities." In *The Study of Ethnomusicology: Thirty-One Issues and Concepts*, by Bruno Nettl, 419–30. Chicago, IL: University of Illinois Press.
Noyes, Dorothy. 2003. "Group." In *Eight Words for the Study of Expressive Culture*, edited by Burt Feintuch, 7–41. Chicago: University of Illinois Press.
Szego, C.K. 2003. "Singing Hawaiian and the Aesthetics of (In)Comprehensibility." In *Global Pop, Local Language*, edited by Harris M. Berger and Michael Thomas Carroll, 291–328. Jackson: University Press of Mississippi.

Louise Wrazen

Chapter 12

A View from Toronto: Local Perspectives on Music Making, Ethnocultural Difference, and the Cultural Life of a City

This chapter stems from the research I began with an ethnocultural group in Toronto in the 1980s. During this period, public awareness of and political support for cultural diversity have been reflected in the growing prominence of narratives of difference in defining the life of the city, in part to keep pace with changes in demographics. This discussion addresses limitations in current discourses of difference in defining today's urban arts sector, in particular. Drawing on Anthony Shay's idea of layering as a metaphor for the cultural activities found within the city (2006), I foreground some of the more hidden layers of local newcomer[1] and immigrant musical subcultures from among the many that constitute the cultural life of the city. Two performances, drawn from my research among the Polish Górale (Highlanders), expose inner layers that are hidden from a broader public consciousness to illustrate shortcomings in the understanding of diversity as leveraged within the city's dominant narrative. A close reading of contrasting performances in the history of Górale in Toronto offers only one view, from among many possible in the city, to undermine what persists as the "clichéd language of 'diversity today'" (Diamond 2000, 54).[2] In uncovering these inner spaces, I seek to reposition these musical layers as recognizable components of a city's sounds and to locate them within the ontologies of displacement that contribute to local and national diversities. In elaborating on the music culture of one community, this chapter establishes ethnocultural performance as part of a national soundscape and situates the creative work of migrants (here, specifically, immigrants and newcomers) within discourses of cultural diversity both locally and nationally.

I begin with a brief overview of demographics and consider the word "diversity" as it is applied to Toronto. I then introduce the Górale into this setting, and turn to two events to explore contrasting constructions of belonging and difference within ethnocultural layers largely invisible as constituents of a recognized diversity in this broader urban framework.

Orientation to the Demographic Setting and the Language of Difference

Canada's debt to immigration has been officially recognized at least since 1971 with the introduction of multiculturalism as policy, which was then followed by the Canadian Multiculturalism Act in 1988.[3] Current political support for refugees and recent population statistics confirm immigration's growing importance to Canada.[4] Statistics Canada has identified international migration as the main lever of population growth in Canada, accounting for 60.8 percent of growth from 2014 to 2015. As of 2011, 51 percent of those living in Toronto were born outside Canada (as opposed to 22 percent in the rest of Canada) and 49 percent self-identified as immigrants, with 33 percent arriving between 2001 and 2011 (Toronto 2013).[5] Although analysis of the 2016 census was not available at the time of this writing, these trends do not appear to be changing; the current population of the metropolitan area of Toronto, at about 5.93 million, continues to account for approximately 17 percent of Canada's population.

Although such monikers as multiculturalism, cultural diversity, and pluralism are used as progressive banners of inclusion within political discourse, their use has also garnered criticism. For example, in her article "Diversity Is a White Word," Tania Cañas (2017) argues that such terms "only normalise whiteness as the example of what it means to be and exist in the world." Diversity discourse within the cultural sector is a means of control, where diversity "is given 'permission' to exist under conditional inclusion. This is inclusion that is conditional on predefined palatable criteria; a means to frame, describe and ultimately prescribe diversity through constructed visibilities" (Cañas 2017). Instead, she argues for diversity in cultural leadership as the means to challenge the very terms of engagement and enunciation (Cañas 2017). Similar concerns are shared in urban studies. In the recent volume devoted to Toronto, *Subdivided: City-Building in an Age of Hyper-diversity*, Jay

Pitter is cautious about the over-reliance on the concept of diversity from the perspective of urban planning and development. As she explains, diversity "is inherent in the urban project's built environment and natural ecology. But when it comes to the human beings who collectively make up a global city like Toronto – a place with accelerating social, economic and ethnocultural division – the over-emphasis placed on diversity is lazy social shorthand, an attempt to smooth over ragged edges we struggle to understand. Civic leaders endlessly repeat the catchphrase 'Diversity is our strength,' as if it could resolve our issues or conclude difficult discussions" (Pitter 2016, 6). Instead, the book suggests hyper-diversity as a way to replace a tired word with a more dynamic conceptual response to current demands of Toronto. In a recent article in the *New York Times Magazine*, "Has 'Diversity' Lost Its Meaning?," Anna Holmes suggests that the word "has become both euphemism and cliché, a convenient shorthand that gestures at inclusivity and representation without actually taking them seriously" (Holmes 2015, 2/5). In a similar vein, Sara Ahmed argues that an institutional preference for the term "diversity" can signal an actual lack of commitment to change (Ahmed 2014, 53).

The City of Toronto's current motto is "Diversity Our Strength." Originally chosen to refer to the combined strength of seven municipalities following amalgamation in 1997, the phrase conveniently suits the city's current demographic. This is acknowledged on the city's website, which includes "diversity" among the seven categories on its facts page[6] and a calendar that advertises many events that feature performances by ethnocultural communities.[7] These more widely publicized, larger displays of multicultural diversity animate many of the city's public areas in what Cañas might call aesthetic presentations in spaces for designated self-expression (2017).

In addition to these public performances, however, numerous smaller and more distinctive community-specific music spaces form a part of the city's inner cultural landscape. Here they contribute to a propulsion of identity and cultural life where value is determined by the subjective needs of participants and specific expectations of the local group within larger narratives of displacement. Many of these subcultural sounds (Slobin 2000) remain under the official radar and unacknowledged for their contributions to individual lives, community life, and overall metropolitan vitality.

At another level, through general media coverage, the cultural sector of the city is most often identified with an arts scene defined by dance companies and groups devoted to European-based art traditions; contemporary, often-hybridized and innovative music and dance events; and a widely supported popular urban music and dance scene.[8] These limited categories tend to erase the small and local in our public urban consciousness in favour of mainstream arts scenes, or the more spectacular, curated musical representations of an official diversity[9] that forms part of the city's marketing and tourism strategy within an economic agenda.

At a time when the main driver of population growth rests with immigrants, the cultural vitality of these urban subcultures is overlooked in public discourse, which instead favours mainstream events that feature prominent performers associated with a global "world music" network. For example, a 2011 report by the City of Toronto (*Creative Capital Gains: An Action Plan for Toronto*) focused explicitly on Toronto's cultural and creative profile, yet largely overlooked ethnocultural contributions.[10] The report describes Toronto as "alive with culture" (Toronto 2011, 5) with "a wealth of creative capital to exploit – from its training centres, skilled workers, and great cultural institutions and festivals, to its unrivalled diversity and exciting cultural scenes" (Toronto 2011, 6). This "unrivalled diversity," however, remains largely undefined, and this category makes little substantive contribution to the body of the report. Rather, the report tends to identify "exciting cultural scenes" with commercially prominent events and artists. For example, it describes Toronto as "home to Canada's largest and most diverse music economy" and "a platform for unique cross-cultural blends (think Jane Bunnett's Cuban jazz or the African Guitar Summit) with a strong reputation for developing artists who go on to global fame" (Toronto 2011, 25), and lists international launches in the categories of urban artists, pop artists, opera stars, world artists, and "top-drawer classical ensembles." It focuses on the economic potential of these musicians: "Toronto's music scene is one of the most attractive aspects of its cultural life. Because of its ability to bridge culture and engage with other industry clusters (film, television, gaming, fashion, and web design all rely heavily on sound tracks), music has the potential to generate real wealth" (Toronto 2011, 25).

The 2015 annual report of the Economic Development & Culture Division of Toronto reflects a similar approach in its update to the 2011 *Action Plan*. Its single reference to diversity appears when listing annual signature and special project arts and cultural events (such as Cavalcade of Lights, Doors Open Toronto, Nuit Blanche Toronto, and Summer in the Squares), which are "free and celebrate the vibrancy and diversity of Toronto, enrich the quality of life for residents, attract world-wide tourist audiences and promote professional local, national and international artists, co-producers and presenters in every artistic discipline" (Toronto 2015, 13). Where economic metrics are the primary determinants of cultural value, world music (as one component of a broader global music industry) may achieve some recognition as part of "cross-cultural blends," but more locally created musical activities remain overlooked. Although regarded as an advantageous and desirable attribute of the city, diversity here remains a cliché.

Several recent events present an opportunity for a more substantive rendering of diversity. For example, at the national level, the Canada Council for the Arts is launching a new funding model in April 2017 that explicitly highlights diversity.[11] As reported in the press, "the most striking change may be the direct tying of diversity to funding for large arts organizations" (Nestruck 2016). This marks an explicit recognition of Canada's changing demographics and places a responsibility on arts organizations to reflect this reorientation of priorities in programming as well as administration, backstage, and in their audiences – a mandate that may have an impact on Toronto's cultural scene. Elsewhere, Toronto has recently been distinguished in the international press in a feature article in the *Guardian* newspaper (UK) that describes the city as coming "into its own by becoming a city of others," noting that people from over 230 countries make Toronto their home (March 2016). Similarly, a study by BBC radio has identified Toronto as the most diverse city in the world, a designation noted by several local news sources (see, for example, Flack 2016). Stephen Marche, in his *Guardian* article, elaborates on this designation and notably suggests that "diversity is not what sets Toronto apart; the near-unanimous celebration of diversity does. Toronto may be the last city in the world that unabashedly desires difference" (Marche 2016). However disputed the methodologies behind this ranking may be, this international attention focuses unequivocally on Toronto's ethnocultural demographic and inclusivity during a time when many countries and cities are moving in the opposite direction.

This "celebration of diversity" may reflect the proportion of city spaces now used for the cultural display of ethnocultural difference. These have expanded significantly from the time when occasions such as Canada Day, the CHIN picnic,[12] and Ontario Place or CNE "international days" provided the main occasions for a public display of heritage. To illustrate, a quick search of listings for Sunday, 20 July 2016 shows at least eight large public events devoted to immigrant subcultures across the Greater Toronto Area (GTA) on that single day (ten including Scarborough and Mississauga), including a Turkish festival, Bhangra dance competition, Afrofest, and Latin Arts festival.[13] Many of these build on smaller local initiatives, such as groups and ensembles formed by community members who rely on local support and resources. Such public events in shared urban spaces not only expose some of the inner cultural layers of the city but also support broader interactions and alliances. Despite their growing presence, however, it remains for these and other such events to be acknowledged in arts discourse as part of the diversities of urban cultural life, rather than relegated to reductive categories such as heritage production or world music.

Orientation to the Ethnographic Setting

The remainder of this chapter maps the activities of one ethnocultural community onto the discursive framework explored above – activities that reductive clichés tend to erase. Polish immigrants came to Canada in six waves, beginning in 1854. By 1971, there were over 300,000 Poles in Canada. In the 2011 census 1,010,705 identified with full or partial Polish ethnic origin, with Toronto accounting for 214,460.[14] The Highlanders, or Górale, form a distinctive subculture within the larger group of Polish immigrants who now live in the GTA. Although the word Górale can refer generically to any group of people from the hills or mountains (*góry*), those featured in this chapter come from Podhale, a small region on the northern side of the Tatra Mountains bordering Slovakia. With their own local dialect and material and expressive culture, these Górale distinguish themselves from larger Polish communities in diaspora (e.g., Chicago, New Jersey, Toronto), just as they promote a strong regionalism within the national discourse of Poland (Cooley 2005). Although they contributed to earlier waves of Polish and Galician immigration at the beginning of the twentieth century and following the Second World War, those who arrived during the communist period of the 1960s and 1970s[15] consolidated their presence to be distinct from the general Polish community (or *Polonia*[16]) in the Toronto area by forming the Polish Highlanders Association of Toronto in 1978. This may be regarded as the first generation of deliberately defined "Górale" activity in Canada.[17]

The primary musical index of Górale regional identity is a string ensemble, polyphonic singing, and a dance form (known as the *góralski*) for a single couple that combines singing with the ensemble. The string ensemble features a *prym* (first fiddle, who plays the melody), and includes one or more *sekund*(s) (second fiddle[s], who follow with chords or countermelody), and *basy* (a three-string cello-like instrument, worn with a strap over the shoulder, that provides the bass and rhythmic foundations). Dance tunes are in duple metre, with strong repeated chord patterns of either four- or five-measure phrases. The polyphonic singing style, which can be a cappella or accompanied, metric or non-metric, is based on a single couplet of text, and the music consists of either a single melodic phrase repeated or two phrases. One person (man or woman) begins singing the tune, then others join in on the lower part(s), mostly in thirds with some fourths or fifths, using a loud, resonant vocal quality, with men and women singing in the same register.

Vocal and instrumental repertoires are linked, with many shared tunes related to dance. The góralski dance was traditionally a dance for a single couple, and an important forum for courtship (Wrazen 2004). Briefly outlined, in this dance a man approaches the musicians, sings a tune and text, then turns and waits for his partner to arrive on the dance floor while the string ensemble begins to play the tune. His partner is brought to the floor by a friend (following prescribed dance movements) who then leaves. The woman then begins to dance with her partner, following his moves with her own corresponding steps. The couple dances, without physical contact, for as long as the man chooses, and the musicians follow his lead. When the man decides to stop dancing to this tune, he stops, leaves the dance floor, and returns to the musicians to sing another tune. The woman returns to the side to wait until she is again brought to the floor, where they dance again. A single set usually comprises from three to five separate tunes and dances. The man indicates that he is finished his turn by swinging his partner in a circular motion. Only then can another man approach the musicians for his dance.

During my fieldwork in Toronto, I have followed the transition of this music and dance from a spontaneous practice to its more formalized presentations by ensembles on stage (e.g., 2005, 2007a, 2007b). The two examples I consider below represent different points along this continuum. Both feature the string ensemble, while the second also includes singing and dancing. The first is a scene of intimate music making that features some impromptu playing that I recorded at a Górale family Christmas party in the 1980s. The party was held in a community hall on the second floor of a Polish credit union. About sixty people enjoyed a full meal, some general dancing, a visit from Santa, and performance by the group's newly formed song and dance ensemble, Harnasie. The second features a formalized song and dance performance in 2011 by the well-established Polish ensemble Biały Orzeł (White Eagle, henceforth BO) that included Górale. This well-publicized event was held in a large university auditorium for a wider, predominantly Polish audience of over 1,000 that contrasts with the intimacy of the first example.

Together, these two ethnographic moments offer contrasting perspectives on performance practice and aesthetics in an immigrant history of Toronto, and reposition past regional identities within shifting dual nationalist discourses of homeland and Canada.[18] By invoking expressive cultures associated with homelands real and imagined, individuals performatively assert themselves to build new identities and forge alliances in a complex urban setting. As both strategic and positional, the process of subjectification is tied to such discursive practices, or "specific enunciative strategies" (Hall 2005 [1996], 2–4). The two performances discussed below are examples of discursive practices that negotiate personhood and community with difference and belonging. While spanning a thirty-year period, they represent examples that can also occur as synchronous layers.

Scene 1: Off the Stage in 1985

This section takes its point of departure from a recording I made in 1985. It captures a special form of insider participation nurtured within the cracks of urban immigrant life that is not represented in any official planning documents, but is essential to individual lives. I address this performance (and my role in it) from a perspective within a specific newcomer musical experience at an event on 22 January 1985:

> The Górale Christmas party (*Opłatek*) is tucked into the second-floor hall of the Polish credit union on Roncesvalles Avenue in the heart of the Polish district. We're here to accompany Harnasie and to play for dancing after the show. It's a flexible group led by Franek Mrowca on prym, including Józef Ratułowski and Józef Podczerwiński (sekund), and Józef Leja (basy). Any other musicians who want to join in can add to the accompanying fiddles. I'm here to play sekund, as usual. It's not clear when the performance will begin, so we wait at a table with our instruments ready – drinking, eating, talking. At a certain point, unexpectedly, Franek Mrowca starts to play a tune. We're not all here, but those of us at the table pick up our instruments and begin to accompany him, following his lead with our chords. I quickly turn on my recorder.

Part of what I recorded at that moment can be heard on the CD compilation *Bellows and Bows* devoted to Canadian fiddle and accordion traditions (Johnson 2012, CD1 Track 35). In response to the request for a recording of Górale fiddling in Canada to include in this anthology, I looked for something representative and well recorded. This became a challenge, however, since my recordings from Canada often featured discrepant tunings, a poorly positioned microphone, and various interruptions and background sounds that overshadowed a featured performer or ensemble. As a result, I included a performance that was not ideally recorded and could be heard as relatively unpolished.

The playing on this recording dates from a time of growing confidence among the Górale as a distinct community within Toronto. Having recently formed the Polish Highlanders Association of Canada, the group sponsored several community events during the year and was working to locally establish its music and dance ensemble Harnasie.[19] During this period, however, there were relatively few experienced traditional musicians from Podhale in the GTA to provide the music, essential as a sonic marker at any gathering. Franek Mrowca, heard in the recording, was one of only two experienced first fiddlers (pryms). Although he admitted that advancing age prevented him from playing as he once did, he accepted every invitation to perform, and was kept busy playing from the time of his arrival in Canada in 1984. He relied on anyone else in the community who could play to join him in the essential accompanying ensemble. This typically consisted of a core group, of which I was a member, but it also could expand to include anyone else who wanted to join in. These were usually older village musicians with limited experience. Since the time of this recording, several accomplished fiddlers have arrived in Toronto from Podhale (as I also explained in the liner notes on *Bellows and Bows* [Johnson 2012, 86]). The playing of these more recently arrived musicians (heard in the second example) is characterized by technical agility, harmonic cohesion, and a highly polished style that contrasts with the players heard in 1985.

The track on this CD recording, therefore, features musicians from the older generation of Górale performance in Canada characterized by a more idiosyncratic and flexible quality of playing (see figure 12.1 for a picture of some of the musicians at this event). The three tunes performed are part of a standard repertoire of traditional melodies that accompany the góralski dance (which can be seen in the second example). The tunes are generally called by their tune type rather than by a distinctive name (this was Franek Mrowca's

Figure 12.1 | Józef Podczerwiński, Józef Ratułowski, and Franek Mrowca in 1985.

practice). The recording begins with a *wierchowa* (peak) melody. This tune type is built on a duple-time, five-bar (ten-beat) repeated chord pattern with a repeated bass of DD EE DE AA DD (or some variation) above which the sekunds play corresponding chords. (This is not exactly what is played on the recording, since [among other reasons] the prym tuned his violin above A440 and the other instruments were not reliably tuned together.) Franek Mrowca referred to the melody he plays in the recording as a *zwykła* (ordinary one), and he played it often. There is a brief break after the first tune and at 1'04" the prym begins the second tune, *krzesana po s'tyry/cztery*, (striking in four); this is based on a brisk two-bar pattern (bass AA AA DD DD, with occasional change to GG) that corresponds to changes in dance steps. On the recording at 1'50," he then leads immediately to the final green (*zielona*) tune, which is in seven-measure phrases and marks the end of the dance set – in this case the playing sequence. Each short tune can be repeated for as long as the first fiddler chooses, with ornaments and elaborations added in the personal style of the prym. The other musicians follow. As heard in the 1985 recording of this ensemble, however, they do so with varying degrees of success, and the relationships between parts are not always clear. Rhythmic insecurity and tuning discrepancies further suggest different levels of experience on the part of the players. The strong tapping of feet heard on the recording, however, confirms the spirit of the dance in these tunes.

This 1985 recording draws attention to four issues. First, it suggests a level of competence that is strikingly different from the virtuosity and exceptionality that we have grown to expect from recorded performances – even those made during fieldwork and then released to the public. In so doing, it questions our reliance on exceptional musicians in research and learning. Thomas Solomon has suggested that "we need to take so-called 'lesser' performers seriously as holders of musical knowledge" (2010, 1), and argues for the overall merits of performing music – even if at a lower level of competency. Applying ideologies from Western performance aesthetics to these musicians risks dismissing them and overlooking the social efficacy and affective value of their playing. It also overlooks the possibility of local aesthetic preference based on discrepancy and variation, where "participatory discrepancies" are an integral component of a music (Keil 1994). In his article "Participatory Discrepancies and the Power of Music," Charles Keil refers explicitly to the Górale when he notes changes in style brought by Western aesthetics, so that "the driving dissonance of Goral singing and strong playing from the Tatras have been gradually 'toned down' in the New World" (Keil 1994, 100). Although I have heard what Keil calls "driving dissonance" on recordings from the 1950s from Poland, the kind of playing that I recorded in 1985 may be less the result of a deliberate aesthetic than lack of performing experience of some of the players.[20] Nonetheless, it serves to question our codified expectations of listening. Such different performance aesthetics also draw our attention to different ways of sounding local (Diamond 2013, 157).

When I have played this recording in class, some students wince in response to the playing. To them, it sounds wrong – it sounds bad. Their response could belong to the category of "*real* experiences of auditive discomfort," but, as Washburne and Derno point out in their volume *Bad Music: The Music We Love to Hate*, passing an aesthetic judgment is also a strategic act that is the result of "positioning oneself within a given *discursive* landscape" (italics in the original, 2004, 3). As they argue, "Anytime anyone makes a discursive judgment of 'good' or 'bad' this is first and foremost a positioning gesture, which serves to construct or reimagine specific modes of subjectivity or to restructure social relationships by asserting deliberate musical agency ... The very act of passing an aesthetic judgment assumes and bestows authority upon the judge. By disaffiliating ourselves with certain forms of musical expression, we make a claim for being 'in the know' about things, we demonstrate an educated perspective and activate a wide range of underlying assumptions about what is 'good'" (Washburne and Derno 2004, 3).

Performances of this repertoire today – in Poland and North America – draw on highly polished performers who play in finely tuned synchrony and who have expanded their harmonic language beyond the essential primary chords from playing other repertoires (e.g., Slovakian, Hungarian, Romanian tunes) and from formal musical training. Such performances would be more consistent with today's dominant discursive listening perspectives. This performance, however, is a visceral reminder that difference resides in many aspects of performance within our urban setting.

Second, the recording draws attention to insider expectations of what it means to play together. Franek Mrowca often told me that he plays because it makes him feel happy. Whatever the occasion, he would go for the chance to play with others. When he picked up his fiddle at the time of this recording, the basy player was not around, so one of the sekund players switched to play the basy even though he rarely played the instrument: providing the bass function was more important here than adding another harmonic filler. Other fiddlers joined in, as they did later when we played for the performance of the dance ensemble. When I played with Franek Mrowca, he was never certain who would turn up to play for an event, and no one was turned away in his inclusive approach to playing. In contrast to other more recent Górale contexts where ensembles are the result of more restrictive membership based on experience and proficiency, during this time in Toronto the ensemble was much more fluid, and playing became a performative expression of friendship and belonging. This aligns with Thomas Turino's category of participatory music and dance, which "is more about the social relations being realized through the performance than about producing art that can somehow be abstracted from those social relations" (2008, 35). The recording, therefore, captures a specific time when priority was "placed on encouraging people to join in regardless of the quality of their contributions" (Turino 2008, 35). Writing of Western popular music, Simon Frith questions the role of judgment in this context, suggesting that collective music offers musical pleasures as social pleasures, and is "not subject to the same sort of aesthetic judgment" (Frith 2004, 35), which would risk undermining the credibility of alternative bases for aesthetic judgment.

Third, this recording provides a glimpse into an intimate moment of spontaneous music making. We had been sitting around one of the many tables set up in the hall, waiting to be called to play for the ensemble when Franek Mrowca began. While those in the immediate vicinity of our table heard our playing, this musical gesture was not necessarily directed at an external public ear. Rather, it served as an enunciative strategy of Górale regionalism among friends. Franek Mrowca reached out to his fellow players in a moment of musical inspiration to create a space of understanding and kinship. This resonated beyond our circle to sonically enclose those who shared this expressive vocabulary in this closed space, and in so doing reintroduced the sounds and memories of a past world that many older Górale in the room had experienced. The recording, therefore, offers a glimpse into some of the richness and diversity present on the very inside of migrant communities – within places unknown to policymakers and most reporting on the cultural sector.

Finally, the quality of the recording itself highlights certain expectations. While digital editing diminished some of the background noise and attempted to address the balance between the parts, the melody remains in the background in this recording. Whereas in performance the prym should be the most prominent part, here the first fiddler's tune is overpowered by the chordal accompaniment of the other instruments. My microphone was in the wrong place, hastily positioned to quickly begin recording so that I could join in the playing. For me this was a learning session, a chance to play and possibly record some spontaneous playing that could help me later. This was an opportunity afforded to me by this inclusive group because of the circumstances in this small Górale community at that time, where an absence of proficient instrumentalists left a gap that the less experienced could fill, myself included. The spontaneous performance in this recording reflects an intimate moment of music making within a particular period in the history of Górale immigration in Canada. It comes at a time of consolidation and assertion of a regional diasporic identity as separate from the predominant Polish-Canadian presence; it also coincides with a period when these Górale saw themselves as independently contributing to the growing multicultural consciousness then prevalent in Canadian discourse.

Scene 2: On the Stage in 2011

My second example focuses on a public performance that is tied to a more confident and established assertion of difference within a city increasingly drawn to diversity for its branding. This post-millennial performance by a well-established Polish dance ensemble on 3 December 2011 marks a different moment in a community's history in Canada. It contrasts with the first in performance context and style, recording quality, and my subject position.

The *White Eagle/Biały Orzeł Forty-Fifth Anniversary Gala Concert* is at the Ryerson Theatre in downtown Toronto. The 1,250-seat theatre seems full, and I hear snatches of conversations in Polish and English around me. I sit next to a video tripod, and one of the professional cameramen stands next to me. The program presents different ethnographic regions of Poland and features Podhale in the first half. For this set, BO is joined by the current version of the ensemble Harnasie and is accompanied by Górale musicians. This dynamic playing is led by *prym* Janusz Gąsienica, who deftly leads the other four musicians through tunes that they obviously know very well and can present effectively for this important concert. I see Mayor Rob Ford in the front row with his family (the show was delayed because of his late arrival).

This concert was a major event in BO's season and was professionally video recorded and edited into a two-DVD set. Highly polished choreography and singing to both recorded music and live musicians created a seamless, visually stunning concert that aspired to, and achieved, a high level of professionalism (see figure 12.2). BO is a prominent Toronto-based ensemble that has worked closely with Górale repertoire and musicians while also performing other regional Polish styles. My connection to this ensemble is through its artistic director, Ted Zdybał, who was a member of Harnasie in the 1980s and has remained musically active within the Górale community in addition to his work with BO. A strong musician and dancer, he continues to play with Górale musicians in Toronto (some of whom also accompany BO) and has led the Górale ensemble Harnasie at various times. This concert was conceived and largely choreographed by Ted, who also arranged and played much of the music. Below I introduce the ensemble and its role in the community as part of a larger network of identity politics to expose another layer of ethnocultural music and dance activities found in Toronto.

The Biały Orzeł/White Eagle Polish Song and Dance Ensemble was formed in 1966 by Paul and Maria Dubicki and today is a well-established ensemble within and beyond the Toronto-area Polish community.[21] Current membership rests at approximately seventy members of Polish extraction (eighty-one members are listed in the program accompanying the 2011 concert), subdivided into three groups: the older "representative" group (ages about sixteen and up), the intermediate group (nine to fifteen), and the junior group (four to eight). The ensemble has been active nationally and internationally since its early days: for example, in 1969 it took part in the Nova Scotia Multicultural

Figure 12.2 | The ensembles Biały Orzeł and Harnasie presenting the Podhale region in 2011.

Festival, and in 1972 it travelled to Rzeszów, Poland, for the biennial World Festival of Polonian Folk Ensembles (it has returned on a regular basis). Ted Zbybał has worked with the ensemble since 1996, first as consultant, then as artistic director. Formerly on the board of directors of Folklore Canada (an affiliate of CIOFF, the International Council of Organizations of Folklore Festivals and Folk Arts), Ted has expanded the ensemble's repertoire and travelled widely with it to develop its international profile. BO has performed not only in Poland but also at various international festivals (e.g., in Mexico, Turkey, China [Macau], Hong Kong), where the ensemble presents a version of (multiethnic) Canada on an international stage.

In contrast to the first example where I was one of the players, my perspective on BO is drawn from conversations with Ted and from watching the older group rehearse, talking to its members afterward, and distributing brief questionnaires. Many members (now in their twenties) have been part of the ensemble since they were eight or nine, moving up through the different age groups. It becomes a family tradition for those who have (or had) siblings or parents as members. Direct ties to Poland remain strong: some are first-generation Canadian-born whereas others were born in Poland or have siblings who were born there. Members belong to the ensemble for the chance to travel, to make friends, to develop confidence, and to perform. They see it as a way to keep "the Polish-ness alive within," to develop an "appreciation for other cultures," or "to help reconnect [myself] with my culture and make some friends on the way." The ensemble is close, reported long-time member Anna Światkiewicz (now in university studying biology), who referred to "my BO family." Like many who responded to my questions, she named the forty-fifth anniversary concert as the most important performance for her: "this concert allowed me to show the audience just how much we love BO, folklore, Ted, and Poland."

The Forty-Fifth Anniversary Gala Concert presented an ambitious program characteristic of the ensemble's range and approach. The two-and-a-half-hour concert was thematically organized around the four seasons of the year and divided into twenty-three separate numbers featuring different Polish regions, dances, and calendrical customs and rituals. Four features of this performance stand out. First, the ensemble aims not only to entertain, but also to educate its audience and dancers. As stated in the program, "It is our strong hope that Bialy Orzel [sic] – our White Eagle Polish Song and Dance Ensemble – can serve to regenerate these forgotten traditions and rekindle the spirit with which our Forefathers lived their lives; with the rituals and folklore that once shaped the years and life cycle of every Pole" (Biały Orzeł 2011, 29). The concert DVDs build on this goal by including additional footage of historic photographs and films featuring the life and customs of rural Poland, sometimes as part of an introduction or conclusion to a set, sometimes superimposed over the performance on stage. These digitally align BO's contemporary representations directly with past practices. The ensemble's didactic mandate fulfills a larger role, therefore – to perpetuate, promote, and disseminate rural traditional culture, and to maintain the collective memory of a community now settled in its new urban home.

Second, in aspiring to revisit the traditions of the past in their performances, BO uses sophisticated theatrical narratives to structure many of these tightly choreographed performances, thus imparting a starkly different aesthetic intention from the first example. Although here realized through the creative leadership of, first, the Dubickis and now, Ted Zdybał, the historical provenance of this form of ensemble-based performance can be traced to a style known throughout Eastern bloc countries during the Soviet era. Colin Quigley aptly describes these folk dance performance ensembles: "The choreographies used folk dance steps within a theatrical dance presentational framework. Dancers performed largely in unison or in large groupings moving through floor patterns designed as audience spectacle. There was little room for individuality in the dancing, much less any improvisation. These choreographies were set to composed suites of folklore music played by large ensembles of professional musicians in an orchestral manner ... [or] performed to recordings" (Quigley 2014, 185). Although this generation of state-sponsored ensembles was ideologically connected to the apparatus of Soviet-imposed communism, those they inspired aesthetically outside their homeland (such as BO) have strikingly different aims and objectives that are tied to an assertion and display of heritage in very different contexts. This is suggested when the voice-over at the beginning of the Forty-Fifth Anniversary Gala Concert DVD introduces BO as shaping and enhancing members' skills "into the passionate representation of Polish culture you see today." This representation of culture now becomes a heritage available for display, and follows Barbara Kirshenblatt-Gimblett's valuable definition of heritage as a new mode of cultural production in the present that is based on the past: "Despite a discourse of conservation, preservation, restoration, reclamation, recovery, re-creation, recuperation, revitalization, and regeneration, heritage produces something new in the present that has recourse to the past" (Kirshenblatt-Gimblett 1998, 149).

This concert is a newly conceived, creatively realized performance based on a set arrangement of dances and music performed by a well-rehearsed and pre-selected group of performers. It is a form of presentational music, which contrasts with participatory music in its reliance on closed prearranged forms where entire programs may be conceived as set artistic items (Turino 2008, 58). This is an effective way to present heritage, positioned now strategically for multiple audiences. At this concert, the audience included an appreciative Polonia (including the president of the Canadian Polish Congress), the broader folk arts community (including members of the Community Folk Arts Council), and other political elites who were either present (mayor of the city, consul general of the Republic of Poland), or whose letters of acknowledgment graced the program booklet (premier of Ontario, minister of Canadian Heritage and Official Languages).

A third feature of the event concerns the special attention placed on the region of Podhale. An ambitious Górale set (sixth on the program) drew on a narrative of an Easter-time custom (*polewacka*) where young men douse unmarried girls with water in a courting ritual. This combined the senior group of BO with members of Harnasie and was accompanied by Górale musicians who play together in an established ensemble called Hyr (Janusz Gąsienica on prym, Józef Siuty and Józek Prusak Ciupaga on sekund, and Ted Zdybał on basy).[22] The Górale musicians playing here exhibit a harmonic security, synchrony, and sonic presence that reflect a newer generation of musicians that form part of a larger community of Górale in the Toronto area today.[23] They also share a stylistic knowledge and performing experience that allows them to flexibly and adroitly follow the series of dance and song sequences on the stage from the time of their entrance for this set (around 4'31") to the end (around 12'54").

A segment of a solo góralski dance within this longer set illustrates some of the flexibility characteristic of Górale performance genres, and so departs from the tightly scripted performance aesthetics described above and featured in the choreographed group versions of traditional steps also included in this longer set. (It also illustrates the dancing that accompanies the tunes that were played by the musicians in the first example.) At around 8'00 the prym transitions from accompanying the group singing, which has just finished, to speed up the same tune for dancing. This is articulated by a young man who stamps his feet at the right of the screen at 8'02"; he begins dancing and a young woman emerges from the group of dancers to dance "po góralsku" with him. The musicians by now are playing a *wierchowa* (peak) tune of ten-beat phrases (tuned to concert pitch, this tune is different from the one played in the earlier recording, with the basy and sekunds adjusting accordingly). The change to the next dance in four – *po cztery* – is called out by the dancer, who changes steps in front of the musicians without pausing. The change to the corresponding tune is realized following some adjustments so that musicians and dancers are all together around 8'37" (this is the same tune played in the first example, but with a slightly elaborated bass pattern).[24] The change to a new dance would have traditionally required a full break and new tune to be sung to the musicians (see Cooley 2005, Wrazen 2004). At 8'54" the young man shouts out *"zielona"* (green) to indicate that he has finished, and the prym seamlessly leads the musicians into a five-measure-phrase tune (8'59") as the couple moves to the side to make way for all the young men to dance. The overall musical density is complicated from 8'14" to 8'50" by women singing a different tune a cappella over the dancing and playing (see Wrazen 2013, 132 for this as gendered practice). The set ends after the women have joined the men (around 12'44") and all exit singing; the video clip concludes the segment with iconic pastoral images of sheep and shepherds.

This sequence departs from some of the other highly choreographed segments in the program. For example, the dancers have the flexibility to determine the length of the dance and to develop their personal style (even while omitting the sung breaks between steps), and the musicians' playing attends to the steps of the dancers. Similarly, the first fiddler plays with an imaginative use of variation and elaboration that is well supported by the other players. Ted has explained that he wants to hold back on the styling to keep the góralski "clean" – to uphold a village style in the dances (personal communication, 5 November 2015). This distinctive performance style inscribed a regional sensibility onto the event to highlight the Górale presence within the representation of wider Polish national heritage. As performed here by this group of Górale musicians,[25] and dancers, this enunciative strategy brings a secure sense of regional identity to the public, now confidently displayed for a large external audience.

Finally, the BO ensemble itself engaged with a discourse of ethnocultural diversity. Having already chosen a downtown venue and invited important public officials as a way to assert its presence more broadly within the city, the ensemble performatively acknowledged inter-group relationships in a couple of ways. First, in its program devoted to an overview of Poland, BO performed a set called "Dances of the Roma" (with choreography and assistance from Csenge Posa and Andrew Komaromy) that represented a marginalized group in Poland and drew attention to a historic relationship with a broader Romani population. By referencing a Polish past characterized by a higher degree of ethnic diversity,[26] the performance recognized ethnocultural difference as a part of the homeland it was representing. In addition, BO addressed the ethnic pluralism of the community's current home when it invited a guest set by the Academy of Serbian Folk Dancing. By including this Toronto-based Serbian group in its program, the Polish group positioned itself within a broader local network of immigrant subcultures and expanded the demographic of its audience in an inclusive gesture of shared belonging within the city.[27]

This event marked a secure sense of belonging in the immigrant history of this community that contrasts with the first example. Not only do the Górale here participate in a discursive practice aimed to mark their presence in the city but they contribute substantively to a larger ensemble (BO) that performatively aligns itself with other groups in Toronto. Whereas the first example focused on a closed insider moment of subcultural performance, this scene has introduced community interrelationships and alliances as essential components of a city's cultural activity. Together, they allow us to explore some of the resonances characterizing lesser-known layers of cultural activities in the city. And even while limited to a single ethnocultural community of European provenance, these scenes afford a view hinting at the fuller scope and nuance that characterizes urban musical life.

Conclusions

This chapter has reflected on limitations in current discourses of difference as found in urban arts narratives, and introduced two events drawn from Górale performances in the city over a thirty-year period as evidence of hidden layers of diversity thriving in the city. These ethnographic scenes identify insider spaces of cultural activity that contribute to a broader urban soundscape yet receive little or no broader recognition. Situated within local ethnocultural neighbourhoods, such performances remain largely unknown outside the communities themselves. Many are not intended for large audiences. Yet even those held in more public venues escape mention by mainstream media, and so are not widely acknowledged as contributing to an urban arts sector. And seldom do such events receive public funding.[28] They all contribute essentially, however, to the diversities that constitute urban cultural life.

I have turned to these specific local immigrant musical subcultures of Toronto to guard against a reductive narrative of diversity that risks an erasure of the small and local in favour of the convened public spectacle. Events such as those discussed in this essay highlight a small segment of the many ethnocultural communities founded on displacement that form part of a complex layering of musical initiatives driving the vitality of the city. As explored here, in some events, the performative focus inward reaffirms personal experiences associated with familiar sounds and performance aesthetics of newcomers and recent immigrants, while others may enunciate a more complex set of relations in identity politics and self-representation within a relational urban public sphere. The details contained in each instance are reminders that difference and diversity reside in many aspects of performance.

This chapter also positions these examples of ethnocultural performance as belonging to a more inclusive national soundscape. These two scenes detail some specific musical styles, aesthetics, and experiences from among the many communities that add to the layers of a Canadian musical landscape and contribute to "shifting demographics of a pluralizing national soundscape" where "not everyone shares the same sense of self" (Mason 2007, 95). Although these specific examples focus on older European layers of migrants at a time of urgent debate related to racialized groups, Indigenous populations, those identified with (dis)abilities, and other marginalized communities, this discussion participates in the broader project of destabilizing tokenistic references to diversity in favour of an inclusive ideology that acknowledges difference as normative and includes it as an essential part of sounding and feeling local.

Notes

1 The term "newcomer" is now used to refer to an immigrant or refugee who has been in Canada for a relatively short time, that is, less than three to five years (see http://www.newyouth.ca/immigration/settlement-services/what-immigrant-refugee-newcomer-undocumented-person, accessed 15 August 2016).
2 This discussion owes much to the influential work of Beverley Diamond, who has long been engaged with concepts of difference and diversity in Canada (e.g., 2000, 2001, among others).
3 While relevant, a detailed discussion and critique of multiculturalism is beyond the scope of this paper. For a cogent summary of some of these issues, see "Mere 'Song and Dance': Complicating the Multicultural Imperative in the Arts" (Bakht 2012, 1–2).
4 Between 4 November 2015 and 2 January 2017, the Government of Canada resettled more than 39,000 Syrian refugees (http://www.cic.gc.ca/english/refugees/welcome/milestones.asp, accessed 22 January 2017).
5 Completing the 2011 National Household Survey was voluntary, leading to some critiques. A comparable document based on the 2016 census is not yet available, though some statistics appear at http://www12.statcan.gc.ca/census-recensement/2016/dp-pd/hlt-fst/pd-pl/Tables.cfm?Lang=Eng&T=200 (accessed 29 May 2017).
6 http://www1.toronto.ca/wps/portal/contentonly?vgnextoid=57a12cc817453410VgnVCM10000071d60f89RCRD (accessed 29 May 2017).
7 These are listed on the City of Toronto website: http://www1.toronto.ca/wps/portal/contentonly?vgnextoid=376a3293dc3ef310VgnVCM10000071d60f89RCRD (accessed 9 July 2016) as well as in various online and print publications. See, for example, *Now Magazine*, BlogTO (http://www.blogto.com/events/, accessed 9 July 2016).
8 Some aim for more inclusive coverage of events, and include some "world" music listings (e.g., *The Wholenote* and *Now Magazine*).
9 One of the most elaborate and spectacular of such displays was the closing ceremony of the 2015 Pan American Games in Toronto, which took place in the Rogers Centre.
10 The language of this report suggests the influence of urban studies theorist Richard Florida, who first published *The Rise of the Creative Class* in 2003. In a new edition of this book, Florida continues to argue for the economic force of creativity and the rise of a new creative class. However, despite his call to promote diversity as "an openness to all kinds of people, no matter their gender, race, nationality, sexual orientation, or just plain geekiness" (Florida, 2012, ix), his discussion largely overlooks ethnocultural contributions to the cultural life of a city.

11 Since the time of this writing, the Canada Council has released its Arts Equity Policy, which can be viewed here: https://canadacouncil.ca//media/Files/CCA/Corporate/Governance/Policy/CCA/CCAEquityPolicy.pdf. More details are available on the new website: https://canadacouncil.ca/commitments (accessed 8 July 2018).
12 The three-day CHIN picnic features both international and local performers from ethno-cultural communities. It was founded in 1966 by Johnny Lombardi, who was also a pioneer in multicultural broadcasting in Canada with the first CHIN radio station in 1966.
13 These are (in no particular order): Heritage Toronto tour: A Glimpse of the Ward: Toronto's First Immigrant Neighbourhood (10:30 walking tour of St John's Ward); Anatolia Fest: Celebrating Turkish Culture (10am–11pm Dundas Square); Toronto Bastille Day: Celebrate Bastille Day (10am–8pm Wychwood Barns); Tarana Indian Dance Showcase (3–5pm Winchester Street Theatre); Chak De Bhangra Workshops and Dance Competition (1:30–5pm Harbourfront); Salsa on St Clair (12–8:30pm St Clair Ave West); Afrofest (12–8pm Woodbine Park); Ontario Latin Arts Festival, The Hispanic Canadian Arts and Cultural Association (1–4pm Mel Lastman Square); Taste of Lawrence, International Food, Music and Cultural Festival (11am–7pm Lawrence and Warden); Japan Festival (12–8pm Celebration Square Mississauga). There were also many other concerts (e.g., Sunidhi Chauhan and Ayushman Khurana Live in Concert, Bollywood playback singer with actor/singer; 6:00pm Hershey Centre, Mississauga).
14 Information from http://www.thecanadianencyclopedia.ca/en/article/poles/ and various Statistics Canada sites (e.g., http://www.bac-lac.gc.ca/eng/discover/immigration/history-ethnic-cultural/Pages/polish.aspx, accessed 9 December 2016).
15 See Wnuk (1985) for a history, and Znaniecki and Thomas (1996) for an abridged version of the classic early twentieth-century study of Polish emigration to North America. Although appearing to be geographically isolated, Górale have had a long history of association with the outside world through tourism, ethnographic inquiry, and the seasonal or permanent departure from home in search of work, leading many to other areas of Europe and eventually to North America in the 1870s and 1880s.
16 Latin for Poland, *Polonia* is often used to refer to the larger Polish diaspora. The first Polish-Canadian umbrella organization, the Federation of Polish Societies in Canada, was formed in 1933, and renamed the Canadian Polish Congress in 1944.
17 Following the Polish government's restriction of movement in the 1980s (culminating with the imposition of martial law in 1981), emigration increased after the fall of communism and the first democratic elections in Poland in 1989. Movement has increased since that time, including among the Górale.
18 They also present two different approaches to fieldwork: the first is based on my first-person experience of playing with a group of musicians, whom I knew well, and recording the result; the second revolves around a performance I attended that was recorded professionally, and includes my interviews and questionnaires for performers.
19 This was affirmed by identifying Harnasie as a Górale ensemble when it performed at public events in Toronto.
20 None of the players mentioned in this chapter are professional musicians who make their primary living through music, though they all play/have played at events where they are paid, however casually (i.e., passing of the hat).

21 There are many similar Polish dance ensembles in the Toronto area as well as throughout Canada. For a detailed and insightful analysis of two ensembles in Manitoba, see Smith 2013. A fuller consideration of Biały Orzeł is beyond the scope of this paper.
22 This sequence, which is taken from the DVD, is available at https://www.youtube.com/watch?v=RL6rUslXET8 (accessed 1 December 2016). The clip begins at 1'56" with some historical footage from Podhale with voice-over of two women reminiscing about the past. There is much to discuss in this full clip, which includes a variety of singing and dancing.
23 Research with this ensemble is based on conversations and some playing with members Janusz Gąsienica and Ted Zdybał.
24 On the DVD, the fluency of this dance step is visually reinforced as analogous to the flowing of a mountain stream, and a video of this is superimposed over the dancing from 8'30" to 8'45."
25 These musicians also perform repertoire from the other regions for other parts of the program.
26 Ted Zdybał's commitment to present different ethnicities associated with Poland guides his ongoing planning for the ensemble, which includes a grouping to represent the Lemko (originally from the northern Carpathians of southeastern Poland) and Jewish minorities (with help from a European colleague with this expertise).
27 As a way to acknowledge Francophone culture and First Nations presence in Canada, the ensemble's repertoire also includes "La Danse Quebecois [sic]" and "First Nations Dance," which it performed at its thirty-fifth anniversary concert in 2001. I have not seen these performed, and therefore cannot comment on the performances.
28 Although the Toronto Arts Council can offer funding in some areas, many groups are not aware of it as an option (http://www.torontoartscouncil.org/Grant-Programs, accessed 26 July 2016). A separate study would be needed to determine the potential influences of changing arts policies.

References

Ahmed, Sara. 2014. *On Being Accepted: Racism and Diversity in Institutional Life*. Durham, NC: Duke University Press.

Bakht, Natasha. 2012. "Mere 'Song and Dance': Complicating the Multicultural Imperative in the Arts." In *Pluralism in the Arts in Canada: A Change Is Gonna Come*, edited by Charles C. Smith, 1–15. Montreal, QC: RR Donnelley.

Biały Orzeł. 2011. *Seasons of Biały Orzeł: 4 Pory Roku*. Program for the Forty-Fifth Anniversary Gala Concert.

Cañas, Tania. 2017. "Diversity Is a White Word." In *ArtsHub* (9 January). Accessed 29 May 2017. http://www.artshub.com.au/education/news-article/opinions-and-analysis/professional-development/tania-canas/diversity-is-a-white-word-252910.

Cooley, Timothy J. 2005. *Making Music in the Polish Tatras*. Bloomington: Indiana University Press.

Diamond, Beverley. 2000. "What's the Difference? Reflections on Discourses of Morality, Modernism, and Mosaics in the Study of Music in Canada." *Canadian Music Review* 21 (1): 54–75.

— 2001. "Identity, Diversity, and Interaction." In *The Garland Encyclopedia of World Music*. Vol. 3, *The United Stated and Canada*, edited by Ellen Koskoff, 1056–65. New York and London: Garland Publishing, Inc.

— 2013. "The Power of Stories: Canadian Music Scholarship's Narratives and Counter-Narratives." *Intersections* 33 (2): 155–65.

Flack, Derek. 2016. "Toronto Named Most Diverse City in the World." In *BlogTO*. 15 May. Accessed 6 July 2016. http://www.blogto.com/city/2016/05/toronto_named_most_diverse_city_in_the_world/.

Florida, Richard. 2012. *The Rise of the Creative Class, Revisited*. New York, NY: Basic Books.

Frith, Simon. 2004. "What Is Bad Music?" In *Bad Music: The Music We Love to Hate*, edited by Christopher J. Washburne and Maiken Derno, 15–36. New York, NY: Routledge.

Hall, Stuart. 2005 (1996). "Introduction: Who Needs 'Identity'?" In *Questions of Cultural Identity*, edited by Stuart Hall and Paul du Gay, 1–17. London, UK: Sage Publications.

Holmes, Anna. 2015. "Has 'Diversity' Lost Its Meaning?" *New York Times Magazine*. 27 October. Accessed 18 December 2015. http://www.nytimes.com/2015/11/01/magazine/has-diversity-lost-its-meaning.html?_r=0.

Johnson, Sherry. 2012. *Bellows and Bows: Historic Recordings of Traditional Fiddle and Accordion Music from Across Canada*. 2 CD set and book. St John's, NL: Research Centre for the Study of Music, Media and Place.

Keil, Charles. 1994. "Participatory Discrepancies and the Power of Music." In *Music Grooves*, edited by Charles Keil and Steven Feld, 96–108. Chicago, IL: University of Chicago Press.

Kirshenblatt-Gimblett, Barbara. 1998. *Destination Culture: Tourism, Museums, and Heritage*. Berkeley: University of California Press.

Marche, Stephen. 2016. "Welcome to the New Toronto: The Most Fascinatingly Boring City in the World." *Guardian* (4 July). Accessed 6 July 2016. https://www.theguardian.com/cities/2016/jul/04/new-toronto-most-fascinatingly-boring-city-guardian-canada-week.

Mason, Kaley. 2007. "Situating Musical Lives in Multiethnic Canada: Listening for the Non-Western 'I.'" In *Folk Music, Traditional Music, Ethnomusicology: Canadian Perspectives, Past and Present*, edited by Anna Hoefnagels and Gordon E. Smith, 95–101. Newcastle, UK: Cambridge Scholars.

Nestruck, J. Kelly. 2016. "Canada Council's Diversity Focus Brings New Opportunities, Challenges." *Globe and Mail*. 15 January. Accessed 11 July 2016. http://www.theglobeandmail.com/arts/theatre-and-performance/canada-councils-diversity-focus-brings-new-opportunities-challenges/article28212718/.

Pitter, Jay. 2016. "Introduction." In *Subdivided: City-Building in an Age of Hyper-diversity*, edited by Jay Pitter and John Lorinc, 5–12. Toronto, ON: Coach House Books.

Quigley, Colin. 2014. "The Hungarian Dance House Movement and Revival of Transylvanian String Band Music." In *The Oxford Handbook of Music Revival*, edited by Caroline Bithell and Juniper Hill, 182–202. Oxford, UK: Oxford University Press.

Shay, Anthony. 2006. *Choreographing Identities: Folk Dance, Ethnicity and Festival in the US and Canada*. Jefferson, NC: McFarland & Co.

Slobin, Mark. 2000 (1993). *Subcultural Sounds: Micromusics of the West*. Hanover, CT and London, UK: Wesleyan University Press.

Smith, Muriel. 2013. "The Polish Folk Ensembles of Winnipeg: Shaped by Atlantic Cultural Currents." *MUSICultures* 40 (1):145–77.

Solomon, Thomas. 2010. "On Playing Badly and the Limits of Musical Knowledge." Unpublished paper presented at the British Forum for Ethnomusicology, 8–11 April.

Toronto, City of. 2011. *Creative Capital Gains: An Action Plan for Toronto*. Accessed 18 December 2015. http://www.livewithculture.ca/creative-capital-initiative/an-action-plan-for-toronto/.

— 2013. *2011 National Household Survey: Immigration, Citizenship, Place of Birth, Ethnicity, Visible Minorities, Religion and Aboriginal Peoples (Backgrounder)*. Accessed 18 December 2015. https://www1.toronto.ca/city_of_toronto/social_development_finance__administration/files/pdf/nhs_backgrounder.pdf.

— 2015. *Making Toronto a Place where Business and Culture Thrive*. Economic and Development and Culture Division Annual Report 2015. Accessed 9 July 2016. https://www.toronto.ca/legdocs/mmis/2016/ed/bgrd/backgroundfile-92000.pdf.

Turino, Thomas. 2008. *Music as Social Life: The Politics of Participation*. Chicago, IL: University of Chicago Press.

Washburne, Christopher J., and Maiken Derno. 2004. "Introduction." In *Bad Music: The Music We Love to Hate*, 1–14. New York, NY and London, UK: Routledge.

Wnuk, Wlodzimierz. 1985. *Górale za Wielką Wodą*. Warsaw, Poland: Ludowa Spółdzielnia Wydawnicza.

Wrazen, Louise. 2004. "Men and Women Dancing in the Remembered Past of Podhale Poland." *The Anthropology of East Europe Review* 22 (1): 145–54.

— 2005. "Diasporic Experiences: Mediating Time, Memory and Identity in Górale Performance." *The Canadian Journal for Traditional Music* 32: 43–51.

— 2007a. "Relocating the Tatras: Place and Music in Górale Identity and Imagination." *Ethnomusicology* 51(2): 185–204.

— 2007b. "Privileging Narratives: Singing, the Polish Tatras, and Canada." *Intersections: Canadian Journal of Music* 27 (2): 60–80.

— 2013. "A Place of Her Own: Gendered Singing in Poland's Tatras." In *Performing Gender, Place, and Emotion: Global Perspectives*, edited by Fiona Magowan and Louise Wrazen, 127–44. Rochester, NY: University of Rochester Press.

Znaniecki, Florian, and William I. Thomas. 1996. *The Polish Peasant in Europe and America: A Classic Work in Immigration History*. Abridged and edited by Eli Zaretsky. Urbana: University of Illinois Press.

Rebecca Draisey-Collishaw

Chapter 13

Re-imagining the Nation: The CBC as a Mediator of Ethnocultural Encounter in St John's, Newfoundland and Labrador

> In a complicated and perverse world, action which is not informed with vision, imagination, and reflection, is more likely to increase confusion and conflict than to straighten things out. (Dewey 1993, 7)

This chapter considers the role of the Canadian Broadcasting Corporation (CBC) as a producer and curator of culture. During the first decade of the twenty-first century, examples of what I call "fusion programming" aired from regional broadcast centres across Canada.[1] Premised on encounters between musics and musicians from different genres, styles, and ethnocultural traditions, this category of music programming embodied objectives outlined in Canada's Broadcasting Act (Government of Canada 1991) and Multiculturalism Act (Government of Canada 1988), and responded to internal pressures at the CBC for content to be "more multicultural."[2] Here I focus on just one example of this type of programming – a radio concert series produced between 2007 and 2008 in St John's, Newfoundland – to explore how a specific approach to arranging voices on-air relates to perceptions of belonging and Otherness within a multicultural nation.

Produced under the umbrella of *Musicraft*, the "Come By Concerts" brought together musicians from a variety of traditions to "rub shoulders," "combining" the musics of newer immigrant communities with "Newfoundland tunes and songs" performed by "natives of Newfoundland."[3] With a mandate to reflect the musical life of Newfoundland and Labrador, *Musicraft* typically broadcast "pickups" of concerts already happening in communities, performances of in-studio guests, and selections of commercial recordings.[4] The

"Come By Concerts" stood apart from *Musicraft*'s regular musical offerings since they involved a production role for the CBC, community partnerships, and an active society-building agenda that drove decisions about voicing and content. The broadcasts targeted regional audiences, though selections from the concerts were also heard across Canada, representing the nation's most easterly region to the rest of the country. My analysis considers the "Come By Concerts" as tools for reflecting and renegotiating Canada's social order, but also raises concerns about potentially hierarchical readings that perpetuate the marginalization of particular voices.

I begin with the policies, priorities, and social trends that contextualized programming decisions during the early twenty-first century. Produced as part of the CBC's regional programming lineup and in step with the introduction of new provincial-level policies on immigration in 2007 and multiculturalism in 2008, the "Come By Concerts" sought to create spaces of ethnocultural encounter by facilitating musical collaborations between prominent traditional Newfoundland musicians and musicians from more recent immigrant communities resident in the St John's area. As actors working in service to the public, producers engage the systems in which they are embedded. The ways in which they think creatively about how to abet top-down agendas and grassroots challenges, or even when they engage without conscious contemplation, are important variables in an ongoing policy process.[5]

Notably, I focus on the broadcaster as an active agent in the production of audiences. In a study exploring the production of national culture via comic books, Jason Dittmer and Soren Larsen suggest that audiences are "interpellated" through the ways in which they are addressed. They explain, "When a subject acknowledges a call to a particular identity by an ideological state apparatus, they then become beholden to certain ideological imperatives that are associated with that identity. Thus, interpellation can result in the seduction of audiences into active participation in collective fantasies, such as nationhood" (Dittmer and Larsen 2007, 737). Accordingly, I analyze the ways in which producers/hosts conceptualize audiences "by the foregrounding of some narratives and the silencing of others" (ibid., 738). This means that I have given less weight to the perspectives of audiences. Similarly, while musicians typically are active participants in constructing and contesting the discourses that surround them and their music(s), producers have curatorial control over the content of broadcast concerts: the production team ultimately decides which songs and conversations make it to air. Indeed, anecdotal accounts by members of the production team for *Fuse*, another example of fusion programming, about what was excluded from broadcasts make clear the extent of the producer's narrative authority (see Draisey-Collishaw 2017).[6] In this context, musician intention is almost incidental.

The notion of "producing an audience" or "producing culture" comes from Stuart Hall's call for public broadcasters to "re-imagin[e] the nation" by "becoming the 'theatre' in which cultural diversity is produced, displayed and represented, and the forum in which the terms of its associative life together are negotiated" (1993, 36). This demand relies on the premise that social realities are discursively constructed. "Discourse" refers to the unvoiced rules and categorizations that are assumed as natural elements of knowledge and that function to protect structural inequalities by delegitimizing and stigmatizing perspectives that threaten the established order (Foucault 1981; cf. Hall 1986, 1993). Taking this definition a step further, "discursive formations" refer to the ways in which bodies of discourse – including words, music, and approaches to curation and mediation – are ordered and articulated. Discursive formations are hierarchical, reinforcing the dominance of established identities and subjectivities, and shaping the perceived nature of reality within societies. This is not to imply that such formations are marked by an inherent unity, totality, or finiteness; rather, they are cross-cut with conflicts and their negotiated nature contains persistent potential for change and reordering (Hall 1986, 1993). Indeed, "re-imagining the nation," to use Hall's formulation, relies on this potential for change.

From the contexts that supported production of the "Come By Concerts," my discussion turns to the broadcasts themselves. Through descriptions of content, analysis of the "Come By Concerts" as spaces of encounter, and consideration of the assumptions and intentions that shaped production decisions, I suggest that fusion programming may perpetuate some of the inequalities that it is intended to redress. I am not the first to point to the capacity of the rhetorical deployment of multiculturalism to mask injustices and shore up existing hegemonies (see Mackey 1999; Bannerji 2000; Roberts 2011). However, I follow dancer and legal scholar Natasha Bakht's suggestion that a solution lies not in dismantling the structures of multiculturalism but in engaging them critically: "that is, to be conscious of its flaws and to infuse within it an analysis that reveals its limits" (2012, 131). This case study, particularly when read against a backdrop of other broadcasts crafted according to similar agendas in parallel circumstances, is a call to recognize the invisible boundaries that are subtly reinforced through programming decisions as a foundation for exploring alternatives.

Contextualizing Programming for Multicultural Newfoundland

While often cloaked in platitudes about openness and the value of diversity, the legalities of multiculturalism in Canada enact a pragmatic strategy of management intended to depoliticize difference. Multiculturalism, in this sense, is about social organization, interpreting law, and protecting human rights (Fleras and Kunz 2001, 5–7). According to social geographer Audrey Kobayashi (1993), multiculturalism in Canada can be understood as existing in three stages: demographic (pre-1970), symbolic (1970s to c. 1980s), and structural (c. 1980s to present). When Prime Minister Pierre Elliott Trudeau announced a policy of official multiculturalism in 1970, he was legitimizing a "demographic" reality, but only through the celebration of symbols that lacked real scope to address actual structural injustices. This "symbolic stage" of multiculturalism did, however, create the conditions (and some funding) for minority groups to organize. One of the results was the founding of the Canadian Ethnocultural Council, an influential political lobby dedicated to representing the interests of minorities.

The "structural" stage of multiculturalism dates to the patriation of the Canadian Constitution (i.e., the Canadian Charter of Rights and Freedoms) in 1982 and the implementation of the Multiculturalism Act in 1988. This stage also incorporates all subsequent legislative and policy moves focused on the protection and promotion of human rights through strategies that target racism, inequity, and lack of official representation (Ley 2007). These structural moves include regional deployment of the principles of multiculturalism through provincial-level laws and policies on multiculturalism and human rights. Saskatchewan, for example, was the first province to enact official multiculturalism in 1974, updating this legislation in 1997 to better address structural inequalities (Dewing and Leman 2006). The rest of the provinces and territories of Canada have subsequently followed suit with their own versions of multiculturalism and/or anti-discrimination laws (Dewing 2009).

There are definite pitfalls in conflating conversations about multiculturalism, immigration, and visible minorities. While these concepts intersect, they are not synonymous: multiculturalism is an overarching framework that applies to all Canadians and residents, immigration is a legal process through which residency and/or citizenship is sought, and minority groups often have been in Canada for generations. Nevertheless, Newfoundland and Labrador's history of colonization and its approach to implementing a strategy on immigration and a related policy on multiculturalism have resulted in points of overlap that are difficult to avoid.

While the island of Newfoundland originally was home to significant Indigenous populations, by the nineteenth century these groups had been decimated by settler populations and pushed to the region's geographic fringes.[7] French settlers were the majority population in Newfoundland through to the eighteenth century, and people of French descent remain the majority population on the island's west coast. Still-isolated settlements of Scots are scattered across Newfoundland's south coast and the Codroy Valley. Though a significant Portuguese community was never permanently established in Newfoundland, there was sustained contact through the fisheries from the sixteenth century through to 1974 when the last ship of the White Fleet left St John's Harbour. And, too, West Country English and Irish immigrants settled the outports from Notre Dame Bay to the Burin Peninsula during the eighteenth and nineteenth centuries. During the twentieth century, while many regions of Canada experienced successive waves of migration from a variety of locales, for political and economic reasons Newfoundland and Labrador became a place that people emigrated from, not to. Indeed, in 2006 only 1.67 percent of Newfoundland and Labrador's total population (500,605) were defined as immigrants (Statistics Canada 2007a): individuals who are or have been "landed immigrant[s]/permanent resident[s] ... Some immigrants have resided in Canada for a number of years, while others have arrived recently. Most immigrants are born outside Canada, but a small number are born in Canada" (Statistics Canada 2015). Visible minorities – "persons; other than Aboriginal peoples; who are non-Caucasian in race or non-white in colour" (Statistics Canada 2007b) – made up only 1.14 percent of Newfoundland and Labrador's total population (Statistics Canada 2007a). In this context, "traditional" Newfoundlanders tend to be imagined as simply Anglo-Irish, reflecting the dominance of particular voices in provincial identity discourses.[8]

In 2007, the provincial government of Newfoundland and Labrador launched an immigration strategy with the goal of attracting between 1,200 and 1,500 new immigrants annually within five years and boosting retention levels from 36 percent – the lowest rate among Canadian provinces – to 70 percent (Office of Immigration and Multiculturalism 2007; Immigration Policy and Planning 2005, 6). This strategy acknowledged the province's changing economic fortunes and the potential opportunities that prosperity afforded for both the recruitment of an entrepreneurial and skilled labour work force, and the development of post-secondary education opportunities. Significantly, the province's declining birthrate, aging population, and traditional dependence on out-migration for work created structural conditions that necessitated an alternative approach to sustaining the local populace. With the goal of educating the general public about the benefits of an increased immigrant presence in the province, Newfoundland and Labrador's 2007 immigration strategy emphasized partnerships between governmental bodies (federal and provincial) and community stakeholders. These partnerships also provided practical assistance for settlement and integration within communities, including access to education, healthcare, and social services; translation services; English as a Second Language training for children and adults; housing support services; information services; and recognition of foreign credentials.[9]

Further support for accomplishing the goals of the 2007 immigration strategy came in 2008 with the introduction of Newfoundland and Labrador's first official multiculturalism policy. The new policy explicitly focused on promoting greater intercultural understanding between new Canadians and established Newfoundlanders (Government of Newfoundland and Labrador 2014). The combined result of these initiatives has been an increase in the rate of new Canadians choosing to settle in Newfoundland for professional, academic, and other reasons. Indeed, the results of the 2016 Census of Canada reveal increased levels of immigration to Newfoundland, particularly from Asia and Africa. The level of immigration in the period between 2011 and 2016 (3,680 immigrants) is almost double that of the period between 2006 and 2010 (1,870 immigrants). As well, just over 60 percent of immigrants in the later period are economic immigrants (i.e., admitted according to the terms of worker, business, and provincial programs), up from 55.6 percent in the 2006–2010 period. Notably, these changes concentrate in St John's, the provincial capital (Statistics Canada 2017a). While it remains to be seen whether this growth will continue and whether immigrant populations will opt to remain in the province, the presence of growing immigrant and visible minority populations challenges dominant notions of provincial identity.

Encounters in Audiotopic Space

Ethnomusicologist Parmela Singh Attariwala observes that the structures of music making (and the arts more generally) in Canada are directly implicated by the Multiculturalism Act and related legislation: "By spelling out the responsibility of the Government of Canada and its institutions to uphold multiculturalism in the second part of the 1988 Multicultural Policy, the government placed its own institutions (including Crown Corporations such as the CBC, the Canada Council and the National Film Board) at the heart of structural change, effectively imposing a kind of affirmative action" (2013, 133). While the principles of multiculturalism are deployed regionally through provincial-level legislation and strategies, those principles also are operationalized in sector specific laws and mandates. For example, the Broadcasting Act (1991) provides the regulatory framework for Canada's broadcasting system, defining the roles of public, commercial, and educational components.[10] Among other responsibilities, the CBC is obliged to provide programming that "reflect[s] Canada and its regions to national and regional audiences," "actively contribute[s] to the flow and exchange of cultural expression," "contribute[s] to shared national consciousness and identity," and "reflect[s] the multicultural and multiracial nature of Canada" (Canada 1991, 3[1][m]).[11] The inclusion of this final clause brings the CBC's mandate in line with some of the more broadly ideological justifications for the ongoing relevance of public service broadcasting in the twenty-first century – including Hall's call for public broadcasting to become a forum for "re-imagining the nation."[12]

This is no simple task. Unprecedented media proliferation and technological innovation leading to media convergence, ubiquitous social networking media, and emphasis on DIY approaches to production combine with increasingly transnational populations to foster the proliferation of micro-publics and niche audiences – formations that challenge traditional models for broadcasting. Raboy and Taras report that the Canadian media have responded to these conditions by becoming one of the most diverse in the world (2007, 84). Entire commercial networks cater to a wide variety of language and cultural affiliations, sometimes reaching transnational markets. And, too, community and educational broadcasters provide scheduling blocks for communities – defined according to a variety of criteria – to address their members (Fleras 2009; Fleras and Kunz 2001). The CBC plays a role in this rapidly changing media system through infrastructure rollout in a geographically vast country that lacks the population base to support commercial development.[13] It has also pioneered new approaches to content production during a period of media convergence, including taking an early lead in the development of online public broadcast services (O'Neill 2006) and more recently following industry trends in the production of podcasts and digital streaming services (Fautaux 2017a, b). While the mediascape has never been more diversified, niche audiences for specialty programming rarely have cause to overlap or interact, and the vagaries of scheduling potentially reinforce the marginalization of particular communities within the national landscape. With its public service remit and its almost universal coverage in Canada, the CBC remains one of the few available platforms for bringing diverse and geographically dispersed communities into dialogue.

"Fusion programming" can be understood as an attempt at reimagining the nation – or, in the case of the "Come By Concerts," an attempt to reimagine the province. At its core, fusion programming is about encounter between communities, embodied and ensounded in the meeting of disparately positioned musics and musicians. This coinage references the name of the longest running example of this type of programming (*Fuse*), but the idea of "fusion" – reaction, ignition, energy – emphasizes the dynamism of moments of encounter in a way that terms like "hybridity" may obscure (cf. Brinner 2009, 215–16; Stanyek 2004). Some producers stressed that they were trying to capture the energy of extemporaneous encounters – unexpected moments of synergy between performers and co-present audiences referenced metaphorically by sparks and lit fuses – a goal that sometimes superseded emphasis on the production of polished musical objects. Though appearing in various guises over a variety of network platforms, the general template for this type of programming involved bringing together musicians/musical groups from differing scenes (distinguished along genre, generational, cultural, or geographic lines) to perform and discuss the challenges of collaboration. Conversations framing the music often referenced diversity and multiculturalism (or, at least, involved extensive discussion of differences), and frequently included some sort of mapping of musicians onto Canada's social geography.

The arrangement of voices and the negotiation of difference are inherent in fusion programming. Episodes, accordingly, can be thought of as microcosmic discursive formations that comprise words, sounds, modes of interaction, and affective responses to the structures of meaning realized through "musicking" (cf. Small 1998). The discursive field encompasses interpersonal engagements between musicians and audiences, but also includes interactions with members of production teams and with the spaces and places occupied in performance. Sociologist Christopher Small explains that performance spaces are constructed with particular relationships and understandings of normativity in mind, simultaneously encouraging desirable behaviours while "closing off the possibility of behaviours of a different kind" (1998, 20). He later contends that "those taking part in a musical performance are in effect saying – to themselves, to one another, and to anyone else who may be watching or listening – *This is who we are*" (1998, 134). Participating in a performance is a means of articulating complex relationships between people, places, and sounds. Relationships are musicked into relief, allowing them to be modelled, reinforced, and learned through enactment (1998, 9).

However, there are distinctions between musicking *within* versus *across and between* cultures. Though not speaking directly to broadcasting, Josh Kun's theorization of "audiotopias" provides a relevant frame for understanding what was attempted through fusion programming. He explains that audiotopias are places in which sound, space, and identity converge, "offer[ing] the listener and/or the musicians new maps for re-imagining the present social world" (2005, 23). Cultures are "contest[ed]" and "consolidat[ed]," "sound[ed]" and "silenc[ed]" in these produced spaces, revealing possibilities that either disrupt or confirm existing national narratives (2005, 22). By using this term, I am describing potential for perception that moves beyond an impossible utopian desire for unified harmony to a space in which difference matters. Music has a productive capacity, creating spaces in which difference may be introduced, negotiated, and accepted without insistence on resolution by consensus. These are spaces in which sound does not appeal to the rational, but instead works on the emotional.

Notably, the analysis presented in this chapter speaks to the structures of meaning realized in spaces mediated by the broadcaster. As analytics, "musicking" and "audiotopias" encourage attention to the positionality of actors and observers. However, there are important interpretive distinctions to be made between attentive listening in a live performance space and distracted encounters with radio sounds overheard while driving to work or doing housework. Similarly, local knowledge provides important contextual cues that are unavailable to audiences more distant – physically and/or culturally – from sources. Jody Berland notes that "through radio, music mediates our interactions with space and our contradictory senses of belonging. Each spatial organization and scale of locality – the city, the nation, the ancestral home, and the space between the ears – is organized by cultural technologies of space, and each offers its imprimatur to the mix" (2009, 191). Proximity between sound and source, the intimacy of relationships between musicians and audiences, and the mediating voice of the broadcaster are all elements of the audiotopic space.[14] The limits of this chapter and lack of access to the live performances, however, make it impossible to tease out all of these elements and the interpretive possibilities that proximity, perspective, and mediating voice each pose.[15] While I acknowledge that this range exists, my focus remains on the agency of the broadcaster and her mediating voice as a producer and interpellator of audiences.

Musicking the New St John's?

Between December 2006 and February 2008, CBC host and producer Francesca Swann produced three broadcasts that explicitly explored the changing ethnocultural profile of Newfoundland and Labrador.[16] Swann explained: "I was noticing that we encounter people from different ethnicities when we go to the university, or go to the hospital but we don't really see or hear that reflected in the music here. And ... I had this feeling that we weren't actually hearing the full range of the evolving musical life of the province on my show and that to do that I should really try to include some of those newer ethnicities in our community. And they weren't generally being presented in traditional presentation series so I had to go seeking them out in their various communities" (2010). Swann's comments reference her awareness of Newfoundland's changing social landscape and implications for the province's musical life. However, representing these trends meant taking a more hands-on approach to organizing performances; traditional concert venues that tended to appear in *Musicraft*'s programming schedule rarely featured performers from newer immigrant communities.[17]

Produced by and for the CBC, the "Come By Concerts" came with higher than usual price tags. In addition to the more typical task of recording concerts and mixing them for broadcast on *Musicraft*, producing the "Come By Concerts" involved hiring the musicians, organizing the venues, researching the audiences, and a host of other responsibilities that go along with being an impresario. These extra costs and responsibilities exceeded Swann's operating budget so she sought out partnerships. For example, Memorial University's School of Music donated the use of the concert venue, called Petro-Canada Hall at the time, a contribution that helped to offset some of the production costs.

Conceptually, the concerts proved appealing to the local CBC administration and the national network. This meant that Swann could access "co-funding" from other sources within the CBC. She explained that the extra financial support had much to do with the CBC's mandate to reflect the diversity of local communities: "I think there was a desire from the network side and also from our own station's side, to start reflecting more of a realistic cross-section of how the community here is evolving with different people coming in and I think there was a wish to get that on the air. It works well into CBC's mandate of reflecting the country back to itself and telling people's stories from our communities and reflecting the changes in our society" (Swann 2010). Funding from the national network came from *Canada Live*, at the time a daily radio program that was the CBC's primary platform for broadcasting live performance content. When *Canada Live* came on air in 2007 it was given a mandate – and a significant budget – to broadcast concerts recorded in locations across Canada to a national audience. Equitable representation of the regions was an important element of that mandate, but so was demonstration of Canada's multicultural nature through inclusion of a diverse range of musics. The CBC Music Department and *Canada Live* allotted each region a quota of concerts. They also set guidelines: approximately 25 percent of recorded concerts should qualify as "world music" (MacKeigan 2012). Pressure for music programming to be "more multicultural" influenced content decisions for *Canada Live*, but also had a trickledown effect: regional producers could access supplemental production funds (as well as national exposure for local musicians) if a proposed performance met the appropriate criteria and recording standards. Regional producers increased their odds of accessing co-funding from network-level programs like *Canada Live* by pitching performances that could be framed as "multicultural" or by arranging concerts that featured a nationally recognized musician/group in collaboration with a local artist.[18]

Although Swann was unable to comment specifically on the reception of the broadcasts by members of her radio audience, she indicated that the concerts generally were well received. Petro-Canada Hall, which has a seating capacity of 120, was full for each performance and audiences comprised both established Newfoundlanders and members of minority communities. Indeed, Swann emphasized the value of engaging a new listenership through the "Come By Concerts" as a means of expanding audiences and more fully reflecting the nature of the region's many communities. Featuring musicians from Balkan, Indian, and Bangladeshi communities introduced so-called traditional Newfoundlanders to the music of more insular neighbours, but also served as an invitation to both recent immigrant and longstanding minority communities to tune in.[19] Though she was unable to comment on whether this strategy worked, Swann reported receiving positive feedback and requests for information about future events.

When I spoke with Swann in 2010, she expressed an interest in producing more "Come By Concerts." She felt a professional obligation to provide this type of programming for listeners. Production, however, depended on the availability of musicians who were both willing and able to perform at a professional standard. Moreover, the concerts required an unusually high level of commitment from musicians; in order to perform effectively together, musicians had to acquire new repertoire and be willing to explore unfamiliar musical styles. Budget cuts and related reductions in live music recording initiatives ultimately curtailed any possibility of further additions to the "Come By Concert" series (see CBC 2012).

Broadcast 1: Sveti Ivan and Pamela Morgan

The first of the "Come By Concerts" aired on 24 December 2006. It features a Balkan choir called Sveti Ivan alongside Newfoundland singer, songwriter, and producer Pamela Morgan. Sveti Ivan ("St John's" in a number of Eastern European languages) formed in January 2006 under the leadership of ethnomusicologist Kathleen Wiens. Drawn from local immigrant communities, the choir also included singers who were interested in Eastern European choral repertoire.[20] Some of Sveti Ivan's songs feature as a soloist George Miminis, president of the Greek Community of Newfoundland and Labrador and founding musician of the Forgotten Bouzouki and Acousmata.[21] The house band for the concert includes Graham Blair on mandolin, Tom Power on guitar, Matthew Hender on bass, and Heather Wright on violin, all students affiliated with Memorial University's music and folklore departments. The overall effect of including so many voices from a range of traditions and performance styles is a broadcast that approaches the idea of "fusion" through the juxtaposition of repertoires, timbres, and ensembles.

The broadcast begins with a set of four Balkan songs: a Croatian lullaby, a traditional Hungarian dance tune, and two songs by Greek songwriter Mikis Theodorakis.[22] Each is sung by the choir and accompanied by the instrumental ensemble (see figure 13.1).[23] Following the choir's set, Morgan sings four traditional Newfoundland songs ("I'll Hang My Harp on a Willow Tree," "Seven Years," "Who Is at My Window," and "To Drive the Cold Winter Away") and, marking the date of broadcast, the performance concludes with the choir performing a set of four Christmas songs.

The broadcast cut of the concert emphasizes song and music, though it includes spoken introductions that provide contextual details about the songs and represented traditions. Swann provides an opening and closing frame for the broadcast, describing the musicians and performance space, and relating the conceptual principles that inspired this particular coming together of voices. Within and between sets, members of each ensemble (principally Kathleen Wiens and Pamela Morgan) narrate the music, describing forms and instruments, local histories, and song traditions. However, there are narrative distinctions in the contextual commentary that mark differing assumptions about the performers and their musics – slight differences but nevertheless worth considering. For example, the introductory commentary provided by representatives of Sveti Ivan focuses on defining the sounds, appearance, and usage of presumably exotic instruments for listeners.[24] Morgan's comments, in contrast, establish the history of her repertoire and describe her forays into intercultural musical collaborations. Presumptions about the types of information audiences will need to interpret the singers' respective performances have the potential to influence the approach to curating content.

The juxtapositions of repertoires and related traditions demonstrate differences, but also highlight similarities. During the final set, for example, members of the choir tell stories about Christmas traditions in distant homelands. They describe practices unique to far-off locales, but emphasize a similarity of purpose that resonates with more proximate local customs. Like "traditional" Newfoundlanders, the choristers are celebrating a holiday with festivities based around food, family, and spirituality. Reinforcing the sense of familiarity, Wiens relates details of house visiting practices that parallel Newfoundland's mummering traditions.[25]

In this program, juxtaposition is the main approach to fusion, placing repertoires, traditions, and performers side by side to enable comparison. However, there are two notable exceptions to this pattern: at each transition point in the program the musicians perform together, combining – fusing – distinctive elements of their musical styles (see figure 13.1). At the end of the first set, Morgan joins on a reprise of the choir's opening song: a Croatian lullaby called "Senjico Senjala." Rather than singing along, Morgan transforms the choral lullaby by layering in a song that, in its own right, speaks to the constructed nature of traditions. Widely heard as an iconic Newfoundland song, "She's Like the Swallow" likely was not sung with great frequency in the province until after 1930. Collected by Maud Karpeles and subsequently canonized through dissemination by Edith Fowke and Richard Johnston in *Folksongs of Canada* (1954) and by Kenneth Peacock in *Songs of the Newfoundland Outports* (1965), the song symbolizes the vitality of Old World – in this case British – traditions in Newfoundland (see Rosenberg 2007). The

"Traditional music from Eastern Europe rubs shoulders with
the folk songs of Newfoundland and Labrador as these
two musical worlds converge."

Sveti Ivan Set

Senjico Senjala (trad. Croatian lullaby)
Somogyi Karaikazao (trad. Hungarian folk dance)
Mother and Mary (Mikis Theodorakis), featuring George Miminis
Sorrow (Mikis Theodorakis), featuring George Miminis
**Senjico Senjala / She's Like the Swallow (trad., arr. Pamela Morgan),
featuring Pamela Morgan**

Pamela Morgan Set

I'll Hang my Harp on a Willow Tree (trad., Fogo Island, NL)
Seven Years (trad., Bell Island, NL)
Who is at my Window (trad., NL)
To Drive the Cold Winter Away (trad.)

Sveti Ivan Set

Kolenda (trad., Croatian[?] house visiting song)
**We Three Kings (John Henry Hopkins Jr., arr. Pamela Morgan and Sveti Ivan),
featuring Pamela Morgan**
Silent Night (Franz Gruber), with narration by members of Sveti Ivan
Hej Mili Moj (trad., Polish[?])

Figure 13.1 | Program for Come By Concert 1. Banded titles indicate performers, specifically indicating the dominant voice and style of the set. Bolded song titles indicate specific points of collaboration within the overall broadcast program.

broadcast introduction to Morgan's arrangement of "Senjico Senjala" / "She's Like the Swallow" features Wiens explaining that something new is created when two musics come together, in this case totally recasting the characters of, respectively, a lullaby and a lament. Later in the broadcast, Morgan and Sveti Ivan rejoin to sing the second song of Sveti Ivan's second set: the musicians perform an arrangement of the Christmas song "We Three Kings." Their version features the choir singing an ostinato based on a Romanian melody and the words for "star of wonder, star of night" while Morgan soars over the choir, singing the more familiar version of the Christmas carol.

In each case – "Senjico Senjala" / "She's like the Swallow" by Morgan and "We Three Kings" by the combined resources of the performers – the arrangement of the songs is quite original and the performers present a compelling combination of textures and harmonies. And yet the hierarchical relationship of the voices – their discursive ordering – is inescapable: the choir is cast in a supportive role while Morgan remains the star performer. This relationship probably has more to do with Western choral performance practices that privilege solo voices as audible focal points than with the ethnocultural identities of the performers. Choristers typically work to blend their individual voices to create a unified sound, while soloists emphasize different harmonics in their voices or add vibrato to distinguish themselves from the ensemble. Moreover, the solo voice often carries the melody or is made sonically dominant through volume, timbre, and tessitura. Indeed, even when no clear markers of sonic dominance are included, listeners accustomed to Western choral performance practices become conditioned to hear these distinctions.[26] Accordingly, the possibility of perceiving the terms of the musicians' encounter as anything other than hierarchical is limited from the outset.

Broadcast 2: Reels and Ragas

Just over a month later, a second broadcast aired on 28 January 2007. Described as a performance in which "reels and ragas meet as Indian and Newfoundland musics fuse," the broadcast combines three distinct repertoires: traditional Newfoundland-Irish sets performed by Graham Wells (accordion); sets of Karnatic Indian music sung by Sobhana Venkatesan; and Hindustani music performed by Dr Arya and Bani Bal (vocals) and Sanchita Chakraborty (tabla). Percussionist Curtis Andrews provides the voice that unites the performers and crosses between musical worlds (see figure 13.2). Specializing in various West African and Indian drumming styles, Andrews accompanies Wells for part of the broadcast and Venkatesan for the rest.

Using sets of Newfoundland-Irish accordion tunes to bookend the broadcast has the potential to suggest an arrangement of voices not unlike that established in the previous "Come By Concert." However, this narrative in which the immigrant community is framed within the dominant culture (see Fast and Pegley 2012, 5–7, 23–6) is disrupted and complicated by Andrews's accompaniment for the tunes. Rather than relying on the traditional rhythmic patterns used to reinforce the danceability of tunes (in this case, a set of singles[27] to begin and reels to end), Andrews improvises an accompaniment that

"Reels and ragas meet as Indian and Newfoundland music fuse at a MUSICRAFT Come By Concert in the PetroCanada Hall at Memorial University. Natives of Newfoundland: accordion player, Graham Wells and percussionist, Curtis Andrews perform with members of St John's Indian community: co-vocalists, Dr. Arya Bal, Bani Bal and Sobhana Venkatesan with tabla player Sanchita Chakraborty."

Newfoundland-Irish Set (featuring Graham Wells and Curtis Andrews)

Mahers / Broderick / Mussels in the Corner (trad.)
Jigs: Garry Shannans / Geese in the Bog (trad.)

Sobhana Venkatesan Set (featuring Curtis Andrews)

Swaminatha Paripalaya (Muthuswamy Dikshithar)
Vara Narada (Tyagaraja Swami)
Palihncu Kamakshi Pavani (Shyaamaa Shaastree)

Newfoundland-Irish Set (featuring Graham Wells and Curtis Andrews)

Conamara Stocking / Chattering Magpie (trad.)
Kitty Jones (trad.)

North Indian Set (featuring Arya and Bani Bal, Sanchita Chakraborty)

In Praise of Lord Ganesh
Your Enchanting Music
Season is Passing By, featuring Graham Wells and Curtis Andrews

Newfoundland-Irish Set (featuring Graham Wells and Curtis Andrews)

Reels (trad.)

Figure 13.2 | Program for Come By Concert 2. Banded titles indicate the dominant voice and style of the set. Bolded song titles indicate specific points of collaboration within the overall broadcast program.

draws on the repertory of rhythms used later in the broadcast to accompany Venkatesan. The tunes instantly became both exotic – that is, distinct from the expected range of timbres, textures, and metric configurations of traditional Newfoundland-Irish dance music – and familiar. Andrews embodies and ensounds ambiguities. A native of Carbonear, Newfoundland, Andrews is sonically marked as part of the dominant culture by the light Newfoundland accent that inflects his speech. But this dominance is complicated by the musical and personal ambiguities that allow him to cross between affiliations as a traditional Newfoundland musician and Indian drummer: his specialization in the musical practices of South India and Ghana, choices of dress, and a slightly swarthy complexion sometimes have supported mistaken perceptions of a non-existent South Asian heritage.[28]

Broadcast 3: Ballads to Bangladesh!

The final "Come By Concert," "Ballads to Bangladesh!," went to air a year later on 17 February 2008. Featuring Bangladeshi singer Shahana Begum Islam[29] and Newfoundland-born singer-songwriter Leanne Kean, this broadcast also includes Graham Wells, Billy Sutton, and Curtis Andrews performing traditional Newfoundland-Irish tunes and filling the role of backing band for the singers. Much like the "Reels and Ragas" broadcast from a year earlier, Newfoundland-Irish tunes provide supposedly familiar frames for the presumably more exotic sound of Begum Islam's singing.

Although weighted to feature Begum Islam, whose musical prestige is suggested when she is introduced as a "regular" on Bangladeshi radio, a single set of Western pop songs placed at the temporal midpoint of the broadcast inflects this focus. Leanne Kean performs two of her own compositions before being joined by the instrumentalists in a rendition of Newfoundland's unofficial anthem, "Song for Newfoundland." Unlike Begum Islam's performance, there is minimal interaction between Kean and the other musicians. She largely remains a solo voice, suggesting little need for her music to be altered through collaboration – or, just as likely, revealing a lack of experience in performing repertoire not her own.[30] In contrast, during Begum Islam's performance there is a clear negotiation of styles at work: Wells's accordion sounds remarkably like a harmonium and Begum Islam's singing overlaps and elaborates the diatonic fixed scale of his instrument with the microtonal variations of the modes in which her songs are composed.

The language used to introduce the musicians contains subtle tensions and contradictions that shape understandings of how musicians belong (see figure 13.3; cf. figures 13.1 and 13.2). In her study of the ways in which Canadian literary prize-winners are received based on their citizenship and perceived "Canadianness," Gillian Roberts observes that there are tensions and discursive contradictions that result in a simultaneous claiming of authors as belonging while distancing them as from elsewhere. She analyzes a *Toronto*

"Ballads to Bangladesh! A CBC Come By Concert...combining Shahana Begum from Bangladesh with Newfoundland natives: Graham Wells on accordion and whistle, Billy Sutton, bouzouki and fiddle, Curtis Andrews, percussion and 18-year-old Torbay singer/songwriter Leanne Kean. This is a line-up of Newfoundland tunes and songs together with songs that Shahana has written and inherited from her father and sister. Shahana, who now lives in St John's (and has raised a family here), used to be a regular performer on Bangladesh radio."

Newfoundland-Irish Set (featuring Graham Wells, Billy Sutton, and Curtis Andrews)

Crowleys / Exile of Erin (trad.)

Shahana Begum Set (featuring Graham Wells, Billy Sutton, and Curtis Andrews)

Heaven Among Dinosaurs (Shahana Begum)
Young Emotions (Akm Abdul Aziz)

Newfoundland-Irish Set (featuring Graham Wells, Billy Sutton, and Curtis Andrews)

Cat in the Corner / [untitled] / Biddy Dalys (trad.)

Leanne Kean Set

Pretending (Leanne Kean)
Solid Ground (Leanne Kean)
Song for Newfoundland (Wayne Chaulk), featuring Graham Wells and Billy Sutton

Shahana Begum Set (featuring Graham Wells, Billy Sutton, and Curtis Andrews)

Undying Affection (Nadira Begum)
Blind Ambition (Shahana Begum)

Newfoundland-Irish Set (featuring Graham Wells, Billy Sutton, and Curtis Andrews)

Frank Maher's Singles / Running the Goat (trad.)

Shahana Begum Set (featuring Graham Wells, Billy Sutton, and Curtis Andrews)

Longing for Another's Return (Akm Abdul Aziz)

Figure 13.3 | Program for Come By Concert 3. Banded titles indicate the dominant voice and style of the set. Bolded song titles indicate specific points of collaboration within the overall broadcast program.

Star editorial celebrating Michael Ondaatje's receipt of the Booker Prize, noting how the language of the announcement moves the author "from being a guest in Canada, as suggested by the metaphor of adoption, to encapsulating Canadian cultural success and values, not only occupying the Canadian host position, but also acting as Canadian culture's representative, an exemplary figure held up for emulation" (2011, 4). A similar pattern appears in the narratives that frame the musicians featured in the "Come By Concerts." For example, Begum Islam "from Bangladesh" is juxtaposed with "Newfoundland natives," but also inscribed as an heir to family traditions (she sings songs "inherited from her father and sister"). Importantly, she is acknowledged as having established roots within Newfoundland (she's "raised a family here"). This narrative approach distances Begum Islam as an exotic import to Newfoundland, but simultaneously shows her to possess values that are familiar and even prized in the insular communities of "traditional" Newfoundland.

Indeed, this approach to describing and positioning the musicians in relation to each other, to audiences, to geographies, and to established sociocultural structures and institutions exemplifies a particular approach to describing travel and mobility that I have labelled "transit narratives" (see Draisey-Collishaw 2018). These are narrative frames that often (though not exclusively) appear in conjunction with musicians who were born outside Canada, frequently emphasizing the exoticism of the musician and/or her music, and suggesting that primary influences exist outside Canada. Musicians, accordingly, are narrated as Other, even when Canadian and/or North American muses are cited or formative years are spent in Canada. The legitimacy of the singer and her music is established through references to awards and institutional affiliations within Canada, but a subtle distinction is drawn between simply being a *Canadian*-Canadian, to use Mackey's (1999) turn of phrase, and being a hyphenated Canadian – Bangladeshi-Canadian in Begum Islam's case. Such hyphenate identities reflect the complexity of identity politics, functioning as a claim to trans-/extra-national identities when adopted by the bearer, but a hegemonic mechanism for maintaining the status quo when ascribed by representatives of the dominant culture.

Re-imagining the Nation: The Discursive Con-"fusions" of Multiculturalism

This chapter began with Kobayashi's (1993) observation that Canada has entered a structural stage of multiculturalism in which legislation and policy are directed at the equitable protection and promotion of human rights (also see Ley 2007). Since being enshrined in the Charter (Government of Canada 1982) and the Multiculturalism Act (Government of Canada 1988), the principles of multiculturalism have become the basis for interpreting and deriving other legislation and policy – including the terms of provincial-level strategies, the Broadcasting Act, and the CBC's mandate. As Attariwala observes, multiculturalism effectively puts the government's own institutions, including Crown corporations like the CBC, "at the heart of structural change" (2013, 133). Accordingly, the CBC has a mandated responsibility to "re-imagine the nation" (Hall 1993, 36). The "Come By Concerts" celebrated the changing ethnocultural profile of Newfoundland and Labrador – or, more accurately, the greater St John's area – in terms of a dynamic "convergence of musical worlds" (Broadcast 1; see figure 13.1) and a "fusing" of native Newfoundlanders with St John's' well-established Indian community (Broadcast 2; see figure 13.2). Analyzing these broadcasts in terms of production motives, issues of voicing, and how broadcasts contribute to wider conversations about the nature of regional communities, is a means of assessing how multicultural Canada is being re-imagined.

The "Come By Concerts" emerged in dialogue with specific local conditions and were designed with the needs of a regional audience in mind: they acknowledged demographic changes within Newfoundland and Labrador and a new public mandate to become a more open and inclusive society (see Immigration Policy and Planning 2005; Office of Immigration and Multiculturalism 2007; Government of Newfoundland and Labrador 2014). In this sense, these case studies suggest the difficulties of navigating Canada's cultural policies and are revealing of the ethics of program production. In organizing the concerts that provided the source materials for broadcasts on *Musicraft* and *Canada Live*, the producer of the "Come By Concerts" was responding to a lack of public spaces in which difference might effectively be modelled and engaged. Despite intentions, distinctions between communities were maintained through the arrangement of voices and address of musicians in the broadcasts; the unintended outcome was a discursive formation that tended to shore up an imagining of national identity in which visible minorities remain guests of a dominant Anglo-Canadian and white culture (cf. Roberts 2011).

The "Come By Concerts" are demonstrative of the CBC's ongoing potential as a producer and curator of culture. Indeed, they might even be considered "symptomatic" of wider discourses relating to the nature of Canada's social order (Conway 2011). In his study of the journalistic coverage of the constitutional debates leading up to the Meech Lake and Charlottetown Accords, communications scholar Kyle Conway points to the dialectic relationship between context, production, reception, artifact, and discursively formed reality. "Journalists," he explains, "were influenced by the broader debates taking place, and their coverage in turn influenced those debates. However, journalists covered only a subset of the broader debates – how could they do otherwise?" (2011, 9). As one-off broadcasts with limited audience penetration at regional levels, the "Come By Concerts" are not "representative of" the CBC's total programming output. Nor did they represent and influence Newfoundland and Labrador's many communities.[31] However, as "symptomatic examples" of an approach to programming and the discourses of a particular moment, these broadcasts are useful tools for thinking through the naturalized assumptions privileged in their encodings: they function as catalysts for discussing the role of the media in constructing, maintaining, and "re-imagining" the nation.

In my introductory comments, I mentioned that this case study forms part of a larger study of fusion programming in Canada. As part of this larger project, I analyzed eight examples of fusion programming (in addition to the "Come By Concerts") produced in different CBC broadcast centres. Each case study addressed programming motives, production and funding (where this information was available), live versus broadcast elements, audience and reach, and the content of broadcasts (see Draisey-Collishaw 2017). These fusion programming examples all followed similar conceptual principles and tended to use similar vocabularies for describing motives, discussing musicians, and narrating audiotopic encounters. In some cases, fusion programming was presented as an extemporaneous, unplanned, and live encounter of inherently different voices. Performances were intentionally un-/under-rehearsed with the goal of highlighting the process of intercultural communication rather than the outcome(s) of such meetings. At the opposite extreme, commissioned compositions tended to emphasize sleek production values and the creation of an object of assumed aesthetic worth. Projects planned specifically with regional audiences in mind tended to involve a strong community outreach agenda: free concerts; in-person meetings of producers, musicians, and audiences; and inclusion of musicians with varied levels of performance experience. Projects that prioritized the national audience, in contrast, did not have the same potential for direct community engagement, and tended to give precedence to professional performance standards. As well, the size and scope of the national audience influenced decisions about what musics were deemed appropriate for inclusion. Distinctions in levels of investment, community engagement, production values, and how producers understood their audiences are potentially productive for thinking through the limits and alternatives to existing programming models.

My analysis in this chapter points to fusion programming's potential to perpetuate a discursive ordering of voices that bolsters entrenched divides and normalizes the dominance of a typically white settler population. However, the process of preparing the "Come By Concerts" deserves further consideration, particularly since it details a level of investment and community engagement that distinguishes these broadcasts from some other examples of fusion programming. In the weeks leading up to each of the "Come By Concerts," the musicians crossed between each other's musical and social worlds. They learned about new musics and styles of performing, and gleaned glimpses into their collaborators' private lives. Swann reported positively on feedback she received from participating musicians. She told stories about invitations and warm receptions into the homes of performers. She also indicated that this engagement extended beyond the musicians and into the performers' respective communities. In my analytical terms, the process of preparing for the concerts involved actors musicking in audiotopic spaces that made available alternative perspectives to their lived realities.

The fusion programming premise and its execution did not stagnate over the period of the "Come By Concerts'" production: there was ongoing experimentation with voicing that complicated hierarchical orderings. For example, in the first broadcast a star of traditional Newfoundland song fronted a choir of "new" voices at designated points. The second broadcast featured a single musician who assumed the role of mediator between musical worlds, crossing and bridging the gap between traditional Newfoundland dance music and South Indian Karnatic song. And finally, the form of the third broadcast placed less emphasis on framing new voices with traditional Newfoundland-Irish tunes. With the "Come By Concerts," the broadcaster attempted to reach across ethnocultural divides as a means of bringing communities into dialogue, envisioning a space in which differences could be negotiated and a diverse public re-imagined at the regional level. Though imperfect – and even problematic – in their realization, the production of the broadcasts indicates an awareness of the changing needs of audiences in Newfoundland and Labrador and an important attempt to engage a wider public across ingrained ethnocultural and community lines.

Natasha Bakht argues for the necessity of critically engaging the effects of multiculturalism through "an analysis that reveals its limits" (2012, 131).

This sort of engagement is not about dismantling the mechanisms of multiculturalism, but about providing a basis for moving debates, policies, and realizations forward. My analysis in this chapter focuses on the agency of the producer as a silent voice that speaks through the broadcasts. Though not heard directly, this voice determines the narrative arc of broadcasts, the language used to frame performances, and the terms of engagement between communities that are modelled through musical interactions.

Focus on the agency of the broadcaster as a curator and producer of culture also demonstrates one of the limits of fusion programming. As Swann's account attests, face-to-face encounters between musicians were affective experiences that influenced individual and community reception of Other musics and performers. Musicians had opportunities to define for themselves the terms of their engagement with partnering musicians, rather than relying on "inaccurate assumptions based upon ethnocultural generalities" (Attariwala 2013, 113). I suspect (though cannot confirm) that the live concerts, with their potential for direct communication between musicians, communities, and broadcaster, held similar potential for encounter and new forms of engagement with cultural Others. The possibility for spatial co-presence and direct contact – elements that Jason Stanyek (2004) defines as essential for intercultural encounter – are limited by the broadcast medium.[32] Musician voices are mediated by the broadcaster: voices are translated and meanings shaped by naturalized assumptions about the nature of musics, national and/or regional identities, and institutional biases. Might assigning musicians greater agency for self-expression be a way forward? Is there an argument for granting musicians a more significant role in the production process (e.g., as partnering producers and co-editors)? Might there be a way of using multi-platform content delivery as a means of providing performers with space to curate their own performances? Re-imagining the nation in more equitable terms requires vision, imagination, and reflection on where programming models have taken us. An absence of these elements, as pragmatist philosopher John Dewey points out, "is more likely to increase confusion and conflict than to straighten things out" (1993, 7). Asking questions about who possesses the agency to communicate is one path toward alternative programming models and new perspectives on how Canada's many communities might be re-imagined.

Notes

1 Examples of fusion programming produced by the CBC between 2000 and 2012 include selections from the *True North Concerts* and *True North Concert Series* (produced by Peter Skinner, CBC North); "Burning to Shine" on zeDTV (produced by Jon Siddall, Vancouver); the "Combo to Go" concert series (produced by Catherine McClelland, Calgary); *Mundo Montréal* and *Rendez-Vous* (produced by Sophie Laurent, Montreal); The Roots Project, *Playing through Changes*, and the Slean-Hatzis project (produced by Jeff Reilly, Halifax); and *Fuse* (produced by Caitlin Crockard, Ottawa). For case studies of these programs, see Draisey-Collishaw 2017.
2 CBC/Radio-Canada's 2006–2007 strategic plan lists eight priorities to be accomplished by 2011. The second of these priorities is "reflecting regional and demographic diversity." Evaluation of this priority was based on the creation of "programs produced in regions for regions; programs produced in regions for network; visible minority staff; stories about visible minorities" (CBC/Radio-Canada 2006, 29).
3 The quoted fragments come from the broadcast introductions to the three broadcasts that are the focus of this case study. Full transcripts of these statements can be found in figures 13.1, 13.2, and 13.3.
4 In 2012, the CBC's St John's–based mobile broadcast unit was decommissioned following punitive budget cuts. These cuts dramatically curtailed the broadcaster's capacity to record concerts happening in communities throughout the province. Until 2015, most regions offered programming similar to that of *Musicraft*, according to a mandate to reflect the musical life of the area. In the wake of cuts to CBC's annual parliamentary allocation in 2015, *Musicraft* (and similar programs in other regions) was cut from the regular program roster. "Regions" – as is the case with Newfoundland and Labrador – sometimes align with provincial borders, but sometimes include only a portion of a province (e.g., the Toronto and Ottawa broadcast centres service different parts of Ontario) or reach across provincial borders (e.g., Thunder Bay's catchment reaches into Manitoba). Regions are defined by the broadcaster and include the geographical range of stations scattered across Canada. A list of current regional centres is available from http://www.cbc.ca/news/canada#region-nav (accessed 4 January 2017).
5 I am not suggesting a linear relationship between policies and the actions of producers. Political, cultural, and social systems are complexly interrelated, meaning that policies rarely act in a straightforward manner. Programming decisions, such as those that gave rise to "fusion programming," result from a combination of conscious and unconscious awareness and ongoing negotiations within those systems.
6 *Fuse* broadcast as part of CBC Radio One's national lineup between 3 July 2005 and 20 September 2008. At various points during its four-season, seventy-six-episode run, it was also available on Radio 2, Radio 3, Sirius Satellite Radio, and Bold TV. Production was based in Ottawa, though a number of episodes were recorded in other centres across Canada, including Halifax, Sackville, Toronto, Regina, Calgary, Vancouver, and Whitehorse.
7 The 2016 Census of Canada indicates that approximately 8.9 percent of Newfoundland and Labrador's total population (512,255) identify as Aboriginal (Statistics Canada 2017b).

8   For discussion of the construction of Newfoundland's ethnocultural identity as Irish, see Everett 2016, Farquharson 2008, Harris Walsh 2015, Keough 2008, Osborne 2013, and Trew 2005.
9   See Office of Immigration and Multiculturalism 2007 for a description of the seventeen goals that are the basis of the provincial immigration strategy. For discussion of the conditions supporting development of this plan, see Immigration Policy and Planning 2005.
10 For discussion of the components that make up the Canadian broadcasting system and their functions see Armstrong 2010 and Salter and Odartey-Wellington 2008. For an account of the historical development of these policies, see Raboy 1990.
11 This is a hefty – and perhaps even unmanageable – mandate, particularly in the context of perpetual budgetary crisis. Indeed, Conway's analysis of issues of representation in the news coverage of the Meech Lake and Charlottetown accords points to the effect of budget cuts on the capacities of journalists to engage the demands of their mandate (2011, 68). Very little appears to have changed in twenty-five years. Though a thorough assessment of policy, programming, and actions taken by the CBC should account for fiscal circumstances, for reasons of space – not to mention the challenges of access – detailed accounts of budgets have been omitted from my analysis.
12 Other characteristics of public service broadcasting include being publicly funded but not state run; existing for the public good; being based on principles of universal access and diversity (in programming, audiences, and opinions); and maintaining independence from political or commercial influence, while remaining distinct from other broadcasting services (World Radio and Television Council 2000; see also Raboy 2006; Raboy and Taras 2007; Chignell 2009; and Hendy 2013).
13 The physical size of Canada combined with low population density means that it is not commercially viable to service rural and remote communities. Historically, the public broadcaster – the CBC – has taken a leading role in building and maintaining the infrastructure necessary to provide equitable broadcast coverage of Canada.
14 I address these issues in Draisey-Collishaw 2017.
15 My access was limited to the broadcast cuts for *Musicraft*; I did not have access to unedited recordings or the versions created for broadcast on the national network. As well, I was not present at the live performances that provided the source materials for the concert broadcasts.
16 Many thanks to Francesca Swann for facilitating my access to archival recordings of the "Come By Concerts," and to CBC archivist Christine Davies for alerting me to the series in the first place.
17 Accessing mainstream public venues is an ongoing challenge for so-called "multicultural" groups. In her 1994 study of multiethnic dance groups in Ontario (defined as non-Western dance of all types, including classical, sacred, ritual, and folk), De Shane notes the tendency to ghettoize these groups by restricting access to performance spaces and events. Distinctions in access are also addressed in Bakht 2012 and Attariwala 2012. More recently, the 27 January 2016 edition of *Now* featured a series of editorials about racism in the music industry, several of which pointed to persistent issues of access to mainstream facilities and support (Gillis et al. 2016).

18 Although all three of Swann's "Come By Concerts" were funded in part by *Canada Live*, only two were broadcast nationally (Sveti Ivan and Pamela Morgan, and Ballads to Bangladesh!). Several other fusion programs produced at this time received funding from *Canada Live* (or other national programs). Examples include "Combo to Go" (produced in Calgary), selections from *True North Concert Series* (produced in Yellowknife), and *Mundo Montréal* (produced in Montreal).

19 My data on the promotional strategies employed for reaching beyond the CBC's established audience(s) is limited. Swann referred to the exchanges between musicians as, in certain cases, involving receptions in private homes that included musicians' friends and families. These direct forms of contact may have supported recruitment of audiences who were not CBC regulars.

20 For discussion of the complexities of identity formations in diasporic folkloric groups like Sveti Ivan, see Chong's case study of the choir (2006).

21 In an interview published in *The Scope*, a St John's-based arts magazine, Miminis stated that the Newfoundland Greek Community had a membership of thirty to thirty-five. At the time, the province of Newfoundland and Labrador had a total population of eighty to one hundred Greeks (Smellie 2008). I have cited these numbers because they speak to why the concert series had potential to reach "new" audiences. The small size of certain population groups and the existence of ethnic clubs/societies meant that not only were there existing networks for promoting events, there were often established audiences for the performers who featured in the "Come By Concerts."

22 Mikis Theodorakis (b. 1925) is considered Greece's best-known living composer. He has written more than a thousand songs, worked as a film composer (including scores for *Zorba the Greek* [1964] and *Serpico* [1973]), and composed "The Ballad of Mauthausen" about the Holocaust.

23 The instrumental ensemble for this portion of the broadcast also included Morgan on the *baglamas*, a long-necked lute used in Greek music. The *baglamas* is somewhat similar to the bouzouki though higher pitched. It is distinct from the *bağlama* (sometimes known more simply as *saz*), another lute-type instrument used widely in Turkish entertainment and dance music and to accompany sung poetry, particularly in Turkey and Azerbaijan.

24 Diamond describes constructions of the Other as intentionally ambiguous and capable of application to many forms of difference, ranging from gendered divides to (post/de)colonial contexts. Others, she explains, "were seen as localized, totalized and ahistorical; they were exotic inversions, hence confirmations of normalcy, and they were clearly regarded as unequal" (1994, 11). My use of "exotic," here and throughout this chapter, relies on this notion of inversion as a confirmation of the normative. As a label, it is contingent and constructed, available for a range of decodings that rely on the subjectivities, priorities, and often-unexamined worldviews of broadcasters and listeners.

25 Mummering is a Newfoundland Anglo-Irish house-visiting tradition that involves dressing in costumes and calling on neighbours to perform plays, music, and jokes at Christmas time. In recent years, this predominantly rural tradition has been revived as a festival that involves workshops, entertainment, and a parade in St John's.

26 Cf. Douglas 2004 for related arguments about how particular types of radio programming condition the listening habits and expectations of listeners.
27 "Singles" are a type of dance tune performed in Newfoundland. Similar to Irish polkas (though with their own idiomatic metric emphases), they are generally played in a fast 2/4.
28 Details about Andrews's varied specializations can be found on his personal website: http://www.curtisandrews.ca/about.htm (accessed 17 November 2015).
29 Shahana Begum Islam (1954–2010).
30 Broadcasters often have very pragmatic reasons for the ways in which they arrange voices on air – reasons that have little to do with ideologies and everything to do with the limits of production schedules, the abilities of performers, the quality of recordings, and the duration of available air time.
31 In 2017, the CBC cited an 18.5 percent all-day audience share for their Radio One and Radio 2 services (their terrestrial broadcast networks). Ratings for individual programs, timeslots, and regions are not available; this is protected information (CBC/Radio-Canada 2017). Audience share varies across Canada. For example, in metropolitan centres it tends to be lower because the market is fragmented by a large range of options. In contexts such as these, an 18.5 percent share is considered a very good level of penetration. Historically, rural and remote regions – including Newfoundland and Labrador – have fewer (and sometimes no) alternatives so audience share may be closer to 45 percent (Skinner 2012; Bergfeldt 2012).
32 See Stanyek 2004 for discussion of "co-presence" as an element of intercultural encounter and music making.

References

Armstrong, Robert. 2010. *Broadcasting Policy in Canada*. Toronto, ON: University of Toronto Press.

Attariwala, Parmela Singh. 2013. "Eh 440: Tuning into the Effects of Multiculturalism on Publicly Funded Canadian Music." PhD diss., University of Toronto.

Bakht, Natasha. 2012 [2011]. "Mere 'Song and Dance': Complicating the Multicultural Imperative in the Arts." In *Pluralism in the Arts in Canada: A Change Is Gonna Come*, edited by Charles C. Smith, 1–14. Our School/Our Selves, vol. 5. Ottawa, ON: Canadian Centre for Policy Alternatives.

Bannerji, Himani. 2000. *The Dark Side of the Nation: Essays on Multiculturalism, Nationalism, and Gender*. Toronto, ON: Canadian Scholars' Press.

Bergfeldt, Wendy. 2012. Interview with author (CBC Sydney Broadcast Centre, Sydney, Cape Breton, Nova Scotia). 28 June.

Berland, Jody. 2009. *North of Empire: Essays on the Cultural Technologies of Space*. Durham, NC: Duke University Press.

Brinner, Benjamin. 2009. *Playing across a Divide: Israeli-Palestinian Musical Encounters*. New York, NY: Oxford University Press.

CBC. 2012. "CBC to Cut Jobs, Programs over Next 3 Years." *CBC News*, 4 April. Accessed 11 April 2012. http://www.cbc.ca/news/canada/story/2012/04/04/cbc-budget-cuts.html.

CBC/Radio-Canada. 2006. *Making a Place for All Canadians: Public Broadcasting in the Digital Era, Summary of CBC/Radio-Canada's Corporate Plan for 2006–2007 to 2010–2011.* Ottawa, ON: Canadian Broadcasting Corporation.

– 2017. "Accountability Plan: Our Performance – Media Lines, English Services Highlight." *Celebrating Canadian Culture: Annual Report 2016–2017.* Accessed 14 July 2018. http://www.cbc.radio-canada.ca/site/annual-reports/2016-2017/accountability-plan/our-performance-media-lines-english-services-highlights-en.html.

Chignell, Hugh. 2009. *Key Concepts in Radio Studies.* London, UK: Sage.

Chong, Carolyn. 2006. "Constructing Identities in a Women's Balkan Folklore Ensemble." *MUSICultures* 33: 32–47.

Conway, Kyle. 2011. *Everyone Says No: Public Service Broadcasting and the Failure of Translation.* Montreal & Kingston: McGill-Queen's University Press.

De Shane, Nina. 1994. "'Multiethnic' Dance in Ontario: The Struggle over Hegemony." In *Canadian Music: Issues of Hegemony and Identity*, edited by Beverley Diamond and Robert Witmer, 75–88. Toronto, ON: Canadian Scholars' Press.

Dewing, Michael. 2009. "Canadian Multiculturalism." Publication No. 2009–20–E. Ottawa, ON: Library of Parliament, Parliamentary Research Branch. (15 September; revised 14 May 2013).

Dewing, Michael, and Marc Leman. 2006. "Canadian Multiculturalism." 16 March. Ottawa, ON: Library of Parliament, Parliamentary Research Branch.

Dewey, John. 1993 [1917]. "The Need for a Recovery of Philosophy." In *The Political Writings*, edited by Debra Morris and Ian Shapiro, 1–9. Indianapolis, IN: Hackett Publishing Company.

Diamond, Beverley. 1994. "Introduction: Issues of Hegemony and Identity in Canadian Music." In *Canadian Music: Issues of Hegemony and Identity*, edited by Beverley Diamond and Robert Witmer, 1–22. Toronto, ON: Canadian Scholars' Press.

Dittmer, Jason, and Soren Larsen. 2007. "*Captain Canuck*, Audience Response, and the Project of Canadian Nationalism." *Social & Cultural Geography* 8 (5): 735–53.

Douglas, Susan J. 2004. *Listening In: Radio and the American Imagination.* Minneapolis: University of Minnesota Press.

Draisey-Collishaw, Rebecca. 2017. "Curating Canadianness: Radio, Fusion Programming, and Hierarchies of Difference." PhD diss., Memorial University of Newfoundland.

– 2018. "'Traveling-in-Dwelling, Dwelling-in-Traveling': Producing Multicultural Canada through Narrations of Mobility on CBC Radio's *Fuse.*" *Ethnomusicology Forum* 27 (3): 323–43.

Everett, Holly. 2016. "Do You Play Newfoundland Music? Tracking Traditional Music in the Tourist Imaginary." *MUSICultures* 43 (1): 112–31.

Farquharson, Danine. 2008. "Introduction: How Irish Is Newfoundland?" *The Canadian Journal of Irish Studies* 34 (2): 10–11.

Fast, Susan, and Kip Pegley. 2012. *Music, Politics, and Violence.* Middletown, CT: Wesleyan University Press.

Fauteux, Brian. 2017a. "The Radio Host and Piloted Listening in the Digital Age: CBC Radio 3 and Its Online Listening Community." *Journal of Canadian Studies* 51 (2): 338–61.

— 2017b. "'Songs You Need to Hear': Public Radio Partnerships and the Mobility of National Music." *Radio Journal: International Studies in Broadcast & Audio Media* 15 (1): 47–63. DOI: 10.1386/rjao.15.1.47_1.

Fleras, Augie. 2009. "Theorizing Multicultural Media as Social Capital: Crossing Borders, Constructing Buffers, Creating Bonds, Building Bridges." *Canadian Journal of Communication* 34 (4): 725–30.

Fleras, Augie, and Jean Lock Kunz. 2001. *Media and Minorities: Representing Diversity in a Multicultural Canada*. Toronto, ON: Thompson Educational Publishing.

Foucault, Michel. 1981. "The Order of Discourse: Inaugural Lecture at the Collège de France (2 December 1970)." In *Untying the Text: A Post-Structuralist Reader*, edited by Robert Young, 48–78. London, UK: Routledge.

Gillis, Carla, Tabassum Siddiqui, Michelle da Salva, Vish Khanna, and Tanya-Tiziana. 2016. "Real Talk about Racism in the Toronto Music Scene." *Now*. 27 January. Accessed 16 March 2017. https://nowtoronto.com/music/real-talk-about-racism-in-the-toronto-music-scene/.

Government of Canada. 1982. Constitution Act. Canadian Charter of Rights and Freedoms. Department of Justice. Ottawa, ON: Minister of Justice.

— 1988. Multiculturalism Act. Department of Justice. Ottawa, ON: Minister of Justice.

— 1991. Broadcasting Act. Department of Justice. Ottawa, ON: Minister of Justice.

Government of Newfoundland and Labrador. 2014. Multiculturalism. 6 March. Accessed 6 November 2015. http://www.nlimmigration.ca/en/live/multiculturalism.aspx.

Hall, Stuart. 1986. "Gramsci's Relevance for the Study of Race and Ethnicity." *Journal of Communication Inquiry* 10 (2): 5–27.

— 1993. "Which Public, Whose Service?" In *All Our Futures: The Changing Role and Purpose of the BBC*, edited by Wilf Stevenson, 23–8. [London, UK]: British Film Institute.

Harris Walsh, Kristin. 2015. "Irishness and Step Dancing in Newfoundland and Labrador." In *Global Movements: Dance, Place and Hybridity*, edited by Adam Pine and Olaf Kuhlke, 23–38. Lanham, MD: Lexington Books.

Hendy, David. 2013. *Public Service Broadcasting*. New York, NY: Palgrave Macmillan.

Immigration Policy and Planning. 2005. "An Immigration Strategy for Newfoundland and Labrador: Opportunity for Growth." 30 September. Discussion Paper, Department of Human Resources, Labour and Employment, Government of Newfoundland and Labrador. Accessed 4 October 2016. http://www.aes.gov.nl.ca/publications/immigration/ImmigrationStrategy.pdf.

Keough, Willeen. 2008. "Creating the 'Irish Loop': Cultural Renaissance or Commodification of Ethnic Identity in an Imagined Tourist Landscape?" *The Canadian Journal of Irish Studies* 34 (2): 12–22.

Kobayashi, Audrey. 1993. "Multiculturalism: Representing a Canadian Institution." In *Place/Culture/Representation*, edited by James Duncan and David Ley, 205–31. London, UK: Routledge.

Kun, Josh. 2005. "Introduction: Strangers among Sounds." In *Audiotopia: Music, Race, and America*, 1–28. Berkeley: University of California Press.
Ley, David. 2007. *Multiculturalism: A Canadian Defence*. Research on Immigration and Integration in the Metropolis Working Paper Series, 7.4. Vancouver, BC: Vancouver Centre of Excellence. Accessed 11 November 2015 http://mbc.metropolis.net/assets/uploads/files/wp/2007/WP07-04.pdf.
Mackey, Eva. 1999. *The House of Difference: Cultural Politics and National Identity in Canada*. London, UK: Routledge.
MacKeigan, Ann. 2012. Telephone interview with author. 26 August.
Office of Immigration and Multiculturalism. 2007. *Opportunity and Growth: An Immigration Strategy for Newfoundland and Labrador*. St John's, NL: Newfoundland and Labrador Department of Human Resources, Labour and Employment.
O'Neill, Brian. 2006. "CBC.ca: Broadcast Sovereignty in a Digital Environment." *Convergence: The International Journal of Research into New Media Technologies* 12 (2): 179–97.
Osborne, Evelyn. 2013. "The Most (Imagined) Irish Place in the World? The Interaction between Irish and Newfoundland Musicians, Electronic Mass Media, and the Construction of Musical Senses of Place." PhD diss., Memorial University of Newfoundland.
Raboy, Marc. 1990. *Missed Opportunities: The Story of Canada's Broadcasting Policy*. Montreal & Kingston: McGill-Queen's University Press.
– 2006. "Creating the Conditions for Communication in the Public Good." *Canadian Journal of Communication* 31: 289–306.
Raboy, Marc, and David Taras. 2007. "On Life Support: The CBC and the Future of Public Broadcasting in Canada." In *How Canadians Communicate*. Vol. 2, *Media, Globalization, and Identity*, edited by David Taras, 83–103. Calgary, AB: University of Calgary Press.
Roberts, Gillian. 2011. *Prizing Literature: The Celebration and Circulation of Nation Culture*. Toronto, ON: University of Toronto Press.
Rosenberg, Neil V. 2007. "'She's Like the Swallow': Folksong as Cultural Icon." *Newfoundland and Labrador Studies* 22 (1): 75–113.
Salter, Liora, and Felix N.L. Odartey-Wellington. 2008. *The CRTC and Broadcasting Regulation in Canada*. Toronto, ON: Carswell.
Skinner, Peter. 2012. Telephone interview with author. 23 August.
Small, Christopher. 1998. *Musicking: The Meanings of Performing and Listening*. Hanover, CT: Wesleyan University Press.
Smellie, Sarah. 2008. "People: George Miminis." *The Scope*. 28 February. Accessed 8 January 2017. http://thescope.ca/people/george-miminis.
Stanyek, Jason. 2004. "Diasporic Improvisation and the Articulation of Intercultural Music." PhD diss., University of California, San Diego.
Statistics Canada. 2007a. "2006 Community Profiles." *2006 Census*. Statistics Canada Catalogue no. 92-591-XWE. Ottawa. Released 13 March 2007. Accessed 11 November 2015. http://www12.statcan.ca/census-recensement/2006/dp-pd/prof/92-591/index.cfm?Lang=E.

- 2007b. "Visible minority groups 2006 counts for Canada provinces and territories – 20% sample data (table)." *Ethnocultural Portrait of Canada Highlight Tables: 2006 Census*. Statistics Canada Catalogue no. 97–562–XWE2006002. Ottawa. Released 2 April 2008.
- 2015. "Immigrant." *Definitions, Data Sources and Methods*. 4 April. Accessed 5 October 2016. http://www.statcan.gc.ca/eng/concepts/definitions/immigrant.
- 2017a. "Immigrant population by selected places of birth, admission category and period of immigration, Canada, provinces and territories, census metropolitan areas and areas outside of census metropolitan areas, 2016 Census." *Data products, 2016 Census*. 27. Accessed 9 July 2018. https://www12.statcan.gc.ca/census-recensement/2016/dp-pd/dv-vd/imm/index-eng.cfm.
- 2017b. "Canada [Country] and Newfoundland and Labrador [Province] (table). Census Profile." *2016 Census*. Catalogue no. 98–316–X2016001. 29 November. Accessed 9 July 2018. https://www12.statcan.gc.ca/census-recensement/2016/dp-pd/prof/index.cfm?Lang=E.

Swann, Francesca. 2010. Interview with author (CBC St John's Broadcast Centre, St John's, Newfoundland). 24 November.

Trew, Johanne Devlin. 2005. "'The Forgotten Irish': Contested Sites and Narratives of Nation in Newfoundland." *Ethnologies* 27 (2): 43–77.

World Radio and Television Council. 2000. *Public Broadcasting: Why? How?* Accessed 4 December 2010. http://portal.unesco.org/ci/en/ev.php-URL_ID=18796&URL_DO=DO_TOPIC&URL_SECTION=201.html.

Judith Klassen

Chapter 14

Music, Mimesis, and Modulation among Mennonites in Rural Manitoba

Despite diverse manifestations of ethnocultural Mennonite identity in transnational contexts – and indeed among and within Mennonite congregations and families – assumptions about rural Mennonite communities as religiously conservative and insular persist in contemporary Canada.[1] While diversity within ethnocultural communities is increasingly recognized and acknowledged in academic and popular spheres (Diamond and Witmer 1994; among Mennonites in particular, see Dueck 2017; Klassen 2016), and the notion of "ethnicity" as it pertains to Mennonite identity has been problematized (Sawatsky 1991; Werner 2005; Winland 1993), public stereotypes of stasis and homogeneity frequently inform the way that Mennonites are portrayed in historical and contemporary contexts.[2] The narratives of Mennonites who grew up in Mennonite villages in rural Manitoba, Bolivia, and Mexico, and who now call southern Manitoba home, complicate these portrayals. Historical and contemporary engagement with expressive culture – including mimesis, translation, and modulation (to follow Toynbee and Dueck's vocabulary [2011, 12]) – demonstrates that community boundaries are more permeable than frequently conceived, and that Mennonite engagement with "the world" is not a new concept. Instead, while nonconformity has functioned as an important aspect of ethnocultural Mennonite identity, it is part of a gentle cosmopolitanism that has been manifested historically through music, dance, visual art, and recitation, and is also evident in language, foodways, clothing, and other aspects of so-called traditional life.

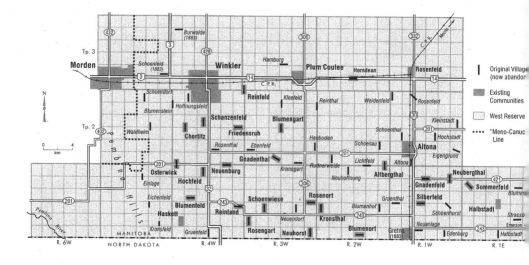

Figure 14.1 | Villages of the West Reserve Mennonite settlement in southern Manitoba.

It is this process of adoption (mimesis) and adaptation (translation), occurring alongside a constant negotiation of values and lived belief (modulation), that forms the basis of this chapter. I examine several forms of expressive culture that demonstrate heterogeneity and permeability within the context of Mennonite experiences in southern Manitoba: a collection of folk dances known as Mennonite circle games, a New Year's Eve mumming tradition, and popular song repertoires within the context of home.

I grew up in Altona, Manitoba, and spent my formative years attending the Altona Bergthaler Mennonite Church. Thus research for this chapter has been shaped by my connection to Mennonites in southern Manitoba; it has also involved archival research, interviews, and participant observation at community events and worship services. Fieldwork has focused on West Reserve settlements of Mennonites in Manitoba (see figure 14.1).[3] The villages established in these settlements were founded, and until the late twentieth century almost exclusively populated, by Anabaptist Mennonites who left Russia/Ukraine in the 1870s seeking religious freedom in Canada.[4]

Mennonite History and Boundary Maintenance

While Christianities are historically connected with one another, and thus many musical repertoires are shared among Christianities, many of the key linkages and expansions within Christian history are the products of schism and difference, which often are marked by the intentional use of musical differentiation as well. (Riley and Dueck 2016, 5)

Yeah, I think we should ask an outsider about our church. They would know better. I would say it's very open, like everybody's welcome and – yikes, I don't know what to say. (Neufeld 2015)

Boundary maintenance has been a central shaping force in the history of ethnocultural Mennonites in Canada, and indeed globally. In each of the major historical Mennonite migrations – from the Netherlands to the Vistula Delta in the sixteenth century, to Russia/Ukraine in the eighteenth century, to Canada in the nineteenth century, and from Canada to Mexico and Paraguay, and on to Bolivia and Belize, in the twentieth century – a primary reason for relocation has been a perceived loss of independence due to government interference in community affairs. Divergent ideas about which boundaries are negotiable and which are not have led to significant tensions within and among Mennonite churches as well.

In Manitoba, the years following the initial 1870s migration represented a period of change. Frictions among conserving[5] and less conserving groups were amplified as Mennonites from different colonies and denominations in Russia/Ukraine began interacting in new Canadian contexts. Some points of divergence were negotiated informally as part of daily interactions while others became divisive and resulted in significant changes such as church mergers, splits, and the creation of new Mennonite denominations.[6]

Negotiations about boundary maintenance and what it means to live faithfully have persisted. In some cases, these negotiations have been tied to social values and priorities that have historically served as distinguishing markers for Mennonites within Manitoba's broader population. For example, Sommerfelder, Old Colony, and Reinland churches[7] continue to be associated with more conserving worship practices (e.g., they do not use musical instruments in the sanctuary), and questions about what it means to live simply continue to inform views on clothing choices, language use, and other lifeways within Mennonite towns and villages. Divergent views about how these aspects of ethnocultural life should be played out have not always been explicit; instead, unspoken interpretations of humility, simplicity, and being "in but not of the world" have often shaped perceptions of Mennonites in and outside of Mennonite communities.

In other cases, negotiating boundaries has put Mennonite communities into direct conflict with government authorities. Perhaps the most significant factor in drawing Mennonites to Manitoba in the nineteenth century was the provision of a *Privilegium* – a promise from the Canadian government of special privileges that would enable Mennonites to live "apart" upon settling in Canada. In addition to exemption from military service and the swearing of oaths, Mennonites were promised free land and the right to manage their own schools (Krahn and Ens 1989, 3). During the course of the First World War, however, many of these privileges came under scrutiny, amplified in no small part by Mennonite pacifism and their use of High and Low German in school, church, and home. Public schools were established by the Manitoba government in Reinländer Mennonite districts at this time, and were perceived by conserving Mennonites as a dangerous encroachment into a primary aspect of church life – the education of its children. According to historian Cornelius Krahn, "not a single [Mennonite] child attended the schools" (1989, 9), only increasing animosity between conserving Mennonites and government authorities. As a result of these and subsequent tensions, a majority of Manitoba's Reinländer Mennonites relocated to Mexico in the 1920s, where they (again) sought to establish communities free from government interference.[8]

During this period of upheaval another wave of Mennonites arrived in Canada, this time the result of civil war in the Soviet Union.[9] Many of these new immigrants, known as Russländer, had been wealthy landowners in Russia who held strong views on matters such as education, music, and other aspects of expressive culture.[10] Their arrival created fertile ground for the continued negotiation of boundaries, values, and priorities between Kanadier Mennonites from the 1870s migration and their new neighbours.[11] Many Russländer settled on farms recently vacated by conserving Reinländer families and, soon after arrival in Canada, took on prominent roles in the public sphere. Victor Carl Friesen notes that on this account "there was a tendency to take them [Russländer Mennonites] as representative of all Mennonites in western Canada even though they were a minority" (1989, 16–17). He goes on to suggest that this was cause for antipathy between some Russländer and Kanadier groups.

This historical portrait of diversity is not contradicted by current expressions of Mennonite-ness in Manitoba. In recent decades new questions and themes have been introduced into Mennonite debates about what faithful living looks like, including, for example, the ordination of women, same-sex marriage, and other LGBTQ issues. Tensions with government authorities continue to arise (though less frequently than in the early twentieth century),[12] and the demographic make-up of so-called "Mennonite communities" continues to shift.[13] Indeed, the negotiation of boundaries amid shared and sometimes conflicting values remains a salient aspect of Mennonite experience.

Permeability and Song Practice: Mimesis, Translation, Modulation

Contestations of clear-cut cultural boundaries are not limited to denominational affiliation and political encounter, but also extend to language and other aspects of expressive culture. In her pivotal 1989 book, *Singing Mennonite*, ethnomusicologist Doreen Helen Klassen examines Low German song practice among Mennonites in Manitoba. This collection of approximately 200 songs is significant not only as a compilation of orally transmitted music that had been largely overlooked in previous studies, but also for Klassen's contextualization of the repertoire and its use of Low German: "It may seem obvious that the singing of Low German songs in Russian and southern Manitoba Mennonite village contexts expresses ethnicity because it includes those who speak the language and excludes those who do not. However, Low German songs convey Mennonite identity in less explicit but equally significant ways, such as through references to ethnic outsiders or through selective borrowing of musical materials from these outsiders" (Klassen 1989, 8). Klassen goes on to suggest that "Mennonites have consistently borrowed melodies from cultures they respected, and ignored the melodies of people they considered culturally inferior" (10). While addressing a specific body of Low German songs, Klassen's allusion to selective cultural borrowing ties in to broader concepts of cultural encounter and imitation. Writing about music and migration, Jason Toynbee and Byron Dueck propose that musical borrowing and appropriation do not necessarily indicate movement toward homogeneity, but can, by contrast, be strategies for cultural persistence (2011, 7). Drawing on Taussig's (1993) theory of mimesis (imitation) and alterity (cultural difference), they suggest that "copying does not necessarily result in sameness. Rather, and perhaps particularly in cases of colonial domination, it affirms and reinstates difference" (2011, 8). Imitation may initially serve as an attempt "to contain a threatening alterity," but this is frequently followed by change and elaboration "in response to the most pressing concerns of the people who have appropriated [the copied object]" (2011, 10). For Toynbee and Dueck, then, the process of copying is closely linked to translation, "a creative move ... with the potential to transform musical practices and sounds into ones that operate or signify in ways quite distinct from their old context" (ibid.); in order for adopted forms of expressive culture to make sense within a new context, they must have meaning within the conceptual and aesthetic frameworks of that context. This is not to imply that expressive culture is simply made up of discrete components that can be selected, mimicked, and translated to suit particular new parameters; rather, modulation is at play: "the dynamism of expressive practices, cultures, and societies – the potential fluidity of the traditional objects of the humanities and social sciences. Scholarly discourse still acknowledges genres and structures, but it is increasingly rare that it depicts them in static ways" (Toynbee and Dueck 2011, 12).

The song practices that form the basis of this chapter demonstrate mimesis, translation, and modulation at work, revealing the porosity of socio-cultural boundaries even as those boundaries are intentionally maintained: English-language folk dances become Mennonite circle games in rural Mennonite villages; the *Brommtopp*, an instrument and mumming tradition, evidences a centuries-long history of mimesis and translation; and unique iterations of popular songs such as "You Are My Sunshine" reveal that boundary maintenance and porosity exist not only at the community level but also among individuals and families. In the following sections, I introduce these song practices in further depth, examining mimesis, translation, and the processes of change (modulation) to which they are connected.

Mennonite Circle Games

The origins of Mennonite circle games are difficult to trace. They are often associated with *Schlüsselbund Lieder*, or "key ring songs," a German-language repertoire believed to have been adopted by Mennonites in Russia (see figure 14.2), and sung to accompany games played by Mennonite youth at *Nokjaste* (Low German, literally "after weddings"), or other informal gatherings.[14]

Schlüsselbund Lieder, however, were never ubiquitous among Mennonites in Manitoba: Kanadier Mennonites of Old Colony or Sommerfelder background more often gathered for informal barn and square dances (Klassen 1989, 174), while others disapproved of the games' conspicuous similarity to dancing. Still, by the 1950s and 1960s, a repertoire of English-language "Mennonite circle games" had become an important social activity for many Mennonite youth in southern Manitoba villages. While these games share

Figure 14.2 | Mennonite youth in Halbstadt (Molotschna, Ukraine), 1914.

some characteristics with *Schlüsselbund Lieder*, the Mennonite circle games played in rural southern Manitoba have distinctive features that implicitly demonstrate the porosity of socio-cultural boundaries in Canada; heterogeneity among Mennonite churches, families, and individuals; and adaptation and change over time. In this section, I explore the origins and related repertoire of this predominantly English-language collection of Mennonite circle games, their relation to dancing vis-à-vis Mennonite values within the context of village life, and the eventual decline of the games in the late 1960s.

Like *Schlüsselbund Lieder* in Russia, Mennonite circle games were most often played at youth socials and village *Nokjaste* in southern Manitoba.[15] In the 1950s and 1960s, when the games were most popular, wedding ceremonies were often held in the mid-afternoon. After the wedding, guests would remain at the church for a shared meal before relocating to the yard of the bride's family where the *Nokjast* was held. This gathering was an opportunity for visiting, eating, performances of music and/or recitations, and the opening of gifts. Circle games were not pre-arranged, but rather happened spontaneously. Songs were sung in unison, and each had a specific set of patterned movements or actions, usually beginning with the formation of a circle. Games could be adapted to larger and smaller groups (numbers usually ranged from twenty to fifty participants), though most involved some partnering and required, variously, even or uneven numbers of men and women. Linking arms, weaving in and out of circle formations, joining raised hands to create arches, creating circles within circles, and shifting between clockwise and counter-clockwise motion were all part of the movement vocabulary. Competence for circle games was not taught, but was rather learned through observation and participation.

A wedding invitation was not required to participate in *Nokjast* activities, which meant that circle games were open to all village youth, whether or not they were directly connected to the wedding pair. Describing her own coming of age in Blumenort, Anne Kehler recalls that "You needed to be a teenager for sure before you started playing. It was frowned on if the younger kids tried to get in there. Like, they could stand at the side and watch and sing, but no way did you get in there! ... It was terribly exciting. Oh, now I'm grown up; I can quit playing with dolls and play adult games! [Laughter]" (2016). For some who grew up watching the games, the shift from observation to participation was relatively easy; for others it proved more challenging. Regional variation was also a potential cause for confusion when youth from different villages gathered (Ens 2016).[16] This was especially evident in "Bingo," where the linking of elbows near the beginning of the game precedes a complete turn with one's partner, followed by a pattern of weaving. If participants differed on which elbow should be linked at the outset, the entire pattern could be thrown off.

Mary Derksen recalls, "'Bingo' was always my favourite, but you had to know how to play it or else you would mess it all up ... And when it works nicely then it looks nice. But, it didn't always because some didn't know how to play it, and then it got mixed up ... That's why I didn't go into 'Bingo' because sort of, sometimes I thought I did it" (2016). Other commonly mentioned songs in the circle game repertoire include "Topsy," "The Old Man Goes a Courting," "Grünes Gras," "Susie Brownie," "Captain Jinks," "Four in a Boat," and "The Old Dusty Miller."[17] "Auld Lang Syne" functioned as a closing song, with participants creating an inward-facing circle, crossing arms, joining hands, and rocking back and forth while singing together.[18]

That most of these songs are English, rather than German, is a significant departure from *Schlüsselbund Lieder*, and speaks to the permeability of community boundaries in rural Mennonite villages. In fact, the only German song associated with circle games in Manitoba that was named during the course of my research was "Grünes Gras" ("Green Grass"). By contrast, two other songs from the repertoire – "Bingo" and "Captain Jinks" – are included in *Dance a While: A Handbook for Folk, Square, Contra, and Social Dance* (Pittman et al. 2009), a provocative link to English-language folk dancing, and

Figure 14.3 | Mennonite circle games at a wedding in southern Manitoba, 2008.

away from any particularly Mennonite roots. When considering the games through a lens of Mennonite pacifism and nonconformity, "Captain Jinks" stands out: it appears in a dance handbook, the military imagery in the song text is blatant, and the circle game that accompanies it includes a salute to one's partner during the first verse:

> When Captain Jinks comes home at night
> He claps his hands with all his might
> Salute your partner so polite
> For that's the style of the army.
>
> Join your hands and forward all
> Forward all, forward all
> Join your hands and forward all
> For that's the style of the army.[19]

While this apparent defiance of Mennonite pacifism and its expression within a dance idiom seem incongruous with Mennonite belief, participants with whom I spoke did not recall concerns being raised about the text or its accompanying movement. Mary Derksen puts it succinctly: "that was just a song and we sang that" (2016).[20]

Despite the prevalence of English-language songs, their unclear origins, and the inclusion of texts (such as "Captain Jinks") that seem inconsistent with Mennonite values, circle games were and continue to be considered "Mennonite" by those familiar with them. As the lack of controversy around the use of military imagery suggests, the significance of the games was tied less to themes and origins than it was to their particular social role within village communities. It is to this social role – and the related question of whether the games were appropriate entertainment for village youth – that I now turn.

Circle Games: "We had to call them something –"

"Mennonites don't have sex because it could lead to dancing." This joke, while crude, points to a longstanding discrepancy between how dance is perceived among various Mennonite groups and how it has functioned historically. Mennonite circle games provide a provocative window into this debate – turning on questions of conformity, sexuality, and faith – as it played out in southern Manitoba during the 1950s and 1960s.

Despite rhetoric that Canadian Mennonites have long viewed dancing as sin and therefore *verboten* (forbidden), narratives from those who grew up in rural communities in Canada, Mexico, and Bolivia suggest that dancing has often been an important social activity for youth. In many conserving Mennonite villages, square dances and other forms of social dance were common. Frieda Sawatzky, for example, describes the openness to dancing experienced by her mother-in-law in Sommerfeld, Manitoba, in the 1930s: "Sunday afternoon is when they danced. Whoever went along [in] the village, and whoever's parents had gone visiting for the day, that's where they cleaned out the living room ... and they danced to their heart's content. But then by 5 o'clock everybody had to go home and do the chores. So they had to put all the furniture back, and they were done" (2016). Responding to Frieda's description, Joyce Falk and Edna Letkeman laugh:

JF: Then we really weren't so far out in my teen years [1960s] when we would be at the Reimer's[21] right?
EL: Dancing up a storm –

JF: But we didn't clean out the living room – we just danced up a storm!
EL: But that was also when Mom and Dad were gone –
JF: That's right. They went to some church function [laughter], and the kids took over. (2016)

For Sara,[22] who grew up as part of the Sommerfeld church in Bolivia before moving to Canada in the late 1980s, dancing was not forbidden, provided that "no gospel songs [were] mixed up with the dancing" (2015). Helena Martens, too, recalls dances from her youth in Bolivia, where she and her sister accompanied dancers with *Putseleeda*[23] on their accordions in the 1990s (2015).

This apparent openness to kitchen and barn dances among conserving Mennonites in rural spaces, however, does not indicate that dancing was not contentious. The story told by Sara about why gospel music and dancing should never mix suggests a complex relationship between sacred and profane within her Bolivian community. In Manitoba, it was dancing itself that came to be suspect, and many who speak of their parents' participation in social dance in the 1930s and 1940s were not, themselves, encouraged to do the same as youth in the 1950s and 1960s:

GRACE HARMS: For us, we weren't encouraged to dance. And yet that was totally [my mother's] past. So where does that come from?
EDNA LETKEMAN: I don't know, there seems to have been a generational thing sort of where all of the sudden it just seemed wrong. Right? 'Cause I know my dad knew how to dance ... But other than that I was never encouraged. Not told *not* to, but I just –
MARGARET KLASSEN: Melvin's dad,[24] he would play [the fiddle] at dances, until a certain point. And then he quit. [Melvin] always says there was a Brunk crusade,[25] and after that they [his family] started going to Sunday school and they quit with dances. (2016)

Evangelical tent meetings such as the Brunk Revivals had a significant impact on communities in rural Manitoba. While emphases on personal salvation, piety, and experiences of conversion were not unfamiliar (especially among those with ties to Mennonite Brethren and other Russian Mennonite churches), for those whose belief systems had long been grounded in faithful living and *gelassenheit* (yieldedness) within the church community, the individualism and moral emphases of revivalist movements led to the questioning of cultural practices not previously considered to be tied to one's faith. Playing the fiddle at barn dances became a "sin."[26]

By the end of the 1950s, the idea that "Mennonites don't dance" was well established in many Mennonite communities. Werner Ens recalls that when he attended teacher's college in Winnipeg in the 1950s, Mennonite students could opt out of the folk dance class. In his words, "I know there were a few of the Mennonite kids who took them, and most of us didn't. At age eighteen, nineteen you are not always that mature that you know what you want or shouldn't do, or do [laughs]" (2016).

During this same period, the navigation of Mennonite values vis-à-vis dance was also underway for postwar European immigrants to urban Canada. Historian Marlene Epp describes how many 1940s immigrants grew up with dancing as part of their lives in Germany, only to discover that it was considered to be at odds with Christian values in much of North America: "even if enjoyed by Canadian Mennonite lay people, dancing was something definitely frowned upon by the leadership, increasingly so in the 1950s" (2000, 172). The debate continued into the 1960s, in some cases leading to the possible loss of church membership (ibid., 173).

Against this backdrop, the popularity of Mennonite circle games takes on added significance. The trick of semantics that made continued involvement in the games possible is not lost on many who participated. When asked for a general description of the games, Werner Ens begins by calling the name a misnomer: "It's not games because in a game you have winners and losers. So they were more like ... we had to call them something because we couldn't call them dances" (2014). Pressed as to whether it was explicit that the word "dance" not be used, Ens goes on: "Well, dancing was wrong so we didn't dance. And some people, there were some groups of Mennonites who frowned on this because this was way too close to dancing" (2014).

It is this tension – between viewing circle games as a healthy and socially sanctioned environment for teenaged youth to interact, and as "too close to dancing" – that has shaped discussions about their propriety. Marlene Ens, who is married to Werner and grew up in the village of Gnadenthal, describes a personal struggle about whether or not to participate in the games when she was a teenager. While Werner jokes that he "corrupted her," Marlene is sincere in her memory of having felt pressure not to participate: "I guess there were some people in my life that suggested that that was not a good idea" (2014). As Werner observed, this "peer pressure of a kind" (2016) could impact one's friendships; no small matter in the context of village life, where social circles are closely knit.

Whereas the "potential for sexual stimulation" associated with dancing was cited as a point of concern among Mennonite churches as late as 1990 (Becker 1990), circle games seem to have occupied a middle ground. A discussion with several women who grew up in rural Manitoba about why circle games were considered acceptable and dancing was not elicited an exchange that playfully illustrates the multiple and varied ways that the games could be interpreted:

SUSAN DUECK: Just remember, dancing wasn't allowed, but circle games were. The alternative to dancing…
JUDITH KLASSEN: So how did that work?
GRACE HARMS: Well you never were together like this [gestures with her hands facing each other]. Your bodies were never together. Side by side, arms linking, or backs turning –
EDNA LETKEMAN: Except that it was dark and there were cars and – [laughter]. There was "together" all right! (2016)

A similar playfulness emerges in Anne Kehler's memory of her husband, Menno Kehler, and his impression of the games. While he initially considered them "childish" when compared with the social dancing in his home village of Neubergthal, Anne describes how he and his friends "enjoyed it as much as anybody else did" once they joined in. She goes on: "And if they weren't participating they were standing and watching. Like there was usually a yard light in the middle, and in those days those very thin dresses were in style, those nylon ones? I know Henry Fehr[27] ... he would say exactly which girls all had nice legs [laughs]. So they had their own fun!" According to Anne, "coupling" was closely watched, and if two people were together for every game, "oh ja, [daut] jeft bald kjast"[28] (2016).

"If cars wouldn't have been invented, maybe we would still be doing circle games –"[29]

By the mid-1960s, the popularity of Mennonite circle games had begun to wane in southern Manitoba. While the view that they were considered "too much like dancing" and the increasing popularity of evening weddings (and resulting decrease in *Nokjaste*) are both cited as potential contributors to their decline, the most common reason offered can be summed up in a single word: cars. "Well, when we were growing up it was rare to have somebody who was 18, 16, or 17 to have a car, or access to a car. And if they did, then 'OK, there's a wedding in Gnadenthal, let's go and play games over there – Albert, can you get the car tonight?' And we'd pile in and go, type of stuff. When … in the late 50s it became fairly popular for guys to get their car, they could pick up their girl and go and whatever … Yeah they were still at weddings but it seemed to be petering down a little bit" (Werner Ens 2016). This sentiment was repeated frequently when discussing the decline of circle games in southern Manitoba villages, as decisions about entertainment and social engagement were no longer shaped by what was within reasonable distance for walking, biking, or horseback. Of course, this impact was not limited to circle games: "I mean, country stores have all closed because everybody goes to town because it's cheaper, and there's more variety, and so on. And you can't compete. And you have less community activity because, 'I can go and watch this here in Winkler,' 'I can go to the ball game,' 'I can go to the hockey game – I can do this, I can do that.' So yeah, the transportation certainly has made a huge difference" (ibid.).

The impact of transportation demonstrates more than the presence of permeability, change, and adaptation in rural Mennonite communities in Manitoba. It also illustrates the close, though often unnamed, links between values and daily life in those communities. The increased traffic out of rural villages for entertainment was not an intentional weakening of community ties, but interviews suggest that it nevertheless resulted in an increasingly individualistic understanding of social engagement and activity. This is not to say that the end of circle game popularity was considered a dire reflection on the state of rural communities, but many describe related changes in terms of loss.

Circle games demonstrate the constant navigation of values within the context of Mennonite community life in rural Manitoba. While the predominance of English-language repertoires and the presence of military imagery clearly indicate twentieth-century adaptations to earlier traditions, Mennonite circle games have nevertheless been perceived (and celebrated) as "Mennonite" among participants. Tensions regarding the propriety of the games reflect heterogeneity at community, family, and individual levels, but it is noteworthy that these are framed by participants as negotiating what faithful living looked like, rather than being tied to boundary maintenance. That is to say, the mimetic act was not questioned; rather, it was the nature of translation and modulation that required navigation. Here, the integration and elaboration of circle games within the context of rural village life demonstrates the translation of English-language repertoires to a new context. In this case, the modulation, or "potential fluidity of traditional objects," is em-

Figure 14.4 | Jacob K. Schwartz with the *Brommtopp* he built for Neubergthal's centennial celebration in 1976.

bodied in the adoption and subsequent decline of Mennonite circle games in rural communities.

Brommtopp

The *Brommtopp* is a type of friction drum that was used by Mennonite youth in parts of southern Manitoba as part of a New Year's Eve mumming tradition. While specific details vary from one account to another, most *Brommtopp* troupes were made up of young men (numbering from four to "as many as you could get"), who would build a *Brommtopp*, learn several seasonal songs and verses, and spend New Year's Eve making village house visits and performing for those willing to invite them in. *Brommtoppspäla* (*Brommtopp* players) wore costumes that disguised their identities and usually travelled by sleigh or by foot.[30] This meant that they could not travel a great distance in a single night and, according to some, stayed warm by consuming alcohol en route. Upon arrival at a house, *Brommtoppspäla* would knock on a window to request entry: *"Kjanen dee nei joasch sanga nan kommi?"*[31] Once inside, they would lean the *Brommtopp* against an interior door to begin their performance. The instrument – made from a barrel and requiring resin and water to activate its horsehair tassel – made a loud rumbling sound and was used to accompany "The *Brommtopp* Song." The noise that ensued, combined with performer disguises, elicited responses ranging from fear to fascination, irritation to amusement. Following a performance, members of the household would usually offer the *Brommtoppspäla* some *Porzeltje* (New Year's fritters), liquor, and, in some instances, a few coins in thanks.

A precise history of the *Brommtopp* is difficult to trace; however, both the instrument and Mennonite mumming are believed to have roots that extend to the sixteenth century. Barbara Boock, of the Deutsches Volksliedarchiv in Freiburg, Germany, affirms that the *"Brummtopf"* (or *"Rummelpott"*) is connected to New Year's Eve and *Fastnacht* (eve of Lent) in northern Germany and the Netherlands (personal communication 2004); friction drums are also found in Poland and Ukraine, and the most common versions of "The *Brommtopp* Song" in Canada are variants on a Werder Platt text that has been traced back to the Vistula Delta.[32] It is believed that the custom travelled with the Mennonites to the Vistula Delta from the Netherlands in the mid-sixteenth century, from the Vistula Delta to Prussia in the 1780s, and finally to Canada in the 1870s.[33]

Not all Mennonites in Manitoba are familiar with the *Brommtopp*. The custom is most closely tied to those associated with the 1870s Bergthaler migration from Russia; on Manitoba's West Reserve, this includes Bergthaler and Sommerfelder Mennonites.[34] In the course of my field research on the West Reserve in 2004 and again in 2014–16, the villages identified with the *Brommtopp* included Blumenfeld, Blumenthal, Gnadenthal, Halbstadt, Hochfeld, Neubergthal, Neuenburg, Plum Coulee, Schoenthal, and Sommerfeld (see figure 14.1), as well as the Amsterdam School District (located near Rosenfeld).[35] Despite a history extending over four centuries and dating back to the earliest days of the Mennonite church, the popularity of the *Brommtopp* dwindled in Manitoba by the late 1950s; in the twenty-first century, the instrument is performed only rarely, and predominantly at public events.

Despite the relative brevity of the *Brommtopp*'s active life in Manitoba when compared with its centuries' long history, the music, clothing, and performance associated with the custom in twentieth-century Canada demonstrate mimesis, translation, modulation, and the permeability of community boundaries.

"The Brommtopp Song"

During the course of my fieldwork, I came across numerous iterations of "The *Brommtopp* Song." Despite differences in spelling, each maintains strong connections to the Werder Platt version (Rosenberg's "*Brommtopps Leet*"), with variation occurring in dialect, verse order, and thematic content.[36]

"Brommtopps Leet"[37]	"The *Brommtopp* Song"
Wie kome hia häa one irjent Spott,	We come here to you without making fun,
En scheena good'nowent jeft ons Gott;	A nice good evening give us God;
En scheena good'nowent, ne freelijche Tiet,	A nice good evening and a happy time,
Dee ons dee Brommtopp haft jeliet.	Which the *Brommtopp* can provide.
Wie wensche däm Harn en gooden Desch,	We wish the master a well-laden table,
Opp aule fea Akje en jebrodna Fesch;	On all four corners a good fried fish;
Enne Medd 'ne Kruck met goldna Wien,	In the middle a jug with golden wine,
Doa kjemt dee Har met Lost doabie.	With that the master may jolly be.
Wie wensche de Frü 'ne goldne Kroon,	We wish the mistress a golden crown,
Onn ferr't Joa en junga Sän.	And in the coming year a fine young son.
Wie wensche däm Sän en jesoldeldet Peat,	We wish the son a saddled horse,
En poa Pistoole onn en blanket Schweat.	A pair of pistols and a shining sword.
Wie wensche daut Mäakje selwane Fadadoos,	We wish the daughter a silver pencil case,
Onn näakjst Joa en junga Matroos.	In the coming year, a fine young general.
Wie wensche däm Kjnajcht ne Schrop onn ne Schea,	We wish the hired man a currycomb and shears,

Daut hee kaun putse däm Har siene Pead.	So he may groom the master's horse.
Wie wensche dee Kjäakjsche en rooda Rock,	We wish the kitchen maid a red skirt,
Onn dan omm'n Joa eent mett'm Bassemstock.	And during the year (a licking with) the broomstick.
Wie wensche däm Koohoad ne Scheffel enne Henj,	We wish the cowherd a shovel in hand,
Daut hee kaun foare dän Growe felengd.	So he can work the length of the ditch.

When comparing Manitoba Mennonite variants to the Werder Platt text, a notable adaptation can be observed in the removal of military imagery. Whereas the Werder Platt version wishes the daughter *"en junga Matroos"* ("a fine young general"), southern Manitoba variants in High German remove the general from the text, usually replacing him with *"einen hübsch jungen Mann"* ("a handsome young man"). This alteration is in keeping with Mennonite pacifism, and could be read as a translation of the text to reflect Mennonite non-violence and the separation of church and state. However, because the song has been predominantly passed on through oral transmission, most Mennonites in Manitoba are unfamiliar with the earlier Werder Platt text and would not be aware of this shift. Additionally, this interpretation does not fully account for the retention of references to "pistol and sword" as wishes for the son. While not explicitly militaristic, these are nonetheless weapons of violence and somewhat weaken a reading of the Mennonite variant as explicitly pacifist.

Other textual variants subvert the power structure presented in the Werder Platt text. For example, while the wishes expressed in the *"Brommtopps Leet"* strengthen the position of the family in power (e.g., good things for the master, his wife, and their children; work equipment for the hired hands, and a "licking" with the broom for the hired girl), the version known to Agnes Toews[38] places the hired hand in a defiant position that disrupts the existing authority structure:

Den Knecht den wünschen wir eine Schaufel in der Hand,
das er kann schmettern den Kuhscheis an der Wand.

The farmhand we wish a shovel in the hand,
so that he can dash cow shit on the wall.

When read within the context of Mennonite values that emphasize humility, community, and the priesthood of all believers, this alteration stands out. Whether intentionally political or not, the variant's subversive text is provocative and speaks to the dynamic nature of expressive forms and the varied contexts in which *translation* becomes meaningful. Here, the parameters of Mennonite village life are shown to extend beyond church and home, beyond family and congregation, to encompass critiques of class and power.

Perhaps the most noteworthy alteration to the text appears in the final stanza of a common variant identified in southern Manitoba. Again, quoting the version known to Agnes Toews:

Wir ziehen das Schnur wohl über das Haus, wohl über das Haus,
Da sprangen drei schwarz braune Mädchen heraus.
Die Mädchen wollen wir lieben und ehren,
Auf das sie uns gute Gaben verehren.

We draw a band across the house, across the house,
And three brown maidens bounded out.
These maidens we want to love and honour,
So that they will admire our gifts.

The origins of this stanza are not clear; however, references to *schwarz braune Mädchen*, *schwarzbraune Jungfern*, or *schwart-braune Maddels*, appear in three of five (known) variants associated with southern Manitoba *Brommtopp*.[39] Interactions between Mennonites and First Nations and Metis people in Manitoba were frequent when Mennonites first immigrated to Canada and may explain this reference to "*schwarz braune Mädchen.*" Folklorists Fehr and Greenhill describe the text and its performance as implying "cross-ethnic, or cross-racial identity" (2011, 164) and potentially racist, particularly when paired with early twentieth-century costume choices that at times reflected cultural stereotypes. Such an analysis underscores the complex history of migration in southern Manitoba and the settling of Canada's western provinces more broadly, as well as the upheaval and displacement to which that colonial history is linked. This context also draws attention to the social and political significance of textual variants in so-called traditional song forms. As a result of increasing sensitivity to the impacts of cross-cultural encounter, several staged performances of the *Brommtopp* in recent years have seen *Brommtopp-späla* alter this stanza of the text such that three *pretty* maidens (drei *hübsche* Mädchen), rather than three brown maidens (drei *schwarz braune* Mädchen), appear.[40] Again, translation and modulation play out in relation to shifting social, cultural, and geographic contexts.

Melodically, it is more difficult to analyze relationships, as only two published accounts (Friesen 1989, 82–3, and Toews 1977, 305), one archival recording (MHA 1976),[41] and several recent field recordings of Manitoba revival performances include melodies. While the lyrical phrase lengths in various song texts are consistent (implying metrical symmetry in musical performance), and each of the recorded versions follows a similar chord structure (moving from the dominant to the tonic each time "*den Brommtopp*" is sung), the rhythmic patterns and melodies presented by Friesen, Toews, and in the Mennonite Heritage Archives recordings differ from one another, suggesting regional variation.

Interviews support this hypothesis. Recalling Neubergthal's centennial celebration in July 1976, Menno Kehler observes that the participants his troupe had recruited from Halbstadt "[came] from only eight miles away, yet their song was different" (2004). Johnny Kehler also alludes to variation, even within a single troupe: "It was more, almost like when you sing hymns, like the end of a sentence, some guys would draw it out a little further than the other people ... and you see that even in churches, some of the songs, some people will sing a little different than the other ones but the words would be the same" (2004).

Clothing: Disguise

The costumes worn by *Brommtoppspäla* are said to have significantly shaped the reception of the *Brommtopp* and its players. Some accounts assign very specific roles to participants;[42] others, such as those that emerged in the course of my own field research, suggest a much less formal relationship between specific roles and costumes. Many referred to masks or painted faces; also described were clowns and men wearing dresses. "Everyone would dress up [so] that nobody would know them. And I know that Uncle Dave, he usually dressed up like a cowboy. And he would make himself something that looked a bit like a horse, you know, put a horse's head on top of it, and then he would be strictly in gear, with all, put all the gear that they needed as a cowboy, and he would ride that horse into this house ... And one would be an RCMP, one would be something else. Whatever they wanted, whatever they wanted to be ... then of course, you didn't know them ... They'd paint up their faces. They would paint them up so that you wouldn't have a clue who

Figure 14.5 | *Brommtopp* troupe from Amsterdam School District near Rosenfeld, Manitoba, in the late 1920s.

they were" (Schulz 2004). For Johnny Kehler, who participated in a troupe in Neubergthal as a youth, the ability to conceal one's identity was more important than the specific details of a costume: "Of course ... you would dress up, eh? You know, you would get your face painted – wear different clothes. It was sort of a New Year's tradition type of thing that people wouldn't really know who you were ... You'd put an old shirt on, or coveralls – look like an old farmer. Or, you'd paint your face – whatever, you know? Whatever suited. Just to look different" (2004). Anne Kehler's account reflects an even less formal impetus: "Well, sometimes it was as simple as turning your jacket inside out. And then maybe putting something weird on, pinning something weird on there. Or they would find an old toque and poke holes into it, and pull it over their face so they just had the holes, and then, when they were singing that toque would always move [laughs], and yeah, things like that ... Their faces were usually covered. And if they weren't covered they had painted them" (2016). Describing changes that she observed in Neubergthal starting in the

1960s, Anne goes on to suggest that the emphasis on costumes as disguise declined gradually, as house visits ended and the performance context for *Brommtopp* troupes shifted to staged performances at community events: "And I know for some of them, at the beginning, they still got dressed up and did the face painting and all that, but as the men grew older, they didn't want to do that anymore ... Did they think it was childish or what? I don't know. Or was it just too much work?" (2016).

Fehr and Greenhill frame the clothing and character choices of *Brommtoppspäla* in terms of gender drag and ethnic drag (2011, 147).[43] Describing revival performances of the *Brommtopp* in southern Manitoba, they suggest that "the transgendered costumed men mark their performative non-performance of womanhood by wearing their jeans or dress pants under their skirts and aprons, as well as by leaving on their everyday men's shoes" (2011, 159). Taking this a step further, they assert that "racial and ethnic anxieties were ... manifested through imitation in historical *Brommtopp* performances," and that images of historical troupes "invoke the actual marginalisation of ethnoracial minorities in historic and present-day Manitoba" (2011, 165). This critique draws attention to sensitive aspects of cultural performance and power. Cognisance of the multifaceted impacts of permeable boundaries and cross-cultural encounter is an important aspect of any related analysis. Still, it is imperative that social markers such as class, as well as individual experience(s) and expressions, are taken into account. Here, the concept of mimetic processes as those "by which musical styles move across cultural boundaries and power differentials" (Dueck 2011, 201) is valuable, as it accounts for shifting and variable power relationships. Images of *Brommtoppspäla* from the early twentieth century are jarring for the disguised and sometimes racialized bodies they present, but the power differentials at play within the context of rural Manitoba in the early twentieth century are more complex than simple charges of racism and homophobia allow.

Responses to disguised performers were varied and sometimes intense. While some anticipated the arrival and performance of the *Brommtoppspäla* with amusement, others – especially children – resented the fear that came with the transformation of a familiar environment into one of uncertainty:[44] "It just put the fear of the Lord in you because you just didn't know why they were dressed so – they were really awful, there was nothing pretty about the costumes, and they wore facemasks and stuff and made a lot of noise. And as children we weren't allowed to do that, and then for these adults to come and dominate a place or a space, that was yours ..., then it was like – what is this all about? What is the point of this, you know?" (Harms 2016).

Brommtopp *Decline*

The decline of the *Brommtopp* in Manitoba has been attributed to several factors, each consistent with a concept of modulation that recognizes the dynamic nature of expressive forms. As with circle games, an increase in entertainment options afforded by the influx of automobiles among youth lessened the need for collective, village-initiated activities – *Brommtoppspäla* no longer needed to create their own fun. Youth were not the only actors in this shift, however. The custom of New Year's Eve house visiting required not only performers who would prepare a *Brommtopp*, dress up in disguise, and make the journey through the village; *Brommtoppspäla* also needed to be invited in, and this became less common. As the quality of village homes improved, there was less interest in cleaning up the water, resin, and melted snow tracked in with the *Brommtoppspäla*.[45] At the same time, as villages diversified and Mennonites from various denominations came to live next to one another, familiarity with, and a common understanding of, the custom could no longer be assumed: why invite strangers into your home to make a mess, frighten your children, all the while in disguise and possibly under the influence of alcohol? Thus the decline of *Brommtopp* marks the changing face of village life, not only among youth but also among the broader village population. Whether tied to moral values (e.g., alcohol consumption) or less tangible shifts such as increasing individualism and changing demographics, it is evident that permeability vis-à-vis populations, technologies, and beliefs led to an alteration in the village fabric; what was once a playful, if at times bawdy, custom could no longer be translated into a form that was comprehensible to its community.

"You Are My Sunshine": Mimesis and Translation in Popular Music

In both Mennonite circle games and *Brommtopp*, access to entertainments outside the village and a related shift toward individualism have been cited as factors in their decline. It is simplistic, however, to assume a facile causal relationship. While engagement with popular entertainment such as music is often linked to individual experience and preference (particularly when juxtaposed with collective song practices that require the involvement of multiple participants), it is also possible for popular repertoires to be adopted, translated, and made dynamically meaningful within familial and community contexts. That music making among many Mennonite families is important is not a new observation (Klassen 1989; Klassen 2007/2008; 2009), and there are numerous popular genres and repertoires that have been used by Mennonites within the context of home. During the course of my fieldwork in southern Manitoba, "You Are My Sunshine" emerged as an example of modulation wherein engagement with a popular song was both individually meaningful and supportive of family and community ties.

I focus here on "You Are My Sunshine" because it was named, without prompting, by many of the people with whom I spoke during the course of my research. While not identified as particularly "Mennonite," the popularity of the song, combined with its multivalence within the context of home and family, demonstrates the continued mimesis and translation, adoption and adaptation, of diverse expressive forms among diasporic Mennonites in new environments.

History and Context

Historically, the relationship between Mennonites and "music" has proven complex. During the Christian Reformation of the sixteenth century, Anabaptists felt that Martin Luther had not gone far enough in separating church and state, and that church should be enacted through a daily life of voluntary obedience, grounded in pacifism, discipleship, and Christian community.[46] Within the context of worship, musical instruments and even singing in parts were rejected as a distraction from humility before God; also rejected were the icons, hierarchy, liturgy, and rituals of the Roman Catholic Church, resulting in persecution and charges of heresy. Among some conserving Mennonite groups, the forbidding of *Musik* (High German, "music") – referring to music that involves musical instruments, recorded musical sound, and related technologies – has continued for centuries. In southern Manitoba, *Musik* was forbidden among Reinländer/Old Colony Mennonites in the first half of the twentieth century, though it was not uncommon for musical instruments, gramophones, and radios to be kept secretly. While access to popular repertoires through live performances and diverse media (including radios, CDs, and other digital formats) in daily life is now commonplace, some conserving churches in southern Manitoba continue to avoid the use of instruments and electronic amplification in their sanctuaries.

How does this connect with "You Are My Sunshine"? While simplistic readings often associate popular music with individualism and so-called mainstream culture, the adoption of popular repertoires in the context of Mennonite family life echoes, in many instances, the processes of mimesis, translation, and modulation that have shaped the historical development of Mennonite expressive culture. As in the Netherlands and Russia, permeable boundaries create opportunity not only for access to alternative modes of expression but also for the adoption and shaping of those modes such that they become meaningful in the context of individual, family, and community life. It is here that "You Are My Sunshine" becomes compelling. First recorded by the Pine Ridge Boys in 1939,[47] the song has since been recorded by musicians as diverse as Gene Autry, Bing Crosby, Aretha Franklin, Anne Murray, and Brian Wilson, among many others. While the ubiquity of "You Are My Sunshine" in English North America is significant, it is the song's translation into the context of Mennonite family life and the related assignation of diverse meanings within local, individual, and familial spaces that make it relevant to this study. Associated variously with collective listening to gramophone records, with family music making, and with the use of music to articulate what was difficult to say in plain language, the varied and multiple adaptations of "You Are My Sunshine" demonstrate the heterogeneity of Mennonite communities and families in the process of translation.

"You Are My Sunshine": Vignette #1

In 1963, Andrew Hamm of Neubergthal, Manitoba, was recorded by Kenneth Peacock for the National Museum of Canada (now the Canadian Museum of History). Transcriptions of several High and Low German folk songs were subsequently included in Peacock's *Twenty Ethnic Songs from Western Canada* (1966). Writing about this encounter, Peacock describes Hamm as "one of the liveliest and most witty informants I have met anywhere," and suggests that his pre-conceived idea of Mennonites as "serious, even dour, people" was challenged in southern Manitoba (1966, 49). During my own conversation with Hamm's daughter, Susan Fehr, in 2014, the vital place of music within the context of village and family was substantiated. In addition to descriptions of square dances and memories of her father singing together with his sister, Mary Loewen, Susan recalls with laughter, "our house was a singing house. We had a gramophone with records and we played records and sang from records and stuff like that." When asked if she could recall songs that they would have listened to, "You Are My Sunshine" is the first that Susan names.

"You Are My Sunshine": Vignette #2

Bill Stoesz grew up on a farm near Lowe Farm, Manitoba, and does not remember singing together as a family, except at the Christmas gathering when it was important to his mother that they sing Christmas songs. He does recall, however, his mother playing the chord organ and his father, the harmonica. (Bill's father would secretly practise his songs in the barn after Bill and his siblings had finished the chores and were not around.) When asked what sorts of music his parents would play, the first song that Bill names is "You Are My Sunshine" (2016).

"You Are My Sunshine": Vignette #3

Margaret Neufeld moved from Mexico to Manitoba as a new mother in the early 2000s. Recounting her childhood in Mexico's northern region, she describes how her father played the *Trajchharmonie* (accordion/concertina) while singing with her and her siblings. Most of the songs were Spanish, but Margaret also recalls an English song in this repertoire: "Yeah, he played that very beautiful. And my favourite song that we all would sing together when Dad would play the *Trajchharmonie*, it would be 'You Are My Sunshine'" (2015).

"You Are My Sunshine": Vignette #4

For Margaretha Friesen, who moved to Canada from Mexico as a teenager in the 1980s, *"Dü bess mien Sonneschien"* (Low German; "You Are My Sunshine") is a lullaby. "My mom often, when we were sick, then she often sat beside our bed and sang that song in Low German, 'You Are My Sunshine.' And that I always kept singing to our children" (2015). The Low German version of the song that Margaretha has carried with her over the years resembles the chorus of the English original in places, but also reflects variation within the context of family nurture:

Dü bess mien Sonneschien, mien leewja Sonneschien,	You are my sunshine, my dearest sunshine,
Dü moakst mie schaftijch wann dee Sonne schient,	You make me happy when the sun shines,
Dü moakst mie schaftijch wann dü [lach no] mie,	You make me happy when you [smile at] me,
Dü bess mien Sonneschien, mien leewja Sonneschien,	You are my sunshine, my dearest sunshine,
Dü moakst mie schaftijch wann dü erschlaft,	You make me happy when you sleep,
Dü moakst mie schaftijch wann dü opp'stähst,	You make me happy when you awake,
Dü moakst mie schaftijch wann ekj dü see.	You make me happy when I see you.
Dü bess mien Sonneschien, mien leewja Sonneschien,	You are my sunshine, my dearest sunshine,
Dü moakst mie schaftijch soo daut ekj mott roarn,	You make me happy so that I must cry,
Dü bess mien Sonneschien, dü bess mien Sonneschien,	You are my sunshine, you are my sunshine,
Mien eewje, leewje Sonneschein.[48]	My eternal, dearest sunshine.

Like the original, Margaretha's variation juxtaposes happiness and sunshine with tears. Read within the context of a conserving Mennonite home, however, the repeating line "*Dü bess mien Sonneschien, mien leewja Sonneschien,*" takes on additional significance. In Jack Thiessen's *Mennonite Low German Dictionary*, the verb *leewe* – from which *leewja* takes its meaning – is defined as "to love, but this verb is never used by [Mennonite Low German] speakers" (2003, 139). Margaretha's subsequent explication of the importance of the song in her own life echoes this commentary: "That is my mom's way of saying; the way we grew up we didn't learn to tell people how much we loved each other. So I guess when I think back, I think that was my mom's way of letting us know how much she loved us... So that was very special. That's, I guess, the reason I have written it down and I want to remember it forever" (2015).

Margaretha's association with "You Are My Sunshine" is highly personal, while at the same time demonstrating diasporic movement, modulation, and persistence across generations. The popular American song was introduced to Margaretha by her mother in Mexico, then travelled with her to Canada where she continued to sing it to her own children. The expression of affection that was not possible in plain language is enabled here through the Low German translation of the song. On one hand, the translation is literal: an English song (loosely) rendered in Low German. Also at play, however, is the creative transformation of musical practices and sounds "into ones that operate or signify in ways quite different from their old context" (Toynbee and Dueck 2011, 8). Here, the popular song "becomes familiar" and is "elaborated in response to the most pressing concerns of the people who have appropriated it" (ibid., 10). In their adoption and adaptation of "You Are My Sunshine," Margaretha and her mother not only translate the text for a new linguistic (Low German) and contextual use (as a song of comfort in the setting of home); they also challenge the norms of that very language and context by using the song to express affection in settings of familial intimacy.

Conclusions

> The creative uses of sound, then, will be recognized both for their potential to mark boundaries and to cross them, to facilitate entitivity and to shift the emphasis to connectivity. (Diamond 1994, 16)

> And we still don't do any dancing. But I do look on it different now than I have been raised. I think there's absolutely good dancing and there's bad dancing. Like we have gone to the [First Nations] reserve a few times and watched their powwows. It's very beautiful dancing and it's good dancing. (Neufeld 2015)

> Something that's tradition, has a beginning and an end, right?... And I often feel, like even with the *Brommtopp* and a lot of these things, like there is a beginning and there's an end. You know? And then things change. (Letkeman 2016)

Challenging the notion that cosmopolitanism is unique to urban spaces, Byron Dueck writes, "unacknowledged cosmopolitanisms are hidden everywhere, all the more easily ignored when they seem to be manifestations of the traditional, the rural or the sacred" (2011, 199). In this chapter, Mennonite circle games, the *Brommtopp*, and a popular song from the 1930s demonstrate the dynamism of expressive forms within the context of ethnocultural Mennonite life in rural Manitoba. In each case, a series of mimetic acts led to the adoption of a particular practice or repertoire that was subsequently translated such that it could be comprehended and made meaningful in new social and cultural spaces. In the case of "You Are My Sunshine," this involved the literal and performative translation of a popular song into Mennonite contexts; with Mennonite circle games, it was the reconfiguring of conceptual space that enabled a translation of the games that side-stepped a direct link to dancing and thus rendered them palatable to the broader community; the *Brommtopp*, by contrast, faced challenges in translation as the custom became increasingly less comprehensible to a shifting body of village members.

Of course, these translations were not singular and discrete happenings that occurred along a linear trajectory. Rather, they contribute to larger processes of social and cultural engagement, of change and modulation. While the *Brommtopp* and Mennonite circle games are no longer tangibly linked to specific seasonal festivals or rites of passage among southern Manitoba Mennonites, the modulation of their place within the communities in which they were once formative evidences "the potential fluidity" to which Toynbee and Dueck refer (2011, 12). Here, "You Are My Sunshine" is significant not only for its adoption in heterogeneous Mennonite family settings (though this stands out), but also for its ability to become meaningful in a new context while shaping and challenging the normative parameters of that context. This is not a question of exposure to influences from outside a particular Mennonite community, but rather a demonstration of the active engagement of individuals and families in dynamically creating the communities they inhabit – being influenced by, but also exerting influence upon, the environments around them. As Toynbee and Dueck observe, and as Diamond and Witmer have articulated before, it is not only expressive practices that are dynamic but also social identities (Diamond and Witmer 1994, 303) and the cultural and societal frameworks in which they become meaningful (Toynbee and Dueck 2011, 12).

Notes

1 I use "ethnocultural" here to refer to Mennonites whose historical connection to the early Mennonite church is manifested through shared aspects of lifeways and expressive culture.
2 Consider, for example, *Pure*, a mini-series on CBC television's 2017 line-up. The series conflates ethnocultural characteristics from diverse and distinct Mennonite communities (clothing, language, etc.), while depicting a sensationalized narrative of drug smuggling among conserving rural Mennonites in Canada, framed as the collision of

"religious vs secular, rural vs urban, plain vs materialistic" worlds (Nova Scotia Business Inc. 2016).

3   During the course of my fieldwork, I interviewed Mennonites with past or current associations with the West Reserve villages of Blumenfeld, Blumenort, Gnadenthal, Halbstadt, Kronsthal, Neubergthal, Reinfeld, Reinland, Sommerfeld, the town of Altona, and the city of Winkler. Church affiliations were varied, including past or present connections to Mennonite denominations such as Bergthaler, Blumenorter, Old Colony, Reinland, Kleine Gemeinde, Sommerfelder, Evangelical Mennonite Mission Church (EMMC), and Rudnerwieder congregations, in addition to several churches that formed as a result of more recent congregational splits (e.g., Seeds Church in Altona, established in the 1990s; Zion Mennonite Church in Schanzenfeld, established in 1980). Special thanks to all those who welcomed me into their homes and archives, and to Jaime Friesen Pankratz and the adult English literacy class at Regional Connections in Winkler, MB; it was a gift to meet and to learn from you.

4   For a detailed historical overview of Mennonite settlements in Manitoba, see Friesen 2007.

5   Drawing on the work of John J. Friesen (2004, 140), and as I have done in previous publications (2009; 2016), I use "conserving" rather than "conservative" to emphasize the intentional and ongoing nature of boundary maintenance among conserving Mennonites.

6   For example, disagreements between Bergthaler and Reinländer Mennonites (two groups who migrated to southern Manitoba in the 1870s) over the use of songbooks and style of singing in worship became divisive and resulted in their inability to worship together (Krahn and Ens 1989, 5).

7   The initial conserving Mennonites of the West Reserve were known as Reinländer Mennonites. After the majority of this group relocated to Mexico from Canada in the 1920s, those who remained behind eventually reorganized and came to be known as Old Colony Mennonites (Friesen 2007, 29). The Reinland Mennonite Church currently active in Manitoba is not directly related to these Reinländer and Old Colony groups (Loewen Reimer 2008, 75).

8   Two-thirds of Reinländer church members left Canada at this time. Old Colonists who remained in Manitoba were initially without leadership, but reorganized in 1937 under the direction of Jacob J. Froese (Friesen 2007, 77).

9   See Friesen (2007, 64–71) for an overview of the unrest (c. 1918–20) that led to Russian Mennonites seeking immigration to Canada in the 1920s.

10 Choral singing and orchestral music received a strong boost with the arrival of Russländer immigrants in the 1920s (Berg 1985; Friesen 2007, 94–6).

11 Mennonites who left Russia in the 1920s are frequently referred to as Russländer Mennonites, while those who arrived in the earlier 1870s migration are called Kanadier Mennonites.

12 A 2012 warning from the Canada Revenue Agency (CRA) to the *Canadian Mennonite* magazine underscores the ongoing potential for tensions between Mennonites and federal authorities. Citing articles in the magazine (including an editorial that encouraged readers to keep Mennonite values of pacifism, social justice, and environmentalism in mind when voting in an upcoming federal election), the CRA reminded the *Canadian*

Mennonite that "partisan political activities" could jeopardize its charitable status. The response of editor and publisher Dick Benner encapsulates the tension between church and state, between lived belief and political activism, precisely: "I didn't see this as political advocacy because we were speaking out of our core beliefs" (CBC News Manitoba 2012; see also DeGurse 2012).

13 The town of Altona, Manitoba, for example, welcomed five Syrian refugee families in 2016, increasing its population by 1 percent (Anderssen 2016).

14 *Schlüsselbund Lieder* were sung primarily in High German, with Low German verses added "usually with the intent of teasing an individual or a couple" (Klassen 1989, 173). Doreen Klassen suggests that the name may have come from the rattling of keys that signalled the choosing of partners in these games (ibid.). A similar origin is described by Norma Jost Voth, who suggests that during the *Schlüsselbund* game, a girl with keys on a ring traversed a circle of youth to seek out a male partner; when chosen, she started a song and jingled the key ring to signal that all girls should find a boy with whom to walk. When she dropped the keys, all rushed for a seat and the one left without a chair took the keys to start the game again (1991, 147–8).

15 During the course of my fieldwork, interviewees remembered circle games being part of wedding celebrations in Blumenfeld, Blumenort, Gnadenthal, Kronsgart, Kronsthal, Reinfeld, and Reinland. I was unable to locate any photos of circle games from the 1950s and 1960s. One respondent wondered if this was, perhaps, a result of their being frowned upon for their association with dancing and therefore not documented. The photo in figure 14.3 is from a 2008 wedding in Altona, MB, where Werner and Marlene Ens were invited to lead the games at the reception hall.

16 Werner Ens, who participated extensively in the games as a youth and who led them while a teacher at the Mennonite Collegiate Institute in Gretna, Manitoba, recalls that "those from the west [Boissevain, Killarney] did them differently than we did them" (2016).

17 A published collection of Mennonite circle games does not exist; however, Werner Ens has compiled an unpublished selection of circle games songs and descriptions of their accompanying movements.

18 "Bingo" and "Auld Lang Syne," led by Werner and Marlene Ens as part of a 2010 event at the Mennonite Heritage Village in Steinbach, MB, can be seen and heard at https://youtu.be/gKxinDmZn9g.

19 Excerpt from an unpublished manuscript of "*Mennonite Circle Games*, compiled and explained by Werner Ens."

20 The presence of military referents in Mennonite folk song in southern Manitoba is not unprecedented. The well-known Low German song "*Onns Noba Klosse haud ne Koa*" ("Our Neighbour Klassen Had a Car"), for example, borrows its tune from the popular First World War song "Mademoiselle from Armentières" (Klassen 1989, 131).

21 Pseudonym.

22 Surname has been removed for privacy.

23 Herman Rempel defines *Putseleeda* (Low German) as "vigorous folk songs reflecting humour and or satire" (1995).

24 Margaret Klassen was part of the focus group discussion where this exchange took place. Margaret is my mother, Melvin is my father, and his father was David Klassen.

25 The Brunk Revivals visited southern Manitoba in 1957. Emphasizing the wrath of God and personal confrontations with evil, revivalist movements were seen variously as energizing for the greater church, and undermining of Mennonite emphases on God's love and community discipleship. This resulted in the adoption of "A Statement of Concerns on Revivalism and Evangelism" by the General Council of Mennonite Church General Conference in 1953 (see Bender, Crous, van der Zijpp, and Hostetler 1990).

26 Barn dances and associated activities (e.g., dancing, playing the fiddle) were considered sinful to some due to alcohol consumption at some of those dances.

27 Pseudonym.

28 Low German; "it soon gives a wedding."

29 M. Ens 2016.

30 Interviewees also mentioned the use of cars and trucks in later years, a transition consistent with that described by Fehr and Greenhill (2011, 147); Petkau suggests that *Brommtoppspäla* would park their vehicle near the edge of a village and visit homes by foot (1981, 92).

31 Low German, "Can the New Year's singers come in?" From Johnny Kehler, personal communication, 2004. Spelling his.

32 Werder Platt is a Low German vernacular developed by Mennonites during their time in West Prussia (Werner 2007, 20). Citing the Werder Platt version of the text found in Siegfried Rosenberg's 1930 book, *Geschichte des Kreises Grosses Werder*, Norma Jost Voth includes this song in her 1991 *Mennonite Foods and Folkways from Southern Russia* text (1991, 110).

33 It has been suggested that Mennonites brought the *Rummelpott* (or *Brommtopp*) to the Vistula Delta when they came to the region between 1550 and 1570. The presence of the instrument in many parts of northern Germany and surrounding regions, however, weakens any hypothesis of it spreading solely through settlement (Preuß 1994, 14).

34 According to Julius Toews, *Brommtoppspäla* usually came from villages in the West Reserve that had been settled by people of Bergthaler background (1977, 301). Irene Friesen Petkau suggests that the custom was maintained in both East and West Reserves, and that it is not clear whether this suggests a unique association with Manitoba's Bergthaler settlement (1981, 92).

35 While Voth suggests that southern Manitoba Mennonites were the only Mennonite contingent to carry on with the *Brommtopp* custom upon reaching North America (1991, 112), the towns and villages I have mentioned here reflect the boundaries of my research and fieldwork and are not necessarily the only spaces wherein New Year's Eve house visits occurred. I have heard accounts of the *Brommtopp* among Mennonites with conserving, primarily Sommerfelder, roots in Mexico and Bolivia as well. For example, Helena (Penner) Martens, who grew up as part of the Sommerfelder community in Bolivia and who now calls Winkler home, remembers her father singing "The *Brommtopp* Song" to her and her siblings when they were children. Her version of the melody and text bears much in common with that used by revival *Brommtoppspäla* in southern Manitoba (2015).

36 Variations of the song title include "*Brommtopp Leed*," "*Brommtop Lied*," "*Bromm Topp Leabd*," "*Brummtopflied*," "The *Brummtupp* Song," and "The *Brommtopp* Song." A 2010

performance can be seen at https://youtu.be/o4t3SXEP-eE; a melodic variant and a description of the making of a *Brommtopp* from a 1976 performance can be heard at https://youtu.be/7eOUijgMmho.

37 Werder Platt version of the *"Brommtopps Leet"* from Rosenberg's *Geschichte des Kreises Grosses Werder* (as printed and translated in Voth 1991, 110).

38 This version of the song, titled *"Brommtop Lied,"* was told to Marge Friesen by her aunt, Agnes Toews (1913–2002). Toews was from the Altona area; I received the text from Friesen in 2004. Spelling as received.

39 In addition to the Agnes Toews variant, a 1977 text published by Julius Toews references *"drei schwarzbraune Jungfern"* (303; this text is also referenced in Petkau 1981, 92), and an unpublished version from Johnny Kehler refers to *"drei schwart-braune Maddels"* (letter, 2004). Not all of these variants include the final two lines of the stanza, and Victor Carl Friesen's version of the text, published in 1989, makes no reference to "dark brown maidens" (82–3).

40 A 2010 concert series prepared by the Mennonite Heritage Village (featuring *Brommtopp* performances) is one such example. Here, the *Brommtoppsäla* proposed using *"drei hübsche Mädchen"*; notably, singers were heard to sing *"drei schwarz braune Jung-frauen,"* perhaps indicating the relatively new introduction of this variant.

41 Mennonite Heritage Archives, Cassette 99, XXV–B–10. *"Mennonites in Manitoba: Neu Bergthal*. Performances by Neu Bergthal of the traditional song & music assoc with the bromm Topp," 1 July and 31 July 1976. An excerpt from this performance can be heard at https://youtu.be/7eOUijgMmho.

42 See, for example, *Blumenfeld: Where Land and People Meet* (Petkau 1981, 90–1).

43 Fehr and Greenhill's use of "ethnic drag" follows that of Katrin Sieg in *Ethnic Drag: Performing Race, Nation, Sexuality in West Germany* (2005).

44 This is echoed in descriptions relayed by others, such as Fehr and Greenhill (2011, 162–3) and Chornoboy (2007, 61–2).

45 This concern for the mess created by *Brommtopp* visitors was suggested by several interviewees; Fehr and Greenhill also refer to the significant shift from linoleum and wood floors to carpet and broadloom (2011, 157).

46 Anabaptists did not support infant baptism, believing instead that baptism should be received voluntarily upon confession of faith (Loewen and Nolt 1996, 86–7). Menno Simons, after whom Mennonites are named, was a Roman Catholic priest who went on to become a leader in the Anabaptist movement, starting in 1536 (ibid., 111).

47 Jimmie Davis and Charles Mitchell are believed to have purchased the rights to "You Are My Sunshine" from Paul Rice in 1939. The song's authorship, however, has been disputed over the years, with Oliver Hood considered its most likely author (*Sub-Q* 2015; Pappas 1990). A 1939 recording by the Pine Ridge Boys (Bluebird, B–8263–A) can be found at
https://www.youtube.com/watch?v=xvPolI-pBCw.

48 *"Dü bess mien Sonneschien,"* as sung by Margaretha Friesen, can be heard at https://youtu.be/dphHwJf_1lA.

References

Anderssen, Erin. 2016. "Welcome to the Country." *Globe and Mail*, 13 July. Accessed 1 December 2016. http://www.theglobeandmail.com/news/national/welcome-to-the-country/article30820904/.

Becker, Ann Weber. 1990. "Dance." *Global Anabaptist Mennonite Encyclopedia Online*. Accessed 24 November 2016. http://gameo.org/index.php?title=Dance&oldid=103739.

Bender, Harold S., Ernst Crous, Nanne van der Zijpp, and Beulah Stauffer Hostetler. 1990. "Revivalism." *Global Anabaptist Mennonite Encyclopedia Online*. Accessed 12 October 2016. http://gameo.org/index.php?title=Revivalism&oldid=135773.

Berg, Wesley. 1985. *From Russia with Music: A Study of the Mennonite Choral Singing Tradition in Canada*. Winnipeg, MB: Hyperion Press.

CBC News Manitoba. 2012. "Mennonite Magazine Warned about 'Political' Articles." 9 November. Accessed 24 November 2016. http://www.cbc.ca/news/canada/manitoba/mennonite-magazine-warned-about-political-articles-1.1170274.

Chornoboy, Eleanor Hildebrand. 2007. *Faspa with Jast: A Snack of Mennonite Stories Told by Family and Guests*. Sanford, MB: Interior Publishing.

DeGurse, Carl. 2012. "*Canadian Mennonite* Warned of Political Activities." *Canadian Mennonite* 16/22. Accessed 24 November 2016. http://www.canadianmennonite.org/articles/canadian-mennonite-warned-political-activities.

Diamond, Beverley. 1994. "Introduction: Issues of Hegemony and Identity in Canadian Music." In Diamond and Witmer, *Canadian Music: Issues of Hegemony and Identity*, 1–21.

Diamond, Beverley, and Robert Witmer, eds. 1994. *Canadian Music: Issues of Hegemony and Identity*. Toronto, ON: Canadian Scholars' Press Inc.

Dueck, Byron. 2011. "Cities: Introduction." In Toynbee and Dueck, *Migrating Music*, 197–201.

Dueck, Jonathan. 2017. *Congregational Music, Conflict, and Community*. Oxford, UK: Routledge.

Ens, Werner. n.d. "Mennonite Circle Games, compiled and explained by Werner Ens." Unpublished Manuscript.

Epp, Marlene. 2000. *Women without Men: Mennonite Refugees of the Second World War*. Toronto, ON: University of Toronto Press.

Fehr, Marcie, and Pauline Greenhill. 2011. "'Our *Brommtopp* Is of Our Own Design': (De)Constructing Masculinities in Southern Manitoba Mennonite Mumming." *Ethnologies* 33 (2): 143–77.

Friesen, John J. 2004. "Old Colony Theology, Ecclesiology and Experience of Church in Manitoba." *Journal of Mennonite Studies* 22: 131–44.

– 2007. *Building Communities: The Changing Face of Manitoba Mennonites*. Winnipeg, MB: CMU Press.

Friesen, Victor Carl. 1989. *The Windmill Turning: Nursery Rhymes, Maxims, and Other Expressions of Western Canadian Mennonites*. Edmonton: University of Alberta Press.

Klassen, Doreen Helen. 1989. *Singing Mennonite: Low German Songs among the Mennonites*. Winnipeg: University of Manitoba Press.

Klassen, Judith. 2007/2008. "You Call That 'Christian'? Language Use and Evangelism in the Music of a Mennonite Family in Mexico." *MUSICultures* 34/35: 1–25.

— 2009. "Under the Bed and behind the Barn: Musical Secrets and Familial Vitality in Mennonite Mexico." *Journal of Mennonite Studies* 27: 229–47.

— 2016. "The Politics of Pronunciation among German-Speaking Mennonites in Northern Mexico." In *The Oxford Handbook of Music and World Christianities*, edited by Suzel Ana Reily and Jonathan M. Dueck, 208–27. New York, NY: Oxford University Press.

Krahn, Cornelius, and Adolf Ens. 1989. "Manitoba (Canada)." *Global Anabaptist Mennonite Encyclopedia Online*. Accessed 16 August 2016. http://gameo.org/index.php?title=Manitoba_(Canada)&oldid=132850.

Loewen, Harry, and Steven Nolt. 1996. *Through Fire & Water: An Overview of Mennonite History*. Waterloo, ON: Herald Press.

Loewen Reimer, Margaret. 2008. *One Quilt, Many Pieces: A Guide to Mennonite Groups in Canada*. Waterloo, ON: Herald Press.

Nova Scotia Business Inc. 2016. "Choosing Nova Scotia: Spotlight on Pure." Accessed 24 November 2016. http://www.novascotiabusiness.com/en/home/articles/film-and-creative/post.aspx/choosing-nova-scotia-spotlight-on-pure/.

Pappas, Theodore. "The 'Theft' of an American Classic." Accessed 24 November 2016. http://www.rosemontrecords.com/historical.html. [This article first appeared in the November 1990 issue of *Chronicles: A Magazine of American Culture*, a publication of the Rockford Institute (www.ChroniclesMagazine.org).]

Peacock, Kenneth. 1966. *Twenty Ethnic Songs from Western Canada*. National Museum of Canada. Bulletin No. 211, Anthropological Series No. 76.

Petkau, Irene Friesen. 1981. *Blumenfeld: Where Land and People Meet*. Winkler, MB: Blumenfeld Historical Committee.

Pittman, Anne M., Marlys S. Waller, and Cathy L. Dark. 2009. *Dance a While: A Handbook for Folk, Square, Contra, and Social Dance*. 10th ed. Toronto, ON: Pearson.

Preuß, Hans. 1996. "Sitten und Bräuche zwischen Weihnachten und Neujahr." *Pangritz-Kurier* 4: 12–14, 37.

Rempel, Herman. 1995. *Kjenn Jie Noch Plautdietsch? A Mennonite Low German Dictionary*. 2nd rev. ed. Rosenort, MB: PrairieView Press.

Riley, Suzel Ana, and Jonathan M. Dueck. 2016. "Introduction." In *The Oxford Handbook of Music and World Christianities*, edited by Suzel Ana Riley and Jonathan M. Dueck, 1–30. New York, NY: Oxford University Press.

Sawatsky, Rodney J. 1991. "Mennonite Ethnicity: Medium, Message and Mission." *Journal of Mennonite Studies* 9: 113–21.

Sieg, Katrin. 2005. *Ethnic Drag: Performing Race, Nation, Sexuality in West Germany*. Ann Arbor: University of Michigan Press.

Sub-Q: The Interactive Magazine for Interactive Fiction. 2015. "Who Owns 'You Are My Sunshine'?" Accessed 24 November 2016. https://sub-q.com/who-owns-you-are-my-sunshine/.

Taussig, Michael. 1993. *Mimesis and Alterity: A Particular History of the Senses*. London, UK: Routledge.

Thiessen, Jack. 2003. *Mennonite Low German Dictionary / Mennonitisch-Plattdeutsches Wörterbuch*. Madison, WI: Max Kade Institute for German-American Studies.
Toews, Julius G. 1977. "Traditional Pastimes." In *Mennonite Memories: Settling in Western Canada*, edited by Lawrence Klippenstein and Julius G. Toews, 300–5. Winnipeg, MB: Centennial Publications.
Toynbee, Jason, and Byron Dueck, eds. 2011. *Migrating Music*. New York, NY: Routledge.
– 2011. "Migrating Music." In Toynbee and Dueck, *Migrating Music*, 1–17.
Voth, Norma Jost. 1991. *Mennonite Foods & Folkways from South Russia*, vol. 2. Intercourse, PA: Good Books.
Werner, Hans P. 2005. "Peoplehoods of the Past: Mennonites and the Ethnic Boundary." *Journal of Mennonite Studies* 23 (1): 23–35.
– 2007. *Imagined Homes: Soviet German Immigrants in Two Cities*. Winnipeg: University of Manitoba Press.
Winland, Daphne Naomi. 1993. "The Quest for Mennonite Peoplehood: Ethno-Religious Identity and the Dilemma of Definitions." *Canadian Review of Sociology and Anthropology* 30 (1): 110–38.

Interviews

Derksen, Mary. 2016. Interview by author. Reinfeld, MB, 22 July.
Ens, Werner and Marlene. 2014. Interview by author. Winkler, MB, 23 June.
– 2016. Interview by author. Winkler, MB, 18 July.
Fehr, Susan. 2014. Interview by author. Altona, MB, 25 June.
Friesen, Margaretha. 2015. Interview by author. Telephone, 30 December.
Kehler, Anne. 2016. Interview by author. Altona, MB, 20 July.
Kehler, Johnny. 2004. Interview by author. Telephone, 2 February.
– 2004. Personal communication. Letter, 4 February.
Kehler, Menno. 2004. Interview by author. Telephone, 20 February.
Martens, Helena. 2015. Interview by author. Winkler, MB, 28 October.
Neufeld, Margaret. 2015. Interview by author. Reinland, MB, 27 October.
Sara. 2015. Interview by author. 27 October.
– 2016. Interview by author. 21 July.
Schulz, Waldo. 2004. Interviews by author. Telephone, 2 March and 5 April.
Stoesz, Bill and Ruth. 2016. Interview by author. Altona, MB, 22 July.
Susan Dueck, Joyce Falk, Grace Harms, Margaret Klassen, Edna Letkeman, Frieda Sawatzky. 2016. Focus group facilitated by author. Altona, MB, 18 July.

Marcia Ostashewski

Chapter 15

Ukrainian Catholic Congregational Singing in Canada: Sounds in Service and Celebration

As priests, clothed in layers of embroidered vestments, open the central Royal Doors of the iconastasis,[1] they welcome parishioners to celebrate weekly Byzantine Ukrainian Catholic worship services in parishes across Canada.[2] As the Royal Doors are opening, a priest begins censing the altar while parishioners sing an opening hymn (see appendix, track 1). Then, he begins intoning, or singing, the prayers that commence the liturgy; the congregation responds in song. The term "celebration" is used in both English and Ukrainian for the Byzantine Ukrainian religious practice of performing liturgy. Even in sombre services, congregants' senses, especially of sight, hearing, and smell, but in some circumstances also of touch and taste, are stimulated in many ways, resulting in a heightened experience in communion with others. The sounds of celebration may include bright, small bells chiming while a melismatic *Amin'* (Amen) is sung (see Appendix, Track 3); they may also include the voices of children, with parents whispering in reply. During certain occasions, such as weddings, instruments or recorded popular musics may be heard in Byzantine Ukrainian Catholic churches. During services on Good Friday (the Friday preceding Easter Sunday), the knocking of the *kalatalo*, or wooden knocker, can be heard, symbolizing the hammer driving the nails through the hands and feet of Jesus onto the cross. Carols at Christmas and joyous Easter hymns, sometimes accompanied by the ringing of handbells, provide a cheerful counterpoint to an often hushed and sometimes melancholic soundscape. If the parish has large outdoor bells, and a member of the congregation knows how to ring them (or how to work an automated

Figure 15.1 | Interior, Holy Ghost Ukrainian Church, Sydney, Nova Scotia, 12 July 2012. To provide some visual context for the reader, this photo was taken in the Holy Ghost Ukrainian Church (Sydney, Nova Scotia) on 12 July 2012 during a liturgy in which some young parishioners received their First Holy Communion (as evidenced by the young girls in veils and white dresses, in the lower right-hand corner). It depicts the priest, Father Roman Dusanowskyj, while he is delivering his homily. Father Roman often comes close to the congregation to speak with them and even engages in discussion when he delivers his homily. Behind him, up the stairs, is the iconastasis, which separates the altar area from the rest of the church. The Royal Doors are the central, large doors. Both the central and smaller side doors have been removed from their hinges and are missing from this photo; at the time of the photo, they were being used in a museum exhibit celebrating the parish's centenary.

machine), they may be rung to punctuate the liturgy at special prayers (see Appendix, Track 3). These outdoor bells may also be used to call the congregation to service, or to share news of a death or an emergency. They sound through the church and over prairie landscapes, small towns, and large urban centres across the country.

While Byzantine Ukrainian worship across Canada shares many common elements, differences also exist within this sacred soundscape. Addressing the breadth of Ukrainian history in Canada, from the earliest period of immigration just prior to 1900, historian Frances Swyripa has noted that Ukrainian Orthodox and Catholic churches have long been "central in preserving the language, culture and identity of Ukrainian Canadians" (2012). While there are important theological, political, and organizational differences between Catholic and Orthodox faiths, both of which are of Byzantine origin, many aspects of their liturgical practice are very similar.[3]

One core component of Byzantine Ukrainian practice across the country is cantor-led congregational responsorial singing (see Appendix for a description of the audio examples that accompany this chapter). In this chapter, I focus on the eastern-rite Byzantine Ukrainian Catholic faith tradition that is common across much of Canada. Byzantine Ukrainian Catholicism has its roots in the early Christian centre of Byzantium, or Constantinople, now called Istanbul. Although Byzantine Ukrainian Catholic and Orthodox rites are very similar in practice, and various aspects of their histories in Canada overlap and intertwine, these are two separate political-religious entities. Yet, due to their great similarity in practice, I draw on some useful points of comparison. A cantor-led congregational responsorial singing practice is common to both; I have more personal and field research experience with Catholic traditions. In cantor-led congregational responsorial practice, a priest (also known as the celebrant) leads prayer in dialogue with a cantor, who is supported by members of the congregation who wish to sing at a given service.[4]

Dialogic cantor-led congregational responsorial singing is an essential aspect of the celebration of a Byzantine Ukrainian Catholic liturgy, and it has served – and continues to serve – in the creation and sustenance of communities across Canada. It is a distinct practice, different from that of a "choir," as I describe in more detail below. Cantor-led congregational singing is the most basic aspect of congregational liturgical musical practice in Ukrainian Catholic churches. It is, at the same time, a shared practice that connects all Byzantine Ukrainian Catholics across Canada and around the world; it is also a practice that demonstrates the uniqueness of each community, to the degree that it may even reveal details about individual congregants who are participating in any given liturgy at a particular place and time.

In this chapter, I draw on ethnographic observations and interview data, as well as literature on history and material culture reviewed and collected over the last twenty years while working with Ukrainians in disparate diasporic communities. This includes my own participation in the practice as a child and young adult, regularly attending Ukrainian Byzantine liturgies with my family, and my more recent role as a cantor at Holy Ghost Ukrainian Catholic Church in Sydney, Nova Scotia since 2014. Building on the work of Klymasz and others, this chapter draws on my research with Ukrainian Canadians across Canada and in Ukraine, specifically on my research and participation in congregational responsorial singing in Byzantine Ukrainian Catholic churches in different regions of Canada. Some aspects of the practice have changed in the more than 125 years since it has come to Canada, but it continues to be a cherished music through which communities are created and celebrated. Although involvement in Ukrainian Byzantine Catholic parish communities is largely in decline across the country, religious practices continue to be a central and iconic aspect of Ukrainian culture and experiences, albeit among smaller numbers of people. Commenting on the community in which I have been living since 2013, folklorist Elizabeth Beaton observed that well into the 1980s at least, "in the case of Ukrainians in the industrial urban community of Sydney, Nova Scotia, religion [was] the operative link in the reciprocity between human action and the socio-political environment" (1989). My more recent observations concur with Beaton's regarding the continued central importance of religion and, more specifically, of the Holy Ghost Ukrainian Catholic parish, in Ukrainian community life and experience in the region.

Ukrainians and Ukrainian Culture in Canada

Although Ukrainian Canadian experiences on the prairies are somewhat well known, knowledge of their experiences elsewhere in the country is less so. Canadians of Ukrainian ancestry, like many ethnocultural groups in Canada, are typically viewed homogeneously;[5] however, this chapter shows some of the varying experiences and expressions within their communities and across the nation, focusing on Christian traditions.

Today, many Canadians of Ukrainian ancestry are involved in distinctive cultural practices in their local communities. In the mid-2010s, communities across the country prepared to celebrate the one hundred and twenty-fifth anniversary of Ukrainian immigration to Canada in 2016. They simultaneously began organizing celebrations for the 150th anniversary of Canadian Confederation in 2017. In preliminary planning meetings for these celebrations, community leaders for national Ukrainian Canadian organizations expressed their desire to educate the public about and celebrate the diverse ways in which Ukrainians and Ukrainian cultural expressions have affected other Canadians. Ukrainian sounds and celebrations have long been a vibrant component of Canadian cultural landscapes; these sounds and celebrations are the focus of this chapter, particularly related to Christian traditions.

Ethnomusicology (particularly in North America) has conventionally been concerned with writing "generalizations" about music and culture (Rice 2010, 105). The existence of a "group" of Ukrainian Canadians is taken as self-evident in public discourses of Canadian history (e.g., Swyripa 2012; "Ukrainian Canadians" 2016), yet Ukrainian Canadians have rightly lamented this. Those who identify today as Ukrainian Canadian or of Ukrainian heritage in Canada come from a great diversity of geographies, lineages, religions (or no religion), and dialects and languages, including evolved languages that are very different from the Ukrainian spoken by the earliest immigrants to Canada. Influenced by personal histories, local conditions, and encounters and relations with other ethnocultural groups, Ukrainian customs and culture are also reconfigured, expressed, and practised multifariously.

Byzantine Ukrainian Catholic Worship Practices in Canada: Sounds, Celebration, and Significance

Liturgical music, including cantor-led congregational responsorial singing, is one vital dimension of Byzantine Ukrainian Catholic religious practice that was foundational for immigrants as they created their new communities in Canada. In their early writings, church leaders in Canada, including Canada's first Metropolitan Sheptyc'kyj (Bishop of the Archeparchy, or the highest level of Church official in the region), highlighted the importance of congregational responsorial singing:

> By His own sublime example the Savior sanctified the exclusive use of vocal music (i.e., music without instrumental accompaniment) during the divine services. (As in Lambertson 1994, translation of 1916 text *The Churchsinger's Companion*; Klymasz 2000, 157)

> He who sings the liturgy, prays twice over. (Metropolitan A. Sheptyc'kyj, "To the Cantors" [1939]; Klymasz [2000, v])

The musical setting for the singing of prayers and responses is chosen by a cantor based on various factors, such as the type of service (e.g., funeral or memorial service [see appendix, track 4], Vespers, or Matins), and common practice in a given parish. Cantor-led congregational responsorial singing is largely based on chant and involves improvised three- or four-part harmony. Historically, Ukrainian Byzantine religious ceremonies have been led by a priest (the celebrant), who performs the service in dialogue with a *djak*,[6] a cantor (Klymasz 2000). Any members of the congregation who wish to, can join these two singers in three- or four-part harmony. Traditionally, both the priest and cantor are male; however, singing by women has always been welcome as a part of congregational responsorial practice.

The chant that forms the basis of responsorial congregational singing has historically arisen from two complementary bodies of musical material: (1) a group of chant melodies, or Tones (relative pitch clusters that provide the basis for chant melodies), that are used for the changeable parts of the liturgy, including Propers (including *Troparion*, *Kontakion*, and *Theotokion* as in appendix, track 2), which are the parts of the liturgy that change according to occasion or season; and (2) *samoyilka* (literally, self-expressed music) melodies for the fixed portion of liturgical responses (e.g., "Lord, have mercy"). Whatever the basis of the melody, the focus in cantor-led congregational responsorial practice is typically on the declamation of the text of the prayer; occasionally, some particularly important words (e.g., "Amen"), phrases, or prayers will be sung with more ornate or even melismatic treatment (see appendix, track 3).[7]

Tones are a collection of pitches, melodic contours, and fragments; and different chant music dialects dictate different ways of creating melodies in practice. They are similar to Indian *ragas* or Western musical modes, in that they provide foundational melodic and structural content. The Tones most commonly used among Byzantine Ukrainian Catholics in Canada are based on chant prescribed in a Galician (or, Western Ukrainian) compendium transcribed in 1894.[8] Each Tone provides a basic structural formula according to which the priest, cantor, and congregation will sing a prayer. This formula includes starting pitches and intervallic structures (that use a movable tonic in practice), as well as semi-cadential and cadential phrase structures, all of which are drawn upon in each improvised "performance" during a liturgy or service.

Melodic content for cantor-led congregational responsorial singing may also be derived from samoyilka melodies that are easily adapted to any text. The sources of these musics are varied, and sometimes unknown. Neither the existing literature nor my research consultants can pinpoint the origins of most common samoyilka melodies in use in Ukrainian Canadian Catholic practice today. Even Peter Galadza, one of the most highly regarded scholar-practitioners on the topic, simply says that the music involved in congregational responsorial singing involves "settings for the Divine Liturgy [that] follow the chant of the Ukrainian Church, with several pieces from other traditions" (Galadza 2004, x).[9] Although some modern texts provide notation for three- or four-part harmony to support the practice of part singing, members of the congregation have traditionally created their own harmonies (drawing on what they have heard others sing, and their own capacities and skills) as they sing along with samoyilka melodies.[10] They often learn the text and melodies of this repertoire by ear through repeated exposure to the liturgies. Although it is now common to see members of the congregation reading along with notated music while singing hymns, very few of the congregation members whom I have interviewed can read music. This suggests that the harmonies they sing for hymns are either learned by ear or independently created.

I have observed yet another source of congregational responsorial singing material in Byzantine Ukrainian Catholic churches in Canada. A choral practice,[11] distinct from cantor-led congregational responsorial singing, is also common in this faith tradition. Many Byzantine Ukrainian Canadian churches have their own conductor-led choirs, made up of parishioners (some or all of whom may regularly participate in cantor-led responsorial singing), that may provide the responses during services. For example, in our Cape Breton parish, the choir sings liturgies on a few special occasions, such as Easter and Christmas; during the rest of the liturgies in a given year, responses are either spoken by members of the congregation or sung by a cantor and *krylos* (congregational singers) together. Choral singing practice is based on music that has been formally composed and scored for a multi-part choir;[12] like cantor-led responsorial liturgical singing, this choral liturgical responsorial singing is typically unaccompanied, as per the standards of Byzantine practice. Entire choral settings have been composed for liturgies; these are sung in whole or in part (most often pieced together), and directed by a conductor. Some through-composed choral settings of liturgical music have been folded into common congregational practice and may have been altered according to local practice, often accounting for capacities or preferences of local singers. In other cases, choral compositions of liturgical responses are based on pre-existing chant melodies. Thus there is some relationship between the cantor-led and choral practices, but they are distinct.

Language and Transmission: Modifying Practices in New Contexts

Cantor-led congregational responsorial singing among Ukrainian Canadians is an enduring cultural practice. Nevertheless, exposure to a variety of changes, including newer choral musics, has influenced and modified it over time. The formulaic nature of the Tones has also lent itself to adaptation from Ukrainian into English. Many Byzantine Ukrainian churches in Canada – particularly Catholic churches – are adapting Tones to accommodate English-language prayer (see Appendix, tracks 1, 2, and 4). Language is one element of congregational responsorial singing that has changed repeatedly during the history of the practice in Canada; it has been a cultural element at the core of many discussions and debates about Ukrainian identity in diaspora.[13]

Since the first wave of Ukrainian immigration to Canada over a century ago, Ukrainian churches have experienced major changes related to language that continue to reshape contemporary sacred musical practice and congregational responsorial singing. The first significant change was a shift from the use of the conservative Slavic liturgical language called Church Slavonic to the vernacular Ukrainian. A related challenge has to do with a recent update in the Ukrainian vernacular. That is, the current official version of the Ukrainian liturgical text uses idiosyncratic language and is frequently awkward;[14] it is often more jarring than even the English translation. This leads to the second significant change related to language: the use of an English translation of the liturgical text. This change appears to have occurred at different times in different parts of North America, beginning after the 1960s.[15] As Myroslaw Tataryn has noted, the debate around language in liturgical contexts is highly charged, tied as it is to ideas and values about the maintenance of culture and identity. Yet, in Ukrainian Catholic churches in Canada,[16] the use of English has been increasingly common (along with the use of the Gregorian calendar rather than Julian) since the 1960s (2009, 311).

In my research with Ukrainian Canadians on the Canadian prairies, all participants noted that their parishes began to integrate an increasing amount of English in services as a way of keeping young Canadian families involved in parish activities. One cantor reported that he and the priest collaboratively determine which language to use (or whether to oscillate between Ukrainian and English) in a given service based on who is in attendance: generally, this means he will sing more English when more young people are present (Orleski 2014). Father Roman Dusanowskyj of Sydney's Ukrainian parish informed me that, in the 1950s and 1960s, individual parishes began creating their own translations; eventually, clergy began to create and publish official translations that are now available nationwide. However, no research has been carried out to test the assumption that using (more) English results in greater participation by young(er) people. Another aspect that has not yet been explored is the role of Ukrainian as a ritual language; several parishioners with whom I regularly attend and sing liturgy join me in maintaining that singing in Ukrainian intensifies our (desired) experience of a sense of ritual in the liturgy.

Using English rather than Ukrainian in congregational music necessitates some adaptation. Formulaic and improvisational aspects of congregational musical practice must be considered, and occasionally a cadential pattern will indicate an emphasis on a syllable that would not typically be emphasized in spoken English. While some congregational responsorial singers may demonstrate mild forms of resistance to these sometimes awkward musical moments, members of the congregation by and large appear to accept them.

Transmission: Cantors and Other Guides for Congregational Responsorial Singing

Expert *djaks* – the above-mentioned cantors who are in dialogue with the priest – possess an enormous amount of learning and years of experience. Indeed, in 1881, Tchaikovsky, whose music drew on the melodies of Byzantine religious practice, commented on the amount of knowledge required to serve as cantor:

> I am completely lost in this ocean of Eimos, Sedalions, Theotokions, Troparions, Kontakions, etc [sic], first and secondary ones, and sometimes I feel I am going off my head. When I asked Father Alexander again how his cantor manages when he sings the canon with sticheras[17] and how does he know what he has to read and sing (for the church has extremely exact rules about what to sing and read on particular days, in what mode and how many times); he answered: "I don't know, before each service he looks something up the book." If the clergy don't know, what am I, a sinner to do? (in Klymasz 2000, v)

Inspired by the enormous challenges of a cantor's practice while sometimes serving as cantor in my home parish in Sydney, Nova Scotia, in 2015 I began to formally conduct research with learned, experienced cantors in Alberta. I also began to interview and study with Father Roman Dusanowskyj, who has taught liturgical musics to Ukrainian Catholic seminarians in Rome.

Some cantors I interviewed learned the practice in childhood, usually from their fathers. In 2015, I interviewed cantor Steve Orleski (b. 1926) and his wife, Olga (b. 1933). Steve serves as a cantor in his home parish, the Kaleland Ukrainian Orthodox Church of Saints Peter and Paul, in northeastern Alberta, and Olga is an active singer in her parish. Steve also serves as a cantor in at least ten nearby rural parish communities. Steve and other cantors have indicated that parishioners will be acknowledged if they have "a good voice," and may be invited to serve as cantor. I asked the Orleskis what makes a cantor's voice "good"; Steve explained, and Olga agreed: "one who can carry the tune, you know, has a good voice. Because otherwise, if you're out [of tune], then everything is out" (Orleski, 7 June 2015). A strong, clear voice is needed to lead the congregation in response to the priest's prayers. The Orleskis also discussed the importance of the capacity to harmonize with other singers. Their comments demonstrate that they personally value the practice of singing with other members of the congregation. Although he did not receive formal training, Steve turns now and again to a trunkful of liturgical and prayer service books he inherited from his father, some of which include musical transcriptions. Steve "gets by," he says, using only three or four Tones; many other cantors with whom I have conducted informal and formal interviews also indicate this is the common practice. The numerous research participants I spoke with in Orleski's area revere his singing and confirm that his practice, if limited, is more than satisfactory.

The Orleskis provided information about Steve's individual experiences as a cantor of Byzantine Ukrainian Orthodox faith in present-day western Canada in an interview form; however, other cantors have published material about their experiences and cantorial knowledge, including Joseph Roll. More than thirty years ago, in 1984, Roll published *Music of the Ukrainian Catholic Church for Congregational Singing* in which he compiled and notated fundamental components of congregational responsorial practices of the Ukrainian Catholic Church in Canada. Roll also included music from "Basilian[18] and popular sources according to current practice" (1984, v). In his foreword, Roll explains his reasons for creating the work: "The revitalization of congregational singing in the Ukrainian Catholic Church is long overdue. In August 1979, Bishop Basil Losten established a Cantors' Institute at St Basil's Seminary in Stamford, Connecticut. We have seen by the enthusiasm and numbers

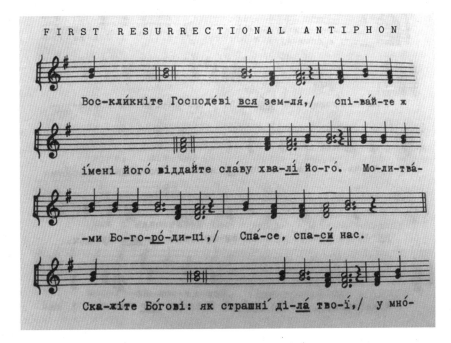

Figure 15.2 | Facsimile of Joseph Roll's transcription of the First Resurrectional Antiphon (Roll 1984).

of the participants of this first institute that the faithful of the Church are eager for such a program of learning church music. The Cantors' Institute was continued and expanded in 1980. Hopefully it will grow in years to come" (1984, v). Roll created the text as a guide to the practice, hoping it would support a revitalization of congregational responsorial singing. Roll's comments reveal that the practice had already been in decline since the 1970s.

Roll's cantorial style was to lead and support the congregation in responding to the priest during services. The text he published was, in essence, a written and tangible guide. It served the same helping function as a cantor might do in person. In transcribing the practice, he recorded not only the cantor's parts (his role), but also some of the potential voices of the congregational singers. Figure 15.2 is a facsimile of Roll's transcription of the First Resurrectional Antiphon, which, in the current English liturgical translation, begins, "Shout to the Lord, all the Earth, sing now to His name, give glory to His praise. Through the prayers of the Mother of God, O Saviour, save us" (Synod 1988). The declamatory style of the practice and common harmonies are evident in this example. Roll also includes directions about rhythm and

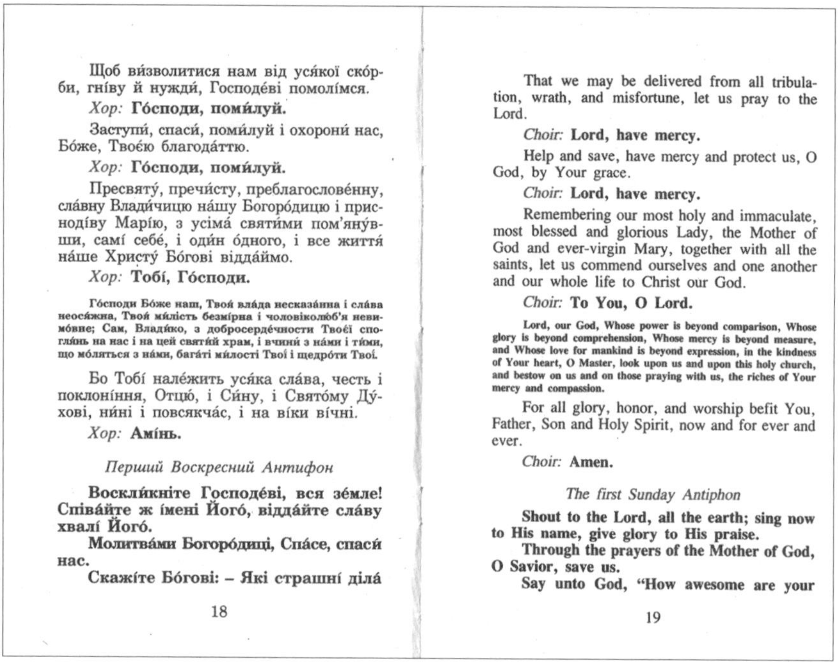

Figure 15.3 | Facsimile of The Divine Liturgy of St John Chrysostom (Synod 1987). The "First Antiphon" at the bottom of the page is precisely the same liturgical component shown in figure 15.2.

syllabic stresses to those who are reading the text alone, with underlined text and overhead accents.

As in this example, much of the music in Roll's volume is written for three voices. The three voices represent the role of the cantor and the potential voices of congregants. Roll encourages the involvement of the congregation (rather than focusing on the cantor). Although I was not aware of this publication until I was studying music at university, the music contained therein is a familiar part of my childhood experiences of liturgy and prayer, as it is for many Ukrainian parishioners in western Canada. We heard it, learned it by ear, and sang it as part of religious practice associated with the Eastern Rite. However, then, as now, members of the congregation may not sing precisely the pitches that Roll has notated.

Roll's volume is not widely used in Byzantine Ukrainian Catholic churches in Canada, except perhaps by cantors. This may be because it presents the liturgy only in Ukrainian, which increasingly fewer people are able to read and speak. It is worth noting, however, that such a note-by-note liturgical guidebook has never been in common use. Liturgical guidebooks that support congregational responsorial practice are commonly used in churches today, but they do not contain notated music. Rather, they contain only the text of the liturgy (see figure 15.3), and, in the case of Catholic churches, the text is presented with Ukrainian alongside the English on the opposite facing page. Except perhaps in occasional special services such as Easter or funerals, where the music is less familiar, and for which clergy may provide notated music for congregational responses, the congregation does not usually follow a musical score. The only notated regularly sung congregational music is that of paraliturgical hymns, which are usually sung either before or after the liturgy.[19] Most parishes have hymnals that contain notated three- or four-part choral settings. As with the sung responses to the priests' incantations, a cantor usually leads these hymns. Further, most research participants from across the country, including cantors, admit that they have never learned to read musical scores; if they refer to them, they do so largely as a guideline for the shape of melodies and distinction of rhythmic values.

Changing Gender Roles in Music Practices across Canada

Above, I have delineated some changes in Byzantine Ukrainian congregational responsorial practice in Canada. I have used examples of local practices to illustrate national trends that have been modified in specific places according to that locale's idiosyncrasies and needs. Often these modifications are related to language. In the following paragraphs, I turn to examples that complicate the issue of the gender of the cantor in Byzantine Ukrainian Catholic responsorial singing. Any priest or parishioner with whom I have spoken has said that the role of cantor is traditionally prescribed for and filled by a male. However, at least one instance drawn from the earliest years of immigration to Canada challenges this convention. In Sydney, Cape Breton, prior to 1915 and the arrival of a learned man who could serve as cantor, "the first Sydney cantor was a woman by the name of Mrs Pashkarenka" (Huk 2011, 39). Countless parishioners in Sydney's Holy Ghost Ukrainian Catholic Parish have also extolled the abilities of two women who led the sung responses to services in the 1970s and 1980s, warmly referred to in the community as "Mrs (Anne) Hawrylak" and Maria Delorenzo. Both women were recognized to have lovely, strong, and unique voices; though they both died several years ago, their memories are cherished, and parishioners frequently recall their beautiful musical contributions both in church and in theatrical performances in the hall.

Some may argue that these examples come from Cape Breton, a relatively isolated group of Ukrainians in Canada. However, female cantors may be more common than previously understood, both historically and recently. Other isolated groups may have faced the same challenges related to a paucity of capable male cantors. However, isolation is not the only factor that has determined the gender of the person in this traditionally male role. While conducting research in Ukrainian Byzantine churches across northeastern Alberta, I learned of several women in different communities who serve as cantors in their parishes. They all noted that they assumed their cantorial roles when there was a need and no men had filled the position. They typically highlighted that the majority of the parish attendees were elderly and that the learned men had either died or become too ill to sing. In each case, these women said that they like to sing, that they were encouraged by others in the parish to lead responses, and, usually, that they had taken some lessons provided by clergy in the context where fewer and fewer parishioners had the confidence to sing out or even knew how to respond in dialogue with the priest during liturgies.

My own experience further substantiates the broadening scope of who is considered for the roles of cantor in contemporary cantorial practice. When I was a teenager and young adult in the 1990s, parish priests and parishioners sometimes invited me to lead responses in special ceremonies being conducted in the area (e.g., marriages, commemoration ceremonies, funerals) because of my strong singing voice. At that time, however, the regular Sunday cantor role was reserved for an older learned man of the community. Contemporary occurrences of female cantors, as well as the early twentieth-century example from Sydney, point to women filling the role when no knowledgable men have been available. However, in my own experience in Alberta, it was not men's availability that was necessarily at issue. Those who contracted me to sing at weddings had the option to hire any number of men to fulfill the role, but they selected me because they knew me to be a competent singer and enjoyed hearing me sing. In those cases, it appears that personal relationships, a desire for a particular aesthetic, or perhaps a wish to have the role filled by a trained and professional musician may have influenced the parishioners' preferences and in turn challenged the traditional gender of the cantor.

In discussions with Sydney's parishioners about Mrs Hawrylak and Maria Delorenzo, a lack of learned men was not necessarily the sole reason for their singing as cantors. Both women were revered for their voices (especially Delorenzo, who came from a family of strong singers). Also, my own singing in Sydney's parish is encouraged because it is appreciated both aesthetically and in terms of my ability to serve as a strong lead supporting those in the congregation who wish to sing. Until now, the parish has been functioning with spoken responses and still does on regular occasions, including weekday morning and Saturday night English liturgies. However, Father Roman has repeatedly stated, both publicly and personally, that responsorial singing makes the services much more enjoyable for him personally, and he shares that many congregants have also indicated so to him. These specific cases of women cantors should be examined further. They also encourage the interrogation of how frequently and under what circumstances the "tradition" of a learned man serving as cantor may actually have been/be challenged. This in turn leads to questions of how we are to understand this "tradition," other Ukrainian traditions, and "tradition" more generally, when what seems to be the official or normative practice is varied.

Since moving to Sydney in 2013, I have been invited to lead the congregation in responsorial singing during the regular Sunday liturgies as well as special services. The role of cantor that I and the other women cantors occupy, however, is far less formalized than it is for Orleski or Roll. In addition to my role as *djak*, I am also identified as a part of the *krylos* (the group of parishioners that leads the singing); indeed, I am recognized by Father Roman Dusanowskyj as a leader within this small group. And, while I am fairly confident with my singing, I sometimes need direction from the priest or other congregants. For example, at a few points in each service,[20] I quietly check details of the changeable parts of the liturgy with parish elders who have celebrated liturgies nearly every day for decades; special services that are rarely performed demand additional attention. In this way, the role of cantor is served by multiple people: a strong singer, congregants who enjoy singing, and people who are knowledgable about different detailed aspects of the music and liturgical structures. While this means that the "cantor" (referring to me in this case) has less specialized knowledge of the practice than someone like Orleski or Roll, it also means that the practice is decidedly more collaborative, communal, and participatory.

Despite an aging and generally declining population, numerous members at my home parish in Sydney have noted that Father Roman's positive relationship with community members has brought many parishioners back to the church. The revived practice of congregational responsorial singing has also brought members of the congregation back into regular attendance;

these members say they have returned to regularly attending the church's sung services because they enjoy hearing the singing in church and they appreciate being able to sing, which they remember doing in years past.

Conclusion

In this chapter I have drawn attention to a cherished and iconic musical practice that is not widely known outside Ukrainian communities. I have done so as a means of informing a wider public of the practice's rich history and the ways in which it endures. As historian Greg Kealey has noted, material presented in a language other than English typically gets less attention in Canada, if only because relatively few people have the language capacity to attend to it (personal communication). In the case of Byzantine Ukrainian cantor-led congregational singing in Canada, an even smaller number of people will have both the language and the musical training to apply themselves to mastering this expressive form.

While some with whom I sing in my Nova Scotia parish are concerned with continuing the practice as a means of "continuing the culture," what we all enjoy most is singing together as part of a community. Indeed, this collaborative practice assists in *creating* a sense of community and belonging. Over the decades of my research, the children of immigrants have frequently told me that such a sense of belonging was vital to Ukrainian immigrants as they endeavoured to make a new home. Relocating my own family across the continent many times for work has brought sharply into focus the essential role such regular practices and community activities can play in our lives. We appreciate coming together regularly for contemplative time; we also take pleasure in singing for others at special times in their lives. We enjoy singing music that others tell us they not only value but also enjoy participating in. We hold the opportunity to speak the language of our families and to preserve our heritage in high regard. It is an exquisite musical practice through which we create and celebrate our relationships and our community every time we sing.

Byzantine Ukrainian Catholic cantor-led congregational responsorial singing is a locus of traditions and practices that have historically been invoked as evidence of ethnocultural group boundaries and immutability (Noyes 2003, 14). Although numerous research participants in my study of congregational responsorial singing have articulated that they engage in such practices to "keep up the culture," they also maintain that they enjoy its social aspect. It appears that the involvement of individuals in group activities may be shaped by a person's individual inclinations as much as their ancestry, language, or geography. Scholars have observed that religious practice can serve as "a resource for individuals and communities to negotiate their identities and actions" (Swindler 1986, in Tataryn 2009, 308), adding that it can be part of a kind of cultural toolkit during immigration, settlement, and subsequent community activity. Father Roman notes, "It doesn't matter which church you go to, if they use samoyilka, you're home. If they don't use familiar music that you can sing along with, then you are an audience member" (personal communication, 11 March 2016). As he eloquently points out, relationships, intimacies, and communities are created and maintained through the sounds and practice of this music.

In the introduction to his edited collection of a variety of cantorial traditions in Canada, Klymasz wrote that he hoped the volume would "suggest avenues for future research into this rich yet neglected aspect of musical creativity" (2000, 3). To date, very little has been published in the way of critical examinations of cantorial practices in Canada, and about Ukrainian cantorial practice in particular. While the current chapter makes only the most fundamental of inroads, it does begin to carve a path. There are many other dimensions of Ukrainian liturgical musics and cantors in Canada that have yet to be explored, including the aesthetics of sound and a "good voice" in a liturgical context; economies of exchange (monetary and otherwise);[21] the recording and commercial production of liturgical musics and how that impacts tradition and practice; and structures of sound and language in the musics, past and current, and related performance practices.

While Ukrainian sacred music practices in Canada may, like so many religious activities across the country, be waning, I observe and value the changing nature of culture and expressive practices over time and space. Congregational responsorial singing is a practice that continues to be cherished as an iconic component of Ukrainian cultural expression in Canada. It is one of many traditions, practices, and worldviews valued by Ukrainians around the world. Although Ukrainian traditions, practices, and worldviews show evidence of specific histories and are practised in distinctive ways in communities across Canada, they connect Ukrainian Canadians with Ukrainians living elsewhere. Indeed, they are a historical and vital part of broader communities of Eastern Christian practice, some of which are now drawing much international attention.[22]

Rather than assimilation and homogeneity, the research presented in this chapter demonstrates a singing practice that is inclusive of distinctiveness and difference, and of change. Even this brief examination of Byzantine

Ukrainian Catholic congregational responsorial music in Canada demonstrates that amid various challenges and affordances, musical practices are able to accommodate constraining pressures; they also demonstrate that local and specific resources and individuals can play significant roles in shaping distinctive local practices.

Ukrainians have lived rich and complex individual lives and created rich and complex communities. They have worked alongside other Canadians toward greater inclusivity regarding gender and political values, and they have enriched many musical cultures in a variety of positive ways. How might our understanding of Ukrainian histories, culture, and expression in Canada be different if, rather than beginning from the position of *dissolution*, we contended that concomitant processes of *acquisition* and other change are to be valued? How might we comprehend Ukrainian histories in Canada if we focused on the evidence of new forms of agency, vibrancy, and vitality in the face of extraordinary circumstances and amid tremendous trials faced through immigration, settlement, and making a living in a new land? What might our actions and values regarding newer immigrant cultures and expressive forms (including their religious practices) be, if we moved forward together with an understanding that these practices are vital adaptive tools? Finally, how might our understandings of culture, expression, and experiences be productively enriched if we began from a position of valuing the place of music and musicians in our critical examinations of history and culture? These are prescient questions to consider as we continue to welcome new Canadians, and as we begin the next 150 years and a new chapter in Canada's history.

Appendix

On 17 September 2017, a recording was made of the weekly liturgy at Holy Ghost Ukrainian Catholic Church in Sydney, Nova Scotia. This liturgy includes some special prayers in honour of the memory of the deceased members of the Ukrainian Catholic Men's Club. Each year, a liturgy is dedicated to the memory of these men and their contributions to the parish and community. Some of these prayers are in English, in an effort to ensure that everyone in the congregation understands them. As is typical for Sunday morning liturgies in this parish, Father Roman Dusanowskyj served as the main celebrant, or priest, and Marcia Ostashewski led the congregation in singing hymns and liturgical responses. Four excerpts appear on a YouTube channel. See "Accompanying Video and Audio Examples," in this volume. They include the following content.

Track 1 (6:00)
Father Roman has opened the Royal Doors to begin the Liturgy, and greets the congregation with instruction for the morning's opening hymn. He begins censing the altar, with a censor that has tiny bells that can be heard in the recording. Father Roman then begins the opening prayers; the congregational singers respond. A special prayer, in English, in honour of the deceased is inserted into the Great Litany of prayers, demonstrating the application of the chant in both languages. This segment ends as the cantor and congregational singers are singing the First Antiphon.

Track 2 (1:02)
Father Roman calls a prayer aloud at the Prayer of Entrance. Here, the cantor and congregational singers sing some of the Propers for this liturgy, the *Troparion*, *Kontakion*, and *Theotokion*. The introductory prayer, which remains the same for each liturgy, is sung in Ukrainian. However, the text that changes from service to service is sung in English because it is sung without rehearsal, in an improvisatory manner, and very few members of the congregation read Ukrainian well enough to be able to manage sight reading and singing.

Track 3 (2:54)
This segment opens as the congregational singers are singing "Hosanna" prior to the Prayer of Consecration of the Eucharist. Father Roman sings in a lower, more solemn tone than he does during the rest of the service, and more slowly. The cantor and congregation's "Amen" responses to these Consecration prayers are somewhat melismatic and ornamented. As well, the priest's assistant rings a set of small, handheld bells three times (signifying the Holy Trinity) during each "Amen" to emphasize the importance of these prayers. These distinctive sounds in this segment of the service, with respect to the singing and bells, are intended to emphasize this especially important moment in the Liturgy when, according to the faith, the bread and wine are transformed into the Body and Blood of Jesus Christ. Also, a prayer is sung shortly after the Consecration to the Mother of God. At this time, Father Roman is censing the consecrated Bread and Wine at the altar; as well, the outside bells are rung and can be heard in the background.

Track 4 (4:59)
At the end of the Liturgy, a short prayer service is sung in honour of the memory of the deceased members of the Holy Ghost Ukrainian Catholic Church Men's Club. As is evident, the tonality of the music that is sung in memoriam is dramatically distinct from the regular liturgy chant. Some parts of this excerpt are sung in Ukrainian and others in English, showing another aspect of the chant practices in the different languages.

Notes

1 The iconastasis is a wall composed of various icons that separates the congregation in the nave from the clergy at the altar. These walls are built, traditionally, in such a way as to entirely obscure the altar from the congregation. However, in more modern churches, this wall is often symbolically constructed, with simple framing that includes some icons. In some churches, there is no iconastasis. This reflects local value and interest in bringing the congregation, priests, and God closer to one another in liturgical practice.
2 Both Ukrainian Catholic and Ukrainian Orthodox religions are Eastern Christian traditions. They practise many similar doxologies; however, they are governed by separate, complex political entities, and operate with some distinctive theological aspects. While the lived experiences of those who practise these religions and are part of these faith communities have often been more complicated than a dualistic split might suggest, the music described in this chapter is nonetheless tied to the very long and complicated human histories that have been shaped by religious rites, movements of people, politics enacted on grand and local scales, and cultural changes in modern times. For more detailed information about these traditions as they have existed, and are practised and governed in Canada, see Goa 1989. Many Byzantine Ukrainian churchgoers in Canada will use the English word "Mass" to refer to regular prayer services (usually held on Sunday mornings, though sometimes on Saturday afternoons); however, the regular service in Byzantine Ukrainian practice is not, in fact, a Mass, a term that refers to a specific ritualized service of prayers in the Roman Catholic Church. Instead, the parallel prayer service in Byzantine Ukrainian practice is called the Liturgy, which refers to the regular rituals and prayers – liturgies – performed in Ukrainian Catholic churches as "The Divine Liturgy of St John Chrysostom." Other liturgies (e.g., of St Basil the Great, performed on Easter Saturday) are performed at special times of the year.
3 Father Roman Dusanowskyj of Cape Breton's Holy Ghost Ukrainian Catholic Parish has noted that due to their specific histories, Orthodox churches typically use Kievan chant dialects and Catholic churches customarily use Galician.
4 As Father Roman Dusanowskyj explains, the congregational singers that support the cantor in dialogue with the celebrant are sometimes referred to as the *krylos*. *Krylos* is also the word for the wooden cabinet table or podium in which cantors may store their books, and upon which they may lay them open for reference as they respond during a liturgy. The connection between the two uses of the word *krylos* draws attention to a supportive role played by the congregational singers.

5   For a discussion of the problematic notion of cultural homogeneity in the context of western Ukrainian music and culture in Canada, see the work of folklorist Robert Klymasz (e.g., 1994).
6   *Djak* is a transliteration of the Cyrillic, in English. It is pronounced "dyak," in a single syllable.
7   While clergy with whom I have sung have advised me that a clear declamation of the text at a speed at which the congregation can follow is important, I have witnessed a cantor progress through the responses too quickly to allow the congregation to join in. As a member of the congregation, I found it frustrating not to be able to participate. I did not have an opportunity to discuss this cantor's hasty style with either him or the priest. However, Father Roman Dusanowskyj explains that cantors must negotiate a complicated politics regarding their craft. For example, he notes that some cantors have been known to change the key in which they are singing mid-phrase to discourage too many members of the congregation from singing along, thereby preserving their special role in the practice of prayer. Father Roman also relates growing up in a church in Toronto where an expert and revered cantor is well known to have carefully guarded his practice. This cantor, Father Roman says, did not like to share his role or his resources, nor was he inclined to teach others. In life, the cantor said he would take his cantor books with him to the grave, which Father Roman notes he literally did, being buried with his books. In light of the special role that cantors have in a parish community – and the central role these parishes have had for many immigrants and their descendants – it is understandable that a cantor might want to guard his craft.
8   The 1894 compendium of Galician chant, the *Hlasopisnets'*, or *Book of Tones*, is the basis of the liturgical chanting with which I am most familiar in Ukrainian Catholic churches throughout western and central Canada. I received an unbound copy about a decade ago from the Basilian Fathers Monastery in Mundare, Alberta. I examined the chants transcribed therein, which are notated in a similar fashion to early Western music's neumes.
9   Ethnomusicologist Brian Cherwick writes about the importance of both choral and chant-based music in Ukrainian churches (2001, 1241).
10 Singing in three- or four-part harmony is also a common practice in Ukrainian traditional vernacular (folk) song.
11 Ukrainian Canadian churches have long been a locus for choir formation (in the church for sacred music, and/or in the parish hall for other music and theatrical performance). In 1942, music researcher Laura Bolton observed that choral singing was among the most popular activities of early Ukrainian settlers to Canada (Boulton in Cherwick, 2001, 1241). Cherwick's description of Ukrainian music practices in Canada includes choral singing as an enduring and popular activity (2001, 1241).
12 Although it has become more common to include instrumental music or pre-recorded music for special services, such as weddings, baptisms, and funerals, since at least the 1990s, unaccompanied singing continues to be the main practice in Byzantine Ukrainian liturgical practice in Canada. Ethnographic research in Cape Breton has provided evidence that a few parish members around the 1980s

regularly played instruments during services at Sydney's Holy Ghost Ukrainian parish: Steve Hasiuk, organ; Tony Stetch and John Nalepa, violin. While many details have yet to be gathered on the integration of instrumental music in our parish, these factors indicate the existence of unique local parish histories where instrumental music has been part of religious practice in some form.

13 Sociologist Wsevolod Isajiw notes that "ethnic language has been often considered one of the most socially significant ethnic patterns" – an assertion that religious studies scholar Myroslaw Tataryn rightly interrogates (Isajiw 1990, 49 in Tataryn 2009, 311). As a scholar of multiple aspects of cultural expression, and having heard from Ukrainian Canadians in the theatrical dance industry that they "dance Ukrainian" rather than speak Ukrainian, I share an interest in interrogating relationships of language, culture, and identity. While language is a significant entry point into other aspects of culture and community relationships, Klymasz also noted as early as 1970 that "the [Ukrainian Canadian] folklore complex has begun to stress, instead, the remaining non-verbal elements ... acoustic, optical and tactile manifestations" (1970, 2). These include the sound of Ukrainian music, the visual art of Easter egg ornamentation, and dance.

14 As noted by historian John-Paul Himka, "The Ukrainian text is also a translation, from Church Slavonic [an older linguistic form previously used by the Church]. The Ukrainian vernacular [everyday language] only began to replace Church Slavonic in Ukrainian Catholic liturgical practice after Vatican II, i.e., in the mid-1960s [at the same time as local vernacular languages were used instead of Latin in Roman Catholic churches around the world]. Ukrainian Orthodox churches introduced Ukrainian in 1918. Of course, the Church Slavonic was a translation from the Greek [as it would have been used as part of Byzantine practice] (but new melodies were created for it)" (Himka, personal communication, 4 April 2016). This is to say that the language and linguistic varieties used in liturgies have changed many times since immigration to Canada over a century ago; as long-time practitioners will note, singing practice has had to be adjusted with each change. Father Roman Dusanowskyj has also commented on these changes.

15 Based on informal interviews.

16 I have not conducted extensive research in Orthodox parishes so I am unable to provide parallel information about those contexts.

17 A particular genre of hymn integrated into specific services (in contrast to a paraliturgical hymn which is sung outside the bounds of the liturgy).

18 The Basilians are one of two predominating monastic orders of priests who serve communities in western Canada and who originate in the western Ukrainian province of Galicia (though there have always been more secular or non-monastic Ukrainian Catholic priests in Galicia). The prevalence of Basilian materials in North America is largely due to Basilians' ownership of publishing companies; they are the most prolific Ukrainian publishers of religious materials on the continent. Basilians were the most experienced Ukrainian Catholic missionaries (Martynowych, email communication, 23 March 2016).

19 Mudri-Zubacz, who has studied paraliturgical repertoire in Ukrainian Catholic churches in diaspora in North America, also draws attention to the ways in which some liturgical

and sensory experiences are shared across parishes, while other aspects of repertoire may be used to invoke a uniqueness of expression and practice (2008, 66).
20 A Catholic service usually lasts between forty-five and sixty minutes, and Orthodox services usually between seventy-five and ninety minutes.
21 The only specific information on economic implications of cantors that I have found is about a cantor in Sydney, Nova Scotia who received nominal compensation that would have barely covered relevant costs, such as travel (Huk 2011, 40).
22 As I write this chapter, global audiences are focused on two historic international meetings that have involved and addressed Canadians, Ukrainians, and Eastern Christianity. The first is between the current heads of the Roman Catholic and Russian Orthodox churches whose leaders have not met since the schism of these Western and Eastern branches of Christianity a thousand years ago (BBC 2016). The second spotlight is focused on Ukrainians in the face of the current violent conflicts with Russian troops in Ukraine. Canada's government, beginning with former prime minister Stephen Harper, tried to address the concerns Ukrainian Canadians feel for their relations in the homeland. These concerns continue to be addressed under the current prime minister, Justin Trudeau (CBC 2016).

References

Beaton, Elizabeth. 1989. "Ukrainians in Cape Breton: Radicalism and Religion." Paper presented at *Atlantic Canada Studies Conference*, University of Edinburgh, Edinburgh, Scotland.

CBC News. 2016. *Obama and Trudeau at the White House: The Complete Speeches*. Video. Accessed 27 January 2017. https://www.youtube.com/watch?v=9NZbJ11Hz7c.

Cherwick, Brian. 2001. "Ukrainian Music." In *Garland Encyclopedia of World Music*, edited by Ellen Koskoff, 3: 1241–4. New York, NY: Garland.

Galadza, Peter, Joseph Roll, J. Michael Thompson, Roman Galadza, and John Sianchuk. 2004. *The Divine Liturgy: An Anthology for Worship*. Ottawa, ON: The Metropolitan Andrey Sheptytysky Institute of Eastern Christian Studies.

Goa, David J., ed. 1989. *The Ukrainian Religious Experience: Tradition and the Canadian Cultural Context*. Edmonton: Canadian Institute of Ukrainian Studies, University of Alberta.

Huk, John. 2011. *Strangers in the Land: The Ukrainian Presence in Cape Breton*. 2nd ed. Sydney: Cape Breton University Press.

Klymasz, Robert, 1970. "Ukrainian Folklore in Canada: An Immigrant Complex in Transition." PhD diss., Department of Folklore, Indiana University.

– 1994. "From Immigrant to Ethnic Folklore: A Canadian View of Process and Transition." In *Canadian Music: Issues of Hegemony and Identity*, edited by Beverley Diamond and Robert Witmer, 351–8. Toronto, ON: Canadian Scholars' Press.

– ed. 2000. *From Chantre to Djak: Cantorial Traditions in Canada*. Hull, QC: Canadian Museum of Civilization.

Lambertsen, Isaac, translator. 1994. *The Church Singer's Companion,* 3rd ed. [*Sputnik psalomshchnika*]. New York, NY.

Mudri-Zubacz, Melita. 2008. "Ukrainian Catholic Paraliturgical Hymns: A Closer Look." In *Winnipeg Papers on Ukrainian Music,* edited by R. Klymasz, 51–69. Winnipeg, MB: The Centre of Ukrainian Canadian Studies Press.

Noyes, Dorothy. 2003. "Group." In *Eight Words for the Study of Expressive Culture,* edited by Burt Feintuch, 7–41. Urbana: University of Illinois Press.

Orleski, Steve. 2014. Sanctuary Project Interview. Interview by author, 7 June. Kaleland Ukrainian Orthodox Church, Kaleland, AB.

Rice, Timothy. 2010. "Ethnomusicological Theory." *Yearbook for Traditional Music* 42: 100–34.

Roll, Joseph. 1984. *Music of the Ukrainian Catholic Church for Congregational Singing.* Stamford, CT.: Basileos Press.

Sheptyc'kyj, Metropolitan Andrej. 1939/1961. "Do djakiv [To the cantors]." In *Pys'ma-poslannja mytropolyta Andreja (Z chasiv bol'shevyc'koji okupaciji) [Letters-epistles of Metropolitan Andrej (during Bolshevik occupation)]*. Yorkton, SK: Lohos.

Swyripa, Frances. 1993. *Wedded to the Cause: Ukrainian-Canadian Women and Ethnic Identity, 1891–1991*. Toronto, ON: University of Toronto Press.

– 2012. "Ukrainian Canadians," *The Canadian Encyclopedia*. Accessed 15 March 2016. http://www.thecanadianencyclopedia.ca/en/article/ukrainian-canadians/.

Synod of the Hierarchy of the Ukrainian Catholic Church. 1988. *The Liturgy of St John Chrysostom*. Etobicoke, ON: The Basilian Press.

Tataryn, M. 2009. "Canada's Eastern Christians." In *Christianity and Ethnicity in Canada*, edited by Paul Bramadat and David Seljak. 1st ed., 287–329. Toronto, ON: University of Toronto Press.

"Ukrainian Canadians." *Wikipedia*. Last updated 14 August 2016. Accessed 17 August 2016. https://en.wikipedia.org/wiki/Ukrainian_Canadians.

"Unity Call as Pope Francis Holds Historic Talks with Russian Orthodox Patriarch – BBC News." 2016. Accessed 14 February 2016. *BBC News*. http://www.bbc.com/news/world-latin-america-35565085.

Anna Hoefnagels

Chapter 16

(Re)Presenting Indigenous Activism in the Nation's Capital: Signifying Resistance across Time and Place through Music in Alanis Obomsawin's *Trick or Treaty?* (2014)

For many Canadians, Idle No More was a short-lived political movement that drew national and international attention to environmental issues and Indigenous rights in Canada, peaking in the winter of 2012–13. Organization around Idle No More was quick and efficient, with grassroots organizers using social media to coordinate events and to swiftly disseminate information, gaining the attention of national media outlets and the general public. First Nations activists Jessica Gordon (Cree/Saulteaux, Treaty Four), Nina Wilson (Nakota and Plains Cree, Treaty Four), and Sylvia McAdam (Cree, Treaty Six) and their non-Indigenous ally Sheelah McLean are recognized as the founders of Idle No More through their organization of a teach-in in Saskatoon, Saskatchewan on 10 November 2012. The teach-in was in response to Bill C45, an omnibus bill proposed by the federal government that included language that took away First Nations control of their land and waterways. From this teach-in, the hashtag Idle No More (#IdleNoMore) was circulated on social media and became the movement's rallying cry. The National Day of Solidarity and Resurgence across Canada on 10 December and the announcement of Chief Theresa Spence's hunger strike on 11 December catapulted Idle No More into mainstream media, inspiring thousands of people to become involved (see table 16.1). Activists L. Jane McMillan, Janelle Young, and Molly Peters summarized the emergence of Idle No More and the continued resonance of its core concerns:

Table 16.1 | Timeline of key Idle No More events

4 November 2012	Jessica Gordon posts a message on Twitter using #IdleNoMore
10 November 2012	Teach-in in Saskatoon in response to Bill C-45, which had been introduced to House of Commons on 18 October 2012
10 December 2012	First Day of Action ("A National Day of Solidarity and Resurgence")
11 December 2012	Theresa Spence begins her hunger strike on Victoria Island, in Ottawa
17 December 2012	The start of the "Round Dance Revolution"; flash mob in Regina shopping mall
21 December 2012	Second National Day of Action: massive rally on Parliament Hill in Ottawa, with supporting protests nationally and internationally, including large round dance at the major intersection of Yonge and Dundas Streets in Toronto
11 January 2013	Most concentrated day of protest: #J11
28 January 2013	International Day of Action ("World Day of Action"): #J28

Note: See the Kino-ndo-niimi Collective 2014, 389–409 for a detailed timeline of events related to Idle No More.

> The great vision of Nina Wilson, Sheelah McLean, Sylvia McAdam, and Jessica Gordon, the founders of Idle No More, blossomed against the barren landscape of failed federal policies, sanitized Canadian history, and blatant rejection of Indigenous treaty rights. Through teach-ins, Facebook, and Twitter, they formed an Indigenous/non-Indigenous alliance and generated a grassroots movement to protest the Conservative government's failure to consult Aboriginal people on the *Jobs and Growth Act*, legislation that directly impacts Indigenous rights and title. The Idle No More movement became a national call to action to stop such colonial practices, and it now serves as a platform for collective cultural resurgence and environmental protection activism. (2013, 430)

As Marc Woons notes, Idle No More activities also extended beyond Canada's borders, notably on the International Day of Action, which saw events "in over a dozen countries including a one-man protest outside the Canadian embassy in Sri Lanka and events in Cairo, London, and even Warsaw" (2013, 173).

Also referred to as "Canada's Native winter" (Wotherspoon and Hansen 2013, 21), Idle No More activities included rallies and demonstrations that featured First Nations music – powwow songs, hand-drumming songs, and round dance songs; together these repertoires serve as the sonic rendering of Indigenous activism and cultural pride. As a form of nonviolent resistance, the songs and dances also fostered a sense of unity and equality of participants, and highlighted the importance of the arts in protest across time and place. Selena Couture's discussion of the round dance also applies to these performative aspects of Idle No More: "The round dance is both a metaphor for the decentralized nature of INM [Idle No More] and a method for connecting the present with the past. The centrality of this culturally expressive practice reveals *performance to be at the symbolic heart of this movement*" (2014, 119, italics mine).

Many of the images of Idle No More – in which drums and musicians feature prominently – were taken at massive rallies in cities throughout Canada, and at marches to, and speeches at, Parliament Hill in Ottawa. Complementing these images depicting people in typical Ottawa winters of −20°C temperatures and snowfall are others that were taken indoors, at flash-mob style round dances in major shopping malls in cities across Canada, ad hoc performances nicknamed "the Round Dance Revolution" (McMahon 2014, 98–100). The musical and physical disruption of mainstream capitalist consumption in major shopping centres during the busiest season for shopping – that is, the season leading up to Christmas – interrupted settler colonial patterns, reasserting the place and sounds of Indigenous people in unexpected spaces. In his discussion of Idle No More, historian and self-identified settler activist Adam J. Barker suggests these were acts of resurgence: "[Idle No More is an] Indigenous movement that reject[s] the politics of recognition in favour of asserting Indigenous place-relationships and social spaces challeng[ing] the core of both Canadian political economy and Settler identity. Just as settler colonialism is created by settler collectives spreading through places, building spatially stretched relationships, Indigenous resistance simultaneously disrupts settler colonial space while reasserting Indigenous spaces, altering the spatialities of both" (2015, 46). In this quotation Barker references the work of Dene scholar Glen Coulthard, who asserts that many of the "recognition" practices that are intended to give voice to Indigenous people in Canada are instead a replication of colonial power structures, and

Figure 16.1 | Musicians, demonstrators, flags, and drums at an Idle No More march in Ottawa.

that resurgence from within Indigenous communities is the most effective strategy for change.[1]

Popular images associated with Idle No More during this period often included musicians holding drums, or dancers in regalia (see figure 16.1). Although viewers rarely learn the names and meanings of the songs that those musicians are singing and to which the dancers are moving, music is a significant tool in Indigenous activism, uniting people in song, raising awareness of issues, and empowering and impacting musicians and listeners; it has the capacity to travel across time and place, and to be heard in public and private: "The strength and power of Indigenous music lies in its capacity to build community, culture and identity as Indigenous musicians communicate across, between and within their communities. Indigenous music is a critical foundation for the larger schema of Indigenous resistance and protest practices" (McKinnon 2010, 268–9).

The sounds and images associated with Idle No More activities in Ottawa were captured by participants and shared in online forums; they are also included in Alanis Obomsawin's 2014 documentary *Trick or Treaty?*[2] A feature-length documentary (one hour and twenty-four minutes), *Trick or Treaty?* examines the historic negotiations that led to the establishment of Treaty No. 9 (the land that is now considered part of Northern Ontario). Framed within the activism in Ottawa during the Idle No More movement, it articulates the geographic links between Idle No More as a national movement, Indigenous land rights (in general, and in specific locations), and the spaces that are inhabited by Indigenous people in Canada. Produced by award-winning Abenaki filmmaker Alanis Obomsawin through the National Film Board of Canada (NFB), this documentary complements the wide range of recently generated materials that comment on Idle No More.[3]

Particularly striking in *Trick or Treaty?* is the way that Obomsawin uses music to reinforce the various "places" of Indigenous activism as both local and global, while also asserting the temporal connections of Indigenous activism of the nineteenth century with contemporary activism and hope for the future. In this chapter I examine how Obomsawin uses music vignettes from Idle No More (diegetic music)[4] to frame the narrative of *Trick or Treaty?* and Idle No More as based largely in Ottawa, while also using non-diegetic music to position this movement within broader geographic and temporal boundaries. This analysis creates a deeper understanding of the roles of music in fostering a sense of inclusivity and belonging, and in calling out injustices suffered by Indigenous peoples in Canada historically and presently.

A "Movement Moment": Idle No More in Context

Idle No More belongs within the context of recent global engagement and ongoing Indigenous activism. While it would be easy to conclude that Idle No More was inspired by the Occupy Movement that began in the fall of 2011, the Arab Spring of December 2010–12, and domestic movements such as the university student protests in Quebec during the spring and summer of 2012, the lineage of resistance for Idle No More spans a far longer period than these few concentrated years, and cannot be viewed in isolation from the Truth and Reconciliation Commission (TRC) of 2010–15.[5] Indeed, it could be argued that Idle No More challenged non-Indigenous people in Canada to consider the meanings and implications of "reconciliation" and their own complicity as "perpetrators of intergenerational irresponsibility" (Robinson 2016, 63) in maintaining privileged positions inherited from their families and community. Likewise, the slogan "Idle No More" sought to engage Indigenous people across the nation in acts of resurgence and survivance. The "aesthetic actions" that emerged during Idle No More, similar to those that were presented and experienced at the TRC hearings, "perform a similar political function as artistic practice: they unsettle us, provoke us, and make us reconsider our assumptions" (Robinson and Martin 2016b, 3). *Trick or Treaty?* serves to document the peak of Idle No More activities in the winter of 2012–13, to engage non-Indigenous viewers with the issues of land and dishonest treaty negotiations, and to incite audiences to claim responsibility to future generations.

Idle No More's concerns of environmentalism, relationships of respect, and a desire for nation to nation negotiations with non-Indigenous Canadians have been priorities for Indigenous people for generations (see Woons 2013, 173); First Peoples have frequently organized themselves politically, building alliances for war and survival; more recently, the late twentieth and early twenty-first centuries witnessed significant events that are part of a larger movement of resistance. The Red Power Movement of the 1960s, resistance to the White Paper in 1969 in Canada, and the Massacre at Wounded Knee on the Pine Ridge Reservation in South Dakota in 1973 inspired many Indigenous people in Canada to become more politically active, in some cases identifying strongly with the US-based American Indian Movement. Since at least 1990, the year of the Oka Crisis (at Kahnasatake, a Mohawk community near Montreal), there have been a number of confrontations based on land rights and stewardship that could be considered local precursors to Idle No More in Canada. In the immediate wake of Idle No More were anti-fracking demonstrations in Elsipogtog First Nation (Mi'kmaw), New Brunswick; in the United States, Indigenous activists and their allies resisted the development of the Dakota Access Pipeline (#NoDAPL) from April 2016 until early 2017 to protect the water and resist the use of Indigenous land for the pipeline, continuing the environmentally focused activism of Idle No More. Also receiving mainstream media attention since the release of the TRC's final report have been the disproportionate number of murdered and missing Indigenous women and children, and victims of the so-called '60s Scoop.[6] The National Inquiry into Murdered and Missing Indigenous Women and Girls was launched in September 2016.

Adam Barker identifies Idle No More as a "movement moment" (2015, 44) within the long history of Indigenous activism. Wotherspoon and Jansen comment: "The Idle No More movement is widely interpreted to be a contemporary movement. However, while the movement of that specific name is relatively recent, it is grounded in longstanding historical roots located within struggles to define and maintain Indigenous identity and foster effective Indigenous nationhood. Its core vision is articulated in terms of objectives to work with allies to recognize First Nations sovereignty and nationhood and to employ an effective nation to nation relationship to foster social justice and protect the environment and lands in a respectful way" (2013, 22–3). They emphasize the Indigenous responsibility to protect the land and water: "The movement is important because it is rooted in old Indigenous laws that speak of our duty to protect the water and land for the future generations. It marks the reawakening of an Indigenous tradition and culture grounded in respect for the environment, fostering resistance to the kinds of exploitation of land and water conveyed through many of the terms of Bill C-45" (2013, 23).

Throughout these episodes in recent Indigenous history in Canada, music has featured prominently, heard on the front lines of activism, included in television footage shown on news programs, and documented by those in attendance.[7] Although rarely addressed by participants or academics, the soundscape associated with contemporary activism offers important insight into the role that music plays in Indigenous activism; it crosses cultural and geographic boundaries and, through social media and online forums, it is not contained to the place or time of its performance.

Alanis Obomsawin's Activism and *Trick or Treaty?*

Widely regarded as an excellent filmmaker, Alanis Obomsawin has established herself as an iconic and highly respected Indigenous documentarian. Born in 1932 in Lebanon, New Hampshire, Obomsawin spent her formative years on the Odanak First Nation near Sorel, Quebec; she lived in Trois-Rivières, Quebec, from the age of nine to twenty-two, where she experienced racism and discrimination. Obomsawin's first career was as a singer and storyteller beginning in the 1960s; she performed covers of popular tunes as well as traditional Abenaki songs and original songs, accompanying herself on hand-drum or rattle. Much of her work as a musician was activist in nature, performing at schools to teach about Indigenous culture, at jails to empower imprisoned Indigenous adults, and at festivals, where she offered an Indigenous perspective on life in Canada. In 1984 she released *Bush Lady* through CBC Radio-Canada.[8] This album comprises four original tracks and two traditional songs, liner notes in which Obomsawin indicates the sources, inspiration, and goals for each song, and a longer text in which she recounts the discrimination she faced as a youth in the predominantly white community of Trois-Rivières. Obomsawin's background as a musician is evident in much of her film work, where sound and music figure prominently, often creating additional layers of meaning in the narratives of the films.

During her campaign to have a swimming pool built in her home community, Obomsawin drew the attention of the National Film Board of Canada with her strong activism, and in 1967 the NFB approached her to serve as a consultant for work on Indigenous subject matter. She quickly decided, however, to create her own documentaries in order to have artistic control, and to avoid simply serving as the NFB's "in" to Indigenous communities. Obomsawin's first NFB film was a thirteen-minute video titled *Christmas at Moose Factory* (1971), featuring drawings and narration from a child's perspective about Christmas experiences in this northern Cree community; her best known documentary is *Kanehsatake: 270 Years of Resistance* (1993), which documented the conflict and activities around the Oka Crisis in 1990. Obomsawin has produced over fifty documentary films, all of which detail aspects of Indigenous life in Canada and have been described as "projects of resistance" (Cornellier 2012, 3), infused with "lyrical sensibility" in a medium usually characterized as "didactic, pedagogical and utilitarian" (White 1999, 33). Her body of work is noted for its activist topics, its narrative approach, and the subjective position taken by Obomsawin as narrator, interviewer, and social actor. Obomsawin is widely recognized as a pioneer in Indigenous film in Canada who merges the aesthetic practices of documentary film with traditional storytelling to educate and inform audiences about the historic and ongoing injustices faced in Canada by Indigenous people.[9]

Trick or Treaty?, released in 2014, was the first film by an Indigenous filmmaker to be screened as part of the Masters program at the Toronto International Film Festival (TIFF). The title of the documentary draws from the opening sentence of historian John Long's book *Treaty No. 9: Making the Agreement to Share the Land in Far Northern Ontario in 1905*; it reads: "Was it a trick or a treaty? Was treaty-signing in far northern Ontario simply a ruse, whereby the Indigenous signatories were fooled into signing a complex legal document that took away their rights? Or do their signatures signify their agreement to more general promises that constitute an oral agreement, misunderstood by most Canadians?" (2010, 3). Much of *Trick or Treaty?* focuses on the historic negotiations around Treaty 9 (1905) and the work of Stan Louttit, Grand Chief of the Mushkegowuk Council, to demonstrate that the oral agreements of this treaty were not represented in the written text.[10] It includes footage from a series of conferences that were organized for Indigenous leaders and community members to explore the conditions under which historic treaties were negotiated. These conditions resulted in the establishment of reserves and treaty agreements between the federal government and local First Nations. Juxtaposed with these materials is footage taken from Idle No More demonstrations and marches in Ottawa in the winter of 2012–13, as well as footage of the Nishiyuu Walkers,[11] a group of Cree youth who walked over 1,600 kilometres from their home community of Whapmagoostui, located on James Bay in northern Quebec, to deliver their concerns to Ottawa. Within the narrative created through video footage of these events and the information provided by John Long through classroom discussion sessions included in the film, a continuum is created between historic manipulation of Indigenous leaders during treaty negotiations, contemporary environmental concerns, and hopes for the future envisaged by and for Indigenous youth.

Creating a Sense of Place-Based Activism through Images, Sounds, and Words

Trick or Treaty? opens with a view of the cloud-covered sun on a cold winter's morning, a statue of Samuel de Champlain, located on Nepean Point in Ottawa, in the foreground. The camera pans to the buildings and land that constitute Parliament Hill, atop a cliff overlooking the frozen Ottawa River, with the sound of birds in the background. The symbolism of this opening scene is clear: Samuel de Champlain, credited as the "Father of New France," is looking toward the political epicentre of Canada, both perched on land that is recognized as unceded Algonquin territory. Land rights, sovereignty, respect: these are the centrepieces of Idle No More. The sound cuts to a question from a reporter, posed to then-national chief of the Assembly of First Nations Shawn A-in-chut Atleo, asking about the appropriateness of a reporter being escorted off the Attawapiskat First Nation during the water crisis there. The camera catches up to pan the audience of reporters in the National Press Theatre, watching intently as Atleo responds, flanked by Perry Bellegarde, chief of the Federation of Saskatchewan Indian Nations, on his left, and, on his right, Jody Wilson-Raybould, regional chief of the Assembly of First Nations of British Columbia.[12] Clearly agitated and passionate, Atleo responds by questioning the appropriateness of the ongoing mistreatment of Indigenous people in Canada, saying, "poverty is killing our people; the history of colonization and unilateral action on the part of governments will stop now." He warns, "We said we would be at a tipping point with the growth in our population exploding with over half under the age of twenty-five ... that tipping point is now. We have arrived at the fork in the road." Atleo is referencing the history of colonial mistreatment of Indigenous people in Canada, the activism of Idle No More, and the future that is envisioned by Indigenous leaders and settler activist allies. This poignant opening to *Trick or Treaty?*, emblematic of Obomsawin's effective directorial work, serves to position this documentary in a very specific time and place.

Idle No More is national in scope. Still, Ottawa's position as the site where change can be legislated by the federal government places this city – and particularly Parliament Hill and Victoria Island – as central to Idle No More activities and the ongoing political activism of Indigenous communities in Canada. Ottawa is both a meeting ground and the "arrival" point for Indigenous activists. Following the opening scene of *Trick or Treaty?* in which Chief Atleo addresses reporters in the National Press Theatre, viewers are taken along the 1.5 km journey of people walking from Victoria Island, a site in downtown Ottawa that is considered sacred to local Indigenous people, to Parliament Hill, the epicentre of national politics (see figure 16.2). Walkers of all ages, including babies in strollers, move forward on this cloudy winter day, most dressed for the cold with winter coats and toques, some wearing powwow regalia or other clothing with icons associated with their Indigenous heritage, such as the distinct purple and white symbol of the Haudenosaunee Confederacy. Other icons of Indigenous identity and sovereignty can be seen, including flags (Canada, United States, POW/MIA,[13] the Mohawk warrior flag), eagle staffs and coup sticks with eagle feathers and ribbons attached to them (the ribbons are often of the four sacred colours – red, black, yellow, white – associated with the four colours of humanity and the four colours of the medicine wheel). Numerous marchers carry placards with text emblazoned on them: "Unified and standing together for Indigenous sovereignty"; "Honour our Treaties"; "Algonquin Unceded"; "Idle No More – what did we do to deserve this, Harper?" Close-ups show people stoic and thoughtful, some are smiling, others seemingly concerned; police officers can be seen in the background, watching and chatting among themselves. Many of the walkers are holding or playing hand drums. A line of women is seen walking together, playing their hand drums, some wearing leather medicine pouches around their necks, others canteens of water (see figure 16.2). In front of the walkers is a wall of photographers, eagerly documenting this peaceful march eastward along Wellington Street to Parliament Hill. Another scene features Gilbert Whiteduck, then chief of the Kitigan Zibi Anishnabek First Nation,

Figure 16.2 | Women musicians in an Idle No More march in Ottawa.

one of the Algonquin Nations asserting that Ottawa is located on their traditional and unceded lands. There is also a group of community leaders holding their community staffs, many moving in sync to the beat of the drum. The powwow drum, carried by singers and accompanied with their distinct melodies, is the sonic underpinning of this sequence of images; noteworthy is the sound of eagle whistles, one of the most spiritually meaningful sounds for traditionalist First Nations people. Marchers close to the drum move to its incessant beat; some wearing powwow regalia dance to the music while others dance on the spot. One woman is holding up an upturned flag of British Columbia, shouting "Today. The sun rises for our people. Forever. For our children," while there are other occasional shouts from the crowd: "We're coming, Harper. We're getting closer!" This opening march serves to frame the content of *Trick or Treaty?* as directly connected to Idle No More, which is geographically centred in Ottawa and characterized by music, movement, and collective engagement with the arts and politics.

Obomsawin also privileges Ottawa as a primary site for Indigenous activism in *Trick or Treaty?* through the inclusion of footage from the marches that took place in Ottawa in the early 1970s in response to the appropriation of

Indigenous land for resource development. These images are shown during the oration of Metis leader Tony Belcourt, first president of the Native Council of Canada, 1971–74 (starting at 00:17:36). Belcourt identifies Ottawa as a key site for Indigenous activism, saying, "I want to recall and remember all the other leaders that have come since I first came here forty-one years ago. And when I look out here now, I remember that forty-one years ago, we never had crowds like this. We have the same arguments. Our lands were being taken away from us. Our environment was being destroyed. Our way of life was being threatened. The health and safety of our peoples were all at risk." The documentary shifts from footage of Belcourt speaking to the large crowd at Parliament Hill to an interview exchange in which he reiterates that treatment of Indigenous issues by the Canadian government has not changed in over forty years. The interview ends on a high note, with Belcourt stating that the main difference between activism in the 1970s and that of 2012–13 is that the government can no longer get away with the mistreatment of Indigenous peoples, implying that the national scope of Idle No More and its significant media coverage will force government accountability. By juxtaposing historic images of Indigenous protest in Ottawa in the 1970s with Belcourt's assertion that the federal government must take responsibility for Indigenous issues, Obomsawin links Indigenous communities' concerns about land and resource development with the site at which legislation is negotiated – Parliament Hill in Ottawa.

Creating the Local "Movement Moment" and a Sense of Solidarity through Music: Two Vignettes

At various points throughout *Trick or Treaty?* Obomsawin includes video footage of Idle No More demonstrations in Ottawa that features musicians performing as part of a march or at a rally. The music that predominates at these events is often intertribal in nature, meaning that it is First Nations music that is not specific to a particular nation and can be performed by all Indigenous people. Although a variety of songs were performed by activists at Idle No More,[14] the song that forms the foundation for much of the live footage in *Trick or Treaty?* is the intertribal song "Come Out Fighting."[15] Performed by Ottawa River Singers, it is heard during the opening scenes showing the march from Victoria Island to Parliament Hill (starting at 00:02:05) and also near the end of the documentary, at the arrival of the Nishiyuu Walkers to Parliament Hill on 25 March 2013 (the song begins at 1:04.55, following the completion of another intertribal song). Characteristic of powwow songs, "Come out Fighting" is performed by men, accompanying themselves on a large hand-made powwow drum. It opens with a short musical phrase sung solo, which is then repeated by the other singers, extending the phrase, followed by a second phrase. The repetition, as well the use of vocables instead of text, allows listeners to quickly learn the song and join in. In *Trick or Treaty?* members of the Ottawa River Singers can be seen carrying the drum as they strike it, surrounded by walkers, joining in singing when they can, or dancing as they move along. The performance of this intertribal song during Idle No More rallies served to unite the people who were there, synchronizing their movements with the inescapable beat of the drum.

A second musical moment featured at the end of *Trick or Treaty?* – a round dance on Parliament Hill – reinforces the role of music and dance in fostering a sense of solidarity and inclusion at demonstrations in Ottawa. Following the arrival of the Nishiyuu Walkers, Obomsawin uses footage of the round dance that took place after the oration of Indigenous leaders complimenting the walkers. The speakers emphasized the importance of youth to future generations and solidarity among Indigenous people. Chief Theresa Spence welcomed the walkers with these words of recognition:

> And there's one important message that we received from this journey, is to love each other and take care of each other. That was the purpose of this treaty, is to ... walk together. He [Nishiyuu Walker leader David Kawapit] showed us that they did that together. They walked together with hands in hands. When they met a lot of challenges during that journey, they didn't walk away from each other. They stayed together. They take care of each other. And this is what we need to do, with this Parliament government: we have to walk together. It's time to walk together. The treaty's going to be there, it's never going to go away, so we have to honour that and protect that treaty. But we can't do it alone, we need our partners. You're leading us to be together and to work with the government. You're going to lead us into that journey. And I want to thank you from the bottom of my heart. Gchi meegwetch.

While the text of the speeches that close *Trick or Treaty?* unify the threads of narrative in the documentary – Idle No More, Treaty No. 9 negotiations, concern for Indigenous youth and future generations – the images of the round dance reinforce the messages of unity and solidarity, messages that permeate speeches included in *Trick or Treaty?* While the huge crowd assembled on Parliament Hill claps and cheers for the walkers and the speeches of community leaders, the camera briefly pans to the underside of a hand drum being held in one hand; viewers see the silhouette of the drum stick as it moves to create the sound of the drum (1:15:06). The camera quickly shifts back to the grounds at Parliament Hill, where the impromptu round dance is taking place. People have joined hands and are stepping in a clockwise direction to the long-short beat of the drum, arms swaying as they face toward the centre of the growing circle of dancers. People run to join in the circle, arms outstretched as they meet the others, openly welcomed. The line of dancers faces the middle of the circle, with more and more people joining in. Next is a close-up of the singers – a group of men standing in a circle on the steps of Parliament Hill, loudly and enthusiastically singing the round dance song, accompanying themselves on their hand drums; later women can be heard joining in the song at the ends of phrases, with a close up of their faces. The round dance circle grows, so that the perimeter of the grounds at Parliament Hill is lined with dancers. The symbolism of these images – strangers joining together in dance on Parliament Hill, dancing to the long-short ("heartbeat") rhythm of the drum – cannot be lost on participants or viewers of *Trick or Treaty?* Indeed, the peaceful demonstration through a round dance – a traditional social dance that celebrates inclusivity and equality – illustrates a sense of solidarity among all participants, Indigenous and non-Indigenous, youth and elders.[16]

While emotions were heated during the intense early months of Idle No More, and Indigenous people in Canada continue to contend with many critical issues, Obomsawin ends the documentary with a sense of hope; the speeches of the Indigenous leaders coupled with the round dance reiterate the spirit of solidarity that characterized much of the activism around Idle No More. Nishiyuu walker David Kawapit, the seventeen-year old who initiated the walk, says over the sounds of the music, "Change doesn't just come overnight, it takes time. And we're just kick-starting something larger than our journey. And it's slowly getting there. Change is going to come. Soon" (01:15:54). Finally, drawing the connection between Idle No More and the concerns around treaty rights, the words of one of the participants in Dr Long's classes are juxtaposed over the sound of the round dance song: "Treaties are a very sacred ... sacred thing. That's why we know we are still here. That resilience, that belief, that hope, to think that someday we will have what we want. Because, to me, I look around and we're still very much alive. We're still trying to get people to understand what those agreements, what those promises mean. But it hasn't changed who we are inside. That's the important piece. That, to me, is the hope" (01:16:33). As these words are being spoken, Obomsawin juxtaposes footage of singers performing the round dance with that of Grand Chief Stan Louttit talking with a small group of people, with treaty documents in front of him; rounding out this collage of images is a return to the singers, ending with a close-up of Ottawa River Singers' Brock Lewis as he sings the round dance song. The links between musicians, activists, and youth are brought together in this closing sequence, unified by a shared sense of hope for the future; the round dance song ends, followed by cheers and strikes on the drums. The camera pans up to the Peace Tower with a Canadian flag perched on top, returning to the symbolism of place that opened the documentary; then, a seagull flies in the sky.

During the film's closing credits, Obomsawin speaks the words "The drum will always call," and the text "To all the marchers, Drummers and Singers: 'You have made a mark in history – change has arrived'" scrolls across the screen. By documenting the involvement of the Ottawa River Singers and other musicians during Idle No More activities in Ottawa, Obomsawin demonstrates her awareness of the teachings of the drum for peace and positive relations, the importance of the drumbeat as a symbol for Mother Earth, and the unifying call of intertribal First Nations music. At a screening of *Trick or Treaty?* at Carleton University, Ottawa, in January 2017, Obomsawin recognized members of the Ottawa River Singers in the audience, inviting them to the front of the auditorium and thanking them for their ongoing work; after performing a song for the packed room, they were greeted with a standing ovation.

Music to Link Activists across Time and Place: John Trudell's "Crazy Horse"

Throughout *Trick or Treaty?* Obomsawin shows the links between the activism associated with previous Indigenous issues in Canada and the United States with those of today and tomorrow. This musical narrative of continuity is particularly striking in Obomsawin's choice of John Trudell's song "Crazy Horse" at the conclusion of the documentary, following the footage of the round dance at Parliament Hill. For those familiar with the legacies of Trudell and Crazy Horse, the use of this song as the closing music for *Trick or Treaty?* positions Idle No More in dialogue with broader Indigenous activism – both geographically (across North America) and diachronically (since the late nineteenth century).

John Trudell was born in Omaha, Nebraska, in 1946, the son of a Santee Sioux father and Mexican mother, and he died in Santa Clara County, California in 2015. He spent his childhood on the Santee Reservation in Nebraska and in early adulthood he joined the American military. Trudell's name is directly associated with Indigenous activism, and specifically the Red Power movement of the 1960s and 1970s; he is well known for his very public role in the All Tribes occupation of Alcatraz Island in San Francisco in November 1969,[17] and for his leadership within the American Indian Movement (1973–79). During the 1960s and 1970s Indigenous activists across North America were drawing attention to their experiences of discrimination, poverty, poor living conditions, and marginalization, and the ongoing disregard by the federal government of their treaty obligations. As Trudell stated, "This is a country where all men are created equal and it's the land of the free and the home of truth and justice and liberty for all. But we want to know why that doesn't apply to us" (2017). Because of his political leadership and activism, Trudell was closely monitored by the FBI. In 1979, twelve hours after Trudell had burned an American flag in front of the FBI headquarters as a protest, his pregnant wife Tina Manning, three children, and mother-in-law were killed in a suspicious house fire. After the loss of his family, Trudell turned his attention to a different form of activism through his creative writing; he gained accolades as a poet, actor, speaker, and musician, but his role as an Indigenous activist remained. In his own words, "When I started writing, ... my lines were my bombs; these were the bombs I was throwing, these were my explosions. These were, almost in a way, my acts of violence against society. That was the only way I could act" (2017).

Trudell's reputation as an activist, artist, actor, and literary figure make him a recognizable icon of Indigenous activism. Turning his attention to protest through writing, Trudell eventually met musician and accomplished guitarist Jesse Ed Davis, who had performed with Bob Dylan and Jackson Browne. Davis offered to set Trudell's words to music, and through this collaboration, music became an alternative platform for Trudell's activism. Trudell released his first album, *Tribal Voice*, in 1983, and he went on to release ten more albums, gaining the praise of notable recording artists, including Kris Kristofferson and Bob Dylan. The themes of his creative output include the earth and our relationship to it, resistance and decolonization, traditional gender roles, kinship and the importance of women to society, and the importance of language (Lee 2007, 91–5). Trudell's music is a combination of his speaking voice supported with solo guitar, synthesized chordal accompaniment, and for some pieces, drums, shakers, and Indigenous flute. He expresses his poetry with rhythmic and lyrical nuance, with the focus on the text; the style of his creative output continues the centrality of storytelling and the importance of oral traditions to many Indigenous nations; as literary scholar Jan Johnson writes, "Native music could tell the stories that textbooks weren't teaching and newspapers weren't covering ... Through their songs, these [Indigenous pop] musicians asserted ethical demands for fairness and justice to listeners who understood that much of the discourse of the times was occurring on record players and radios" (2016, 94).

Trudell's creative output and activist voice heighten the impact of Obomsawin's use of "Crazy Horse" to close *Trick or Treaty?*, linking the themes of the documentary with cross-continental Indigenous concerns of the late nineteenth and early twentieth centuries.[18] The text of "Crazy Horse" immediately summons Crazy Horse, the late nineteenth-century celebrated war leader and noted Oglala Lakota who led the resistance against the surrender of traditional Lakota lands to the American government for settlement by non-Indigenous people, and sought to preserve the traditional ways of life of his people. As a respected war hero, Crazy Horse (in Lakota, his name is Tȟašúŋke Witkó) has come to be seen as an icon of Indigenous resistance: he rejected negotiations with non-Indigenous colonizers, he opposed the imposition of Euro-American lifeways, and he condemned the devastation rendered by the wholesale slaughter of buffalo herds and the encroachment of Euro-American settlement on traditional Lakota lands. Historian Kingsley Bray asserts, "For modern Lakota people he has remained a compelling symbol of resistance ... The public at large recognizes the name of Crazy Horse as a touchstone of freedom, of integrity and bravery against the odds" (2006, xvi).

By invoking Crazy Horse, Trudell's text links contemporary activism to early Indigenous activism. The song opens with the words "Crazy Horse, we hear what you say,"[19] before turning attention to the specific issues affecting Indigenous peoples. Trudell's narration questions how the earth, the stars, and the air can be sold, before acknowledging the confrontation between people, as land and lifestyle were taken from Indigenous people for the material gain of the "predators." The text directly addresses the colonization efforts of settlers and the resilience of Indigenous people in lines such as "Predators face he possessed a race; Possession a way that doesn't end,"

"Children of God feed on children of Earth," and "Predator tries civilising us, but the tribes will not go without return." The text also links the concerns of this nineteenth-century leader with the issues plaguing Indigenous peoples at the start of the twenty-first century, reinforcing the teaching that one must consider the impact of all decisions on future generations.

Trudell draws further links between nineteenth-century and contemporary activism by invoking the teaching of the seven generations, saying "we are the seventh generation." As Anishinabe/Ojibway law professor John Burrows summarizes, many First Nations people recognize that now is the time of the seventh generation, tracing contemporary demands for change to the imposition of the Indian Act in Canada in the late 1800s, the period in which Crazy Horse was living. Burrows writes:

> For my family, it is now the seventh generation since the Indian Act was introduced. The seventh generation! This generation holds special significance for Indigenous people. Decisions about the future are not supposed to occur without taking them into account. Unfortunately, the Indian Act cuts most deeply at this very point. The Indian Act is purposely designed to assimilate us. It is meant to sever the generations. The Act is working its purpose, through provisions concerning land, elections, membership, commerce and education. It cuts us from those future relationships. We cannot take account of the seventh generation if the Indian Act continues to remove them from us. (Burrows 2008, 3)

By referencing the teachings of the seven generations, the exploitation of land and resources, and environmental concerns, the text of Trudell's song "Crazy Horse" invokes the same issues that fueled Idle No More: protection of the land, the rights of Indigenous people, dispossession, and sovereignty. These parallels make Obomsawin's choice to use it as the non-diagetic music accompanying the closing sequences of *Trick or Treaty?* especially poignant.

The closing images of *Trick or Treaty?*, accompanied by Trudell's "Crazy Horse," are mostly aerial views of forests and waterways and footage of various animals and birds moving freely in their natural environment; similar vignettes of wildlife and the wilderness appear throughout *Trick or Treaty?* as transition frames, reminding viewers of the centrality of land to Idle No More. However, when the song text shifts to the topic of possession, the lack of concern for people, and the materialism that fuels development, there is a concomitant shift in the video footage toward human abuses of the land

(1:19:26): aerial views of an oil refinery, a close-up of some large vehicles used in the oil sands, and a giant hole in the ground with a tanker moving toward the site of activity in the sand pit. Indeed, the images that correspond with Trudell's text reiterate that "these days are the hardest." The final sequences of *Trick or Treaty?* feature historic still photos of various Indigenous peoples: a family in a canoe, a man on a sled pulled by dogs, three decorated chiefs, a family outside a tepee wearing Western clothes. As one photo fades into another, Trudell again invokes Crazy Horse and his prophecy of the seven generations, closing with "We are the seventh generation" before Obomsawin's voice reminds viewers that "the drum will always call."

The ways in which Obomsawin juxtaposes the closing sequence of images with the lyrics of "Crazy Horse" and the haunting voice of John Trudell encourage viewers to reflect on the links between the pillaging and destruction of land and the environment for resource extraction, Indigenous treaty rights and the deceitful negotiations that took place during the nineteenth century, and the energy and vision of activists involved in Idle No More during the winter of 2012–13. The activism with which Trudell was associated – particularly his involvement in the American Indian Movement in the 1970s and his subsequent creative output – clearly positions him as an influential figure among Indigenous activists. By using "Crazy Horse" to close *Trick or Treaty?* Obomsawin makes tangible the links between Idle No More, nineteenth-century resistance, the priority for protection of land and lifeways of Indigenous people across North America, and the need to think of future generations.

Narrative Interconnectivity and Indigenous Storytelling: Conclusions

As a "movement moment" on the trajectory of Indigenous resistance in North America, Idle No More is linked with previous activist "moments," building on the momentum of, and sharing many core issues with other conflicts and resistances involving Indigenous people. The Truth and Reconciliation Commission, like Idle No More, was a forwarding-looking, energizing measure for improved education around Indigenous history and issues, and the introduction of programs and initiatives to better support Indigenous peoples. Both drew attention to important longstanding issues, such as the disproportionate number of murdered and missing Indigenous women, and most recently, survivors of the '60s scoop.

The music that Alanis Obomsawin features in *Trick or Treaty?* reinforces the interconnectedness of contemporary activism with the ongoing resistance against dispossession and assimilation in the nineteenth century. Music selections also connect the activism coming out of the Red Power movement in the 1960s and 1970s with ongoing struggles for acknowledgment of land and treaty rights, and the protection of traditional culture and values; indeed, music links the local nature of much activism with efforts across Turtle Island, showing the connections between the local and the global.

The interweaving of narratives – of corrupt negotiations during the late nineteenth-century establishment of Treaty No. 9 in northern Ontario, the Idle No More movement, and the Nishiyuu Walkers's long trek – reminds audiences of the importance of storytelling to Indigenous cultures. As Steve Loft writes, "Obomsawin is a storyteller, a carrier of history, and a creator of history. She weaves her stories slowly and deliberately, revealing the connections that lie beneath the surface. Her films lead us on journeys beyond the superficial, perfunctory attention normally accorded the topics she chooses. Obomsawin examines critically, ethically, and morally, the clash of cultures and their repercussions on Native people through the lives and stories of those most often voiceless" (2005, 62).

Stories to teach and to remember; stories to change. Storytelling imparts the traditional teachings that remind people of the interconnectedness of all things – people, land, water, our ancestors, and future generations. Indeed, in viewing *Trick or Treaty?* and understanding how Obomsawin weaves these priorities throughout the documentary through images, text, and song, we are able to better understand how Idle No More is not a single "moment" in time; rather it is part of a longer trajectory of Indigenous resistance and resurgence. We can also see how music serves to narrate the multiplicity of issues plaguing First Peoples today, while also empowering and enriching the lives of those who hear and perform these songs. Putting a sound to the images of Idle No More, and understanding the meaning of the songs that are heard in the soundscape of Indigenous resistance and cultural renewal, adds layers of meaning to the moments of Indigenous activism, geographically and diachronically.

Since its release, *Trick or Treaty?* has been screened at numerous Indigenous Friendship Centres and urban community centres, at educational institutions of all levels, and in film festivals across Canada, often featuring opportunities to discuss the film and other topics with Obomsawin during a question and answer period. The film can be live streamed on the NFB and CBC websites and educators are using it to teach about treaties, oral histories, and Indigenous peoples in Canada in general (Baker and Maki 2018, Indspire 2018). Many songs and narratives have been created following the initial Idle

No More activities, continuing to draw attention to Indigenous resurgence. As musicians, artists, writers, and filmmakers continue to raise awareness of Indigenous issues in North America, the output of Alanis Obomsawin, and her creative and meaningful selection of subject matter, sounds, and imagery, will continue to resonate and inspire others.

In the few years following the peak of Idle No More, its impact continues to resonate with Indigenous leaders and the Canadian public, particularly regarding social justice issues and land and sovereignty debates. Governmental and educational institutions are responding to the ninety-four recommendations of the Truth and Reconciliation Commission, seeking ways of engaging Indigenous people and communities as political leaders and educators. New forms of storytelling by Indigenous artists and their allies – including ballets, theatre pieces, and film –contribute to understanding the rich history of the people living in Canada; likewise, school curricula are changing to give a more critical account of colonization, settlement, and contemporary issues. *Trick or Treaty?* closes with a spirit of hope, healing, and change, and a call to take care of the earth and each other that speaks to the priorities of Indigenous youth. Viewers are left with a clearer understanding of the interconnectedness of the historic mistreatment of Indigenous peoples, contemporary concerns for the environment, and priorities for future generations.

Notes

1 See Coulthard 2014.
2 Films by Alanis Obomsawim, including *Trick or Treaty?*, can be found on and streamed through the National Film Board of Canada website (https://www.nfb.ca).
3 Books that focus on Idle No More include Kino-ndo-niimi Collective 2014 and Coates 2015. Various YouTube videos and online playlists have also been created (see, for example Alexis 2013, RPM 2013, and Woodward 2013), as have new songs such as Ulali's "Idle No More," Rellik's "Idle No More," and Drezus's "Red Winter," among others.
4 The terms diagetic and non-diagetic originate in film studies; diagetic music is incorporated in a film as part of the action or scene on the screen, as part of the film's action, whereas non-diagetic music is superimposed and is added to the film for dramatic effect.
5 The National Truth and Reconciliation Commission examined the history of Indian Residential Schools in Canada. The commission ran from 1 June 2008 until December 2015 when the final report was issued. Chaired by the Honourable Justice Murray Sinclair, with Dr Marie Wilson and Chief Wilton Littlechild serving as commissioners, it involved testimonials from survivors of residential schools and their family members, documenting the abuse suffered by students and the intergenerational impact of the

cultural genocide that took place in these state-endorsed, mostly church-run institutions. Thousands of Indigenous children were forced to attend residential schools, separating them from their families and home communities. In addition to increasing public awareness of the genocidal goals and impacts of Indian Residential Schools on Indigenous peoples and cultures in Canada, the commission's final report included ninety-four recommendations that seek to facilitate reconciliation between Indigenous individuals and communities and Canadian society more broadly. See Dylan Robinson and Keavy Martin 2016 for an examination of some of the artistic expressions that were performed at, generated around, or comment on the Truth and Reconciliation Commission.

6   The '60s Scoop refers to the period during which Indigenous children were apprehended from their communities and adopted into homes of Euro-Canadians.

7   Some songs have become iconic of contemporary Indigenous activism, such as the "AIM Song" and "The Women's Warrior Song," as have songs in popular music idioms such as the EDM/powwow music blend of A Tribe Called Red, Buffy Sainte Marie's folk-inspired songs, and Tanya Tagaq's unique creations using traditional Inuit throat singing techniques.

8   Information about this LP can be obtained through the Museum of Canadian Music. See http://citizenfreak.com/titles/294247-obomsawin-alanis-bush-lady to access online sound files of this recording and the accompanying print materials (accessed 6 September 2017); information about various singles that were also released in 1984 can also be found on this site.

9   See Gauthier 2010 and Cornellier 2012 for a discussion of how Obomsawin's oeuvre fits within the NFB and Indigenous filmmaking. See Pick 1999 for a discussion of the links between Obomsawin's documentary filmmaking and Indigenous storytelling traditions.

10 This council comprises the chiefs of eight Cree First Nation communities in northern Ontario.

11 Nishiyuu is Cree for "human beings."

12 Wilson-Raybould is Kwakwaka'wakw and a member of the We Wai Kai Nation in British Columbia. In November of 2015 she was sworn in as minister of justice of Canada, the first Indigenous person to hold that post.

13 The POW/MIA flag recognizes prisoners of war (POW) and soldiers who went missing in action (MIA). Although it is more widely associated with American soldiers who were imprisoned, went missing, or were unaccounted for during conflicts in Southeast Asia during the 1970s, the flag is often used in Indigenous gatherings to acknowledge First Peoples who were likewise lost due to conflicts.

14 Throughout *Trick or Treaty?* are scenes that illustrate the importance of music to Indigenous life. For example, two hand-drummers sing an honour song to open a meeting in Moose Factory organized by Chief Stan Louttit in which people are invited to look at historic Treaty 9 documents (00:22:33); there is footage of a traditional song by male singers accompanying themselves on hand drums as they stand on the steps of Parliament, greeted with enthusiastic applause and cheering when they finish (00:30:50–00:31:51); impromptu dancing to a hand-drum song marks the arrival of the Nishiyuu Walkers to Ottawa (1:04:20); and a giant round dance is held on the grounds

of Parliament Hill, led by a group male singers on hand drums with women singers supporting them (1:15:06). The music and dance featured in *Trick or Treaty?* remind viewers of the diversity of Indigenous forms of cultural expression that are practised throughout Canada.

15   Brock Lewis, member of Ottawa River Singers, identified this song for me. Other songs that were often sung during Idle No More and other rallies, vigils, and demonstrations (and found on various YouTube videos of these events) include the "Strong Woman's Song," "Women's Warrior Song," and "AIM Song," but these are not featured in *Trick or Treaty?* Each of these songs has a particular teaching attached to it about its origins, purposes, and meanings.

16   For additional details about the symbolic meaning of the round dance and how it relates to Idle No More activism, see Amanda Morris's 2014 article. Citing Carleton University's Centre for Aboriginal Culture and Education (now Centre for Indigenous Initiatives), she writes, "As an inspirational protest action against the legislative injustices perpetrated by colonial governments on Indigenous nations, the round dance was likely chosen because of its inclusive nature. According to the Centre for Aboriginal Culture and Education (2013): 'This dance was a healing ceremony that became a social dance for Aboriginal people and is held in the winter season ... We join hands in a circle and dance around the drummers and singers. The beat of the drum is like the heartbeat of the community, and everyone moves as one. It's a dance for everyone: children, friends, families, youth and Elders.' Clearly, the choice of dance for these protest rallies was a wise selection on the part of the organizers" (2014, 253).

17   This nineteen-month-long occupation drew national and international attention to Indigenous issues in the United States and is recognized for both catapulting Indigenous rights into mainstream media and for uniting Indigenous people across the continent.

18   Trudell wrote "Crazy Horse" in the summer of 1997; it was released on his album *Bone Days* in 2001.

19   John Trudell lyrics provided courtesy of Poet Tree Publishing c/o Drive Music Publishing.

References

Alexis, Brandon. 2013. "Idle No More (Documentary)" YouTube video. Accessed 8 November 2017. https://youtu.be/WyuUU4VohDM.

Baker, Brad, and Stephanie Maki. 2018. "An Educator's Guide to *Trick or Treaty?* and *Hi-Ho Mistahey!*" Accessed 10 July 2018. https://indspire.ca/wp-content/uploads/2017/03/NFB-Educator-Guide-Trick-or-Treaty.pdf.

Barker, Adam J. 2015. "'A Direct Act of Resurgence, and Direct Act of Sovereignty': Reflections on Idle No More, Indigenous Activism, and Canadian Settler Colonialism." *Globalizations* 12 (1): 43–65.

Burrows, John. 2008. *Seven Generations, Seven Teachings: Ending the Indian Act*. Ottawa, ON: National Centre for First Nations Governance. Accessed 5 September 2017. http://fngovernance.org/resources_docs/7_Generations_7_Teachings.pdf.

Bray, Kingsley. 2006. *Crazy Horse: A Lakota Life*. Norman: University of Oklahoma Press.
Coates, Ken. 2015. *#IdleNoMore and the Remaking of Canada*. Regina, SK: University of Regina Press.
Cornellier, Bruno. 2012. "The Thing about Obomsawin's Indianness: Indigenous Reality and the Burden of Education at the National Film Board of Canada." *Canadian Journal of Film Studies – Revue canadienne d'études cinématographiques* 21 (2): 2–26.
Coulthard, Glen Sean. 2014. *Red Skin White Masks: Rejecting the Colonial Politics of Recognition*. Minneapolis: University of Minnesota Press.
Couture, Selena. 2014. "Performativity of Time, Movement and Voice in Idle No More." Review of the Kino-nda-niimi Collective, *The Winter We Danced*, in *Performance Research* 19 (6): 118–20.
Gauthier, Jennifer L. 2010. "Dismantling the Master's House: The Feminist Fourth Cinema Documentaries of Alanis Obomsawin and Loretta Todd." *Post Script: Essays in Film and the Humanities* 29 (3): 27–43.
Indspire. 2018. "Successful Practices: Showcasing Strategies That Work." Accessed 10 July 2018. https://indspire.ca/successfulpractices/trick-or-treaty/.
Johnson, Jan. 2016. "'We Were All Wounded at Wounded Knee': The Engaged Resistance of Folk and Rock in the Red Power Era." In *Indigenous Pop: Native American Music from Jazz to Hip Hop*, edited by Jeff Berglund, Jan Johnson, and Kimberli Lee, 92–106. Tucson: University of Arizona Press.
The Kino-nda-niimi Collective, eds. 2014. *The Winter We Danced: Voices from the Past, the Future and the Idle No More Movement*. Winnipeg, MB: Arbeiter Ring Publishing.
Lee, Kimberli. 2007. "Heartspeak from the Spirit: Songs of John Trudell, Keith Secola, and Robbie Robertson." *Studies in American Indian Literatures* 19 (3): 89–114.
Lewis, Brock. 2015. Interview with author. Ottawa, Ontario, 11 May.
Loft, Steven. 2005. "Sovereignty, Subjectivity, and Social Action: The Films of Alanis Obomsawin." In *Transference, Tradition, Technology: Native New Media Exploring Visual and Digital Culture*, edited by Dana Claxton, Steve Loft, and Melanie Townsend, 6–67. Banff, AB: Walter Phillips Gallery.
Long, John. 2010. *Treaty No. 9: Making the Agreement to Share the Land in Far Northern Ontario in 1905*. Montreal & Kingston: McGill-Queen's University Press.
McKinnon, Crystal. 2010. "Indigenous Music as a Space of Resistance." In *Making Settler Colonial Space: Perspectives on Race, Place and Identity*, edited by Tracey Banivanua Mar and Penelope Edmonds, 255–72. New York, NY: Palgrave Macmillan.
McMahon. Ryan. 2014. "The Round Dance Revolution: Idle No More." In Kino-nda-niimi Collective, *The Winter We Danced*, 98–100.
McMillan, L. Jane, Janelle Young, and Molly Peters. 2013. "Commentary: The 'Idle No More' Movement in Eastern Canada." *Canadian Journal of Law and Society / Revue Canadienne Droit et Société* 28 (3): 429–31.
Morris, Amanda. 2014. "Twenty-First-Century Debt Collectors: Idle No More Combats a Five-Hundred-Year-Old Debt." *WSQ: Women's Studies Quarterly* 42 (1 & 2): 242–56.
Museum of Canadian Music. "Obomsawin, Alanis – Bush Lady." Accessed 6 September 2017. http://citizenfreak.com/titles/294247-obomsawin-alanis-bush-lady.

Obomsawin, Alanis. 1971. *Christmas at Moose Factory*. Ottawa, ON: National Film Board of Canada.
— 1993. *Kanehsatake: 270 Years of Resistance*. Ottawa, ON: National Film Board of Canada.
— 2012. *Trick or Treaty?* Ottawa, ON: National Film Board of Canada.
"Ottawa River." Tribal Spirit Music. Accessed 8 September 2017. https://tribalspiritmusic.com/artists/ottawa-river/.
Pick, Zuzana. 1999. "Storytelling and Resistance: The Documentary Practice of Alanis Obomsawin." In *Gendering the Nation: Canadian Women's Cinema*, edited by Kay Armatage, Kass Banning, Brenda Longfellow, and Janine Marchessault, 76–93. Toronto, ON: University of Toronto Press.
Robinson, Dylan. 2016. "Intergenerational Sense, Intergenerational Responsibility." In Robinson and Keavy, *Arts of Engagement*, 43–65.
Robinson, Dylan, and Keavy Martin, eds. 2016a. *Arts of Engagement: Taking Aesthetic Action In and Beyond the Truth and Reconciliation Commission of Canada*. Waterloo, ON: Wilfrid Laurier University Press.
Robinson, Dylan, and Keavy Martin. 2016b. "Introduction: 'The Body Is a Resonant Chamber.'" In Robinson and Keavy, *Arts of Engagement*, 1–20.
RPM (Revolutions per Minute). 2013. "Indigenous Music Culture," website. Accessed 8 November 2017. http://rpm.fm/music/download-idle-no-more-songs-for-life-vol-1/.
Trudell, John. 2015. "We Have the Power (1974)." *Akwesasne Notes* 6 (3): 10–11 (1973), reprinted in *Say We Are Nations: Documents of Politics and Protest in Indigenous America Since 1887*, edited by Daniel M. Cobb, 163–6. Chapel Hill: University of North Carolina Press.
— 2017. "John Trudell: A Blue Indian." YouTube video. Accessed 18 September 2017. https://www.youtube.com/watch?time_continue=616&v=foQKPMGA1Ws.
White, Jerry. 1992. "Alanis Obomsawin, Documentary Form and the Canadian Nation(s)." *Cineaction* 49, 25–36; reprinted in 1999 in *North of Everything: English-Canadian Cinema Since 1980*, edited by Jerry White and William Beard, 364–75. Edmonton: University of Alberta Press.
Woodward Syd. 2013. "Idle No More Short Documentary." YouTube video. Accessed 8 November 2017. https://youtu.be/IzXI7aznBtc.
Woons, Marc. 2013. "The 'Idle No More' Movement and Global Indifference to Indigenous Nationalism." *AlterNative: An International Journal of Indigenous Peoples* 9 (2): 172–7.
Wotherspoon, Terry, and John Hansen. 2013. "The 'Idle No More' Movement: Paradoxes of First Nations Inclusion in the Canadian Context." *Social Inclusion* 1 (1): 21–36.

Accompanying Video and Audio Examples

Readers are encouraged to access the video and audio files that supplement chapter contents on the following YouTube playlist. The numbering of items in this list corresponds with the numeration found below.
https://www.youtube.com/playlist?list=PL5b8Om_bWObhPSBMOsZiOpWjPKdH63IRq.

Part One | Transforming Musical Traditions

Chapter 3, Margaret E. Walker, "Kathak in Canada: Classical and Contemporary"

1. *NextSteps 2014–15*, Bageshree Vaze. Published 20 April 2015.
   A short promotional video published by Harbourfront Next Steps dance series, featuring kathak dancer/choreographer Bageshree Vaze talking about her new work *Paratopia*, with clips of the Raagini dance company in rehearsal.
   https://youtu.be/uFO8MUZO86o
2. Kathak Recital by Sanjay Bhattacharya. Published 19 February 2010.
   Sanjay Bhattacharya provides a ten-minute example of a "traditional kathak solo" beginning with an invocatory Sanskrit piece (in this case a *stotra* praising the Hindu God Ram), followed by the string of *nritt* or non-representational dance items, and ending with an expressional item or *abhinaya* telling a well-known story of the Hindu God Krishna teasing a maiden who is fetching water.
   https://youtu.be/BBycSHTaT7A
3. Kathak and Tabla *Jugalbandi*. Published 16 July 2015.
   Mukta Joshi (dancer) with Kishore Pane on tabla: this excerpt from the end of a longer performance provides a good example of a *jugalbandi*, with the tabla player responding to the patterns of the kathak dancer's feet. The video ends with footwork and a *tihai* that finishes with the characteristic left-heel spins.
   https://youtu.be/rS1OBXT7Eec
4. *Shakuntala – A Dance Drama*, by Panwar Music and Dance. Published 7 August 2013.
   Toronto-based Hemant and Vaishali Panwar's 2014 creation *Shakuntala*.
   https://youtu.be/6J8V5MtppmU
5. *Firedance: Kathak/Flamenco Collaboration*. Published 28 January 2008.
   Joanna de Souza's collaboration with flamenco dancer Esmeralda Enrique.
   https://youtu.be/FoNjpIezVVQ

6 Delhi2Dublin Canada Day 2007. Published 2 July 2007.
Saveeta Sharma and some of her students performing with Irish step dancers, breakdancers, and popular fusion group Delhi2Dublin on Canada Day at Parliament Hill, Ottawa in 2007.
https://youtu.be/AcFWOdDg_rk

7 Dance Fusion – Kathak, Flamenco, and Canadian Step Dance. Published 24 May 2009.
April Verch, Ilsa Godino, and Amika Kushwaha performing Ottawa Valley step dancing, flamenco, and kathak in an improvised *sawal-jawab* or question and answer selection at the Vancouver Island Music Festival in 2008.
https://youtu.be/rcEiSV1fFqA

Chapter 4, Heather Sparling, "Taking the Piss Out: Presentational and Participatory Elements in the History of the Cape Breton Milling Frolic"

8 *Eriskay, 1934.* Published 26 April 2011.
A video shot in 1934 about life on the Scottish Western Isle (with audio later overdubbed).
Watch from 14'30" for the waulking (although the whole video is relevant since it shows how the wool was shorn, spun, and woven before the cloth was ready to be waulked).
https://youtu.be/O9_tOh6NYOs

9 Traditional Gaelic Waulking songs at Soldiers of Killiecrankie, July 2014. Published 8 August 2014.
A contemporary re-enactment of waulking.
https://youtu.be/mKbbURJSM58

10 Waulking at Noth Harris Show, 2010. Published 9 May 2011.
A contemporary re-enactment of waulking.
https://youtu.be/EjslTMBwRTA

11 Explanation of a Milling Frolic. Published 10 October 2012.
A description of Cape Breton milling frolics provided by Jim Watson, one of the foremost experts on traditional Gaelic song in Cape Breton. This video was shot at the Highland Village, which includes milling frolics as part of its tourist activities.
https://youtu.be/q8rDRuuYMe8

12 Milling song at *Celtic Heart of North America* Launch. Published 11 June 2010.
Video shows many well-known older milling singers.
https://youtu.be/BWnfGXwRyCw

13 Gaelic Milling Frolic. Published 14 November 2009.
People of mixed generations participating at a milling frolic.
https://youtu.be/XHax-NPP2v0

Chapter 5, Meghan C. Forsyth, "Improvising on the Margins: Tradition and Musical Agency in les Îles-de-la-Madeleine"

14 Vishtèn, "Reel du pendu." Published 5 November 2017.
This track from Vishten's 2009 *Live* album features fiddler Pascal Miousse of Cap-aux-Meules, Îles-de-la-Madeleine, accompanied by his father, Bernard Miousse, on guitar. The tune, "Reel du pendu" ("Hanged Man's Reel," "Hangman's Reel," "Devil's Reel") is

widely known for its individualized and often virtuosic interpretations and the legend that surrounds its origins. The most common version of the legend suggests that, while standing on the gallows, a man condemned to death by hanging was given a badly tuned fiddle and, despite never having touched a fiddle before, played this tune from memory so expertly that he was granted his freedom. The tune is normally played with the violin cross-tuned (*scordatura*) in the key of A. One of the most famous recordings of this tune is by the Québécois fiddler Jean "Ti-Jean" Carignan in 1973. A 1972 film by André Gladu, *Le reel du pendu* (National Film Board of Canada), traces the tune through Quebec, Acadia, and Louisiana.
https://youtu.be/sPDBP_8073o

15 Bertrand Déraspe, musicien traditionnel. Published 29 March 2012.
Fisherman and fiddler Bertrand Déraspe of Pointe-aux-Loups, Îles-de-la-Madeleine, demonstrates the Madelinot fiddle style inherited from his father, Arnold Déraspe. Bertrand and Arnold play several tunes together. To learn more (in French):
http://irepi.ulaval.ca/fiche-bertrand-deraspe-189.html
https://youtu.be/aGU9YRH-9o8

Part Two | Rethinking Genres and Artistic Practices

Chapter 7, Monique Giroux, "Metis (Style) Fiddling: From Historical Roots to Contemporary Practice"

16 Ivan Spence plays "Buffalo Gals." Published 9 October 2008.
The A part (00:00–00:16) of this version of "Buffalo Gals" by Metis fiddler Ivan Spence provides a comparison to Lavallee's version of the same tune. Although there are similarities, especially in his use of repeated notes, Spence does not use ghosted notes to the same degree as Lavallee.
https://youtu.be/2bLUq5S3V2c

17 Garry Lepine, "Andy Roussin Reel." Published 2 December 2017.
Recording of a performance in 2012 on the mainstage at Metisfest, Killarney, Manitoba. Lepine blurs the beginnings/endings of phrases in the B part, uses strongly accented offbeats, and repeated sixteenth notes to "fill in" beats. Ends of phrases are marked by one or two strongly accented notes, longer note values, and low bows. He uses a great deal of droning throughout.
https://youtu.be/ejcy9WWPEdo

18 Shawn Mousseau, "Buck Skin Reel." Published 2 December 2017.
Recording on the mainstage at Metisfest, Killarney, Manitoba. Like Lepine, Mousseau's playing features strongly accented offbeats, but he uses more detached bowings and greater rhythmic variety than Lepine. Mousseau has an aggressive, "in-the-string" approach to bowing. The use of ghosted notes followed by an accented note creates a lilt and forward motion. Mousseau's heel-toe foot tapping recalls traditional clogging.
https://youtu.be/FXsop9iuQJo

19 JJ Lavallee, "Buffalo Gals." Uploaded 2 December 2017.
Impromptu performance in 2012 on the "halfstage" at Metisfest, Killarney, Manitoba. Lavallee encouraged the boy on spoons to join him so that he could learn to play the spoons, imitating how a child might have traditionally learned. The playing features

very prominent use of filler sixteenth notes (adding the "jiggy jiggy"). Drone notes are often played as loudly as the melody, emphasizing the percussive element of his playing (i.e., rhythm is more important than melody). Ghosting of notes is especially prominent in the A section (00:16–00:31).
https://youtu.be/dKUnLXE7QFU

Chapter 8, Colin P. McGuire, "War Drums in Chinatown: Chinese Canadian Lion Dance Percussion as Martial Art"

20 Hong Luck Kung Fu Club, Chinese Lion Dance. Published 25 November 2016. Members of the Hong Luck Kung Fu Club are lion dancing at the reception banquet of a Chinese Canadian nuptial celebration in Toronto, Ontario. There are two lion costumes, each animated by two martial artists. A percussion ensemble consisting of a drum, a gong, and cymbals accompanies the performers. The lion dance is believed to disperse negative energy, thus making room for good fortune to flourish; it is also a form of entertainment and a symbol of identity.
http://youtu.be/wAKfjY0cBvk

Chapter 9, Ian Hayes, "'Holy jeez, I can hear everything': Liveness in Cape Breton Fiddle Recordings"

21 Ashley MacIsaac, "Devil in the Kitchen." Published 12 August 2011.
This is the music video for "Devil in the Kitchen," a traditional Scottish fiddle and pipe tune, from Ashley MacIsaac's 1995 album, *Hi, how are you today?* This album was known for its fusion of grunge rock with traditional Cape Breton fiddling and achieved double-platinum status.
https://youtu.be/QP3P0EUb92s

22 Natalie MacMaster, "Catharsis." Published 9 April 2010.
"Catharsis" was featured on Natalie MacMaster's Juno-nominated album *No Boundaries* (1996). This is an excellent example of how in the 1990s Cape Breton fiddlers began including influences of pop and rock to create a more commercially focused genre of Cape Breton fiddling.
https://youtu.be/-jn4yHnSh6o

23 Chrissy Crowley, "Parmars" (East Coast Live). Published 9 April 2014.
This is an example of a modern studio recording of Cape Breton fiddling.
https://youtu.be/Md-SPrFsFsI

24 Andrea and Kinnon Beaton Set, Part Two. Published 6 March 2007.
This is a set of strathspeys and reels played by Andrea and Kinnon Beaton at a house party – a typical traditional performance and setting for Cape Breton fiddling.
https://youtu.be/k4r1Gv4z42U

25 Cape Breton fiddler Kimberley Fraser at the Red Shoe Pub. Published on 1 March 2007. The Red Shoe Pub (Mabou, Cape Breton) is an important music venue that regularly features traditional Cape Breton fiddling in a relaxed social setting for both locals and tourists.
https://youtu.be/g41Ww5tB8QM

Chapter 10, Jesse Stewart and Niel Scobie, "Fantastic Voyage: The Diasporic Roots and Routes of Early Toronto Hip Hop"

26   Michie Mee and L.A. Luv, "Jamaican Funk Canadian Style." Published 7 August 2010.
     Michie Mee and L.A. Luv's first official music video (1991) features rapper Michie Mee dressed in colourful "dancehall queen" fashion. Visually, the video displays other Jamaican cultural signifiers such as the Jamaican flag and a visual colour palette dominated by black, green, yellow, and red.
     https://youtu.be/ObqLwv7UtP8

27   Maestro Fresh-Wes, "Let Your Backbone Slide." Published 17 January 2011.
     In his second music video (first as a signed artist), Maestro Fresh-Wes performs on stage dressed in his signature tuxedo. Other shots include him surrounded by his manager Farley Flex, DJ LTD, and dancers. The video received regular airplay on MuchMusic which helped his album *Symphony In Effect* receive platinum sales status in Canada.
     https://youtu.be/CsPSO1N-uIY

28   Maestro Fresh-Wes, "Nothin' At All." Published 19 June 2008.
     From Maestro Fresh-Wes's sophomore LP, *The Black Tie Affair* (1991), the video for "Nothin' At All" features the artist rapping alone in a dark room in which multiple chains hang from the ceiling. These shots are interspersed with scenes of Maestro sitting among children of multiple cultural backgrounds. The video also features images of Indigenous drummers, Bishop Desmond Tutu, boxers Egerton Marcus and Lennox Lewis, dub poet Lillian Allen, and fellow Toronto-based hip hop artists such as Michie Mee, Dream Warriors, K-4rce, HDV, and Devon.
     https://youtu.be/oUy9QPzXnkY

29   Dream Warriors, "My Definition of a Boombastic Jazz Style." Published 12 April 2013.
     This video features group members King Lou and Capital Q performing on stage, interspersed with black-and-white shots of the duo walking through apartment courtyards, as well as a faux game show – a nod to *Definition*, a Canadian television program of the 1970s–80s. The "winner" of the game receives a trip to "the projects." Notably, King Lou carries a six-foot staff made of dried sugarcane stalk, an item associated with Caribbean sugarcane plantations during the slave trade.
     https://youtu.be/LoE5yHMrP0A

30   Dream Warriors, "Ludi." Published 16 December 2016.
     The video begins with King Lou and Capital Q playing the board game Ludi. A graphic indicates they are on the Caribbean island of St Kitts. The duo performs on a catamaran, the beach, and village streets. Other shots feature lush, green island landscapes, a sunset, and a cameo by King Lou's mother who can be seen holding the group's signature dried sugarcane stalk.
     https://youtu.be/V6BATfeJirQ

31   Devon, "Mr. Metro." Published 21 May 2010.
     Footage of Toronto police officers is interspersed with black-and-white archival footage from American Civil Rights-era demonstrations including Black Panther Party rallies. Devon raps and plays keyboard in front of a television displaying the images mentioned above, as well as on the streets of Toronto near police cars.
     https://youtu.be/GA-H9DwqnWw

508 | Accompanying Video and Audio Examples

32 Dance Appeal, featuring Devon, "Can't Repress the Cause." Published 1 February 2010.
    Dance Appeal was a supergroup formed in 1991 that included many Toronto performers of Caribbean and West Indian heritage, including hip hop artists Michie Mee, Maestro Fresh-Wes, Dream Warriors, Devon, B-Kool, HDV, and Self Defense; reggae artists Leroy Sibbles, Carla Marshall, and Messenjah; dub poet Lillian Allen; and singers Dionne, Thando Hyman, Jillian Mendez, Lorraine Scott, and Zama; as well as white performers Eria Fachin, Lorraine Segato, and Thyron Lee White. Each performer receives camera time, performing in a variety of spaces such as a neighbourhood street corner, a darkened alley, a recording studio, and a TTC subway station.
    https://youtu.be/mF4GL2dOeJA

Chapter 11, Janice Esther Tulk, "Identity, Aesthetics, and Place in Medicine Dream's 'In This World'"

33 Medicine Dream, "In This World." Published 8 February 2008.
    The song "In This World" was released on Medicine Dream's third CD, *Tomegan Gospem*, in 2002. A few years later, it was chosen for their first music video, which was produced in collaboration with Alaska Native Heritage Center and the Peabody Essex Museum under the direction of Megann C. Lemieux.
    https://youtu.be/BBlzAXobSvY

Part Three | Heterogeneity, Diversity, and the Possibility of Alternatives

Chapter 12, Louise Wrazen, "A View from Toronto: Local Perspectives on Music Making, Ethnocultural Difference, and the Cultural Life of a City"

34 Three Górale tunes from Podhale, Poland. Published 10 November 2017.
    A recording of some spontaneous playing by Polish Highlander (Górale) musicians sitting around a table at a Christmas party in Toronto, 1985. Franek Mrowca (on lead fiddle) plays three dance tunes with others joining in to accompany.
    https://youtu.be/qdJtzdlzReE

35 Harnasie Toronto Kanada Polewacka. Published 20 April 2013.
    Górale musicians (Hyr) and ensemble (Harnasie) with members of White Eagle/Biały Orzeł ensemble presenting music and dance of the Podhale region as part of a larger performance at Ryerson Theatre, Toronto, 2011. Segment begins at 1'49" with historical footage and recreation of Easter customs before young men sing (3'55") and musicians enter (4'31"). Sequence discussed in chapter begins at 8'01".
    https://youtu.be/RL6rUslXET8

Chapter 14, Judith Klassen, "Music, Mimesis, and Modulation among Mennonites in Rural Manitoba"

36 Mennonite Circle Games. Published 5 November 2017.
    "Bingo" and "Auld Lang Syne" led by Werner and Marlene Ens at the Mennonite Heritage Village in Steinbach, Manitoba, 2010.
    https://youtu.be/gKxinDmZn9g

37 "Brommtopp Leed" (excerpts). Published 12 March 2019.
Performances in Neubergthal, Manitoba and at the Canadian Mennonite University, Winnipeg, Manitoba, as part of a concert series held in connection with the Mennonite Heritage Village exhibition *Singing in Time: Mennonites and Music*, 2010.
https://youtu.be/o4t3SXEP-eE

38 Brommtopp. Published 8 November 2017.
Jacob K. Schwartz describes how the instrument is made at a 1976 community event in Neubergthal, Manitoba, celebrating the village's one-hundredth anniversary. This is followed by an excerpt of a performance of the song. (Source: Mennonite Heritage Archives, Cassette 99, XXV–B–10. "*Mennonites in Manitoba: Neu Bergthal.* Performances by Neu Bergthal of the traditional song & music assoc with the bromm Topp." 1 and 31 July 1976.)
https://youtu.be/7eOUijgMmho

39 Pine Ridge Boys, "You Are My Sunshine." Published 8 August 2014.
A 1939 recording of "You Are My Sunshine" by the Pine Ridge Boys (Bluebird, B–8263–A).
https://youtu.be/xvPolI-pBCw

40 "Dü bess mien Sonneschien" (Low German, "You Are My Sunshine"). Published 12 March 2019.
Sung by Margaretha Friesen, 2015.
https://youtu.be/dphHwJf_1lA

Chapter 15, Marcia Ostashewski, "Ukrainian Catholic Congregational Singing in Canada: Sounds in Service and Celebration"

41 Opening Hymn. Published 18 October 2017.
Father Roman Dusanowskyj has opened the Royal Doors to begin the liturgy, and greets the congregation with instruction for the morning's opening hymn. He begins censing the altar, with a censor that has tiny bells which can be heard in the recording. Father Roman then begins the opening prayers; the congregational singers respond. A special prayer, in English, in honour of the deceased is inserted into the Great Litany of prayers, demonstrating the application of the chant in both languages. This segment ends as the cantor and congregational singers are singing the First Antiphon.
https://youtu.be/N4ABF1vXd4Q

42 Prayer of Entrance. Published 18 October 2017.
Father Roman Dusanowskyj calls a prayer aloud at the Prayer of Entrance. Here, the cantor and congregational singers sing some of the Propers for this liturgy, the *Troparion*, *Kontakion*, and *Theotokion*. The introductory prayer, which remains the same in each liturgy, is sung in Ukrainian. However, the text that changes from service to service is sung in English because it is sung without rehearsal, in an improvisatory manner, and very few members of the congregation read Ukrainian well enough to manage sight reading and singing.
https://youtu.be/s3ztEcJy3Mo

510 | Accompanying Video and Audio Examples

43 Bells, Chant. Published 18 October 2017.
    This segment opens as the congregational singers are singing "Hosanna" prior to the Prayer of Consecration of the Eucharist. Father Roman Dusanowskyj sings in a lower, more solemn tone than he does during the rest of the service, and more slowly. The cantor and congregation's "Amen" responses to these consecration prayers are somewhat melismatic and ornamented. As well, the priest's assistant rings a set of small, handheld bells three times (signifying the Holy Trinity) during each "Amen" to emphasize the importance of these prayers. These distinctive sounds in this segment of the service are intended to emphasize this especially important moment in the Liturgy when, according to the faith, the bread and wine are transformed into the Body and Blood of Jesus Christ. Also, a prayer is sung shortly after the consecration to the Mother of God. At this time, Father Roman is censing the consecrated Bread and Wine at the altar; as well, the outside bells are rung and can be heard in the background.
    https://youtu.be/Ou8mh3dhxjw

44 "That the Lord God." Published 18 October 2017.
    At the end of the Liturgy on this particular day, a short prayer service is sung in honour of the memory of the deceased members of the Holy Ghost Ukrainian Catholic Church Men's Club. As is evident, the tonality of the music that is sung in memoriam is dramatically distinct from the regular liturgy chant. Some parts of this excerpt are sung in Ukrainian and others in English, demonstrating another aspect of the chant practices in the different languages.
    https://youtu.be/DwnqNq6TJoY

Chapter 16, Anna Hoefnagels, "(Re)Presenting Indigenous Activism in the Nation's Capital: Signifying Resistance across Time and Space through Music in Alanis Obomsawin's Trick or Treaty? *(2014)"*

45 *Trick or Treaty?* (Trailer). Published 1 August 2014.
    Trailer for Alanis Obomsawin's documentary *Trick or Treaty?* published by the National Film Board of Canada. The full video is available for streaming and downloading through the National Film Board website: https://www.nfb.ca/film/trick_or_treaty/.
    https://youtu.be/g34TyonH8O8

46 Idle No More short documentary, *Grounded News*. Published 10 January 2013.
    Short documentary by Syd Woodward featuring various people speaking about the importance of Idle No more to Indigenous rights and sovereignty, and showing footage from Idle No More.
    https://youtu.be/IzXI7aznBtc

47 Idle No More short documentary. Published 19 April 2013.
    Short documentary directed by Brandon Alexis in which speakers address concerns that ignited the Idle No More movement, including footage from flash mob round dances in shopping malls and interviews with various activists.
    https://youtu.be/WyuUU4VohDM

Contributors

REBECCA DRAISEY-COLLISHAW is a SSHRC postdoctoral fellow at the Dan School of Drama and Music, Queen's University. Building on her doctoral work in ethnomusicology at Memorial University of Newfoundland, her current research focuses on relationships between public policy, music programming on Canada's national public broadcaster (CBC), and intercultural communications between musicians. Draisey-Collishaw was the curator for the Irish Traditional Music Archive's digital exhibition *A Grand Time: The Songs, Music, and Dance of Newfoundland's Cape Shore* (2018) and the co-guest-editor of the 2018 volume of the *Yearbook for Traditional Music*.

MEGHAN C. FORSYTH is assistant professor of ethnomusicology at Memorial University of Newfoundland. Her research focuses on instrumental music and dance traditions of the Acadian diaspora. Forsyth is co-author, with Ursula A. Kelly, of *The Music of Our Burnished Axes: Songs and Stories of the Woods Workers of Newfoundland and Labrador* (ISER Books, 2018), and produced the travelling exhibit *Songs and Stories of the "Forgotten Service."* She is also the producer of *Dansez!*, an award-winning, multimedia exhibit and website on Acadian dance traditions on Prince Edward Island.

MONIQUE GIROUX holds the Canada Research Chair in Indigenous Music, Culture, and Politics at the University of Lethbridge. Her research explores Metis cultural revival and resurgence, critically exploring how music is used to negotiate relationships between Indigenous nations and settler populations. She has undertaken ethnographic research in the Canadian Prairies, Ontario, North Dakota, and Montana, as well as extensive archival research focused on public discourse around, and settler appropriation of, Metis culture. Her publications include articles on Metis music festivals (*MUSICultures*), on Metis bard Pierre Falcon (*Ethnologies*), and on Indigenous/settler relations at old time fiddle contests (*Ethnomusicology*).

IAN HAYES has a background in Celtic music and jazz performance. In his doctoral work at Memorial University of Newfoundland, he examined how Cape Breton fiddlers negotiate economic and representational aspects of their careers, as well as how they conceive tradition and cultural identity in both private and commercial contexts. His research interests include discourse analysis, technology studies, and tourism. He has published articles in the journals *Ethnologies* and *MUSICultures*. Hayes also serves on the executive of the Folklore Studies Association of Canada.

ANNA HOEFNAGELS is an ethnomusicologist whose areas of research include Indigenous music in Canada, women's music, music and gender, and Canadian traditional music. With Beverley Diamond she co-edited the award-winning *Aboriginal Music in Contemporary Canada: Echoes and Exchanges* (McGill-Queen's University Press, 2012) and she is author of numerous journal articles and book chapters. Anna is associate professor of music in Carleton University's School for Studies in Art and Culture.

SHERRY JOHNSON is associate professor in music at York University, as well as a step dancer, fiddler, educator, and researcher. She is interested in the interrelationships between music and dance in a variety of contexts, gender in performance, and issues of globalization in relation to vernacular music and dance. She was the guest editor of *Bellows & Bows: Historic Recordings of Fiddle & Accordion Music from across Canada* (2012), a double CD with accompanying booklet. Her writing has been published in the *Canadian Journal for Traditional Music*, *American Anthropologist*, *Ethnologies*, *Ethnomusicology*, and the *British Journal of Music Education*.

JUDITH KLASSEN is an ethnomusicologist and curator of cultural expression at the Canadian Museum of History. In addition to research and collection development in various aspects of expressive culture, she is currently undertaking a research project on the complex and sometimes mythologized histories of popular music in Canada. Klassen's ongoing research among Mennonites in Manitoba and northern Mexico led to her collaboration on *Singing in Time: Music and Mennonites*, an exhibition produced by the Mennonite Heritage Village in Steinbach, Manitoba (2010). Klassen is past president of the Canadian Society for Traditional Music/Société canadienne pour les traditions musicales and has worked as a violist and string instructor in Canada, Mexico, and Paraguay.

CHRIS MCDONALD is associate professor of music at Cape Breton University. He is the author of *Rush, Rock Music, and the Middle Class: Dreaming in Middletown* (Indiana University Press, 2009). In addition to his work on popular music and social class, he researches popular and traditional music in Atlantic Canada. His recent focus has been the piano accompaniment style in Cape Breton's fiddle tradition. He has taught guitar and piano, and performs in a wide range of styles.

COLIN P. MCGUIRE holds a PhD in ethnomusicology from York University. His work focuses on listening to music and martial arts, particularly Chinese kung fu, examining sonic being-in-the-world and somaesthetic meaning. In particular, he is interested in hearing connections between movement and sound that shape relationships, values, and beliefs. Through intermedia investigations of heroic display, McGuire contributes to broader discussions of diaspora, transnation, community, identity, resistance, and tradition. His articles have been published in *Ethnomusicology Forum*, *MUSICultures*, and the *International Journal of Sport and Society*. Currently, McGuire is revising the manuscript of a book titled *Martial Sound*.

MARCIA OSTASHEWSKI is associate professor of ethnomusicology and director of the Centre for Sound Communities at Cape Breton University, which she established as part of her prior appointment as Canada Research Chair in Communities and Cultures. This state-of-the-art digital arts and humanities facility supports community-engaged research programs for Ostashewski and affiliated researchers. These programs result in innovative outcomes, including intensive public outreach, the production of diverse digital media, and both popular press and academic publications. Ostashewski also teaches a variety of courses on music, dance, performance, tourism, and research methods.

LAURA RISK is assistant professor of music and society in the Department of Arts, Culture and Media at the University of Toronto Scarborough, with a cross appointment in the Faculty of Music at the University of Toronto. Her research explores the intersection of musical genre, nationalism, recording technologies, and performance practice in fiddling cultures from Quebec to the British Isles. She has published articles in *Ethnomusicology*, *MUSICultures*, and the SAGE *Encyclopedia of Music and Culture*, and is a co-author of *The Glengarry Collection: The Highland Fiddle Music of Aonghas Grant*. She received the 2014 Prix Mnémo for her co-production of the CD *Douglastown: Music and Song from the Gaspé Coast*.

NIEL SCOBIE, a PhD candidate in media studies at Western University, examines diasporic cultural expressivity in Canadian hip hop music. He is the recipient of a doctoral scholarship from the Social Sciences and Humanities Research Council of Canada. He has presented his research at conferences hosted by the International Association for the Study of Popular Music, the Canadian University Music Society, and the Royal Music Association, among others. In addition to co-authoring a chapter for this anthology, he is contributing an essay on Canadian hip hop pioneer Michie Mee for a forthcoming edited volume on Canadian popular culture.

GORDON E. SMITH is professor of ethnomusicology at Queen's University. Formerly director of the School of Music, he is currently vice-dean in the Faculty of Arts and Science. In addition to journal articles and book chapters, his publications include collaborative book projects, such as *Istvan Anhalt: Pathways and Memory* (2001), *Folk Music, Traditional Music, Ethnomusicology: Canadian Perspectives Past and Present* (2007), *Marius Barbeau: Modelling Twentieth-Century Culture* (2008), *Music Traditions, Cultures, and Contexts* (2010), and *Territoires musicaux mis en scène* (2011). His current research is focused on music in Indigenous contexts, with particular emphasis on intergenerational connections around music, resurgence, and healing in Mi'kmaq communities in Cape Breton Island, Nova Scotia.

HEATHER SPARLING is the Canada Research Chair in Musical Traditions and associate professor of ethnomusicology at Cape Breton University. Her research interests include Gaelic songs of Nova Scotia, vernacular dance traditions of Cape Breton, and disaster songs of Atlantic Canada, focusing on questions of genre, the intersections between language and music, and memory and memorialization. She is the author of *Reeling Roosters & Dancing Ducks: Celtic Mouth Music* (Cape Breton University Press, 2014) and the editor of the journal *MUSICultures*. She is a fluent Gaelic learner as well as the principal flutist with the Cape Breton Orchestra.

JESSE STEWART is a composer, percussionist, visual artist, writer, and educator. He is associate professor of music in Carleton University's School for Studies in Art and Culture and an adjunct professor in the Visual Arts program at the University of Ottawa. His writing has appeared in such journals as *American Music*, *Black Music Research Journal*, *Contemporary Music Review*, *Intermedialities*, *Music and Arts in Action*, and in many edited anthologies. He is the recipient of numerous awards and honours including the 2012 Instrumental Album of the Year Juno award for Stretch Orchestra's self-titled debut album, the D2L Innovation Award in Teaching and Learning, and the Order of Ottawa.

JANICE ESTHER TULK is senior researcher, prospect and development at Cape Breton University. Her research of the past five years has focused on Indigenous economic development, wise business practices, the role of technology in mentorship, and expressive culture of the Mi'kmaq, particularly in Newfoundland. Tulk has published in *MUSICultures*, *Newfoundland and Labrador Studies*, *Ethnologies*, *Culture & Tradition*, *Journal of Aboriginal Economic Development*, and various anthologies, including the *Oxford Handbook of Musical Repatriation*. She is co-editor of *Indigenous Business in Canada: Principles and Practices* and producer/author of the CD/book set *Welta'q "It Sounds Good": Historic Recordings of the Mi'kmaq*.

MARGARET E. WALKER is professor of ethno/musicology at Queen's University. Her research crosses disciplinary boundaries, and includes ethnomusicology, historiography, teaching and learning, and dance studies. Her primary research has centred around North Indian dance and her 2014 monograph, *India's Kathak Dance in Historical Perspective*, proposes an alternate historiography to the dominant nationalist narrative. She has participated on two international research teams: the European Research Council–funded "Musical Transitions to European Colonialism in the Eastern Indian Ocean" project at King's College London, and the Balzan "Towards a Global History of Music" project based at Oxford University. She is currently working on curriculum revision with respect to global and decolonized music history.

LOUISE WRAZEN is associate professor in the Department of Music at York University, Toronto. Her research explores adaptations of traditional music within diasporic and transnational contexts; music and gender, memory and place with a focus on the Polish Tatra mountain region of Podhale; music, identity, and post-socialism; and music and disability. Her publications include the co-edited volume *Performing Gender, Place, and Emotion in Music: Global Perspectives* (with Fiona Magowan), and articles in *Women Singers in Global Contexts* and the journals *Ethnomusicology*, *Yearbook for Traditional Music*, and *Intersections*, among others.

Index

An italic *f* following a page reference indicates a figure.

Aboriginal Peoples Television Network (APTN), 348
Acadian fiddling tradition, 41, 157, 166, 167
Acadian settlers and culture, 140n12, 147–9, 168n5, 180
accordions and accordion music: with fiddling, 150*f*, 153, 169; in Mennonite communities, 427, 442; for Newfoundland-Irish tunes, 400, 401; research on, 20; with South Asian music and musicians, 400–1, 402, 403; at *veillées*, 43, 45, 48
African diasporic cultures and communities: call-response trope, 308; Caribbean diasporas, 207; hip hop roots in, 207, 306–9, 331n15; history of slavery and colonialism, 306, 320; memory, signifyin(g), and code-switching, 307–9
Afrika Bambaataa, 309–10
Afrological musics and forms, 307–9, 326–8, 330n3, 331n21
AIM. *See* American Indian Movement (AIM)
Alarie, Sylva, 59
Alaska Native Heritage Center, 338, 343, 344
Alexis, Brandon, 510
Alfa Rococo (pop duo), 44
Alfred, Taiaiake, 237n31
Allard, Joseph, 162, 170n28
Allen, Lillian, 323, 325, 328, 507
alterity, 421
Altona (Manitoba), 418, 446n3, 447n13, 447n15

Alvarez, Steven, 338, 343, 344
American Folklore Society: Quebec Section, 46, 49, 52, 56, 58–60, 80n9; *veillées* in Montreal, 46, 48, 52
American Indian Movement (AIM), 482, 492, 495, 498n7, 499n15
American/Texas contest-style fiddling, 160, 170n24
Amsterdam School District (Manitoba), 432, 437
Anabaptists. *See under* Mennonites: communities and practices
Anderson, Cea, 337
Anderson brothers (Pete, Lawrence, and Gilbert, Enoch Cree Nation), 212–13
Andrews, Curtis, 400–3
Anklewicz, Mike, 22
Appadurai, Arjun, 133
Arcand, John, 215, 221, 225, 232, 235n16, 236n30
Archambault, Tim, 18
articulation: cultural articulation, 188, 201n2; Hall's concept of, 80n8
Asham Stompers (dance group), 230
Atleo, Shawn A-in-chut, 485–6
atonic, 124, 140n11
Attariwala, Parmela Singh, 391, 405, 408, 410n17
Attawapiskat First Nation, 485
audiotopic space, 391–5, 406, 407
Augustine, Stephen, 350, 351

Austin, Gene, 285, 298
A.Y.E. (rapper): "Can I Live," 331n20

Back to Batoche Days (Saskatchewan), 215, 218, 227, 233
Baggins, Cameron, 216
Bakht, Natasha, 92, 102, 388, 407
Bal, Arya, 400–1
Bal, Bani, 400–1
Bal, Mieke, 307
ballads, 179–84, 187–90, 194, 197
Ballantyne, R.M., 211
Bannerji, Himani, 5
Banton, George, 318
Barbeau, Marius: folklore collection and research, 49, 55, 56, 61; and Gauthier, 59; and *veillées* in Montreal, 46, 48, 49–50, 52, 55–9
Barker, Adam J., 479, 482
Barra MacNeils, 188, 198, 280
Bartlett, Cheryl, 350
Basilian order, 462, 473n8, 474n18
Bates, Elliot, 282
battles, battle raps, 310–11, 330n6
Baudouin, Gustave, 52
Bauman, Richard, 159
Beat Factory (production company), 310
Beaton, Andrea, 506
Beaton, Elizabeth, 456
Beaton, Kinnon, 300n6, 506
Beaulieu, Albert, 237n36
Beckwith, John, 22
Bedard, Mel, 214
Beethoven, Ludwig van, 87, 91
Belcourt, Tony, 488
Bellegarde, Perry, 485
Bellemare, Luc, 49, 58, 80n9
Belly, 329
Bennett, Margaret, 140nn12–13, 141n17
Bennett, Mikey, 311
Bentahila, Abdelali, 311
Beothuk, 339, 352n15
Bergthaler Mennonites, 418, 432, 446n3, 446n6
Berland, Jody, 394
Berry, Ivan, 310
Bey, Salome, 318

bhangra music and dance, 22, 365
bharatanatyam (South Indian dance genre), 92, 93, 101
Bhattacharya, Sanjay, 110n14, 503
Biały Orzeł (BO, White Eagle), 367–8, 374–8, 375f, 508
Big Daddy Kane, 305
Bishop, Stephen, 312
B-Kool, 325
Blacking, John, 254
Black Lives Matter, 331n20
Black Music Association of Canada, 326
Blair, Graham, 397, 399
Blumenfeld, 432, 446n3, 447n15
Blumenort (Manitoba), 424, 446n3, 447n15
Blumenthal (Manitoba), 432
blurred genres, 245
BO. *See* Biały Orzeł (White Eagle)
Boardmore, Liz and Harry: *The Rise and Follies of Cape Breton*, 193
Bolivia: Mennonite communities, 419, 426, 427, 448n35
Les bonnes soirées canadiennes (CHCR radio), 45
Boock, Barbara, 432
Boogie Down Productions, 305, 310, 330n7
Boretz, Avron, 265
La Bottine Souriante (band), 43, 46, 195
Boulton, Laura, 473n11
Boyd, Colin, 300n1
Boyd, Luke (Classified), 199
Brackett, David, 47–8, 53, 66
Bradley, Bruce, 326
Bramadat, Paul, 91
breakdancing, 330n5
Breathnach, Breandán, 161
British North America (Quebec) Act (1774), 148
Brommtopp. *See* Mennonites: mumming tradition
Brown, James, 312
Browne, Jackson, 492
Browner, Tara, 18
Brunk Revivals, 427, 448n25
Burrows, John, 494
"Bye Bye 2008" (television sketch), 43–5, 46, 67

Cadence Weapon (rapper), 329
Café de la Grave (Havre-Aubert), 150*f*, 151, 153
Calabrese, Donnie, 298
Cameron, John Allan, 188–90, 197
Campbell, John Lorne, 121–2, 140n8
Campbell, Mairi, 301n12
Campbell, Mark V., 331nn14–15
Canada Council for the Arts, 101, 365, 382n11, 392
Canada Science and Technology Museum, 25
Canadian Broadcasting Corporation (CBC): archives, 25; audience share, 412n31; broadcasting infrastructure, 392–3, 410n13; fusion programming, 386, 388, 393–4, 397–8, 406–8; mandate, 392, 395–6, 405, 409n4; multiculturalism, 359, 392, 405, 410n11; online digital services, 392–3. *See also* radio broadcasts
– programs: "Bye Bye 2008," 43–5, 46, 67; *Canada Live*, 396, 405, 411n18; *Fuse*, 387, 393, 409n1, 409n6; *Musicraft*, 386–7, 395, 405, 409n4 (*see also* "Come By Concerts"); *Pure*, 445–6n2
– regional centres, 386, 387, 409n2, 409n4; Halifax, 187, 409; St John's, 359, 386–408
Canadian Centre for Ethnomusicology (University of Alberta), 23
The Canadian Encyclopedia, 15
Canadian Ethnocultural Council, 326, 389
Canadian Film Development Corporation, 189
Canadian Folk Music Journal, 17, 26n5
Canadian Journal for Traditional Music/La Revue de musique folklorique canadienne, 26n5
Canadian legislation: Canadian Multiculturalism Act (1988), 4–5, 318, 362, 386, 391–2, 405; Charter of Rights and Freedoms (1982), 389, 405; Chinese Exclusion Act (1923), 254–5; Chinese Immigration Act (1884), 254–5; Immigration Act (1967), 255, 257; Indian Act, 213, 494
Canadian Museum of Civilization, 27n13
Canadian Museum of History, 24, 27n13, 441

Canadian Native Friendship Centre (Edmonton), 213
Canadian Polish Congress, 377, 382n16
Canadian Radio-television and Telecommunications Commission (CRTC), 325–6, 329
Canadian Society for Traditional Music/La Société canadienne pour les traditions musicales (CSTM/SCTM), 17
Canadian University Music Review: "Canadian Perspectives in Ethnomusicology," 16–17
La Canadienne (magazine), 52, 57, 58
Cañas, Tania, 363
Cantonese opera, 268n3
"Can't Repress the Cause," 325–9
Cape Breton: Acadian population, 180; Celtic Colours International Festival, 178; Gaelic speakers and culture, 115, 116–17, 126, 180; labour songs, 19; *The Rise and Follies of Cape Breton*, 193, 195. *See also* Nova Scotia
Cape Breton fiddling tradition: accompaniment, 278, 280; amateur recordings (dance tapes), 279, 283, 287, 288–9, 292, 300n7; audience or crowd for, 286, 288–9; Celtic Boom (1990s), 280; commercial recordings, 275, 278–81, 300n1; correctness and accuracy, 269; foot stomping, 295–6; history and performance practice, 276–81; liveness in studio recordings, 206, 275–6, 284–300; live performances, 275–6; live (on-location) recordings, 278, 287–90, 291; and Madelinot fiddling, 166, 167; melodic variation, 159–60; participatory discrepancies, 237n40, 284, 286, 297–9, 371; radio broadcasts of, 157; recordings of Cape Breton fiddlers, 9, 206, 275–300; revival of (1970s), 278; social contexts, 275; staged performance style, 279–81; violin tone or timbre, 291–3. *See also* recordings; *individual fiddlers*
Cape Breton milling frolics. *See* milling (waulking) frolics
Cape Breton University, 24, 141n16
Capital Q (rapper), 319, 507
Caplan, Rod, 129.

Carignan, Jean, 162, 505
Carter, Michael, 237n37
Carter, Wilf, 190, 194
Casgrain, Henri-Raymond: *Légendes canadiennes*, 53
Catchaway, Frank, 224
ceilidh, 131, 135–6, 141n19
Celtic Colours International Festival (Cape Breton), 178, 199
Celtic Wave (Celtic Boom), 20, 195–8, 280
Centre Mnémo (Quebec), 25
Chafe, Winnie, 300n6
Chakrabarty, Dipesh, 248
Chakraborty, Sanchita, 400–1
Chakravorty, Ashok, 90
Chakravorty, Pallabi, 88–9, 90
Champlain, Samuel de (statue), 485
Chan, Arlene, 246
Chan, Jim, 258, 261, 262
Chan, Ka Nin: *Harmonious Interest*, 268n3
Chan, Margaret, 21
Chan, Paul, 257, 258, 270n23
Chan Dau, 249
Chan Heung, 249
Chapman, Stan, 152
Chartier, Émile, 55–6
Chauveau, Pierre J.O., 54
Cherwick, Brian, 21, 473n9, 473n11
Chez Isidore (CFTM Montreal), 45
Child, Francis, and Child Ballads, 178, 179, 187, 188
China: Guangdong Province, 206, 246, 249, 254, 256–7, 269n8; Henan Province, 248; languages and dialects, 256–7, 269n9; People's Republic of, 251, 252, 257; Republican Era (1911–49), 258; *Romance of the Three Kingdoms*, 251–2, 270n16; Taishan region, 256, 258, 268n2. *See also* lion dancing
Chinese Canadians: Cantonese opera, 268n3; Chinatowns, 243, 245–9, 255, 267–8, 270n21; history and experience of, 254–7, 267–8, 270n21; languages and dialects, 246, 256–7, 264, 269n9; racism against, 206, 245–7, 254–5, 257, 267, 268n3. *See also* lion dancing

Chinese New Year, 243, 252, 259–61, 263, 271n33
Chisholm, Angus, 153
Choquette, Ernest, 56
Chow Lin, 271n31
Chow-Morris, Kim, 21
Christmas at Moose Factory (film), 484
Church Slavonic, 460, 474n14
citationality, 47–8, 53
Ciupaga, Józek Prusak, 378
Classified (rapper), 329
Claude, Louis, 50
clogging. *See under* Metis fiddle traditions
Cloutier, Véronique, 43–4
Cockburn, Bruce, 188
code-switching, 307, 309, 311, 327
Cohen, Judith R., 15, 21
Collinson, Francis, 122, 140n8
"Come By Concerts" (CBC), 386–408; audiences, 396, 405, 407; as fusion programming, 386, 388, 393–4, 397–8, 406–8; multicultural mandate, 386; musicians for, 397, 407; narrative distinctions or hierarchies, 398, 400; production and funding, 387, 395–7, 411n18; promotional strategies, 411n19; significance and value, 405–7; programs: Ballads to Bangladesh!, 402–4; Reels and Ragas, 400–2; Sveti Ivan and Pamela Morgan, 397–400
"Come Out Fighting" (Ottawa River Singers), 488–9
Connected by Blood (group), 331n20
Connerton, Paul, 307
contest-style (American/Texas) fiddling, 160, 170n24
Conway, Kyle, 406, 410n11
Cooke, Jesse, 280
Cooley, Timothy, 169n22, 366
Coplan, David, 39, 106
Cormier, J.P., 292, 294–5, 296, 302n20
Couture, Selena, 479
Creighton, Helen: career as a folksong collector, 177–80, 183–6; definition of folksong, 178; documentary on, 197; festival named for, 199; influence of, 188–9, 190–1, 197

- publications, 182–4; *Folk Songs of Nova Scotia*, 183; *Maritime Folksongs*, 183; *Songs and Ballads of Nova Scotia*, 183, 184; *Songs of Nova Scotia* (film), 184
- songs collected by: "Ged a Sheòl Mi air M' Aineol," 127–9; "Oran do Cheap Breatainn," 194; "The Nova Scotia Song," 187

Croft, Clary, 19, 188, 194
cross tuning (*scordatura*): in French-Canadian fiddling, 162, 209, 505; in Metis fiddling, 224–5, 234n3
Crowley, Chrissy, 506
CRTC. *See* Canadian Radio-television and Telecommunications Commission
cultural memory, 307–8, 319–23

Dance Appeal ("Can't Repress the Cause"), 325–9, 508
The Dances of the Metis (film), 227
DanceWorks, 102
Daney, Buz, 337, 344
DANs/CE KAPITAL (festival), 91f, 99
Das, Ritesh, 90
Davidson, Estwood, 296
Davies, Eirlys E., 311
Davis, Jesse Ed, 492
Deep Roots Music Festival (Annapolis Valley), 199
Dejarlis, Andy, 212, 235n9
Deleuze, Gilles, 198
Delorenzo, Maria, 465, 466–7
Densmore, Frances, 223
Déraspe, Alexandre, 161
Déraspe, Arnold, 505
Déraspe, Bertrand, 153, 155, 157, 158f, 163–5, 505
Derksen, Mary, 424, 426
Derno, Maiken, 371
De Shane, Nina, 410n17
de Souza, Joanna (née Joanna Das), 90; *Firedance*, 99, 503
De Temps Antan (band), 46
deterritorialization, 198
Devon (Mr. Metro, Devon Martin), 313–15, 318, 323–5, 328, 329; "Mr. Metro," 323–4, 331n20, 507

Dewey, John, 386, 408
Dhiman, Palak, 92, 100, 105
Diamond, Beverley, 7, 10, 13–19, 350, 381n2, 411n24, 444
Dionne (singer), 325
disaster songs, 19, 190, 191
discursive formations, 388, 393, 405
Dittmer, Jason, 387
DJ LTD (Alva Swaby), 316
DJ/sound system culture, 330n7
Doane, Melanie, 198
Dodd, Coxsone, 327
Douglastown (Quebec), 61, 63–5, 66, 67
Doyle, Peter, 285
Draisey-Collishaw, Rebecca, 10, 22, 359, 386–416
Drake, 315, 329
Dream Warriors, 319–23; in Dance Appeal, 325, 328, 329; "Ludi," 319, 321–2, 323, 507; "My Conversation," 331n19; "My Definition of a Boombastic Jazz Style," 319, 320, 323, 507; "Very Easy to Assemble but Hard to Take Apart," 319, 322–3
Drops of Brandy (anthology), 227
Dubicki, Paul and Maria, 374, 376
Dubinsky, Leon, 194
Dueck, Byron, 18, 223–4, 234–5nn5–6, 421–2, 444–5
Duncan, James, 193
Dunn, Charles, 120, 126
Dusanowskyj, Father Roman: at Holy Ghost Ukrainian Church, 454f, 470–2, 509–10; on language of liturgy, 460–1, 474n14; on liturgical music, 462, 467, 469, 472nn3–4, 473n7
Duval, Jean, 80n9
Dylan, Bob, 492

eagle whistles, 487
Earth, Wind and Fire (band), 312
East Coast Music Awards, 199–200, 301n16
Ebony MC (Marlon Bruce), 316
L'École des arts de la veillée, 45
Education through Cultural and Historical Organizations (ECHO), 343, 348
Edwardson, Ryan, 4, 189
Eggleton, Art, 326

Elmastukwek Mi'kmaq Mawio'Mi (gathering), 339
Elsipogtog First Nation, 482
Encyclopedia of Music in Canada/Encyclopédie de la musique au Canada, 15
The Encyclopedia of Native American Music of North America, 18
English song traditions: ballads, 179, 181–3, 188, 190, 194, 197; in Nova Scotia, 8–9, 177–201; used for Mennonite circle games, 422, 424–5
Enrique, Esmeralda, 99, 503
Ens, Werner and Marlene, 428, 430, 447nn16–19, 508
Epp, Marlene, 428
Eric's Trip (band), 199
Essiambre, Sister Henriette, 61–3, 64, 66, 67
ethnocultural performances, 366–80
ethnomusicology in Canada, 13–26; current trends in, 10; Diamond's contribution to, 7, 11n5; institutional engagement with, 22–5; key sources on, 15–22; and microhistories, 3, 6, 14; music traditions and cultures, 11n6; sources on, 15–22
Eurological (term), 330n3
Evangelical Mennonite Mission Church, 446n3
Evangelical tent meetings, 427

Fachin, Eria, 325, 326, 327
Faerrell, Jesse, 231
Falk, Joyce, 426–7
Fantastic Voyage (CKLN radio), 305, 316
Faucher de Saint-Maurice, Narcisse, 54
Federation of Newfoundland Indians, 339, 352n9
Fehr, Marcie, 435, 438, 449nn43–5
Fehr, Susan, 441–2
Feintuch, Burt, 133, 281, 301n8
Feld, Steven, 282
Feltham, Heleanor, 264–5, 270n15
Ferand, Ernst, 168n12
Festival Chants de Vielles, 162, 170n26
Festival de musique traditionnelle (Parc de Gros-Cap), 151
The Fiddle Tree (album), 289, 301n12

Fiddle Wall of Fame, 227, 237n39
fiddling traditions and practices: Acadian fiddling tradition, 41, 157, 166, 167; with accordion, 150f, 153, 169; contest-style (American/Texas), 160, 170n24; cross tuning (*scordatura*), 162, 209, 224–5, 234n3, 505; with flamenco, 380; Gaspesian, 62–6, 157; Inuit, 234n1; Irish tunes, 63–5, 390, 400–5, 407; in Mennonite communities, 427–8; Newfoundland fiddling and dance tunes, 237n31, 390, 400–5, 407, 412n27; Norwegian fiddle tradition, 163, 223; old-time, 160, 214, 234n2, 235n14, 238n42; Ottawa Valley fiddle and step dance tradition, 20, 111n22, 142n23, 504; in Prince Edward Island, 151, 153, 156, 157; Québécois, 19, 20, 41, 44, 53–4, 166, 167. *See also* Cape Breton fiddling tradition; Madelinot-style fiddling; Metis fiddle traditions
Field, John, 338, 344
Figgy Duff (band), 201n3
Fitzgerald, Winston ("Scotty"), 153, 296, 297
flamenco: with fiddling, 380; with kathak dancing, 99, 111n22, 503, 504
Fleck, Béla, 280
Flett, Lawrence, 224, 237n36
Florida, Richard, 381n10
Floyd, Samuel A., 308–9, 330n4
folksong(s): and art music, 186; and authenticity, 177; and commercial folk revival, 187–90; commercial genre, 178; fused with pop and rock, 195–8; singer-songwriters, 187–8, 190–5; sources for, 19–20; use in schools, 184; variability spectrum, 159–60
folksong canons, 178, 180–6, 200–1
folksong collecting: context for, 42, 53, 177, 179; of French-Canadian songs, 52; in Nova Scotia, 177–86; of occupational and protest songs, 185; and social class, 181–2, 184–5
Forsyth, Meghan, 8, 41, 145–76
Fowke, Edith, 177, 185; *Folk Songs of Canada*, 186, 398

Fraser, Kimberley, 284, 296, 506
Fréchette, Louis, 56
friction drums, 431f, 432
Fridal, Farley ("Flex"), 316, 507
Friesen, John J., 446n5
Friesen, Margaretha, 442–4, 449n48, 509
Friesen, Marge, 449n38
Friesen, Victor Carl, 420, 449n39
Frith, Simon, 282, 372
Froese, Jacob J., 446n8
frolic (term), 139n1
Frontier Fiddle Program, 216–18
fusion programming, 386, 388, 393–4, 397–8, 406–8, 409n1, 411n18

Gabriel's Lake (Newfoundland), 338, 339
Gaelic language and culture: milling (waulking) songs, 8, 41, 114–17, 119, 125–39, 504; songs collected by Creighton, 179, 180, 186, 197; songs performed by folk singers, 188, 197
Gagnon, Ernest, 59; *Chansons populaires du Canada*, 53, 55
Gaillard, Slim, 322
Galadza, Peter, 459
Gallaugher, Annemarie, 15
Gangani, Rajendra, 97
Gąsienica, Janusz, 374, 378, 383n23
Gaspé peninsula: fiddling traditions, 62–6, 157; *veillées* and informal music making, 40, 44, 47, 61–6
Gates, Henry Louis, Jr, 308, 330n4
Gauthier, Cathy, 43
Gauthier, Conrad, 46, 48–9, 58–60, 80n9
Gauthier, Robert, 44
Gauthier Mercier, Catherine, 22
Geertz, Clifford, 245
Genthon, Del, 212
Genthon, Frederick, 212, 235n8
Genticorum (band), 46
Gibbons, Roy, 214, 215, 218
Giddens, Anthony, 198
Gillis, Alex, 300n1
Gilroy, Paul: *The Black Atlantic*, 306
Giroux, Monique, 9, 206, 209–33

Gladu, André, 45
Glenbow Museum (Calgary), 25
glocalization, 198
Gluska, Virginia, 216–18
Gnadenthal (Manitoba), 428, 430, 432, 446n3, 447n15
Godino, Ilsa, 110n22, 504
Goertzen, Chris, 160, 163
Gomez, Danny, 104
Goodon, Dan, 219, 220–1, 222
Górale (Highlanders). *See* Polish Górale
Gordon, Jessica, 477, 478
Gould, Glenn, 285–6
Gow, Joe, 336, 346–7
Graham, Glenn, 277, 295–6
Gramsci, Antonio, 201n2
Grant, Colin, 297–9
Grapes of Wrath (band), 195
Gravel, Ludger, 50
Great Big Sea (band), 195, 196, 197
Green, Thomas, 248
Greenhill, Pauline, 435, 438, 449nn43–5
Greenough, Ann, 187
Gregory, David, 19
Guattari, Felix, 198
Guigné, Anna Kearney, 19
Guilbault, Jocelyne, 201n2
Guilbert, Daniel, 48, 80n9
Gulyani, Manisha, 95f
Gunning, Dave, 188
Gupta, Deepti, 90, 99–100; *Collision/Collusion*, 99
Guthro, Bruce, 198

Halbstadt (Manitoba), 432, 436, 446n3
Halbstadt (Ukraine), 423f
Haley, Alex: *Roots*, 316, 330n10
Hall, Michael (Mike), 288–9, 301n9
Hall, Stuart, 47, 80n8, 388, 392
Hamm, Andrew, 441
Handler, Richard, 45
Hanscomb, C.W., 212
Hansen, John, 479, 482–3, 501
Harbourfront Centre (Toronto), 102, 108
Hardship Post (band), 199

Harms, Grace, 427, 429, 439
Harnasie (Górale ensemble), 367–74, 382n19
Harper, Stephen, 267, 475n22, 487
Hartlan, Enos, 183
Hasiuk, Steve, 474n12
Hatcher, Annamarie, 350
Hatten, Robert, 151
Hawrylak, Anne, 465, 466
Hayes, Ian, 9, 160, 206, 275–300
Helen Creighton Folklore Festival (Dartmouth), 199
Helzer, David, 351n8
Hender, Matthew, 397, 399
Henderson, Jocko, 306, 329n1
Henman, Chuck, 344, 351n8
Henneberry, Ben, 183
Heptones (trio), 327
Herder, Johann Gottfried, 134, 182–3, 185–6, 191–2, 200
Hernàndez i Martí, Gil-Manuel, 198
heterogeneity, 9–10, 357, 418
Hill, Juniper, 151, 152–3
Himka, John-Paul, 474n14
Hindustani vocal music, 101, 400, 401
hip hop, 207, 305–29; Afrological forms and cultural memory, 308–9; and breakdancing, 330n5; and Dance Appeal, 325–9; *Fantastic Voyage*, 305, 316; in Indigenous communities, 331n15, 341; in New York, 306, 309–10; research on, 229n2; in Toronto, 9, 305–29. *See also specific rappers and groups*
Hobsbawm, Eric, 39, 89, 106, 249
Hochfeld (Manitoba), 432
Hoefnagels, Anna, 3–10, 13–26, 39–42, 359–60, 477–97
Holland, Jerry, 279, 293–4
Holmes, Anna, 363
Holy Ghost Ukrainian Catholic Church (Sydney). *See under* Ukrainian Catholic Church
Hong Kong, 206, 251, 256–7, 261
Hood, Mantle, 170n23
Hood, Oliver, 449n47

Houle, Lawrence, 237n36
How the Fiddle Flows (documentary), 227
Hu, William C.C., 250
Hyman, Thando, 325, 326
Hynes, Ron, 195
hyper-diversity, 363
hyper-realism, 286–7
Hyr (ensemble), 378, 508

iconastasis, 453, 454, 472n1
Idle No More: context for, 18, 481–3, 496–8; emergence and organization, 477–9; and hip hop artists, 331n15; music featured in, 10, 479, 480*f*, 483, 488–95, 497n3, 499n15; National Day of Solidarity and Resurgence (2012), 477, 478*f*; photographs, 480*f*, 487*f*; portrayed in *Trick or Treaty?*, 10, 359–60, 480–2, 485–97, 498–9n14, 510; round dance on Parliament Hill, 489–91, 498–9n14, 499n16; round dances at shopping malls, 478*f*, 479, 510; significance, 497; and storytelling, 496; timeline, 478*f*
Les Îles-de-la-Madeleine, 145–76; Madelinots (term), 145, 168n2; map and name, 146–7*f*, 167–8nn1–2; Acadian population, 147–9; English-speaking population, 147, 148, 167n1, 168n7; fishery, 147–8, 149, 158, 168n9; Indigenous peoples, 147, 168n4; sea, landscape, and isolation, 148, 149, 155, 165–6; tourism and cultural events, 149–51. *See also* Madelinot-style fiddling
India: bharatanatyam, 92, 93, 101; Hindu traditions, 88, 96, 98, 107; Karnatic music, 400–2; kathak associated with, 41, 87–9, 92–3, 99–100; postcolonial nationalism and cultural revival, 88–9, 92, 106; vocal music, 101, 400, 402–4
Indian and Métis Friendship Centre (Winnipeg), 213
Indigenous activism: music featured in, 10, 359–60, 483, 491–5, 498n7; treaty negotiations, 10, 481, 485, 489, 496, 498n14. *See also* Idle No More; *Trick or Treaty?*

Indigenous instruments: drums, 335, 336; eagle whistle, 487; flutes, 335, 336, 338, 352n10, 493
Indigenous music and dance: decoding of, 341–2, 349–50; distribution on YouTube, 349; elements of, 337, 355, 366; intertribal music, 336–7, 338, 488–9, 491; Inuit music, 19, 234n1, 341, 349, 498n7; middle ground and two-eyed seeing, 350–1; music videos, 207, 335–6; research on, 18–19, 26n6, 225–6; as site of empowerment, 335. *See also* Metis fiddle traditions
Indigenous resurgence, 210, 234–5n6, 237n31, 477–8, 496–7
Institute for Canadian Music (University of Toronto), 24
Inter-Media Services. *See* Miller, Dave, and Inter-Media Services
International Council for Traditional Music, 26n5
Inuit music: fiddling, 234n1; hip hop and rap, 341, 349; research, 19; throat singing, 498n7
Inverness Serenaders (band), 300n1
Irish fiddle tunes, 63–5, 390, 400–5, 407
Isajiw, Wsevolod, 474
Islam, Shahana Begum, 402–404

Jale (band), 199
Jamaican dancehall culture, 312–14, 328
Jamaican Patois (Patwa), 311–13, 328, 330n8
Jamaican ska, 321
Jamaican sound system culture, 306, 327, 330n7
James, Simon, 134
jam formats (fiddling), 118, 150*f*, 153, 221
jigging, 20, 159, 169n20, 213
jiggy jiggy, 231–2, 238n44, 506
John Arcand Fiddle Festival. *See* Arcand, John
Johnson, Jan, 493
Johnson, Sherry, 3–10, 13–26, 160, 205–7
Johnston, Richard: *Folk Songs of Canada*, 186, 398
Johnstown (Nova Scotia), 138
Joly, Dianne, 48, 49

Jones, Quincy: "Soul Bossa Nova," 319–20, 331n17
Joseph, Clifton, 323
Joshi, Mukta, 110n14, 503

Kaleland Ukrainian Orthodox Church of Saints Peter and Paul (Alberta), 462
Kallmann, Helmut, 15, 26n1
Kanadier Mennonites, 420, 422, 446n11
Kanehsatake (film), 484
Kardinal Offishall, 315, 329, 331n19
Karpeles, Maud, 177, 398
kathak dance, 87–108; artistic recognition and funding, 41, 101–2, 108–9; as classical or traditional, 87, 89, 92–4, 105–8; contemporary choreography and productions, 97–100, 104–5; creativity and innovation, 8, 41, 87, 96; debut performances, 96*f*; elements from Hindu mythology, 96–7, 103; and flamenco, 99, 111n22, 503, 504; hybrid and syncretic origins, 8, 41, 88, 108–9; items in sequence, 94–6, 109n3; as multicultural or ethnic, 87, 89, 91–3, 100, 102; in Pakistan, 109n1, 110n17; tabla accompaniment, 101, 104, 110nn13–14
Kathak Mahotsav Canada (festival), 100
Kawapit, David, 490–1
Kealey, Greg, 468
Keali'inohomoku, Joann, 107, 111n29
Kean, Leanne, 402, 403
Kehler, Anne, 424, 429, 437
Kehler, Johnny, 436, 437, 449n39
Kehler, Menno, 429, 436
Keil, Charles, 237n40, 286, 371
Keillor, Elaine, 15–16, 18
Kelly, John M.H., 18
Kelly, Laoise, 301n12
Keplin, Ryan, 236n23
Keplinfest, 218, 227
Killabeatz (Cj Mairs), 104
Kinderman, William, 151
Kinew, Wab, 349
King, Rodney, 323
King Lou, 311, 319, 322, 507
Kirshenblatt-Gimblett, Barbara, 377
Kitigan Zibi Anishnabek First Nation, 486–7

Kittredge, George Lyman, 181
Klassen, Doreen Helen, 421–2, 447n14
Klassen, Judith, 3–10, 13–26, 357–60, 417–45
Klassen, Margaret, 427, 447n24
Klassen, Melvin, 427, 447n24
Kleine Gemeinde Mennonites, 446n3
Klippenstein, Blaine, 216–17, 236n19
Klymasz, Robert B., 21, 456–8, 461, 469, 474n13
K'naan, 315, 329
Kobayashi, Audrey, 389, 404
k-os (Kevin Brereton), 329
Koskoff, Ellen, 6, 15, 358
Kothar, Sunil, 107
Krahn, Cornelius, 420
Kristofferson, Kris, 492
Kronsgart (Manitoba), 447n15
Kronsthal (Manitoba), 446n3, 447n15
krs-One (Lawrence Parker), 310, 311
Kun, Josh, 394
Kushwaha, Amika, 110n22, 504

LaFever, K.C., 337
Lafleur, Donat, 58
Lakewind Sound Studios (Nova Scotia), 290–7, 298, 301nn15–16
Lakhia, Kumudini, 97
L.A. Luv, 311–12, 313, 314; "Elements of Style," 311; "Jamaican Funk," 311–14, 507; "On This Mic," 311; "Run for Cover," 311; "Victory Is Calling," 311
Lamond, Mary Jane, 196
Langevin, Roger: *Les Pêcheurs*, 154*f*
Langille, Claudine, 301n12
Lapierre, Arthur, 58–60
Larsen, Soren, 387
LaRue, François-Alexandre-Hubert, 53, 55
Latin Quarter (New York club), 310
Lavalee, Darren, 230
Lavallee, JJ: "Buffalo Gals," 226, 230–2, 238n45, 505; "Metchif Reel," 231
Lavery, Fred, 290, 301nn15–16
LaVonne, Don, 352n23
Leahy (band), 195
LeBlanc, Avila à Alfred, 153, 154*f*

LeBlanc, Félix, 155
LeBlanc, Pastelle, 150*f*
Lederman, Anne: on cross tunings and clogging, 224–5; on Metis fiddling, 209, 214, 216–18; recordings made by, 235n8, 236n17, 237n36; on Red River Jig, 238n45; on Scottish fiddling, 211, 223; on tune forms, 347n44
Lefebvre, Armand, 59
Legendre, Joël, 43, 45
Legendre, Napoléon, 54
Leja, Józef, 368
Lemieux, Megann C., 344, 508
Lepine, Garry: career and recordings, 227, 236n28, 237n38; rendition of "Andy Roussin Reel," 227, 228*f*, 230, 236n37, 238n40, 505
Letkeman, Edna, 426–7, 444
Létourneau, Henri, 235n8
Levin, Robert, 151
Levine, Victoria Lindsay, 18
Lewis, Brock, 491, 499n15
Lewis, George, 330n3
Lewis, Lennox, 318
Li, Peter, 246, 254
Lieu, David, 271n29
lion dancing: in Canada, 243–5; components, 261–3; costumes, 242, 250, 251–2, 260; interdisciplinarity, 206, 244–5; origins, 249–53; parades and presentations, 259–61, 265–6, 270n26; Southern lion, 250, 251, 259. *See also* China; Chinese Canadians
 – Hong Luck Kung Fu Club: fieldwork at, 243–5; founding and mandate, 245–6, 248, 257–9, 267–8; lion dance parades, 242–3, 506; lion dance team, 250*f*, 251, 252*f*, 257, 260, 261–4
 – kung fu: in Canadian Chinatowns, 245–9; origins and heritage, 247–9; percussion rhythms for, 253–4; practice and teaching, 244–7, 258–9; styles, 247–8, 249, 269n12
 – percussion ensemble: instruments, 242–3; percussion rhythms, 248, 253–4; sound and movement intersection, 259–64; vocables, 261–4

Littlechild, Chief Wilton, 497n5
Liu, Wanyu, 252
Lo, Henry, 268–9n5
Loft, Steve, 496
Lomax, John, 179
Lombardi, Johnny, 382n12
Long, John, 484, 485, 490
Losten, Basil (bishop), 462
Louttit, Stan, 484–5, 491, 498n14
Lucas, Ralph, 65
Ludacris (rapper), 331n17
lumber camps: songs and music making, 50, 52, 54, 62–6
Lunenburg Folk Harbour Festival, 178, 199

McAdam, Sylvia, 477, 478
McArthur, Danny, 104
MacCannell, Dean, 132
MacCormack, Rosemary, 141nn14–15
McCurdy, Howard, 326
MacDonald, Angus L., 180, 184
MacDonald, Chris, 8–9, 42, 177–201
MacDonald, Dan Alex, 194
McDonald, John, 63–6
McDonald, Norma, 64–6
MacDonald, Paul, 287–90, 291–4, 296, 298, 301n12
McDonald, William, 63–6
MacEachen, Frances, 134, 136
MacEachern, Dan Hughie, 300n1
McFayden, Sarah, 301n12
MacGillivray, Allister, 188, 193–4; *The Nova Scotia Song Collection*, 194, 195
McGuire, Colin, 9, 21, 206, 242–68
MacIsaac, Ashley, 195, 196, 280–1, 300–1n8, 301n15, 506
McKay, Ian, 178, 180, 184–5
MacKeel (group), 197
MacKenzie, Carl, 300n6
MacKenzie, W. Roy, 178, 179, 181–3, 195, 198; *Ballads and Sea Songs of Nova Scotia*, 181, 183; *The Quest of the Ballad*, 181–2, 184
MacKinnon, Catherine, 187, 188
McKinnon, Crystal, 480
McKinnon, Ian, 275, 278–9
McLean, Sheela, 477

MacLeod, Malcolm Angus, 141n14
MacMaster, Alex and Minnie, 289, 301n10
MacMaster, Natalie, 195, 197, 280, 281, 300–1n8, 301n10, 506
McMillan, L. Jane, 477–8
MacNeil, Kenzie, 193, 194
MacNeil, Rita, 193, 194, 301n15
MacPhee, Doug, 300n6
Madelinot-style fiddling: accompaniment for, 153; Cape Breton influence on, 153, 157; distinctive rhythm, 155–6, 157–9, 158*f*; extra-musical elements, 165–6; flexible style and improvisation, 145–6, 156–65, 170n30; influenced by sea and landscape, 155, 165–6; oral tradition and transcriptions, 163–5, 164*f*; recordings of, 162, 505; *scordatura*, 162; tune sources, 153, 157–9; venues and performances, 150*f*, 151, 153, 161–2; virtuosity, 156, 162, 167, 170n28; young professional musicians, 156, 159, 161, 167. *See also* Îles-de-la-Madeleine
Maestro Fresh-Wes (Maestro). *See* Williams, Wes
Magdalen Islands. *See* Îles-de-la-Madeleine
Mahabharata (Sanskrit epic), 98
Maharaj, Birju, 97
Major, Charlie, 231
Mangaldas, Aditi, 97, 98
Manitoba Fiddle Association, 227; Fiddle Wall of Fame, 237n39
Manitoulin Island (Ontario), 238n45
Manning, Tina, 492
Manny, Louise, 177
Manuel, Peter, 107
Marchand, Charles, 59
Marche, Stephen, 365
Marcus, Egerton, 318
Mariposa Folk Festival, 20, 24
Markoff, Irene, 21
Marley, Bob, 309, 316
Marsh, Charity, 341, 349, 351n2
Marshall, Albert, 350
Marshall, Carla, 325, 328
Marshall, Murdena, 350
Martens, Helena, 427, 448n35

martial virtue, 249
Mason, Vaughan, 316
Massicotte, Édouard-Zotique, 46, 48–52, 56–60, 80n9, 81–2n30
Matsue, Jennifer Milioto, 205
Mattax Moersch, Charlotte, 151
Maulik, Sudeshna, 90
Maynard, Dave, 216
Maytwayashing, Cliff, 220, 221, 229
Maz (quartet), 46
Maziade, Marc, 46
Medicine Dream (band): Alaska base, 9, 336, 337, 339, 340, 343; audiences for, 340–1, 348–9; formation and members, 337, 344; Pike's leadership and Mi'kmaw culture, 336–40, 352n14; political issues, 339–41; touring and awards, 338; songs: "Hurtful Stories," 341, 352n18; "If We Were Wolves," 341, 352n18; "If You Dream of Eagles," 341; "In This World," 207, 336, 340, 342–9, 508; "Lightning Flashes the Sky," 337; "True Friends," 337; "We Belong," 341, 344, 352n18. *See also* Pike, Paul
Meintjes, Louise, 283–4
Memorial University of Newfoundland, 23, 24, 395, 396, 397
Mendez, Jillian, 325, 327
Mennonite Brethren, 427
Mennonites
– circle games, 422–31; decline of, 429–31, 439; features and movement vocabulary, 423–4; as "Mennonite," 359, 430–1; occasions for, 422, 423–4, 429, 447n15; songs for, 418, 424–6, 447n17, 508
– communities and practices: Anabaptist origins, 418, 440, 449; conserving groups, 419, 420, 426–7, 440–3, 445n2, 445n5, 445n7; German vernacular, 420, 432, 433–4, 448n32; and government authorities, 419, 420, 421, 446–7n12; and Indigenous peoples, 435; migrations, 419–20, 446n9; pacifism and social justice, 420, 425–6, 434, 440, 447n12; permeability of boundaries, 10, 359, 417, 418–21, 424, 430, 432, 439; and revivalism, 427–8, 448n25; transportation access, 429–31, 439; values in daily life, 430, 435, 440; views on dancing, 422, 426–9; views on music and songs, 359, 418, 439–44, 446n6
– mumming tradition (*Brommtopp*), 431–9; drum for, 359, 422, 431f, 509; origins of, 432; players and costumes, 431–2, 436–9, 437f; responses to, 438–9; song for, 433–6, 509

Mercier, Jean-François, 44
Messenjah, 325
Messer, Don, and *Don Messer's Jubilee*, 169n14, 187, 189, 200
Metisfest (Manitoba), 215, 218–22, 227, 230, 235n16, 236n23, 236n28, 505
Metis fiddle traditions, 209–338: definition and style, 209–10, 214, 215, 234n1; accompaniment and collaboration, 211, 215, 223–4, 225, 226; asymmetry (crooked tunes) and metric irregularity, 209, 211, 222, 223–4, 226, 237nn31–2; Cajun elements, 233; clogging with, 209, 211, 215, 222, 224–5, 234n2; contemporary practice and relevance, 9, 209–10, 232–3; cross (altered) tunings, 209, 222, 224, 234n3; danceability, 222, 226; descending melodic lines, 211, 222, 225; diversity, 226–7; double-stringing, 222, 225; festival circuit and contest events, 28, 214–15, 227; filler notes (jiggy jiggy), 231–2; historical background, 211–15; Indigenous influences, 211, 223, 234n1; individuality and creativity, 211, 214–15, 217–18, 222, 225–6; learning and teaching, 216–18; vs old-time styles, 214; recordings, 212, 236n17; Red River style, 212; resurgence and revival, 206, 210, 234–5n6; social and stylistic complexity, 233; standardization, 217–18; tablature for, 217; transcriptions, 222, 228–9f, 231f
– Metis fiddle tunes: "Andy Roussin Reel," 227, 228f, 230, 505; "Big John McNeil," 214, 220; "Buck Skin Reel," 229f, 230, 505; "Buffalo Gals," 230–2, 231f, 505; "Devil's Reel," 224, 237n35; "Devil's Waltz," 224; "Drops of Brandy," 114, 223; "Duck Dance,"

213, 214, 223, 224; "Faded Love," 214, 220; "Metchif Reel," 231; "Orange Blossom Special," 233, 238n45; "Red River Jig," 212, 213, 214, 220, 223, 224; "Reel of Eight," 213; "St Anne's Reel," 214, 220; "Whiskey before Breakfast," 214, 219; *Drops of Brandy* (anthology), 227

Metis Heritage Celebration (Oshawa), 218

Metis jigging, 20

Metis Music Festival (St Laurent), 218

Metis Music Hall of Fame, 227, 237n39

Metis people and culture: friendship centres, 213; impact of Western settlement, 211–12; and Mennonite communities, 435; and multiculturalism, 213–14

Michie Mee (Michelle McCullock), 307, 309–15, 318, 324, 327, 330n7, 330n9; "Canada Large," 314; and Dance Appeal, 325, 327, 328, 329; "Elements of Style," 311; "Jamaican Funk," 311–14, 507; "On This Mic," 311; "A Portion from Up North," 314; "Run for Cover," 311; "Victory Is Calling," 311

microhistories, 3, 6, 14, 22, 42, 360

Middleton, Richard, 201n2

Mi'kmaw: Mi'kmaq and Mi'kmaw (orthography), 351n3; Beothuk people and mercenary myth, 339–40, 341, 352, 352n15; eight-point star, 339, 344; Elmastukwek Mi'kmaq Mawio'Mi, 339; Elsipogtog First Nation, 482; in Magdalen Islands (*Munagesunok*), 168n4; in Nova Scotia, 179–80, 186; Paul Pike's identification with, 9, 207, 336–42, 344; Qalipu First Nation, 339, 352n9; two-eyed seeing and middle ground metaphors, 207, 349–51

Mi'kmwesu (flute-playing trickster), 352n10

Miller, Dave, and Inter-Media Services, 278, 279, 300n6

Miller, Derek, 348

milling (waulking) frolics: defined, 139; Acadian *fouleries*, 140n12; in Cape Breton, 114, 125–38; change and continuity in, 129, 134; as a communal labour activity, 114; and Gaelic culture, 115, 126, 130–8; in Newfoundland, 140n12; participatory/presentational aspects, 41, 115–18, 125, 137–8, 142n21; in Scotland, 41, 114, 119, 125–6; for tourists, 41, 115, 118, 130–2, 137–8; traditional practices, 114–15, 119, 120f; urine used in, 114–15, 130, 139, 141n17

milling (waulking) songs: collections and literature on, 117; English language in, 131; extemporizing in, 121; format, 119–20, 126–7, 140n8; Gaelic texts, 116, 122–4, 127–9; recordings, 504; song repertoire, 114, 126–7, 130; split chorus, 122, 124

mimesis and alterity (theory), 421

Miminis, George, 397, 399, 411n21

Miousse, Bernard, 170n26, 504

Miousse, Pascal, 150f, 156–7, 162–3, 166, 170n26, 504

Miro, Henri, 52

Mishra, Anuj, 102

Monson, Ingrid, 282

Montmarquette, Alfred, 58

Moore, Allan, 350

Moose Factory (Ontario), 498n14

Moreau, Ives, 21

Moreau, Sylvie, 43

Morgan, Pamela, 397–400, 411n18, 411n21

Morin, Victor, 48

Morris, Amanda, 499n16

Morrisette, Louise, 42, 44

Morrison, Roderick, 127

Mousseau, Lawrence, 229

Mousseau, Shawn, 229f, 230, 505

Mousseau, Willie, 229, 238n41

mouth music (*turlutte*), 169n20

Mrowca, Franek, 368, 369, 370f, 372–3, 508

MuchMusic, 196, 316, 329, 347

Mudri-Zubacz, Melita, 475n19

multiculturalism issues: with broadcasting, 359, 382n12, 388, 392, 410n11; with kathak dance, 91–2, 101–2, 108–9; with Metis fiddling, 213; with nationalism, 4–5; policies and legislation (Canadian Multiculturalism Act), 4–5, 201n5, 213, 318, 362–3, 386, 391–2

mumming (mummering) traditions, 398, 411n25, 418, 431–9

Munro, Henry, 183, 184
Murray, Anne, 187, 188, 196, 441
musicking, 393–4
MUSICultures, 17, 26n5

Nahachewsky, Andriy, 21
Nalepa, John, 474n12
Narváez, Peter, 194–5, 340, 352n16
Nataraj, Madhu, 98
National Film Board of Canada (NFB): Creighton's work with, 184, 197; and multiculturalism, 392; Obomsawin's work with, 481, 484; role in promoting Canadian musicians, 189; *A Sigh and a Wish*, 197; *Songs of Nova Scotia*, 184. See also *Trick or Treaty?*
National Inquiry into Missing and Murdered Indigenous Women and Girls, 18, 482, 496
nationalism: and art music, 48–9, 57; English Canadian, 196, 200, 201n5; and folklore collecting, 55, 56–7; and multiculturalism, 4–5; postcolonial, 106; transnationalism, 21
nationalist composers, 186
National Museum of Man, 27n13
National Music Centre (Calgary), 25
Native American Music Awards, 338, 349
Native Council of Canada, 488
Nelson, Ron, 305, 310, 316
Netherlands: Mennonites communities in, 419, 432, 441
Nettl, Bruno, 151–2, 162, 168–9n12, 357
Neubergthal (Manitoba): *Brommtopp*, 431f, 432, 436, 437–8, 509; fieldwork interviews in, 446n3; songs and dances in, 429, 441
Neuenburg (Manitoba), 432
Neufeld, Margaret, 442, 444
New Delhi Kathak Kendra (dance school), 90
Newfoundland (island) and Newfoundland and Labrador (province): colonization and settlement, 389, 390, 398; Greek community, 397, 411nn21–3; immigrants and visible minorities, 390, 397; immigration strategy, 390–1; Magdalen Islands annexed to, 148; mummering tradition, 398, 411n25; population, 390–1. See also "Come By Concerts"
– folk music: fiddling and dance tunes, 237n31, 390, 400–5, 407, 412n27; folksongs, 186, 386, 397–400; milling frolics, 140nn12–13, 141n17; recording archive, 19; song collectors, 177, 398
– Indigenous peoples: Beothuk and mercenary myth, 339–40, 341, 352, 352n15; at Gabriel's Lake, 338, 339; population of, 390, 409n7; Qalipu First Nation, 339, 352. See also Mi'kmaw
Newton, Abby, 301n12
Newton, George, 337, 340–1, 344, 345, 346
Nimjee, Ameera, 22
Nishiyuu Walkers, 485, 488–9, 490, 496, 498n11, 498n14
Nokjaste, 422, 423–4, 429
nomad aesthetic, 323–5
nonviolence, 434, 479
North Shore Gaelic Singers, 126
Northwest Resistance, 214
Norwegian fiddle tradition, 163, 223
Nova Scotia: Celtic Wave, 195–8; diversity, 180, 181; Gaelic speakers and culture, 116–17, 131–5, 186; industrialization and urbanization, 178, 181; plurality of musical traditions, 186; settlement of, 179–81; tourism and folklore image, 177–8, 184–5, 200
– folksong tradition: English folksong tradition, 8–9, 42, 177–201; and folk revival, 187–90; folksong collecting and canon, 177–86, 200–1; singer-songwriters, 188–90, 191–2. See also Cape Breton

Obomsawin, Alanis: career, 483–4; *Bush Lady* (album), 483–4; *Christmas at Moose Factory* (film), 484; *Kanehsatake* (film), 484; *Trick or Treaty?* (film), 10, 359–60, 480–1, 485–97, 498–9n14, 510
Observatoire interdisciplinaire de création et de recherche en musique, 24
Old Colony Mennonites, 419, 422, 440, 446n3, 446n7, 446n8

old-time fiddling tradition, 160, 214, 234n2, 235n14, 238n42
Ondaatje, Michael, 404
oral notation systems, 90, 94, 104, 109n7, 109n10
Orleski, Olga, 462
Orleski, Steve, 462, 467
Ornstein, Lisa, 153, 162
Ostashewski, Marcia, 10, 21, 359, 453–72
Ottawa River Singers: "Come Out Fighting," 488–9, 491, 499n15
Ottawa Valley step dancing, 20

"Paddy on the Turnpike," 157, 158f
Page, Dorothy Azure, 225
Painchaud, Carole, 165–6
Painchaud, Sonia, 153
Pane, Kishore, 110n14, 503
Pankratz, Jaime Friesen, 446n3
Panwar, Hemant and Vaishali: *Shakuntala*, 98, 503
participatory music practices. *See* Turino, Thomas, participatory/presentational model
Pashkarenka, Mrs (cantor), 465
patrimonialisation, 48
Peabody Essex Museum, 338, 343, 344
Peacock, Kenneth, 177, 201n3, 398, 441
Pegley, Kip, 320, 347, 348–9, 353n30
People's Republic of China. *See under* China
performance spaces: normativity and relationships, 393–4, 410n17
Peters, Molly, 477–8
Peterson, Oscar, 318
Petipa, Marius: *La Bayadère*, 110n20
Petkau, Irene Friesen, 448n34
Pike, Paul: career, 337–9; leadership of Medicine Dream, 336–40, 352n14; Mi'kmaw identification and heritage, 9, 207, 336–42, 344, 349–51. *See also* Medicine Dream
Pitter, Jay, 362–3
Plum Coulee (Manitoba), 432
Podczerwiński, Józef, 368, 370f
Poi Suk, 258, 270n24

Poitras, Frank, 235n8
Poland, 366–77, 382n15, 382n17
Polish diaspora (*Polonia*), 21, 366, 369, 377–8, 382n16
Polish Górale (Highlanders), 358–9, 361–85; diversity, 379; fieldwork with, 361, 367–8, 371–2, 382n18; polyphonic singing, 366, 367; string ensembles, 366, 368–70, 377–8, 382n16; as a subculture, 366–8, 382n15; Toronto community, 358–9, 366–7
– *góralski* dance performances: at a party, 368–73, 370f, 508; at a public gala, 373–80, 375f, 508
Polish Highlanders Association of Canada, 366, 369
Porcello, Thomas, 282, 283, 284, 286
Posen, Sheldon, 184, 189
Potskin, Brent, 238n45
Power, Tom, 397, 399
powwows: drums and vocals, 335, 336, 351n7, 479, 487, 489; Mennonites at, 444; recordings of, 282, 301n11, 347, 348, 349; traditions in Pike's work with Medicine Dream, 339, 344–5, 347, 348
Pratibha Arts, 102
pre-composition, 152, 169n13
presentational music practices. *See* Turino, Thomas, participatory/presentational model
Prince, J.-E., 55, 56
Prince Edward Island: Gaelic speakers, 116; kitchen parties, 82n33; traditional fiddle music, 151, 153, 156, 157
Prögler, J.A., 297–8
protest songs, 19, 185
Provost, Monique, 22

Qalipu First Nation, 339, 352
QuébéAsia Dance Collective, 87
Québécois fiddling and folk music, 19, 20, 41, 44, 53–4, 166, 167. *See also veillées*
Quick, Sarah, 213, 222, 226, 232–3, 234–5nn5–6
Quigley, Colin, 376–7
Quinn, Bob, 194

Raagini Dance Company, 102
rabostan, 153
Raboy, Marc, 392
racism and racial discrimination: in Canada, 317–19; against Chinese Canadians, 245–7, 254–5, 257, 267, 268n3; police harassment and brutality, 323–4, 331n20; Williams's response to, 315–19
radio broadcasts: audiences for, 387; of diasporic musics, 325–9; of fiddle music, 157, 158–9, 169n19; of fiddling, 212; of hip hop, 305, 316; infrastructure for, 392–3, 410n13; limitations of, 408; multicultural programs, 382n12; and production of audiences, 387; public service broadcasts, 392, 410n12; role of producers, 387–8, 409n5; as "theatre" for cultural diversity, 388; urban radio stations, 325, 329, 331n21; of *veillées*, 45. See also Canadian Broadcasting Corporation (CBC)
Rahn, Jay, 26n3
Ramzy, Carolyn, 22
Ranger, Terence, 39, 89, 106, 249
Rankin, Raylene, 193, 197
Rankin Family (band), 188, 194, 195, 197, 198, 280
Rao, Nancy, 268n3
Rascalz, 329
Ratułowski, Józef, 368, 370*f*
Raulin, Anne, 265–6
recordings: amateur or home-made (dance tapes), 279, 283, 287, 288–9, 292, 300n7; audience or crowd noise, 286, 288–9; audio quality of, 282, 373; of Cape Breton fiddlers, 9, 206, 275–300; engineers and producers, 283, 290–1, 296–9; extra-musical sound, 279, 301n11; fiddlers' active role, 296–7; for field research, 370–3; foot stomping, 295–6, 302n21; hyper-realism, 206, 284, 286–7, 290, 294, 296, 298, 299; liveness in, 206, 275–6, 284–300; microphone placement, 286–7, 294–5, 296, 302n23; minor imperfections, 289; on-location, 278, 287–90, 291; participatory discrepancies, 237n40, 284, 286, 297–9, 371; powwow aesthetic, 347; professional video recordings, 374;

punch-in, 290, 297, 300n17; "raw–polished" spectrum, 276, 281, 282–4, 290, 299–300; reverb and ambient sound, 284–6, 289–90; techniques to add liveness, 276, 290–9; and vernacular vs commercial viability, 284; violin sound or timbre, 291–3, 294–5. See also Cape Breton fiddling tradition
Red Power Movement, 482, 492, 496
"Red River Jig," 212, 213, 214, 220, 223, 238n45
Red River Jig tuning, 224
Red River Resistance, 214
Red River style, 212, 233
"Reel à Célestin à Jos," 155
"Reel à Jean-Joseph à Avila," 157, 158*f*
"Reel du pendu" (Hanged Man's Reel), 162–3, 170n26, 170nn28–9, 504
reggae, 310–12, 315, 322, 326–7, 330n7
Reid, Johnny, 231
Reinfeld (Manitoba), 446n3, 447n15
Reinländer Mennonites, 420, 440, 446n6, 446n8
Reinland Mennonites, 419, 446n3, 446n7, 447n15
Rellik (rapper), 331n15
residential schools (Indian Residential Schools), 18, 497–8n5
resistance (vs rebellion), 214, 235n13, 236n24
resurgence, 210, 234–5n6, 237n31, 477–8, 496–7
reterritorialization, 198
revivalism, 427–8, 448n25
Rice, Paul, 449n47
Rice, Timothy, 244, 457
Richard, Patricia, 156
The Rise and Follies of Cape Breton (musical theatre), 193, 195
Risk, Laura, 8, 40, 43–68
Roach, Jason, 290
Robbins, James, 11n5
Roberts, Gillian, 402
Robertson, Roland, 198
Robinson, Dylan, 18, 19, 481–2
Rogers, Stan, 190–2, 194, 195; Stan Rogers Folk Festival, 178, 199

Roll, Joseph, 462–4, 463f, 467
Roman Catholic Church, 472n2, 474n14, 475n22
Roots (television mini-series), 316, 330n10
Rosenberg, Neil, 186, 189, 200, 398
Rosenberg, Siegfried, 433, 448n32
Rosenfeld (Manitoba), 432, 437
round dances, 478–9, 489–91, 498–9n14, 499n16, 510
Rouse, Ervin Thomas, 233
Roy, Camille, 54
Roy, Régis, 59
Rudnerwieder congregation, 446n3
Run-D.M.C., 305
Rushton, John Philippe, 317
Russia: Mennonite communities, 418, 419, 420, 427, 432, 446nn9–11; Russian churches, 475n22. *See also* Ukraine
Ryerson Polytechnical Institute (now Ryerson University): CKLN, 305; Ryerson Theatre, 374

St Basil's Seminary (Connecticut), 462–3
St Basil the Great (liturgy), 472n2
Sainte-Marie, Buffy, 498n7
Saint-Godefroi (on Gaspé coast), 61–3
Saint-Pierre et Miquelon, 147f, 168n5
Sampson, Gordie, 198, 290, 301nn15–16
Sanden, Paul, 281, 285–6
Sara, Ralph, 344, 351n8
Savard, Louis-Martin, 19
Sawatzky, Frieda, 426
Saxena, Sushil Kumar, 109n3
Scales, Christopher, 282, 301n11, 341–2, 347, 348
Schafer, R. Murray, 27n9, 186
Schechner, Richard, 265
Schlesse, Samantha, 104
Schlüsselbund Lieder (key ring songs), 422–3, 424, 447n14
Schoenthal (Manitoba), 432
Schofield, Katherine, 106
Schwartz, Jacob K., 431f
Scobie, Niel, 9, 207, 305–29, 341
Scobie, Willow, 341
Scott, Lorraine, 325, 327
Scott La Rock (Scott Sterling), 310, 311

Segato, Lorraine, 325, 327
Self Defence (rapper), 325
Sen, Saswati, 97
Senior, Doreen, 187
Seth, Dakàsha, 97
seventh generation, 494–5
Shad (Shadrach Kabango), 329
Shaolin Temple (China), 248–9, 268
Sharma, Saveeta, 90, 99–100, 110n22, 504
Sharp, Cecil, 179
Shaw, John, 134
Shaw, Margaret Fay, 139n3
Shay, Anthony, 362
Sheppard, Mike, 290–1, 293, 294–6, 298, 300n16
Shore, Marlene, 13
Sibbles, Leroy, 325, 327
Signifyin'/Signifyin(g)/signifyin(g), 307, 308–9, 319–23, 330n4
Simons, Menno, 449n46
Sinclair, Murray, 497n5
Singa, Rina, 90, 99, 100, 108
Singalong Jubilee (CBC Halifax), 187–8, 189, 194
singer-songwriters (folk entrepreneurs), 187–8, 190–5
Siuty, József, 378
60s Scoop, 18, 482, 495, 498n6
Sloan (group), 195, 199
Small, Christopher, 393
Smallwood, Joey, 340, 343
Smetana, Bedřich, 186
Smith, Christina, 237n33
Smith, Gordon E., xiii–xv, 16, 17
Smith, Muriel, 21
Smithsonian Center for Folklife and Cultural Heritage, 24, 25
Snow, Hank, 190
Société du parler français au Canada, 54–5, 56, 57
Société historique de Montréal, 49
Société pour la promotion de la danse traditionnelle québécoise, 45
Society for Ethnomusicology, 13, 14, 17
Soirée Canadienne (CHLT Sherbrooke), 40, 45
Solis, Gabriel, 151, 152, 168n11
Solomon, Thomas, 371

Somaduroff, Justin, 351n8
Sommerfelder Mennonites, 419, 422, 426–7, 432, 446n3, 448n35
Soucy, Isidore, 58, 162
Sparling, Heather, 8, 41, 114–42
Spence, Emile, 238n44
Spence, Ivan, 238n44
Spence, Chief Theresa, 477, 478f, 489
Spicer, Keith, 326
Spirit of the West (band), 195
Sprag Session (band), 297–8
Spring, Howard, 152, 169n13
square dancing: with Cape Breton fiddling, 276, 277, 280; in Mennonite communities, 422, 426; with Metis fiddling, 213, 230, 235n16; at *veillées*, 62, 63
Stanbury, Alan, 194
Stan Rogers Folk Festival (Canso), 178, 199
Stardust (NYC club), 309
Sterne, Jonathan, 282
Stetch, Tony, 474n12
Stévance, Sophie, 19
Stevens, Paul, 54
Stewart, Jesse, 9, 207, 305–29
Stoesz, Bill, 442
Stomperfest (Reedy Creek/Kinosota, Manitoba), 230
storytelling, 7, 341, 484, 493, 495–7
"Strong Women's Song," 499n15
The Sugarhill Gang: "Rapper's Delight," 309, 316
Sugar Love (rapper), 310
Suroît (band), 155, 166
Sutton, Billy, 402–3
Sveti Ivan (Balkan choir), 397–400, 411n18
Swann, Francesca, 395–7, 407, 408
Świątkiewicz, Anna, 376
Swollen Members (hip hop group), 329
Swyripa, Frances, 455
Szego, Kati, 22, 358

Taché, Joseph-Charles, 53, 56, 81n23
Tagaq, Tanya, 19, 498n7
Taras, David, 392
Tataryn, Myroslaw, 460, 474n13
Taussig, Michael, 421

Taylor, George, 278
Tchaikovsky, Pyotr Il'yich, 450
Tellier, Paul M., 326
Temperley, Nicholas, 151
Theodorakis, Mikis, 411n22
Thibert, Marie-Élaine, 43
Thiessen, Jack, 443
Thobani, Sitara, 109n5, 110n18
Thomas, Otis: *The Fiddle Tree*, 301n12
Thompson, Richard H., 255
Thrush Hermit (band), 99
Tobias, Ken, 187, 188
Toews, Agnes, 434, 435, 449n38
Toews, Julius, 448n34, 449n39
Tomlinson, John, 198
Toronto: Chinatown, 243, 247, 268n4, 270n22; CHIN picnics, 382n12; cultural sector, 363–6; Góvale community, 9, 358–9, 366–7; Harbourfront Centre, 102, 108; hip hop culture, 9, 305–29; urban radio stations, 325, 329
tourism and tourists: term, 141n18; in Cape Breton for milling frolics, 41, 115, 130–2, 137–9; in Les Îles-de-la-Madeleine for fiddling, 149–51; in Nova Scotia for folk music, 177–8, 184–5, 200
Toynbee, Jason, 417, 421–2, 444, 445
tradition(s): term, 39–40, 106, 300n2, 336–7, 351nn6–7; and citationality, 47–8; and creativity, 160–1, 167; and genre, 205; and Indigenous popular music, 336–7; invented traditions, 39–40, 89, 106, 249
Trag (Tragedy Khadafi), 319, 331n16
The Tragically Hip (band), 195
transit narratives, 404
Travers, Mary (La Bolduc), 58
A Tribe Called Red (band), 498n7
Trick or Treaty? (documentary by Obomsawin), 10, 359–60, 480–1, 485–97, 498–9n14, 510. *See also* Indigenous activism
Trudeau, Justin, 475, 475n22
Trudeau, Pierre Elliott, 101, 189, 389
Trudell, John, 491–5; "Crazy Horse," 493–5
Truth and Reconciliation Commission (TRC), 5, 18, 481, 482, 495, 497–8n5

Tulk, Janice, 9, 207, 335–55
Turino, Thomas, participatory/presentational model: for Górale ensembles, 372, 377; for Metisfest participants, 221–2; for milling frolics, 41, 115–18, 125, 133, 137–8, 142n21; for musicians making recordings, 282, 283
Turtle Mountain Chippewa Reservation (North Dakota), 218, 219, 233, 236n24
two-eyed seeing (metaphor), 207, 350–1
Tye, Diane, 184

Ukraine: Mennonites in, 418, 419, 423f; province of Galicia, 474n18; Russian troops in, 475n22. *See also* Russia
- Ukrainian diaspora and traditions: in Canada, 454–5, 456–7; choral singing, 473n10, 473n11; dance and music, 21, 474n13; role of church, 455–6, 467–8; young families in, 460

Ukrainian Catholic Church (Byzantine Ukrainian Catholicism): adaptation and change, 460–1, 470; Byzantine origin, 455; cantors, 460–8, 473n6; Galician chant, 458, 472n4, 473n8; gender roles, 465–8; hymns and carols, 453; instruments and recorded music, 453, 473–4n12; liturgy and languages, 460–1, 463–4f, 472n2, 473n8, 474n14; outdoor bells, 453–4; priest (celebrant), 455, 458; *samoyilka* melodies, 458–9, 469; Tones (chant melodies), 458, 460, 462, 473n8
- congregational responsorial singing, 359, 455–9; centrality of, 457; change in, 469–70; enjoyment and community with, 359, 467–9; future research directions, 469; *krylos*, 459, 467, 472n4; male and female participants, 458; settings and harmonies, 457–8, 459, 464–5, 473n10; and Ukrainian culture, 468–70
- Holy Ghost Ukrainian Catholic Church (Sydney), 453–72; cantors, 456, 465; instrumental music, 474n12; photograph, 454f; weekly liturgy, 470–2, 510. *See also* Dusanowskyj, Father Roman

Ukrainian Orthodox Church, 455, 462, 472nn2–3, 474n14, 475n20, 475n22
union songs, 185
United Empire Loyalists, 179
Universal Zulu Nation, 309–10
Université de Montréal, 23, 24
Université Laval, 24
University of Alberta, 23, 24
University of British Columbia, 23
University of Regina, 24
University of Toronto, 23, 24
Upasana School of Dance (Ottawa), 90
urban arts sector, 361, 363–5, 380
urban music (genre), 327
Urban Music Association of Canada, 326
urban radio stations, 325, 329, 331n21

Van Dyke, Henry, 55–6
Vanishing Cape Breton Fiddler (documentary), 278
Varghese, Meera, 92
Vaze, Bageshree, 90, 92, 100, 101–5, 108, 503; *Paratopia*, 102–5, 103f; *Rebel Goddess*, 101, 103, 111n25
veillées, 40, 43–68; term, 44, 48; and art music, 56–7; and citationality, 47–8; fiddling in, 53–4; in Gaspé, 40, 44, 47, 61–6; historicization of, 40, 46–7; as idealized performances, 44, 46, 57; as informal gatherings, 44, 61–6; in literature, 53–6; in Montreal, 49–53, 69–79; and patrimonialisation, 48–9; research on, 48–9; and *Soirée Canadienne*, 40, 45; sources and documentation for, 61–2; stage furnishings for, 51f; in television broadcasts, 40, 44–5; as *terroir* performances, 56–9; as theatrical productions, 58–60. *See also* Québécois fiddling and folk music
"Les Veillées d'automne" (Montreal), 45
"Veillées du bon vieux temps," 46, 58–60, 69, 71–9
Venkatesan, Sobhana, 400–1
Vent'arrière, 155, 158, 169n15
Le Vent du Nord (band), 46
Verch, April, 110n22, 504

Vigneau, Louis Charles, 155
Vigneault, Gilles, 43
Vishtèn (band), 156, 170n26, 504
Vision Crew, 316
Vistula Delta, 419, 432, 448n33
Vollrath, Calvin, 214, 236n17
Voth, Norma Jost, 447n14, 448n35
Vrooman, Nicholas, 211, 223, 225, 235
Vyas, Vineet, 101

Wachowich, Nancy, 341
Walcott, Rinaldo, 307, 323, 324
Walker, Gordon, 3
Walker, Margaret, 8, 41, 87–108
Wallace, Beattie, 296
Washburne, Christopher, 371
waulking. *See* milling
Wells, Graham, 400–3
Werder Platt (Low German vernacular), 432, 433–4, 448n32
West Reserve Mennonite settlement, 418*f*, 432, 446n3, 446n7, 448n34
Whapmagoostui (northern Quebec), 485
White, Thyron Lee, 325, 327
Whiteduck, Gilbert, 486–7
Whittall, Geoff, 196
Wiens, Kathleen, 397, 398, 399
Williams, Wes (Maestro Fresh-Wes, Maestro), 305, 307, 315–19, 329; *The Black Tie Affair*, 317, 507; in Dance Appeal, 325, 328, 329; "I'm Showin' You," 316; "Let Your Backbone Slide," 315, 316–17, 507; "Nothin' At All," 317–19, 331nn14–15, 507; *Stick to Your Vision*, 315; *Symphony in Effect*, 317
Wilson, Brian, 441
Wilson, Marie, 497n5
Wilson, Nina, 477, 478
Wilson, William A., 134, 182, 185, 192
Wilson-Raybould, Jody, 485, 498n12
Wing Suk (nickname), 264, 271n31
Winkler (Manitoba), 430, 446n3
Witmer, Robert, 16, 26n3, 445
Wolters-Fredlund, Benita, 21
"Women's Warrior Song," 498n7, 499n15
Wong, Deborah, 162, 245
Wong Association (Toronto), 247, 255
Woodward, Syd, 510
wool milling (waulking). *See* milling
Woons, Marc, 478, 482
world music: as a category, 195, 365, 396; ensembles in universities, 23; as a network, 364
Wotherspoon, Terry, 479, 482–3
Wounded Knee, 482
Wrazen, Louise, 9, 21, 358–9, 361–85, 508
Wright, Heather, 397, 399
Wright-McLeod, Brian, 18

Yee, Paul: *Jade in the Coal*, 268n3
Yellowbird, Shane, 231
York Factory (Manitoba), 211
York University, 23, 24
"You Are My Sunshine"/"Dü bess mien Sonneschien," 422, 439–44, 445, 449n47, 509

Zama (singer), 325
Zarrili, Philip, 259
Zdybał, Ted, 374–6, 378, 379, 383n23, 383n26
Zulu musicians, 284
Zulu Nation (Universal Zulu Nation), 309–10